MARTIN D. SEYER

RS-232
Made Easy
Connecting
Computers,
Printers, Terminals,
and Modems

Second Edition

PRENTICE HALL
Englewood Cliffs, New Jersey 07632

Library of Congress Cataloging-in-Publication Data

Seyer, Martin D.
   RS-232 made easy : connecting computers, printers, terminals, and
modems / Martin D. Seyer.—2nd ed.
      Includes bibliographical references and index.
      ISBN 0-13-749870-5 (case).—ISBN 0-13-749854-3 (paper)
      1. Computer interfaces—Standards—United States. I. Title.
TK7887.5.S48 1991
004.6—dc20   90-26516
                                                         CIP

Editorial/production supervision
  and interior design: Laura Huber
Manufacturing buyers: Kelly Behr/Susan Brunke
Acquisitions editor: Karen Gettman

 © 1991 by Prentice-Hall, Inc.
A Simon & Schuster Company
Englewood Cliffs, New Jersey 07632

The publisher offers discounts on this book when ordered
in bulk quantities. For more information, write:

Special Sales/College Marketing
College Technical and Reference Division
Prentice Hall
Englewood Cliffs, New Jersey 07632

Printed in the United States of America
10 9 8 7 6 5 4 3 2
10 9 8 7 6 5 4 3   PBK

ISBN 0-13-749870-5 CASE

ISBN 0-13-749854-3 PAPER

Prentice-Hall International (UK) Limited, *London*
Prentice-Hall of Australia Pty. Limited, *Sydney*
Prentice-Hall Canada Inc., *Toronto*
Prentice-Hall Hispanoamericana, S.A., *Mexico*
Prentice-Hall of India Private Limited, *New Delhi*
Prentice-Hall of Japan, Inc., *Tokyo*
Simon & Schuster Asia Pte. Ltd., *Singapore*
Editora Prentice-Hall do Brasil, Ltda., *Rio de Janeiro*

Dedication

This book is dedicated to my wife, Melinda, who has over the past 12 years been a tremendous inspiration. I also wish to thank my children, Nathan, Taylor Macy, and Alex. Alex was not mentioned in any other books because of his late arrival into the family. They all supplied the patience, encouragement, and understanding necessary for me to write this and other publications. Special thanks go to Kevin, my brother, for providing much of the peripheral information and to the Bud Keller family, my in-laws, for providing the collection point for much of the material provided by vendors.

Contents

Foreword

The second edition of *RS-232 Made Easy* is a continuation of my first book, *RS-232 Made Easy*, a text designed to provide the reader with a good, solid understanding of the leads in the RS-232-C interface. It focused on the interaction of these leads between data terminal equipment, DTE, and data communication equipment, DCE. The tutorial was written to allow an easy yet thorough understanding of serial interfacing. This book incorporates some tutorial sections of the first book, but also adds a chapter featuring the most frequently asked questions pertaining to serial connections.

Also, a review of more than eight hundred devices has been included in the appendices. With this information the reader can design a cable in minutes versus the hours that it normally requires. The device information from this book can be combined with the device information contained in the first edition of *RS-232 Made Easy*, or with any of my other books, for many more cable designs. The material necessary to compile this critical information was provided by various vendors, whose contributions are greatly appreciated. The user should consult this information and use it frequently.

Readers should be aware that RS-232 is also known as EIA-232-D. Both terms are used in this text and are interchangeable. Readers and vendors are encouraged to send any supporting information, device pinout information, or other information to Prentice Hall College Book Editorial-Editor, so that it may be incorporated into future revisions. The author and publisher want to continue to provide you the tools necessary for easier connections.

I hope you enjoy it!

Martin D. Seyer

Preface

Have you heard this before?

"Prior to dialing the phone number and connecting to services such as CompuServe, Dow Jones, or Prodigy,[1] ensure that the DTE is connected to the DCE with the RS-232-C cable provided for the serial ports. If you're using a terminal, all that is needed is an RS-232 interface and a modem or acoustic coupler. If you are accessing the system with a computer, laptop, or workstation, merely add a communication package and a modem. The speeds that are supported are 300, 1200, and 2400 bps over a full-duplex facility. The mode being used must support all RS-232-C–compatible signals for proper control of the transmission. The port on your device should be optioned for 8 bits, no parity, ASCII, with only one stop bit. The number you are dialing will be automatically answered. When you get the answer-back tone, go to "data." If you are using a printer with a serial interface, check to make sure that it is optioned for the correct speed, parity, character, length, and polarity. If a null-modem cable is used between the terminal or computer and the printer, does it allow for either hardware or software flow control?"

What is all of this mumbo jumbo about options, communications, DTE, DCE, and RS-232-C? Is it something out of *Star Wars?* is E.T. trying to phone home? Is it a foreign language? No! It is terminology encountered by an increasing number of people involved with various aspects of personal and professional computing and communications. Whether you are providing on-line access to a database, connecting to a time-sharing system or information service, or merely attaching a printer and a personal computer, these terms become extremely important. Where can you find out about connecting devices using serial interfaces, such as computers, printers, terminals, plotters, and modems? Look no further—you have come to the right place!

[1]CompuServe is a trademark of CompuServe Inc.; Dow Jones is a trademark of Dow Jones & Co., Inc.; Prodigy is a trademark of IBM Corp.

A standard for connecting business machines with serial interfaces has been in existence in the data processing and data communications industry for several years. The latest revision of this standard, known as RS-232-D or, technically EIA 232-D, was established by the Electronic Industries Association of Washington, D.C., in 1969. Interfaces adhering to this standard are incorporated into alsmost all mainframe computers, minicomputers, and associated peripherals. Also, as PCs, workstations, and UNIX-based microcomputers, both business and personal, have become widespread, they too are supplying RS-232-type ports. With such increasing popularity, the need for a functional understanding of how to connect devices using RS-232 ports has never been greater.

Although widely used with computers, printers, terminals, and modems, RS-232 is not very well understood. A single source providing functional insights into the definition and characteristic of the standard is needed. This edition of *RS-232 Made Easy* fills the void by providing both a framework for understanding serial communications and a thorough explanation of the functions of each leads of the RS-232 interface.

The international counterpart that resembles RS-232 is known as CCITT V.24. CCITT stands for the International Telegraph and Telephone Consultative Committee. Both CCITT and EIA interfaces are similar. The basic difference is nomenclature. Throughout this book, reference is made only to EIA RS-232 C (see Figure D-1), but the context is equally applicable to the V.24 standard. The reader need only remember that the naming conventions are different between the two.

Components of a communication environment involving RS-232 ports can easily be likened to a railway system. Just as a train is transported along the rails between stations, so is information transferred between business machines. The elements of a railway system, such as the rails, trains, and stations (depots), provide an excellent illustration for comparison with the specifics of an RS-232 communication environment. Utilizing this analogy, both a general and detailed understanding can be achieved.

RS-232 Made Easy, second edition, is organized in a manner that requires no prior knowledge of the subject. Its approach is from the standpoint of a first-time microcomputer buyer who is interested in, among other things, the game-playing capabilities of the computer. Of course, many machines are purchased by individuals, such as teachers, professors, hobbyists, business executives, engineers, analysts, programmers, and others, who have no intention of playing computer games. Nonetheless, a light-hearted approach allows for gradual movement into the seriousness of interfacing with both RS-232 and RS-422.

Specifics of the interface are first described in lay terms, using the railway system analogy. The technical definitions of the terms immediately follow the analogy and are indicated by the heading RS-232. Because data communication requirements dictate the various components of the standard, the analogy generally focuses on communication environments in which the RS-232-C interface is widely used. Communication terminology is denoted by the heading DATA COMMUNICATIONS. This same technique is applied in all chapters as the foundation is gradually expanded to provide the reader with a thorough understanding of both serial interfaces.

Chapters 1 and 2 establish the need for RS-232 and provide an understanding of prevalent communication terminology; thereafter, the explanation evolves into the specifics of RS-232. Support organizations around the world were polled and asked to provide the most frequently asked questions surrounding the connections of computers and peripherals. This collection is featured in Chapter 9. The body of the book is followed by appendices that serve as resources for users. They include excerpts from the RS-232 standard and the RS-449 standard, which was intended to gradually replace RS-232. Also, the tools that are useful when working in these serial environments are described.

Additional material includes a listing of PCs, minicomputers, microcomputers, terminals, modems, and printers and their corresponding RS-232 pin assignments. *RS-232 Made Easy* proceeds to demonstrate, in a step-by-step manner, the interconnecting of the printers, CRTs, and computers employing the RS-232-C interface. The cables for connecting such equipment are described. These pinouts represent information on products not included in the first edition. However this reference can be combined with the first edition's pinout information to expand the number of cables that can be designed. For example, if a user desires to connect an Apple Macintosh to a Hayes Smartmodem, or an HP Laserjet printer to an IBM PC/ AT, IBM PS/2, workstation, or UNIX computer, the charts indicate which leads on the interfaces should be connected. Factors relating to buffering and flow control can be easily addressed. Consulting the options checklist makes installation of the systems easier and simplifies the selection of options in the areas of speed, parity, polarity, flow control, and echoplexing. Should questions or issues arise, the reader can consult Chapter 9, for assistance.

By providing a functional insight into RS-232 (and, correspondingly, CCITT V.24), *RS-232 Made Easy*, second edition, becomes a practical resource for a large spectrum of users. This spectrum includes users of data processing and data communication equipment, sales personnel, installers, technicians, consultants, and hobbyists who deal with all types of computer and communication systems. Although the approach is from the perspective of a microcomputer user, the systems covered range from personal computers to mainframe systems and their associated peripherals. Whatever the specifics, this book provides a single point of reference for all RS-232-related questions.

Note: Whenever RS-232 is mentioned, it refers to the latest revision of the standard, which is EIA 232-D.

This work reflects the author's views only, not those of Tandem Computer, with whom the author is affiliated.

Special thanks is given to all the vendors listed in Appendices F and G who provided the information necessary to compile the charts for this book.

M. D. Seyer

Acknowledgments

The author and publisher would like to extend a special thank you to the support organizations of the companies listed here. Individuals from the support staffs have collected and provided the most frequently asked questions they receive from their customers surrounding the connections of computers, modems, printers, and terminals.

AMP, Inc.
ECZEL Corporation
inmac
Lyben Computer Systems
NCR Direct Marketing Division
R + R Direct
The Drawing Board—Comp. Supp. Div.
TRW
Visible Computer Supply Corp.

Black Box Corporation
Heathkit
Jensen Tools
MiSCO
Pryor Catalog Sales Corp.
Specialized Products Company
Thomas Computer Corporation
Valiant UNIVERSALmicro

Thanks a million!

CHAPTER

1

introduction to
RS-232

So you finally decided to take the plunge! After all those trips to computer stores, many sleepless nights, and perhaps a signature loan or two, your personal computer or workstation is no longer just a dream. You own a computer.

Proudly, you carry your latest toy. Hurriedly, you unpack it. Nestled between pieces of cardboard and styrofoam lies the magic box of plastic, metal, and wires. Excitement and anticipation cause you to ignore your peers, parents, spouse, or progeny hollering in the background. You pull and tug. A sigh of relief escapes you as you lift the new computer from the box and find that it has no broken parts. Technocrat that you are, or assume you are, you debate whether or not to follow the assembly instructions. After coming to your senses and letting your pocketbook override your ego, you proceed to read the step-by-step procedures for device assembling. The instructions are outlined something like this:

1. Pop the top.
2. Scrape off the tape.
3. Guard the cards.
4. Put what you got in the slot.
5. Attach the cord to the mother board.
6. Label the cable.
7. Make sure the drive is alive.
8. Don't be sloppy with the floppy.
9. Twitch the switch.
10. Load the code . . .

Booting the disk, you display the directory for a catalog of available programs. If you're lucky, a game or two will be on the disk and save you a few quarters at the arcades. But more important, you get a feel for the machine's capabilities as you proceed to bang away at the keyboard. You grudgingly scan or read the tutorial manuals that were included with your system. You may even go as far as testing your skills at some Basic or C language programming. Being a novice, the extent of your programming is loop counting from 1 to 1009, adding and subtracting, printing your name on the screen 100 times, tweaking the speaker, or perhaps performing some simple graphics tricks such as drawing lines or randomly displaying dots on the screen.

After many lines of "successful" coding, you recognize that the box truly can do more than you can convince it to do. Yes, not only can this device be used to satisfy entertainment needs, but the literature indicates that it can also serve as a business tool.

For example, a professor may have purchased the system to keep track of students' grades, attendance records, major subjects, and other information. A review of computer periodicals discloses that large number of filing system programs exist to satisfy this need. An example is dBASE IV,[1] which provides an orderly means of computerizing your manual filing system. By entering the different records into the database management system, different reports may be generated—and printed, if a printer can be attached.

What about the financial wizards, such as brokers, accountants, investors, and bankers, who need quickly to calculate and recalculate figures and projections? "What if" questions have never been more easily answered than with the different spreadsheets available today. A program such as Lotus 1-2-3[2] can save countless hours of pencil scribblings and erasures.

An author or clerical person can hardly survive these days unless some type of word processor is utilized. The editing features allow for mistakes to be corrected prior to printing. The letter-quality or laser printer works extremely well, with no loss of text, when properly interfaced and optioned.

How about the terminal user who has a modem or an acoustic coupler connected to the terminal or microcomputer emulating a terminal? Miles or blocks away is a computer containing a variety of information just waiting to be accessed. A service bureau, such as the Dow Jones NEWS/RETRIEVAL databank or G.E. Tymshare systems can be accessed by terminals or computers with modems, properly optioned, supporting serial communications through an RS-232 port.

Whatever the situation, as you read through the supporting documentation provided with the system, you note continual references to computers, printers, plotters, and modems that employ serial interfaces conforming to the RS-232-C standard. The documentation indicates that an expanded set of functions is available to the user if the computer or terminal supports one of these interfaces.

You quickly grab your manuals and skim the table of contents to find the section on input/output. Your eyes light up when you reach the paragraph that confirms that your computer or terminals has a serial port or allows a circuit board to be installed that gives you this capability. Even though you know that RS-232 is available, you still don't know whether it is a cable, a piece of software, a circuit board, or a connector.

Further reading points out the existence of 8, 9, 10, 15, or 25 pins, control leads, connectors, and other components. So you ask again, "What is EIA-232?" Very simply, it is pins, connectors, control signals, timing signals, data signals, ground signals, and many other things. Simplicity has just become complexity. Wouldn't things be nice if we could make things simple again? Perhaps an analogy will help.

[1]dBASE IV is a trademark of Ashton-Tate.

[2]1-2-3 is a trademark of Lotus Corporation.

Let's first review what RS-232 is as outlined by the formal definition of the standard. The EIA standard, EIA-232-D (RS-232), is the interface between data terminal equipment (DTE, typically a computer or computer terminal) and data communication equipment (DCE, typically a modem), employing serial binary data interchange. As the definition states, RS-232 is simply a standard. This standard outlines the set of rules for exchanging data between business machines. These business machines can be terminals, printers, front-end processors, computers, workstations, or other equipment employing serial communications.

Why is there a need for a standard anyway? "Once upon a time," computers and terminals tried to exchange data. These business machines were usually located in different cities or buildings. However, due to their remoteness, a problem existed because one machine didn't know when to transmit characters and expect the receiving machine to get the data. Also, the characters, if not sent at the correct time, would become garbled and subsequently lost. If the characters were sent at the wrong rate of speed, bigger problems occurred. Due to the multitude of vendors supplying the business machines, different connectors came into use. When two business machines, such as a computer and printer or a terminal and modem, were to be connected, they couldn't be physically plugged together. The size and shape of the plugs were not the same. One might say that they were not "plug compatible." It is hard to fit a square peg into a round hole. Electrical incompatibilities were also a risk. It was a "shocking" experience to connect the wrong electrical signals. These problems exemplify the need for a standard to outline the control of when, where, and how the data were to be transferred between machines.

This condition could easily be equated to a train attempting to cross a body of water over a drawbridge. If the bridge is drawn, the train would plunge into the water. Should this occur, all cargo on the train would be lost. Should the train be on the wrong track, a head-on collision with an oncoming train could occur, causing havoc for both the dispatcher and receiver of the train. Another problem occurs if the train is on the wrong track. This could cause the train to miss the station it is trying to reach. The proper speed of travel should also be maintained for smooth operation on the railway system.

Wouldn't life be simpler if the track were in place and the train were on the right track, obeying the speed limit? If all these factors were tended to, the clerk at the destination depot would know when to expect the train, and the train would more than likely arrive at the station as planned.

It is obvious that without a standard set of rules for all trains to follow, transfer of cargo would not be an easy task. If the analogy is applied to our problem of business machines communicating to exchange data, you can begin to understand why the RS-232 standard was needed. Instead of manufacturers building their own unique railroads, a system standard could be established that everyone could follow. If properly adhered to, easy flow of trains could occur. This is the railway system that this book uses to describe the standard that EIA-232-D represents. It provides a thorough description and understanding of what RS-232 is, as well as a detailed functional insight into the components and thier interrelationships. The railway analogy is intended to provide both a layperson's understanding and a technician's resource. Once the analogy is understood, the reader will have obtained a working knowledge of the concepts of an RS-232 interface.

But, first, let us establish a framework for the communication terminology frequently used in serial communications.

2

communication

jargon

This chapter describes data communication terms. If you have a good understanding of such terminology, you may skip this chapter. Recognition of the terms and acronyms presented here is important, as they are very common in the industry today. Although they are not unique to RS-232, their relevance to the EIA-232 standard should be understood. The heading **Data communications** introduces technical communication definitions. These terms can easily be related to various components of the railway system mentioned in Chapter 1. Expressed in this fashion, the communication jargon will quickly become a part of your vocabulary. So, without further delay, let us get on track and start rolling!

Railroads have been exciting to people of all ages. They have been in operation for many years, yet rarely does a train crash or derail. This is even more significant when you consider that trains manage to travel in both directions on a single track without catastrophes. Sometimes there are two sets of tracks, which resolves many potential problems, but numerous single-rail systems still exist today.

What about the trains themselves? Most of them have an engine and a caboose, with the railroad cars between them. It is not uncommon to see trains with several engines and cabooses surrounding the cars. The makeup of the train plays an important role in our analogy, as you will see later.

The prerequisite for a train traveling between stations, or depots, is the construction of a railway system. There are three modes of operation on this system. The following paragraphs outline the way in which these rails can be laid.

The first case is where trains are going to be traveling in one direction only—north to south, for example. One set of rails will usually suffice. With this single track, the train can then only be traveling southbound at any time, as in Figure 2-1.

Data communications: The communication term for this mode is *simplex*. The set of rails (or, in our case, telephone lines) allowing a single direction

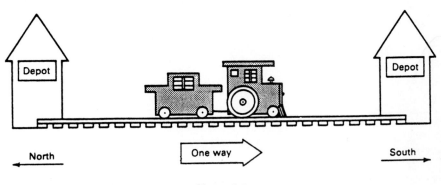

Figure 2-1

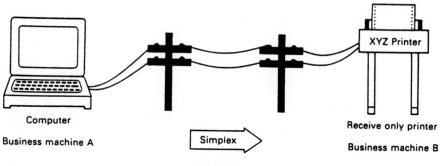

Computer

Business machine A

Simplex

Receive only printer

Business machine B

Figure 2-2

of traffic can be obtained from Ma Rail (Ma Bell) or any other provider of these systems. The providers of telephone lines are commonly referred to as *common carriers*. The pair of rails in our scenario corresponds to a telephone line that is simply a pair of wires. Characters are to be transmitted only from business machine A to business machine B over these lines, as pictured in Figure 2-2. The reverse direction is not allowed in a simplex environment. *Simplex* can now be described as a mode allowing transmission of data in one direction only. This is usually accomplished by using a two-wire facility.

The second type of railway system can be constructed when trains need to travel in both directions, north and south. A single track can still handle the traffic. However, only one train can travel across the rails in a given direction at any given time (nonsimultaneously). Otherwise, a northbound train and a southbound train would collide, causing a derailment. So, train traffic can be either northbound or southbound, but not both simultaneously, as shown in Figure 2-3.

Data communications: The term for this arrangement is *half-duplex*, or *HDX*. Characters may be transmitted in both directions, but not simultaneously, over a single pair of wires, as shown in Figure 2-4. This is also known as two-way

North

Which way now?

South

Figure 2-3

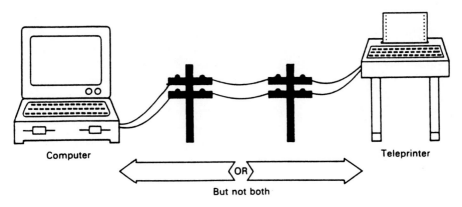

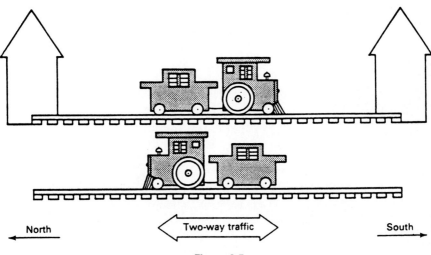

Figure 2-4

alternate transmission. The direction of traffic is alternated to utilize the single pair of wires efficiently.

Sometimes we want both northbound and southbound trains to be able to use the tracks at the same time. This is the stipulation for our third type of railway system. There are two ways of meeting this requirement. A two-track railway system can be built, with one track for northbound trains, and the other for southbound traffic. This system allows trains to travel in both directions simultaneously. The use of separate tracks eliminates the possibility of head-on collisions (Figure 2-5).

Data communications: The term for this transmission mode is *full-duplex*, or *FDX*. Characters can be transmitted in both directions, simultaneously, on a four-wire facility (two sets of tracks require four rails).

Figure 2-5

The only problem with this railway system is that the cost of buying or building the tracks can be very expensive. With a two-track system, more resources are required. The more rails the crew has to spike to the railroad ties, the greater the cost of the system for depot interconnections. Maybe this is what the common carriers are referring to when they warn that "spikes on the lines are costly"? Actually spikes on the lines are unwanted noises that cause errors in the data streams being transmitted. Usually, a retransmission of the errored data is required.

There is a way to allow data to be transmitted in both directions, simultaneously, on a two-wire facility. Because explanation of this technique is beyond the scope of this book, you are encouraged to refer to *Technical Aspects of Data Communications** by John E. McNamara for an explanation of FDX transmission over two-wire facilities.

We have described the requirements for three different railway systems that allow trains to travel between depots. It is important to realize that up to this point we haven't physically connected the depots; we have merely outlined the construction requirements. Later in this discussion we describe how we actually establish the connection of the depots that are separated by a body of water.

Data communications: *Simplex*, *HDX*, *FDX*, and *two-* or *four-wire facilities* relate to the communication modes available through the *common carrier* or telephone networks. The actual types of telephone connections are discussed in greater detail when we outline the procedures for connecting two business machines (or depots).

The goal of our train (character) is to get from station to station (business machine to business machine). These business machines could range from computers or printers to terminals. They are commonly referred to as data terminal equipment (DTE). Between the stations (DTEs) lies a body of water. To allow the trains to travel between stations, the railway system must be established. A decision must be made regarding a permanent or temporary system across the water. This decision is based on the projected number of trains that are expected to cross the water.

If the anticipated traffic load is rather large, we may elect to build a permanent railway structure across the water. The projected heavy traffic loads require that these rails be of good quality and available at all times. Generally, the quality of these tracks is proportional to their cost. The primary advantage of a permanent railway bridge is its full-time availability. The owner has use of the facility 24 hours a day.

Data communications: The technical term for our permanent railway system, or bridge, is a *private line*. Private lines, often called dedicated lines, are generally contracted for on a monthly basis from the different common carriers. The 24-hour availability of these lines allows transmission of large quantities of characters.

*Bedford, Mass.: Digital Press, 1978.

Often, the traffic volume isn't great enough to dictate the need for a permanent structure across the water. In this case, a temporary structure is available: A drawbridge will be accessible by each train station for use as needed. When trains need to cross the water, a connection is established between stations by lowering the drawbridge. This connection is broken by raising the bridge after all trains have crossed. The drawbridge will then be available to other trains. This setup is attractive because the stations pay for the use of the bridge only while it is lowered. Thus, if anticipated traffic volumes are low, a temporary facility should be considered.

Data communications: This drawbridge corresponds to the *dial-up* or *switched lines* that can be used to connect two business machines (DTEs). A call is placed between business machines using the normal telephone network and maintained as long as required for all characters to be transmitted. Upon completion, the connection is broken by hanging up the phones.

Data communications: Thus, data can be transmitted over *dial-up* or *private-line* facilities.

Both of these facilities (bridges) pass through the phone companies' switches, or central offices. These facilities are sometimes referenced as *data communication equipment* (*DCE*). The major component of DCE is a *modem*. The word *modem* is a contraction of *modulator-demodulator*. A modem is a unit incorporating a technique for placing and receiving computer signals over the common carriers' communication facility.

These modems should be viewed in our analogy as booths where traffic dispatchers, or patrolmen, reside. There is a booth at both the origination and destination locations. The dispatcher at the originating booth directs trains onto the tracks of the bridge to allow them to cross the water; the dispatcher at the far-end booth transfers the trains from the bridge to the train station.

The dispatchers also let the depots know if the bridge is available, and sometimes they provide the speed limit at which the trains can travel. The smooth operation of trains between station and dispatcher is accomplished by using common signals. Both the station and dispatcher must have a set of signals that they can generate and recognize to know when the trains can depart or arrive. The signals used to control this traffic are the major topics of the subsequent chapters of this book.

Having established that the railway system can be built in several ways and with different modes of operation, let us explore what the trains consist of and their role in our analogy. The trains are important due to the fact that they contain the cargo. After all, the cargo dictated the need for the railway system in the first place.

In order for cargo to be shipped from one location to another (depot to depot), certain types of railroad cars are needed. The most common cars used today are boxcars and flatcars. We will use these in our comparison.

At the depot, the train is put together with a combination of boxcars and flatcars. The number of cars allowed per train varies between depots. This variance

Figure 2-6

causes problems when cargo is to be shipped on these cars to another depot. The receiving depot, not knowing the number of cars to expect, will never know if the entire shipment was received. So the originator must notify the destination depot of the makeup and number of cars in the train. Knowing this, the destination depot can determine if the number of cars that arrived is the same as the number sent (Figure 2-6).

Data communications: The selection of boxcars and flatcars was intentional. These two car types allow a graphic representation of characters that business machines transmit. A character can be viewed as a specific number of 1s and 0s. The specific number of 1s and 0s representing characters is established by the machine manufacturers. Whether they be terminals, printers, or computers, this number must be consistent at both ends before data can be exchanged between two devices. Typically, these 1s and 0s are viewed as representing two positions, on and off. Pictorially, Figure 2-7 could represent a character.

Understanding what particular character these 1s and 0s represent is not important for now. There exist character code sets that determine the specific makeup of any given character. One of the most prominent is ASCII. Any given set of 1s and 0s represents a specific character. Character makeup can be derived from available ASCII charts. The important point to note is that each 1 and 0 makes up a tiny bit of the whole character. For ease of reference, we will call them *bits*, which just happens to be the official name for them, though this word *bit* originated as a contraction of "binary digit."

If we assume that a boxcar is a 1 bit and the flatcar is a 0 bit, our picture would be very much the same as before (Figure 2-8).

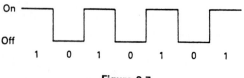

Figure 2-7

Figure 2-8

Data communications: The following discussion is unique to a communication technique termed *asynchronous transmission*, also known as *start/stop transmission*.

A train would not be complete without an engine and a caboose. When you see an engine coming down the track, you know that railroad cars are close behind. This engine signifies the beginning of the train. In our example, the engine would be followed by the specific number of boxcars and flatcars previously discussed. To signify the end of the train, a caboose is attached. The next trains will consist of the same engine-cars-caboose sequence. Often, more than one caboose and engine are attached. But for simplicity, we only will use one engine and one caboose per train, as in Figure 2-9.

Data communications: In technical terms, the engine, which signifies the beginning of the train, represents what is known as a *start bit*. The start bit informs the business machine that data bits (boxcars and flatcars) will follow. After the data bits, a caboose is attached to indicate the end of the character. This caboose is termed a *stop bit*. As you can see in Figures 2-10 and 2-11, our train (or *character*) consists of a *start bit*, *data bits*, and a *stop bit*, which correspond to our engine-boxcar/flatcar-caboose sequence.

Figure 2-9

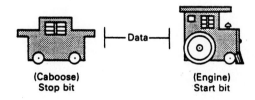

(Caboose)   **(Engine)**
Stop bit   **Start bit**

Figure 2-10

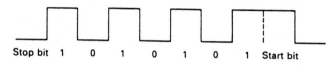

Stop bit 1   0   1   0   1   0   1 Start bit

Figure 2-11

Data communications: The fact that the stop bit may or may not be at the same level as the last bit of the character is not important. Simply keep in mind that the stop bit is a unique bit that trails the data bits.

What happens if the wrong type of car is used in a train, if boxcars are used instead of flatcars? How does the destination depot know that some of the cars are wrong? The problem could be resolved in the following fashion: No matter how many boxcars are in the train, there should always be an odd number of boxcars. In reality, railroad cars are not arbitrarily added to keep the train to a consistent length. But, for ease of understanding, we will assume this in the analogy. The goal is to permit the depot at the destination to confirm that the proper railroad cars were received. The originator of the train makes this possible simply by counting the number of boxcars in the train. If it is an even number, the engineer adds another boxcar, making the number odd. If the number is odd, the engineer adds a flatcar. These actions not only keep the number of boxcars odd but also keep the trains the same length. As long as the receiving depot (computer or terminal) knows that an odd number of boxcars is supposed to arrive, a count can be made to determine if the correct train arrived at the depot. If the boxcar count is an even number at the final destination, the receiving depot knows that the correct cars were not received (Figure 2-12).

Data communications: This concept of keeping an odd number of bits (boxcars) in a character (train) is known as *parity*. The boxcar or flatcar that was added to keep the number odd is known as the *parity bit*. By counting the number of 1s (boxcars), the receiving depot does a *parity check*. If the number of 1

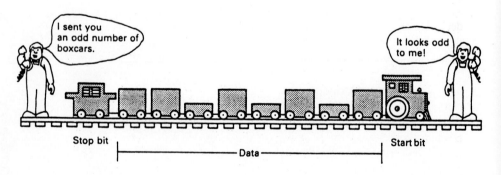

Figure 2-12

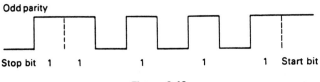

Figure 2-13

bits is even a *parity error* has occurred, making the received character incorrect. The causes of parity errors are numerous, some of the more common causes being poor-quality communication lines, power surges, and poor interface connections. Any of these conditions may cause the flipping of one of the character's bits as it travels over the communication facility. A similar scheme could just as easily have been chosen to check for an even number of 1s. This is how the terms *odd* and *even parity* came into existence (Figure 2-13).

Data communications: The concept of enclosing a character with a *start* and *stop bit* is known as *asynchronous transmission*. The start bit (engine) indicates to the receiving depot the time to start looking for the cars of the train; the stop bit (caboose) lets the depot know when the entire train had arrived. The "timing" for the beginning and end of the train is provided by the engine and caboose. Because of this, it is said that, in asynchronous transmission, the start and stop bits provide the *timing*. Each character (train) is individually *synchronized* (timed).

As the need for shipping more cargo came about, more trains were needed. However, the existing railway system wasn't adequate for these trains. What was needed was a railway system that allowed both longer and faster trains. Also, operational costs skyrocketed because one engine and one caboose were required for every train (character). Valuable time on the track was being wasted for engines and cabooses when it could have been used for more boxcars and flatcars.

So, the railway system was improved to allow faster trains and to provide a means of combining little trains into larger trains. This reduced the number of engines and cabooses required, freeing up more track time. Because of the increased speeds and sizes of the trains, a speed limit was needed for safety purposes. The decision was made to allow the railway system to establish the speed limit. The depots agreed to abide by this limit. If properly adhered to, the depots would know exactly how fast the longer trains should be traveling (Figure 2-14).

Data communications: This transmission scheme is known as *synchronous transmission*. Usually, the communications network component (railway system) established the timing (speed limit) at which the data bits would be transmitted. Better methods of determining whether the data (trains) arrived correctly were also developed. These methods are termed *protocols*. Communication protocols, having no direct bearing on RS-232, are not discussed in this book, as they are extremely complex and would complicate the discussion of RS-232.

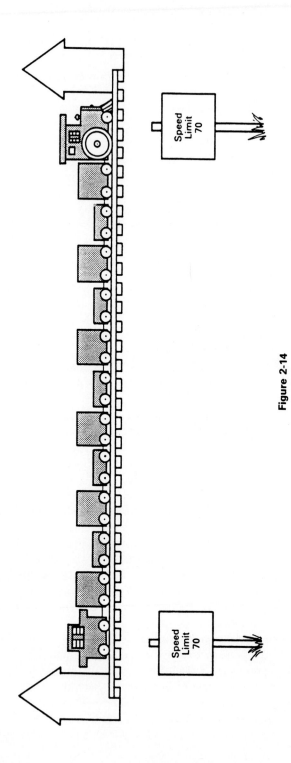

Figure 2-14

16

Furthermore, because the bulk of microcomputers and terminals in the market today use low speeds or unsophisticated protocols, we have chosen to concentrate on asynchronous transmission environments. However, synchronous transmission will be discussed again when the timing elements of RS-232 are explained. Elsewhere, unless specifically mentioned, you can assume that we are discussing an asynchronous environment.

At this point, you should have a general understanding of the *format* and *timing* of *characters* in an *asynchronous* environment. The following is a quick review of our analogy as it relates to data communication jargon.

1. The railroad tracks are the telephone lines or communication facilities.
2. *Data* transmission occurs when the trains travel along the tracks.
3. Tracks allowing trains to go in one direction only are termed *simplex*.
4. Tracks allowing train traffic in both directions but not simultaneously are termed *half-duplex*, or *HDX*.
5. Tracks allowing tracks to travel in both directions simultaneously are referred to as *full-duplex*, or *FDX*.
6. *Asynchronous transmission* takes place in an environment in which *characters* (boxcars and flatcars) have a *start bit* (engine) and a *stop bit* (caboose) to indicate the beginning and end of the *data bits*.
7. *Data terminal equipment* (*DTE*) is considered to be computers, terminals, or printers—depots and stations in our analogy.
8. *Data communication equipment* (*DCE*) is considered to be the *modems* between the computers, terminals, and printers—denoted as booths in our analogy.

Although these terms are not unique to RS-232, their understanding is a prerequisite to a true comprehension of the need for and operation of the RS-232 interface in a communication environment. Now that you are on track, let's proceed on down the rails. All aboard!

REVIEW QUESTIONS*

1. A mode of transmission in which each character is individually timed is _____.
2. _____ facilities allow transmission in one direction only.
3. The distinction between half-duplex and full-duplex is that HDX allows traffic in both directions nonsimultaneously/simultaneously, while FDX allows two-way traffic nonsimultaneously/simultaneously.
4. Common carriers provide _____ for data transmission.

*Answers to Review Questions will be found in Chapter 9.

5. A business machine can be one of many devices. List three of the most prevalent: _____, _____, _____.

6. DTE, potentially either terminals, printers, or computers, is the acronym for _____.

7. DCE, generally modems, is the acronym for _____.

8. The _____ interface is the interface between DTE and DCE employing serial binary data interchange.

9. A type of line that is only temporary in nature is called a _____ line.

10. _____ lines are used when traffic volume between two locations is extremely high.

11. _____ is the contraction for modulator-demodulator.

12. A _____ converts computer signals for transmission over the common carriers' communication facilities.

13. _____ are used to control the exchange of data between DTE and DCE.

14. The scheme of counting the number of bits in a character to determine whether it is odd or even is known as _____.

15. The bits surrounding the data bits of a character are the _____ and _____ bits.

CHAPTER

3

asynchronous modems and RS-232

With a general understanding of some basic communication terminology, we are ready for a detailed explanation of the specifics of the RS-232-C interface. This will be accomplished by building upon our basic railway system analogy. At the end of this chapter is a summary of the railway system and its corresponding communication-environment counterparts.

The function of RS-232-interface leads depends on the type of communication facility used, dial-up or private lines. This chapter focuses on a dial-up environment.

In what areas would a dial-up environment be appropriate? A dial-up connection is normally used, for example, to access a database service, such as The Source.* The information available from The Source, such as commodity and stock quotes, is to be shared by a large terminal or computer population. Typically, access to the service is for short periods of time. For example, a user may desire a small report once each day from the service. Over a dial-up facility, the user connects to a port, retrieves the information, logs off, and then disconnects from the port. The port is now available for other users to access. Dial-up facilities fit nicely where there are low traffic volumes per user. Many different dial-up facilities, such as Telenet† and TYMNET,‡ are available for accessing the different services. Charges for these access services generally are per minute. The cost of these facilities in conjunction with traffic volumes determines when dial-up lines are more economical than other facilities, such as private lines. These two major factors influence the use of dial-up connections in the following types of service offerings:

1. Public databases
2. Service bureaus
3. Message services
4. Computer-to-computer data exchanges

These are but a few of the many areas in which RS-232 is used in a dial-up environment, but they are the ones covered in this chapter.

In our treatment of the interactions of RS-232 leads, the train depots correspond to our computer, terminals, or printers (DTE) and the booths to our modems (DCE). These leads are separated by category, such as data, control, ground, and timing, for ease of learning. Our discussion begins with the data leads necessary for transmitting information.

*The Source is a service mark of Source Telecomputing Corp.
†Telenet is a service mark of GTE Corp.
‡TYMNET is a service mark of McDonnell Douglas Corporation.

A dispatcher knows that there are two kinds of trains at a depot, departing and arriving trains. Departing trains have a preassigned track, say, track 2. All leaving trains will depart on this track.

Once they cross the water and reach the far-end toll booth, the trains are switched to a different track, track 3, which is set aside for arriving trains. The dispatcher, by assigning separate tracks, can monitor each and see if any trains are departing to or arriving from the booths and drawbridge.

RS-232:   In an RS-232 environment, the departing trains are the *transmitted data*, and the arriving trains are the *received data*. All data (trains) departing from the station (business machine) will go across a track called the *transmitted data lead*. A track (lead), known as the *received data lead*, is set aside for all arriving trains (data) to use. In an RS-232 interface, 25 *pins*, or leads, are available for use by the DTE and DCE (see Figure A-1). However, only a limited number of leads are used as "tracks" for data transfer. Each lead has a preassigned function. For example, the transmitted data go across pin 2, whereas the received data arrive on pin 3. By monitoring pin 2, transmitted data can be detected. To check if data are being received, pin 3 should be monitored. The tools available to monitor these and other leads are discussed in Appendix E.

Keep in mind that at one end of the track, the train is considered to be departing, but once it crosses the bridge, it is considered an arriving train at the destination depot.

RS-232:   Transmitted data at the originating DTE are on pin 2 of the *RS-232 interface*, whereas, at the receiving DTE, these same data arrive on pin 3, as shown in Figure 3-1. Transmitted data are "output" at one end and become "input" at the other end.

For example, when a terminal is connected to The Source, the keyboard operator's typed characters are passed from the terminal to the modem on pin 2. These output data are transmitted over the communication line to the far-end

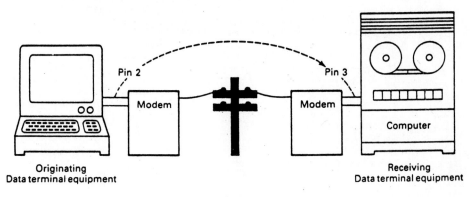

Originating   Receiving
Data terminal equipment   Data terminal equipment

Figure 3-1

modem. At this end, the received data are presented to the computer as input on pin 3.

Our bridge is a drawbridge. Control of the tracks must be maintained. The depot (DTE) must know when the bridge is in place. The booth attendant must inform the dispatcher at the station when the train (data) can be moved (transmitted) over the bridge (communication facilities). To keep our trains from going into the deep, the drawbridge had better be lowered between the two depots when each train reaches it. Lowering the drawbridge corresponds to establishing a telephone connection between DTE locations.

As a train approaches the water, it must let the other depot know that the bridge must be lowered. Each train station is equipped with a bell that produces a loud ring. Let's set up a procedure for indicating when to lower the bridge. Whenever a booth (modem) hears the ringing from the distant station, this should be interpreted as an indication that the bridge should be lowered. We will call this our *ring indicator*. The scenario would be similar to Figure 3-2.

RS-232:   In the actual RS-232 interface, pin 22 is known as the *ring indicator*. When the number of the telephone associated with a modem is dialed, this lead will indicate that ringing is occurring. It will go on and off in direct correlation with the phone rings. This is an indication that a request is being made for establishment of a dial-up connection.

The booth operator at the distant end hears the ringing. However, he doesn't want to lower the bridge for the train to arrive unless he knows for certain that there is someone at the depot ready to receive the train. If the train arrived while the depot was not being operated, no one could receive and inspect it, and the train could get lost in the railroad yard. So, as a rule, the booth will not lower the bridge unless the station is manned.

RS-232:   This signal from the depot (DTE) is termed *data terminal ready* (*DTR*). Pin 20 is a control lead or signal used by the DTE to indicate that the modem

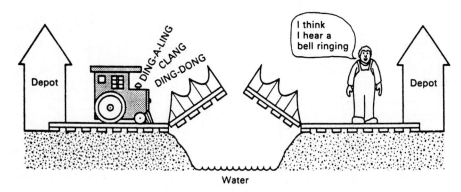

Water

Figure 3-2

should answer the phone. Some modems are equipped with the capability to answer the call automatically if pin 20 is on. This feature, termed *auto-answer*, allows for terminal users to establish a telephone connection with an unmanned computer site. Although not an RS-232 term, *auto-answer* utilizes pins on the RS-232 interface. Generally, if the machine's power is on, DTR will be on, enabling calls to be answered for the connection to be established.

Let's assume that the train station is manned by someone who turns on a light when a request is received to signal that the booth attendant should lower the bridge. When the booth operator hears the bell ringing, he lowers his half of the bridge.

At the originating station, the booth operator can tell that the remote operator has lowered his part of the bridge. He checks to see if his end should be lowered in the same fashion. If his station has given him the proper signal, he lowers the bridge. If the station failed to pass him the signal, he refuses to lower the bridge. The far-end booth operator waits to see if the bridge was actually lowered. If the bridge was not lowered, after a period of time, the operator raises his end so that other trains might have access to the bridge.

RS-232:   This is referred to as *timing out*. Timing out occurs if the proper signal (DTR) is not present at one of the ends. The *communication path* will not be established. However, if the DTR signals are present at both ends, the connection is maintained. To disconnect a dial-up connection, either end merely drops DTR (pin 20).

Generally, most commercially available databases, time-sharing systems, and other services are set up to support auto-answer. This allows for unattended operation of the service. For example, to access Dow Jones services, you merely dial the phone number of a port on the computer. Because the port is optioned for auto-answer, DTR will be on, allowing the modem to answer the call automatically. By answering the call, the modem returns a high-pitched answer-back tone to the originator. Upon detection of this tone, the originator enters data mode manually, or automatically if the modem can accomplish this, completing the connection. DTR determines if the connection is maintained or not.

Some modems offer auto-dial capabilities. If these types of modems are used, the phone number can be dialed automatically. Upon detection of the answer-back tone, the modem automatically completes the connection without human intervention. The Hayes Smartmodem* and Ven-Tel MD212 Plus† are two such modems. The Ven-Tel, for example, allows either keyboard entry of a phone number or a selection of prestored numbers to be dialed. This is accomplished without the need for a telephone handset. The presence of DTR (pin 20) allows the connections to be established and maintained. If the far-end computer or terminal doesn't have DTR on, the modem will not answer the call. In the case of auto-dialers, the ringing will continue forever unless intelligence is added. The originating modem should moni-

---

*Smartmodem is a trademark of Hayes Microcomputer Products.

†MD212 Plus is a trademark of Ven-Tel Inc.

tor the number of rings and abort the call after a preset number of unsuccessful rings. The intelligence in the modem could allow for an alternate number or numbers to be called if a "no answer" condition occurs.

If the dialed number is busy, the modem can retry the call until a successful connection is made. Features such as auto-dial, storing numbers, and counting the number of rings are made possible by putting intelligence, generally microprocessors, into the modems.

This intelligence has to be able to monitor the obvious signal of DTR, pin 20, but also has to take into account previously discussed RS-232 signals. For example, the number to be called, input on the keyboard of the terminal or computer, must be transmitted from the terminal or computer to the modem. This number, output on pin 2 (transmitted data), must be recognized by the modem as a digit to be dialed. The modem must known when all of the digits are received to make a valid call. Usually, the terminal operator ends the number with a carriage return, which serves as a delimiter indicating that the modem should dial that number. These digits from the terminal are standard ASCII representations of numbers. The modem must translate the ASCII characters into dial pulses or Touch-Tone* digits that the standard phone network can understand. This is because the telephone network has no way of knowing whether a machine or a human is placing a call. It only knows Touch-Tone or rotary-dialed pulses.

How does an "intelligent" modem indicate that a busy condition, no answer, some other problem, or a successful call has occurred? Recall that the terminal or computer receives its characters on pin 3, received data, over the RS-232 interface. The modem must interpret the condition and pass the appropriate message to the terminal on pin 3.

Once the call setup has taken place, the intelligence of the modem must become almost transparent and allow the modem to behave like the standard asynchronous modem. In this mode, modulation and demodulation of the character take place as discussed in Chapter 2. The RS-232 signals now are used according to the standard.

Assume that the bridge is successfully lowered to allow trains across. To let each depot know this, each booth gives a signal to the depots indicating that the bridge is lowered.

RS-232:   The term for this lead is *data set ready (DSR)*. This signal is on pin 6. In a dial-up environment, DSR is asserted to the proper voltage, that is, goes high, if a communication path has been established.

RS-232:   The telephone connection is now established. Here is a quick review of the sequence of events.

*Touch-Tone is a trademark of AT&T.

1. The phone number is dialed.
2. *Ring indicator* (pin 22) is on at the distant end.
3. If the terminal or computer is on, DTR is on, allowing the call to be answered. This is termed *auto-answer*. When DTR is on and *ring indicator* is detected, the call will be automatically answered.
4. Once answered, each *modem* will raise its *data set ready* lead as an indication that a line is present for that station.
5. The originating station is on; its DTR lead is on (high), so the connection can be maintained. Usually, if a terminal is involved in originating the call, a data button on the phone must be pushed to maintain the connection.
6. The connection is now established.
7. Data may now be exchanged between the two devices.

When the transfer of information is completed, the connection is broken when either end drops DTR. The terminal operator may drop DTR generally in one of three ways:

1. Manually disconnect (hang up) the call.
2. Place the terminal into a mode known as "local mode." This is contrasted with being "on-line." While in on-line mode, DTR is on. By placing the terminal off-line or in local mode, DTR is lowered, automatically causing the modem to drop the connection.
3. Unplugging or turning off the terminal or computer. Lack of power lowers DTR, causing a disconnect by the modem.

The far-end computer can also generally break the connection in one of several ways:

1. If someone unplugs the computer (heaven forbid!), DTR will go off, causing the modem to hang up.
2. The program executing in the computer can generally control the DTR signal and bring it down at will.
3. Often, the unit handling the communications for the computer, known as a front-end processor (FEP), can recognize a disconnect character from the far-end terminal or computer. Generally, in an asynchronous environment, a Control-D character sequence will be received and interpreted by the host computer or FEP as a disconnect sequence. Once this sequence is received, the FEP will drop DTR, causing the modem to disconnect.

Data terminal ready plays a major role in the establishment, maintenance, and disconnecting of a dial-up connection.

For now, let's keep DTR on to maintain the line. So far, the train is right on schedule. Several types of railway systems have been discussed. One-track, one-way (simplex); one-track, two-way, nonsimultaneous (half-duplex); and one- or two-track, two-way, simultaneous (full-duplex) paths were explained in Chapter 2. For now, ignore the simplex and FDX facilities for transmitting data; we are going to focus on half-duplex (HDX).

In this mode, the bridge across the water has only one set of tracks. Things could really get messy if we didn't control when and in which direction each train would cross the bridge. The booth attendants must maintain control of the situation to prevent trains from colliding and ending up in the water.

The depots, with trains wanting to cross the bridge, are in contention for the right-of-way on the tracks. When they want to send the trains (data), they should turn on the engines' headlights, signaling a request to send the trains across. The headlights can be seen all the way across the water. So, if the local booth attendant sees the lights initiated by the station (DTE), he knows that the right-of-way was desired. However, the booth attendant had better check to see if the far end has the right to the track prior to giving this privilege to the local depot. Because the engine headlights are so bright, he is easily able to see if the far end had control of the track or not. If he detected a light, he would not honor the request to send (Figure 3-3). If, however, no light was detected from the far end, the booth attendant would give a clear-to-send signal to its station. The depot could send as many trains across the bridge as desired because it had control of the bridge.

Once all of the trains had crossed the bridge, the sending depot operator would turn out the headlights as an indication that he was relinquishing control of the track. Either end could then request to send trains across the bridge and be given a clear-to-send signal by the booth attendants. Obviously, the booth attendants play an important role in controlling the smoothness of operation over the railway system.

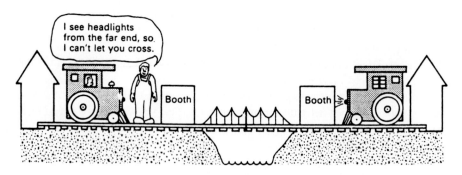

Figure 3-3

RS-232:   In a half-duplex environment, contention for the communication facilities exists. A typical modem found in this class is a 202* type. The 202 is a Bell System modem type that operates in a half-duplex fashion at 1200 bits per second (bps). Modems that operate in the same environment are said to be 202-compatible or look-alikes. Control of this two-way, nonsimultaneous path is handled by a DTE-DCE interaction. DTE-1 raises a *request to send* (*RTS*), pin 4, if it has data to transmit. This causes a signal to be passed across the telephone line, detectable at the other end on pin 8. The signal at the far end is termed *data carrier detect (DCD)* or *received line signal detector*. It is important to note that although separate pins are used for different functions on the interface, this does not imply that a separate communication facility for each is required. In reality, all signals are passed over the same path. Locally, however, the modem first checks its own DCD lead, pin 8. If its DCD is not on, a *clear-to-send* (*CTS*) signal is passed to the local DTE-1. DTE-1 now has control of the facilities and can transmit data on the proper lead (pin 2). However, if the local modem detects that pin 8 is on, a CTS signal will not be given to DTE-1. The fact that DCD is on is an indication that the far end has control of the line. Figure 3-4 pictorially represents the interaction of the leads.

The following summarizes the DTE-DCE interaction.

1. RTS (pin 4) is raised by DTE.
2. DCD (pin 8) is checked by the modem to see if the far-end DTE has its RTS high.
3. If the far end's RTS is high (DCD is on), the modem does not give CTS, and the DTE drops RTs and goes back to step 1. If DCD is off, it proceeds to step 4.
4. If DCD is off, the local modem (DCE), after a slight delay, gives a CTS (pin 5) signal to the DTE.
5. DTE then presents data on the transmitted data lead (pin 2), and the modem transmits this to the far end.
6. The receiving modem puts the received data on pin 3 for presentation to the destination DTE.
7. The originating DTE continues with RTS held high until all data are transmitted. Then it drops its RTS, which drops DCD at the far end and CTS locally, causing the line to be idle once again.
8. Either DTE can now raise RTS to obtain control of the line.

What if our bridge across the water allows two-way simultaneous traffic? We don't have to worry about who has control of the track because each station has its own path across the bridge. To save time and capitalize on our two-way concurrent traffic possibilities, the dispatchers should turn their headlights on and leave them on while the stations are manned. Thus, each booth attendant will always give his

*The 202 is a trademark of the Bell System.

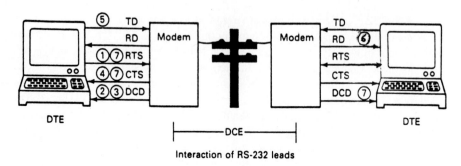

Interaction of RS-232 leads

Figure 3-4

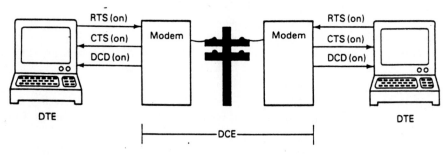

Figure 3-5

depot a clear-to-send signal, even though he detects headlights from across the bridge. Now the stations can send traffic across a bridge without worrying about obtaining the right-of-way on the bridge.

RS-232:   This is termed *full-duplex*. Several modems offer full-duplex capabilities. For example, a 103J*-compatible modem operates FDX at 300 bps. A 212A* look-alike modem generally offers two speeds, 300 and 1200 bps, both available in a full-duplex mode. Both DTEs have RTS held high, both modems give CTS constantly, and both modems have DCD high because the far end's RTS lead is on constantly (Figure 3-5).

The trains are really smokin' along the tracks now. But what happens if the bridge malfunctions or the operators vacate the stations? Obviously, all traffic should cease. The booth attendant turns off his CTS signal and raises the bridge. To start traffic again, the entire procedure must be repeated.

RS-232:   If DTR goes off (loses power, for instance), the modem will disconnect the line. The modem will no longer have DSR high as an indication to

*103J and 212A are trademarks of the Bell System.

the DTE that a connection is established. Whether the communication mode is HDX or FDX, the procedure for the dial-up connection will have to be repeated for further data transmission.

We have just described the role of several RS-232 leads in a dial-up environment. Following is a review of the interface leads, separated by function. By separating the leads into distinct functions and noting their directions, the serial interface can be easily understood. This will become more evident as we proceed into areas of cross connections.

Note the last two interface leads in the chart in Figure 3-6. The *ground leads* are important for electrical reasons. Pin 1 is usually a frame ground to keep people from receiving shocks in the event of electrical shorts or problems. This is the same principle that is applied to the grounded wall outlets of your home. Pin 7 is termed *signal ground* and is used as a reference for all other signals on the interface. For example, the signal on pin 7 establishes the common ground reference potential for all the other circuits except pin 1. The function of these two leads is easily understood.

Throughout this text, abbreviations for the different RS-232 leads are used. These acronyms, such as DTR, DSR, and RTS, are used for ease of recognition of the leads. In practice, the EIA-232-D and CCITT V.24 standards use totally different nomenclatures. For example, in RS-232, the categories of leads, ground, data, control, and timing are referred to as the A, B, C, and D circuits. The international standard denotes the various pins by numbers such as 101, 102, 108.2, and so on. Although these standards outline the precise labeling of the leads, the industry usually refers to them by either pin assignments, such as pin 20, or the acronyms used in this text, such as DTR. This is why only pin numbers and acronyms are used here. Refer to Appendix A (Figure A-1) for the precise circuit nomenclature, if needed.

The remainder of this chapter is devoted to the subject of modem tests. Generally, asynchronous modems offer diagnostics to the user that can aid in a quick determination of problems when they occur in a configuration. Problems are evident when the data being received or transmitted are garbled. Transmission of

Function	Pin	Lead name (abbreviation)	Direction
Data	2	Transmitted data (TD)	From DTE
Data	3	Received data (RD)	From DCE
Control	4	Request to send (RTS)	From DTE
Control	5	Clear to send (CTS)	From DCE
Control	8	Data carrier detect (DCD)	From DCE
Control	6	Data set ready (DSR)	From DCE
Control	20	Data terminal ready (DTR)	From DTE
Control	22	Ring indicator (RI)	From DCE
Ground	1	Protective ground (PG)	N/A
Ground	7	Signal ground (SG)	N/A

Figure 3-6

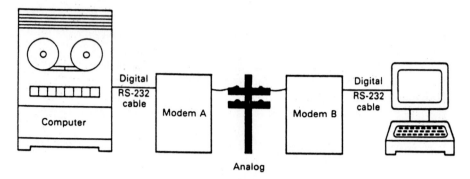

Figure 3-7

the data may be restricted by a faulty modem. To understand the tests available to isolate the problem, a general description of signal forms must be known. In review, the function of a modem, when transmitting, is to convert (modulate) a digital signal from a computer, terminal, or printer onto the analog telephone network. When receiving, the purpose is to convert the received data back into their original digital form (Figure 3-7).

To perform the conversions, each modem is equipped with a transmitter and a receiver (Figure 3-8).

To determine if a modem is faulty, four tests are available: analog loopback, digital loopback, remote digital loopback, and self-test. They are generally activated by pressing buttons on the front of the modems.

Analog Loopback (AL).   If the AL button is pressed at modem A, its transmitter is looped back to its receiver as it is disconnected from the line (Figure 3-9). Anything transmitted through the modem will be immediately echoed back through the receiver. Anything output by the computer on pin 2 will be received on pin 3 (received data). This allows for testing the output and input functions on the analog side of the modem, consequently terms *analog loopback*. If the output by the computer doesn't match the input it receives by the loopback, the local modem has a problem.

Digital Loopback (DL).   If the DL button is pressed at modem A, its receiver is looped back on the RS-232 side to its transmitter (Figure 3-10). Concep-

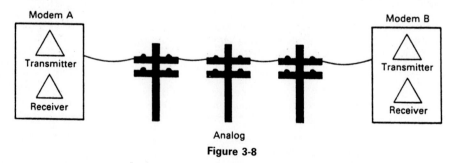

Figure 3-8

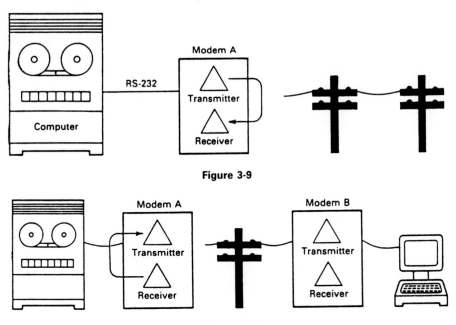

Figure 3-9

Figure 3-10

tually, anything that is received by modem A from the far end (modem B) will be looped from pin 3 on the RS-232 side to pin 2 or will transmit data back to modem B. The data may never actually appear on the RS-232 pins, but the concept applies. Even though the terminal at modem B will be originating the characters to be echoed, someone must be physically present at modem A to push the DL button. From this you can see that coordination at each end is required. This test is normally done after the local modem has passed the AL test. If the results of the DL test are negative—that is, if transmitted characters are not the same as received characters—the far-end modem could have a problem.

Remote Digital Loopback (RDL).   By pressing this button, the need for the manual pressing of the DL button at the far-end modem is eliminated. If the RDL button is pressed on modem A, a signal is passed to modem B that causes it automatically to go into DL mode, functioning as previously described. This capability eliminates a lot of the coordination efforts.

Self-Test (ST).   This button relieves the terminal operator or computer of the requirement of generating a test pattern. By pressing the ST button, a test pattern is generated by the modem. Depending on the setting of the AL, DL, and RDL buttons, different sides of the modems will be tested, analog or digital. Generally, a light or other indication will flash on the front of the modem if an error is received. The difference between a self-test pattern and a computer- or terminal-generated pattern is that the electronics will automatically catch any errors. Normally, the terminal operator or computer would have to compare transmitted patterns with received patterns to determine problems.

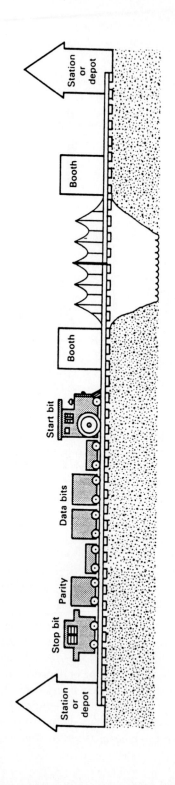

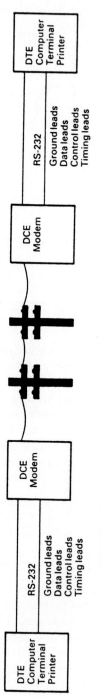

Figure 3-11 Summary of railway system analogy with communication environment equivalents.

REVIEW QUESTIONS

1. Transmitted data are found on pin _____. Once these data arrive at the other end of the facility, they are found on pin _____, known as _____.
2. The lead monitored by the DTE to determine that a call is being received is pin _____, which is _____. Will it stay on constantly? Explain.
3. If the ring indicator is detected, the lead that must be on for the modem to answer and maintain the call is pin _____, which is _____.
4. How can the DTE be assured that the connection is established?
5. If contention for the line exists, the mode of operation is _____.
6. To bid for control of a line, the DTE raises the lead on pin _____, which is _____. If the modem, (DCE) doesn't see _____ on, _____ is given to the DTE.
7. If pin 8 (DCD) is detected, what lead at the other end has been raised?
8. What lead is turned off, or dropped, to disconnect a dial-up line?
9. Protective ground is found on pin _____.
10. Signal ground is a _____ for all other signals and is found on pin _____.
11. Explain how pins 2 and 3 are used by an intelligent modem, above and beyond their normal functions.
12. A terminal can cause a disconnect from a line in a number of ways. Explain the different ways and relate them to the RS-232 pins.
13. Explain the justification for using auto-answer at a remote computer site. Explain the RS-232 significance, such as a no-answer condition. How does the modem or computer sense that a call is being received?
14. When a service bureau or time-sharing system is accessed, generally a log-on prompt occurs upon a successful connection to determine if you are a valid user. The long-on generally consists of an ID and password. How does the host computer know when to prompt the originator for the ID and password? Explain in terms of RS-232 interaction.
15. In RS-232 connections, the importance of perspective of lead direction is often overlooked. Recall that certain signals were output from the DTE, while others were output from the DCE. State a rule of thumb for lead direction and describe it in terms of DTE-DCE interaction.
16. Complete the following chart.

Function	Pin	Lead name (Abbr.)	Direction
Data	_____	Transmitted data (TD)	_____
Data	_____	Received data (RD)	_____
Control	_____	Request to send (_____)	_____
Control	_____	Clear to send (_____)	_____
Control	_____	Data carrier detect (_____)	_____
Control	_____	Data set ready (_____)	_____
Control	_____	Data terminal ready (_____)	_____
Control	_____	Ring indicator (_____)	From DCE
Ground	_____	Protective ground (_____)	N/A
Ground	_____	Signal ground (_____)	N/A

4

EIA-232-D operation in a private-line environment

Chapter 3 dealt with a temporary lowering of the drawbridge. Recall that this corresponded to a dial-up or switched-line environment in the communication business. The reason for the temporary structure is the limited traffic between train stations, as well as cost considerations.

What if traffic volume between stations increases to the point at which it is not economical to keep raising and lowering the drawbridge? The cost of raising and lowering the bridge could become greater than the cost of maintaining a permanent connection. When either high volume or high costs are typical, a permanent structure between depots should be considered.

RS-232:   This arrangement is termed a *private line*, also called a *leased line*. Private lines are permanent connections between terminals, computers, or a mixture of both. Although the cost is sometimes high, these lines are available 24 hours a day for a flat monthly rate. This availability allows for greater data transmission without concern for increased cost.

Typical applications utilizing private lines are on-line data entry or inquiry-response systems with high volumes of data traffic. A terminal operator can input or retrieve data throughout the day. Typically, these applications are found on larger systems of the minicomputer or mainframe size. The higher volumes dictate higher transmission speeds, which until recently have been limited to synchronous transmission. However, technology in asynchronous transmission is evolving to allow much higher speeds than the 1200–1800-bps limitations in the past. Nonetheless, asynchronous or synchronous, the cost of private lines may be restrictive until traffic volumes reach a trade-off level, at which it becomes uneconomical to continue to use dial-up facilities. Private lines may then be justifiable.

For example, an airline reservation agent may have a terminal connected via a private line to a host computer in a distant city. Because of the large number of telephone inquiries handled by the agent daily, a dial-up connection is probably impractical. With this level of traffic, much of the time could be spent dialing and establishing the connections. Also, analysis of typical long-distance rates would indicate that after a certain number of hours each day, it becomes cheaper to procure a leased or private line. Once again, traffic volumes and costs determine whether a dial-up or private line is used.

Although most of the RS-232 signals are the same as in the dial-up environment, some of them are functionally different or not used at all. In our dial-up analogy, the first signal used was the ringing of the bell, indicating that the bridge connection should be made. In a private-line environment, no ringing indication is needed because we have a permanent bridge structure.

This also implies that the data terminal ready (DTR) signal need not interact with the ring indicator. The manned depot, in our analogy, had to turn on a light

(DTR) signaling that the bridge could be lowered. Obviously, there is no bridge lowering, so the booth operator doesn't even check for the light signal from the station.

RS-232:   *Data terminal ready* (pin 20) may be present at the DTE; however, the DCE often ignores this lead in a private-line environment.

As you can see, this cuts out almost 50 percent of our headaches. Without ring indicator (pin 22), and with data terminal ready (pin 20) at both ends, we need only concern ourselves with the data leads (pins 2 and 3), the ground leads (pins 1 and 7), and the remaining control leads: request to send (pin 4), clear to send (pin 5), data set ready (pin 6), and data carrier detect (pin 8). The data and ground leads function in the same manner in either a private-line or dial-up environment, so we don't repeat them.

With a permanent bridge across the water, we have only to make sure that the trains travel when they are supposed to. Thus, we still must maintain control of the direction of traffic. If you recall, in both half-duplex and full-duplex environments, the station needed to know if the booth was in operation. The booth had to give the station a signal indicating that the bridge was present and that it was able to perform the control function. So we must still allow and check for this signal.

RS-232:   *Data set ready* (pin 6) must be present for data to be transmitted. When the private-line modem has power applied to it and the modem is functioning properly, DSR will be on. If the modem is not on, is in a test mode, or is faulty, DSR will not be high. Once the data terminal equipment checks for this signal and finds it on, it can be assured that the modem is available to perform its functions.

Assuming a half-duplex environment, the dispatcher at the depot makes sure that he turns on the engine headlights (RTS) when right-of-way of the facilities is desired. The far end can see the headlights (the *carrier*) and then knows that control of the track is being requested. Locally, the booth attendant gives a clear-to-send signal to the station. This interaction, as you can see, is the same as in the dial-up environment outlined in Chapter 3.

In a full-duplex environment, the signal interaction between the depots and booths is also the same as it was with the temporary bridge. Both stations keep the headlights turned on at all times because traffic can flow in both directions, simultaneously.

RS-232:   As you can see, ground, data, and most of the control leads of the communication facility are the same in either a private-line or dial-up environment. Regardless of whether you're in an HDX or FDX mode, the data and ground leads behave the same. Transmitted data is on pin 2, while received data is on pin 3. Pin 1 is protective ground, and signal ground is found on pin 7. The same interaction between RTS, CTS, and DCD occurs, dictated only by whether the facility is half-duplex or full-duplex. The main RS-232 difference is that pins 22 and 20 have no useful function in a private-line environment because the connection

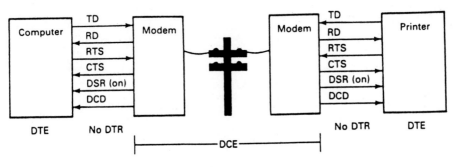

Figure 4-1

between business machines is permanent. Also pin 6, data set ready, is on as long as the modem has power applied to it, whereas in a dial-up environment, it usually came on after the connection was established. The private line is represented in Figure 4-1.

Function	Pin	Lead Name (Abbr.)	Direction
Data	2	Transmitted data (TD)	From DTE
Data	3	Received data (RD)	From DCE
Control	4	Request to send (RTS)	From DTE
Control	5	Clear to send (CTS)	From DCE
Control	8	Data carrier detect (DCD)	From DCE
Control	6	Data set ready (DSR)	From DCE
Control	20	Data terminal ready (DTR)	Not used
Control	22	Ring indicator (RI)	Not used
Ground	1	Protective group (PG)	N/A
Ground	7	Signal ground (SG)	N/A

Figure 4-2

REVIEW QUESTIONS

1. If the modem is off, what lead will not be high on the RS-232 interface?
2. In a private-line environment, how does the DTE know if the modem is not functioning?
3. DTR is used in a private-line environment to maintain the connection. True or false?
4. Because of different levels in a private line, signal ground behaves differently. True or false?
5. The RTS-CTS-DCD interactions are functionally the same in a private-line environment as they are on a dial-up line. True or false?
6. Complete the following chart.

Function	Pin	Lead name (Abbr.)	Direction
Data	2	_____	From DTE
Data	3	_____	From DCE
Control	4	_____	From DTE
Control	5	_____	From DCE
Control	8	_____	From DCE
Control	6	_____	From DCE
Control	20	_____	_____
Control	22	_____	_____
Ground	1	_____	N/A
Ground	7	_____	N/A

5

synchronous

environments

The trains up to now, consisting of boxcars and flatcars, have each had at least one engine and one caboose. The engine and caboose provided the timing of the traffic. At the destination station, once you saw an engine, you could bet that the rest of the train was following, right on time, with the caboose signaling the end of the train. Timing was on a train-by-train basis.

RS-232: This transmission scheme, known as *asynchronous transmission*, has provided the basis for the bulk of our analogy up to this point. Because of start and stop bits, each character was individually *timed*, or *synchronized*. No special timing was needed. A different transmission scheme, known as *synchronous transmission*, will be introduced into the simile. But first, it is important to note a trend in the microcomputer field.

The use of personal computers (PCs) in synchronous environments is flourishing due to the communication software packages being written. De facto standards for terminals operating in synchronous private-line environments exist. Examples are IBM 3270 BSC/SDLC devices and controllers and IBM 2780/3780 BSC terminals.* These terminals and others operate in a synchronous environment, involving the timing aspect of the RS-232 interface. Because of the popularity of these terminal types, vast numbers of applications have been developed specifically for them. As the base of personal computers expands, the desire to access these existing applications also grows. In order for a personal computer to use these application packages, the PC must behave like a synchronous device. That means that if a PC wants to access applications normally intended for an IBM 3270 Binary Synchronous (BSC) device, the software in the PC must emulate all the device characteristics of the BSC terminal. This includes protocols, buffering, screen addressing, keyboard sequences, and other aspects. Software to emulate terminals is readily available for PCs. The specific characteristics of the terminal families are not as important to understanding RS-232 as the timing functions involved between the synchronous devices and their modems. Our scenario will describe the elements necessary for understanding timing in these terminals or emulating devices.

The need for longer and faster trains was discussed in Chapter 2. The basis for this need was that we had an engine and caboose for every seven or eight cars. This resulted in a lot of wasted track time. If you totaled the time on the track required for each engine and caboose, roughly 20 percent of the train was used for timing. Rather than send each train (character) out one at a time, with an engine and caboose, the Railroad Commission decided on a more economical and sophisticated method. The approach was temporarily to hold several small trains traveling to the same station and later ship them all at once as one long train.

---

*2780, 3270, and 3780 are trademarks of IBM Corp.

RS-232:   The communication term for this technique is *buffering*. Characters (trains) are *buffered* at the originating station (business machine) into logical groupings for transmission as a single group. The need for an engine and caboose still exists, but in a different manner, as we shall see in a moment.

Once a method of buffering trains at one location was discovered, several benefits were realized. Money was saved due to the fact that fewer engines and cabooses were needed. Also, more time was available for actual train traffic because of the reduced need for engines and cabooses.

However, a couple of factors must be dealt with in this environment. The longer a train is, the greater the possibility for it to jump the track, causing garbling and derailment of the boxcars and flatcars. The major cause of derailment is either the track or the speed at which the train was traveling. The quality of the track is a major factor influencing the smoothness of train operation. The higher the quality, the less likelihood of derailment. A lower-quality track may collapse, causing a bit of a mess (or, I should say, a mess of bits). The tracks have already been designed by the engineers and established by the installers. So, we must assume that the tracks were built and conditioned for such a traffic load.

However, no one has addressed the actual rate of speed. How fast should a train be allowed to travel and who controls this speed limit over the bridge?

RS-232:   The control of this speed limit is dubbed *timing*. Instead of individually synchronizing each character, the larger group of buffered data is synchronized by means of the timing element. In contrast with asynchronous transmission, this method is known as *synchronous transmission*. The engine and caboose are still present, indicating the beginning and end of the train. However, they assume a different meaning. In asynchronous transmission, the two units were start and stop bits, providing the timing for the individual characters. In a synchronous environment, the engine and caboose represent characters by themselves, indicating the start of a *block* of text and the end of that unit of text. They are not used for the function of timing but for the framing of a block of text. Timing is handled in a totally different fashion in synchronous transmission.

So, how will timing of trains be handled when our trains are longer and faster? First of all, the speed limit for the tracks should be established. How fast can trains successfully travel across the permanent or temporary bridge? The speed limit should be fast enough to allow the maximum number of trains to cross the bridge, yet slow enough to allow the trains to reach their destination safely.

The type and size of tracks used, for the most part, dictate the speed limit to be enforced. Based on the bridge engineers' specifications for the railroad lines, a rate will be established. Once established, enforcement of this limit is all that remains for a smooth flow of high-speed trains.

RS-232:   The speed limit is usually expressed in *bits per second* (*bps*). This rate is the number of 1s and 0s that can be transmitted in the period of one second. Once the speed is known, you can divide it by the number of bits per character to determine how many characters can be transmitted in a second. Typical synchronous speeds are 1200, 2400, 4800, 9600, and 19,200 bps. If the speed of a communication facility is 2400 bps and the length of each character is 8 bits, approximately 300 characters can be transmitted over the line each second. The RS-232 standard allows for speeds up to 20,000 bps. Speeds near the maximum are common in a private-line environment. In a dial-up environment, synchronous speeds of 4800 bps are more typical. However, technology is advancing to the point where speeds approaching the maximum rate allowed by the standard can be attained over dial-up lines.

Having established a speed limit for the rails, somehow we must provide for the regulation or control of the limit over the bridge. Thus, trains need some mechanism for controlling how fast they should proceed down the railroad lines.

RS-232:   Timing must be provided to control the rate at which data are transmitted and received on the lines.

The speed of the trains can be controlled at a number of different points in our bridge connection. Analyzing the various elements in our analogy, an obvious choice is the train station, because one exists at each end of the bridge. The depot at the origination site could regulate the speed of all outgoing trains. Outbound trains would be informed by the station of the correct speed at which to travel. At the same depot, the speed of the inbound trains could be monitored. The depot operator could then determine if the train is traveling at the correct speed (Figure 5-1).

RS-232:   The speed control of the outbound traffic is termed *transmit timing*. Transmit timing is the clocking rate of the data transmission. The characters are "clocked" out onto the line at whatever rate the transmit timing lead is providing. When transmit timing is provided by the train depot (DTE), it is supplied on pin 24. Some business machines have an option of either *internal* or *external timing*. When the DTE is to be the source for the timing, internal timing should be selected. In this case, timing is provided by the computer, terminal, or printer on pin 24 for data transmission.

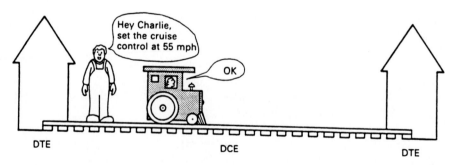

Figure 5-1

Figure 5-2

Another potential location for train speed regulation is the booths. The booths could provide the depot with the speed at which the trains should depart from the depot and cross the bridge. Because the booths are directly connected to the bridge, they are in a better position to know the quality of the facility. Because of this, speed control by the booths is the more common of the two possibilities (Figure 5-2).

RS-232:   The term for this is also *transmit timing*. However, this type of timing provided by the booth (modem) is considered to be a DCE source. A different lead, pin 15, is used to indicate transmit timing from a DCE source. In this case, if we looked at the business machine (DTE), the option for timing would be set for external timing. But from the DCE (modem) point of view, the modem would be optioned for internal timing. It is important to note that this could be a confusing option unless one considers the "source" of the timing. In summary, if the DTE is to provide the transmit timing, this timing will be provided on pin 24; if the DCE will provide it, the timing will be provided on pin 15 (Figure A-1). Thus, we have an option as to who is going to provide the speed limit (*clock rate*) of the data transfer.

At the booth across the bridge, the speed of the train could be monitored for an indication of the speed limit. Why is this required? The receiving depot must know the speed at which the trains will be arriving. This is necessary to allow the receiving station to check the train cars it received to ensure the accuracy of the shipment. To allow for this, we will let the booth derive the speed of the train as it passes by. Then, the booth operator will pass the derived speed limit to the depot for proper reception of the train. When these two components, booth and depot, are working in sync, the trains can be properly received and analyzed (Figure 5-3).

Figure 5-3

RS-232:   This is known as *receiver signal element timing* (DCE source). For ease of reference, we will call it *receive timing*. This timing is found on pin 17. Typically, the modem can generate its own receive timing. However, it is often more efficient to derive the receive timing from the data being received. If the modem can extract the speed limit from the data received, this timing can be passed on pin 17 to the business machine, which uses this clock rate to receive the data properly.

At this end, we also have to allow for the transmit timing function. The fewer sources for timing that are used, the less of a chance for timing problems to occur. To minimize the number of sources for timing, the following connection is possible. If the derived timing on pin 17 is looped up to pin 15 (transmit timing), *synchronization* is usually more easily maintained, because it comes from a single source. We have also satisfied the transmit timing requirement at this end by using the receive timing (Figure 5-4). As you can see, there is a single source for the timing. By looping the receive timing at one end to the transmit timing lead, there is less timing to keep in sync. Often, in modems, this option is known as *slave timing*—the transmit timing (pin 15) at one end is *slaved* (derived) from the receive timing lead

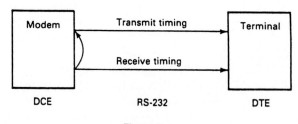

Figure 5-4

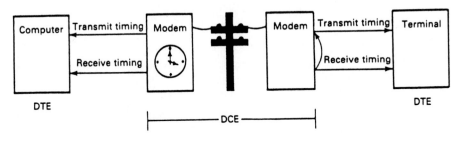

Figure 5-5

(pin 17). If you follow the timing all the way through the network, you can see that a single source can be used to provide both transmit and receive timing at both ends of the facility. This is the ideal environment to set up for synchronous transmission (Figure 5-5).

As we have seen, the key difference between asynchronous and synchronous transmission is the aspect of timing. Asynchronous transmission requires timing on a character basis. A typical example of this is a VT-100* or other async terminal. Each character is surrounded by start and stop bits for the purpose of timing. In most data communications over telephone lines requiring speeds greater than 1200 bps, the synchronous mode of operation will be used. With synchronous transmission, a timing signal is provided by either the DTE or DCE for synchronization of the data transmission. Special leads on the RS-232 interface have been set aside for this timing, as shown in Figure 5-6.

Function	Pin	Lead name	Source
Timing	15	Transmit timing	From DCE
Timing	17	Receive timing	From DCE
Timing	24	Transmit timing	From DTE

Figure 5-6

As a final review note, the more engineers trying to pilot the train, the more possibilities for traffic problems. In a communication environment, the more sources providing the timing, the greater the chances for mismatched clock rates. To limit the potential for errors, use the fewest number of timing sources by deriving the timing (slave timing) from a single source whenever possible.

*VT-100 is a trademark of Digital Equipment Corporation.

REVIEW QUESTIONS

1. A transmission scheme in which characters are individually timed is _____.
2. A transmission scheme in which characters are temporarily stored until a block can be sent out at a predetermined clock rate is _____.
3. Temporarily storing characters for later transmission is known as _____.
4. The aspect that distinguishes asynchronous transmission from synchronous transmission is the _____ element.
5. Transmission rates are generally expressed in _____.
6. The RS-232 standard allows a maximum speed of _____ bps.
7. There are two major types of timing in an RS-232 environment, _____ and _____ timing.
8. If the DTE is providing the transmit timing, it is found on pin _____. If the modem is providing the transmit timing, it is found on pin _____.
9. The receive timing is found on pin _____.
10. The modem option that loops pin 17 to pin 15 is known as _____ timing.
11. Explain the differences between internal and external timing as it relates to RS-232 signals.
12. Explain slave timing and why it is used.
13. Compare asynchronous transmission and synchronous transmission.
14. Complete the following timing chart.

6

secondary signals and flow control

We have been discussing the bridge across the body of water. In these discussions we have implied that only trains can cross the bridge over the tracks. We will now identify other vehicles that may cross the water to maximize the use of the bridge.

As long as we are using the bridge to provide rail service across the water, why not expand the offering to allow smaller objects to cross? For example, the way the bridges are constructed, some unused space exists along the sides of the tracks. Let us optimize the use of the facilities by using the remaining space beside the tracks as a sidewalk for slower-moving traffic such as pedestrians, bicycles, and so on. This narrow strip is a very thin band of concrete or steel. The band width is so narrow that people or bicycles can normally go in only one direction at a time. Have you heard this before? This was the characteristic of HDX. Refer to Figure 6-1 for representation of the extra space along the sides of the bridge.

In our earlier discussions, we outlined the procedure for control of HDX facilities like this. The same concept of requesting to send by the station and getting a clear-to-send signal for crossing is applicable, as is the indication to the other side that a depot is requesting to send something across. However, because of the limited side-band width, these signals are considered secondary and are reserved only for smaller traffic, not the large trains that run on the tracks. Even though the side bands permit only limited traffic, they serve a very useful purpose, as we shall see.

RS-232:   Pins of this nature carry secondary signals. They function in the same manner as their primary counterparts but control secondary channels of the communication facility (Figure A-1). For example, RTS becomes *secondary request to send*. The same *secondary* nomenclature applies to *clear to send* and *data carrier detect*. In addition, there are *secondary transmitted* and *received data* channels. Intelligent modems, capable of transmitting diagnostic information, use these secondary data channels for testing and trouble-reporting purposes. However, unless intelligent devices are being used, these secondary data channels are rarely utilized. Nevertheless, *secondary data carrier detect*, also known as *secondary*

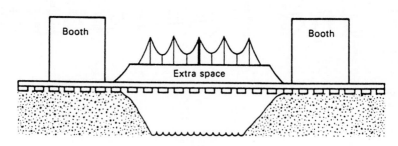

Figure 6-1

Function	Pin	Name	Direction
Data	14	Secondary transmitted data	From DTE
Data	16	Secondary received data	From DCE
Control	19	Secondary request to send	From DTE
Control	13	Secondary clear to send	From DCE
Control	12	Secondary carrier detect	From DCE

Figure 6-2

receive line signal detector, plays an important role in the area of transmission control. See Figure 6-2 for a listing of the *secondary leads* on the RS-232 interface.

In half-duplex environments, these secondary signals have a key role. As you recall, when a half-duplex facility is being utilized, primary data and control signals are used in one direction at a time. Information is transmitted in a single direction with great success under normal circumstances. But what if a problem occurs at one end of the facility? What type of problems could occur? The next few paragraphs define the types of potential problems and describe their solutions using these secondary signals. We will temporarily ignore our analogy and utilize pure RS-232 terminology for the remainder of this chapter.

Let's focus on a specific configuration of a computer transmitting payroll information across the communication facility to a receive-only printer over a half-duplex facility. There is no need to cover how the connection is established between the two devices, as we have been through that sequence in earlier chapters. So let's assume that the connection is established, either dial-up or private line, and the proper signals have been exchanged to allow the computer to transmit data to the printer as shown in Figure 6-3.

Things are going smoothly until, after minutes or hours of data traffic, the supply of paper being fed through the printer begins to get a little low. As the printer continues to chug along, the last sheet of paper rolls through the printer. The problem should now be intuitively obvious to the most casual observer. The computer will continue to throw data at the printer. The printer, however, receives the data but can't transcribe the bits onto the paper. Remember we are out of the

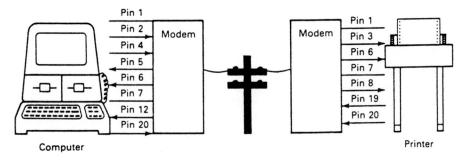

Figure 6-3

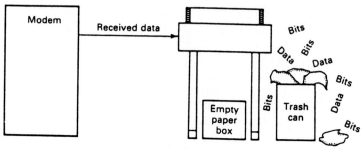

Figure 6-4

pulp. So the data are either printed on the bare printer platen or are lost (Figure 6-4). This could be catastrophic, especially if the next item to be printed would have been your paycheck! Let's solve the problem so we won't shortchange ourselves in the future.

In a half-duplex environment, the primary data path is available in only one direction at a time. However, the secondary data and control signals are available to be used from either the computer or printer end. We'll utilize these secondary signals to control the loss of data and keep the "cards and letters" and checks coming.

The best way to prevent the loss of the received data is to provide a means of notifying the computer, or transmitting end, of the problem. In this case we have what is known as a "paper out" condition. If the computer is aware of a problem at the far-end printer, it can temporarily halt data transmission until the problem is cleared. Once a new batch of paper is threaded through the printer, the printer will be ready to crank out your check. The printing can resume after the printer gives an indication to the computer that all is O.K.

Peripheral manufacturers capitalized on the availability of secondary control signals on the RS-232 interface to prevent the catastrophe. The solution was to have the printer, or receiving device, always give a positive indication when data could be received. This was made possible by having the printer keep its secondary request to send (SRTS) lead high. Because these secondary signals behave the same as our primary ones, this caused secondary carrier to be transmitted back to the computer. The computer was constantly monitoring its secondary data carrier detect (SDCD) lead, pin 12. As long as pin 12 was high on the interface, data could be transmitted.

Should a paper-out or other problem condition occur, the printer would drop its SRTS lead, causing no secondary carrier to be evident at the computer end. If SDCD was low, the computer would cease transmission because of the indication that a problem existed at the far end. Once the problem was cleared, its SDCD/SRLSD pin would come back on because the printer at the far end would once again raise its SRTS signal. The computer could now successfully print your paycheck.

RS-232:   Even though we are in a half-duplex environment, we can still pass these secondary signals in the opposite direction of the primary signals. This is possible because we are using a secondary channel of the communication facility that is separate from the primary channel. The technical term for this operation is *reverse channel*. *Reverse channel* is used for the specific function of supervisory control.

Another frequent use of reverse channel is to prevent buffer overflow. If a device is receiving data, the bits can be placed in the device's buffer for printing at whatever speed the printer is capable of. Depending on the size, the device's buffer may fill up to the point that it overflows, or loses data. Reverse channel can be applied in the same manner as in our paper-out condition to prevent buffer overflow and, consequently, loss of data.

Reverse channel performs what is known as a *hardware XON/XOFF* or hardware flow control function. "Busy" and "DTR" terminology describe the same concept of flow control between a printer or terminal locally attached to a computer. Refer to Chapters 7 and 8 for more details on local connections of devices and hardware flow control.

With FDX, some devices, such as printers, can monitor their buffer or paper supply electronically. If either the paper is getting low or the buffer is reaching its capacity, the printer can transmit a *device control character*. This character is transmitted over the primary-data channel to the computer, indicating that data transmission should be temporarily suspended. The printer then notifies the computer when transmission can resume by transmitting a different device control character. Full-duplex allows for this two-way communication to occur. This is often termed *software* flow control, or *XON/XOFF*. A physical character is transmitted.

In a half-duplex environment, data can be transmitted in only one direction at a time, limiting the printer's ability to transmit a device control character. The RS-232 secondary signals, reverse channel, are used to accomplish the XON/XOFF function. This is termed *hardware XON/XOFF*, because it is handled by the RS-232 interface.

Reverse channel can be used for other purposes in a communication environment, but the preceding examples demonstrate two of the major uses of these secondary control signals.

REVIEW QUESTIONS

1. The main channel of a communication facility is the _____ channel.
2. _____ signals can be used to solve printer control problems. Explain another method of flow control.
3. List the two secondary data signals.
4. List the three secondary control signals.
5. The term for using secondary RTS for supervisory control is _____.
6. Explain the printer or buffer overflow problem and how to solve it.

7

cross connections

Only one more area of discussion is necessary to give you a full understanding of the RS-232 interface, that of *cross connections* between devices when no communication facilities will be used. Cross connections, perhaps the most important item to a microcomputer user, are generally the least understood. How do you connect a serial device, such as a printer, to the serial interface on your computer? By the end of this chapter, this cross connection will seem as easy as powering up your system.

The bridge scenario, thus far, has provided an excellent foundation for a thorough description of a data communication environment. The train depots and booths stood for DTE and DCE, respectively. Between the two booths was the bridge, which represented the telephone lines for communication facilities. Recall that the bridge could be of a permanent or temporary nature, allowing for the distinction between private and dial-up lines.

We have reached the point when the bridge is no longer needed—the big river is now just a trickle of water.

RS-232: DCE is no longer going to be present. Specifically, the modems and telephone lines are not needed to connect two business machines if they are sitting side by side, or at least within 50 feet of each other. Due to electrical capacities, the RS-232 standard limits the cabling distance to 50 feet. Keep this in mind when locally connecting two devices with serial interfaces.

Even though the big river of water is gone, the trickling creek has to be accommodated for. For purposes of discussion we will design a shortcut under the water—a tunnel. This tunnel must have the capability to handle the trains as if they were crossing a bridge. So, the same "handshaking" must occur for the depots to operate as normal stations would, even though we're in a different environment. The tunnel must be built in such a fashion that the depots don't have to change their procedures for train traffic. In short, the tunnel must emulate the booths and the bridge. This is a requirement to allow the standard stations to be built to operate on either a bridge or tunnel type of facility.

RS-232: Business machines are manufactured with *serial* interfaces that normally conform to the EIA-232-D standard. If the standard is adhered to, RS-232 leads (pins) should be similar for any DTE. This also implies that these business machines are set up to expect the standard RS-232 signals normally provided by the DCE. Specifically, a modem would supply the proper signals to allow the DTE to function properly during its data transmission. When a port is configured to expect the signals normally provided by a modem, that port is said to be *emulating* data terminal equipment. While it is expecting to receive these signals, it also will generate signals such as request to send and data terminal ready, which are output signals from DTE. If, on the other hand, the port is emulating data communication equipment, leads such as data set ready, clear to send, and data carrier detect are output signals generated from the port. When either of these categories, DTE or DCE, is being emulated, the proper output signals should be generated and the corresponding input signals can be expected. Recall from earlier chapters that these standard signals fell into four categories, ground, data, control, and timing. When connecting these leads to allow local connections between machines (without modems), all four categories of leads on the RS-232 interface must be crossed to emulate a communication environment as if modems and lines were present. Because the cross-connections cable is used when no modems are present, we generally refer to it as a *null-modem cable*. The following discussion describes the cross connections required to build this type of cable.

We have already outlined the basic need for the tunnel to be built, emulating the booths and the bridge. The easiest way to accomplish this is to divide the requirements of the stations into four categories: ground, train tracks, traffic control, and speed limit. We will always view these categories from the stations' perspectives. The reason for this is that we are currently dealing with only the two depots (Figure 7-1).

RS-232:   The first and easiest category is *ground*. Because these signals are present for protection and signal reference, merely allow for them in the null-modem cable. *Protective ground* (pin 1) is electrically bonded to the machine or equipment frame, while *signal ground* (pin 7) establishes the common reference for all other interchange circuits except pin 1. So, in a null-modem cable, merely provide these two pins straight through from DTE to DTE. No crossovers are required (Figure 7-2).

The second part of the tunnel emulates the tracks used for the departure and arrival of trains. Again, we view these tracks from the stations' perspectives. Trains departing from station A arrive at station B on a track set aside for receiving trains. The converse is also true. The tunnel should allow for a crossover of these tracks to

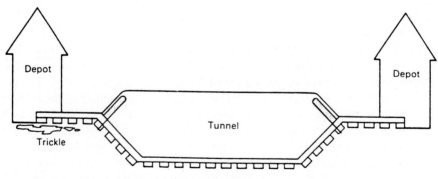

Figure 7-1

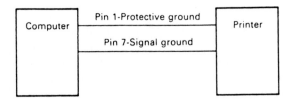

Figure 7-2

prevent head-on collisions of trains. This crossover allows for proper departure and arrival of trains at each station through the tunnel.

RS-232:   This category includes the *data* leads (pins 2 and 3). Pin 2 is used for transmitted data, and pin 3 for received data. Both are normally present at both ends. The exception might be pin 2 at the printer end. Why? You guessed it: Printers do not usually transmit data; they receive only. Data are transmitted over pin 2 from one machine and received on pin 3 at the other. To allow for proper data transmission and reception at both machines, cross pin 2 at one end with pin 3 of the other end. Repeat this at both ends as represented in Figure 7-3.

So far we have accommodated both ground and data leads in the interface—50 percent of our null-modem connection. All that remain are the control and timing leads.

Traffic control was one of the major problems that had to be overcome for proper use of the bridge facilities. Control was used to regulate the flow of trains. The regulation involved both when the bridge would remain lowered for crossing and when a train could actually cross it. We must approach our tunnel connection with the same regulatory concerns, even though a bridge isn't used.

RS-232:   We must allow for actual DTE leads as well as emulated DCE leads in the cross-connection cable. Data terminal equipment (DTE)—provided signals are all that are present in a null-modem cable. This limitation forces us to provide DCE signals with available DTE signals. Specifically, the DTE signals (RTS and DTR) must be used to provide or emulate the DCE-provided signals (DSR, CTS, and DCD) that would have existed in a normal telecommunication environment.

If you consider the configuration, two DTEs are to be locally connected with merely a cable between them. These business machines, built for a communication environment, are expecting the standard RS-232 control signals usually received

Function	Pin	Pin	Function
Transmitted data	2 ⟍ ⟋ 2		Transmitted data
Received data	3 ⟋ ⟍ 3		Received data

Figure 7-3

through the modem. We will now explain how the DCE signals can be emulated by the available DTE-provided signals, RTS and DTR.

We must design the aspect of the tunnel that normally would control the indications and maintenance of the bridge across the water. Because we have no booths to control the bridge and give any indications of status, we use the signal system that is provided by the depot. If the depot is manned to receive trains, an indication is normally given to the booth. This signal lets the booth know that the bridge connection should be maintained and trains could be received.

The depots, even in our tunnel, are still expecting signals indicating that trains have tracks available to them. With no booths available, we have to allow somehow for these signals. To do so, we use the depot's signal at one end of the tunnel to emulate the absent signal at the other end. We duplicate this emulation at the other end of the tunnel. This technique allows depot A to receive the required indication of a connection, even without the presence of a booth.

RS-232:   DTR (pin 20) is ordinarily provided by the DTE (depot) to indicate that power is on at the terminal and is also used to maintain the connection in a dial-up environment. For an indication that the line is established between DTEs, the DCE normally gives a signal on pin 6 (DSR). As long as DSR is on, one can assume that the DCE, both modem and line, is available for data transmission. If pin 6 is not present, the line or connection is not available. To emulate DSR at both ends, we strap the DTR signal at one device across to pin 6 at the other device. The same strapping is done in the other direction. By strapping pin 20 across to pin 6, whenever DTR is high (the machine power is on), the other end will get an indication that the transmission line is available. If power is off, the other end will not have DSR, indicating that the communication path is not established. The pins should be crossed as shown in Figure 7-4.

RS-232:   The other element of the control function on the interface is *path control*. Three leads were necessary for this function (Figure 7-5). RTS was the headlight on the train, turned on by the depot. This light was seen at the far end on pin 8, data carrier detect. CTS was the indication from the booth that a depot had control of the tracks and could send trains across the bridge. When only a single track was available on the bridge (half-duplex), path control was extremely important; when two-way traffic was allowed simultaneously (full-duplex), this concern was somewhat relaxed, but the signals were still present.

In a tunnel, the same track-control signals must be allowed for. The booth

Function	Pin	Pin	Function
Data set ready	6	6	Data set ready
Data terminal ready	20	20	Data terminal ready

Figure 7-4

Function		Pin	
Request to send	RTS	4	
Clear to send	CTS	5	
Data carrier detect	DCD	8	**Figure 7-5**

signals are not present. We must provide these by utilizing available signals from the depot's point of view. Of the three signals necessary for train path control, only one is available at each end. This signal is the headlight indication of a request to send a train to the other depot. How are we going to get three signals from only one? Believe it or not, this can be accomplished rather easily.

Consider the source of each signal. The request to send a train is from the depot. The other two are normally from the two separate booths. The signal indicating that is it clear to send the trains is normally given by the local booth back to the originating depot, whereas the other depot receives its indication of a possible train arrival locally from its booth. Of course, the only time that this signal is given is if the request-to-send signal is raised at the other end by the originating depot.

To allow for this same interaction with neither booths nor bridge, we must once again emulate some signals. The request-to-send and clear-to-send signals occur at the same end of the tunnel. Thus, we can accomplish the RTS-CTS interaction by faking out the depot so that whenever the headlight is turned on, the depot can see it reflected as if it were seeing the signal normally provided by the booth. By placing a mirror or reflector at the entrance to the tunnel, whenever the headlight is on, the depot will see a signal and think it is getting a clear-to-send signal. In this way, at the originating depot, the path-control requirements are met. The far-end depot can still see the headlight through the tunnel and still receives the signals it expects for reception of train traffic.

RS-232:   Technically, we will apply the same concept of mirroring the RTS signal back to the originating machine. RTS (pin 4) is normally generated by the DTE. For data transmission to be allowed, CTS (pin 5) must be received by the same DTE. So, we loop the RTS signal back to the originating DTE by wiring it back to pin 5 (CTS). Pictorially, this is represented as in Figure 7-6.

Whenever the DTE—for example, a computer—raises RTS, it immediately receives a CTS signal indicating that data transmission is now possible. As for the need of the receiving device to have an indication that data will be arriving, we must provide for DCD (pin 8) to be derived from the same source, RTS. Thus, we also connect RTS (pin 4) at the originating DTE to the data carrier detect lead, pin 8, at the far end, as shown in Figure 7-7.

Function	Pin	
Request to send	4	
Clear to send	5	**Figure 7-6**

Function	Pin	Pin	Function
Request to send	4	8	Data carrier detect
Clear to send	5		

Figure 7-7

By making these cross connections, not only will a CTS signal be given, but when RTS is raised, the other end will also receive its DCD signal, indicating that data transmission is possible. Repeat these connections at both DTEs to allow two-way transmission. Whether the terminals are set up for HDX or FDX, path-control requirements have been met in the null-modem cable.

RS-232:   *Timing* leads remain. You will recall that the only situation in which timing leads were required was in a synchronous environment. If the null-modem cable is being built for an asynchronous terminal interconnection, you can ignore this next section and proceed to the discussion on secondary signals. For a synchronous environment, read on.

As booths and bridges were being designed to allow faster trains across them, speed limits were established for smooth train traffic. When possible, a single speed limit was used to regulate trains in both directions, typically controlled by the booth. We are without booths in our tunnel to provide this function. So, we must either provide a traffic cop for this or leave this function up to the depots.

Some depots have the capability to regulate the speed of the traffic, while others do not. If the depots can control the speed limit, let them. Simply decide which depot will regulate the speed, and let the other depot use the same regulation for its train traffic through the tunnel.

In an environment in which neither depot can regulate the speed limit of the train, hire a traffic cop. This patrolman, positioned in the middle of the tunnel, provides speed control in both directions. High-speed train traffic can be regulated without the risk of derailment with the help of this traffic cop.

RS-232:   The two situations just described relate to synchronous environments in which either the DTE can provide timing or an external source of timing is required. In the case of the latter, a null-modem cable cannot be built to satisfy the timing need. In a normal telecommunication environment of this nature, timing must be provided by the DCE or modem. Because there is no DCE when locally connecting two devices, a separate unit must be placed between the devices. This unit is often termed a *synchronous null-modem device* or *synchronous modem eliminator*. It eliminates the modems as the standard null-modem cable does, yet allows for timing. Not only are the ground, data, and control leads taken care of, as previously described, but timing is also provided by the box (Figure 7-8).

What if at least one of the DTEs can provide the timing? We go back to the null-modem cable. There is need for only a single source of timing. If both DTEs have this capability, decide which one will be optioned to provide it. Once

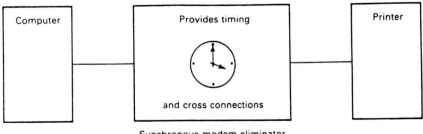

Synchronous modem eliminator

Figure 7-8

optioned, the timing will be provided by the terminal on pin 24, transmit signal element timing (DTE source). This is the timing that will be used for both devices, whether transmitting or receiving. Satisfying the need for timing at both ends is rather simple. Because a single source of timing is required, merely connect all of the associated timing leads together, both transmit and receive. Connect pin 24 to pins 17 and 15 at one end, and connect one of these leads across to pins 15 and 17 tied together at the other end. The fashion in which pins 15 and 17 are connected really doesn't matter as long as both sides are eventually connected to the timing source on pin 24. This is depicted in Figure 7-9.

Now that all timing leads are connected, synchronous transmission can successfully occur. In fact, pin 15 on the DTE side that provides the timing doesn't need to be connected at all. The source DTE is providing its own transmit timing; it will ignore whatever timing is presented to it on pin 15. We have built a synchronous null-modem cable, whereby one of the DTEs is providing the timing.

Figure 7-10 summarizes an asynchronous null-modem cable. To work in a synchronous environment with the DTE providing the timing, add the lead connections shown in Figure 7-11.

In either an asynchronous or synchronous environment, with our null-modem cables, we should still be "on track with RS-232."

RS-232:   One final aspect of a null-modem cable is *printer control*. In Chapter 6, we covered the need for a printer to notify the computer at the distant end of an alarm condition. Specifically, the secondary control signal (reverse channel) was used to indicate that a paper-out condition had occurred. When modems are not used, as in the local attachment of a printer to a computer's serial port, the same

Function	Pin	Pin	Function
Transmit timing	15	15	Transmit timing
Receive timing	17	17	Receive timing
External timing	24		

Figure 7-9

Category	Function	Pin	Pin	Function
Ground	PG	1 ——————— 1		PG
Ground	SG	7 ——————— 7		SG
Data	TD	2	2	TD
Data	RD	3	3	RD
Control	RTS	4	4	RTS
Control	CTS	5	5	CTS
Control	DCD/RLSD	8	8	DCD/RLSD
Control	DSR	6	6	DSR
Control	DTR	20	20	DTR

Figure 7-10

Category	Function	Pin	Pin	Function
Timing	RT	17	15	TT
Timing	EXT-TT	24	17	RT

Figure 7-11

concept is often applied. So, in addition to the standard null-modem cable, cross connections for printer control may be required.

To cross-connect properly between the computer and the printer, the technical specification for the serial ports must be reviewed. First, determine which lead is held high by the printer to indicate that the printer is functioning properly—no paper-out condition. Usually this lead is secondary request to send (pin 19), but often on a printer, pin 20 (DTR) provides this function. Whichever is used, this lead will still function in the same manner. However, the lead must be cross-connected to a lead at the computer end that is required before the computer can transmit.

At the computer end, a lead must be found that is important enough so that the computer can transmit data if it is on. If it is not on, it must prohibit the computer from transmitting data. Secondary data carrier detect is sometimes used for this function. But this signal is not always present on serial interfaces. Data set ready (pin 6) is a lead that is usually monitored by the computer for regulating when data can be transmitted. When modems are used in a dial-up environment, this lead indicates that a line is available for transmission. If this lead (pin 6) is required before the computer can transmit, merely connect it to the lead at the printer end used for printer control. Once connected, the computer and printer behave in a normal fashion, as if there were modems between the devices. Figure 7-12 illustrates this connection. Do not cross-connect pin 20 to pin 6 as previously described. If you did, pin 6 would never fluctuate, defeating the purpose of the cross connection for flow control. Although these two leads may vary, depending on the devices, the same principle for printer control is applied as in a null-modem cable.

There are many ways of building the null-modem cable. Figure 7-13 outlines other possibilities.

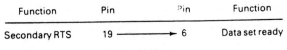

Function	Pin	Pin	Function
Secondary RTS	19 ————▶ 6		Data set ready

Figure 7-12

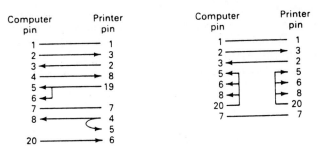

Figure 7-13

The particular null-modem cable used depends on the signals required and provided by the data terminal equipment and is affected by flow-control leads. Consult Appendixes F and G for further possible cross-connections.

REVIEW QUESTIONS

1. The cable that can be built for the local attachment of a printer to a computer's modem port is generally called a _____.

2. _____ connections are used to emulate the leads normally provided by a modem.

3. If the DTE cannot provide the timing, a separate device can be purchased to provide both timing and all other cross connections. This device is a _____.

4. The distance limitation outlined by the EIA-232-D standard is _____ feet.

5. Name the four categories of leads.

6. All signals used in an asynchronous null-modem cable must be emulated or provided by the _____.

7. The two ground leads, normally wired straight through in a null-modem cable, are found on pins _____ and _____.

8. Transmitted data, pin 2, at one end should be crossed over to pin _____ at the receiving end in a null-modem cable.

9. RTS, pin 4, should be looped back, locally, to provide _____, on pin _____, and then across to pin _____ to provide data carrier detect.

10. DTR, pin _____, can be used to provide _____ (pin 6) at the opposite end.

11. The _____ signal normally indicates that a modem was available for use and generally controlled the computer's transmission.

12. If the DTE is providing the timing, it is found on pin _____.

13. In the case of question 12, which three leads should be wired together?

14. Which category of leads differentiates a synchronous null-modem cable from an asynchronous null-modem cable?

15. _____, pin 19, is usually used for printer control and must be crossed to a lead such as data set ready or clear to send at the computer end.

16. Explain, conceptually, how pin 19, secondary request to send, could potentially be used for flow control in a normal communication environment. Assume that the computer at the far end does not monitor any of its secondary signals. (Hint: Use RTS at the printer end and data carrier detect and data set ready at the far end.)

17. What is the "golden rule" when dealing with straight-through RS-232 cables or null-modem cables?

8

interfacing

equipment

The application of the RS-232 interface is widespread in mainframes, minicomputers, microcomputers, printers, and all types of terminals. The basic principles of the standard are implemented in such devices; however; minor variations may occur from device to device. These variations become extremely significant when interfacing different combinations of computers, printers, and terminals. Consequently, several aspects of the specific interfaces, which must be reviewed prior to a successful interconnection, will now be pursued.

Installations of devices to be locally connected may generally be implemented using the previously discussed null-modem cable. This is typically the case when both devices are configured as data terminal equipment (DTE). Recall that such devices generally provide the signals listed in Figure 8-1. The directions of these signals are important as they are output from the DTE. We say that the device is *emulating DTE* in that it generates the signals normally provided by DTE. Also, it is expecting to receive the signals normally generated by data communication equipment (DCE), such as a modem. So, in a null-modem cable, the output signals from the DTE were cross-connected to input signals such as those listed in Figure 8-2.

RS-232: A general rule may be established as follows: When cross-connecting between devices, make sure that an output signal goes to an input signal, and vice versa. A quick review of our null-modem cable shows that transmitted data (output) is cross-connected to received data (input). Also, data terminal ready

Pin	Function	Direction
2	Transmitted data	From DTE
4	Request to send	From DTE
11	Reverse channel (SRTS)	From DTE
19	Reverse channel (SRTS)	From DTE
20	Data terminal ready	From DTE

Figure 8-1

Pin	Function	Direction
3	Received data	To DTE
5	Clear to send	To DTE
6	Data set ready	To DTE
8	Data carrier detect	To DTE
12	Secondary DCD	To DTE

Figure 8-2

IBM PC		PS/2	
Direction	*Pin*	*Pin*	*Direction*
N/A	1 —————— 1		N/A
From PC	2	2	From PS/2
To PC	3	3	To PS/2
From PC	4	4	From PS/2
To PC	5	5	To PS/2
To PC	6	6	Not used
N/A	7	7	N/A
To PC	8	8	To PS/2
From PC	20	20	From PS/2

Figure 8-3

(output) is connected to data set ready (input). Whether dealing with a null-modem cable or any cable for cross connection, the general rule holds true.

For example, when connecting an IBM PC,* using the serial port provided by the asynchronous communications adapter, to an IBM PS/2 computer, a standard null-modem cable will work. This is because both of these machines are configured for connection to a modem (DCE). In other words, they are emulating DTE. This interconnection might be required to allow for a transfer of data files or programs between machines. The cable would connect the pins on the RS-232 interfaces as shown in Figure 8-3. Note that the general rule applies. Output signals are connected to input signals. Specifically, transmitted data (output) on the PC port is connected to received data (input) on the PS/2 port. The same applies to the RTS-CTS-DCD pins as well as the DTR-DSR pin assignments. Ease of implementation can be maintained if the rule is followed.

If the port is configured to emulate DTE, as in the example in Figure 8-3, a modem can be attached to the device with a straight-through cable. From the chart of both computers, one can see the signals that are normally expected by the modem. They are generally ground leads, transmit data, request to send, and data terminal ready. Thus, when connecting a computer, terminal, or printer to a modem, these signals must generally be provided.

What is the significance of a port that, conversely, emulates data communication equipment? The implication is that the device is providing signals normally provided by a modem. These signals are outlined in Figure 8-2. When connecting a standard terminal or printer to a port emulating DCE, the likelihood of cross connections is reduced. By applying our general rule, you can visualize that transmitted data, which is output from the terminal on pin 2, is already input to the port that is emulating DCE. Also, received data is provided by the DCE port as input to the terminal on pin 3. The crossing of a few leads may be required for an item such as flow control, but for the most part, a cable with straight-through leads

*IBM PC and PS/2 are trademarks of International Business Machines.

Direction	Pin		Pin	Direction
N/A	1	———	1	N/A
To DigiCHANNEL	2	———	2	From WY160
From DigiCHANNEL	3	———	3	To WY160
To DigiCHANNEL	4	———	4	From WY160
From DigiCHANNEL	5	———	5	To WY160
From DigiCHANNEL	6	———	6	To WY160
N/A	7	———	7	N/A
From DigiCHANNEL	8	———	8	To WY160
To DigiCHANNEL	20	———	20	From WY160

Figure 8-4

may be used as depicted in Figure 8-4. In this particular instance, a Wyse WY160* Terminal is being connected to a DigiCHANNEL† board from DigiBoard, with a DCE Ocfacable. Note that our rule still applies even though a straight-through cable is being used.

From the preceding examples you can surmise that one of the first factors to consider when interfacing equipment using RS-232 ports is whether a port or terminal is configured to emulate DTE- or DCE-provided signals. The best way to determine this is to review the device documentation. Consult the user's manual for this information. Ordinarily, the manuals that are provided with the equipment contain the information necessary to determine the direction and functions of the RS-232 leads.

If documentation is not available, a device is available for monitoring the RS-232 leads. A *break-out box*, described in Appendix E, may be used to determine which leads are provided by a device. Connect the break-out box to the RS-232 port and make sure that the device is powered and the port in question is active or enabled. The lights on the break-out box should display which leads are being generated from the device. From this display a determination can generally be made as to whether the device is emulating DCE or DTE. For example, if either pin 20, data terminal ready, or pin 4, request to send, is on, the port is more than likely emulating data terminal equipment and is expecting to be connected to a modem or device emulating data communication equipment signals. On the other hand, if the display shows that signals such as clear to send, data set ready, or data carrier detect are present, the port is probably emulating data communication equipment and will allow a straight-through cable to be used when connecting a terminal configured as DTE, as if connecting to a modem.

If neither the documentation nor a break-out box is available, consult Appendix F of this text. The pin assignments with their corresponding directions are listed for a multitude of devices. From the direction of the pins, a determination can be

*WY160 is a trademark of Wyse Technology, Inc.

†DigiCHANNEL is a trademark of DigiBoard, Inc.

made as to how the device is configured. Should all these sources fail, consult the dealer or vendor who markets the product.

Another important aspect of RS-232 interfacing is whether the port is programmable or not. Programmability involves, among other things, the ability to change the directions of the leads. This may be optionable through software or may require some hardware jumping on the I/O board that provides the port. This option may determine if a straight-through cable may be used by allowing the port to be configured to emulate either DTE or DCE. For example, when connecting a printer (DTE) to an optionable port, configure the port to emulate DCE, as this normally allows the use of a straight-through cable as opposed to a null-modem cable. If a modem is to be connected, configure the port as data terminal equipment to allow proper interaction of the signals. Once again, a straight-through cable may be used. If the port offers this flexibility, configure the port to best suit your environment.

Once the pin assignments and directions have been determined, consult Appendix G for a layout of the cables that may be built to interconnect two devices requiring cross connections. Many of the interconnections may be satisfied with a standard null-modem cable; other connections may require specialized cables. Many specialized cables are shown in Appendix G. It is important to note that not all the outlined pin connections in the appendix are required for the cables to work. They are merely provided for completeness. If your device is not listed in the appendix and you are attempting a connection, simply find a device in Appendix F that has the same pin configuration and use this device as a surrogate when referencing Appendix G.

Often, ports will provide signals generally used for testing purposes. These signals normally have a constant voltage on them, such as $+12$ volts or -12 volts. For example, some terminals have a positive voltage output on pin 9 of the interface. This lead may be very helpful in satisfying the requirements of the device to be attached.

Assume that a modem, to be connected to the terminal, requires pin 4 to be on before data may be transmitted. If the terminal doesn't provide pin 4 but does provide a positive voltage on pin 9, pin 9 may be crossed to pin 4, as depicted in Figure 8-5. This will maintain request to send (pin 4) and allow data transmission to occur. Modems may also provide signals like these and may be used to fulfill signal requirements in the same manner. The important factor is that all requirements of the ports, with regard to pins' being on or off, must be met.

The cable between the devices to be connected is important to successful implementation. However, after a cable has been built or supplied, a number of

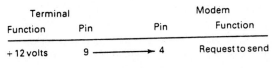

Terminal			Modem
Function	Pin	Pin	Function
+ 12 volts	9 ———————→	4	Request to send

Figure 8-5

Item	Options
Speed	75 bps to 19,200 bps
Flow control	ETX/ACK, XON/XOFF, hardware
Parity	Odd, even, none
Character length	5,6,7,8
# of stop bits	1,1.5,2
Mode	Simplex, half/full duplex
Echoplex	Yes, no
Line feeds	0,1,2
Transmission mode	Async, sync, isochronous
Polarity	Positive, negative

Figure 8-6

other items must be compared and set properly before the interfacing will be complete. Figure 8-6 provides a checklist for options generally found on computers and peripherals. Each element will be discussed as it relates to interfacing equipment.

Speed.   The port speed of both devices should be consistent to prevent data from being garbled. If the maximum rate of operation for a printer is 300 bits per second (bps), the device sending data to the printer must also be set at 300 bps. If both devices may transmit and receive at 4800 bps, set them both at 4800 bps. The speed of transmission through an RS-232 port becomes extremely important when a printer is involved, due to the aspects of buffering and flow control. Refer to the section on flow control for further explanation.

Flow Control.   Flow control, discussed in Chapter 6, involves the regulation of data transferred between two devices. Improper setting of this option could cause data to be lost, garbled, or not transmitted at all. Data flow must be regulated between devices such as a computer and a printer. Although both devices' transmission speeds are set the same, the speed of operation differs. The printer, because it is partially mechanical, may have a printing speed substantially less than the transmission speed, while the computer has the capability of transmitting at a much higher speed. Because of this, either the data must be buffered for delayed printing or flow control must occur to regulate when a printer is capable of receiving more data. For example, if the transmission speed is 4800 bps and each character has 10 bits, 480 characters per second (cps) are being transmitted by the computer (4800 divided by 10). However, the printer may be capable of printing only 100 cps. In these cases, flow control may be used to ensure that no loss of data occurs. Choices for flow control usually involve either XON/XOFF, ETX/ACK, or hardware via one of the RS-232 pins. As discussed in Chapter 6, XON/XOFF is a software flow control method in which characters are transmitted to indicate the status of the printer's condition. ETX/ACK, another software flow control scheme, is similar in concept to XON/XOFF. The connection of pins such as pins 11, 19, and 20 to a required input signal at the computer is termed *hardware flow control*. Flow control, used in conjunction with a buffer in the computer or printer, makes for a very efficient operation at maximum transmission speeds. With or without a buffer, flow control offers a means of overcoming the relatively slow operational speed of a printer. Other devices besides printers require flow control, but the concept is the same. The important aspect is that both ports are configured for the same flow-control method, software or hardware.

Parity.   Any of the parity types discussed in Chapter 2 are acceptable. Simply be consistent at both ends to prevent the garbling of data.

Character Length.   Another factor causing garbled data is the variation of character lengths. For example, there is a five-bit Baudot code and a seven-bit ASCII code. Regardless of the code, if parity is involved, determine if the character-length option includes the parity bit or not, and option accordingly at both ends. Be consistent.

Number of Stop Bits.   Ensure that the same stop bit length is selected at both ends. Check this option if garbled data appears sporadically. Chapter 2 describes the function of the stop bits. The selections are generally 1, 1.5, or 2. Choose the same number for both ends of the configuration.

Mode.   Generally, three modes of operation are available—simplex, half-duplex, and full-duplex. Selection should be consistent, as this option could determine which RS-232 signals are generated or monitored by a port. For example, if a printer is optioned for simplex mode (receive-only), pin 4 may not be generated. In a null-modem cable, this pin may be crossed to pin 8 at the computer end. If the computer requires pin 8 to be on before it will transmit, data transmission will never occur. Choose the mode that suits the environment, and option both ends accordingly.

Echoplex.   This option refers to the displaying of characters. Echoplex is closely related to the modes half- and full-duplex, and the terms are often used interchangeably by vendors to describe options. Some terminals have the option of either locally displaying characters as they are typed or leaving this up to the far end. The terminal may be optioned not to display the characters until they are "echoed" back from the far end, even though they are typed on the keyboard. If the far end is to echo the characters back to the originating device, this is termed *echoplexing*. By its very nature of operation, echoplexing implies that data will be both transmitted and received simultaneously (full-duplex). For example, if a CRT or terminal is connected to a computer that is optioned for echoplexing, a character typed at the keyboard is not displayed until the computer transmits it back. If you think of this in RS-232 terms, the characters that leave on pin 2, transmitted data, are not displayed until they are received on pin 3, received data. This may be used as a form of error detection. If the character displayed is not the same as the one typed, chances are that a parity error has occurred. The terminal operator can then backspace and retype the character.

The device that is to echo the characters should be optioned for echoplexing. As indicated, echoplexing is often confused with the duplexes. If a character is typed, such as *A*, and on the terminal appears *AA*, the far end is echoplexing while the terminal is optioned for local displaying of the characters as they are typed. Sometimes this is the half-duplex option. Half-duplex in this environment means that the terminal is locally generating the typed character. This, in conjunction with the far-end echoplexing, produces the double vision. Change the local terminal to full-duplex or the far end to no echoplexing to alleviate the problem. If, on the other hand, after an *A* is typed, nothing appears, the local device is probably optioned for full-duplex while the far end is not set up to echoplex. Change to half-duplex locally or to enable echoplexing at the far end to resolve the problem. Because they may not always be used interchangeably, the duplexes and echoplexing, as used in your devices, should be thoroughly understood for proper optioning.

Line Feeds.   This option generally offers three choices, 0, 1, or 2. Coordination between the two devices is in order to allow proper spacing on a terminal or printer. Generally, the devices may be optioned to perform a line feed upon the occurrence of a carriage return. If a computer transmits a carriage return to a terminal or printer only, the terminal will perform line feeds according to this option. An option of 0 in this circumstance will produce overwriting on the same line, as no vertical spacing takes place. If 1 is selected, single spacing will occur. Double spacing can be accomplished by selecting 2. Care should be taken in that the computer may already transmit a line feed along with a carriage return. In summary, if unwanted spacing occurs, this option should be checked.

Transmission Mode.   Three choices are generally available for this option: asynchronous, synchronous, or isochronous. Asynchronous implies that start and stop bits are required for timing purposes. In an asynchronous environment, be sure and check the number-of-stop-bits option. Synchronous transmission involves the use of clocks to transmit the data, as covered in Chapters 2 and 5. Option one of the devices in a synchronous environment to provide the timing and check that the proper leads are present in the cables. The third choice is *isochronous*, which is a combination of the other two. Data in an asynchronous format are transmitted synchronously. Ensure that both ends are optioned the same.

Polarity.   Polarity has to do with whether a signal is positive or negative. The important of polarity is generally realized in the area of hardware flow control. For example, if pin 19 is used for the busy signal, an option may exist for the signal on pin 19 to be either positive or negative when the buffer of the device has room available for more data. A determination should be made for the transmitting device's requirements. If the transmitting device requires a positive voltage on the busy signal to enable transmission, option the printer (or receiving device) to generate a positive, or true, signal. Some devices require the reverse or a negative signal for this; however, a positive indication is generally used. Option accordingly.

As these explanations indicate, there are many considerations beyond RS-232 factors that are involved when interfacing serial devices. However, the cable connecting the RS-232 ports is a significant component of the configuration.

In summary, all items should be checked for proper optioning to permit a successful installation. Consult the various user's manuals to determine how to option for DTE or DCE emulation, speed, parity, flow control, character length, number of stop bits, transmission mode, and various other options. Use Appendixes F and G for aids in configuring the proper cable between devices.

For further technical information on the details of the RS-232 and other proposed and existing serial interfaces, such as RS-449, consult Appendixes A, B, and C. The electrical characteristics of the signals, as well as the maximum and minimum voltages allowed on the interfaces, can be found in the standards provided. Another source is John McNamara's *Technical Aspects of Data Communications*, listed in the bibliography.

We hope you enjoy interfacing with EIA-232-D.

REVIEW QUESTIONS

1. Describe DTE emulation versus DCE emulation within an RS-232 port.
2. If data are being transmitted from a computer to a printer but are being garbled, what options should be checked?
3. If data are being lost or printed only sporadically, what options should be checked?
4. A VT-100 terminal operator types in an *M* and sees *MM* on the screen. Describe and solve the problem.
5. If an IBM PC is dumping data to a printer and the printer is double-spacing where it should only be single-spacing, explain the potential causes.

CHAPTER

9

most frequently asked questions about interfacing and answers to questions from chapters 1–8

Several companies specializing in providing support and products for connecting computers, modems, printers, and terminals have collected the most common questions that they are asked when supplying their services and support. This chapter provides the reader with a series of questions and answers for issues surrounding ports, serial cables, and parallel cables. The main topics are highlighted to provide the reader a quick reference for subject matters. Many items may appear to be simple or complex depending on your background. However, they do comprise the list of the "most difficult" to understand and most difficult for which to find answers. Refer to the appendices for specific cable design and port pinout information.

Following the generic questions are the answers to the questions found at the end of Chapters 1–8.

QUESTIONS RELATING TO *PORTS*

Question: What is the difference between **asynchronous and synchronous transmission**?

Answer: Asynchronous transmission is a method of sending and receiving characters by surrounding each of them with a start and stop bit. It is this encapsulation with start/stop bits that provides timing necessary to exchange data. No special timing is needed by the DTE devices and not provided by computers, printers, or terminals, with asynchronous ports, as well as the asynchronous modems. However, in a synchronous environment, timing is required. A clock pulse is used to time the sending and receiving of the characters. Synchronous transmission refers to the use of the timing signal as a means of synchronizing the sending and receiving of data from one device to another. Refer to Chapter 5 for more information about timing and synchronous environments.

Question: What does it mean to be **DTE versus DCE**?

Answer: DTE is an acronym for data terminal equipment, while DCE stands for data communications equipment. Normally the ports of computers, printers, plotters, and terminals are set up as DTE ports. A piece of DTE equipment has the leads as output and those as input that the RS-232 standards suggest. Such leads as output for DTE include Transmit Data, Request to Send, and Data Terminal Ready. Normal DTE input leads are Receive Data, Clear to Send, Data Set Ready, and Data Carrier Detect. DCE equipment has these same leads but with opposite directions. Modems, multiplexors, and any device designed to establish and provide a transmission connection are considered DCE devices.

Question: How can one tell if a port is wired as **DTE or as DCE?**

Answer: The clue as to the port emulation, as it is termed, is the nature of the device. If it is a modem or communication piece of equipment, then it is likely to be data communication equipment. Computers, printers, plotters, and terminals typically provide DTE ports. Be careful not to interpret this universally as some device's ports can emulate a different device. For example, the original Apple II Plus Serial card could be optioned to be either a DTE or DCE port. Many other devices offer similar capabilities. When ordering custom devices, such as print spoolers/buffers, the vendor can generally set up the ports to be either DTE or DCE ports. Hence, noting merely the category of equipment can be misleading. All vendors can provide you the type of port their device offers. Should you lack access to the user's manual or vendor, there is a manual way to determine the port type. By plugging in a breakout box, and enabling the device port, the leads that are on will give an indication of the port type. Use the leads just listed as a measure of the port emulation. If pins 4, 11, 19, or 20 are on (positive), and lead 2 is negative, the port is DTE. If leads 5, 6, or 8, are on (positive), and lead 3 is negative, the port is DCE. For non-DB25–size connectors, it is best to consult the user's manual and view the leads, functions, and directions.

Question: How is a **breakout box** used?

Answer: A breakout box is a test kit for monitoring and jumpering leads in an RS-232 device. The simplest breakout box "breaks out/makes available" the leads of a port, allowing the user to jumper the leads for testing a port or constructing a cable. The more elaborate breakout boxes or activity monitors provide LEDS to indicate the lead polarity (positive/negative) plus provide voltage levels to turn leads on or off. Using a full-featured breakout box, a user can determine which leads are present in an interface, determine positive and negative signals, turn leads on and off, jumper leads for cable design-construction-testing, and monitor the interface lead interaction. Depending on the speed of the interface, you can even see the one- and zero-bit activity (not enough to determine the characters being transmitted). The benefits of a breakout box are testing, port configuration analysis, cable construction, cable testing, and interface monitoring. Other breakout boxes are available for RS-422, Centronics parallel, RS-449, RJ-45, and V.35 ports. Acquire the correct breakout box that meets your port needs.

Question: How can one tell if a port is **serial or parallel?**

Answer: In the case of an IBM PC, the female port on the back is the parallel port, while the male ports are serial ports. The printers typically have a 36-pin connector conforming to an industry standard termed Centronics, due to the Centronics Computer Company's popular interface. All modems use serial communications, as do terminals. Because some terminals, and most computers, offer both serial and parallel ports, the user's manuals should be consulted for a description of each port and the method of transmission supported.

Question: When an IBM PC or compatible has both a **serial and a parallel** port how can a user know the **difference**?

Answer: The serial port on a PC or compatible board is male. The parallel port is female. In the case of an IBM PC/AT or compatible, the serial port is a 9-pin male connector while the parallel port is a 25-pin parallel port.

Question: What are **ABC, ABCDE, EIA, T-switches,** and **X-switches**?

Answer: Devices known as switches can be used to share a port among multiple printers or share a single printer among multiple computers. These switches are referred to as ABC, ABCDE, EIA, T-switches, or X-switches. ABC refers to the ports of a three-port switch connecting one device to two, typically labeled A, B, C, with C being the common device/port to be shared. The computer port would be connected to port C, with the two printers connected to ports A and B. The switch on the box is flipped between the A and B positions to make the various connections. EIA nomenclature arises from the fact that the EIA RS-232 standard dictates the ports that are being switched/shared. T-switch stems from the graphical representation of the leg of the ''T'' being connected to both ends of the bar on top of the letter ''T.'' The term ABCDE switch is used if a single port/device is to be connected to more than two devices. An X-switch cross connects two devices to two different devices depending on the switch setting. Imagine a device connected to port A connected to a device connected to port C with device B connected to device D when the switch is in one position. With the switch flipped to the other position, the connections are crossed (×) with devices attached to ports A and D, as well as B and C, now connected.

Question: How can one computer be connected to **more than one printer**?

Answer: If the computer has more than one port, multiple printers can be attached directly to the ports of the computers. However, if the number of ports on the computers are limited, the ABC-type switches can be used to share a port among multiple printer. The same is true for multiple computers using a single printer. ABC nomenclature is more popular as the same switches are being used to connect parallel devices in an IBM PC environment. Refer to the other questions on ABC switches for explanation of this application.

Question: What is a **port- or modem-sharing device**?

Answer: The idea behind a sharing device is to reduce costs. Typically multiple devices need access to modems for communication with other systems or services. Rather than purchase modems for each computer or terminal, a modem-sharing device can be installed to share the modem easily among all the users. The sharing device has the intelligence to know which computer or terminal is using it and will not allow other users to participate until the current user is finished. Typically, each port is polled by the intelligence in the sharing device. The Request to Send lead is monitored and interpreted to allocate the use of the single modem. If the RTS is on, and controls the modem, other devices are automatically restricted from gaining access until the "owning" device lowers RTS. Typical configurations support from two to eight devices.

Question: Can an **RS-232 ABC switch be used for RS-422 connections**?

Answer: It depends on the port sizes and shapes! If an Apple Macintosh RS-422 port is to be shared by multiple printers using RS-422 ports or RS-232 ports, the Mini-Din or DB-9 port of the Macintoshes are incompatible with the DB-25 ports of most ABC switches. Mini-Din and DB-9 ABC switches can accommodate these connections. RS-422 ports of other devices that are DB-25 in size can use standard RS-232 ABC switches, providing that enough conductors are present in the switch. RS-422 has positive and negative data leads, requiring more conductors than the typical RS-232 interface. Hence, once shape is factored, insure that enough conductors are switched by the ABC device.

Question: Can **pin configurations be changed** in a port?

Answer: It depends—the all-time favorite response to questions. Some ports provide option switches that can alter the direction and function of the leads of a port. The original Apple Super Serial Card for the Apple II models provide a shunt plug that could be plugged in one of two ways to provide DTE or DCE emulation. Breakout boxes are easy means of altering the pin configurations of a port. With breakout boxes, the user can connect any lead to be any other lead. The cable used to connect the port of one device to another can alter the pin configurations of the leads. The cable changes the pin configuration in the cable, but not actually in the port itself.

Question: How many pins are switched on an **RS232 switch box**?

Answer: All of them—at least those that are present in the switch box. When an RS-232 switch is used, typically the following leads at a minimum are switched/ present: 2, 3, 4, 5, 6, 8, 15, 17, 20, 22, 24, and 25 with leads 1 and 7 tied together. Others switch all 25 leads. A good way to determine which leads are switched is to use a voltage/ohmmeter and check each lead for continuity. Using an ABC switch with the switch in the position to connect two ports together, that is, port A to port C, check all the leads of port A, with the same leads of port C, one by one. Those leads that show continuity are switched; those that don't show up are not switched. Log your results as you proceed. Flip the switch to connect port B to port C and double check the continuity. Be aware that switches are available for a multitude of port sizes; hence, the numbering and quantity of leads will vary. However, the same testing technique can be used.

Question: What **gender connectors** are on the back of an ABC/EIA/T-switch?

Answer: Most switches come standard with female connectors on them. However upon request, most vendors will provide male connectors on all or some of the ports of a switch. Refer to the appendix on connectors for gender descriptions.

Question: If using an **IBM PC and two parallel printers,** why can a serial switch be used?

Answer: This is possible due to the usage of a DB-25-size port to provide a parallel port. With the introduction of the IBM PC, a new parallel interfacing technique was spawned, the DB-25 to Centronics 36-pin connection. Prior to the PC introduction, computers had 36-pin or other connectors on the computer, that were to be connected to the same size connector on the printer or peripheral. To save space on the back of the PC, a DB-25S (female) port was used. A cable is used to convert the 25-pin connector to be a 36-pin cable compatible with the ports that are standard on printers. A serial switch has no intelligence pertaining to the activity on the leads, but merely connects two ports together. Hence, the 25 pin ports (i.e., port C) can be connected to the IBM PC. At this point ports A and B on the switch mimic the IBM PC parallel port, DB-25 size. Cables that connect these ports to the printer ports must do the conversion from DB-25 to Centronics (36 pin). It is important that all leads are switched in the ABC switch used because the IBM parallel port uses the bulk of the 25 leads of the port. A single DB-25 cable, along with two DB-25 to 36-pin cables, are needed when a serial switch is used to connect a single PC to multiple parallel peripherals.

Question: Can a computer be connected to a **serial and parallel printer at the same time**?

Answer: Yes! The only requirement is that the computer provide both serial and parallel ports that the operating system or control program recognizes. Multiple connections are common when both a laser and dot matrix printer are connected to an IBM PC. Another example is when a printer and a plotter are connected to the same device. The software merely needs to recognize both ports and offer the ability to send data to either, or both of them.

Question: How can one tell if a port is running **serial or parallel**?

Answer: In the case of an IBM PC, the female port on the back is the parallel port, while the male ports are serial ports. The printers typically have a 36-pin connector conforming to an industry standard termed Centronics, due to the Centronics Computer's popular interface. All modems use serial communications, as do terminals. Because some terminals and most computers offer both serial and parallel ports, the user's manuals should be consulted for a description of each port and the method of transmission supported.

Question: What do **line drivers** do?

Answer: Line drivers are devices that condition digital signals to allow greater distances of transmission. Line drivers can be used instead of modems or extended distance cables to connect two serial devices up to 10 miles apart at speeds of 1200 bps or 2 miles at speeds of 9600. Both asynchronous and synchronous transmission can be supported, with higher speeds possible for the latter. The line drivers have RS-232 ports for connecting either directly to your device, using an RS-232 cable, or to another compatible line driver attached to the other device, using twisted pair cable. Another name for line drivers is short-haul modems.

Question: What is **parallel**? 36 pin?

Answer: Parallel interfaces support the sending and receiving of all the bits of a character at the same time. This requires enough data leads for each bit of the character, plus parity. Hence, a parallel interface has eight separate leads for sending or receiving data. The 36-pin feature is dictated by the industry standard Centronics parallel interface. Centronics Computer Corporation included this interface on its popular devices, with the rest of the industry eventually conforming to the 36-pin interface definition. Each of the leads on the interface has predefined functions. If adhered to properly, the vendors can claim that they have a Centronics-compatible interface. There are other parallel interfaces, but the Centronics is the most popular.

Question: What is **RS-422**, or **EIA-422**?

Answer: RS-422 is a standard outlined by the Electronics Industry Association (EIA) for the serial exchange of digital data between two pieces of equipment. It provides for a balanced interface, as opposed to RS-423 and RS-232, which are unbalanced circuits. Balanced, or differential, transmission uses relative measurements between a positive and negative signal to determine the on/off condition, without reference to a common ground. In contrast, RS-232 interfaces use a common signal ground for reference of signals. Greater distances and higher speeds are possible with RS-422 because these interfaces are less susceptible to noise and interference due to the relative measurements of the data signals.

Question: What is **serial**? 25 pin?

Answer: RS-232, or EIA-232 interfaces are for serial data transmission. This suggests that the bits of a character are sent and received one at a time, serially. Hence, in an RS-232 interface, there is only a single lead for sending data and a single lead for receiving data. The 25-pin feature is dictated by the RS-232 standard, where up to 25 leads can be present in a serial port. Not necessarily all 25 leads are used, but each lead has a predefined function if the port conforms to the standard.

Question: When should a **serial-to-parallel converter** be used?

Answer: Often equipment is already owned that has a particular type of port. For example, a computer may have a serial port, while a printer is equipped with a parallel port. Rather than acquire a board for the computer that provides a parallel port, a serial-to-parallel converter may be used to connect the devices. Furthermore, perhaps parallel ports are not available for a particular computer or terminal; hence, the serial port must be used. In this case, rather than replace the printer or add a serial port to the printer, a converter should be considered. Many converters offer both serial-to-parallel and parallel-to-serial conversion in the same unit. A switch is provided to select between the two. Hence, the above example could be accommodated as well as a computer with a parallel port connected to a printer with a serial port.

Question: Why can't **parallel and serial devices** be used **on the same ABC switch box**?

Answer: The switch merely connects ports together, without regard to logic or intelligence in the signals. The real issue is whether serial ports can be connected to parallel ports. Only with a serial-to-parallel converter is this possible as described in a different question. Hence, without some added intelligence in another device, the two ports are incompatible. Even then, once connected, the computer has to know the type of device it is connected to, that is, a modem or printer.

Question: Why is the **parallel interface** on an IBM PC the **same shape** as the serial interface?

Answer: With the introduction of the IBM PC, a new parallel interfacing technique was spawned, the DB-25 to Centronics 36-pin connection. Prior to the IBM PC introduction, computers had 36-pin or other size connectors for printer connections. These ports were to be connected to the same size port on the printer or peripheral via a cable with 36-pin connectors on each. To save space on the back of the PC, a DB-25S (female) port was used. A cable is used to convert the 25-pin connector to be a 36-pin cable compatible with the ports that are standard on printers. Hence, the parallel interface on the PC is the same size and shape as an RS-232 port. The gender of the parallel connector on the PC is female. The serial connectors for the PC are male. This is the easy way to tell the difference.

Question: What is a **spooler or buffer** for printing?

Answer: A printer is a relatively slow device when compared with a computer's processing capability. The user typically has to wait for the output device to complete the printing and is restricted from performing other processing activities. A spooler/buffer is either software or hardware designed to store temporarily the output information from an application destined for a printer/plotter. This mechanism then interacts with the printer to complete the printing function. The advantage is that the computer or user is free to pursue other functions and not be tied to the relatively slow output device.

Question: When should a **buffer device** be used? How about a buffer device **versus a software spooler**?

Answer: Generally, the amount of printing should dictate whether an external buffer or print spooler is used. Unless a multitasking system, a system that can do more than one thing at a given time, is connected to a printer, the user must wait until the printer completes the output before proceeding to other computer activities. Hence if heavy printing is to be done, an external print spooler or buffer should be considered.

When a multitasking system or software spooler is used, again the amount of printing to be done should dictate whether an external device is used. When a software spooler is used, the same computer resources are used to run the software spooler that are required to do spreadsheet computations, word processing, or database searches. Hence, the computer is shared simultaneously between the spooling function and the current application function. This can slow down the user's computer responsiveness. Rather than tie up the computer's resources, an external buffer can be acquired to free-up the main computer for dedicated operation by the user. The computer merely performs the print function in the normal fashion, with the buffer receiving all the data and storing it in its memory. The computer is then free to perform other user tasks. The buffer then interacts directly with the printer, feeding it information as fast as the printer can print. Even with windowing environments that support multitasking and software spooling, an external buffer should be considered for heavy print environments.

If multiple computers need to share a single printer, an external buffer provides the spooler function, but also provides a device sharing function.

QUESTIONS RELATING TO *SERIAL CABLES*

Question: What is the **distance limitation for RS-232 cables**?

Answer: According to the standard as published by the Electronics Industries Association, the recommended maximum distance is 50 feet. However, longer distances are possible using shielded cabling or line drivers.

Question: Is there a **single cable** that will allow a PC to work with any other device? Why won't one cable work?

Answer: The RS-232 standard was established for the connection of DTE and DCE devices. Normally modems were connected to a computer or terminals using

RS-232 interfaces. With the advent of minicomputers and microcomputers, devices such as terminals and printers, were locally connected to computers using the RS-232 interface. The cable necessary to connect two local devices depends on whether a devices' port emulates DTE or DCE.

Also, printers using hardware flow control with serial interfaces don't all use the same lead for flow control. One of these leads, 4, 11, 19, or 20, could be used. Hence, no one cable can meet all the possibilities.

Question: How do I tell the **sex of a cable**?

Answer: If metal pins are present in the connector or port, the port is a male. If holes/sockets are present, the port or connector is of female gender.

Question: What is a **wire list**?

Answer: When referring to a cable, this refers to the conductor wires in the cable and the way they are connected from one cable end to the other: straight through from 1–1, 2–2, 3–3, and so on or jumpered from 1–1, 2–3, 3–2, 4–5–8, and so on. When referring to a device's port, the wire list is the same as the port pinouts. The pinouts refer to the leads, functions, and directions of leads that are present in a device's port.

Question: What are the **causes of noise or garbled characters**?

Answer: Interference on a signal is the main cause of distortion of data. Electromagnetic and radio frequency interference are typical causes of noise. The concept of noise is similar to that of static on a voice telephone conversation.

Question: The manufacturer of a computer states that the RS-232 cables can only be run up to **50 feet**. Is there a way to **extend this distance** without losing any data?

Answer: The manufacturer is indicating that its port conforms to the RS-232-C standard, which recommends a maximum distance of 50 feet of cable between devices. The reason for limited distance is signal levels, which fade over distance due to loss of signal strength, interference, and so on. Vendors offer extended distance cables that support distances much greater than 50 feet. These cables have extra shielding that reduces signal loss. Hence, greater distance are possible.

Question: What is the difference between a **standard** and **shielded cable**?

Answer: In a standard cable, the leads are individually wrapped and have an outer wrapping that merely contains all of the conductors of a cable. With a shielded cable, a protective layer or sheath surrounds each wire. Also the conductors are grouped in pairs with another protective layer around these pairs of wires with optional additional ground wires for draining interference. Furthermore, some types of extra wrapping (usually foil) is then wrapped around all these pairs of conductors to provide maximum shield from interference.

Question: What are the **benefits of** using a **shielded cable**?

Answer: The interference from electromagnetic and radio frequencies can be avoided or reduced if a cable is shielded. Because of less noise and other interference, signals can be carried much farther; hence, the longer possible distance when using shielded cables.

Question: When is **shielding necessary**?

Answer: The RS-232 allows for limits up to 50 feet. Should the cable distance, not the linear distance, exceed this recommendation, shielded cabling should be considered. The speed of the interface operation will have an impact on this requirement, with lower speeds being less susceptible to interference and hence tolerating greater cable distances. Also the actual location of the cable between the two devices is a critical factor in determining if shielded cables are required. Radio and electromagnetic interference is caused by air conditioners, generators, computer equipment, and other heavy machinery. If the cable is placed next to some of this type of equipment, noise could be a factor. Consider using shielded cabling if this is the environment for your configurations.

Question: With a serial **cable length greater than 50 feet** between a terminal and a computer, what problems can be expected?

Answer: Merely because the cable distance between two devices exceeds 50 feet does not automatically imply that there will be problems with noise and garbled or lost data. However, the greater the distance, the greater potential for loss of data. Distances of up to several hundred feet are possible without data distortion, but the RS-232 does not recommend such distances. However, alternatives exist if the distance exceeds 50 feet. Reduce the speed of the device ports from 19,200 to 9600, to 4800, to 2400, that is, until no data is lost. Use line drivers to regenerate or amplify the signals. Also consider shielded cable.

Question: What exactly does a **null-modem cable** do and when should it be used?

Answer: A straight-through cable, or standard cable, is used to connect a piece of DTE to DCE. Data terminal equipment is a computer, terminal, or printer connected to a piece of data communications equipment, or modem. This configuration can then be connected to another similar configuration via phone lines. When a computer, terminal, or printer is to be locally attached to another computer or terminal, the modems are not needed. The RS-232 interface for the exchange of data between DTE and DCE devices. When no modems are involved to connect two DTE devices together, a cable must be provided with cross-connections to mimic the absent DCE RS-232 lead interactions. Hence, a null-modem cable (no modems) is used to connect two pieces of data terminal equipment locally together. The resulting interface functions just as if there were two modems and a phone connection between the two pieces of DTE.

Question: What is the difference between a **modem and a null-modem** cable?

Answer: A modem cable is one with the leads straight through from one to the other, that is, leads 1 to 1, 2 to 2, 3 to 3, . . ., 25 to 25. A null-modem cable contains the appropriate leads jumpered and crossed over to replicate the normal (but absent) modem lead interactions with the attached DTE.

Questions: Why won't a standard **null-modem cable work in synchronous environments**?

Answer: The previous questions dealt with how a null-modem cable mimics the absent pair of modems. A null modem works great in environments known as asynchronous. No special timing is needed by the DTE devices and is not provided by the asynchronous modems. However, in a synchronous environment, timing is required. Normally the modem has to provide the timing signal. With no modems (null-modem cable), there is no timing source. Hence, a standard null-modem cable will not work. If an alternate timing source can be provided for the synchronous ports, a null-modem cable (slightly modified) can work. Normally, a special device called a synchronous modem eliminator is necessary to provide both a timing source (clock) and the normal null modem cable functions. The exception to this require-ment is if one of the DTE devices can provide a timing source. Typically this is found on lead 24 of the RS-232 interface if it is supported. By connecting this lead to leads 15 and 17 on both ends of the cable, along with the other null-modem cross-connections, two synchronous devices can communicate. Refer to Chapter 5 for more information about timing and synchronous environments.

Question: What information should the customer have prior to purchasing a **nonstandard cable**?

Answer: The purpose of this book is to prepare the user for designing his or her own nonstandard cables. To design a cable properly, the following information about each device port is needed: gender of port, gender size (DB9, DB-25, Mini-DIN, RJ-45, etc.), the number of leads/conductors, lead numbers, functions that are provided on these leads, direction of leads (in/out), and flow control capability (XON/XOFF or hardware lead. Armed with this information for each port, a cable can then be designed, built, or purchased.

Question: What is the difference between a null modem and a **gender changer**?

Answer: A null-modem cable has been described in other questions. A gender changer is a device, or cable, that converts a gender (male/female) into the opposite gender (female/male). These are used to allow the use of existing cables, switches, and other devices. For example, if a cable is already available that has male connectors on both ends, and the user desires to connect an IBM PC port (male) to a Hayes Smartmodem (female), it won't work due to a gender mismatch. Hence, a gender changer could be used to convert the IBM PC port to be female, allowing the male/male cable to be used.

Question: How does a user know **how many conductors** to request in a cable?

Answer: Generally, the user can count the number of leads in each port of the devices to be connected. Select a cable with at least the same number of conductors as the port with the most leads. The only way to know exactly how many conductors are needed in the cable is to design the appropriate cable. Once this is done, the exact number of conductors will be known, factoring in cross-connections and pin-to-pin jumperings.

Question: Why do some vendors provide **modular phone ports for serial connections**?

Answer: Space on a computer or peripheral is precious. Hence, the smaller the connectors on the chassis or boards, the greater the potential for reducing the overall size of the device. This is one of the reasons Apple is providing 8-pin Mini-DIN connectors on its computers and peripherals. Modular cords and connectors provide the same real estate benefits and are readily available at minimum costs. Hence, some computer vendors offer RJ-45 (8–10 pin) connectors or ports for connecting devices together. Typically, the RS-232 signals are used in these ports. Hence, a conversion to connect to devices with DB-25 connectors is needed. Consult the appendices for cross-connections between different ports of devices.

Also, most buildings have excess capacity wiring in the walls and between floors from the telephone wiring. Hence, the wiring for connecting devices on the same floor and between floors could already exist. Also the wiring is very orderly with easy access to wiring closets for any cross-connections.

Question: How can **modular cables** be used **for serial connections**?

Answer: If two devices to be connected have DB-25-size ports, modular cables may be used for the connection. This is accomplished by utilizing modular adapters that have both DB-25 and RJ-45 connectors. One of these adapters is needed for both devices. Jumpering within the adapter accomplished all the cross-connections. Once the connectors are configured, a standard modular (8-pin) cord can be connected to the modular receptacles on each adapter. The only user caution is to ensure that enough conductors are available in the modular cord (generally eight or four) to accommodate the connection. Also there are adapters that convert DB-9, DB-15, and DB-25 to modular connections. Select the one that meets your device's port requirements.

QUESTIONS RELATING TO *PARALLEL CABLES*

Question: What is the **distance limitation for a parallel cable**?

Answer: Normally 6- to 10-foot cables are used. However, distances up to 20 feet are actually allowable.

Question: How can a user obtain the **pinouts** for a printer cable?

Answer: If a cable vendor supplied the cable, and it is an ''off-the-shelf'' cable, they can provide the wire list and cross-connections. If the cable has been custom-made, ask the cable provider for the cable design. If neither of these is available, the user can test the cable conductors and their cross-connections by using a multimeter and testing for conductibility. By using the continuity/conductor test capability of a voltage/ohmmeter, an exact cable layout can be established. By touching one probe to pin 1 of one cable end, and sequentially touching the other probe to all other leads in that connector, as well all leads in the other connector at the other end of the cable, the user can log the connections. Repeat this process for every single pin in both connectors. Although a tedious task, it is very effective for determining the conductor connections. Label the cable with the new found information to save time in the future.

Question: Why can't **RS-232 cables** be used **in parallel connections**?

Answer: RS-232 interfaces are for serial data transmission. This suggests that the bits of a character are sent and received one at a time, serially. Hence, in an RS-232 interface there is only a single lead for sending data, and a single lead for receiving data. By contrast, parallel interfaces support the sending and receiving of all the bits of a character at the same time. This requires enough data leads for each bit of the character, plus parity. Hence, a parallel interface has eight separate leads for sending or receiving data. Because of this fundamental difference in the means of sending and receiving data, the two ports are incompatible. Hence, RS-232 cables cannot be used for parallel connections. The only exception is when ABC switches are used, and this is only for a link in the overall connection, not actually to provide the complete connection. Refer to the questions on ABC switches for further clarification.

QUESTIONS RELATING TO *PRINTERS* WITH *SERIAL INTERFACES*

Question: When a printer/plotter supports **DTR flow control,** what does this mean?

Answer: The connotation is that hardware flow control is supported. RS-232 nomenclature for the lead that is used to provide hardware flow control in this case is Data Terminal Ready (DTR). Other references include SRTS for Secondary Request to Send and Busy for any number of different leads.

Question: How can a user tell if the end of the cable is **male or female**?

Answer: Without exploiting the details of the birds and the bees, a male connector has pins protruding from it, while a female connector has holes (sockets/receptacles) for the pins (up to 25) to fit into.

Question: What is the difference between **hardware and software flow control**?

Answer: Software flow control involves the transmission and reception of an ASCII character to regulate the flow of data. Hence, this technique uses the transmit data lead in an RS-232-C interface. Hardware flow control uses the on/off condition of a port lead to accomplish the same data flow control. A lead in the port will be kept on as long as data can be received, but dropped/lowered when no more may be received. Both accomplish the same goal.

Question: Which is better—**serial or parallel interfaces for printers**?

Answer: If the distance between a printer and attached device exceeds 6 to 10 feet, maybe a serially interfaced printer might be more appropriate. Because the RS-232-C standard allows distances of up to 50 feet, this may be a better selection.

Speeds can be a factor if long documents will be printed and a buffer is involved. Because 9600 or 19,200 bps are the top speeds found in a printer's serial port, a document of 2000 characters would take about 2–3 seconds (2000 characters times 10 bits per character divided by 9600 bps). With a parallel interface, which is typically operating in the 1000s of characters per second range, the same document takes on 1 second. This is not that big of a deal unless you are printing lengthy documents or a large number of documents. The times stated here reflect time required for a computer to send the document to the printer, not the time of the actual printing. Print speed dictates actual throughput rates.

As more print servers are being used with local area networks, the number of users placing demands on a printer increases. Here the speed of the interface could be an issue, but really the buffer size and management of the buffer plays a larger role. Once the printer's buffer is filled, the server cannot send any more data until buffer memory is released. The interface speeds is not that big a factor. But the location of the printer is extremely important. A print server is set up to allow multiple users to share a single printer. The printer is attached to a computer on a network. The computer that is attached to the printer may not be centrally located. With a parallel interfaced printer, the distance of 6–10 feet may not allow easy access to the printer by all users. However, with an RS-232 interface, the distance of 50 feet (or more) could offer the users more flexibility.

Question: What is **polarity**?

Answer: When hardware flow control is used, one of the port's leads of a printer will reflect the readiness of the printer to receive data. Polarity is often an option allowing the user to establish whether an ''on'' or ''off'' condition indicates the printer's readiness. If the attached computer needs leads on to operate, the polarity of the printer should be set to ''HI.'' This implies that it will have a positive voltage on the hardware flow control lead as long as the printer is ready. When it is not ready, a negative or off condition will occur. Because this output control lead is connected to the computer's input leads, the computer will be able to interpret the off condition as a signal to stop sending data. If the computer needs to see a lead come on, or go "HI" to indicate an error condition, then polarity should be set to "low."

Question: When **connecting a printer to a computer,** it is usually necessary to use eight wires in the cable. But to **connect a terminal,** only three wires are required. Why the **difference**?

Answer: A couple of factors determine the number of pins required in a cable. It is possible to use only three pins to connect a printer to a computer. Factors such as flow control, error condition indications, interface indicators, protective grounding requirements, and port requirements dictate the number of required conductors.

Review the known leads that are minimally required for printer connection. These are receive data (usually lead 3) and signal ground (almost always lead 7). Protective ground (pin 1) is not usually needed. Hence only two leads are required thus far.

The use of flow control requires one additional lead. When hardware flow control is used, normally one of the leads 4, 11, 19, or 20 is used. Software flow control uses pin 2 as transmit data to send the XON/XOFF sequences. Hence, flow requires one more lead, bringing the total thus far to three.

Occasionally a printer uses more than one lead to indicate printer conditions when hardware flow control is used. Pin 20 may be used to indicate if the printer lid is open, while pin 19 in the same printer will indicate buffer status and paper out conditions. If multiple printer conditions are indicated on more than one hardware lead, this adds to the pin requirements. However, this is not normally the case, as the flow control lead handles this.

A printer may have input leads that must be on for the printer to receive data or as an indication that there is an attached computer. If the printer provides an output lead, such as 4 or 20, one of these can be locally looped back to the input leads. As long as 4 or 20 is on, the input leads will be on. Hence, no other leads were required. If the printer does not provide any output control leads, then a lead from the computer will have to be used for this purpose, thus requiring another conductor in the cable.

Hence, if the printer uses the flow control technique, software or a single hardware lead, to indicate all error conditions, and any printer input control leads can be satisfied by a printer output control lead, a cable with only three conductors may be used. Local jumpering requires pins/sockets in the connector, not conductors/wires in the cable.

A terminal, on the other hand, normally uses software flow control and, hence, requires no extra leads. The XON/XOFF technique uses the same lead (usually pin 2) as the keyboard operate does for sending data. Hence, pins 2, 3, and 7 are required. Most terminals and computers don't require any input control signals, or they are locally jumpered in the connector.

QUESTIONS RELATING TO *PRINTERS*
WITH *PARALLEL INTERFACES*

Question: Why does the **distance for running parallel Centronics cable** vary for different equipment?

Answer: The distance between devices has to do with signal levels outputted or expected by two attached devices. Because the parallel standards have a signal range for each signal, and signals fade as distances increase, the distance between two devices will vary. If a vendor's port outputs signals that are near the lower level allowed by the standard, then the distance allowed could be reduced.

Another factor is the type of equipment that is cabled, or where the cabling is "ran." Heavy machinery such as air conditioners, compressors, and so on, cause interference that can cause signal power loss. Hence, pay attention to where cabling is ran.

Question: How can a printer with a Centronics-compatible **36-pin port** be connected to a **25-pin port** of an IBM PC/XT/AT? The number of pins don't match.

Answer: The Centronics standard allows for 36 pins, some of which are not used. Also each signal lead has a separate ground lead associated with it. By sharing a common signal ground lead, the number of leads required are reduced. Also several of the leads in the 36-pin interface are not required for the PC connection. By crossing over leads within the cable, in particular the signal ground leads, the number of conductors can be reduced to 25. The reason the printer end has the 36-pin connector is because not all computers will have the 25-pin connector like a PC. Hence, a crossover cable allows most printers with 36-pin connectors to be connected to PCs. These same printers can also be connected to other computers that have 36-pin ports, by using a straight-through cable with 36-pin connectors at each end.

Question: What does it mean to be **HP compatible or Epson compatible**?

Answer: Printer compatibility can mean many things. When referring to interfacing, Centronics compatible implies that a printer conforms to the interface standard that Centronics printer company established. A printer that is HP or Epson compatible typically supports the same escape sequences as the printer they emulate. Hence, if a printer offers Epson compatibility, the same escape sequence used to shrink the print can be used on the non-Epson printer. This is important from an application software standpoint. A variety of printers can be selected for use with a system as long as the application can easily support them. Printer compatibility allows for this. Some printers may offer multiple compatibility modes, that is, both HP and Epson. The reason for this is that not all application programs may support the HP printer, but they almost all support an Epson printer. Hence, the printer with more compatibility modes offers such flexibility.

Question: Why is **software flow control not used in parallel connections**?

Answer: Parallel connections are simplex, implying only a single direction of data transmission. XON/XOFF involves the transmission of a character to the device that is sending data, simultaneous with the reception of data (full duplex). Consequently, a hardware lead is raised and lowered for flow control.

QUESTIONS RELATING TO *MODEMS*

Question: Why can't an **asynchronous modem support synchronous devices**?

Answer: One of the principles of asynchronous transmission is the framing of each character with a start and stop bit. These enclosing bits provide the timing. With synchronous communications, a timing source is used by the attached device for outputting the data. Without a clock pulse, the DTE would never send out data. An asynchronous modem does not provide the timing lead or allow for such transmission. Thus asynchronous modems cannot support synchronous transmission. However, some low-speed dial-up modems now offer both asynchronous and synchronous transmission capabilities. The attached device's transmission technique should match that of the modem.

Question: What is **"AT" compatability** when referring to intelligent modems?

Answer: "AT" compatibility describes a modem's ability to support a standard command set. This standard was established by Hayes Microcomputer Products with its Smartmodem series of modems. The sequence, "AT," short for ATtention, preceded the bulk of the commands that the modem accepted. As software programmers and users made use of this command set in the Hayes modems, other modem vendors offered the same support. Modems with "AT" compatibility support the same, a superset, or subset, of the Hayes Smartmodem series commands.

Question: Why are **all 1200-baud modems not compatible**?

Answer: 1200 bps indicates the speed of the modem. Other factors such as modulation techniques determine if two modems can communicate. AT&T offered the 212A modem that used one modulation technique at 300 bps and a different technique at 1200 bps. Furthermore, the 212A was a full-duplex modem. Some 1200-bps modems are half-duplex only, making them incompatible with a 212A modem.

Question: What is the **normal gender of a modem**?

Answer: Almost all modems are provided with a female connector. This is the recommendation as outlined in the RS-232-C standard. The standard indicates that a female connector should be associated with, but not necessarily physically attached to, the DCE equipment. This implies that a cable could extend from the modem device with a female connector at the end of the cable. However, most modems have the female connector mounted directly on the back of the modem. The standard suggests that DTE devices provide male connectors.

Question: What is **security dial-back,** and how does it work?

Answer: This is a feature of a computer, or possibly a modem, that protects a computer system from illegal access by unauthorized users. The concept stems from the fact that most users access a computer system from stable points, normally their office and/or home. The terminals, or PC, used to access remote computer systems have modems and associated phone numbers. The dial-back feature allows the remote computer system to store information about a user such as their phone number associated with their modem(s). Once a user dials in, the computer system can then accept a login, or immediately prompt the user for the phone number from where they are calling. A disconnect occurs with the computer checking its database and calling the input number. If the number matches a database entry, then the computer knows who the user should be. Once the computer's outbound call is answered by the computer/terminal of the originator of the session, the login prompt is issued. Comparisons are made to determine that logins, passwords, and phone numbers are valid. Otherwise, a disconnect occurs to close out the session.

QUESTIONS RELATING TO *TERMINAL INTERFACING*

Question: What does it mean when a terminal is **ANSI X3.64 compatible**?

Answer: The American National Standards Institute (ANSI) produced a standard that defines "a set of encoded control functions to facilitate data interchange with two-dimensional character-imaging input-output devices." The standard outlines guidelines to allow editing functions, formatting, the specification and control of input areas, as well as certain status setting and interrogation functions, mode selection, and typesetting composition functions. The most common use of the standard, but not limited to, has been by interactive terminal manufacturers.

When a terminal claims ANSI X3.64 compatibility, the implication is that the terminal conforms to the standard. It can handle the escape sequences as outlined in the standard for screen formatting as an example. Hence, any application that uses the appropriate escape sequences can work with the ANSI X3.64 terminal.

Question: Is **DEC VT100 compatibility** the same as ANSI X3.64 compatibility?

Answer: No! The two are very similar, but there are differences. The DEC VT100 terminal is X3.64 compatible, but offers a superset of features. Some of these features include double-height characters, 132-column display of characters, and so on. These features are not found in the X3.64 standard, but are included in the

VT100's capabilities. Hence, vendors will indicate that terminals are VT100 compatible, normally with a few exceptions such as the features just mentioned.

Question: What is the difference between **"print on line" and a screen copy**?

Answer: Print on line (POL) refers to the capability of a terminal simultaneously to print the data it receives as well as display it on the screen. Hence, as a terminal displays data received from an attached or remote computer, a hard copy can be made. The sending computer can control the POL function through escape codes. The computer can cause a terminal to enter POL mode, either displaying or not displaying received data on the screen. Once the data are printed, the computer takes the terminal out of POL mode.

Screen copy, or print local, refers to the capability of a terminal to print a copy of its screen at any given moment. In effect, the printer can produce a picture of the screen contents when the screen copy key is typed. As the data change on the screen, the screen copy key must be typed again to print the new contents.

Question: What significance is a terminal's capability to support **forms**?

Answer: If a terminal can support forms, this implies that memory is available for setting up forms for local data entry. The user can fill out a form and transmit it to a remote or local computer, sending only the variable information. The computer can actually send a sequence to request the sending of this variable information. This offloads the computer.

Question: Why is it better to have the remote computer **echoplex the characters** rather than have the terminal echo them locally?

Answer: This feature has to do with data integrity. Echoplexing is enabled (although it is often referred to as full duplex) to have the computer to which a terminal is attached send back the characters as they are entered on the terminal's keyboard. The terminal displays them only after they are received back through the remote serial port. If users see the same character on the screen that they had typed, they can be assured that the character made it to the computer without error. If, however, the displayed character is different, then an error occurred. This allows the user to backspace and reenter the character(s). If the terminal was merely locally displaying the characters as they were entered, the user would not be aware of any parity errors or other problems that might occur.

Question: What is wrong when a **backspace** key is typed on a terminal's keyboard, with the cursor on the screen backing up, but the data subsequently entered **not appearing correctly** in the computer?

Answer: Chances are that there are two keys on the terminal's keyboard that perform similar functions. One of them is the backspace key, with the other being the delete key. One of them may be a nondestructive backspace that merely locally backs up one space without altering data, while the other may actually delete a character. Depending on the computer system, either key may be correct. Check which key should be used to back up one space to actually correct a character.

Question: What is **line wrap**?

Answer: Line wrap is the ability of a terminal to receive greater than 80 characters (or the maximum line size) of data without losing it. A terminal without line wrap can receive more than 80 characters of data, but will lose the 81st through XX character. The cursor will sit in the 80th position of a line and scroll through the received characters, but the terminal will not display all of them. With line wrap, the cursor advances to the line on the screen automatically and displays the remaining characters.

QUESTIONS RELATING TO *COMPUTERS* WITH *SERIAL INTERFACES*

Question: What is **systems administration** or systems generation?

Answer: These the techniques of defining the parameters necessary to make a computer support attached devices. Systems administration is the term predominantly used for minicomputers or PCs running UNIX. System generation refers to the similar setup that occurs in mainframes.

Question: Most back to back connections require a null-modem cable. How can a **computer to terminal connection use a straight-through cable**?

Answer: A straight-through cable is used to connect a computer to a modem or a DTE device to a DCE device. Hence, the computer is emulating DTE and the terminal emulating DCE, or vice versa. Many computer manufacturers define their ports to emulate DCE ports so terminal connections can use ribbon cables for connections.

Question: When do I need a **protocol converter**?

Answer: Devices communicate with a set of rules, just as humans do. During a conversation with someone, one party listens, while the other talks. If one party didn't hear what was said, they would ask the other party to repeat it. If they don't, that part of the conversation is lost. The words and characters between each party must be the same; otherwise, an interpreter is required. The same is true of devices. If two devices with different communication rules (protocols) or different characters/words (ASCII/EBCDIC) need to communicate, an interpreter (protocol converter) will allow dissimilar devices to communicate. Also the converter will map each device's capabilities to the others.

Question: When a user **disconnects** from a remote computer, how does the computer know?

Answer: Most computers accept the "Control-D" sequence, EOT, as the end of transmission character. Receipt of this character is interpreted to mean that the connection should be broken. The computer then uses the RS-232 leads to disconnect the dial-up connection. By lowering pin 20, DTR, the modem will disconnect the attached line. Hence, the connection is broken by the computer upon receipt of a Control D. Depending on the system, different characters may be used, but the concept is the same.

Question: In the middle of **downloading** a file from an online computer service, onto a local PC, what occurs causing the download to **abort**?

Answer: Many things could happen. The most prominent reason for an abnormal ending to a download is the receipt of a character that closes the file you are receiving into. Several computer service bureaus embed control characters in their data to prevent such downloading. Upon receipt of these control sequences, the terminal emulation or communication software, will act on the received control sequences. Check the emulation package to see if an option exists to receive but not interpret the received control sequences to get around this problem. Another possibility is that noise on the line is bad enough that the modem disconnects. A spike, or hit, on the line could also be interpreted as a disconnect.

Chapter 2

1. asynchronous transmission
2. Simplex
3. nonsimultaneously, simultaneously
4. communications facilities *or* telephone lines
5. terminals, printers, computers
6. data terminal equipment
7. data communication equipment
8. RS-232
9. dial-up *or* switched
10. Private
11. Modem
12. modem
13. Signals
14. parity
15. start, stop

Chapter 3

1. 2, 3, received data
2. 22, ring indicator. No, it correlates to the ringing of the phone.
3. 20, data terminal ready
4. Data set ready will be high.
5. half-duplex (HDX)
6. 4, request to send; data carrier detect, clear to send
7. Request to send (pin 4)
8. Data terminal ready (pin 20)
9. 1
10. reference point, 7
11. Pin 2 is normally the lead used for characters output from the terminal to the modem, while the modem passes the characters it receives off the line to the terminal on pin 3, received data. When an intelligent modem is used, the pins serve the same function, as far as directions of data. What changes are the data. Between the modem and the terminal, the information necessary to dial and establish a connection is transferred. It is up to the modem to interpret the digits for dialing and supply the appropriate responses back to the terminal. A sample interaction on pins 2 and 3 might be as shown in Figure 9–1.
12. DTR, pin 20, is the RS-232 pin determining whether a call is maintained or not. When a terminal is in on-line mode, DTR is asserted. To disconnect, merely place the terminal off-line by either unplugging it, pressing a local mode button, or disabling the RS-232 port in some fashion. By placing the terminal in local mode, DTR is deasserted. The modem, upon detection of this, drops the call.
13. Autoanswer allows unattended operation at a computer or terminal site. Pin 20, DTR, allows the modem to answer the call if it is optioned for this feature. The way a modem knows that a call is arriving is by monitoring pin 22, ring indicator, which fluctuates with the ringing of the phone. Even if autoanswer is optioned in the modem and pin 22 indicates an incoming call, the modem will not answer the call unless pin 20 is on.
14. Reviewing the RS-232 signals, we find that upon entrance of data mode, either manually or automatically, the modem gives an output signal to the computer (DTE) indicating that a connection has been established. Once this occurs, the modem turns on pin 6, data set ready. The computer, upon detection of DSR high, knows it can transmit data across the dial-up connection and promptly prompts the promptee.
15. The golden rule when dealing with RS-232 connections is: An output goes to an input, and vice versa. For example, an output signal from DTE is an input signal to DCE. Transmitted data, output from DTE, are actually input to the modem for transmission over the telephone lines. At the far end, the modem

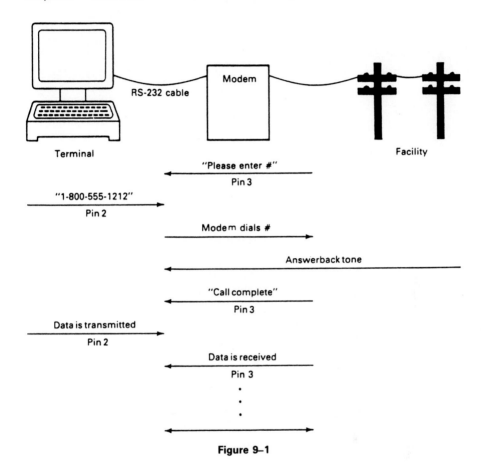

"Please enter #"

Pin 3

"1-800-555-1212"

Pin 2

Modem dials #

Answerback tone

"Call complete"

Pin 3

Data is transmitted

Pin 2

Data is received

Pin 3

Figure 9–1

receives the data and outputs them on pin 3 to the DTE. The DTE accepts them as input, or received data. Perspective becomes extremely important. Viewing pin 4, RTS, from the terminal's perspective, it carries output from the DTE. Viewing this same lead from the modem's angle, it carries input into DCE. Remember: Output to input, input to output.

16. See Figure 3–6.

Chapter 4

1. DSR (pin 6).
2. DSR is off.
3. False
4. False
5. True
6. See Figure 4–2.

Chapter 5

1. asynchronous transmission
2. synchronous transmission
3. buffering
4. timing
5. bits per second (bps)
6. 20,000
7. transmit, receive
8. 24; 15
9. 17
10. slave
11. The issue of internal versus external determines which leads will be used for the clock signal to drive the data. The complicating factor is whether the option of internal or external is being viewed from the perspective of the terminal or computer or the modem. This option is normally viewed from the modem's perspective.

    From the Modem's Perspective: With internal timing, the modem will provide to the DTE on pin 15 the rate at which data will be transmitted. With external timing, the modem will receive its transmit timing from the DTE on pin 24.

    From the Terminal's Perspective: With internal timing, the terminal will provide the clock rate to the DCE on pin 24. With external timing, the terminal will receive the transmitting rate from the DCE on pin 15.

12. Slave timing is a means of reducing the number of timing sources in a network. By deriving the transmit timing from a received signal, the number of clocks is limited, which decreases the likelihood of errors that might normally occur with mismatched clocks. The transmit timing is said to be slaved off the receive timing.
13. Asynchronous transmission, also known as start/stop, is a scheme in which each character is individually timed, by the start and stop bits. Synchronous transmission is a scheme involving the buffering of data to be transmitted at a clock rate, determined by DTE or DCE, at a constant, predictable rate.
14. See Figure 5–6.

Chapter 6

1. primary
2. Secondary. XON/XOFF: An XOFF character is transmitted by the printer to indicate that it can't receive any more data. Once the printer problem condi-

tion clears, an XON character is transmitted. This is an indication to the computer that it can resume data transmission.

3. STD, SRD
4. SRTS, SCTS, SDCD/SRLSD
5. reverse channel
6. If the print speed is less than the transmission (port) speed and the buffer associated with the printer fills up, data could be lost unless a scheme is devised to tell the computer when to temporarily stop transmitting data. This can be accomplished by software or hardware. If both devices support software flow control, the XON/XOFF characters can be transmitted to start and stop data transmission. If XON/XOFF is not supported, reverse channel can be used as a hardware RS-232 flow-control mechanism.

Chapter 7

1. null-modem cable
2. Cross
3. synchronous modem eliminator
4. 50
5. ground, data, control, and timing
6. DTE
7. 1, 7
8. 3
9. CTS, 5, 8
10. 20, DSR
11. data set ready
12. 24
13. pins 24, 15, and 17
14. timing
15. Secondary request to send
16. The connections would be as shown in Figure 9–2. Don't connect pin 4 straight through at the printer end. Connect pin 19 from the printer to pin 4 at the modem. At the computer, don't connect pins 5 and 8 straight through. From the modem, connect pin 8 to pin 5 into the computer. As long as the printer at the far end has pin 19 on, indicating that it can receive data, this indication will be passed over to the computer via the RTS-DCD interaction. Because pin 8 is looped up to pin 5, this will give a clear-to-send indication back to the computer.
17. Output signal to input signal, input signal to output signal

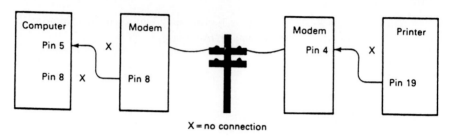

X = no connection

Figure 9–2

Chapter 8

1. When a port is set up to emulate DTE, it is outputting the signals normally output by terminal equipment such as RTS, DTR, and SRTS. At the same time, it is expecting to receive the standard DCE input signals, such as CTS, DSR, and DCD, whereas a port set up as DCE is expecting to be attached to DTE. Signals like TD, RTS, and DTR are input signals, and RD, CTS, DSR, and DCD are output signals for the port.

2. speed, number of stop bits, parity, character length

3. XON/XOFF—either hardware or software, buffer size

4. Find out if the far-end computer is echoplexing. If so, set the VT-100 terminal option to full-duplex or whatever option eliminates the local echo. The local echo in conjunction with the echo causes the double image.

5. The computer board could be adding two line feeds (LF) to each carriage return (CR). Maybe the printer is adding the additional LF. If single spacing is desired, ensure that the computer or printer performs a line feed with each carriage return, but not both devices.

APPENDIX

A

EIA standard
EIA-232-D

This appendix contains extracts from the Electronic Industries Association EIA-232-D Standard, which outlines the interface between data terminal equipment and data communication equipment and data communication equipment employing serial binary data interchange. The standard, in its entirety, is available for order from the following address:

EIA Engineering Department
Standards Sales
2001 Eye Street, N.W.
Washington, D.C. 20006
(202) 457-4966

Notice

EIA engineering standards are designed to serve the public interest through eliminating misunderstandings between manufacturers and purchasers, facilitating interchangeability and improvement of products, and assisting the purchaser in selecting and obtaining with minimum delay the proper product for his particular need. Existence of such standards shall not in any respect preclude any member or nonmember of EIA from manufacturing or selling products not conforming to such standards, nor shall the existence of such standards preclude their voluntary use by those other than EIA members whether the standard is to be used either domestically or internationally.

Recommended standards are adopted by EIA without regard to whether or not their adoption may involve patents on articles, materials, or processes. By such action, EIA does not assume any liability to any patent owner, nor does it assume any obligation whether to parties adopting recommended standards.

1.1   This standard is applicable to the interconnection of data terminal equipment (DTE) and data communication equipment (DCE) employing serial binary data interchange. It defines:

Section 2. Electrical Signal Characteristics
Electrical characteristics of the interchange signals and associated circuitry.
Section 3. Interface Mechanical Characteristics
Definition of the mechanical characteristics of the interface between the data terminal equipment and the data communication equipment.
Section 4. Functional Description of Interchange Circuits
Functional description of a set of data, timing, and control interchange circuits for use at a digital interface between data terminal equipment and data communication equipment.

Section 5. Standard Interfaces for Selected Communication System Configurations

Standard subsets of specific interchange circuits defined for a specific group of data communication system applications.

In addition, the standard includes:

Section 6. Recommendations and Explanatory Notes

Section 7. Glossary of New Terms

1.2   This standard includes thirteen specific interface configurations intended to meet the needs of fifteen defined system applications. These configurations are identified by type, using alphabetic characters A through M and where the configuration of interchange circuits is to be specified, in each case, by the supplier.

1.3   This standard is applicable for use at data signaling rates in the range from zero to a nominal upper limit of 20,000 bits per second.

1.4   This standard is applicable for the interchange of data, timing, and control signals when used in conjunction with electronic equipment, each of which has a single common return (signal ground), that can be interconnected at the interface point. It does not apply where electrical isolation between equipment on opposite sides of the interface point is required.

1.5   This standard applies to both synchronous and nonsynchronous serial binary data communication systems.

1.6   This standard applies to all classes of data communication service, including:

1.6.1   Dedicated leased or private-line service, either two-wire or four-wire. Consideration is given to both point-to-point and multipoint operation.

1.6.2   Switched-network service, either two-wire or four-wire. Consideration is given to automatic answering of calls; however, this standard does not include all of the interchange circuits required for automatically originating a connection. (See EIA Standard RS-366, "Interface Between Data Terminal Equipment and Automatic Calling Equipment for Data Communication.")

1.7   The data set may include transmitting and receiving signal converters as well as control functions. Other functions, such as pulse regeneration, error control, etc., may or may not be provided. Equipment to provide these additional functions may be included in the data terminal equipment or in the data communication equipment, or it may be implemented as a separate unit interposed between the two.

1.7.1   When such additional functions are provided within the data terminal equipment or the data communication equipment, this interface standard shall apply only to the interchange circuits between the two classes of equipment.

1.7.2 When additional functions are provided in a separate unit inserted between the data terminal equipment and the data communication equipment, this standard shall apply to both sides (the interface with the data terminal equipment and the interface with the data communication equipment . . .) of such separate unit.

1.8 This standard applies to all of the modes of operation afforded under the system configurations indicated in Section 5, Standard Interfaces for Selected Communication System Configurations.

Pin number	Circuit	Description
1	AA	Protective ground
2	BA	Transmitted data
3	BB	Received data
4	CA	Request to send
5	CB	Clear to send
6	CC	Data set ready
7	AB	Signal ground (common return)
8	CF	Received line signal detector
9	—	(Reserved for data set testing)
10	—	(Reserved for data set testing)
11		Unassigned
12	SCF	Secondary received line signal detector
13	SCB	Secondary clear to send
14	SBA	Secondary transmitted data
15	DB	Transmission signal element timing (DCE source)
16	SBB	Secondary received data
17	DD	Receiver signal element timing (DCE source)
18		Unassigned
19	SCA	Secondary request to send
20	CD	Data terminal ready
21	CG	Signal quality detector
22	CE	Ring indicator
23	CH/CI	Data signal rate selector (DTE/DCE source)
24	DA	Transmit signal element timing (DTE source)
25		Unassigned

Figure A-1   Interface Connector Pin Assignments

Interchange Circuits

Circuit AA: Protective Ground (CCITT 101)
Direction: Not applicable
This conductor shall be electrically bonded to the machine or equipment frame. It may be further connected to external grounds as required by applicable regulations:

Circuit AB: Signal Ground or Common Return (CCITT 102)
Direction: Not applicable

This conductor establishes the common ground reference potential for all interchange circuits except Circuit AA (Protective Ground). Within the data communication equipment, this circuit shall be brought to one point, and it shall be possible to connect this point to Circuit AA by means of a wire strap inside the equipment. This wire strap can be connected or removed at installation, as may be required to meet applicable regulations or to minimize the introduction of noise into electronic circuitry.

Circuit BA: Transmitted Data (CCITT 103)
Direction: TO data communication equipment
Signals on this circuit are generated by the data terminal equipment and are transferred to the local transmitting signal converter for transmission of data to remote data terminal equipment.

The data terminal equipment shall hold Circuit BA (Transmitted Data) in marking condition during intervals between characters or words, and at all times when no data are being transmitted.

In all systems, the data terminal equipment shall not transmit data unless an ON condition is present on all of the following four circuits, where implemented.

1. Circuit CA (Request to Send)
2. Circuit CB (Clear to Send)
3. Circuit CC (Data Set Ready)
4. Circuit CD (Data Terminal Ready)

All data signals that are transmitted across the interface on interchange circuit BA (Transmitted Data) during the time an ON condition is maintained on all of the above four circuits, where implemented, shall be transmitted to the communication channel. . . .

Circuit BB: Received Data (CCITT 104)
Direction: FROM data communication equipment
Signals on this circuit are generated by the receiving signal converter in response to data signals received from remote data terminal equipment via the remote transmitting signal converter. Circuit BB (Received Data) shall be held in the Binary One (Marking) condition at all times when Circuit CF (Received Line Signal Detector) is in the OFF condition.

On a half-duplex channel, Circuit BB shall be held in the Binary One (Marking) condition when Circuit CA (Request to Send) is in the ON condition and for a brief interval following the ON to OFF transition to Circuit CA to allow for the completion of transmission (see Circuit BA, Transmitted Data) and the decay of line reflections. . . .

Circuit CA: Request to Send (CCITT 105)
Direction: TO data communication equipment
This circuit is used to condition the local data communication equipment for

data transmission and, on a half-duplex channel, to control the direction of data transmission of the local data communication equipment.

On one-way-only channels or duplex channels, the ON condition maintains the data communication equipment in the transmit mode. The OFF condition maintains the data communication equipment in a nontransmit mode.

On a half-duplex channel, the ON condition maintains the data communication equipment in the transmit mode and inhibits the receive mode. The OFF condition maintains the data communication equipment in the receive mode.

A transition from OFF to ON instructs the data communication equipment to enter the transmit code. . . . The data communication equipment responds by taking such action as may be necessary and indicates completion of such actions by turning ON Circuit CB (Clear to Send), thereby indicating to the data terminal equipment that data may be transferred across the interface point on interchange Circuit BA (Transmitted Data).

A transition from ON to OFF instructs the data communication equipment to complete the transmission of all data which was previously transferred across the interface point on interchange Circuit BA and then assume a nontransmit mode or a receive mode, as appropriate. The data communication equipment responds to this instruction by turning OFF Circuit CB (Clear to Send) when it is prepared to respond again to a subsequent ON condition of Circuit CA.

Note: A nontransmit mode does not imply that all line signals have been removed from the communication channel. . . .

When Circuit CA is turned OFF, it shall not be turned ON again until Circuit CB has been turned OFF by the data communication equipment.

An ON condition is required on Circuit CA as well as on Circuit CB, Circuit CC (Data Set Ready), and, where implemented, Circuit CD (Data Terminal Ready) whenever the data terminal equipment transfers data across the interface on interchange Circuit BA.

It is permissible to turn Circuit CA ON at any time when Circuit CB is OFF regardless of the condition of any other interchange circuit.

Circuit CB: Clear to Send (CCITT 106)
Direction: FROM data communication equipment
Signals on this circuit are generated by the data communication equipment to indicate whether or not the data set is ready to transmit data.

The ON condition, together with the ON condition on interchange circuits CA, CC, and, where implemented, CD, is an indication to the data terminal equipment that signals presented on Circuit BA (Transmitted Data) will be transmitted to the communication channel.

The OFF condition is an indication to the data terminal equipment that it should not transfer data across the interface on interchange Circuit BA.

The ON condition of Circuit CB is a response to the occurrence of a simultaneous ON condition on Circuit CC (Data Set Ready) and Circuit CA (Request to Send), delayed as may be appropriate to the data communication equipment for establishing a data communication channel (including the removal of the Mark Hold clamp from the Received Data interchange circuit of the remote data set) to remote data terminal equipment.

When Circuit CA (Request to Send) is not implemented in the data communication equipment with transmitting capability, Circuit CA shall be assumed to be in the ON condition at all times, and Circuit CB shall respond accordingly.

Circuit CC: Data Set Ready (CCITT 107)
Direction: FROM data communication equipment
Signals on this circuit are used to indicate the status of the local data set. The ON condition on this circuit is presented to indicate [all of the following]:

1. The local data communication equipment is connected to a communication channel ("Off Hook" in switched service).
2. The local data communication equipment is not in test (local or remote), talk (alternate voice), or dial* mode. . . .
3. The local data communication equipment has completed, where applicable:
   a. any timing functions required by the switching system to complete call establishment, and;
   b. the transmission of any discreet answer tone, the duration of which is controlled solely by the local data set.

Where the local data communication equipment does not transmit an answer tone, or where the duration of the answer tone is controlled by some action of the remote data set, the ON condition is presented as soon as all the other listed conditions (1, 2, and 3a) are satisfied.

This circuit shall be used only to indicate the status of the local data set. The ON condition shall not be interpreted as either an indication that a communication channel has been established to a remote data station or the status of any remote station equipment.

The OFF condition shall appear at all other times and shall be an indication that the data terminal equipment is to disregard signals appearing on any other interchange circuit with the exception of Circuit CE (Ring Indicator). The OFF condition shall not impair the operation of Circuit CE or Circuit CD (Data Terminal Ready).

When the OFF condition occurs during the progress of a call before Circuit CD is turned OFF, the data terminal equipment shall interpret this as a lost or aborted connection and take action to terminate the call. Any subsequent ON condition on Circuit CC is to be considered a new call.

When the data set is used in conjunction with automatic calling equipment (ACE), the OFF to ON transition of Circuit CC shall not be interpreted as an

*The data communication equipment is considered to be in the dial mode when circuitry directly associated with the call-origination function is connected to the communication channel. These functions include signaling to the central office (dialing) and monitoring the communication channel for call progress or answer-back signals.

indication that the ACE has relinquished control of the communication channel to the data set. Indication of this is given on the appropriate lead in the ACE interface (see EIA Standard RS-366).

> *Note:* Attention is called to the fact that if a data call is interrupted by alternate voice communication, Circuit CC will be in the OFF condition during the time that voice communication is in progress. The transmission or reception of the signals required to condition the communication channel or data communication equipment in response to the ON condition of interchange Circuit CA (Request to Send) of the transmitting data terminal equipment will take place after Circuit CC comes ON, but prior to the ON condition on Circuit CB (Clear to Send) or Circuit CF (Received Line Signal Detector).

Circuit CD: Data Terminal Ready (CCITT 108.2)
Direction: TO data communication equipment
Signals on this circuit used to control switching of the data communication equipment to the communication channel. The ON condition prepares the data communication equipment to be connected to the communication channel and maintains the connection established by external means (e.g., manual call origination, manual answering, or automatic call origination).

When the station is equipped for automatic answering of received calls and is in the automatic answering mode, connection to the line occurs only in response to a combination of a ringing signal and the ON condition of circuit CD (Data Terminal Ready); however, the data terminal equipment is normally permitted to present the ON condition on Circuit CD whenever it is ready to transmit or receive data, except as indicated below.

The OFF condition causes the data communication equipment to be removed from the communication channel following the completion of any "in process" transmission. See Circuit BA (Transmitted Data). The OFF condition shall not disable the operation of Circuit CE (Ring Indicator).

In switched-network applications, when Circuit CD is turned OFF, it shall not be turned ON again until Circuit CC (Data Set Ready) is turned OFF by the data communication equipment.

Circuit CE: Ring Indicator (CCITT 125)
Direction: FROM data communication equipment
The ON condition of this circuit indicates that a ringing signal is being received on the communication channel.

The ON condition shall appear approximately coincident with the ON segment of the ringing cycle (during rings) on the communication channel.

The OFF condition shall be maintained during the OFF segment of the ringing cycle (between "rings") and at all other times when ringing is not being received. The operation of this circuit shall not be disabled by the OFF condition on Circuit CD (Data Terminal Ready).

Circuit CF: Received Line Signal Detector (CCITT 109)

Direction: FROM data communication equipment

The ON condition on this circuit is presented when the data communication equipment is receiving a signal which meets its suitability criteria. These criteria are established by the data communication equipment manufacturer.

The OFF condition indicates that no signal is being received or that the received signal is unsuitable for demodulation.

The OFF condition of Circuit CF (Received Line Signal Detector) shall cause Circuit BB (Received Data) to be clamped to the Binary One (Marking) condition.

The indications on this circuit shall follow the actual onset or loss of signal by appropriate guard delays.

On half-duplex channels, Circuit CF is held in the OFF condition whenever Circuit CA (Request to Send) is in the ON condition and for a brief interval of time following the ON to OFF transition of Circuit CA. (See Circuit BB.)

Circuit CG: Signal Quality Detector (CCITT 110)

Direction: FROM data communication equipment

Signals on this circuit are used to indicate whether or not there is a high probability of an error in the received data.

An ON condition is maintained whenever there is no reason to believe that an error has occurred.

An OFF condition indicates that there is a high probability of an error. It may, in some instances, be used to call automatically for the retransmission of the previously transmitted data signal. Preferably the response of this circuit shall be such as to permit identification of individual questionable signal elements on Circuit BB (Received Data).

Circuit CH: Data Signal Rate Selector (DTE Source) (CCITT 111)

Direction: TO data communication equipment

Signals on this circuit are used to select between the two data signaling rates in the case of dual rate synchronous data sets or the two ranges of data signaling rates in the case of dual range nonsynchronous data sets.

An ON condition shall select the higher data signaling rate or range of rates.

The rate of timing signals, if included in the interface, shall be controlled by this circuit as may be appropriate.

Circuit CI: Data Signal Rate Selector (DCE Source) (CCITT 112)

Direction: FROM data communication equipment

Signals on this circuit are used to select between the two data signaling rates in the case of dual rate synchronous data sets or the two ranges of data signaling rates in the case of dual range nonsynchronous data sets.

An ON condition shall select the higher data signaling rate or range of rates.

The rate of timing signals, if included in the interface, shall be controlled by this circuit as may be appropriate.

Circuit DA: Transmitter Signal Element Timing (DTE Source) (CCITT 113)
Direction: TO data communication equipment

Signals on this circuit are used to provide the transmitting signal converter with signal element timing information.

The ON to OFF transition shall nominally indicate the center of each signal element on Circuit BA (Transmitted Data). When Circuit DA is implemented in the DTE, the DTE shall normally provide timing information on this circuit whenever the DTE is in a power ON condition. It is permissible for the DTE to withhold timing information on this circuit for short periods provided Circuit CA (Request to Send) is in the OFF condition. (For example, the temporary withholding of timing information may be necessary in performing maintenance tests within the DTE.)

Circuit DB: Transmitter Signal Element Timing (DCE Source) (CCITT 114)
Direction: FROM data communication equipment

Signals on this circuit are used to provide the data terminal equipment with signal element timing information. The data terminal equipment shall provide a data signal on Circuit BA (Transmitted Data) in which the transitions between signal elements nominally occur at the time of the transitions from OFF to ON condition of the signal on Circuit DB. When Circuit DB is implemented in the DCE, the DCE shall normally provide timing information on this circuit whenever the DCE is in a power ON condition. It is permissible for the DCE to withhold timing information on this circuit for short periods provided Circuit CC (Data Set Ready) is in the OFF condition. (For example, the withholding of timing information may be necessary in performing maintenance tests within the DCE.)

Circuit DD: Receiver Signal Element Timing (DCE Source) (CCITT 115)
Direction: FROM data communication equipment

Signals on this circuit are used to provide the data terminal equipment with received signal element timing information. The transition from ON to OFF condition shall nominally indicate the center of each signal element on Circuit BB (Received Data). Timing information on Circuit DD shall be provided at all times when Circuit CF (Received Line Signal Detector) is in the ON condition. It may, but need not, be present following the ON to OFF transition of Circuit CF . . .

Circuit SBA: Secondary Transmitted Data (CCITT 118)
Direction: TO data communication equipment

This circuit is equivalent to Circuit BA (Transmitted Data) except that it is used to transmit data via the secondary channel.

Signals on this circuit are generated by the data terminal equipment and are connected to the local secondary channel transmitting signal converter for transmission of data to remote data terminal equipment.

The data terminal equipment shall hold Circuit SBA (Secondary Transmitted Data) in marking condition during intervals between characters or words and at all times when no data are being transmitted.

In all systems, the data terminal equipment shall not transmit data on the secondary channel unless an ON condition is present on all of the following four circuits, where implemented:

1. Circuit SCA (Secondary Request to Send)
2. Circuit SCB (Secondary Clear To Send)
3. Circuit CC (Data Set Ready)
4. Circuit CD (Data Terminal Ready)

All data signals that are transmitted across the interface on interchange Circuit SBA during the time when the above conditions are satisfied shall be transmitted to the communication channel . . .

When the secondary channel is usable only for circuit assurance or to interrupt the flow of data in the primary channel (less than 10 baud capability), Circuit SBA (Secondary Transmitted Data) is normally not provided, and the channel carrier is turned ON or OFF by means of Circuit SCA (Secondary Request to Send). Carrier OFF is interpreted as an interrupt condition.

Circuit SBB: Secondary Received Data (CCITT 119)
Direction: FROM data communication equipment
This circuit is equivalent to Circuit BB (Received Data) except that it is used to receive data on the secondary channel.

When the secondary channel is usable only for circuit assurance or to interrupt the flow of data in the primary channel, Circuit SBB is normally not provided. See interchange Circuit SCF (Secondary Received Line Signal Detector).

Circuit SCA: Secondary Request to Send (CCITT 120)
Direction: TO data communication equipment
This circuit is equivalent to Circuit CA (Request to Send) except that it requests the establishment of the secondary channel instead of requesting the establishment of the primary data channel.

Where the secondary channel is used as a backward channel, the ON condition of Circuit CA (Request to Send) shall disable Circuit SCA and it shall not be possible to condition the secondary channel transmitting signal converter to transmit during any time interval when the primary channel transmitting signal converter is so conditioned. Where system considerations dictate that one or the other of the two channels be in transmit mode at all times but never both simultaneously, this can be accomplished by permanently applying an ON condition to Circuit SCA (Secondary Request to Send) and controlling both the primary and secondary channels, in complementary fashion, by means of Circuit CA (Request to Send). Alternatively, in the case, Circuit SCB need not be implemented in the interface.

When the secondary channel is usable only for circuit assurance or to interrupt the flow of data in the primary data channel, Circuit SCA shall serve to turn ON the secondary channel unmodulated carrier. The OFF condition of Circuit SCA shall turn OFF the secondary channel carrier and thereby signal an interrupt condition at the remote end of the communication channel.

Circuit SCB: Secondary Clear to Send (CCITT 121)

Direction: FROM data communication equipment

This circuit is equivalent to Circuit CB (Clear to Send) except that it indicates that availability of the secondary channel instead of indicating the availability of the primary channel. This circuit is not provided where the secondary channel is usable only as a circuit assurance or an interrupt channel.

Circuit SCF: Secondary Received Line Signal Detector (CCITT 122)

Direction: FROM data communication equipment

This circuit is equivalent to Circuit CF (Received Line Signal Detector) except that it indicates the proper reception of the secondary channel line signal instead of indicating the proper reception of a primary channel received-line signal.

Where the secondary channel is usable only as a circuit assurance or an interrupt channel (see Circuit SCA, Secondary Request to Send), Circuit SCF shall be used to indicate the circuit assurance status or to signal the interrupt. The ON condition shall indicate circuit assurance or a noninterrupt condition. The OFF condition shall indicate circuit failure (no assurance) or the interrupt condition.

B

EIA standard
EIA-449

This appendix contains parts of the Electronic Industries Association EIA-449 Standard, which outlines the general-purpose 37-position and 9-position interface for equipment employing serial binary data interchange. The actual standard may be ordered from:

EIA Engineering Department
Standards Sales
2001 Eye Street, N.W.
Washington, D.C. 20006
(202) 457-4966

Notice

EIA engineering standards are designed to serve the public interest through eliminating misunderstandings between manufacturers and purchasers, facilitating interchangeability and improvement of products, and assisting the purchaser in selecting and obtaining with minimum delay the proper product for his particular need. Existence of such standards shall not in any respect preclude any member or nonmember of EIA from manufacturing or selling products not conforming to such standards, nor shall the existence of such standards preclude their voluntary use by those other than EIA members whether the standard is to be used either domestically or internationally.

Recommended standards are adopted by EIA without regard to whether or not their adoption may involve patents on articles, materials, or processes. By such action, EIA does not assume any liability to any patent owner, nor does it assume any obligation whatever to parties adopting recommended standards.

EIA Standard EIA-449 was developed in close coordination and cooperation with the international standards activities of the CCITT (International Telegraph and Telephone Consultative Committee) and ISO (International Organization for Standardization) and is compatible with CCITT Recommendation V.24, "List of Definitions for Interchange Circuits Between Data Terminal Equipment and Data Circuit-Terminating Equipment," and Recommendation V.54, "Loop Test Devices for Modems," as well as with ISO Draft Proposal DP-4902, "37-Pin and 9-Pin DTE/DCE Interface Connectors and Pin Assignments."

General-Purpose, 37-Position and 9-Position Interface for Data Terminal Equipment and Data Circuit-Terminating Equipment Employing Serial Binary Data Interchange

Foreword. (This Foreword provides additional information and does not form an integral part of the EIA Standard specifying the General-Purpose 37-

Position and 9-Position Interface for Data Terminal Equipment and Data Circuit-Terminating Equipment Employing Serial Binary Data Interchange.)

This Standard, together with EIA Standards EIA-422 and EIA-423, is intended to gradually replace EIA Standard EIA-232-D as the specification for the interface between data terminal equipment (DTE) and data circuit-terminating equipment (DCE) employing serial binary data interchange. With a few additional provisions for interoperability, equipment conforming to this standard can interoperate with equipment designed to EIA-232-D. This standard is intended primarily for data applications using analog telecommunications networks.

EIA Standard EIA-232-D is in need of replacement in order to specify new electrical characteristics and to define several new interchange circuits. New electrical characteristics are needed to accommodate advances in integrated circuit design, to reduce crosstalk between interchange circuits, to permit greater distances between equipments, and to permit higher data signaling rates. With the expected increase in use of standard electrical interface characteristics between many different kinds of equipment, it is now appropriate to publish the electrical interface characteristics in separate standards. Two electrical interface standards have been published for voltage digital interface circuits:

EIA Standard EIA-422 "Electrical Characteristics of Balanced-Voltage Digital Interface Circuits"

EIA Standard EIA-423, "Electrical Characteristics of Unbalanced-Voltage Digital Interface Circuits"

With the adoption of EIA Standards EIA-422 and EIA-423, it became necessary to create a new standard which specifies the remaining characteristics (i.e., the functional and mechanical characteristics) of the interface between data terminal equipment and data circuit-terminating equipment. That is the purpose of this standard.

The basic interchange circuit functional definitions of EIA Standard EIA-232-D have been retained in this standard. However, there are a number of significant differences:

1. Application of this standard has been expanded to include signaling rates up to 2,000,000 bits per second.

2. Ten circuit functions have been defined in this standard which were not part of EIA-232-D. These include three circuits for control and status of testing functions in the DCE (Circuit LL, Local Loopback; Circuit RL, Remote Loopback; and Circuit TM, Test Mode), two circuits for control and status of the transfer of the DCE to a standby channel (Circuit SS, Select Standby, and Circuit SB, Standby Indicator), a circuit to provide an out-of-service function under control of the DTE (Circuit IS, Terminal In Service) a circuit to provide a new signal function (Circuit NS, New Signal), and a circuit for DCE frequency selection (Circuit SF, Select Frequency). In addition, two circuits

have been defined to provide a common reference for each direction of transmission across the interface (Circuit SC, Send Common, and Circuit RC, Receive Common).

3. Three interchange circuits defined in EIA-232-D have not been included in this standard. Protective ground (EIA-232-D Circuit AA) is not included as part of the interface to permit bonding of equipment frames, when necessary, to be done in a manner which is in compliance with national and local electrical codes. However, a contact on the interface connector is assigned to facilitate the use of shielded interconnecting cable. The two circuits reserved for data set testing (EIA-232-D contacts 9 and 10) have not been included in order to minimize the size of the interface connector.

4. Some changes have been made to the circuit function definitions. For example, operation of the Data Set Ready circuit has been changed and a new name, Data Mode, has been established due to the inclusion of a separate interchange circuit (Test Mode) to indicate a DCE test condition.

5. A new set of standard interfaces for selected communication system configurations has been established. In order to achieve a greater degree of standardization, the option in EIA-232-D which permitted the omission of the Request to Send interchange circuit for certain transmit only or duplex primary channel applications has been eliminated.

6. A new set of circuit names and mnemonics has been established. To avoid confusion with EIA-232-D, all mnemonics in this standard are different from those used in EIA-232-D. The new mnemonics were chosen to be easily related to circuit functions and circuit names.

7. A different interface connector size and interface connector latching arrangement have been specified. A larger-size connector (37-position) is specified to accommodate the additional interface leads required for the ten newly defined circuit functions and to accommodate balanced operation for ten interchange circuits. In addition, a separate 9-position connector is specified to accommodate the secondary channel interchange circuits. The 37-position and 9-position connectors are from the same connector family as the 25-position connector in general use by equipment conforming to EIA Standard EIA-232-D. A connector latching block is specified to permit latching and unlatching of the connectors without the use of a tool. This latching block will also permit the use of screws to fasten together the connectors. The different connectors will also serve as an indication that certain precautions with regard to interface voltage levels, signal risetimes, fail-safe circuitry, grounding, etc., must be taken into account before equipment conforming to EIA-232-D can be connected to equipment conforming to the new electrical characteristic standards.

The connector contact assignments have been chosen to facilitate connection of equipment conforming to this standard to equipment conforming to EIA-232-D.

Close attention was given during the development of EIA-449 and EIA-423 to facilitate an orderly transition from the existing EIA-232-D equipment to the next generation without forcing obsolescence or costly retrofits. It will therefore be possible to connect new equipment designed to EIA-449 on one side of an interface to equipment designed to EIA-232-D on the other side of the interface. Such interconnections can be accomplished with a few additional provisions associated

Circuit mnemonic	Circuit name	Circuit direction	Circuit type	
SG	Signal ground	—	Common	
SC	Send common	To DCE		
RC	Receive common	From DCE		
IS	Terminal in service	To DCE	Control	
IC	Incoming call	From DCE		
TR	Terminal ready	To DCE		
DM	Data mode	From DCE		
SD	Send data	To DCE	Data	Primary channel
RD	Receive data	From DCE		
TT	Terminal timing	To DCE	Timing	
ST	Send timing	From DCE		
RT	Receive timing	From DCE		
RS	Request to send	To DCE	Control	
CS	Clear to send	From DCE		
RR	Receiver ready	From DCE		
SQ	Signal quality	From DCE		
NS	New signal	To DCE		
SF	Select frequency	To DCE		
SR	Signaling rate selector	To DCE		
SI	Signaling rate indicator	From DCE		
SSD	Secondary send data	To DCE	Data	Secondary channel
SRD	Secondary receive data	From DCE		
SRS	Secondary request to send	To DCE	Control	
SCS	Secondary clear to send	From DCE		
SRR	Secondary receiver ready	From DCE		
LL	Local loopback	To DCE	Control	
RL	Remote loopback	To DCE		
TM	Test mode	From DCE		
SS	Select standby	To DCE	Control	
SB	Standby indicator	From DCE		

Figure B-1 Interchange Circuits

only with the new EIA-449 equipment. These provisions are discussed in an EIA Industrial Electronics Bulletin (IE Bulletin No. 12), "Application Notes on Interconnection Between Interface Circuits Units EIA-449 and EIA-232-D."

This standard is designed to be compatible with the specifications of the International Telegraph and Telephone Consultative Committee (CCITT) and the International Organization for Standardization (ISO). However, it should be noted that this standard contains a few specifications which are subjects of further study in CCITT and ISO. These are:

1. Use of interchange circuits Terminal In Service and New Signal.
2. Status of interchange circuits during an equalizer retraining period.

The USA is actively participating in CCITT and ISO to gain international agreement on these items.

Work is presently underway, in cooperation with CCITT and ISO, to expand the Remote Loopback test function to include testing on multipoint networks. This augmentation will not affect the point-to-point testing capability specified in this document. Work is also underway to augment this standard to cover direct DTE-to-DTE applications. This augmentation will not affect, in any way, the DTE-to-DCE operation specified in this document. In addition, work will proceed in cooperation with CCITT toward the development of a more efficient all-balanced interface which minimizes the number of interchange circuits. It is expected that EIA-449 will provide the basis for this new work.

APPENDIX

C

industrial electronics bulletin no. 12

This appendix contains extracts from the application notes on interconnection between interface circuits using EIA-449 and EIA-232-D. It may be ordered from:

EIA Engineering Department
Standards Sales
2001 Eye Street, N.W.
Washington, D.C. 20006
(202) 457-4966

Introduction

The new series of digital interface standards, EIA-449, EIA-422, and EIA-423, have been developed to meet the advancing state of the art and greatly enhance the operation between DTEs and DCEs for data communication applications. Since EIA-232-D has been the pervasive digital interface standard for a number of years, close attention was given during the development of EIA-449, EIA-422, and EIA-423 to the selection of parameter values that would facilitate an orderly transition from the existing EIA-232-D equipment to the next generation without forcing obsolescence or costly retrofits. It will, therefore, be possible to connect new equipment designed to EIA-449 on one side of an interface to equipment designed to EIA-232-D on the other side of the interface. Such interconnection can be accomplished with a few additional provisions associated only with the new EIA-449 equipment, and the performance will be that normally experienced between EIA-232-D DTEs and DCEs.

This Industrial Electronics Bulletin provides application notes as guidance for implementing the necessary provisions that will allow continued use of existing EIA-232-D equipment by facilitating a graceful transition to the new equipment using EIA-449. [See Figure C-1].

RS-449			RS-232-C	
		AA	Protective ground	
SG SC RC	Signal ground Send common Receive common	AB	Signal ground	
IS IC TR* DM*	Terminal in service Incoming call Terminal ready Data mode	CE CD CC	Ring indicator Data terminal ready Data set ready	
SD* RD*	Send data Receive data	BA BB	Transmitted data Received data	

TT*
 	
ST*
 	
RT*
	Terminal timing
	
	Send timing
	
	Receive timing
		DA
		
		DB
		
		DD
			Transmitter signal element
			  timing (DTE source)
			Transmitter signal element
			  timing (DCE source)
			Receiver signal element timing	

RS*
CS*
RR*
SQ
NS
SF
SR
 	
SI
	Request to send
	Clear to send
	Receiver ready
	Signal quality
	New signal
	Select frequency
	Signaling rate selector
	
	Signaling rate indicator
		CA
		CB
		CF
		CG
		
		CH
		
		CI
			Request to send
			Clear to send
			Received line signal detector
			Signal quality detector
			
			Data signal rate selector
			  (DTE source)
			Data signal rate selector
			  (DCE source)	

SSD SRD	Secondary send data Secondary receive data	SBA SBB	Secondary transmitted data Secondary received data	
SRS SCS SRR	Secondary request to send Secondary clear to send Secondary receiver ready	SCA SCB SCF	Secondary request to send Secondary clear to send Secondary received line signal detector	
LL RL TM	Local loopback Remote loopback Test mode		Pins 9 & 10 test function	
SS SB	Select standby Standby indicator			

*Category I circuits

Figure C-1 Equivalency Table

D

EIA-232-D circuit summary with CCITT equivalents

Pin	Interchange Circuit	CCITT Equivalent	Description	Gnd	Data		Control		Timing	
					From DCE	To DCE	From DCE	To DCE	From DCE	To DCE
1	AA	101	Protective ground	X						
7	AB	102	Signal ground/common return	X						
2	BA	103	Transmitted data			X				
3	BB	104	Received data		X					
4	CA	105	Request to send					X		
5	CB	106	Clear to send				X			
6	CC	107	Data set ready				X			
20	CD	108.2	Data terminal ready					X		
22	CE	125	Ring indicator				X			
8	CF	109	Received line signal detector				X			
21	CG	110	Signal quality detector				X			
23	CH	111	Data signal rate selector (DTE)					X		
23	CI	112	Data signal rate selector (DCE)				X			
24	DA	113	Transmitter signal element timing (DTE)							X
15	DB	114	Transmitter signal element timing (DCE)						X	
17	DD	115	Receiver signal element timing (DCE)						X	
14	SBA	118	Secondary transmitted data			X				
16	SBB	119	Secondary received data		X					
19	SCA	120	Secondary request to send					X		
13	SCB	121	Secondary clear to send				X			
12	SCF	122	Secondary received line signal detector				X			

Figure D-1 EIA-232 Circuit Summary with CCITT Equivalents

APPENDIX

E

tools of the trade

The RS-232 serial interface leads and their functions should now be very familiar to you. The ground, data, control, and timing leads all release in a logical fashion, as described in the text. But often the description simply is not enough. Is there any way actually to view this logical interaction of the leads? How can a user or service technician monitor the status of a given lead? This appendix explains the different tools available for use on the RS-232-C interface. These tools are available from a multitude of vendors and are offered in many different forms. Consult the ads in various periodicals for actual costs and availability of these devices and cables.

Break-Out Box

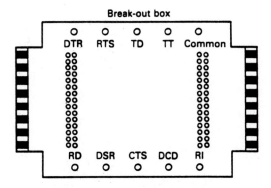

Figure E–1

Description and Functions:

- RS-232 connector(s), both male and female
- LEDs for various RS-232 leads (DSR, DTR, TD, etc.)
- Jumper position for cross connections
- Possibly battery powered
- Allows monitoring of various RS-232 leads to detect whether they are high/low or on/off.
- By connecting this device to an RS-232 interface, one can determine if the port is wired for DCE or DTE emulation.
- Allows for opening of individual pin circuits
- Typical price is $125.

RS-232 Male/Female Adapter

Description and Functions:

- Allows connection of mismatched RS-232-C connectors
- Changes male connector to female connector, or vice versa
- Typical price is $50.

RS-232 ABC/EIA Switch

Description and Functions:

- Box with multiple RS-232 ports
- Usually no power is required.
- Allows interconnection of more than two serial devices
- Switch(es) for changing configuration without changing cables
- Can reduce the number of ports or devices required (e.g., two printers can share the same computer by the mere flip of a switch; also, two computers can share the one modem or printer with the same ease)
- Typical price is $100.

RS-232 Pin Inserter and Extractor

Description and Functions:

- Allows easy insertion and extraction of crimped pins in a connector
- Typical price is $3.

RS-232 Synchronous Modem Eliminator

Description and Functions:

- Box with two RS-232 connectors
- Usually AC-powered
- Replaces synchronous modems between two devices
- Provides clock for timing
- Provides null-modem cable function
- Typical price is $300.

RS-232 Cable Tester

Description and Functions:

- Provides testing of RS-232 cables
- Indicates whether pins are wired straight through or possibly crossed over, as in a null-modem cable
- Typical price is $450.

RS-232 Buffer

Description and Functions:

- Provides buffering or spooling of data (Buffers data being output to a slow-speed printer to free up a computer. The printer can then print at its own speed. This utilizes the computer resource better by allowing other functions to occur simultaneously with the printing operation.)
- Price varies from $150 to $1000, depending on the amount of buffer storage provided.

RS-232 Serial-to-Parallel Adapter

Description and Functions:

- Box with serial and parallel cables attached
- Buffered for greater flexibility
- Allows parallel device—for example, a printer—to be connected to an RS-232 serial interface
- Typical price is $125.

RS-232/RS-449 Adapter

Description and Functions:

- Converts pins from the RS-232 standard to the new RS-449 standard interface
- Allows devices with RS-232 interfaces to be connected to RS-449 ports
- Typical price is $50.

Although there are many more devices available to supplement the support of equipment incorporating an RS-232 interface, these should give you an idea of the array of "tools of the trade" that are available when working with the serial interfaces.

SCS-RS-232 SOFTWARE CABLE DESIGNER DESCRIPTION AND FUNCTIONS

- Software tool for interfacing computers and peripherals
- Designs custom cables in seconds by merely selecting devices to connect
- Automates functionality found in Appendices F and G
- Runs on any IBM PC or compatible
- Easy to use, menu-driven interface
- Lists pinouts for 100s for computers, modems, printers, and terminals
- Includes many different sizes of ports—DB-25, DB-9, Mini-DIN, RJ-45, and so on
- Multiple databases of devices to choose from (with updates)
- Users can add their own devices to software database for easy connection to 100s of other devices
- Available from Significant Systems and distributed by Market Central, Inc. (412) 746-6000 or can be ordered from many of the mail-order catalogs listed in the acknowledgment section of this book.

F

pinouts for serial ports of computers and peripherals

INTRODUCTION

Included in this appendix is information about the ports for many different products. The products are separated by category (computers, modems, ports boards and terminal servers, buffers and data switches, printers, and terminals) and alphabetized within each category for easy reference. The reader can use this information, in conjunction with Appendix G, to quickly design thousands of different cables.

The EIA-232 leads for hundreds of different products are shown, along with functional names and the direction of the leads. Lead direction is either in or out, relative to the port of the device. A critical piece of information is the gender of each port, which is also included. In addition, flow control information and special notes about the ports are listed. The leads listed in the flow control section reflect the signals used to control data flow. Unless specifically noted, the first lead of multiple leads is used for hardware flow control in the cabling diagrams of Appendix G. Also, the supported methods for software flow control is listed.

Different ports are included in this appendix for the same devices. The device ports may be available from the vendor in a variety of forms, including modular connectors, DB-25, DB-9, DB-15, Mini-DIN, octacables, etc. Often either male or female connectors are possible. For example, a ports board may offer a modular connector, but also provide a modular-DB-25 adapter in either male or female form. In many cases, a port can use either control signals, or only the two data leads and a signal ground lead. Some devices support this without any special optioning, while others must be optioned. Entries are included for many ports using both full-control as well as a simplified interface. The reader is encouraged to double check for the correct port and connectors to avoid errors in cabling.

Furthermore, when modular ports are used, different modular cables can be used to connect adapters and other devices. Two choices exist for cabling, either straight-through or reversing cables. The modular cable that is used impacts the pinout numbering and the resulting cable connection. Many devices in this appendix with modular ports have multiple entries to support the use of either straight-through or reversing cables.

Another factor when interfacing with modular ports is the size of modular cord and corresponding number of leads. Physically a four wire connector can be plugged into a six, eight, or ten wire jack. However, only the innermost four leads are being used with this type of cable. The same is true for using six, or eight wire modular cables. The port information in this appendix denotes the number of leads used when a modular cord is physically plugged into a port. Lack of specific mention of a cable represents the physical jack and the inherent pin assignments of the port.

From these lists, devices can be selected to be cabled together. Once the appropriate devices have been identified, note the corresponding "PinConfig:". Use this pin configuration number in conjunction with Appendix G to design the cable necessary to connect two devices.

A software package, "Quick Cabler," from Significant Systems was used as the database for the vendor-provided information. This program runs on any standard PC and contains thousands of devices and their pinouts. From these databases, the cabling solutions in Appendix G were generated. Designing a cable takes only seconds with this software tool. The devices in this appendix are available in computer format with the Quick Cabler databases and can be purchased as a computerized alternative to these appendixes. Consult the "Tools of the Trade" section in Appendix E to locate where to acquire the Quick Cabler.

Every attempt was made to include as many different devices and accurate pin configurations as possible. As this book is the second edition of the original text, *RS-232 Made Easy*, these pin configurations can be used in conjunction with those found in the original textbook. Feel free to mix and match! The author is interested in providing more editions with the latest product and port information. If a device is not included herein, please send the information to Martin D. Seyer, C/O Prentice Hall. Also include any changes to the information found in this appendix. Happy Connections!!!!

computers

```
Altos                                     ALTOS Computer Systems
386 Series 1000, 2000 Computers           386 Series 1000/2000 Computer
Port: COM1/COM2          DB9P             Port: 9-Pin              DB9P
Gender: Male             PinConfig: C16   Gender: Male            PinConfig: C45

Pin  Function(Direction)                  Pin  Function(Direction)
------------------------------------      ------------------------------------
1    Carrier Detect(In)                   5    Signal Ground
2    Receive Data(In)                     3    Transmitted Data(out)
3    Transmit Data(Out)                   2    Received Data(in)
4    Data Terminal Ready(Out)             4    Data Terminal Ready(out)
5    Signal Ground                        7    Request To Send(out)
6    Data Set Ready(In)                   6    Data Set Ready(in)
7    Request to Send(Out)                 8    Clear To Send(in)
8    Clear to Send(In)                    ------------------------------------
9    Ring Indicator(In)                   Flow Control: 4   XON/XOFF
------------------------------------      Note:
Flow Control: 6 & 8
Note:  The flow control leads of the
attached device should be connected to
leads 6 & 8
```

```
ALTOS Computer Systems                    Altos
ALL 9-Pin Based Systems                   386 Series 1000 Computers
Port: 9-Pin              DB9P             Port: SIO/2 (9-pin)     DB25S
Gender: Male             PinConfig: C45   Gender: Female          PinConfig: C16

Pin  Function(Direction)                  Pin  Function(Direction)
------------------------------------      ------------------------------------
5    Signal Ground                        1    Data Carrier Detect(In)
3    Transmitted Data(out)                2    Receive Data(In)
2    Received Data(in)                    3    Transmit Data(Out)
4    Data Terminal Ready(out)             4    Data Terminal Ready(Out)
7    Request To Send(out)                 5    Signal Ground
6    Data Set Ready(in)                   6    Data Set Ready(In)
8    Clear To Send(in)                    7    Request to Send(Out)
------------------------------------      8    Clear to Send(In)
Flow Control: 4   XON/XOFF                9    RIK (In)
Note:                                     ------------------------------------
                                          Flow Control: 6 & 8
                                          Note:  The flow control leads of the
                                          attached device should be connected to
                                          leads 6 & 8
```

```
American Mitac Corp.                      American Mitac Corp.
MPC2386 computer                          MPC2386-003 computer
Port: Serial(DB-9)       DB9P             Port: Serial            DB25S
Gender: Female           PinConfig: C16   Gender: Female          PinConfig: C01

Pin  Function(Direction)                  Pin  Function(Direction)
------------------------------------      ------------------------------------
1    Carrier Detect(In)                   2    Transmit Data(Out)
2    Receive Data(In)                     3    Receive Data(In)
3    Transmit Data(Out)                   4    Request to Send(Out)
4    Data Terminal Ready(Out)             5    Clear to Send(In)
5    Signal Ground                        6    Data Set Ready(In)
6    Data Set Ready(In)                   7    Signal Ground
7    Request to Send(Out)                 8    Data Carrier Detect(In)
8    Clear to Send(In)                    20   Data Terminal Ready(Out)
9    Ring Indicator(In)                   22   Ring Indicator(In)
------------------------------------      ------------------------------------
Flow Control: 6 & 8                       Flow Control: 5 & 6
Note:  Leads 6 & 8 need to be on to send  Note:  Leads 5 & 6 must be on to send &
& receive data Adapters can be used to    receive data. Connect 5 & 6 to other
convert port to DB-25 size                device's flow control lead
```

American Mitac Corp. MPC2400V, 2400VEComputers Port: Serial(2 ports) DB9P Gender: Male PinConfig: C16	American Mitac Corp. MPC 3400E Computer Port: Serial(2 ports) DB9P Gender: Male PinConfig: C16
Pin Function(Direction) ------- 1 Carrier Detect(In) 2 Receive Data(In) 3 Transmit Data(Out) 4 Data Terminal Ready(Out) 5 Signal Ground 6 Data Set Ready(In) 7 Request to Send(Out) 8 Clear to Send(In) 9 Ring Indicator(In)	Pin Function(Direction) ------- 1 Carrier Detect(In) 2 Receive Data(In) 3 Transmit Data(Out) 4 Data Terminal Ready(Out) 5 Signal Ground 6 Data Set Ready(In) 7 Request to Send(Out) 8 Clear to Send(In) 9 Ring Indicator(In)
American Mitac Corp. MPC 4000F/G/H Computer Port: Serial(2 ports) DB9P Gender: Male PinConfig: C16	**American Mitac Corp.** MPS3000F Computer Port: Serial DB25S Gender: Female PinConfig: C01
Pin Function(Direction) ------- 1 Carrier Detect(In) 2 Receive Data(In) 3 Transmit Data(Out) 4 Data Terminal Ready(Out) 5 Signal Ground 6 Data Set Ready(In) 7 Request to Send(Out) 8 Clear to Send(In) 9 Ring Indicator(In)	Pin Function(Direction) ------- 2 Transmit Data(Out) 3 Receive Data(In) 4 Request to Send(Out) 5 Clear to Send(In) 6 Data Set Ready(In) 7 Signal Ground 8 Data Carrier Detect(In) 20 Data Terminal Ready(Out) 22 Ring Indicator(In) ------- Flow Control: 5 & 6 Note: Leads 5 & 6 must be on to send & receive data. Connect 5 & 6 to other device's flow control lead
Amstrad, Inc. PC20, 2086Computer Port: Serial DB25S Gender: Female PinConfig: C01	**Amstrad, Inc.** PC2286, 2386 Computers Port: Serial DB9P Gender: Male PinConfig: C16
Pin Function(Direction) ------- 2 Transmit Data(Out) 3 Receive Data(In) 4 Request to Send(Out) 5 Clear to Send(In) 6 Data Set Ready(In) 7 Signal Ground 8 Data Carrier Detect(In) 20 Data Terminal Ready(Out) 22 Ring Indicator(In) ------- Flow Control: 5 & 6 Note: Leads 5 & 6 must be on to send & receive data. Connect 5 & 6 to other device's flow control lead	Pin Function(Direction) ------- 1 Carrier Detect(In) 2 Receive Data(In) 3 Transmit Data(Out) 4 Data Terminal Ready(Out) 5 Signal Ground 6 Data Set Ready(In) 7 Request to Send(Out) 8 Clear to Send(In) 9 Ring Indicator(In) ------- Flow Control: 6 & 8 Note: Leads 6 & 8 need to be on to send & receive data Adapters can be used to convert port to DB-25 size

```
Apple Computer                          AST
Apple IIC Computer                      Bravo/386SX Computer
Port:  Serial(DIN)      DIN(5)          Port:  RS-232           DB25P
Gender:  Female         PinConfig: C43  Gender:  Male           PinConfig: C01

Pin   Function(Direction)               Pin   Function(Direction)
------------------------------------    ------------------------------------
3     Signal Ground                     2     Transmit Data(Out)
2     Transmitted Data(out)             3     Receive Data(In)
4     Received Data(in)                 4     Request to Send(Out)
1     Data Terminal Ready(out)          5     Clear to Send(In)
5     Data Set Ready(in)                6     Data Set Ready(In)
------------------------------------    7     Signal Ground
Flow Control: 1   XON/XOFF              8     Data Carrier Detect(In)
Note:                                   20    Data Terminal Ready(Out)
                                        22    Ring Indicator(In)
                                        ------------------------------------
                                        Flow Control: 5 & 6
                                        Note:
```

```
AST                                     AT&T
Premium 386SX/16, 486/25 Computers      6286 Computer
Port:  RS-232(2 ports)  DB9P            Port:  RS-232           DB25S
Gender:  Male           PinConfig: C01  Gender:  Female         PinConfig: C01

Pin   Function(Direction)               Pin   Function(Direction)
------------------------------------    ------------------------------------
2     Transmit Data(Out)                2     Transmit Data(Out)
3     Receive Data(In)                  3     Receive Data(In)
4     Request to Send(Out)              4     Request to Send(Out)
5     Clear to Send(In)                 5     Clear to Send(In)
6     Data Set Ready(In)                6     Data Set Ready(In)
7     Signal Ground                     7     Signal Ground
8     Data Carrier Detect(In)           8     Data Carrier Detect(In)
20    Data Terminal Ready(Out)          20    Data Terminal Ready(Out)
22    Ring Indicator(In)                22    Ring Indicator(In)
------------------------------------    ------------------------------------
Flow Control: 5 & 6                     Flow Control: 5 & 6
Note:                                   Note:
```

```
AT&T                                    Austin Computer Systems
6386/16, 20, 6386E Computer             286-12.5, 16, Cache Computer
Port:  RS-232           DB25P           Port:  Serial(2 Ports)  DB9P
Gender:  Male           PinConfig: C01  Gender:  Male           PinConfig: C16

Pin   Function(Direction)               Pin   Function(Direction)
------------------------------------    ------------------------------------
2     Transmit Data(Out)                1     Carrier Detect(In)
3     Receive Data(In)                  2     Receive Data(In)
4     Request to Send(Out)              3     Transmit Data(Out)
5     Clear to Send(In)                 4     Data Terminal Ready(Out)
6     Data Set Ready(In)                5     Signal Ground
7     Signal Ground                     6     Data Set Ready(In)
8     Data Carrier Detect(In)           7     Request to Send(Out)
20    Data Terminal Ready(Out)          8     Clear to Send(In)
22    Ring Indicator(In)                9     Ring Indicator(In)
------------------------------------    ------------------------------------
Flow Control: 5 & 6                     Flow Control: 6 & 8
Note:                                   Note:  Leads 6 & 8 need to be on to send
                                        & receive data Adapters can be used to
                                        convert port to DB-25 size
```

```
Austin Computer Systems                 Austin Computer Systems
386-20, 33 Cache Computer               386-SX, DX-25 Computer
Port: COMM1/COMM2 ports    DB9P         Port: Serial(2 Ports)     DB9P
Gender: Male            PinConfig: C16  Gender: Male           PinConfig: C16

Pin   Function(Direction)               Pin   Function(Direction)
------------------------------------    ------------------------------------
1     Carrier Detect(In)                1     Carrier Detect(In)
2     Receive Data(In)                  2     Receive Data(In)
3     Transmit Data(Out)                3     Transmit Data(Out)
4     Data Terminal Ready(Out)          4     Data Terminal Ready(Out)
5     Signal Ground                     5     Signal Ground
6     Data Set Ready(In)                6     Data Set Ready(In)
7     Request to Send(Out)              7     Request to Send(Out)
8     Clear to Send(In)                 8     Clear to Send(In)
9     Ring Indicator(In)                9     Ring Indicator(In)
------------------------------------    ------------------------------------
Flow Control: 6 & 8                     Flow Control: 6 & 8
Note: Leads 6 & 8 need to be on to send Note: Leads 6 & 8 need to be on to send
& receive data Adapters can be used to  & receive data Adapters can be used to
convert port to DB-25 size              convert port to DB-25 size
```
```
Austin Computer Systems                 Compaq Computer Corp.
486 Cache Computer                      DESKPRO 286e, 386/20e, 386/25, 386/33
Port: COMM1/COMM2        DB9P           Computers
Gender: Male          PinConfig: C16    Port: RS-232              DB9P
                                        Gender: Male           PinConfig: C16
Pin   Function(Direction)
------------------------------------    Pin   Function(Direction)
1     Carrier Detect(In)                ------------------------------------
2     Receive Data(In)                  1     Carrier Detect(In)
3     Transmit Data(Out)                2     Receive Data(In)
4     Data Terminal Ready(Out)          3     Transmit Data(Out)
5     Signal Ground                     4     Data Terminal Ready(Out)
6     Data Set Ready(In)                5     Signal Ground
7     Request to Send(Out)              6     Data Set Ready(In)
8     Clear to Send(In)                 7     Request to Send(Out)
9     Ring Indicator(In)                8     Clear to Send(In)
------------------------------------    9     Ring Indicator(In)
Flow Control: 6 & 8                     ------------------------------------
Note: Leads 6 & 8 need to be on to send Flow Control: 6 & 8
& receive data Adapters can be used to  Note: The flow control leads of the
convert port to DB-25 size              attached device should be connected to
                                        leads 6 & 8
```
```
Compaq Computer Corp.                   Compaq Computer Corp.
DESKPRO 386S, 486/25, Computer          LTE, LTE 286, Computer
Port: RS-232             DB9P           Port: RS-232              DB9P
Gender: Male          PinConfig: C16    Gender: Male           PinConfig: C16

Pin   Function(Direction)               Pin   Function(Direction)
------------------------------------    ------------------------------------
1     Carrier Detect(In)                1     Carrier Detect(In)
2     Receive Data(In)                  2     Receive Data(In)
3     Transmit Data(Out)                3     Transmit Data(Out)
4     Data Terminal Ready(Out)          4     Data Terminal Ready(Out)
5     Signal Ground                     5     Signal Ground
6     Data Set Ready(In)                6     Data Set Ready(In)
7     Request to Send(Out)              7     Request to Send(Out)
8     Clear to Send(In)                 8     Clear to Send(In)
9     Ring Indicator(In)                9     Ring Indicator(In)
------------------------------------    ------------------------------------
Flow Control: 6 & 8                     Flow Control: 6 & 8
Note: The flow control leads of the     Note: The flow control leads of the
attached device should be connected to  attached device should be connected to
leads 6 & 8                             leads 6 & 8
```

```
Compaq Computer Corp.                          Compaq Computer Corp.
PORTABLE 386/20, PORTABLE III Computers        SLT 286, SLT 386 Computers
Port:  RS-232              DB9P                 Port:  RS-232              DB9P
Gender: Male              PinConfig: C16        Gender: Male              PinConfig: C16

Pin   Function(Direction)                      Pin   Function(Direction)
--------------------------------------         --------------------------------------
1     Carrier Detect(In)                       1     Carrier Detect(In)
2     Receive Data(In)                         2     Receive Data(In)
3     Transmit Data(Out)                       3     Transmit Data(Out)
4     Data Terminal Ready(Out)                 4     Data Terminal Ready(Out)
5     Signal Ground                            5     Signal Ground
6     Data Set Ready(In)                       6     Data Set Ready(In)
7     Request to Send(Out)                     7     Request to Send(Out)
8     Clear to Send(In)                        8     Clear to Send(In)
9     Ring Indicator(In)                       9     Ring Indicator(In)
--------------------------------------         --------------------------------------
Flow Control: 6 & 8                            Flow Control: 6 & 8
Note:  The flow control leads of the           Note:  The flow control leads of the
attached device should be connected to         attached device should be connected to
leads 6 & 8                                    leads 6 & 8
--------------------------------------------------------------------------------------
Compaq Computer Corp.                          CompuAdd
SYSTEMPRO Computer                             212, 216, 220 Computers
Port:  RS-232              DB9P                 Port:  Serial 1(9-pin)    DB9P
Gender: Male              PinConfig: C16        Gender: Male              PinConfig: C16

Pin   Function(Direction)                      Pin   Function(Direction)
--------------------------------------         --------------------------------------
1     Carrier Detect(In)                       1     Carrier Detect(In)
2     Receive Data(In)                         2     Receive Data(In)
3     Transmit Data(Out)                       3     Transmit Data(Out)
4     Data Terminal Ready(Out)                 4     Data Terminal Ready(Out)
5     Signal Ground                            5     Signal Ground
6     Data Set Ready(In)                       6     Data Set Ready(In)
7     Request to Send(Out)                     7     Request to Send(Out)
8     Clear to Send(In)                        8     Clear to Send(In)
9     Ring Indicator(In)                       9     Ring Indicator(In)
--------------------------------------         --------------------------------------
Flow Control: 6 & 8                            Flow Control: 6 & 8
Note:  The flow control leads of the           Note:  This computer offers both 9-pin
attached device should be connected to         and 25-pin connectors.  Serial 2 is the
leads 6 & 8                                    DB-25 port
--------------------------------------------------------------------------------------
CompuAdd                                       CompuAdd
212, 216, 220 Computers                        316 Full-Profile Computer
Port:  Serial 2(25-pin)   DB25P                Port:  Serial 1(25-pin)   DB25P
Gender: Male              PinConfig: C01        Gender: Male              PinConfig: C01

Pin   Function(Direction)                      Pin   Function(Direction)
--------------------------------------         --------------------------------------
2     Transmit Data(Out)                       2     Transmit Data(Out)
3     Receive Data(In)                         3     Receive Data(In)
4     Request to Send(Out)                     4     Request to Send(Out)
5     Clear to Send(In)                        5     Clear to Send(In)
6     Data Set Ready(In)                       6     Data Set Ready(In)
7     Signal Ground                            7     Signal Ground
8     Data Carrier Detect(In)                  8     Data Carrier Detect(In)
20    Data Terminal Ready(Out)                 20    Data Terminal Ready(Out)
22    Ring Indicator(In)                       22    Ring Indicator(In)
--------------------------------------         --------------------------------------
Flow Control: 5 & 6                            Flow Control: 5 & 6
Note:  Both 9-pin & 25-pin ports are           Note:  This computer offers both a 9-pin
available on this computer.  Serial 1 is       and 25-pin his as COM1(Serial 1).  Serial
the 9-pin, Serial 2 is DB25                    2 is a DB25 as well
```

CompuAdd
316, 320 325 Full-Profile Computer
Port: Serial 1(9-pin)   DB9P
Gender: Male   PinConfig: C16

Pin   Function(Direction)
----
1   Carrier Detect(In)
2   Receive Data(In)
3   Transmit Data(Out)
4   Data Terminal Ready(Out)
5   Signal Ground
6   Data Set Ready(In)
7   Request to Send(Out)
8   Clear to Send(In)
9   Ring Indicator(In)

Flow Control: 6 & 8
Note: This computer offers both a 9-pin
and 25-pin as COM1(Serial 1). Serial 2
is a DB25 as well

CompuAdd
316, 320, 325 Full-Profile Computers
Port: Serial 2(25-pin)   DB25P
Gender: Male   PinConfig: C01

Pin   Function(Direction)
----
2   Transmit Data(Out)
3   Receive Data(In)
4   Request to Send(Out)
5   Clear to Send(In)
6   Data Set Ready(In)
7   Signal Ground
8   Data Carrier Detect(In)
20   Data Terminal Ready(Out)
22   Ring Indicator(In)

Flow Control: 5 & 6
Note: This computer offers both a 9-pin
and 25-pinhis as COM1(Serial 1). Serial
2 is a DB25 as well

CompuAdd
316s, 320s Low Profile Computer
Port: Serial 1(9-pin)   DB9P
Gender: Male   PinConfig: C16

Pin   Function(Direction)
----
1   Carrier Detect(In)
2   Receive Data(In)
3   Transmit Data(Out)
4   Data Terminal Ready(Out)
5   Signal Ground
6   Data Set Ready(In)
7   Request to Send(Out)
8   Clear to Send(In)
9   Ring Indicator(In)

Flow Control: 6 & 8
Note: This computer offers both 9-pin
and 25-pin connectors. Serial 2 is the
DB-25 port

CompuAdd
316s, 320s Low Profile Computers
Port: Serial 2(25-pin)   DB25P
Gender: Male   PinConfig: C01

Pin   Function(Direction)
----
2   Transmit Data(Out)
3   Receive Data(In)
4   Request to Send(Out)
5   Clear to Send(In)
6   Data Set Ready(In)
7   Signal Ground
8   Data Carrier Detect(In)
20   Data Terminal Ready(Out)
22   Ring Indicator(In)

Flow Control: 5 & 6
Note: Both 9-pin & 25-pin ports are
available on this computer. Serial 1 is
the 9-pin, Serial 2 is DB25

CompuAdd
810 Computer
Port: Serial 1(9-pin)   DB9P
Gender: Male   PinConfig: C16

Pin   Function(Direction)
----
1   Carrier Detect(In)
2   Receive Data(In)
3   Transmit Data(Out)
4   Data Terminal Ready(Out)
5   Signal Ground
6   Data Set Ready(In)
7   Request to Send(Out)
8   Clear to Send(In)
9   Ring Indicator(In)

Flow Control: 6 & 8
Note: This computer offers both 9-pin
and 25-pin connectors. Serial 2 is the
DB-25 port

CompuAdd
810 Computer
Port: Serial 2(25-pin)   DB25P
Gender: Male   PinConfig: C01

Pin   Function(Direction)
----
2   Transmit Data(Out)
3   Receive Data(In)
4   Request to Send(Out)
5   Clear to Send(In)
6   Data Set Ready(In)
7   Signal Ground
8   Data Carrier Detect(In)
20   Data Terminal Ready(Out)
22   Ring Indicator(In)

Flow Control: 5 & 6
Note: Both 9-pin & 25-pin ports are
available on this computer. Serial 1 is
the 9-pin, Serial 2 is DB25

```
CompuAdd
Companion Computer
Port:  RS-232              DB9P
Gender: Male              PinConfig: C16

Pin   Function(Direction)
------------------------------------------
1     Carrier Detect(In)
2     Receive Data(In)
3     Transmit Data(Out)
4     Data Terminal Ready(Out)
5     Signal Ground
6     Data Set Ready(In)
7     Request to Send(Out)
8     Clear to Send(In)
9     Ring Indicator(In)
------------------------------------------
Flow Control: 6 & 8
Note:  The flow control leads of the
attached device should be connected to
leads 6 & 8
```

```
Compuadd Corp.
212W Computer
Port:  RS-232(25 Pin)     DB25P
Gender: Male              PinConfig: C01

Pin   Function(Direction)
------------------------------------------
2     Transmit Data(Out)
3     Receive Data(In)
4     Request to Send(Out)
5     Clear to Send(In)
6     Data Set Ready(In)
7     Signal Ground
8     Data Carrier Detect(In)
20    Data Terminal Ready(Out)
22    Ring Indicator(In)
------------------------------------------
Flow Control: 5 & 6
Note:  Leads 5 & 6 must be on to send &
receive data. Connect 5 & 6 to other
device's flow control lead
```

```
Compuadd Corp.
212W Computer
Port:  RS-232(9-pin)      DB9P
Gender: Male              PinConfig: C16

Pin   Function(Direction)
------------------------------------------
1     Carrier Detect(In)
2     Receive Data(In)
3     Transmit Data(Out)
4     Data Terminal Ready(Out)
5     Signal Ground
6     Data Set Ready(In)
7     Request to Send(Out)
8     Clear to Send(In)
9     Ring Indicator(In)
------------------------------------------
Flow Control: 6 & 8
Note:  Leads 6 & 8 need to be on to send
& receive data Adapters can be used to
convert port to DB-25 size
```

```
Compuadd Corp.
286 Computer (12/16/20)
Port:  RS-232(25 Pin)     DB25P
Gender: Male              PinConfig: C01

Pin   Function(Direction)
------------------------------------------
2     Transmit Data(Out)
3     Receive Data(In)
4     Request to Send(Out)
5     Clear to Send(In)
6     Data Set Ready(In)
7     Signal Ground
8     Data Carrier Detect(In)
20    Data Terminal Ready(Out)
22    Ring Indicator(In)
------------------------------------------
Flow Control: 5 & 6
Note:  Leads 5 & 6 must be on to send &
receive data. Connect 5 & 6 to other
device's flow control lead
```

```
Compuadd Corp.
286 Computer (12/16/20)
Port:  RS-232(9-pin)      DB25P
Gender: Male              PinConfig: C16

Pin   Function(Direction)
------------------------------------------
1     Carrier Detect(In)
2     Receive Data(In)
3     Transmit Data(Out)
4     Data Terminal Ready(Out)
5     Signal Ground
6     Data Set Ready(In)
7     Request to Send(Out)
8     Clear to Send(In)
9     Ring Indicator(In)
------------------------------------------
Flow Control: 6 & 8
Note:  Leads 6 & 8 need to be on to send
& receive data Adapters can be used to
convert port to DB-25 size
```

```
Compuadd Corp.
386 Computer (16/20/25)
Port:  RS-232(25 Pin)     DB25P
Gender: Male              PinConfig: C01

Pin   Function(Direction)
------------------------------------------
2     Transmit Data(Out)
3     Receive Data(In)
4     Request to Send(Out)
5     Clear to Send(In)
6     Data Set Ready(In)
7     Signal Ground
8     Data Carrier Detect(In)
20    Data Terminal Ready(Out)
22    Ring Indicator(In)
------------------------------------------
Flow Control: 5 & 6
Note:  Leads 5 & 6 must be on to send &
receive data. Connect 5 & 6 to other
device's flow control lead
```

```
Compuadd Corp.                          Compulab Corporation
386 Computer (16/20/25)                 DS-345, 375 Computers
Port: RS-232(9-pin)                     Port: RS-232
Gender: Male          DB9P              Gender: Female          DB25S
                     PinConfig: C16                            PinConfig: C01

Pin   Function(Direction)               Pin   Function(Direction)
-------------------------------------   -------------------------------------
1     Carrier Detect(In)                1     Chassis Ground
2     Receive Data(In)                  2     Transmit Data(Out)
3     Transmit Data(Out)                3     Receive Data(In)
4     Data Terminal Ready(Out)          4     Request to Send(Out)
5     Signal Ground                     5     Clear to Send(In)
6     Data Set Ready(In)                6     Data Set Ready(In)
7     Request to Send(Out)              7     Signal Ground
8     Clear to Send(In)                 8     Data Carrier Detect(In)
9     Ring Indicator(In)                20    Data Terminal Ready(Out)
-------------------------------------   -------------------------------------
Flow Control: 6 & 8                     Flow Control: 5 & 6
Note:  Leads 6 & 8 need to be on to send    Note: Leads 5 & 6 must be on to send &
& receive data Adapters can be used to      receive data. Connect 5 & 6 to other
convert port to DB-25 size                  device's flow control lead
```

```
Data Storage Marketing                  Data Storage Marketing
DataStor 286 Computer (12/16D/20D)      DataStor 286 Computer (12/16D/20D)
Port: RS-232 (25 pin)                   Port: RS-232 (9-pin)
Gender: Male          DB25P             Gender: Male          DB9P
                     PinConfig: C01                           PinConfig: C16

Pin   Function(Direction)               Pin   Function(Direction)
-------------------------------------   -------------------------------------
2     Transmit Data(Out)                1     Carrier Detect(In)
3     Receive Data(In)                  2     Receive Data(In)
4     Request to Send(Out)              3     Transmit Data(Out)
5     Clear to Send(In)                 4     Data Terminal Ready(Out)
6     Data Set Ready(In)                5     Signal Ground
7     Signal Ground                     6     Data Set Ready(In)
8     Data Carrier Detect(In)           7     Request to Send(Out)
20    Data Terminal Ready(Out)          8     Clear to Send(In)
22    Ring Indicator(In)                9     Ring Indicator(In)
-------------------------------------   -------------------------------------
Flow Control: 5 & 6                     Flow Control: 6 & 8
Note: Leads 5 & 6 must be on to send &  Note: Leads 6 & 8 need to be on to send
receive data. Connect 5 & 6 to other    & receive data Adapters can be used to
device's flow control lead              convert port to DB-25 size
```

```
Data Storage Marketing                  Data Storage Marketing
DataStor 386 Computer (20/20C/25/25C/SXD)   DataStor 386 Computer (20/20C/25/25C/SXD)
Port: RS-232 (9-pin)                    Port: RS-232(25 Pin)
Gender: Male          DB25P             Gender: Male          DB25P
                     PinConfig: C16                           PinConfig: C01

Pin   Function(Direction)               Pin   Function(Direction)
-------------------------------------   -------------------------------------
1     Carrier Detect(In)                2     Transmit Data(Out)
2     Receive Data(In)                  3     Receive Data(In)
3     Transmit Data(Out)                4     Request to Send(Out)
4     Data Terminal Ready(Out)          5     Clear to Send(In)
5     Signal Ground                     6     Data Set Ready(In)
6     Data Set Ready(In)                7     Signal Ground
7     Request to Send(Out)              8     Data Carrier Detect(In)
8     Clear to Send(In)                 20    Data Terminal Ready(Out)
9     Ring Indicator(In)                22    Ring Indicator(In)
-------------------------------------   -------------------------------------
Flow Control: 6 & 8                     Flow Control: 5 & 6
Note: Leads 6 & 8 need to be on to send     Note: Leads 5 & 6 must be on to send &
& receive data Adapters can be used to      receive data. Connect 5 & 6 to other
convert port to DB-25 size                  device's flow control lead
```

```
Data Storage Marketing                    Data Storage Marketing
DataStor 486 Computer (25D)               DataStor 486 Computer (25D)
Port: RS-232 (9-pin)      DB9P            Port: RS-232(25 Pin)     DB25P
Gender: Male          PinConfig: C16      Gender: Male         PinConfig: C01

Pin  Function(Direction)                  Pin  Function(Direction)
------------------------------------      ------------------------------------
1     Carrier Detect(In)                  2     Transmit Data(Out)
2     Receive Data(In)                    3     Receive Data(In)
3     Transmit Data(Out)                  4     Request to Send(Out)
4     Data Terminal Ready(Out)            5     Clear to Send(In)
5     Signal Ground                       6     Data Set Ready(In)
6     Data Set Ready(In)                  7     Signal Ground
7     Request to Send(Out)                8     Data Carrier Detect(In)
8     Clear to Send(In)                   20    Data Terminal Ready(Out)
9     Ring Indicator(In)                  22    Ring Indicator(In)
------------------------------------      ------------------------------------
Flow Control: 6 & 8                       Flow Control: 5 & 6
Note:  Leads 6 & 8 need to be on to send  Note:  Leads 5 & 6 must be on to send &
& receive data Adapters can be used to    receive data. Connect 5 & 6 to other
convert port to DB-25 size                device's flow control lead
```
```
DEC                                       DEC
316, 320 Computers                        VAX-DMF-32 board
Port: RS-232            DB9P              Port: Ports 0 & 1(RS-232)
Gender: Male          PinConfig: C16      Gender:              PinConfig: C01

Pin  Function(Direction)                  Pin  Function(Direction)
------------------------------------      ------------------------------------
1     Carrier Detect(In)                  1     Protective Ground
2     Receive Data(In)                    2     Transmit Data(Out)
3     Transmit Data(Out)                  3     Receive Data(In)
4     Data Terminal Ready(Out)            4     Request to Send(Out)
5     Signal Ground                       5     Clear to Send(In)
6     Data Set Ready(In)                  6     Data Set Ready(In)
7     Request to Send(Out)                7     Signal Ground
8     Clear to Send(In)                   8     Data Carrier Detect(In)
9     Ring Indicator(In)                  12    Data Rate Select(In)
------------------------------------      20    Data Terminal Ready(Out)
Flow Control: 6 & 8                       22    Ring Indicator(In)
Note:  The flow control leads of the      ------------------------------------
attached device should be connected to    Flow Control: 6          XON/XOFF
leads 6 & 8                               Note:  Ports 2-7 have partial modem
                                          support(missing leads 5 & 8
```
```
DEC                                       Dell Computer Corp.
VAX-DMF-32 board                          210,220, 310 computers
Port: Ports 2-7(RS-232)                   Port: RS-232            DB9P
Gender:              PinConfig: C01        Gender: Male         PinConfig: C16

Pin  Function(Direction)                  Pin  Function(Direction)
------------------------------------      ------------------------------------
1     Protective Ground                   1     Carrier Detect(In)
2     Transmit Data(Out)                  2     Receive Data(In)
3     Receive Data(In)                    3     Transmit Data(Out)
4     Request to Send(Out)                4     Data Terminal Ready(Out)
6     Data Set Ready(In)                  5     Signal Ground
7     Signal Ground                       6     Data Set Ready(In)
12    Data Rate Select(In)                7     Request to Send(Out)
20    Data Terminal Ready(Out)            8     Clear to Send(In)
------------------------------------      9     Ring Indicator(In)
Flow Control: 6          XON/XOFF         ------------------------------------
Note:  Ports 0-1 provides full modem      Flow Control: 6 & 8
support(leads 5 & 8)                      Note:  Leads 6 & 8 need to be on to send
                                          & receive data Adapters can be used to
                                          convert port to DB-25 size
```

```
Dell Computer Corp.
316 LT, 316SX, 320LX Computers
Port: Serial 1              DB9P
Gender: Male               PinConfig: C16

Pin   Function(Direction)
-------------------------------------------
1     Carrier Detect(In)
2     Receive Data(In)
3     Transmit Data(Out)
4     Data Terminal Ready(Out)
5     Signal Ground
6     Data Set Ready(In)
7     Request to Send(Out)
8     Clear to Send(In)
9     Ring Indicator(In)
-------------------------------------------
Flow Control: 6 & 8
Note:  Leads 6 & 8 need to be on to send
& receive data Adapters can be used to
convert port to DB-25 size
```

```
Dell Computer Corp.
325, 425 Computers
Port: Serial 1 & 2         DB9P
Gender: Male               PinConfig: C16

Pin   Function(Direction)
-------------------------------------------
1     Carrier Detect(In)
2     Receive Data(In)
3     Transmit Data(Out)
4     Data Terminal Ready(Out)
5     Signal Ground
6     Data Set Ready(In)
7     Request to Send(Out)
8     Clear to Send(In)
9     Ring Indicator(In)
-------------------------------------------
Flow Control: 6 & 8
Note:  Leads 6 & 8 need to be on to send
& receive data Adapters can be used to
convert port to DB-25 size
```

```
Epson America
APEX 100 Computer
Port: RS-232               DB25P
Gender: Male               PinConfig: C01

Pin   Function(Direction)
-------------------------------------------
2     Transmit Data(Out)
3     Receive Data(In)
4     Request to Send(Out)
5     Clear to Send(In)
6     Data Set Ready(In)
7     Signal Ground
8     Data Carrier Detect(In)
20    Data Terminal Ready(Out)
22    Ring Indicator(In)
-------------------------------------------
Flow Control: 5 & 6
Note:  Leads 5 & 6 must be on to send &
receive data. Connect 5 & 6 to other
device's flow control lead
```

```
Epson America
Equity 386/20, 386/25 Computers
Port: Serial               DB9P
Gender: Male               PinConfig: C16

Pin   Function(Direction)
-------------------------------------------
1     Carrier Detect(In)
2     Receive Data(In)
3     Transmit Data(Out)
4     Data Terminal Ready(Out)
5     Signal Ground
6     Data Set Ready(In)
7     Request to Send(Out)
8     Clear to Send(In)
9     Ring Indicator(In)
-------------------------------------------
Flow Control: 6 & 8
Note:  The flow control leads of the
attached device should be connected to
leads 6 & 8
```

```
Epson America
Equity 386SX Computer
Port: Serial               DB9P
Gender: Male               PinConfig: C16

Pin   Function(Direction)
-------------------------------------------
1     Carrier Detect(In)
2     Receive Data(In)
3     Transmit Data(Out)
4     Data Terminal Ready(Out)
5     Signal Ground
6     Data Set Ready(In)
7     Request to Send(Out)
8     Clear to Send(In)
9     Ring Indicator(In)
-------------------------------------------
Flow Control: 6 & 8
Note:  The flow control leads of the
attached device should be connected to
leads 6 & 8
```

```
Epson America
Equity I+ Computer
Port: Serial               DB25P
Gender: Male               PinConfig: C01

Pin   Function(Direction)
-------------------------------------------
2     Transmit Data(Out)
3     Receive Data(In)
4     Request to Send(Out)
5     Clear to Send(In)
6     Data Set Ready(In)
7     Signal Ground
8     Data Carrier Detect(In)
20    Data Terminal Ready(Out)
22    Ring Indicator(In)
-------------------------------------------
Flow Control: 5 & 6
Note:  Leads 5 & 6 must be on to send &
receive data. Connect 5 & 6 to other
device's flow control lead
```

```
Epson America                         Epson America
Equity II+/III+ Computer              Equity LT, LT 286e, LT 386SX Computer
Port:  Serial           DB9P          Port:  Serial           DB9P
Gender: Male            PinConfig: C16 Gender: Male           PinConfig: C16

Pin   Function(Direction)             Pin   Function(Direction)
------------------------------------  -------------------------------------
1     Carrier Detect(In)             1     Carrier Detect(In)
2     Receive Data(In)               2     Receive Data(In)
3     Transmit Data(Out)             3     Transmit Data(Out)
4     Data Terminal Ready(Out)       4     Data Terminal Ready(Out)
5     Signal Ground                  5     Signal Ground
6     Data Set Ready(In)             6     Data Set Ready(In)
7     Request to Send(Out)           7     Request to Send(Out)
8     Clear to Send(In)              8     Clear to Send(In)
9     Ring Indicator(In)             9     Ring Indicator(In)
------------------------------------  -------------------------------------
Flow Control: 6 & 8                   Flow Control: 6 & 8
Note:  The flow control leads of the  Note:  The flow control leads of the
attached device should be connected to attached device should be connected to
leads 6 & 8                           leads 6 & 8
```

```
Flexible Computer Corporation         Fortune
Flex/32 MultiComputer                 Fortune 9000 Computer
Port:  COMM                           Port:  RS-232           DB25S
Gender:                 PinConfig: C01 Gender: Female         PinConfig: C01

Pin   Function(Direction)             Pin   Function(Direction)
------------------------------------  -------------------------------------
1     Frame Ground                   1     Frame Ground
2     Transmit Data(Out)             2     Transmit Data(Out)
3     Receive Data(In)               3     Receive Data(In)
4     Request to Send(Out)           4     Request to Send(Out)
5     Clear to Send(In)              5     Clear to Send(In)
7     Signal Ground                  6     Data Set Ready(In)
20    Data Terminal Ready(Out)       7     Signal Ground
------------------------------------  8     Data Carrier Detect(In)
Flow Control: 20          XON/XOFF    20    Data Terminal Ready(Out)
Note:                                 -------------------------------------
                                      Flow Control: 20
                                      Note:
```

```
GRiD Systems Corporation              Hewlett-Packard
1450SX, 1537 laptop computer          VECTRA 486 PC, ES/12 Computers
Port:  RS-232           DB9P          Port:  RS-232(1of2)     DB9P
Gender: Male            PinConfig: C16 Gender: Male           PinConfig: C16

Pin   Function(Direction)             Pin   Function(Direction)
------------------------------------  -------------------------------------
1     Carrier Detect(In)             1     Carrier Detect(In)
2     Receive Data(In)               2     Receive Data(In)
3     Transmit Data(Out)             3     Transmit Data(Out)
4     Data Terminal Ready(Out)       4     Data Terminal Ready(Out)
5     Signal Ground                  5     Signal Ground
6     Data Set Ready(In)             6     Data Set Ready(In)
7     Request to Send(Out)           7     Request to Send(Out)
8     Clear to Send(In)              8     Clear to Send(In)
9     Ring Indicator(In)             9     Ring Indicator(In)
------------------------------------  -------------------------------------
Flow Control: 6 & 8                   Flow Control: 6 & 8
Note:  Leads 6 & 8 need to be on to send  Note:  The flow control leads of the
& receive data Adapters can be used to attached device should be connected to
convert port to DB-25 size           leads 6 & 8
```

```
Hewlett-Packard
VECTRA QS, RS/20, RS/25 Computers
Port: RS-232            DB9P
Gender: Male            PinConfig: C16

Pin   Function(Direction)
------------------------------------------
1         Carrier Detect(In)
2         Receive Data(In)
3         Transmit Data(Out)
4         Data Terminal Ready(Out)
5         Signal Ground
6         Data Set Ready(In)
7         Request to Send(Out)
8         Clear to Send(In)
9         Ring Indicator(In)
------------------------------------------
Flow Control: 6 & 8
Note:  The flow control leads of the
attached device should be connected to
leads 6 & 8
```

```
IBM Corp.
PS/2 Model 25, 30, 50, 55, 60, 70, 80
Computers
Port: RS-232            DB25P
Gender: Male            PinConfig: C01

Pin   Function(Direction)
------------------------------------------
1         Protective Ground
2         Transmit Data(Out)
3         Receive Data(In)
4         Request to Send(Out)
5         Clear to Send(In)
6         Data Set Ready(In)
7         Signal Ground
8         Data Carrier Detect(In)
20        Data Terminal Ready(Out)
22        Ring Indicator(In)
------------------------------------------
Flow Control: 5 & 6
Note:  Leads 5 & 6 must be on to send &
receive data. Connect 5 & 6 to other
device's flow control lead
```

```
IBM Corporation
IBM PC/XT
Port: ACA or equivalent   DB25P
Gender: Male             PinConfig: C01

Pin   Function(Direction)
------------------------------------------
2         Transmit Data(Out)
3         Receive Data(In)
4         Request to Send(Out)
5         Clear to Send(In)
6         Data Set Ready(In)
7         Signal Ground
8         Data Carrier Detect(In)
20        Data Terminal Ready(Out)
22        Ring Indicator(In)
------------------------------------------
Flow Control: 5 & 6
Note:  Leads 5 & 6 must be on to send and
receive data. Connect 5 & 6 to other
device's flow control lead
```

```
Int'l Parallel Machines, Inc.
IP-1 Minicomputer
Port: Console(RS-232)    DB25S
Gender: Female           PinConfig: C06

Pin   Function(Direction)
------------------------------------------
2         Receive Data(In)
3         Transmit Data(Out)
7         Signal Ground
------------------------------------------
Flow Control:           XON/XOFF
Note:  This port is configured as DCE
```

```
ITT
PC/HT Computer
Port: RS-232            DB25P
Gender:                 PinConfig: C01

Pin   Function(Direction)
------------------------------------------
2         Transmit Data(Out)
3         Receive Data(In)
4         Request to Send(Out)
5         Clear to Send(In)
6         Data Set Ready(In)
7         Signal Ground
8         Carrier Detect(In)
20        Data Terminal Ready(Out)
22        Ring Indicator(In)
------------------------------------------
Flow Control: 5,6       XON/XOFF
Note:  Leads 5 & 6 must be on
```

```
Kaypro
Kaypro II Computer
Port: RS-232            DB25S
Gender: Female          PinConfig: C01

Pin   Function(Direction)
------------------------------------------
1         Frame Ground
2         Transmit Data(Out)
3         Receive Data(In)
4         Request to Send(Out)
5         Clear to Send(In)
6         Data Set Ready(In)
7         Signal Ground
8         Data Carrier Detect(In)
20        Data Terminal Ready(Out)
------------------------------------------
Flow Control: 20
Note:
```

LASER Computer	LASER Computer
LASER 128 Series	PC3/PC4 Computer
Port: Serial(DIN) DIN(5)	Port: RS-232(15 Pin) DB15S
Gender: Female PinConfig: C43	Gender: Female PinConfig: C44

Pin   Function(Direction) | Pin   Function(Direction)

```
Pin   Function(Direction)               Pin   Function(Direction)
---------------------------------      ---------------------------------
3     Signal Ground                    9     Signal Ground
2     Transmitted Data(out)            11    Transmitted Data(out)
4     Received Data(in)                13    Received Data(in)
1     Data Terminal Ready(out)         10    Data Terminal Ready(out)
5     Data Set Ready(in)               14    Data Set Ready(in)
---------------------------------      ---------------------------------
Flow Control: 1   XON/XOFF             Flow Control: 10   XON/XOFF
Note:                                  Note:
```

Laser Computer	Laser Computer
Laser 286, 386 Computers	Laser 286, 386 Computers
Port: 9-pin RS-232 DB9P	Port: 25-pin RS-232 DB25P
Gender: Male PinConfig: C16	Gender: Male PinConfig: C01

```
Pin   Function(Direction)               Pin   Function(Direction)
---------------------------------      ---------------------------------
1     Carrier Detect(In)               2     Transmit Data(Out)
2     Receive Data(In)                 3     Receive Data(In)
3     Transmit Data(Out)               4     Request to Send(Out)
4     Data Terminal Ready(Out)         5     Clear to Send(In)
5     Signal Ground                    6     Data Set Ready(In)
6     Data Set Ready(In)               7     Signal Ground
7     Request to Send(Out)             8     Data Carrier Detect(In)
8     Clear to Send(In)                20    Data Terminal Ready(Out)
9     Ring Indicator(In)               22    Ring Indicator(In)
---------------------------------      ---------------------------------
Flow Control: 6 & 8                    Flow Control: 5 & 6
Note: The flow control leads of the   Note:
attached device should be connected to
leads 6 & 8
```

Laser Computer	Mitsubishi Electronics
Laser XT	MP286 Computer
Port: 9-pin RS-232 DB25P	Port: RS-232 DB-25 DB25P
Gender: Male PinConfig: C16	Gender: Male PinConfig: C01

```
Pin   Function(Direction)               Pin   Function(Direction)
---------------------------------      ---------------------------------
1     Carrier Detect(In)               2     Transmit Data(Out)
2     Receive Data(In)                 3     Receive Data(In)
3     Transmit Data(Out)               4     Request to Send(Out)
4     Data Terminal Ready(Out)         5     Clear to Send(In)
5     Signal Ground                    6     Data Set Ready(In)
6     Data Set Ready(In)               7     Signal Ground
7     Request to Send(Out)             8     Data Carrier Detect(In)
8     Clear to Send(In)                20    Data Terminal Ready(Out)
9     Ring Indicator(In)               22    Ring Indicator(In)
---------------------------------      ---------------------------------
Flow Control: 6 & 8                    Flow Control: 5 & 6
Note: The flow control leads of the   Note: The flow control leads of the
attached device should be connected to attached device should be connected to
leads 6 & 8                            leads 5 & 6
```

```
Mitsubishi Electronics
MP286L, MP386, MP386s, MP386/25 Computers
Port:  RS-232 9-pin(2)        DB9P
Gender:  Male              PinConfig: C16

Pin   Function(Direction)
-----------------------------------------
1       Carrier Detect(In)
2       Receive Data(In)
3       Transmit Data(Out)
4       Data Terminal Ready(Out)
5       Signal Ground
6       Data Set Ready(In)
7       Request to Send(Out)
8       Clear to Send(In)
9       Ring Indicator(In)
-----------------------------------------
Flow Control: 6 & 8
Note:  The flow control leads of the
attached device should be connected to
leads 6 & 8
```

```
NCR
9300IP, 9400IP, 9500 Computers
Port:  RS-232                 DB25P
Gender:  Male              PinConfig: C01

Pin   Function(Direction)
-----------------------------------------
2       Transmit Data(Out)
3       Receive Data(In)
4       Request to Send(Out)
5       Clear to Send(In)
6       Data Set Ready(In)
7       Signal Ground
8       Data Carrier Detect(In)
15      Transmit Clock(In)
17      Receive Clock(In)
20      Data Terminal Ready(Out)
22      Ring Indicator(In)
-----------------------------------------
Flow Control: 6              XON/XOFF
Note:
```

```
NCR
System 10000 Model 35, 55, 65, 75, 85
Computers
Port:  RS-232                 DB25S
Gender:  Female            PinConfig: C01

Pin   Function(Direction)
-----------------------------------------
2       Transmit Data(Out)
3       Receive Data(In)
4       Request to Send(Out)
5       Clear to Send(In)
6       Data Set Ready(In)
7       Signal Ground
8       Data Carrier Detect(In)
15      Transmit Clock(In)
17      Receive Clock(In)
20      Data Terminal Ready(Out)
22      Ring Indicator(In)
-----------------------------------------
Flow Control: 6              XON/XOFF
Note:
```

```
NCR Corporation
Tower  Computers
Port:  15-Pin                 DB15P
Gender:  Male              PinConfig: C67

Pin   Function(Direction)
-----------------------------------------
11      Signal Ground
1       Transmitted Data(out)
9       Received Data(in)
2       Request To Send(out)
3       Data Set Ready(in)
10      Clear To Send(in)
12      Data Carrier Detect(in)
-----------------------------------------
Flow Control: 2   XON/XOFF
Note:
```

```
NEC
ProSpeed 286 Computer
Port:  RS-232                 DB9P
Gender:  Male              PinConfig: C16

Pin   Function(Direction)
-----------------------------------------
1       Carrier Detect(In)
2       Receive Data(In)
3       Transmit Data(Out)
4       Data Terminal Ready(Out)
5       Signal Ground
6       Data Set Ready(In)
7       Request to Send(Out)
8       Clear to Send(In)
9       Ring Indicator(In)
-----------------------------------------
Flow Control: 6 & 8
Note:  The flow control leads of the
attached device should be connected to
leads 6 & 8
```

```
NEC
UltraLite
Port:  RS-232                 DB25S
Gender:  Female            PinConfig: C19

Pin   Function(Direction)
-----------------------------------------
7       Signal Ground
2       Transmitted Data(out)
3       Received Data(in)
-----------------------------------------
Flow Control:
Note:
```

Pan United Corp
386/16SX, 20L Computers
Port: Port 1(DB-9)   DB9P
Gender: Male   PinConfig: C16

Pin   Function(Direction)
----
1   Carrier Detect(In)
2   Receive Data(In)
3   Transmit Data(Out)
4   Data Terminal Ready(Out)
5   Signal Ground
6   Data Set Ready(In)
7   Request to Send(Out)
8   Clear to Send(In)
9   Ring Indicator(In)

Flow Control: 6 & 8
Note: The flow control leads of the
attached device should be connected to
leads 6 & 8

Pan United Corp.
386/16SX, 20L Computers
Port: Port 2(DB-25 option)DB25P
Gender: Male   PinConfig: C01

Pin   Function(Direction)
----
2   Transmit Data(Out)
3   Receive Data(In)
4   Request to Send(Out)
5   Clear to Send(In)
6   Data Set Ready(In)
7   Signal Ground
8   Data Carrier Detect(In)
20   Data Terminal Ready(Out)
22   Ring Indicator(In)

Flow Control: 5 & 6
Note:

Panasonic
FX-1650, 1750, 1900, 1950 Computers
Port: RS-232   DB9P
Gender: Male   PinConfig: C16

Pin   Function(Direction)
----
1   Carrier Detect(In)
2   Receive Data(In)
3   Transmit Data(Out)
4   Data Terminal Ready(Out)
5   Signal Ground
6   Data Set Ready(In)
7   Request to Send(Out)
8   Clear to Send(In)
9   Ring Indicator(In)

Flow Control: 6 & 8
Note: The flow control leads of the
attached device should be connected to
leads 6 & 8

Sanyo
MBC-16LT, 16LX, 17, 18Plus Computers
Port: RS-232 9-pin   DB9P
Gender: Male   PinConfig: C16

Pin   Function(Direction)
----
1   Carrier Detect(In)
2   Receive Data(In)
3   Transmit Data(Out)
4   Data Terminal Ready(Out)
5   Signal Ground
6   Data Set Ready(In)
7   Request to Send(Out)
8   Clear to Send(In)
9   Ring Indicator(In)

Flow Control: 6 & 8
Note: The flow control leads of the
attached device should be connected to
leads 6 & 8

Sharp
PC-4502, 4600, 4601, 4602 Computers
Port: Serial(SIO Board) DB25P
Gender: Male   PinConfig: C01

Pin   Function(Direction)
----
2   Transmit Data(Out)
3   Receive Data(In)
4   Request to Send(Out)
5   Clear to Send(In)
6   Data Set Ready(In)
7   Signal Ground
8   Data Carrier Detect(In)
20   Data Terminal Ready(Out)
22   Ring Indicator(In)

Flow Control: 5 & 6
Note: Leads 5 & 6 must be on to send &
receive data. An optional board, CE-451B
or modem provides port

Sharp
PC-4641, 5541 Computers
Port: Serial   DB9P
Gender: Male   PinConfig: C16

Pin   Function(Direction)
----
1   Carrier Detect(In)
2   Receive Data(In)
3   Transmit Data(Out)
4   Data Terminal Ready(Out)
5   Signal Ground
6   Data Set Ready(In)
7   Request to Send(Out)
8   Clear to Send(In)
9   Ring Indicator(In)

Flow Control: 6 & 8
Note: Leads 6 & 8 need to be on to send
& receive data Adapters can be used to
convert port to DB-25 size

```
Sharp
PC-4641 Computer
Port:  Serial(SIO Modem)    DB25P
Gender:  Male               PinConfig: C01

Pin   Function(Direction)
---------------------------------------------
2         Transmit Data(Out)
3         Receive Data(In)
4         Request to Send(Out)
5         Clear to Send(In)
6         Data Set Ready(In)
7         Signal Ground
8         Data Carrier Detect(In)
20        Data Terminal Ready(Out)
22        Ring Indicator(In)
---------------------------------------------
Flow Control: 5 & 6
Note:  This optional port is provided by
an SIO(CE-451B) board, or a modem(CE-
445/462).  A DB-9 is standard
```

```
Sharp
PC-6220 Notepad Computer
Port:  RS-232               DB9P
Gender:  Male               PinConfig: C16

Pin   Function(Direction)
---------------------------------------------
1         Carrier Detect(In)
2         Receive Data(In)
3         Transmit Data(Out)
4         Data Terminal Ready(Out)
5         Signal Ground
6         Data Set Ready(In)
7         Request to Send(Out)
8         Clear to Send(In)
9         Ring Indicator(In)
---------------------------------------------
Flow Control: 6 & 8
Note:  The flow control leads of the
attached device should be connected to
leads 6 & 8
```

```
Sharp
PC-7000/7000A, 7100, 7200 Computers
Port:  Serial               DB25P
Gender:  Male               PinConfig: C01

Pin   Function(Direction)
---------------------------------------------
2         Transmit Data(Out)
3         Receive Data(In)
4         Request to Send(Out)
5         Clear to Send(In)
6         Data Set Ready(In)
7         Signal Ground
8         Data Carrier Detect(In)
20        Data Terminal Ready(Out)
22        Ring Indicator(In)
---------------------------------------------
Flow Control: 5 & 6
Note:  Leads 5 & 6 must be on to send &
receive data. Connect 5 & 6 to other
device's flow control lead
```

```
Sun MicroSystems
ALM-1 Board
Port:  0-15                 DB25P
Gender:  Male               PinConfig: C01

Pin   Function(Direction)
---------------------------------------------
1         Frame Ground
2         Transmit Data(Out)
3         Receive Data(In)
4         Request to Send(Out)
5         Clear to Send(In)
6         Data Set Ready(In)
7         Signal Ground
8         Data Carrier Detect(In)
15        Transmit Clock(In)
17        Receive Clock(In)
20        Data Terminal Ready(Out)
---------------------------------------------
Flow Control:              XON/XOFF
Note:
```

```
Sun MicroSystems
ALM-2 Board
Port:  0 to 3 RS-232        DB25S
Gender:  Female             PinConfig: C01

Pin   Function(Direction)
---------------------------------------------
2         Transmit Data(Out)
3         Receive Data(In)
4         Request to Send(Out)
5         Clear to Send(In)
6         Data Set Ready(In)
7         Signal Ground
8         Data Carrier Detect(In)
15        Transmit Clock(In)
17        Receive Clock(In)
20        Data Terminal Ready(Out)
24        External Transmit Clock(Out)
---------------------------------------------
Flow Control:              XON/XOFF
Note:
```

```
Sun MicroSystems
ALM-2 Board
Port:  4 to 15              DB25S
Gender:  Female             PinConfig: C07

Pin   Function(Direction)
---------------------------------------------
2         Transmit Data(Out)
3         Receive Data(In)
7         Signal Ground
8         Data Carrier Detect(In)
20        Data Terminal Ready(Out)
---------------------------------------------
Flow Control:              XON/XOFF
Note:
```

```
Sun MicroSystems                        Sun MicroSystems
MCP Board                               SparcServer 4/370
Port: 2 & 3              DB25S          Port: 9-pin RS-232        DB25P
Gender: Female          PinConfig: C01  Gender: Male             PinConfig: C16

Pin  Function(Direction)               Pin  Function(Direction)
---------------------------------      ---------------------------------
2     Transmit Data(Out)               1     Carrier Detect(In)
3     Receive Data(In)                 2     Receive Data(In)
4     Request to Send(Out)             3     Transmit Data(Out)
5     Clear to Send(In)                4     Data Terminal Ready(Out)
6     Data Set Ready(In)               5     Signal Ground
7     Signal Ground                    6     Data Set Ready(In)
8     Data Carrier Detect(In)          7     Request to Send(Out)
15    Transmit Clock(In)               8     Clear to Send(In)
17    Receive Clock(In)                9     Ring Indicator(In)
20    Data Terminal Ready(Out)        ---------------------------------
24    External Transmit Clock(Out)     Flow Control: 6 & 8
---------------------------------      Note: The flow control leads of the
Flow Control:         XON/XOFF         attached device should be connected to
Note:                                  leads 6 & 8
```

```
Sun MicroSystems                        Sun MicroSystems
SparcStation 4/330                      SparcStation 4/330
Port: 25-pin RS-232     DB25S           Port: 9-pin RS-232       DB25S
Gender: Female          PinConfig: C01  Gender: Female           PinConfig: C16

Pin  Function(Direction)               Pin  Function(Direction)
---------------------------------      ---------------------------------
2     Transmit Data(Out)               1     Carrier Detect(In)
3     Receive Data(In)                 2     Receive Data(In)
4     Request to Send(Out)             3     Transmit Data(Out)
5     Clear to Send(In)                4     Data Terminal Ready(Out)
6     Data Set Ready(In)               5     Signal Ground
7     Signal Ground                    6     Data Set Ready(In)
8     Data Carrier Detect(In)          7     Request to Send(Out)
15    Transmit Clock(In)               8     Clear to Send(In)
17    Receive Clock(In)                9     Ring Indicator(In)
20    Data Terminal Ready(Out)        ---------------------------------
24    External Transmit Clock(Out)     Flow Control: 6 & 8
25    -5V (Out)                        Note: The flow control leads of the
---------------------------------      attached device should be connected to
Flow Control:         XON/XOFF         leads 6 & 8
Note:
```

```
Sun MicroSystems                        Sun MicroSystems
SparcStation SLC 4/20 Workstation       SparcServer 4/370
Port: 25-pin RS-232     DB25S           Port: 25-pin RS-232      DB25S
Gender: Female          PinConfig: C01  Gender: Female           PinConfig: C01

Pin  Function(Direction)               Pin  Function(Direction)
---------------------------------      ---------------------------------
2     Transmit Data(Out)               2     Transmit Data(Out)
3     Receive Data(In)                 3     Receive Data(In)
4     Request to Send(Out)             4     Request to Send(Out)
5     Clear to Send(In)                5     Clear to Send(In)
6     Data Set Ready(In)               6     Data Set Ready(In)
7     Signal Ground                    7     Signal Ground
8     Data Carrier Detect(In)          8     Data Carrier Detect(In)
15    Transmit Clock(In)               15    Transmit Clock(In)
17    Receive Clock(In)                17    Receive Clock(In)
20    Data Terminal Ready(Out)         20    Data Terminal Ready(Out)
24    External Transmit Clock(Out)     24    External Transmit Clock(Out)
---------------------------------      25    -5V (Out)
Flow Control:         XON/XOFF         ---------------------------------
Note: Port B uses leads 12-DCD,13-    Flow Control:         XON/XOFF
CTS,14-TD,16-RD,19-RTS                 Note:
```

```
Sun MicroSystems
Sun 2 Workstation
Port: 25-pin RS-232        DB25S
Gender:  Female            PinConfig: C01

Pin   Function(Direction)
-----------------------------------------------
2     Transmit Data(Out)
3     Receive Data(In)
4     Request to Send(Out)
5     Clear to Send(In)
6     Data Set Ready(In)
7     Signal Ground
8     Data Carrier Detect(In)
15    Transmit Clock(In)
17    Receive Clock(In)
20    Data Terminal Ready(Out)
24    External Transmit Clock(Out)
25    -5V (Out)
-----------------------------------------------
Flow Control:              XON/XOFF
Note:
```

```
Sun MicroSystems
Sun 2 Workstation
Port: 9-pin RS-232         DB25P
Gender:  Male              PinConfig: C16

Pin   Function(Direction)
-----------------------------------------------
1     Carrier Detect(In)
2     Receive Data(In)
3     Transmit Data(Out)
4     Data Terminal Ready(Out)
5     Signal Ground
6     Data Set Ready(In)
7     Request to Send(Out)
8     Clear to Send(In)
9     Ring Indicator(In)
-----------------------------------------------
Flow Control: 6 & 8
Note:  The flow control leads of the
attached device
```

```
Sun MicroSystems
Sun 3 Workstations
Port: 25-pin RS-232        DB25P
Gender: Male               PinConfig: C01

Pin   Function(Direction)
-----------------------------------------------
2     Transmit Data(Out)
3     Receive Data(In)
4     Request to Send(Out)
5     Clear to Send(In)
6     Data Set Ready(In)
7     Signal Ground
8     Data Carrier Detect(In)
15    Transmit Clock(In)
17    Receive Clock(In)
20    Data Terminal Ready(Out)
24    External Transmit Clock(Out)
25    -5V (Out)
-----------------------------------------------
Flow Control:              XON/XOFF
Note:
```

```
Sun MicroSystems
Sun 4 Workstations
Port: 25-pin RS-232        DB25P
Gender: Male               PinConfig: C01

Pin   Function(Direction)
-----------------------------------------------
2     Transmit Data(Out)
3     Receive Data(In)
4     Request to Send(Out)
5     Clear to Send(In)
6     Data Set Ready(In)
7     Signal Ground
8     Data Carrier Detect(In)
15    Transmit Clock(In)
17    Receive Clock(In)
20    Data Terminal Ready(Out)
24    External Transmit Clock(Out)
25    -5V (Out)
-----------------------------------------------
Flow Control:              XON/XOFF
Note:
```

```
Sun MicroSystems
Sun 3, 4 Workstations
Port:  9-pin RS-232        DB9P
Gender:  Male              PinConfig: C16

Pin   Function(Direction)
-----------------------------------------------
1     Carrier Detect(In)
2     Receive Data(In)
3     Transmit Data(Out)
4     Data Terminal Ready(Out)
5     Signal Ground
6     Data Set Ready(In)
7     Request to Send(Out)
8     Clear to Send(In)
9     Ring Indicator(In)
-----------------------------------------------
Flow Control: 6 & 8
Note:  The flow control leads of the
attached device should be connected to
leads 6 & 8
```

```
Sun MicroSystems
Sun386i CPU
Port:  Port A-RS232        DB25P
Gender:  Male              PinConfig: C01

Pin   Function(Direction)
-----------------------------------------------
2     Transmit Data(Out)
3     Receive Data(In)
4     Request to Send(Out)
5     Clear to Send(In)
6     Data Set Ready(In)
7     Signal Ground
8     Data Carrier Detect(In)
15    Transmit Clock(In)
17    Receive Clock(In)
20    Data Terminal Ready(Out)
22    Ring Indicator(In)
24    External Transmit Clock(Out)
25    -5V (Out)
-----------------------------------------------
Flow Control:              XON/XOFF
Note:
```

```
Sun MicroSystems
SunLink Communications Processor
Port: 1 & 3  RS-232      DB25S
Gender: Female          PinConfig: C01

Pin   Function(Direction)
----------------------------------------
1     Frame Ground
2     Transmit Data(Out)
3     Receive Data(In)
4     Request to Send(Out)
5     Clear to Send(In)
6     Data Set Ready(In)
7     Signal Ground
8     Data Carrier Detect(In)
15    Transmit Clock(In)
17    Receive Clock(In)
20    Data Terminal Ready(Out)
24    External Transmit Clock(Out)
25    +5V (Out)
----------------------------------------
Flow Control:            XON/XOFF
Note:
```

```
Tandem Computers
6100 COMM Subsystem
Port: RS-232            DB25P
Gender: Male            PinConfig: C01

Pin   Function(Direction)
----------------------------------------
1     Protective Ground
2     Transmit Data(Out)
3     Receive Data(In)
4     Request to Send(Out)
5     Clear to Send(In)
6     Data Set Ready(In)
7     Signal Ground
8     Data Carrier Detect(In)
12    Secondary DCD(In)
13    Secondary Cl'r to Send(In)
14    Supervisory Trans.Data(Out)
15    Transmit Clock(Out)
16    Supervisory Rec. Data(In)
17    Receive Clock(Out)
19    Secondary Req. to Send(Out)
20    Data Terminal Ready(Out)
21    SQ  (In)
22    Ring Indicator(In)
23    Data Rate Select(Out)
24    External Transmit Clock(Out)
25    SYNC(Out)
----------------------------------------
Flow Control:            XON/XOFF
Note:
```

```
Tandem Computers
6600 Scorpion
Port: RS-232            DB25P
Gender: Male            PinConfig: P03

Pin   Function(Direction)
----------------------------------------
1     Protective Ground
2     Transmit Data(Out)
3     Receive Data(In)
4     Request to Send(Out)
5     Clear to Send(In)
6     Data Set Ready(In)
7     Signal Ground
8     Data Carrier Detect(In)
15    Transmit Clock(In)
17    Receive Clock(In)
20    Data Terminal Ready(Out)
24    External Transmit Clock(Out)
----------------------------------------
Flow Control: 20         XON/XOFF
Note:  RS-422 is also supported
```

```
Tandem Computers
CLX-RMI port (MFC)
Port: RS-232            DB25P
Gender: Male            PinConfig: C01

Pin   Function(Direction)
----------------------------------------
1     Protective Ground
2     Transmit Data(Out)
3     Receive Data(In)
4     Request to Send(Out)
5     Clear to Send(In)
6     Data Set Ready(In)
7     Signal Ground
8     Data Carrier Detect(In)
12    Data Rate Select(In)
15    Transmit Clock(Out)
17    Receive Clock(Out)
18    AL  (Out)
20    Data Terminal Ready(Out)
21    RDL (Out)
22    Ring Indicator(In)
23    Data Rate Select(Out)
----------------------------------------
Flow Control: 20         XON/XOFF
Note:
```

```
Tandem Computers
OSP
Port: RS-232              DB25P
Gender:                   PinConfig: C01

Pin   Function(Direction)
-------------------------------------------
1      Protective Ground
2      Transmit Data(Out)
3      Receive Data(In)
4      Request to Send(Out)
5      Clear to Send(In)
6      Data Set Ready(In)
7      Signal Ground
8      Data Carrier Detect(In)
20     Data Terminal Ready(Out)
-------------------------------------------
Flow Control: 20              XON/XOFF
Note:  Current loop is also supported
```

```
Tandem Computers
PSX Computer
Port: RS-232              DB25P
Gender:                   PinConfig: C01

Pin   Function(Direction)
-------------------------------------------
2      Transmit Data(Out)
3      Receive Data(In)
4      Request to Send(Out)
5      Clear to Send(In)
6      Data Set Ready(In)
7      Signal Ground
8      Carrier Detect(In)
20     Data Terminal Ready(Out)
-------------------------------------------
Flow Control: 5,6             XON/XOFF
Note:  Leads 5 & 6 must be on
```

```
Tandem Computers
TCC interface
Port: MAIN               DB25P
Gender: Male             PinConfig: P03

Pin   Function(Direction)
-------------------------------------------
1      Protective Ground
2      Transmit Data(Out)
3      Receive Data(In)
4      Request to Send(Out)
5      Clear to Send(In)
6      Data Set Ready(In)
7      Signal Ground
8      Data Carrier Detect(In)
15     Transmit Clock(Out)
17     Receive Clock(Out)
20     Data Terminal Ready(Out)
-------------------------------------------
Flow Control: 20              XON/XOFF
Note:
```

```
Tandy
1000 SL/TL Computers
Port: RS-232             DB9P
Gender: Male             PinConfig: C16

Pin   Function(Direction)
-------------------------------------------
1      Carrier Detect(In)
2      Receive Data(In)
3      Transmit Data(Out)
4      Data Terminal Ready(Out)
5      Signal Ground
6      Data Set Ready(In)
7      Request to Send(Out)
8      Clear to Send(In)
9      Ring Indicator(In)
-------------------------------------------
Flow Control: 6 & 8
Note:  The flow control leads of the
attached device should be connected to
leads 6 & 8
```

```
Tandy
1100/1400 FD Computers
Port: RS-232             DB9P
Gender: Male             PinConfig: C16

Pin   Function(Direction)
-------------------------------------------
1      Carrier Detect(In)
2      Receive Data(In)
3      Transmit Data(Out)
4      Data Terminal Ready(Out)
5      Signal Ground
6      Data Set Ready(In)
7      Request to Send(Out)
8      Clear to Send(In)
9      Ring Indicator(In)
-------------------------------------------
Flow Control: 6 & 8
Note:  The flow control leads of the
attached device should be connected to
leads 6 & 8
```

```
Tandy
1400/1500/2800 HD Computers
Port: RS-232             DB9P
Gender: Male             PinConfig: C16

Pin   Function(Direction)
-------------------------------------------
1      Carrier Detect(In)
2      Receive Data(In)
3      Transmit Data(Out)
4      Data Terminal Ready(Out)
5      Signal Ground
6      Data Set Ready(In)
7      Request to Send(Out)
8      Clear to Send(In)
9      Ring Indicator(In)
-------------------------------------------
Flow Control: 6 & 8
Note:  The flow control leads of the
attached device should be connected to
leads 6 & 8
```

```
Tandy                                    | Tandy
3000 NL, 4000, 4000SX/LX Computers       | 4020/4025 LX , 5000 MC Computers
Port: RS-232            DB9P             | Port: RS-232            DB9P
Gender: Male            PinConfig: C16   | Gender: Male            PinConfig: C16

Pin   Function(Direction)                | Pin   Function(Direction)
------------------------------------     | ------------------------------------
1     Carrier Detect(In)                 | 1     Carrier Detect(In)
2     Receive Data(In)                   | 2     Receive Data(In)
3     Transmit Data(Out)                 | 3     Transmit Data(Out)
4     Data Terminal Ready(Out)           | 4     Data Terminal Ready(Out)
5     Signal Ground                      | 5     Signal Ground
6     Data Set Ready(In)                 | 6     Data Set Ready(In)
7     Request to Send(Out)               | 7     Request to Send(Out)
8     Clear to Send(In)                  | 8     Clear to Send(In)
9     Ring Indicator(In)                 | 9     Ring Indicator(In)
------------------------------------     | ------------------------------------
Flow Control: 6 & 8                      | Flow Control: 6 & 8
Note:  The flow control leads of the     | Note:  The flow control leads of the
attached device should be connected to   | attached device should be connected to
leads 6 & 8                              | leads 6 & 8
```

```
Tandy                                    | Texas Instruments
RS-232 Board(1000 series computers)      | LT2000 Computer
Port: RS-232            DB25P            | Port: RS-232(9-pin)    DB9P
Gender: Male            PinConfig: C01   | Gender: Male            PinConfig: C16

Pin   Function(Direction)                | Pin   Function(Direction)
------------------------------------     | ------------------------------------
2     Transmit Data(Out)                 | 1     Carrier Detect(In)
3     Receive Data(In)                   | 2     Receive Data(In)
4     Request to Send(Out)               | 3     Transmit Data(Out)
5     Clear to Send(In)                  | 4     Data Terminal Ready(Out)
6     Data Set Ready(In)                 | 5     Signal Ground
7     Signal Ground                      | 6     Data Set Ready(In)
8     Data Carrier Detect(In)            | 7     Request to Send(Out)
20    Data Terminal Ready(Out)           | 8     Clear to Send(In)
22    Ring Indicator(In)                 | 9     Ring Indicator(In)
------------------------------------     | ------------------------------------
Flow Control: 5 & 6                      | Flow Control: 6 & 8
Note:  The flow control leads of the     | Note:  The flow control leads of the
attached device should be connected to   | attached device should be connected to
leads 5 & 6                              | leads 6 & 8
```

```
Texas Instruments                        | Texas Instruments
LT286/12, 25, 45 Computers               | LT286/12, 25, 45 Computers
Port: RS-232(25-pin)    DB25P           | Port: RS-232(9-pin)    DB9P
Gender: Male            PinConfig: C01   | Gender: Male            PinConfig: C16

Pin   Function(Direction)                | Pin   Function(Direction)
------------------------------------     | ------------------------------------
2     Transmit Data(Out)                 | 1     Carrier Detect(In)
3     Receive Data(In)                   | 2     Receive Data(In)
4     Request to Send(Out)               | 3     Transmit Data(Out)
5     Clear to Send(In)                  | 4     Data Terminal Ready(Out)
6     Data Set Ready(In)                 | 5     Signal Ground
7     Signal Ground                      | 6     Data Set Ready(In)
8     Data Carrier Detect(In)            | 7     Request to Send(Out)
20    Data Terminal Ready(Out)           | 8     Clear to Send(In)
22    Ring Indicator(In)                 | 9     Ring Indicator(In)
------------------------------------     | ------------------------------------
Flow Control: 5 & 6                      | Flow Control: 6 & 8
Note:                                    | Note:  The flow control leads of the
                                         | attached device should be connected to
                                         | leads 6 & 8
```

```
Toshiba
T1000, 1200, 1600, 3100, 3200, 5100, 5200
Laptops
Port:  RS-232            DB9P
Gender: Male             PinConfig: C16

Pin    Function(Direction)
-----------------------------------------
1       Carrier Detect(In)
2       Receive Data(In)
3       Transmit Data(Out)
4       Data Terminal Ready(Out)
5       Signal Ground
6       Data Set Ready(In)
7       Request to Send(Out)
8       Clear to Send(In)
9       Ring Indicator(In)
-----------------------------------------
Flow Control: 6 & 8
Note:  The flow control leads of the
attached device should be connected to
leads 6 & 8
```

```
Toshiba America, Inc.
T8500 Personal Computer
Port:  RS-232(DB-9)         DB9P
Gender: Male               PinConfig: C16

Pin    Function(Direction)
-----------------------------------------
1       Carrier Detect(In)
2       Receive Data(In)
3       Transmit Data(Out)
4       Data Terminal Ready(Out)
5       Signal Ground
6       Data Set Ready(In)
7       Request to Send(Out)
8       Clear to Send(In)
9       Ring Indicator(In)
-----------------------------------------
Flow Control: 6 & 8
Note:  Leads 6 & 8 need to be on to send
& receive data Adapters can be used to
convert port to DB-25 size
```

```
Tredex California
MAXAR 386 Computer
Port:  RS-232(2 ports)      DB9P
Gender: Male               PinConfig: C16

Pin    Function(Direction)
-----------------------------------------
1       Carrier Detect(In)
2       Receive Data(In)
3       Transmit Data(Out)
4       Data Terminal Ready(Out)
5       Signal Ground
6       Data Set Ready(In)
7       Request to Send(Out)
8       Clear to Send(In)
9       Ring Indicator(In)
-----------------------------------------
Flow Control: 6 & 8
Note:  The flow control leads of the
attached device should be connected to
leads 6 & 8
```

```
UNISYS Corporation
5000/20,30,40,50 Computer
Port:  15-Pin              DB15P
Gender: Male               PinConfig: C67

Pin    Function(Direction)
-----------------------------------------
11      Signal Ground
1       Transmitted Data(out)
9       Received Data(in)
2       Request To Send(out)
3       Data Set Ready(in)
10      Clear To Send(in)
12      Data Carrier Detect(in)
-----------------------------------------
Flow Control: 2    XON/XOFF
Note:
```

```
UNISYS Corporation
5000/85 Computer
Port:  RJ-12               RJ11
Gender: Female             PinConfig: C69

Pin    Function(Direction)
-----------------------------------------
4       Signal Ground
3       Transmitted Data(out)
2       Received Data(in)
1       Data Terminal Ready(out)
6       Data Carrier Detect(out)
5       Data Set Ready(in)
-----------------------------------------
Flow Control: 1    XON/XOFF
Note:
```

```
UNISYS Corporation
5000/85 EGC-8 DCE Board
Port:  RJ-12               RJ11
Gender: Female             PinConfig: C69

Pin    Function(Direction)
-----------------------------------------
4       Signal Ground
3       Transmitted Data(out)
2       Received Data(in)
1       Data Terminal Ready(out)
6       Data Carrier Detect(out)
5       Data Set Ready(in)
-----------------------------------------
Flow Control: 1    XON/XOFF
Note:
```

```
UNISYS Corporation                        UNISYS Corporation
5000/85 GC-16 DCE Board                   Products W/RJ-11 Ports
Port:  RJ-12            RJ11              Port:  RJ-11(4-WIRE)    RJ11
Gender:  Female         PinConfig: C69   Gender:  Female         PinConfig: C70

Pin    Function(Direction)               Pin    Function(Direction)
-------------------------------------    -------------------------------------
4      Signal Ground                     4      Signal Ground
3      Transmitted Data(out)             2      Transmitted Data(out)
2      Received Data(in)                 3      Received Data(in)
1      Data Terminal Ready(out)          5      Data Terminal Ready(out)
6      Data Carrier Detect(out)          -------------------------------------
5      Data Set Ready(in)                Flow Control: 5   XON/OFF
-------------------------------------    Note:  the above does not assume a cross-
Flow Control: 1   XON/XOFF               over cable
Note:
```

```
UNISYS Corporation                        Unisys Corporation
5000/85, EGC-8(DTE), GC-16(DTE) Computer 5000/60, 80, 90 Computers
Port:  RJ-12            RJ11              Port:  DTE              DB25P
Gender:  Female         PinConfig: C22   Gender:  Male           PinConfig: C14

Pin    Function(Direction)               Pin    Function(Direction)
-------------------------------------    -------------------------------------
4      Signal Ground                     1      Frame Ground
2      Transmitted Data(out)             2      Receive Data(In)
3      Received Data(in)                 3      Transmit Data(Out)
5      Data Terminal Ready(out)          4      Clear to Send(In)
1      Data Set Ready(in)                5      Request to Send(Out)
6      Data Carrier Detect(in)           6      Data Terminal Ready(Out)
-------------------------------------    7      Signal Ground
Flow Control: 5   XON/XOFF               20     Data Terminal Ready(In)
Note:                                    -------------------------------------
                                         Flow Control: 20          XON/XOFF
                                         Note:
```

```
Unisys Corporation                        Unisys Corporation
6000/30, 31, 50, 50-SCP, 55 Computers    6000/30, 31, 50, 55 Computers
Port:  COM             DB9P              Port:  ECOM2/ECOM3      DB25P
Gender:  Male          PinConfig: C16    Gender:  Male           PinConfig: C01

Pin    Function(Direction)               Pin    Function(Direction)
-------------------------------------    -------------------------------------
1      Carrier Detect(In)                1      Chassis Ground
2      Receive Data(In)                  2      Transmit Data(Out)
3      Transmit Data(Out)                3      Receive Data(In)
4      Data Terminal Ready(Out)          4      Request to Send(Out)
5      Signal Ground                     5      Clear to Send(In)
6      Data Set Ready(In)                6      Data Set Ready(In)
7      Request to Send(Out)              7      Signal Ground
8      Clear to Send(In)                 8      Carrier Detect(In)
9      Ring Indicator(In)                15     Transmit Clock(In)
-------------------------------------    17     Receive Clock(In)
Flow Control: 6 & 8                      20     Data Terminal Ready(Out)
Note:  The flow control leads of the     22     Ring Indicator(In)
attached device should be connected to   24     External Transmit Clock(Out)
leads 6 & 8                              -------------------------------------
                                         Flow Control: 20          XON/XOFF
                                         Note:
```

Unisys Corporation
7000/40 Computer
Port: RS-232   DB25P
Gender: Male   PinConfig: C01

Pin	Function(Direction)
1	Chassis Ground
2	Transmit Data(Out)
3	Receive Data(In)
4	Request to Send(Out)
5	Clear to Send(In)
6	Data Set Ready(In)
7	Signal Ground
8	Carrier Detect(In)
15	Transmit Clock(In)
17	Receive Clock(In)
20	Data Terminal Ready(Out)
22	Ring Indicator(In)
24	External Transmit Clock(Out)

Flow Control: 20   XON/XOFF
Note:

Unisys Corporation
PW2 300 Computer
Port: RS-232   DB9P
Gender: Male   PinConfig: C16

Pin	Function(Direction)
1	Carrier Detect(In)
2	Receive Data(In)
3	Transmit Data(Out)
4	Data Terminal Ready(Out)
5	Signal Ground
6	Data Set Ready(In)
7	Request to Send(Out)
8	Clear to Send(In)
9	Ring Indicator(In)

Flow Control: 6 & 8
Note: The flow control leads of the attached device should be connected to leads 6 & 8

Unisys Corporation
PW2 500/12, 16, 20A Computers
Port: RS-232   DB25P
Gender: Male   PinConfig: C01

Pin	Function(Direction)
2	Transmit Data(Out)
3	Receive Data(In)
4	Request to Send(Out)
5	Clear to Send(In)
6	Data Set Ready(In)
7	Signal Ground
8	Data Carrier Detect(In)
15	Transmit Clock(In)
17	Receive Clock(In)
20	Data Terminal Ready(Out)
22	Ring Indicator(In)

Flow Control: 6 & 8
Note: The flow control leads of the attached device should be connected to leads 6 & 8

Unisys Corporation
PW2 500/16, 20A Computers
Port: RS-232(9-pin)   DB9P
Gender: Male   PinConfig: C16

Pin	Function(Direction)
1	Carrier Detect(In)
2	Receive Data(In)
3	Transmit Data(Out)
4	Data Terminal Ready(Out)
5	Signal Ground
6	Data Set Ready(In)
7	Request to Send(Out)
8	Clear to Send(In)
9	Ring Indicator(In)

Flow Control: 6 & 8
Note: The flow control leads of the attached device should be connected to leads 6 & 8

Unisys Corporation
PW2 800, 800/20/26/33 Computers
Port: RS-232(1of2)   DB9P
Gender: Male   PinConfig: C16

Pin	Function(Direction)
1	Carrier Detect(In)
2	Receive Data(In)
3	Transmit Data(Out)
4	Data Terminal Ready(Out)
5	Signal Ground
6	Data Set Ready(In)
7	Request to Send(Out)
8	Clear to Send(In)
9	Ring Indicator(In)

Note: The flow control leads of the attached device should be connected to leads 6 & 8

Unisys Corporation
PW2 800/486-25A, 850 Computers
Port: RS-232(1of2)   DB9P
Gender: Male   PinConfig: C16

Pin	Function(Direction)
1	Carrier Detect(In)
2	Receive Data(In)
3	Transmit Data(Out)
4	Data Terminal Ready(Out)
5	Signal Ground
6	Data Set Ready(In)
7	Request to Send(Out)
8	Clear to Send(In)
9	Ring Indicator(In)

Flow Control: 6 & 8
Note: The flow control leads of the attached device should be connected to leads 6 & 8

```
┌─────────────────────────────────────────┬─────────────────────────────────────────┐
│ Unisys Corporation                       │ Wang Laboratories                        │
│ PW2 LAN Workstation/286                  │ Professional & Advanced Personal         │
│ Port: RS-232              DB9P           │ Computers                                │
│ Gender: Male             PinConfig: C16  │ Port: RS-232              DB25P           │
│                                          │ Gender: Male             PinConfig: C01  │
│ Pin   Function(Direction)                │                                          │
│ ---------------------------------------  │ Pin   Function(Direction)                │
│ 1     Carrier Detect(In)                 │ ---------------------------------------  │
│ 2     Receive Data(In)                   │ 2     Transmit Data(Out)                 │
│ 3     Transmit Data(Out)                 │ 3     Receive Data(In)                   │
│ 4     Data Terminal Ready(Out)           │ 4     Request to Send(Out)               │
│ 5     Signal Ground                      │ 5     Clear to Send(In)                  │
│ 6     Data Set Ready(In)                 │ 6     Data Set Ready(In)                 │
│ 7     Request to Send(Out)               │ 7     Signal Ground                      │
│ 8     Clear to Send(In)                  │ 8     Carrier Detect(In)                 │
│ 9     Ring Indicator(In)                 │ 20    Data Terminal Ready(Out)           │
│ ---------------------------------------  │ 22    Ring Indicator(In)                 │
│ Flow Control: 6 & 8                      │ ---------------------------------------  │
│ Note:  The flow control leads of the     │ Flow Control: 5,6         XON/XOFF        │
│ attached device should be connected to   │ Note:  Leads 5 & 6 must be on             │
│ leads 6 & 8                              │                                          │
├─────────────────────────────────────────┼─────────────────────────────────────────┤
│ Wang Laboratories                        │ Wang Laboratories                        │
│ Professional & Advanced Personal         │ Laptop Computer                          │
│ Computers                                │ Port: RS-232              DB25P           │
│ Port: RS-232(9-pin)       DB9P           │ Gender: Male             PinConfig: C01   │
│ Gender: Male             PinConfig: C16  │                                          │
│                                          │ Pin   Function(Direction)                │
│ Pin   Function(Direction)                │ ---------------------------------------  │
│ ---------------------------------------  │ 1     Protective Ground                   │
│ 1     Carrier Detect(In)                 │ 2     Transmit Data(Out)                 │
│ 2     Receive Data(In)                   │ 3     Receive Data(In)                   │
│ 3     Transmit Data(Out)                 │ 4     Request to Send(Out)               │
│ 4     Data Terminal Ready(Out)           │ 5     Clear to Send(In)                  │
│ 5     Signal Ground                      │ 6     Data Set Ready(In)                 │
│ 6     Data Set Ready(In)                 │ 7     Signal Ground                      │
│ 7     Request to Send(Out)               │ 8     Data Carrier Detect(In)            │
│ 8     Clear to Send(In)                  │ 15    Transmit Clock(In)                 │
│ 9     Ring Indicator(In)                 │ 17    Receive Clock(In)                  │
│ ---------------------------------------  │ 20    Data Terminal Ready(Out)           │
│ Flow Control: 6 & 8                      │ 22    Ring Indicator(In)                 │
│ Note:  The flow control leads of the     │ 24    External Transmit Clock(Out)       │
│ attached device should be connected to   │ ---------------------------------------  │
│ leads 6 & 8                              │ Flow Control: 5 & 6                       │
│                                          │ Note:                                    │
├─────────────────────────────────────────┼─────────────────────────────────────────┤
│ Wyse Technology                          │ Yamaha                                   │
│ WY-2012, 3116SX Computers                │ C1 Music Computer                        │
│ Port: Serial 2-9-pin      D9P            │ Port: RS-232              DB9P            │
│ Gender: Male             PinConfig: C16  │ Gender: Male             PinConfig: C16  │
│                                          │                                          │
│ Pin   Function(Direction)                │ Pin   Function(Direction)                │
│ ---------------------------------------  │ ---------------------------------------  │
│ 1     Carrier Detect(In)                 │ 1     Carrier Detect(In)                 │
│ 2     Receive Data(In)                   │ 2     Receive Data(In)                   │
│ 3     Transmit Data(Out)                 │ 3     Transmit Data(Out)                 │
│ 4     Data Terminal Ready(Out)           │ 4     Data Terminal Ready(Out)           │
│ 5     Signal Ground                      │ 5     Signal Ground                      │
│ 6     Data Set Ready(In)                 │ 6     Data Set Ready(In)                 │
│ 7     Request to Send(Out)               │ 7     Request to Send(Out)               │
│ 8     Clear to Send(In)                  │ 8     Clear to Send(In)                  │
│ 9     Ring Indicator(In)                 │ 9     Ring Indicator(In)                 │
│ ---------------------------------------  │ ---------------------------------------  │
│ Flow Control: 6 & 8                      │ Flow Control: 6 & 8                      │
│ Note:  The flow control leads of the     │ Note:  The flow control leads of the     │
│ attached device should be connected to   │ attached device should be connected to   │
│ leads 6 & 8                              │ leads 6 & 8                              │
└─────────────────────────────────────────┴─────────────────────────────────────────┘
```

```
Zenith
ProSpeed 386SX Computer
Port: RS-232              DB9P
Gender: Male             PinConfig: C16

Pin   Function(Direction)
-------------------------------------------
1       Carrier Detect(In)
2       Receive Data(In)
3       Transmit Data(Out)
4       Data Terminal Ready(Out)
5       Signal Ground
6       Data Set Ready(In)
7       Request to Send(Out)
8       Clear to Send(In)
9       Ring Indicator(In)
-------------------------------------------
Flow Control: 6 & 8
Note:  The flow control leads of the
attached device should be connected to
leads 6 & 8
```

```
Zenith
SuperSport, SX, & SuperSport 286
Computers
Port: RS-232              DB9P
Gender: Male             PinConfig: C16

Pin   Function(Direction)
-------------------------------------------
1       Carrier Detect(In)
2       Receive Data(In)
3       Transmit Data(Out)
4       Data Terminal Ready(Out)
5       Signal Ground
6       Data Set Ready(In)
7       Request to Send(Out)
8       Clear to Send(In)
9       Ring Indicator(In)
-------------------------------------------
Flow Control: 6 & 8
Note:  The flow control leads of the
attached device should be connected to
leads 6 & 8
```

```
Zenith
TurboSport 386 Computers
Port: RS-232              DB9P
Gender: Male             PinConfig: C16

Pin   Function(Direction)
-------------------------------------------
1       Carrier Detect(In)
2       Receive Data(In)
3       Transmit Data(Out)
4       Data Terminal Ready(Out)
5       Signal Ground
6       Data Set Ready(In)
7       Request to Send(Out)
8       Clear to Send(In)
9       Ring Indicator(In)
-------------------------------------------
Flow Control: 6 & 8
Note:  The flow control leads of the
attached device should be connected to
leads 6 & 8
```

```
Zenith
Z-386, Z-386SX, Z-386/20, 386/25
Computers
Port: RS-232              DB9P
Gender: Male             PinConfig: C16

Pin   Function(Direction)
-------------------------------------------
1       Carrier Detect(In)
2       Receive Data(In)
3       Transmit Data(Out)
4       Data Terminal Ready(Out)
5       Signal Ground
6       Data Set Ready(In)
7       Request to Send(Out)
8       Clear to Send(In)
9       Ring Indicator(In)
-------------------------------------------
Flow Control: 6 & 8
Note:  The flow control leads of the
attached device should be connected to
leads 6 & 8
```

modems + multiplexors

```
Anchor Automation, Inc.
VM520 modem
Port:  female              DB25S
Gender:  Female            PinConfig: C14

Pin   Function(Direction)
------------------------------------------
1     Frame Ground
2     Transmit Data(In)
3     Receive Data(Out)
5     Clear to Send(Out)
7     Signal Ground
8     Data Carrier Detect(Out)
20    Data Terminal Ready(In)
22    Ring Indicator(Out)
------------------------------------------
Flow Control:
Note:
```

```
Anderson Jacobson
AJ 4048-2 Modem
Port:  RS-232              DB25S
Gender:  Female            PinConfig: C09

Pin   Function(Direction)
------------------------------------------
1     Protective Ground
2     Transmit Data(In)
3     Receive Data(Out)
4     Request to Send(In)
5     Clear to Send(Out)
6     Data Set Ready(Out)
7     Signal Ground
8     Carrier Detect(Out)
15    Transmit Clock(Out)
17    Receive Clock(Out)
19    DLB (In)
20    Data Terminal Ready(In)
21    SQD (Out)
22    Ring Indicator(Out)
23    Data Rate Select(Out)
24    External Transmit Clock(In)
25    AL (In)
------------------------------------------
Flow Control:
Note:
```

```
Anderson Jacobson Inc.
AJ2441-2 Modem
Port:  EIA(RS-232)         DB25S
Gender:  Female            PinConfig: C14

Pin   Function(Direction)
------------------------------------------
1     Protective Ground
2     Transmit Data(In)
3     Receive Data(Out)
4     Request to Send(In)
5     Clear to Send(Out)
6     Data Set Ready(Out)
7     Signal Ground
8     Carrier Detect(Out)
9     +12V(Out)
10    -12V(Out)
12    Speed Select(In)
13    Speed Select(In)
15    Transmit Clock(Out)
17    Receive Clock(Out)
18    LL (In)
20    Data Terminal Ready(In)
21    RDL (In)
22    Ring Indicator(Out)
23    Data Rate Select(In)
24    External Transmit Clock(In)
25    LL (In)
------------------------------------------
Flow Control:
Note:  This card plugs into card
cage(rack mount), or can be put in an AJ-
UCSA-03 enclosure to be standalone
```

```
Anderson Jacobson, Inc.
A242A Acoustic Coupler
Port:  RS-232              DB25S
Gender:  Female            PinConfig: C10

Pin   Function(Direction)
------------------------------------------
1     Protective Ground
2     Transmit Data(In)
3     Receive Data(Out)
5     Clear to Send(Out)
6     Data Set Ready(Out)
7     Signal Ground
8     Data Carrier Detect(Out)
------------------------------------------
Flow Control:
Note:  This port emulates a DCE device
This port can be optioned for 20mA
current loop
```

```
Anderson Jacobson, Inc.              Anderson Jacobson, Inc.
AJ1212-ST Modem                      AJ1232 Modem
Port: EIA(RS-232)      DB25S         Port: RS-232          DB25S
Gender: Female         PinConfig: C14 Gender: Female       PinConfig: C14

Pin   Function(Direction)            Pin   Function(Direction)
-------------------------------      -------------------------------
1     Chassis Ground                 1     Frame Ground
2     Transmit Data(In)              2     Transmit Data(In)
3     Receive Data(Out)              3     Receive Data(Out)
4     Request to Send(In)            5     Clear to Send(Out)
5     Clear to Send(Out)             6     Data Set Ready(Out)
6     Data Set Ready(Out)            7     Signal Ground
7     Signal Ground                  8     Carrier Detect(Out)
8     Carrier Detect(Out)            15    Transmit Clock(Out)
9     +8V (Out)                      17    Receive Clock(Out)
10    -8V (Out)                      20    Data Terminal Ready(In)
15    Transmit Clock(Out)            24    External Transmit Clock(In)
17    Receive Clock(Out)            -------------------------------
20    Data Terminal Ready(In)        Flow Control:
22    Ring Indicator(Out)            Note: DTR must be high for modem
24    External Transmit Clock(In)    operation.  If the attached device can't
-------------------------------      provide DTR, option it high.
Flow Control:
Note:

Anderson Jacobson, Inc.              Anderson Jacobson, Inc.
AJ1234A Acoustic Coupler/Modem       AJ1259-AD
Port: EIA                DB25S       Port: EIA(RS-232)      DB25S
Gender: Female           PinConfig: C14 Gender: Female      PinConfig: C14

Pin   Function(Direction)            Pin   Function(Direction)
-------------------------------      -------------------------------
1     Protective Ground              1     Chassis Ground
2     Transmit Data(In)              2     Transmit Data(In)
3     Receive Data(Out)              3     Receive Data(Out)
4     Request to Send(In)            4     Request to Send(In)
5     Clear to Send(Out)             5     Clear to Send(Out)
6     Data Set Ready(Out)            6     Data Set Ready(Out)
7     Signal Ground                  7     Signal Ground
8     Data Carrier Detect(Out)       8     Carrier Detect(Out)
9     +12V(Out)                      9     +12V(Out)
10    -12V(Out)                      10    -12V(Out)
15    Transmit Clock(Out)            12    Speed Select(In)
17    Receive Clock(Out)             15    Transmit Clock(Out)
20    Data Terminal Ready(In)        17    Receive Clock(Out)
24    External Transmit Clock(In)    18    Busy(In)
-------------------------------      20    Data Terminal Ready(In)
Flow Control:                        21    RDL (In)
Note: This port emulates a DCE device 22   Ring Indicator(Out)
This modem supports leased line operation 23 Data Rate Select(In)
                                     24    External Transmit Clock(In)
                                     25    Busy(In)
                                    -------------------------------
                                     Flow Control:
                                     Note:
```

```
Anderson Jacobson, Inc.
AJ347 Acoustic Coupler/Modem
Port:  RS-232c                DB25S
Gender:  Female               PinConfig: C14

Pin    Function(Direction)
----------------------------------------
1      Protective Ground
2      Transmit Data(In)
3      Receive Data(Out)
4      Request to Send(In)
5      Clear to Send(Out)
6      Data Set Ready(Out)
7      Signal Ground
8      Data Carrier Detect(Out)
20     Data Terminal Ready(In)
----------------------------------------
Flow Control:
Note:  This port emulates a DCE device
Port can be optioned for 20MA operation
```

```
AT&T
103JR modem
Port:  female (DTE port)      DB25S
Gender:  Female               PinConfig: C14

Pin    Function(Direction)
----------------------------------------
2      Transmit Data(In)
3      Receive Data(Out)
5      Clear to Send(Out)
6      Modem Ready(Out)
7      Signal Ground
8      Data Carrier Detect(Out)
9      +12V(Out)
10     -12V(Out)
20     Data Terminal Ready(In)
22     Ring Indicator(Out)
25     Busy(In)
----------------------------------------
Flow Control:
Note:
```

```
Bizcomp Corporation
1012 Intelligent Modem
Port:  RS-232                 DB25S
Gender:  Female               PinConfig: C14

Pin    Function(Direction)
----------------------------------------
2      Transmit Data(In)
3      Receive Data(Out)
5      Clear to Send(Out)
6      Data Set Ready(Out)
7      Signal Ground
8      Data Carrier Detect(Out)
12     Data Rate Select(Out)
15     Transmit Clock(Out)
17     Receive Clock(Out)
20     Data Terminal Ready(In)
21     RDL (In)
22     Ring Indicator(Out)
24     External Transmit Clock(In)
----------------------------------------
Flow Control:
Note:  This port emulates a DCE device
```

```
Bizcomp Corporation
4120 IntelliModem EXT
Port:  RS-232                 DB25S
Gender:  Female               PinConfig: C14

Pin    Function(Direction)
----------------------------------------
2      Transmit Data(In)
3      Receive Data(Out)
5      Clear to Send(Out)
6      Data Set Ready(Out)
7      Signal Ground
8      Data Carrier Detect(Out)
12     HS  (Out)
20     Data Terminal Ready(In)
22     Ring Indicator(Out)
----------------------------------------
Flow Control:
Note:  Lead 5 is on at all times Lead 6 &
8 are exactly the same-Check optioning
```

```
Bizcomp Corporation
IntelliModem 2400/4124/4134/9600 Modems
Port:  RS-232              DB25S
Gender:  Female            PinConfig: C14

Pin    Function(Direction)
-------------------------------------------
2      Receive Data(In)
3      Transmit Data(Out)
5      Clear to Send(Out)
6      Data Set Ready(Out)
7      Signal Ground
8      Data Carrier Detect(Out)
12     HS  (Out)
15     Transmit Clock(In)
17     Receive Clock(In)
20     Data Terminal Ready(In)
22     Ring Indicator(Out)
24     External Transmit Clock(Out)
-------------------------------------------

Flow Control:
Note:  The leads and their
condition(on/off) vary based on async or
sync operation--consult manual
```

```
CXR Telcom
AJ 1951 Modem
Port:  RS-232              DB25S
Gender:  Female            PinConfig: C02

Pin    Function(Direction)
-------------------------------------------
1      Frame Ground
2      Transmit Data(In)
3      Receive Data(Out)
4      Request to Send(In)
5      Clear to Send(Out)
6      Data Set Ready(Out)
7      Signal Ground
8      Data Carrier Detect(Out)
9      +12V(Out)
10     -12V(Out)
11     RDL (In)
12     Data In(Out)
14     DC  (In)
15     Transmit Clock(Out)
17     Receive Clock(Out)
18     LAL (In)
20     Data Terminal Ready(In)
21     SQD (Out)
22     Ring Indicator(Out)
23     Data Rate Select(In)
24     External Transmit Clock(In)
25     TEST(In)
-------------------------------------------

Flow Control:
Note:  This port emulates a DCE device
```

```
CXR Telcom
AJ 9601-MD, 9641  Modems
Port:  RS-232              DB25S
Gender:  Female            PinConfig: C09

Pin    Function(Direction)
-------------------------------------------
1      Protective Ground
2      Transmit Data(In)
3      Receive Data(Out)
4      Request to Send(In)
5      Clear to Send(Out)
6      Data Set Ready(Out)
7      Signal Ground
8      Carrier Detect(Out)
9      +12V(Out)
10     -12V(Out)
11     RDL (In)
12     DMI (Out)
14     DMC (In)
15     Transmit Clock(Out)
17     Receive Clock(Out)
18     AL  (In)
19     DLB (In)
20     Data Terminal Ready(In)
21     SQD (Out)
22     Ring Indicator(Out)
23     Data Rate Select(Out)
24     External Transmit Clock(In)
25     TEST(Out)
-------------------------------------------

Flow Control:
Note:
```

```
CXR Telcom
AJ 9631-SA Modem
Port:  RS-232              DB25S
Gender:  Female            PinConfig: C09

Pin    Function(Direction)
-------------------------------------------
1      Protective Ground
2      Transmit Data(In)
3      Receive Data(Out)
4      Request to Send(In)
5      Clear to Send(Out)
6      Data Set Ready(Out)
7      Signal Ground
8      Carrier Detect(Out)
9      +12V(Out)
10     -12V(Out)
11     RDL (In)
12     Data In(Out)
15     Transmit Clock(Out)
17     Receive Clock(Out)
18     LAL (In)
19     Data In(Out)
20     Data Terminal Ready(In)
21     SQD (Out)
22     Ring Indicator(Out)
23     Data Rate Select(In)
24     External Transmit Clock(In)
25     TEST(Out)
-------------------------------------------

Flow Control:
Note:  Lead 4 & 20 must be high for modem
to operate
```

```
CXR Telcom                              CXR Telcom
AJ 9632 Modem                           AJ 9651 Modems
Port: RS-232            DB25S           Port: RS-232             DB25S
Gender: Female          PinConfig: C02   Gender: Female         PinConfig: C14

Pin   Function(Direction)              Pin   Function(Direction)
-------------------------------------  -------------------------------------
1     Frame Ground                     1     Protective Ground
2     Transmit Data(In)                2     Transmit Data(In)
3     Receive Data(Out)                3     Receive Data(Out)
4     Request to Send(In)              4     Request to Send(In)
5     Clear to Send(Out)               5     Clear to Send(Out)
6     Data Set Ready(Out)              6     Data Set Ready(Out)
7     Signal Ground                    7     Signal Ground
8     Data Carrier Detect(Out)         8     Carrier Detect(Out)
9     +V (Out)                         12    Data Rate Select(In)
10    -V (Out)                         15    Transmit Clock(Out)
11    RDL (In)                         17    Receive Clock(Out)
12    Data Rate Select(In)             18    LAL (In)
15    Transmit Clock(Out)              20    Data Terminal Ready(In)
17    Receive Clock(Out)               21    SQD (Out)
18    LAL (In)                         22    Ring Indicator(Out)
20    Data Terminal Ready(In)          23    Data Rate Select(In)
21    RDL (In)                         24    External Transmit Clock(In)
22    Ring Indicator(Out)              25    TEST(Out)
23    Data Rate Select(In)           -------------------------------------
24    External Transmit Clock(In)      Flow Control:
25    TEST(In)                         Note:  Lead 4 & 20 must be high for modem
-------------------------------------  to operate
Flow Control:
Note:  This port emulates a DCE device


CXR Telcom                              CXR Telcom
AJ UCCA-01 Modems                       AJ2412-AD3H Modem
Port: DTE Terminal      DB25S           Port: TERMINAL           DB25S
Gender: Female          PinConfig: C09   Gender: Female         PinConfig: C14

Pin   Function(Direction)              Pin   Function(Direction)
-------------------------------------  -------------------------------------
1     Protective Ground                1     Protective Ground
2     Transmit Data(In)                2     Transmit Data(In)
3     Receive Data(Out)                3     Receive Data(Out)
4     Request to Send(In)              4     Request to Send(In)
5     Clear to Send(Out)               5     Clear to Send(Out)
6     Data Set Ready(Out)              6     Data Set Ready(Out)
7     Signal Ground                    7     Signal Ground
8     Carrier Detect(Out)              8     Carrier Detect(Out)
12    Secondary DCD(Out)               12    Speed Select(In)
13    Secondary Cl'r to Send(Out)      15    Transmit Clock(Out)
14    Supervisory Trans.Data(Out)      17    Receive Clock(Out)
15    Transmit Clock(Out)              18    Busy(In)
16    Supervisory Rec. Data(Out)       20    Data Terminal Ready(In)
17    Receive Clock(Out)               21    RDL (In)
19    Secondary Req.to Send(In)        22    Ring Indicator(Out)
20    Data Terminal Ready(In)          23    Data Rate Select(In)
21    SQD (Out)                        24    External Transmit Clock(In)
22    Ring Indicator(Out)              25    Busy(In)
23    Data Rate Select(In)           -------------------------------------
24    External Transmit Clock(In)      Flow Control:
-------------------------------------  Note:
Flow Control:
Note:  This cage with port, holds AJ
modem cards
```

```
CXR Telcom
AJ2412-STH Modem
Port: TERMINAL              DB25S
Gender: Female             PinConfig: C14

Pin   Function(Direction)
-------------------------------------
1         Protective Ground
2         Transmit Data(In)
3         Receive Data(Out)
4         Request to Send(In)
5         Clear to Send(Out)
6         Data Set Ready(Out)
7         Signal Ground
8         Carrier Detect(Out)
9         +V  (Out)
10        -V  (Out)
12        Speed Select(In)
15        Transmit Clock(Out)
17        Receive Clock(Out)
18        Busy(In)
20        Data Terminal Ready(In)
21        RDL (In)
22        Ring Indicator(Out)
23        Data Rate Select(In)
24        External Transmit Clock(In)
25        Busy(In)
-------------------------------------
Flow Control:
Note:
```

```
CXR Telcom
AJ2441-1 Modem
Port: DTE Interface        DB25S
Gender: Female             PinConfig: C14

Pin   Function(Direction)
-------------------------------------
1         Chassis Ground
2         Transmit Data(In)
3         Receive Data(Out)
4         Request to Send(In)
5         Clear to Send(Out)
6         Data Set Ready(Out)
7         Signal Ground
8         Carrier Detect(Out)
12        Secondary DCD(Out)
13        Secondary Cl'r to Send(Out)
14        Supervisory Trans.Data(In)
15        Transmit Clock(Out)
16        Supervisory Rec. Data(Out)
17        Receive Clock(Out)
20        Data Terminal Ready(In)
21        SQD (Out)
22        Ring Indicator(Out)
23        Data Rate Select(In)
24        External Transmit Clock(In)
-------------------------------------
Flow Control:
Note:  This card plugs in a rack mount(AJ
UCCA-01) or equivalent--also can be made
standalone(AJ UCSA01)
```

```
DEC
DHU-11 Statistical Multiplexor
Port: Ports 00-15          DB25P
Gender: Male               PinConfig: C01

Pin   Function(Direction)
-------------------------------------
1         Protective Ground
2         Transmit Data(Out)
3         Receive Data(In)
4         Request to Send(Out)
5         Clear to Send(In)
6         Data Set Ready(In)
7         Signal Ground
8         Data Carrier Detect(In)
20        Data Terminal Ready(Out)
22        Ring Indicator(In)
-------------------------------------
Flow Control:             XON/XOFF
Note:  The DHU-11 factory options aren't
set to support the control leads
4/5/6/8/20/22.  Set options
```

```
Gandalf Data
DM 49 HOL, LDM 409419, 192 & 3192 Modems
Port: RS-232               DB25S
Gender: Female             PinConfig: C14

Pin   Function(Direction)
-------------------------------------
1         Frame Ground
2         Receive Data(In)
3         Transmit Data(Out)
4         Request to Send(In)
5         Clear to Send(Out)
6         Data Set Ready(Out)
7         Signal Ground
8         Data Carrier Detect(Out)
15        Transmit Clock(Out)
17        Receive Clock(Out)
18        LAL (In)
20        Data Terminal Ready(In)
21        RDL (In)
24        External Transmit Clock(In)
25        TEST(Out)
-------------------------------------
Flow Control:
Note:  This port emulates a DCE device
```

```
Gandalf Data
LDS 309A Modem
Port: RS-232            DB25S
Gender: Female          PinConfig: C14

Pin   Function(Direction)
---------------------------------------------
1       Frame Ground
2       Receive Data(In)
3       Transmit Data(Out)
4       Request to Send(In)
5       Clear to Send(Out)
6       Data Set Ready(Out)
7       Signal Ground
8       Data Carrier Detect(Out)
9       +10V(Out)
10      -10V(Out)
15      Transmit Clock(Out)
17      Receive Clock(Out)
18      LAL (In)
20      Data Terminal Ready(In)
21      RDL (In)
24      External Transmit Clock(In)
25      TEST(Out)
---------------------------------------------
Flow Control:
Note:  This port emulates a DCE device
```

```
Gandalf Technologies
ACCESS Series 24A24EC Modems
Port: RS-232            DB25S
Gender: Female          PinConfig: C14

Pin   Function(Direction)
---------------------------------------------
1       Frame Ground
2       Transmit Data(In)
3       Receive Data(Out)
4       Request to Send(In)
5       Clear to Send(Out)
6       Data Set Ready(Out)
7       Signal Ground
8       Data Carrier Detect(Out)
12      Serial In(Out)
15      Transmit Clock(Out)
17      Receive Clock(Out)
20      Data Terminal Ready(In)
22      Ring Indicator(Out)
24      External Transmit Clock(In)
25      TEST(Out)
---------------------------------------------
Flow Control:
Note:  This port emulates a DCE device
```

```
Gandalf Technologies
LDS 120E, RM 3120E Local Data Sets
Port: RS-232            DB25S
Gender: Female          PinConfig: C14

Pin   Function(Direction)
---------------------------------------------
1       Frame Ground
2       Transmit Data(In)
3       Receive Data(Out)
4       Request to Send(In)
5       Clear to Send(Out)
6       Data Set Ready(Out)
7       Signal Ground
8       Data Carrier Detect(Out)
9       +10V(Out)
10      -10V(Out)
18      AL (In)
20      Data Terminal Ready(In)
21      RDL (In)
25      TEST(Out)
---------------------------------------------
Flow Control:
Note:  This port emulates a DCE device
```

```
Hayes Microcomputer Products
InterBridge
Port: DCE configuration  DB25P
Gender: Male             PinConfig: C14

Pin   Function(Direction)
---------------------------------------------
1       Protective Ground
2       Transmit Data(In)
3       Receive Data(Out)
4       Request to Send(In)
5       Clear to Send(Out)
6       Data Set Ready(Out)
7       Signal Ground
8       Data Carrier Detect(Out)
15      Transmit Clock(Out)
17      Receive Clock(Out)
20      Data Terminal Ready(In)
22      Ring Indicator(Out)
24      External Transmit Clock(In)
---------------------------------------------
Flow Control:
Note:  This port can be configured to be
either DTE or DCE.  The above port
assumes it is optioned-DCE
```

```
Hayes Microcomputer Products
InterBridge
Port: DTE configuration   DB25P
Gender: Male              PinConfig: C01

Pin   Function(Direction)
-------------------------------------------
1     Protective Ground
2     Transmit Data(Out)
3     Receive Data(In)
4     Request to Send(Out)
5     Clear to Send(In)
6     Data Set Ready(In)
7     Signal Ground
8     Data Carrier Detect(In)
15    Transmit Clock(In)
17    Receive Clock(In)
20    Data Terminal Ready(Out)
22    Ring Indicator(In)
24    External Transmit Clock(Out)
-------------------------------------------
Flow Control:
Note:  This port can be configured to be
either DTE or DCE.  The above port
assumes it is optioned-DTE
```

```
Hayes Microcomputer Products
Smartmodem 2400
Port: RS-232              DB25S
Gender: Female           PinConfig: C14

Pin   Function(Direction)
-------------------------------------------
1     Frame Ground
2     Receive Data(In)
3     Transmit Data(Out)
4     Request to Send(In)
5     Clear to Send(Out)
6     Data Set Ready(Out)
7     Signal Ground
8     Data Carrier Detect(Out)
12    Data Rate Select(Out)
20    Data Terminal Ready(In)
23    Data Rate Select(Out)
-------------------------------------------
Flow Control:
Note:  This modem can support async &
sync modes.  Lead 4 is ignored(async).
User can option leads 4/6/8
```

```
Hayes Microcomputer Products
Smartmodem 2400(V-Series)
Port: RS-232              DB25S
Gender: Female           PinConfig: C14

Pin   Function(Direction)
-------------------------------------------
1     Frame Ground
2     Transmit Data(In)
3     Receive Data(Out)
4     Request to Send(In)
5     Clear to Send(Out)
6     Data Set Ready(Out)
7     Signal Ground
8     Data Carrier Detect(Out)
12    Data Rate Select(Out)
15    Transmit Clock(Out)
17    Receive Clock(Out)
20    Data Terminal Ready(In)
22    Ring Indicator(Out)
23    Data Rate Select(Out)
24    External Transmit Clock(In)
-------------------------------------------
Flow Control:
Note:
```

```
Hayes Microcomputer Products
Smartmodem 9600 V.32
Port: RS-232              DB25S
Gender: Female           PinConfig: C14

Pin   Function(Direction)
-------------------------------------------
1     Frame Ground
2     Transmit Data(In)
3     Receive Data(Out)
4     Request to Send(In)
5     Clear to Send(Out)
6     Data Set Ready(Out)
7     Signal Ground
8     Data Carrier Detect(Out)
12    Data Rate Select(Out)
15    Transmit Clock(Out)
17    Receive Clock(Out)
18    LAL (In)
20    Data Terminal Ready(In)
21    RDL (In)
22    Ring Indicator(Out)
23    Data Rate Select(Out)
24    External Transmit Clock(In)
25    TEST(Out)
-------------------------------------------
Flow Control:
Note:  Leads 12, 15, 17, 23, & 24, are
not typically used in async operation.
Leads 18,21,23,& 24-optional
```

```
Hayes Microcomputer Products
Ultra Smartmodem 9600
Port: RS-232              DB25S
Gender: Female            PinConfig: C14

Pin   Function(Direction)
---------------------------------------------
1     Chassis Ground
2     Transmit Data(In)
3     Receive Data(Out)
4     Request to Send(In)
5     Clear to Send(Out)
6     Data Set Ready(Out)
7     Signal Ground
8     Carrier Detect(Out)
20    Data Terminal Ready(In)
22    Ring Indicator(Out)
---------------------------------------------
Flow Control:              XON/XOFF
Note:
```

```
inmac
1200SD Modem(Clear Signal)
Port: RS-232              DB25S
Gender: Female            PinConfig: C14

Pin   Function(Direction)
---------------------------------------------
1     Frame Ground
2     Transmit Data(In)
3     Receive Data(Out)
4     Request to Send(In)
5     Clear to Send(Out)
6     Data Set Ready(Out)
7     Signal Ground
8     Data Carrier Detect(Out)
9     +12V(Out)
10    -12V(Out)
12    Data Rate Select(Out)
20    Data Terminal Ready(In)
22    Ring Indicator(Out)
---------------------------------------------
Flow Control:
Note:  This port emulates a DCE device
```

```
inmac
Standard V.32 Modem
Port: RS-232              DB25S
Gender: Female            PinConfig: C14

Pin   Function(Direction)
---------------------------------------------
1     Frame Ground
2     Receive Data(In)
3     Transmit Data(Out)
4     Request to Send(In)
5     Clear to Send(Out)
6     Data Set Ready(Out)
7     Signal Ground
8     Data Carrier Detect(Out)
15    Transmit Clock(Out)
17    Receive Clock(Out)
20    Data Terminal Ready(In)
22    Ring Indicator(Out)
24    External Transmit Clock(In)
---------------------------------------------
Flow Control:
Note:  This modem supports MNP protocol.
Default options have CTS/DSR always on--
change for true modem ops.
```

```
inmac
V.32 Modem(Clear Signal) 8042-8 & 9
Port: DTE                 DB25S
Gender: Female            PinConfig: C14

Pin   Function(Direction)
---------------------------------------------
1     Chassis Ground
2     Transmit Data(In)
3     Receive Data(Out)
4     Request to Send(In)
5     Clear to Send(Out)
6     Data Set Ready(Out)
7     Signal Ground
8     Carrier Detect(Out)
9     +10V(Out)
10    -10V
15    Transmit Clock(Out)
17    Receive Clock(Out)
18    AL  (In)
20    Data Terminal Ready(In)
21    RDL (In)
22    Ring Indicator(Out)
23    Data Rate Select(In)
24    External Transmit Clock(In)
25    TEST(Out)
---------------------------------------------
Flow Control:
Note:  Some of the leads in the modem can
be optioned so they are ignored, or are
constantly on
```

```
Supra Corporation
SupraModem 2400/2400 Plus
Port:  RS-232              DB25S
Gender:  Female           PinConfig: C14

Pin   Function(Direction)
------------------------------------------
1       Frame Ground
2       Receive Data(In)
3       Transmit Data(Out)
4       Request to Send(In)
5       Clear to Send(Out)
6       Data Set Ready(Out)
7       Signal Ground
8       Data Carrier Detect(Out)
12      Serial In(Out)
15      Transmit Clock(Out)
17      Receive Clock(Out)
20      Data Terminal Ready(In)
22      Ring Indicator(Out)
23      Serial In(Out)
24      External Transmit Clock(In)
------------------------------------------
Flow Control:
Note:  This port emulates a DCE device
```

```
XECOM
FeedThru XE24FT Modem
Port:  RS-232              DB25S
Gender:  Female           PinConfig: C14

Pin   Function(Direction)
------------------------------------------
2       Transmit Data(In)
3       Receive Data(Out)
4       Request to Send(In)
5       Clear to Send(Out)
6       Data Set Ready(Out)
7       Signal Ground
8       Data Carrier Detect(Out)
12      Serial In(Out)
15      Transmit Clock(Out)
17      Receive Clock(Out)
20      Data Terminal Ready(In)
22      Ring Indicator(Out)
24      External Transmit Clock(In)
------------------------------------------
Flow Control:
Note:  This port has an extra serial
port, that passes through the signals
from the connected port
```

```
XECOM
Newport XE24NP5 Modem(internal)
Port:  Built-in DB9 port   DB9P
Gender:  Male             PinConfig: C16

Pin   Function(Direction)
------------------------------------------
1       Carrier Detect(In)
2       Receive Data(In)
3       Transmit Data(Out)
4       Data Terminal Ready(Out)
5       Signal Ground
6       Data Set Ready(In)
7       Request to Send(Out)
8       Clear to Send(In)
9       Ring Indicator(In)
------------------------------------------
Flow Control: 6 & 8
Note:  The flow control leads of the
attached device should be connected to
leads 6 & 8
```

ports boards + terminal servers

```
ALTOS Computer Systems
SIO/2, TCU/2, TCU-8 Board(for 386)
Port: 9-Pin              DB9P
Gender: Male             PinConfig: C45

Pin   Function(Direction)
----------------------------------------------
5     Signal Ground
3     Transmitted Data(out)
2     Received Data(in)
4     Data Terminal Ready(out)
7     Request To Send(out)
6     Data Set Ready(in)
8     Clear To Send(in)
----------------------------------------------
Flow Control: 4   XON/XOFF
Note:
```

```
Arnet Corporation
Multiport & other Boards
Port: DB-25 with 2/3/7    DB25S
Gender: Female            PinConfig: C19

Pin   Function(Direction)
----------------------------------------------
7     Signal Ground
2     Transmitted Data(out)
3     Received Data(in)
----------------------------------------------
Flow Control:   XON/XOFF
Note: Other leads besides 2/3/7 are
supported
```

```
Arnet Corporation
Modular SMARTPORT
Port: RJ-11(6 leads)     RJ11
Gender: Female           PinConfig: C50

Pin   Function(Direction)
----------------------------------------------
1     Protective Ground
2     Signal Ground
3     Transmitted Data(out)
4     Received Data(in)
----------------------------------------------
Flow Control:   XON/XOFF
Note:  Connections with TD/RD/SG only
will work
```

```
Arnet Corporation
Multiport,Multiport/2 W/RJ-45 Optional
Ports
Port: RJ-45              RJ45
Gender: Female           PinConfig: C52

Pin   Function(Direction)
----------------------------------------------
1     Protective Ground
7     Signal Ground
3     Transmitted Data(out)
5     Received Data(in)
2     Request To Send(out)
4     Data Terminal Ready(out)
6     Data Carrier Detect(in)
8     Clear To Send(in)
----------------------------------------------
Flow Control: 4   XON/XOFF
Note:  This assumes no reversing cable
```

```
Arnet Corporation
Smartport/2, Octaport W/RJ-45 OPTIONAL
Ports
Port: RJ-45              RJ45
Gender: Female           PinConfig: C52

Pin   Function(Direction)
----------------------------------------------
1     Protective Ground
7     Signal Ground
3     Transmitted Data(out)
5     Received Data(in)
2     Request To Send(out)
4     Data Terminal Ready(out)
6     Data Carrier Detect(in)
8     Clear To Send(in)
----------------------------------------------
Flow Control: 4   XON/XOFF
Note:  This assumes no reversing cable
```

```
AT&T
StarServer FT Async Controller
Port: RJ-45              RJ45
Gender: Female           PinConfig: C55

Pin   Function(Direction)
----------------------------------------------
1     Signal Ground
2     Transmitted Data(out)
4     Received Data(in)
3     Data Terminal Ready(out)
5     Request To Send(out)
6     Clear To Send(in)
8     Data Set Ready(in)
----------------------------------------------
Flow Control: 3   XON/XOFF
Note:
```

```
Boca Research                        Boca Research
BOCARAM AT I/O Plus                  BOCARAM AT I/O Plus, boards
Port:  DB-25 cable(port 2) DB25S     Port:  9-pin RS-232        DB9S
Gender:  Female        PinConfig: C01 Gender:  Female       PinConfig: C16

Pin   Function(Direction)            Pin   Function(Direction)
-----------------------------------  -----------------------------------
2      Transmit Data(Out)            1      Carrier Detect(In)
3      Receive Data(In)              2      Receive Data(In)
4      Request to Send(Out)          3      Transmit Data(Out)
5      Clear to Send(In)             4      Data Terminal Ready(Out)
6      Data Set Ready(In)            5      Signal Ground
7      Signal Ground                 6      Data Set Ready(In)
8      Data Carrier Detect(In)       7      Request to Send(Out)
20     Data Terminal Ready(Out)      8      Clear to Send(In)
22     Ring Indicator(In)            9      Ring Indicator(In)
-----------------------------------  -----------------------------------
Flow Control: 5 & 6                  Flow Control: 6 & 8
Note:  A cable extends from the board Note:  The flow control leads of the
to provide this DB-25 port. A 9-pin   attached device should be connected to
AT connector is also provided         leads 6 & 8
```

```
Boca Research                        Boca Research
IO-AT, IO-XT boards                  IO-AT, IO-XT boards
Port:  Port A(9-pin)    DB9P         Port:  B-25-pin option    DB25S
Gender:  Male         PinConfig: C16 Gender:  Female      PinConfig: C01

Pin   Function(Direction)            Pin   Function(Direction)
-----------------------------------  -----------------------------------
1      Carrier Detect(In)            2      Transmit Data(Out)
2      Receive Data(In)              3      Receive Data(In)
3      Transmit Data(Out)            4      Request to Send(Out)
4      Data Terminal Ready(Out)      5      Clear to Send(In)
5      Signal Ground                 6      Data Set Ready(In)
6      Data Set Ready(In)            7      Signal Ground
7      Request to Send(Out)          8      Data Carrier Detect(In)
8      Clear to Send(In)             20     Data Terminal Ready(Out)
9      Ring Indicator(In)            22     Ring Indicator(In)
-----------------------------------  -----------------------------------
Flow Control: 6 & 8                  Flow Control: 5 & 6
Note:  The flow control leads of the Note:
attached device should be connected to
leads 6 & 8
```

```
cisco Systems                        cisco Systems
Terminal Servers                     Terminal Servers
Port:  RJ11-(rev-cable)  RJ11        Port:  RJ11-(no rev-cable) RJ11
Gender:  Male         PinConfig: C66 Gender:  Female      PinConfig: C65

Pin   Function(Direction)            Pin   Function(Direction)
-----------------------------------  -----------------------------------
1      Clear to Send(In)             1      Data Terminal Ready(out)
2      Ring Indicator(In)            2      Receive Data(In)
3      Signal Ground                 3      Transmit Data(Out)
4      Transmit Data(Out)            4      Signal Ground
5      Receive Data(In)              5      Ring Indicator(In)
6      Data Terminal Ready(out)      6      Clear to Send(In)
-----------------------------------  -----------------------------------
Flow Control: 1        XON/XOFF      Flow Control: 1        XON/XOFF
Note:  Different connectors are      Note:  Different connectors are
possible, including enclosed ports,  possible, including enclosed ports,
octacables, & RJ11 ports             octacables, & RJ11 ports
```

cisco Systems ASM/MSM Terminal Servers (Champ to D Octopus cable) Port: DCE-DB25-female DB25S Gender: Female PinConfig: C13	cisco Systems ASM/MSM Terminal Server (Champ to D Octopus Cable) Port: DTE-DB25-male DB25P Gender: Male PinConfig: C07

Left table 1:

Pin   Function(Direction)

Pin	Function(Direction)
2	Receive Data(In)
3	Transmit Data(Out)
5	Data Terminal Ready(In)
7	Signal Ground
20	Clear to Send(Out)
22	Ring Indicator(Out)

Flow Control: 20   XON/XOFF
Note: Different connectors are possible,
including enclosed ports, octacables, &
RJ11 ports

Right table 1:

Pin	Function(Direction)
2	Transmit Data(Out)
3	Receive Data(In)
5	Clear to Send(In)
7	Signal Ground
20	Data Terminal Ready(Out)
22	Ring Indicator(In)

Flow Control: 20   XON/XOFF
Note: Different connectors are possible,
including enclosed ports, octacables, &
RJ11 ports

---

cisco Systems ASM/MSM Terminal Server (Enclosed DB25 ports) Port: DCE-DB25-female DB25S Gender: Female PinConfig: C13	cisco Systems ASM/MSM Terminal Server (Enclosed DB25 ports) Port: DCE-DB25-male DB25P Gender: Male PinConfig: C13

Left table 2:

Pin	Function(Direction)
2	Receive Data(In)
3	Transmit Data(Out)
5	Data Terminal Ready(In)
7	Signal Ground
20	Clear to Send(Out)
22	Ring Indicator(Out)

Flow Control: 20   XON/XOFF
Note: Different connectors are possible,
including enclosed ports, octacables, &
RJ11 ports

Right table 2:

Pin	Function(Direction)
2	Receive Data(In)
3	Transmit Data(Out)
5	Data Terminal Ready(In)
7	Signal Ground
20	Clear to Send(Out)
22	Ring Indicator(Out)

Flow Control: 20   XON/XOFF
Note: Different connectors are possible,
including enclosed ports, octacables, &
RJ11 ports

---

cisco Systems ASM/MSM Terminal Server (Enclosed DB25 ports) Port: DTE-DB25-female DB25S Gender: Female PinConfig: C07	cisco Systems ASM/MSM Terminal Server (Enclosed DB25 ports) Port: DTE-DB25-male DB25P Gender: Male PinConfig: C07

Left table 3:

Pin	Function(Direction)
2	Transmit Data(Out)
3	Receive Data(In)
5	Clear to Send(In)
7	Signal Ground
20	Data Terminal Ready(Out)
22	Ring Indicator(In)

Flow Control: 20   XON/XOFF
Note: Different connectors are possible,
including enclosed ports, octacables, &
RJ11 ports

Right table 3:

Pin	Function(Direction)
2	Transmit Data(Out)
3	Receive Data(In)
5	Clear to Send(In)
7	Signal Ground
20	Data Terminal Ready(Out)
22	Ring Indicator(In)

Flow Control: 20   XON/XOFF
Note: Different connectors are possible,
including enclosed ports, octacables, &
RJ11 ports

cisco Systems
CSC-16 serial line card(Champ to D
Octopus Cable)
Port: DCE-DB25-female   DB25S
Gender: Female   PinConfig: C13

Pin   Function(Direction)
----
2   Receive Data(In)
3   Transmit Data(Out)
5   Data Terminal Ready(In)
7   Signal Ground
20   Clear to Send(Out)
22   Ring Indicator(Out)

Flow Control: 20   XON/XOFF
Note: Different connectors are possible,
including enclosed ports, octacables, &
RJ11 ports

cisco Systems
CSC-16 serial line card(Champ to D
Octopus Cable)
Port: DTE-DB25-male   DB25P
Gender: Male   PinConfig: C07

Pin   Function(Direction)
----
2   Transmit Data(Out)
3   Receive Data(In)
5   Clear to Send(In)
7   Signal Ground
20   Data Terminal Ready(Out)
22   Ring Indicator(In)

Flow Control: 20   XON/XOFF
Note: Different connectors are possible,
including enclosed ports, octacables, &
RJ11 ports

CMC-Rockwell
TranServer
Port: Cable To-DCE(female)DB25P
Gender: Male   PinConfig: C01

Pin   Function(Direction)
----
1   Protective Ground
2   Transmit Data(Out)
3   Receive Data(In)
4   Request to Send(Out)
5   Clear to Send(In)
6   Data Set Ready(In)
7   Signal Ground
8   Carrier Detect(In)
20   Data Terminal Ready(Out)
22   Ring Indicator(In)

Flow Control: 6   XON/XOFF
Note: The cable connects the device to
the TranServer port. It is and RJ-45 to
DB-25 cable

CMC-Rockwell
TranServer
Port: Cable To-DTE(female)DB25P
Gender: Male   PinConfig: C14

Pin   Function(Direction)
----
1   Protective Ground
2   Receive Data(In)
3   Transmit Data(Out)
4   Clear to Send(In)
5   Request to Send(Out)
6   Data Terminal Ready(Out)
7   Signal Ground
8   Carrier Detect(Out)
20   Data Set Ready(In)
22   Ring Indicator(Out)

Flow Control: 6   XON/XOFF
Note: The cable connects the device to
the TranServer port. It is and RJ-45 to
DB-25 cable

CMC(ROCKWELL)
TRANSERVER-DCE MODE
Port: 0-9(RJ45-DCE)   RJ45
Gender: Female   PinConfig: C38

Pin   Function(Direction)
----
2   Protective Ground
7   Signal Ground
3   Transmitted Data(out)
8   Received Data(in)
1   Data Carrier Detect(out)
5   Clear To Send(out)
6   Data Set Ready(out)
10   Ring Indicator(out)
4   Request To Send(in)
9   Data Terminal Ready(in)

Flow Control: 5   XON/XOFF
Note: This assumes no reversing cable.-
DCE MODE

COMPUTONE
ATCC/ATvantage 4 & 8 boards
Port: DB25-RS232   DB25P
Gender: Male   PinConfig: C14

Pin   Function(Direction)
----
2   Receive Data(In)
3   Transmit Data(Out)
4   Clear to Send(In)
5   Request to Send(Out)
7   Signal Ground
8   Data Terminal Ready(Out)
20   Carrier Detect(In)

Flow Control: 20
Note:

COMPUTONE
ATCC//ATvantage Board
Port: RJ-45(8lead)   RJ45
Gender: Female   PinConfig: C26

```
Pin   Function(Direction)
------------------------------------
5     Signal Ground
4     Transmitted Data(out)
7     Received Data(in)
3     Data Terminal Ready(out)
8     Request To Send(out)
2     Clear To Send(in)
6     Data Carrier Detect(in)
------------------------------------
```
Flow Control: 3   XON/XOFF
Note: This entry assumes no reversing
cable is used

COMPUTONE
IntelliPort AT6/AT8/AT16 BOARDS
Port: DB25-RS232   DB25P
Gender: Male   PinConfig: C14

```
Pin   Function(Direction)
------------------------------------
2     Receive Data(In)
3     Transmit Data(Out)
4     Clear to Send(In)
5     Request to Send(Out)
7     Signal Ground
8     Data Terminal Ready(Out)
20    Carrier Detect(In)
------------------------------------
```
Flow Control: 20
Note:

COMPUTONE
IntelliPort PS8 boards
Port: DB25-RS232   DB25S
Gender: Female   PinConfig: C14

```
Pin   Function(Direction)
------------------------------------
2     Receive Data(In)
3     Transmit Data(Out)
4     Clear to Send(In)
5     Request to Send(Out)
7     Signal Ground
8     Data Terminal Ready(Out)
20    Carrier Detect(In)
------------------------------------
```
Flow Control: 20
Note:

COMPUTONE
IntelliPort AT6/AT8/AT16/PS8 Board
Port: RJ-45(8lead)   RJ45
Gender: Female   PinConfig: C26

```
Pin   Function(Direction)
------------------------------------
5     Signal Ground
4     Transmitted Data(out)
7     Received Data(in)
3     Data Terminal Ready(out)
8     Request To Send(out)
2     Clear To Send(in)
6     Data Carrier Detect(in)
------------------------------------
```
Flow Control: 3   XON/XOFF
Note: This entry assumes no reversing
cable is used

COMTROL Corporation
XP, XP PLUS Board
Port: RJ45   RJ45
Gender: Female   PinConfig: C28

```
Pin   Function(Direction)
------------------------------------
3     Signal Ground
4     Transmitted Data(out)
5     Received Data(in)
1     Request To Send(out)
2     Data Terminal Ready(out)
6     Data Carrier Detect(in)
7     Data Set Ready(in)
8     Clear To Send(in)
------------------------------------
```
Flow Control: 2   XON/XOFF
Note: A NUMBER OF Ports are possible,
DB25,DB9,RJ45

COMTROL Corporation
ULTRA CONTROLLER & 186/MC Board
Port: RJ45   RJ45
Gender: Female   PinConfig: C28

```
Pin   Function(Direction)
------------------------------------
3     Signal Ground
4     Transmitted Data(out)
5     Received Data(in)
1     Request To Send(out)
2     Data Terminal Ready(out)
6     Data Carrier Detect(in)
7     Data Set Ready(in)
8     Clear To Send(in)
------------------------------------
```
Flow Control: 2   XON/XOFF
Note: A NUMBER OF Ports are possible,
DB25,DB9,RJ45

COMTROL Corporation HOSTESS, HOSTESS/MC Board Port: RJ45 RJ45 Gender: Female PinConfig: C28 Pin Function(Direction) --- 3 Signal Ground 4 Transmitted Data(out) 5 Received Data(in) 1 Request To Send(out) 2 Data Terminal Ready(out) 6 Data Carrier Detect(in) 7 Data Set Ready(in) 8 Clear To Send(in) --- Flow Control: 2 XON/XOFF Note: A NUMBER OF Ports are possible, DB25,DB9,RJ45	COMTROL Corporation HOSTESS 500, SMART HOSTESS,500/MC, Board Port: RJ45 RJ45 Gender: Female PinConfig: C28 Pin Function(Direction) --- 3 Signal Ground 4 Transmitted Data(out) 5 Received Data(in) 1 Request To Send(out) 2 Data Terminal Ready(out) 6 Data Carrier Detect(in) 7 Data Set Ready(in) 8 Clear To Send(in) --- Flow Control: 2 XON/XOFF Note: A NUMBER OF Ports are possible, DB25,DB9,RJ45
Comtrol Corporation HOSTESS, HOSTESS/MC, 550, 550/MC Controllers Port: DB-9 DB9P Gender: Male PinConfig: C16 Pin Function(Direction) --- 1 Carrier Detect(In) 2 Receive Data(In) 3 Transmit Data(Out) 4 Data Terminal Ready(Out) 5 Signal Ground 6 Data Set Ready(In) 7 Request to Send(Out) 8 Clear to Send(In) 9 Ring Indicator(In) --- Flow Control: 6 & 8 Note: The flow control leads of the attached device should be connected to leads 6 & 8	Comtrol Corporation HOSTESS, HOSTESS/MC, 550, 550/MC Controllers Port: RS-232 DB25S Gender: Female PinConfig: C01 Pin Function(Direction) --- 1 Protective Ground 2 Transmit Data(Out) 3 Receive Data(In) 4 Request to Send(Out) 5 Clear to Send(In) 6 Data Set Ready(In) 7 Signal Ground 8 Data Carrier Detect(In) 15 Transmit Clock(In) 17 Receive Clock(In) 20 Data Terminal Ready(Out) 22 Ring Indicator(In) 24 External Transmit Clock(Out) --- Flow Control: 6 & 8 Note:
Comtrol Corporation SMART HOSTESS, XP, XP PLUS Controllers Port: DB-9 DB9P Gender: Male PinConfig: C16 Pin Function(Direction) --- 1 Carrier Detect(In) 2 Receive Data(In) 3 Transmit Data(Out) 4 Data Terminal Ready(Out) 5 Signal Ground 6 Data Set Ready(In) 7 Request to Send(Out) 8 Clear to Send(In) 9 Ring Indicator(In) --- Flow Control: 6 & 8 Note: The flow control leads of the attached device should be connected to leads 6 & 8	Comtrol Corporation SMART HOSTESS, XP Controllers Port: RS-232 DB25S Gender: Female PinConfig: C01 Pin Function(Direction) --- 1 Protective Ground 2 Transmit Data(Out) 3 Receive Data(In) 4 Request to Send(Out) 5 Clear to Send(In) 6 Data Set Ready(In) 7 Signal Ground 8 Data Carrier Detect(In) 15 Transmit Clock(In) 17 Receive Clock(In) 20 Data Terminal Ready(Out) 22 Ring Indicator(In) 24 External Transmit Clock(Out) --- Flow Control: 5 & 6 Note: Leads 5 & 6 must be on to send & receive data. Connect 5 & 6 to other device's flow control leads

```
Comtrol Corporation                       Comtrol Corporation
ULTRA, ULTRA 186/MC Boards                ULTRA, ULTRA 186/MC Board
Port:  DB-25 interface     DB25S          Port:  DB-9 interface      DB9P
Gender: Female         PinConfig: C01     Gender: Male          PinConfig: C16

Pin   Function(Direction)                 Pin   Function(Direction)
-------------------------------------     -------------------------------------
1     Signal Ground                       1     Carrier Detect(In)
2     Transmit Data(Out)                  2     Receive Data(In)
3     Receive Data(In)                    3     Transmit Data(Out)
4     Request to Send(Out)                4     Data Terminal Ready(Out)
5     Clear to Send(In)                   5     Signal Ground
6     Data Set Ready(In)                  6     Data Set Ready(In)
7     Signal Ground                       7     Request to Send(Out)
8     Carrier Detect(In)                  8     Clear to Send(In)
20    Data Terminal Ready(Out)            9     Ring Indicator(In)
22    Ring Indicator(In)                  -------------------------------------
-------------------------------------     Flow Control: 6 & 8        XON/XOFF
Flow Control: 20        XON/XOFF          Note:  The flow control leads of the
Note:  Check for proper gender option     attached device should be connected to
                                          leads 6 & 8
Comtrol Corporation                       Comtrol Corporation
Universal Interface Box                   Universal Interface Box
Port:  RS-232            DB25S            Port:  RS-232(DB-9)       DB9P
Gender: Female       PinConfig: C01       Gender: Male         PinConfig: C16

Pin   Function(Direction)                 Pin   Function(Direction)
-------------------------------------     -------------------------------------
2     Transmit Data(Out)                  1     Carrier Detect(In)
3     Receive Data(In)                    2     Receive Data(In)
4     Request to Send(Out)                3     Transmit Data(Out)
5     Clear to Send(In)                   4     Data Terminal Ready(Out)
6     Data Set Ready(In)                  5     Signal Ground
7     Signal Ground                       6     Data Set Ready(In)
8     Data Carrier Detect(In)             7     Request to Send(Out)
15    Transmit Clock(In)                  8     Clear to Send(In)
17    Receive Clock(In)                   -------------------------------------
20    Data Terminal Ready(Out)            Flow Control: 6 & 8
22    Ring Indicator(In)                  Note:  Leads 6 & 8 need to be on to send
24    External Transmit Clock(Out)        & receive data Adapters can be used to
-------------------------------------     convert port to DB-25 size
Flow Control: 5 & 6
Note:  Leads 5 & 6 must be on to send &
receive data. Connect 5 & 6 to other
device's flow control leads
Consensys Corp.                           CONSENSYS Corporation
Powerports board                          POWERPORTS
Port:  9-pin ports       DB9P             Port:  RJ45               RJ45
Gender: Male         PinConfig: C16       Gender: Female       PinConfig: C39

Pin   Function(Direction)                 Pin   Function(Direction)
-------------------------------------     -------------------------------------
1     Carrier Detect(In)                  7     Signal Ground
2     Receive Data(In)                    4     Transmitted Data(out)
3     Transmit Data(Out)                  5     Received Data(in)
4     Data Terminal Ready(Out)            1     Data Terminal Ready(out)
5     Signal Ground                       6     Request To Send(out)
6     Data Set Ready(In)                  3     Clear To Send(in)
7     Request to Send(Out)                8     *Lead Of Unknown Function*(in)
8     Clear to Send(In)                   -------------------------------------
-------------------------------------     Flow Control: 1   XON/XOFF
Flow Control: 6 & 8                       Note:  This assumes no reversing cable
Note:  This is an optional DB9 connector
panel.  The standard panel is an RJ45
connector panel
```

```
Datability Software Systems
VISTA VCP-1000 Terminal Server
Port:  8 Port RS-232 Card  DB25P
Gender:  Male              PinConfig: C01

Pin   Function(Direction)
------------------------------------------
1     Frame Ground
2     Transmit Data(Out)
3     Receive Data(In)
4     Request to Send(Out)
5     Clear to Send(In)
6     Data Set Ready(In)
7     Signal Ground
8     Data Carrier Detect(In)
20    Data Terminal Ready(Out)
22    Ring Indicator(In)
------------------------------------------
Flow Control: 5 & 6        XON/XOFF
Note:  Flow control is optionable
```

```
Datability Software Systems
VISTA VCP-1000 Terminal Server
Port:  RS-232 Line Card   DB25P
Gender:  Male             PinConfig: C01

Pin   Function(Direction)
------------------------------------------
1     Frame Ground
2     Transmit Data(Out)
3     Receive Data(In)
4     Request to Send(Out)
5     Clear to Send(In)
6     Data Set Ready(In)
7     Signal Ground
8     Carrier Detect(In)
20    Data Terminal Ready(Out)
22    Ring Indicator(In)
------------------------------------------
Flow Control: 20          XON/XOFF
Note:  Other Line cards that are RS-423
compatible are offered
```

```
DEC
VAX with DMF-32
Port:  00-07(leads 2/3/7  DB25P
Gender:  Male             PinConfig: C19

Pin   Function(Direction)
------------------------------------------
7     Signal Ground
2     Transmitted Data(out)
3     Received Data(in)
------------------------------------------
Flow Control:   XON/XOFF
Note:
```

```
DEC
VAX with DHU-11
Port:  00-15(leads 2/3/7  DB25P
Gender:  Male             PinConfig: C19

Pin   Function(Direction)
------------------------------------------
7     Signal Ground
2     Transmitted Data(out)
3     Received Data(in)
------------------------------------------
Flow Control:   XON/XOFF
Note:
```

```
Diamond Flower
MS-400, MU-440 Cards
Port:  J3 as DCE--9-pin    DB9P
Gender:  Male              PinConfig: C18

Pin   Function(Direction)
------------------------------------------
1     Carrier Detect(Out)
2     Receive Data(Out)
3     Transmit Data(In)
4     Data Terminal Ready(In)
5     Signal Ground
6     Data Set Ready(Out)
7     Request to Send(In)
8     Clear to Send(Out)
9     Ring Indicator(Out)
------------------------------------------
Flow Control: 4
Note:  Port can be optioned to be DTE or
have CTS/DSR/DCD forced high.  Always
connect RI lead to something
```

```
Diamond Flower
MS-400, MU-440 Cards
Port:  J3 as DTE--9-pin    DB9P
Gender:  Male              PinConfig: C16

Pin   Function(Direction)
------------------------------------------
1     Carrier Detect(In)
2     Receive Data(In)
3     Transmit Data(Out)
4     Data Terminal Ready(Out)
5     Signal Ground
6     Data Set Ready(In)
7     Request to Send(Out)
8     Clear to Send(In)
9     Ring Indicator(In)
------------------------------------------
Flow Control: 6 & 8
Note:  Port can be optioned to be DCE or
have CTS/DSR/DCD forced high.  Always
connect RI lead to something
```

```
Diamond Flower(DFI)
MS-400, MU-400 Multi-Serial Cards
Port:  J1/J2 cables as DTE DB25P
Gender:  Male                 PinConfig: C01

Pin   Function(Direction)
------------------------------------------
2       Transmit Data(Out)
3       Receive Data(In)
4       Request to Send(Out)
5       Clear to Send(In)
6       Data Set Ready(In)
7       Signal Ground
8       Data Carrier Detect(In)
20      Data Terminal Ready(Out)
22      Ring Indicator(In)
------------------------------------------
Flow Control: 5,6,8        XON/XOFF
Note:  Port can be optioned to be a DCE
or have leads CTS//DSR/DCD forced high.
You must connect RI lead
```

```
Diamond Flower(DFI)
MS-400, MU-440 Multi-Serial Card
Port:  J1/J2 DCE cables    DB25S
Gender:  Female               PinConfig: C14

Pin   Function(Direction)
------------------------------------------
2       Transmit Data(In)
3       Receive Data(Out)
4       Request to Send(In)
5       Clear to Send(Out)
6       Data Set Ready(Out)
7       Signal Ground
8       Data Carrier Detect(Out)
20      Data Terminal Ready(In)
22      Ring Indicator(Out)
------------------------------------------
Flow Control: 4,20         XON/XOFF
Note:  Port can be optioned to be a DTE
or have leads CTS//DSR/DCD forced high.
You must connect RI lead
```

```
Diamond Flower(DFI)
MS-400, MU-440 Multi-Serial Cards
Port:  J4-DTE no 5/6/8     DB25S
Gender:  Female               PinConfig: C08

Pin   Function(Direction)
------------------------------------------
2       Transmit Data(Out)
3       Receive Data(In)
4       Request to Send(Out)
7       Signal Ground
20      Data Terminal Ready(Out)
22      Ring Indicator(In)
------------------------------------------
Flow Control:             XON/XOFF
Note:  Port can be optioned to be a DCE
or have leads CTS//DSR/DCD active. You
must connect RI lead
```

```
Diamond Flower(DFI)
MS-400 Multi-Serial Card
Port:  J4-Primary as DCE   DB25S
Gender:  Female               PinConfig: C14

Pin   Function(Direction)
------------------------------------------
2       Transmit Data(In)
3       Receive Data(Out)
4       Request to Send(In)
5       Clear to Send(Out)
6       Data Set Ready(Out)
7       Signal Ground
8       Data Carrier Detect(Out)
20      Data Terminal Ready(In)
22      Ring Indicator(Out)
------------------------------------------
Flow Control: 4, 20        XON/XOFF
Note:  Port can be optioned to be a DTE
or have leads CTS//DSR/DCD forced high.
You must connect RI lead
```

```
Diamond Flower(DFI)
MS-400 Multi-Serial Card
Port:  J4-Primary as DTE   DB25S
Gender:  Female               PinConfig: C01

Pin   Function(Direction)
------------------------------------------
2       Transmit Data(Out)
3       Receive Data(In)
4       Request to Send(Out)
5       Clear to Send(In)
6       Data Set Ready(In)
7       Signal Ground
8       Data Carrier Detect(In)
20      Data Terminal Ready(Out)
22      Ring Indicator(In)
------------------------------------------
Flow Control: 5,6,8        XON/XOFF
Note:  Port can be optioned to be a DCE
or have leads CTS//DSR/DCD forced high.
You must connect RI lead
```

```
Diamond Flower(DFI)
MS-422 Dual RS-422/232 Async Adapter
Port:  J2-as RS-232 25-pin DB25S
Gender:  Female               PinConfig: C05

Pin   Function(Direction)
------------------------------------------
2       Transmit Data(Out)
3       Receive Data(In)
4       Request to Send(Out)
5       Clear to Send(In)
7       Signal Ground
------------------------------------------
Flow Control: 5           XON/XOFF
Note:
```

```
Diamond Flower(DFI)
MU-440 Multiuser Adapter board
Port:  J1/J2 cables as DCE DB25P
Gender:  Male                  PinConfig: C14

Pin   Function(Direction)
----------------------------------------------
2        Transmit Data(In)
3        Receive Data(Out)
4        Request to Send(In)
5        Clear to Send(Out)
6        Data Set Ready(Out)
7        Signal Ground
8        Data Carrier Detect(Out)
20       Data Terminal Ready(In)
22       Ring Indicator(Out)
----------------------------------------------
Flow Control: 4,20         XON/XOFF
Note:  Port can be optioned to be a DTE
or have leads CTS//DSR/DCD forced high.
You must connect RI lead
```

```
Diamond Flower(DFI)
MU-440 Multiuser Adapter board
Port:  J1/J2 cables as DTE DB25S
Gender:  Female                PinConfig: C08

Pin   Function(Direction)
----------------------------------------------
2        Transmit Data(In)
3        Receive Data(In)
4        Request to Send(Out)
7        Signal Ground
20       Data Terminal Ready(Out)
22       Ring Indicator(In)
----------------------------------------------
Flow Control: 5,6,8        XON/XOFF
Note:  Port can be optioned to be a DCE.
Leads CTS/DSR & DCD are forced on above.
You must connect RI lead
```

```
Diamond Flower(DFI)
MU-440 Multiuser Adapter board
Port:  J4-Primary as DCE   DB25P
Gender:  Male                  PinConfig: C14

Pin   Function(Direction)
----------------------------------------------
2        Transmit Data(In)
3        Receive Data(Out)
4        Request to Send(In)
5        Clear to Send(Out)
6        Data Set Ready(Out)
7        Signal Ground
8        Data Carrier Detect(Out)
20       Data Terminal Ready(In)
22       Ring Indicator(Out)
----------------------------------------------
Flow Control: 4,20         XON/XOFF
Note:  Leads CTS/DSR/DCD can be forced
high.  This port can be optioned to be a
DTE port.  Connect RI lead
```

```
Diamond Flower(DFI)
MU-440 Multiuser Adapter board
Port:  J4-Primary as DTE   DB25P
Gender:  Male                  PinConfig: C01

Pin   Function(Direction)
----------------------------------------------
2        Transmit Data(Out)
3        Receive Data(In)
4        Request to Send(Out)
5        Clear to Send(In)
6        Data Set Ready(In)
7        Signal Ground
8        Data Carrier Detect(In)
20       Data Terminal Ready(Out)
22       Ring Indicator(In)
----------------------------------------------
Flow Control: 5,6,8        XON/XOFF
Note:  Port can be optioned to be a DCE
or have leads CTS//DSR/DCD forced high.
You must connect RI lead
```

```
Diamond Flower(DFI)
MU-440 Multiuser Adapter board
Port:  J4-Primary as DTE   DB25S
Gender:  Female                PinConfig: C01

Pin   Function(Direction)
----------------------------------------------
2        Transmit Data(Out)
3        Receive Data(In)
4        Request to Send(Out)
5        Clear to Send(In)
6        Data Set Ready(In)
7        Signal Ground
8        Data Carrier Detect(In)
20       Data Terminal Ready(Out)
----------------------------------------------
Flow Control: 5,6,8        XON/XOFF
Note:  This port can be optioned to be a
DCE port and have leads CTS/DSR/DCD
forced to be on.
```

```
Diamond Flower Inc.
MS-422 Async Adapter
Port:  RS-232(9-Pin)       DB9P
Gender:  Male                  PinConfig: C46

Pin   Function(Direction)
----------------------------------------------
5        Signal Ground
3        Transmitted Data(out)
2        Received Data(in)
7        Request To Send(out)
8        Clear To Send(in)
----------------------------------------------
Flow Control: 7  XON/XOFF
Note:
```

```
DigiBoard
Boards using AT connectors
Port: AT Connector         DB25P
Gender: Male               PinConfig: C16

Pin   Function(Direction)
-------------------------------------------
1        Carrier Detect(In)
2        Receive Data(In)
3        Transmit Data(Out)
4        Data Terminal Ready(Out)
5        Signal Ground
6        Data Set Ready(In)
7        Request to Send(Out)
8        Clear to Send(In)
9        Ring Indicator(In)
-------------------------------------------
Flow Control: 6 & 8
Note: The flow control leads of the
attached device should be connected to
leads 6 & 8
```

```
DigiBoard
COM/4i, COM/8i DigiCHANNEL Boards
Port: DCE RS-232 Octacable    DB25P
Gender: Male                  PinConfig:
C14

Pin   Function(Direction)
-------------------------------------------
2        Transmit Data(In)
3        Receive Data(Out)
4        Request to Send(In)
5        Clear to Send(Out)
6        Data Set Ready(Out)
7        Signal Ground
8        Carrier Detect(Out)
20       Data Terminal Ready(In)
22       Ring Indicator(Out)
-------------------------------------------
Flow Control:              XON/XOFF
Note: Ports can be provided for modular
connectors, octacables, or I/O Mate
Connection Boxes
```

```
DigiBoard
COM/4i, COM/8i DigiCHANNEL Boards
Port: DTE Octacable        DB25P
Gender: Male               PinConfig: C01

Pin   Function(Direction)
-------------------------------------------
2        Transmit Data(Out)
3        Receive Data(In)
4        Request to Send(Out)
5        Clear to Send(In)
6        Data Set Ready(In)
7        Signal Ground
8        Carrier Detect(In)
20       Data Terminal Ready(Out)
22       Ring Indicator(In)
-------------------------------------------
Flow Control: 5           XON/XOFF
Note: Modular connectors, octacables,
and I/O Mate Connection Boxes are
available
```

```
DigiBoard
DigiCHANNEL COM/4i,8i Boards
Port: RJ-45(10 lead)       RJ45
Gender: Female             PinConfig: C29

Pin   Function(Direction)
-------------------------------------------
4        Protective Ground
7        Signal Ground
5        Transmitted Data(out)
6        Received Data(in)
3        Request To Send(out)
9        Data Terminal Ready(out)
1        Ring Indicator(in)
2        Data Set Ready(in)
8        Clear To Send(in)
10       Data Carrier Detect(in)
-------------------------------------------
Flow Control: 9  XON/XOFF
Note: This entry assumes ALL 10 leads
are used
```

```
Digiboard
DigiCHANNEL COM/4i,8i,4,8 Boards
Port: RJ-45(8 lead)        RJ45
Gender: Male               PinConfig: C30

Pin   Function(Direction)
-------------------------------------------
3        Protective Ground
6        Signal Ground
4        Transmitted Data(out)
5        Received Data(in)
2        Request To Send(out)
8        Data Terminal Ready(out)
1        Data Set Ready(in)
7        Clear To Send(in)
-------------------------------------------
Flow Control: 8  XON/XOFF
Note: This entry assumes only
8(innermost) leads are used
```

```
DigiBoard
MC/4, MC/8, MC/4i, MC/8i DigiCHANNEL
Boards
Port: DCE Octacable        DB25P
Gender: Male               PinConfig: C14

Pin   Function(Direction)
-------------------------------------------
2        Transmit Data(In)
3        Receive Data(Out)
4        Request to Send(In)
5        Clear to Send(Out)
6        Data Set Ready(Out)
7        Signal Ground
8        Carrier Detect(Out)
20       Data Terminal Ready(In)
22       Ring Indicator(Out)
-------------------------------------------
Flow Control:              XON/XOFF
Note: Ports can be provided for modular
connectors, octacables, or I/O Mate
Connection Boxes
```

DigiBoard
MC/4, MC/8, MC/4i, MC/8i DigiCHANNEL
Boards
Port: DTE Octacable   DB25P
Gender: Male   PinConfig: C01

Pin   Function(Direction)
----
2   Transmit Data(Out)
3   Receive Data(In)
4   Request to Send(Out)
5   Clear to Send(In)
6   Data Set Ready(In)
7   Signal Ground
8   Carrier Detect(In)
20   Data Terminal Ready(Out)
22   Ring Indicator(In)

Flow Control: 5   XON/XOFF
Note: Modular connectors, octacables,
and I/O Mate
         Connection Boxes are available

DigiBoard
MC/4i, MC/8i DigiCHANNEL Board
Port: DCE RS-232 I/O Mate DB25S
Gender: Female   PinConfig: C14

Pin   Function(Direction)
----
2   Transmit Data(In)
3   Receive Data(Out)
4   Request to Send(In)
5   Clear to Send(Out)
6   Data Set Ready(Out)
7   Signal Ground
8   Carrier Detect(Out)
20   Data Terminal Ready(In)
22   Ring Indicator(Out)

Flow Control: XON/XOFF
Note: Ports can be provided for modular
connectors,
         octacables, or I/O Mate Connection
Boxes

DigiBoard
MC/4ii DigiCHANNEL Boards
Port: DTE RS-232 I/O Mate DB25P
Gender: Male   PinConfig: C01

Pin   Function(Direction)
----
2   Transmit Data(Out)
3   Receive Data(In)
4   Request to Send(Out)
5   Clear to Send(In)
6   Data Set Ready(In)
7   Signal Ground
8   Carrier Detect(In)
20   Data Terminal Ready(Out)
22   Ring Indicator(In)

Flow Control: 5   XON/XOFF
Note: Modular connectors, octacables,
and I/O Mate
         Connection Boxes are available

DigiBoard
MC/8i DigiCHANNEL Boards
Port: DTE RS-232 I/O Mate DB25P
Gender: Male   PinConfig: C01

Pin   Function(Direction)
----
2   Transmit Data(Out)
3   Receive Data(In)
4   Request to Send(Out)
5   Clear to Send(In)
6   Data Set Ready(In)
7   Signal Ground
8   Carrier Detect(In)
20   Data Terminal Ready(Out)
22   Ring Indicator(In)

Flow Control: 5   XON/XOFF
Note: Modular connectors, octacables,
and I/O Mate
         Connection Boxes are available

Digiboard
DigiCHANNEL MC/4i,8i,4,8,16 Boards
Port: RJ-45(10 lead)   RJ45
Gender: Female   PinConfig: C29

Pin   Function(Direction)
----
4   Protective Ground
7   Signal Ground
5   Transmitted Data(out)
6   Received Data(in)
3   Request To Send(out)
9   Data Terminal Ready(out)
1   Ring Indicator(in)
2   Data Set Ready(in)
8   Clear To Send(in)
10   Data Carrier Detect(in)

Flow Control: 9   XON/XOFF
Note: This entry assumes
         ALL 10 leads are used

Digiboard
DigiCHANNEL MC/4i,8i,4,8,16 Boards
Port: RJ-45(8 lead)   RJ45
Gender: Male   PinConfig: C30

Pin   Function(Direction)
----
3   Protective Ground
6   Signal Ground
4   Transmitted Data(out)
5   Received Data(in)
2   Request To Send(out)
8   Data Terminal Ready(out)
1   Data Set Ready(in)
7   Clear To Send(in)

Flow Control: 8   XON/XOFF
Note: This entry assumes only
         8(innermost) leads are used

```
DigiBoard                            DigiBoard
NU/4i, NU/8i DigiCHANNEL Board       NU/4i, NU/8i DigiCHANNEL Board
Port: DCE RS232 Octacable DB25S      Port: DCE RS232 Octacable DB25P
Gender: Female        PinConfig: C14 Gender: Male         PinConfig: C14

Pin   Function(Direction)            Pin   Function(Direction)
-----------------------------------  -----------------------------------
2     Transmit Data(In)              2     Transmit Data(In)
3     Receive Data(Out)              3     Receive Data(Out)
4     Request to Send(In)            4     Request to Send(In)
5     Clear to Send(Out)             5     Clear to Send(Out)
6     Data Set Ready(Out)            6     Data Set Ready(Out)
7     Signal Ground                  7     Signal Ground
8     Carrier Detect(Out)            8     Carrier Detect(Out)
20    Data Terminal Ready(In)        20    Data Terminal Ready(In)
22    Ring Indicator(Out)            22    Ring Indicator(Out)
-----------------------------------  -----------------------------------
Flow Control:          XON/XOFF      Flow Control:          XON/XOFF
Note: 2 of these ports can be        Note: 2 of these ports can be
synchronous                          synchronous
```

```
DigiBoard                            DigiBoard
NU/4i, NU/8i DigiCHANNEL Board       NU/4i, NU/8i DigiCHANNEL Board
Port: DTE RS232 Octacable DB25P      Port: DTE RS-232 OctacableDB25S
Gender: Male          PinConfig: C01 Gender: Female       PinConfig: C01

Pin   Function(Direction)            Pin   Function(Direction)
-----------------------------------  -----------------------------------
2     Transmit Data(Out)             2     Transmit Data(Out)
3     Receive Data(In)               3     Receive Data(In)
4     Request to Send(Out)           4     Request to Send(Out)
5     Clear to Send(In)              5     Clear to Send(In)
6     Data Set Ready(In)             6     Data Set Ready(In)
7     Signal Ground                  7     Signal Ground
8     Carrier Detect(In)             8     Carrier Detect(In)
20    Data Terminal Ready(Out)       20    Data Terminal Ready(Out)
22    Ring Indicator(In)             22    Ring Indicator(In)
-----------------------------------  -----------------------------------
Flow Control: 5        XON/XOFF      Flow Control: 5        XON/XOFF
Note: 2 of these ports can be        Note: 2 of these ports can be
synchronous                          synchronous
```

```
DigiBoard                            DigiBoard
NU/4, NU/4i DigiCHANNEL Board        PC/4, PC/4e, PC/8, PC/8e, PC/16
Port: Synchronous DTE    DB25P       DigiCHANNEL Board
Gender: Male          PinConfig: C01 Port: DCE Octacable      DB25P
                                     Gender: Male         PinConfig: C14
Pin   Function(Direction)
-----------------------------------  Pin   Function(Direction)
2     Transmit Data(Out)             -----------------------------------
3     Receive Data(In)               2     Transmit Data(In)
4     Request to Send(Out)           3     Receive Data(Out)
5     Clear to Send(In)              4     Request to Send(In)
6     Data Set Ready(In)             5     Clear to Send(Out)
7     Signal Ground                  6     Data Set Ready(Out)
8     Carrier Detect(In)             7     Signal Ground
15    Transmit Clock(In)             8     Carrier Detect(Out)
17    Receive Clock(In)              20    Data Terminal Ready(In)
20    Data Terminal Ready(Out)       22    Ring Indicator(Out)
22    Ring Indicator(In)             -----------------------------------
-----------------------------------  Flow Control:          XON/XOFF
Flow Control: 5        XON/XOFF      Note: Ports can be provided for modular
Note: 2 of these ports can be        connectors, octacables, or I/O Mate
synchronous                          Connection Boxes
```

```
DigiBoard
PC/4, PC/4e, PC/8, PC/8e, PC/16
DigiCHANNEL Board
Port:  DTE Octacable        DB25P
Gender:  Male               PinConfig: C01

Pin   Function(Direction)
----------------------------------------
2        Transmit Data(Out)
3        Receive Data(In)
4        Request to Send(Out)
5        Clear to Send(In)
6        Data Set Ready(In)
7        Signal Ground
8        Carrier Detect(In)
20       Data Terminal Ready(Out)
22       Ring Indicator(In)
----------------------------------------
Flow Control: 5             XON/XOFF
Note:  Modular connectors, octacables,
and I/O Mate Connection Boxes are
available
```

```
DigiBoard
PC/4i, PC/8i DigiCHANNEL Boards
Port:  DCE RS-232 I/O Mate DB25P
Gender:  Male               PinConfig: C14

Pin   Function(Direction)
----------------------------------------
2        Transmit Data(In)
3        Receive Data(Out)
4        Request to Send(In)
5        Clear to Send(Out)
6        Data Set Ready(Out)
7        Signal Ground
8        Carrier Detect(Out)
20       Data Terminal Ready(In)
22       Ring Indicator(Out)
----------------------------------------
Flow Control:               XON/XOFF
Note:  Ports can be provided for modular
connectors, octacables, or I/O Mate
Connection Boxes
```

```
DigiBoard
PC/4i, PC/8i DigiCHANNEL Boardx
Port:  DCE RS-232 I/O Mate DB25P
Gender:  Male               PinConfig: C14

Pin   Function(Direction)
----------------------------------------
2        Transmit Data(In)
3        Receive Data(Out)
4        Request to Send(In)
5        Clear to Send(Out)
6        Data Set Ready(Out)
7        Signal Ground
8        Carrier Detect(Out)
20       Data Terminal Ready(In)
22       Ring Indicator(Out)
----------------------------------------
Flow Control:               XON/XOFF
Note:  Ports can be provided for modular
connectors, octacables, or I/O Mate
Connection Boxes
```

```
Digiboard
DigiCHANNEL PC/4,8,16,4i,8i,4e,8e Boards
Port:  RJ-45(10 lead)       RJ45
Gender:  Female             PinConfig: C29

Pin   Function(Direction)
----------------------------------------
4        Protective Ground
7        Signal Ground
5        Transmitted Data(out)
6        Received Data(in)
3        Request To Send(out)
9        Data Terminal Ready(out)
1        Ring Indicator(in)
2        Data Set Ready(in)
8        Clear To Send(in)
10       Data Carrier Detect(in)
----------------------------------------
Flow Control: 9   XON/XOFF
Note:  This entry assumes ALL 10 leads
are used
```

```
Digiboard                                    Eicon Technology Corp.
DigiCHANNEL PC/4,8,16,4i,8i,4e,8e Boards     EiconCard/PC
Port: RJ-45(8 lead)          RJ45            Port: V.24                    DB25P
Gender: Male             PinConfig: C30      Gender: Male             PinConfig: C01

Pin   Function(Direction)                    Pin   Function(Direction)
------------------------------------         -----------------------------------------
3     Protective Ground                      1     Protective Ground
6     Signal Ground                          2     Transmit Data(Out)
4     Transmitted Data(out)                  3     Receive Data(In)
5     Received Data(in)                      4     Request to Send(Out)
2     Request To Send(out)                   5     Clear to Send(In)
8     Data Terminal Ready(out)               6     Data Set Ready(In)
1     Data Set Ready(in)                     7     Signal Ground
7     Clear To Send(in)                      8     Data Carrier Detect(In)
------------------------------------         11    STBY(Out)
Flow Control: 8   XON/XOFF                   15    Transmit Clock(In)
Note:  This entry assumes only               17    Receive Clock(In)
8(innermost) leads are used                  18    TEST(Out)
                                             20    Data Terminal Ready(Out)
                                             21    RL  (Out)
                                             22    Ring Indicator(In)
                                             23    Data Rate Select(Out)
                                             24    External Transmit Clock(Out)
                                             25    TEST(In)
                                             -----------------------------------------
                                             Flow Control: 5, 6, & 8
                                             Note:  Leads 5,6&8 must be on to send &
                                             receive data. Connect 5,6&8 to other
                                             device's flow control leads
------------------------------------------   -----------------------------------------
Everex Systems                               Everex Systems
Magic I/O Adapter                            Magic I/O Adapter
Port: RS-232            DB25S                 Port: RS-232(Optional 2nd)DB25S
Gender: Female      PinConfig: C16           Gender: Female           PinConfig: C01

Pin   Function(Direction)                    Pin   Function(Direction)
------------------------------------         -----------------------------------------
1     Carrier Detect(In)                     2     Transmit Data(Out)
2     Receive Data(In)                       3     Receive Data(In)
3     Transmit Data(Out)                     4     Request to Send(Out)
4     Data Terminal Ready(Out)               5     Clear to Send(In)
5     Signal Ground                          6     Data Set Ready(In)
6     Data Set Ready(In)                     7     Signal Ground
7     Request to Send(Out)                   8     Data Carrier Detect(In)
8     Clear to Send(In)                      20    Data Terminal Ready(Out)
9     Ring Indicator(In)                     22    Ring Indicator(In)
------------------------------------         -----------------------------------------
Flow Control: 6 & 8                          Flow Control: 5 & 6
Note:  Leads 6 & 8 need to be on to send     Note:  Leads 5 & 6 must be on to send &
& receive data Adapters can be used to       receive data. Connect 5 & 6 to other
convert port to DB25 size                    device's flow control lead
```

```
Hayes Microcomputer Products
Enhanced Serial Port for
MicroChannel(ESP-PS/2)
Port:  Serial(2 ports)      DB25P
Gender:  Male               PinConfig: C01

Pin   Function(Direction)
----------------------------------------
2        Transmit Data(Out)
3        Receive Data(In)
4        Request to Send(Out)
5        Clear to Send(In)
6        Data Set Ready(In)
7        Signal Ground
8        Data Carrier Detect(In)
20       Data Terminal Ready(Out)
22       Ring Indicator(In)
----------------------------------------
Flow Control: 5 & 6
Note:  Leads 5 & 6 must be on to send &
receive data. Connect 5 & 6 to other
device's flow control lead
```

```
Hayes Microcomputer Products
Enhanced Serial Port for PC/XT/AT(ESP-AT)
Port:  Serial(2 ports)      DB25P
Gender:  Male               PinConfig: C01

Pin   Function(Direction)
----------------------------------------
2        Transmit Data(Out)
3        Receive Data(In)
4        Request to Send(Out)
5        Clear to Send(In)
6        Data Set Ready(In)
7        Signal Ground
8        Data Carrier Detect(In)
20       Data Terminal Ready(Out)
22       Ring Indicator(In)
----------------------------------------
Flow Control: 5 & 6
Note:  Leads 5 & 6 must be on to send &
receive data. Connect 5 & 6 to other
device's flow control lead
```

```
IBM Corporation
ARTIC Board
Port:  RS232(15-Pin)        DB15P
Gender:  Male               PinConfig: C20

Pin   Function(Direction)
----------------------------------------
1        Protective Ground
8        Signal Ground
2        Transmitted Data(out)
4        Received Data(in)
6        Trmtr Sig Elmnt Time <DTE>(out)
13       Trmtr Sig Elmnt Time <DCE>(out)
14       Recvr Sig Elmnt Time <DCE>(in)
3        Request To Send(out)
9        Data Sig Rate Slctr <DTE>(out)
12       Data Terminal Ready(out)
5        Clear To Send(in)
7        Data Carrier Detect(in)
10       Data Set Ready(in)
11       Ring Indicator(in)
----------------------------------------
Flow Control: 12   XON/XOFF
Note:
```

```
IBM
ARTIC Board(A RealTime Interface Co-
Processor)
Port:  DirectConnect Cable DB25S
Gender:  Female             PinConfig: C14

Pin   Function(Direction)
----------------------------------------
1        Frame Ground
2        Transmit Data(In)
3        Receive Data(Out)
4        Request to Send(In)
5        Clear to Send(Out)
6        Data Set Ready(Out)
7        Signal Ground
8        Data Carrier Detect(Out)
15       Transmit Clock(Out)
17       Receive Clock(Out)
20       Data Terminal Ready(In)
----------------------------------------
Flow Control: 5 & 6
Note:  This cable converts the 15 pin
port of the ARTIC to emulate DCE, for
direct connection to device
```

```
IBM
ARTIC Board(A RealTime Interface Co-
Processor)
Port:  Modem Cable          DB25S
Gender:  Female             PinConfig: C01

Pin    Function(Direction)
--------------------------------------
1      Protective Ground
2      Transmit Data(Out)
3      Receive Data(In)
4      Request to Send(Out)
5      Clear to Send(In)
6      Data Set Ready(In)
7      Signal Ground
8      Data Carrier Detect(In)
15     Transmit Clock(In)
17     Receive Clock(In)
20     Data Terminal Ready(Out)
22     Ring Indicator(In)
23     Data Rate Select(Out)
24     External Transmit Clock(Out)
--------------------------------------
Flow Control: 5 & 6
Note:  This cable converts the 15 pin
port on the ARTIC to emulate a DTE
device, for modem connections
```

```
LANTRONIX
EPS-4 Server(RJ12/MMJ to DB25 female
adapter)
Port:  DB25 female adapter DB25S
Gender:  Female             PinConfig: C07

Pin    Function(Direction)
--------------------------------------
1      Protective Ground
2      Transmit Data(Out)
3      Receive Data(Out)
6      Data Set Ready(In)
7      Signal Ground
20     Data Terminal Ready(Out)
--------------------------------------
Flow Control: 6          XON/XOFF
Note:  This adapter converts the RJ12 or
MMJ modular port to be a DB25 RS-232
port(female)
```

```
LANTRONIX
EPS-4, EPS-8, EPS-16 Server(
Port:  DB25(male adapter)  DB25P
Gender:  Male              PinConfig: C07

Pin    Function(Direction)
--------------------------------------
1      Protective Ground
2      Transmit Data(Out)
3      Receive Data(Out)
6      Data Set Ready(In)
7      Signal Ground
20     Data Terminal Ready(Out)
--------------------------------------
Flow Control: 6          XON/XOFF
Note:  This adapter converts the RJ12 or
MMJ modular port to be a DB25 RS-232
port(male)
```

```
LANTRONIX
EPS-4, EPS-8, EPS-16 Server(
Port:  DB25 female adapter DB25S
Gender:  Female            PinConfig: C07

Pin    Function(Direction)
--------------------------------------
1      Protective Ground
2      Transmit Data(Out)
3      Receive Data(Out)
6      Data Set Ready(In)
7      Signal Ground
20     Data Terminal Ready(Out)
--------------------------------------
Flow Control: 6          XON/XOFF
Note:  This adapter converts the RJ12 or
MMJ modular port to be a DB25 RS-232
port(female)
```

```
Lantronix
EPS-4/8/16 Server
Port:  RJ45 OR MMJ         RJ11/MMJ
Gender:  Female            PinConfig: C49

Pin    Function(Direction)
--------------------------------------
3      Protective Ground
4      Signal Ground
2      Transmitted Data(out)
5      Received Data(in)
1      Data Terminal Ready(out)
6      Data Set Ready(in)
--------------------------------------
Flow Control: 1   XON/XOFF
Note:  Multiple port sizes are possible
RJ45-MMJ-DB25, etc.
```

```
Nixdorf
3300 Computer Async Controller
Port:  RJ-45              RJ45
Gender:  Female          PinConfig: C55

Pin    Function(Direction)
--------------------------------------
1      Signal Ground
2      Transmitted Data(out)
4      Received Data(in)
3      Data Terminal Ready(out)
5      Request To Send(out)
6      Clear To Send(in)
8      Data Set Ready(in)
--------------------------------------
Flow Control: 3   XON/XOFF
Note:
```

Sharp
1200 Modem & Serial Port
Port: Serial   DB25S
Gender: Female   PinConfig: C01

Pin   Function(Direction)
----
2   Transmit Data(Out)
3   Receive Data(In)
4   Request to Send(Out)
5   Clear to Send(In)
6   Data Set Ready(In)
7   Signal Ground
8   Data Carrier Detect(In)
20   Data Terminal Ready(Out)
22   Ring Indicator(In)

Flow Control: 5 & 6
Note: This modem card(CE-451M) provides
a modem and a DB-25 serial port for
4500/4600/5500 laptops

Sharp
2400 Modem and Serial Port
Port: Serial   DB25S
Gender: Female   PinConfig: C01

Pin   Function(Direction)
----
2   Transmit Data(Out)
3   Receive Data(In)
4   Request to Send(Out)
5   Clear to Send(In)
6   Data Set Ready(In)
7   Signal Ground
8   Data Carrier Detect(In)
20   Data Terminal Ready(Out)
22   Ring Indicator(In)

Flow Control: 5 & 6
Note: This board(CE-462M) provides a
modem and a DB-25 serial port for
4500/4600/5500 laptops

Sharp
SIO board(for 4500/4600/5500 laptops)
Port: Serial   DB25P
Gender: Male   PinConfig: C01

Pin   Function(Direction)
----
2   Transmit Data(Out)
3   Receive Data(In)
4   Request to Send(Out)
5   Clear to Send(In)
6   Data Set Ready(In)
7   Signal Ground
8   Data Carrier Detect(In)
20   Data Terminal Ready(Out)
22   Ring Indicator(In)

Flow Control: 5 & 6
Note: This port is provided by a serial
board(CE-451B) and can be installed in
the 4500/4600/5500 laptops

Specialix Inc.
SI/4, 8, 16, 32 cards w/Terminal Adapter
4
Port: RS-232   DB25S
Gender: Female   PinConfig: C03

Pin   Function(Direction)
----
2   Receive Data(In)
3   Transmit Data(Out)
4   Request to Send(In)
5   Clear to Send(Out)
6   Data Set Ready(Out)
7   Signal Ground
8   Data Carrier Detect(In)
20   Data Terminal Ready(In)

Flow Control:
Note: This port emulates a DCE device
The port is on the TA, not the Host card

Specialix Inc.
SI/4, 8, 16, 32 cards w/Terminal Adapter
8
Port: RS-232   DB25S
Gender: Female   PinConfig: C03

Pin   Function(Direction)
----
2   Receive Data(In)
3   Transmit Data(Out)
4   Request to Send(In)
5   Clear to Send(Out)
6   Data Set Ready(Out)
7   Signal Ground
8   Data Carrier Detect(In)
20   Data Terminal Ready(In)

Flow Control:
Note: This port emulates a DCE device
The port is on the TA, not the Host card

Specialix Inc.
SI/PS4, 8, 16, 32 cards w/Terminal
Adapter 4
Port: RS-232   DB25S
Gender: Female   PinConfig: C03

Pin   Function(Direction)
----
2   Receive Data(In)
3   Transmit Data(Out)
4   Request to Send(In)
5   Clear to Send(Out)
6   Data Set Ready(Out)
7   Signal Ground
8   Data Carrier Detect(In)
20   Data Terminal Ready(In)

Flow Control:
Note: This port emulates a DCE device
The port is on the TA, not the Host card

Specialix Inc.
SI/PS4, 8, 16, 32 cards w/Terminal
Adapter 8
Port: RS-232   DB25S
Gender: Female   PinConfig: C03

Pin   Function(Direction)
----
2   Receive Data(In)
3   Transmit Data(Out)
4   Request to Send(In)
5   Clear to Send(Out)
6   Data Set Ready(Out)
7   Signal Ground
8   Data Carrier Detect(In)
20   Data Terminal Ready(In)

Flow Control:
Note: This port emulates a DCE device
The port is on the TA, not the Host card

Specialix Inc.
Terminal Adapter 4(TA4), 8(TA8)
Port: RS-232   DB25S
Gender: Female   PinConfig: C03

Pin   Function(Direction)
----
2   Receive Data(In)
3   Transmit Data(Out)
4   Request to Send(In)
5   Clear to Send(Out)
6   Data Set Ready(Out)
7   Signal Ground
8   Data Carrier Detect(In)
20   Data Terminal Ready(In)

Flow Control:
Note: This port emulates a DCE device
The port is on the TA, not the Host card

Stargate Technologies
ACL, ACL II, ACL MC Boards
Port: RS-232   DB25S
Gender: Female   PinConfig: C19

Pin   Function(Direction)
----
7   Signal Ground
2   Transmitted Data(out)
3   Received Data(in)

Flow Control: XON/XOFF
Note:

Star Gate Technologies
ACL II, MC board I/O remote panel(ports
1-8)
Port: P1-P8(RS-232)   DB25P
Gender: Male   PinConfig: C01

Pin   Function(Direction)
----
2   Transmit Data(Out)
3   Receive Data(In)
4   Request to Send(Out)
5   Clear to Send(In)
6   Data Set Ready(In)
7   Signal Ground
8   Data Carrier Detect(In)
20   Data Terminal Ready(Out)

Flow Control: 5, 6 & 8   XON/XOFF
Note: Leads 5, 6 & 8 must be on to send
& receive data. Connect these to other
device's flow control lead

Star Gate Technologies
ACL-Advanced Communication Link board
Port: P1-P8 on I/O Panel DB25P
Gender: Male   PinConfig: C01

Pin   Function(Direction)
----
2   Transmit Data(Out)
3   Receive Data(In)
4   Request to Send(Out)
5   Clear to Send(In)
6   Data Set Ready(In)
7   Signal Ground
8   Data Carrier Detect(In)
20   Data Terminal Ready(Out)
22   Ring Indicator(In)

Flow Control:
Note: If the attached devices doesn't
require handshake signals, only pins
2/3/7 can be used.

Star Gate Technologies
MP2-Adapter for PS/2s
Port: Serial(DB-9rts)   DB9P
Gender: Male   PinConfig: C16

Pin   Function(Direction)
----
1   Carrier Detect(In)
2   Receive Data(In)
3   Transmit Data(Out)
4   Data Terminal Ready(Out)
5   Signal Ground
6   Data Set Ready(In)
7   Request to Send(Out)
8   Clear to Send(In)
9   Ring Indicator(In)

Flow Control: 6 & 8
Note: Leads 6 & 8 need to be on to send
& receive data Adapters can be used to
convert port to DB-25 size

```
Star Gate Technologies
PLUS 8/8 MC board I/O remote panel(ports
1-8)
Port: RS-232              DB25P
Gender: Male              PinConfig: C01

Pin   Function(Direction)
-------------------------------------------
2       Transmit Data(Out)
3       Receive Data(In)
4       Request to Send(Out)
5       Clear to Send(In)
6       Data Set Ready(In)
7       Signal Ground
8       Data Carrier Detect(In)
20      Data Terminal Ready(Out)
22      Ring Indicator(In)
-------------------------------------------
Flow Control: 5 & 6
Note:  Leads 5 & 6 must be on to send &
receive data. Connect 5 & 6 to other
device's flow control lead
```

```
STARGATE TECHNOLOGIES
MH800, Cluster Controller
Port: RJ-12              RJ12
Gender: Female          PinConfig: C53

Pin   Function(Direction)
-------------------------------------------
4       Signal Ground
3       Transmitted Data(out)
5       Received Data(in)
6       Request To Send(out)
-------------------------------------------
Flow Control: 6    XON/XOFF
Note:
```

```
StarGate Technologies
ACL IIR Board
Port: RJ-12              RJ12
Gender: Female          PinConfig: C53

Pin   Function(Direction)
-------------------------------------------
4       Signal Ground
3       Transmitted Data(out)
5       Received Data(in)
6       Request To Send(out)
-------------------------------------------
Flow Control: 6    XON/XOFF
Note:
```

```
STB Systems
Dual Serial, Dual Serial/Parallel boards
Port: RS-232(2 9pin)    DB9P
Gender: Male            PinConfig: C16

Pin   Function(Direction)
-------------------------------------------
1       Carrier Detect(In)
2       Receive Data(In)
3       Transmit Data(Out)
4       Data Terminal Ready(Out)
5       Signal Ground
6       Data Set Ready(In)
7       Request to Send(Out)
8       Clear to Send(In)
9       Ring Indicator(In)
-------------------------------------------
Flow Control: 6 & 8
Note:  The flow control leads of the
attached device should be connected to
leads 6 & 8
```

```
STB Systems
Serial 2, Serial/Parallel 2 boards
Port: RS-232(2 9pin)    DB9P
Gender: Male            PinConfig: C16

Pin   Function(Direction)
-------------------------------------------
1       Carrier Detect(In)
2       Receive Data(In)
3       Transmit Data(Out)
4       Data Terminal Ready(Out)
5       Signal Ground
6       Data Set Ready(In)
7       Request to Send(Out)
8       Clear to Send(In)
9       Ring Indicator(In)
-------------------------------------------
Flow Control: 6 & 8
Note:  The flow control leads of the
attached device should be connected to
leads 6 & 8
```

```
Systech
HPS-7080/7080A Cluster Controllers
Port: RS-232            DB25P
Gender: Male            PinConfig: C01

Pin   Function(Direction)
-------------------------------------------
2       Transmit Data(Out)
3       Receive Data(In)
4       Request to Send(Out)
5       Clear to Send(In)
6       Data Set Ready(In)
7       Signal Ground
8       Data Carrier Detect(In)
20      Data Terminal Ready(Out)
-------------------------------------------
Flow Control:              XON/XOFF
Note:  This controller connects to an HPS
Host Adapter to provide the interfaces
```

```
Systech Corporation                      Systech Corporation
HPS-7082/7082A 8-line Cluster Controller HPS-7088/7088A 16-line Cluster Controller
Port: RS-232         DB25S               Port: RS-232         DB25P
Gender: Female       PinConfig: C01      Gender: Male         PinConfig: C01

Pin   Function(Direction)                Pin   Function(Direction)
-----------------------------------      -----------------------------------
2     Transmit Data(Out)                 2     Transmit Data(Out)
3     Receive Data(In)                   3     Receive Data(In)
4     Request to Send(Out)               4     Request to Send(Out)
5     Clear to Send(In)                  5     Clear to Send(In)
6     Data Set Ready(In)                 6     Data Set Ready(In)
7     Signal Ground                      7     Signal Ground
8     Data Carrier Detect(In)            8     Data Carrier Detect(In)
20    Data Terminal Ready(Out)           20    Data Terminal Ready(Out)
-----------------------------------      -----------------------------------
Flow Control:        XON/XOFF            Flow Control:        XON/XOFF
Note: This controller connects to an HPS Note: This controller connects to an HPS
Host Adapter to provide the ports.       Host Adapter to provide the ports.
-----------------------------------------------------------------------------
Systech Corporation                      Systech Corporation
VMEbus Multiplexors(8 & 16 ports)        VMEbus Multiplexors(8 & 16 ports)
Port: RS-232         DB25P               Port: RS-232         DB25P
Gender: Male         PinConfig: C14      Gender: Male         PinConfig: C01

Pin   Function(Direction)                Pin   Function(Direction)
-----------------------------------      -----------------------------------
2     Transmit Data(In)                  2     Transmit Data(Out)
3     Receive Data(Out)                  3     Receive Data(In)
4     Request to Send(In)                4     Request to Send(Out)
5     Clear to Send(Out)                 5     Clear to Send(In)
6     Data Set Ready(Out)                6     Data Set Ready(In)
7     Signal Ground                      7     Signal Ground
8     Data Carrier Detect(Out)           8     Data Carrier Detect(In)
20    Data Terminal Ready(In)            20    Data Terminal Ready(Out)
-----------------------------------      -----------------------------------
Flow Control:        XON/XOFF            Flow Control:        XON/XOFF
Note: These ports can be ordered to be   Note: These ports can be ordered to be
either DTE or DCE ports.  The above      either DTE or DCE ports.  The above
assumes DCE emulation.                   assumes DTE emulation.
-----------------------------------------------------------------------------
Tandem Computers                         UNISYS Corporation
Integrity S2 Async Controller            DB-15 Terminal Adapter
Port: RJ-45          RJ45                Port: 15-Pin         DB15P
Gender: Female       PinConfig: C55      Gender: Male         PinConfig: C67

Pin   Function(Direction)                Pin   Function(Direction)
-----------------------------------      -----------------------------------
1     Signal Ground                      11    Signal Ground
2     Transmitted Data(out)              1     Transmitted Data(out)
4     Received Data(in)                  9     Received Data(in)
3     Data Terminal Ready(out)           2     Request To Send(out)
5     Request To Send(out)               3     Data Set Ready(in)
6     Clear To Send(in)                  10    Clear To Send(in)
8     Data Set Ready(in)                 12    Data Carrier Detect(in)
-----------------------------------      -----------------------------------
Flow Control: 3    XON/XOFF              Flow Control: 2    XON/XOFF
Note:                                    Note:
```

Western Telematic
LASERNET QwikShare 9 Pin AT Adapter
Port: RS-232(AT)   DB9S
Gender: Female   PinConfig: C47

```
Pin   Function(Direction)
------------------------------------------
5     Signal Ground
2     Transmitted Data(out)
3     Received Data(in)
6     Data Set Ready(out)
8     Clear To Send(out)
------------------------------------------
```
Flow Control: 6   XON/XOFF
Note:

Western Telematics
INCS with RJ-11R Splitter
Port: RJ11   RJ11
Gender: Female   PinConfig: C54

```
Pin   Function(Direction)
------------------------------------------
5     Signal Ground
2     Transmitted Data(out)
4     Received Data(in)
1     Print Control(out)
6     Clear To Send(in)
------------------------------------------
```
Flow Control: 1   XON/XOFF
Note: This assumes no reversing cable

Western Telematics
INCS with RJ-11R Splitter
Port: RJ11(rev-cable)   RJ11
Gender: Male   PinConfig: C71

```
Pin   Function(Direction)
------------------------------------------
2     Signal Ground
5     Transmitted Data(out)
3     Received Data(in)
6     Data Terminal Ready(out)
1     Clear To Send(in)
------------------------------------------
```
Flow Control: 6   XON/XOFF
Note: This entry assumes a reversing
cable is used

Wyse Technology
WY-995 Multiuser Interface Board
Port: RJ11(STRAIGHT)   RJ11
Gender: Female   PinConfig: C63

```
Pin   Function(Direction)
------------------------------------------
3     Protective Ground
4     Signal Ground
2     Transmitted Data(out)
5     Received Data(in)
6     Data Terminal Ready(out)
1     Data Carrier Detect(in)
------------------------------------------
```
Flow Control: 6   XON/XOFF
Note: This entry assumes no reversing
cable

Wyse Technology
WY-995 Multiuser Interface Board
Port: RJ11(rev-cable)   RJ11
Gender: Male   PinConfig: C64

```
Pin   Function(Direction)
------------------------------------------
4     Protective Ground
3     Signal Ground
5     Transmitted Data(out)
2     Received Data(in)
1     Data Terminal Ready(out)
6     Data Carrier Detect(in)
------------------------------------------
```
Flow Control: 1   XON/XOFF
Note:

Wyse
Serial/Parallel Adapter
Port: RS-23m   DB25S
Gender: Female   PinConfig: C16

```
Pin   Function(Direction)
------------------------------------------
1     Carrier Detect(In)
2     Receive Data(In)
3     Transmit Data(Out)
4     Data Terminal Ready(Out)
5     Signal Ground
6     Data Set Ready(In)
7     Request to Send(Out)
8     Clear to Send(In)
9     Ring Indicator(In)
------------------------------------------
```
Flow Control: 6 & 8
Note: Leads 6 & 8 need to be on to send
& receive data Adapters can be used to
convert port to DB-25 size

```
Xyplex                                        Xyplex
1100 Server(RJ-45 to male adapter)            1500 Server(RJ-45 to male adapter)
Port:  1-16              DB25S                 Port:  1-16              DB25S
Gender:  Female         PinConfig: C01         Gender:  Female         PinConfig: C01

Pin   Function(Direction)                      Pin   Function(Direction)
-------------------------------------          -------------------------------------
2      Transmit Data(Out)                      2      Transmit Data(Out)
3      Receive Data(In)                        3      Receive Data(In)
4      Request to Send(Out)                     4      Request to Send(Out)
5      Clear to Send(In)                        5      Clear to Send(In)
6      Data Set Ready(In)                       6      Data Set Ready(In)
7      Signal Ground                            7      Signal Ground
8      Data Carrier Detect(In)                  8      Data Carrier Detect(In)
20     Data Terminal Ready(Out)                 20     Data Terminal Ready(Out)
22     Ring Indicator(In)                       22     Ring Indicator(In)
-------------------------------------          -------------------------------------
Flow Control: 6         XON/XOFF               Flow Control: 6         XON/XOFF
Note:  A straight-through modular cable &      Note:  A straight-through modular cable &
this adapter provide a DB25 port(from the      this adapter provide a DB25 port(from the
modular 1100 port)                             modular 1100 port)
```

```
Xyplex                                        Xyplex
MAXserver 4500/5000(Distribution panel)       MAXserver 4500/5000(Distribution panel-
Port:  1-16 ports       DB25P                 female)
Gender:  Male           PinConfig: C07         Port:  1-16 ports(to DTE)  DB25S
                                               Gender:  Female         PinConfig: C17
Pin   Function(Direction)
-------------------------------------          Pin   Function(Direction)
2      Transmit Data(Out)                       -------------------------------------
3      Receive Data(In)                        2      Receive Data(In)
7      Signal Ground                            3      Transmit Data(Out)
8      Data Carrier Detect(In)                  7      Signal Ground
20     Data Terminal Ready(Out)                 8      Data Terminal Ready(Out)
22     Ring Indicator(In)                       20     Data Carrier Detect(In)
-------------------------------------          22     Ring Indicator(Out)
Flow Control: 8         XON/XOFF               -------------------------------------
Note:  Octopus cables, distribution           Flow Control: 8         XON/XOFF
panels, or modular splitters provide the      Note:  Octopus cables, distribution
ports to attach devices                       panels, or modular splitters provide the
                                               ports to attach devices
```

```
Xyplex                                        Xyplex
MAXserver 4500/5000(Octopus cable-female)     MAXserver 4500/5000(Octopus cable-male)
Port:  1-8 connectors    DB25P                 Port:  1-8 connectors    DB25P
Gender:  Male           PinConfig: C17         Gender:  Male           PinConfig: C07

Pin   Function(Direction)                      Pin   Function(Direction)
-------------------------------------          -------------------------------------
2      Receive Data(In)                        2      Transmit Data(Out)
3      Transmit Data(Out)                       3      Receive Data(In)
7      Signal Ground                            7      Signal Ground
8      Data Terminal Ready(Out)                 8      Data Carrier Detect(In)
20     Data Carrier Detect(In)                  20     Data Terminal Ready(Out)
22     Ring Indicator(Out)                      22     Ring Indicator(In)
-------------------------------------          -------------------------------------
Flow Control: 8         XON/XOFF               Flow Control: 8         XON/XOFF
Note:  Octopus cables, distribution           Note:  Octopus cables, distribution
panels, or modular splitters provide the      panels, or modular splitters provide the
ports to attach devices                       ports to attach devices
```

XYPLEX Incorporated MAXSERVER 1100/1500/1800 Terminal Server Port: RJ-45 RJ45 Gender: Female PinConfig: C40 Pin Function(Direction) -- 4 Signal Ground 3 Transmitted Data(out) 6 Received Data(in) 2 Data Terminal Ready(out) 1 Ring Indicator(in) 7 Data Terminal Ready(in) -- Flow Control: 2 XON/XOFF Note: This assumes no reversing cable	XYPLEX Incorporated MAXSERVER 4500/5000 with Modular Splitter Port: RJ-12 RJ11 Gender: Female PinConfig: C72 Pin Function(Direction) -- 5 Signal Ground 2 Transmitted Data(out) 4 Received Data(in) 1 Data Terminal Ready(out) 3 Data Carrier Detect(in) 6 Ring Indicator(in) -- Flow Control: 1 XON/XOFF Note: This assumes no reversing cable
XYPLEX Incorporated MAXSERVER 4500/5000 with Modular Splitter Port: RJ-12(reversing) RJ11 Gender: Male PinConfig: C73 Pin Function(Direction) -- 2 Signal Ground 5 Transmitted Data(out) 3 Received Data(in) 6 Data Terminal Ready(out) 1 Ring Indicator(in) 4 Data Carrier Detect(in) -- Flow Control: 6 XON/XOFF Note: This entry assumes a reversing cable is used	

buffers + data switches

```
Altek Corporation                    | Altek Corporation
AC30 DataTab Controller              | AC30 DataTab Controller
Port:  RS-232 RTS/CTS off  DB25S     | Port:  RS-232 RTS/CTS on  DB25S
Gender: Female      PinConfig: C07   | Gender: Female      PinConfig: C01

Pin   Function(Direction)            | Pin   Function(Direction)
-----------------------------------  | -----------------------------------
1       Protective Ground            | 1       Protective Ground
2       Transmit Data(Out)           | 2       Transmit Data(Out)
3       Receive Data(In)             | 3       Receive Data(In)
7       Signal Ground                | 4       Request to Send(Out)
20      Data Terminal Ready(Out)     | 5       Clear to Send(In)
-----------------------------------  | 7       Signal Ground
Flow Control:         XON/XOFF       | 20      Data Terminal Ready(Out)
Note:  Leads RTS & CTS can be        | -----------------------------------
enable. The above configuration      | Flow Control: 4      XON/XOFF
assumes they are inactive            | Note:  Leads RTS & CTS can be
                                     | disabled. The above configuration
                                     | assumes they are active
```

```
Altek Corporation                    | Altek Corporation
AC40 DataTab Controller              | AC40 DataTab Controller
Port:  DCE-RTS/CTS off  DB25S        | Port:  DCE-RTS/CTS on  DB25S
Gender: Female      PinConfig: C14   | Gender: Female      PinConfig: C14

Pin   Function(Direction)            | Pin   Function(Direction)
-----------------------------------  | -----------------------------------
2       Transmit Data(In)            | 2       Transmit Data(In)
3       Receive Data(Out)            | 3       Receive Data(Out)
6       Data Set Ready(Out)          | 4       Request to Send(In)
7       Signal Ground                | 5       Clear to Send(Out)
8       Data Carrier Detect(Out)     | 6       Data Set Ready(Out)
20      Data Terminal Ready(In)      | 7       Signal Ground
-----------------------------------  | 8       Data Carrier Detect(Out)
Flow Control:         XON/XOFF       | 20      Data Terminal Ready(In)
Note:  Ports 1 & 2 can be set to be  | -----------------------------------
either DCE(above) or DTE.  The above | Flow Control:         XON/XOFF
pinouts assume rts/cts inactive      | Note:  Ports 1 & 2 can be set to be
                                     | either DCE(above) or DTE.  The above
                                     | pinouts assume rts/cts are active
```

```
Altek Corporation                    | Altek Corporation
AC40 DataTab Controller              | AC40 DataTab Controller
Port:  DTE Mode-RTS/CTS offDB25S     | Port:  DTE Mode-RTS/CTS on DB25S
Gender: Female      PinConfig: C07   | Gender: Female      PinConfig: C01

Pin   Function(Direction)            | Pin   Function(Direction)
-----------------------------------  | -----------------------------------
2       Transmit Data(Out)           | 2       Transmit Data(Out)
3       Receive Data(In)             | 3       Receive Data(In)
6       Data Set Ready(In)           | 4       Request to Send(Out)
7       Signal Ground                | 5       Clear to Send(In)
20      Data Terminal Ready(Out)     | 6       Data Set Ready(In)
-----------------------------------  | 7       Signal Ground
Flow Control:         XON/XOFF       | 20      Data Terminal Ready(Out)
Note:  The above assumes RTS/CTS is  | -----------------------------------
inactive. Ports 1 & 2 can be set to  | Flow Control: 4      XON/XOFF
either DTE(above) or DCE             | Note:  The above assumes RTS/CTS is
                                     | active.  Ports 1 & 2 can be set to
                                     | either DTE(above) or DCE
```

```
Architectural Comm
StarBus Network
Port:  RS-232(Peripheral)  DB25S
Gender:  Female            PinConfig: C07

Pin   Function(Direction)
---------------------------------------
2      Transmit Data(Out)
3      Receive Data(In)
5      Clear to Send(In)
6      Data Set Ready(In)
7      Signal Ground
8      Data Carrier Detect(In)
20     Data Terminal Ready(Out)
---------------------------------------
Flow Control: 6          XON/XOFF
Note:  The switch in the peripheral
position causes the port to emulate DTE--
for connection of DCE devices
```

```
Architectural Comm.
StarBus Network
Port:  RS-232(Comp/Term)   DB25S
Gender:  Female            PinConfig: C14

Pin   Function(Direction)
---------------------------------------
2      Transmit Data(In)
3      Receive Data(Out)
5      Clear to Send(Out)
6      Data Set Ready(Out)
7      Signal Ground
8      Data Carrier Detect(Out)
20     Data Terminal Ready(In)
---------------------------------------
Flow Control: 20         XON/XOFF
Note:  The switch in computer/terminal
position, causes the port to emulate DCE-
-for connecting DTE device
```

```
Barcode Industries
MaxiBar Reader
Port:  J6                  RJ45
Gender:  Female            PinConfig: C05

Pin   Function(Direction)
---------------------------------------
2      Transmit Data(Out)
3      Receive Data(In)
4      Request to Send(Out)
5      Clear to Send(In)
7      Signal Ground
---------------------------------------
Flow Control:
Note:
```

```
Barcode Industries
MaxiBar reader
Port:  Modem Conn.(Type T2)DB25P
Gender:  Male              PinConfig: C11

Pin   Function(Direction)
---------------------------------------
1      Frame Ground
2      Transmit Data(Out)
3      Receive Data(In)
4      Request to Send(Out)
5      Clear to Send(In)
7      Signal Ground
8      Data Carrier Detect(In)
20     Data Terminal Ready(Out)
---------------------------------------
Flow Control:
Note:
```

```
Barcode Industries
MaxiBar Reader
Port:  Terminal Conn-T2 cblDB25S
Gender:  Female            PinConfig: C14

Pin   Function(Direction)
---------------------------------------
1      Frame Ground
2      Receive Data(In)
3      Transmit Data(Out)
4      Clear to Send(In)
5      Request to Send(Out)
7      Signal Ground
20     Data Terminal Ready(In)
---------------------------------------
Flow Control:
Note:
```

```
Barcode Industries
MaxiBar Reader
Port:  Terminal Conn-T1 cblDB25P
Gender:  Male              PinConfig: C14

Pin   Function(Direction)
---------------------------------------
1      Frame Ground
2      Receive Data(In)
3      Transmit Data(Out)
4      Clear to Send(In)
5      Request to Send(Out)
7      Signal Ground
20     Data Terminal Ready(In)
---------------------------------------
Flow Control:
Note:
```

```
Barcode Industries, Inc.
MaxiBar Reader
Port: RS-232-T1 cable(J6) DB25S
Gender: Female          PinConfig: C01

Pin   Function(Direction)
-------------------------------------
1     Frame Ground
2     Transmit Data(Out)
3     Receive Data(In)
4     Request to Send(Out)
5     Clear to Send(In)
7     Signal Ground
20    Data Terminal Ready(Out)
-------------------------------------
Flow Control: 5              XON/XOFF
                             ACK/NAK
Note: Different cables, such as the
above are available, RJ-45 for the J6
Modem port & a DB-25 on other end
```

```
Barcode Industries, Inc.
MaxiBar Reader
Port: RS-232-Type t1 cableDB25P
Gender: Male            PinConfig: C13

Pin   Function(Direction)
-------------------------------------
1     Frame Ground
2     Receive Data(In)
3     Transmit Data(Out)
4     Request to Send(Out)
5     Clear to Send(In)
7     Signal Ground
-------------------------------------
Flow Control: 5              XON/XOFF
Note: Terminal connector is port J7.
The above cable has RJ-45 & DB-25
connectors--others available
```

```
Barcode Industries, Inc.
MaxiBar Reader
Port: rs-232-Type T2 cableDB25S
Gender: Female          PinConfig: C13

Pin   Function(Direction)
-------------------------------------
1     Frame Ground
2     Receive Data(In)
3     Transmit Data(Out)
4     Request to Send(Out)
5     Clear to Send(In)
7     Signal Ground
-------------------------------------
Flow Control:
Note:
```

```
Buffalo Products
SL peripheral sharing device
Port: Channels 4-9        DB25S
Gender: Female          PinConfig: C07

Pin   Function(Direction)
-------------------------------------
2     Transmit Data(Out)
3     Receive Data(In)
5     Clear to Send(In)
6     Data Set Ready(In)
7     Signal Ground
8     Data Carrier Detect(In)
19    Data Carrier Detect(Out)
20    Data Terminal Ready(Out)
-------------------------------------
Flow Control: 20             XON/XOFF
Note: These ports are configurable as
input or output
```

```
Clone Technologies
CompuRegister 1, 2, 3, 4 Cash Registers
Port: RS-232              DB25P
Gender: Male            PinConfig: C01

Pin   Function(Direction)
-------------------------------------
2     Transmit Data(Out)
3     Receive Data(In)
4     Request to Send(Out)
5     Clear to Send(In)
6     Data Set Ready(In)
7     Signal Ground
8     Data Carrier Detect(In)
20    Data Terminal Ready(Out)
22    Ring Indicator(In)
-------------------------------------
Flow Control: 5 & 6
Note: This cash register incorporates
industry standard PCs
```

```
Dresselhaus Computer Products
SmartPrint/LSS printer sharing system
Port: input(computer-top) DB25S
Gender: Female          PinConfig: C10

Pin   Function(Direction)
-------------------------------------
2     Receive Data(In)
5     Request to Send(Out)
6     Clear to Send(Out)
7     Signal Ground
-------------------------------------
Flow Control: 5,6
Note: There are multiple inputs & a
single output for printer. Above port
connects to computer
```

```
Dresselhause Computer Products
SmartPrint /LSS printer sharing system
Port: output(printer-end) DB25S
Gender: Female              PinConfig: C12

Pin   Function(Direction)
----------------------------------------
3        Transmit Data(Out)
7        Signal Ground
20       Data Terminal Ready(In)
----------------------------------------
Flow Control: 20
Note: Above port is for printer
connection. There are multiple ports
also for computer connection
```

```
Equinox Systems
210022 Modular Splitter(LM Muxes)
Port: 6 lead modular      RJ11
Gender: Female              PinConfig: C56

Pin   Function(Direction)
----------------------------------------
3        Protective Ground
5        Signal Ground
4        Transmitted Data(out)
2        Received Data(in)
1        Print Control(out)
6        Print Control(in)
----------------------------------------
Flow Control: 1    XON/XOFF
Note: This does not assume a reversing
cable
```

```
Equinox Systems
210022 Modular Splitter(LM Muxes)
Port: 6 lead rev-cable    RJ11
Gender: Male               PinConfig: C57

Pin   Function(Direction)
----------------------------------------
4        Protective Ground
2        Signal Ground
3        Transmitted Data(out)
5        Received Data(in)
6        Data Terminal Ready(out)
1        Data Set Ready(in)
----------------------------------------
Flow Control: 6
Note: This assumes a reversing modular
cable is used
```

```
Equinox Systems
210016 Modular Splitter(DS Switches)
Port: 6 lead Modular      RJ11
Gender: Female              PinConfig: C56

Pin   Function(Direction)
----------------------------------------
3        Protective Ground
5        Signal Ground
4        Transmitted Data(out)
2        Received Data(in)
1        Print Control(out)
6        Print Control(in)
----------------------------------------
Flow Control: 1    XON/XOFF
Note: This does not assume a reversing
cable
```

```
Equinox Systems
210016 Modular Splitter(DS Switches)
Port: 6 lead rev-cable    RJ11
Gender: Male               PinConfig: C57

Pin   Function(Direction)
----------------------------------------
4        Protective Ground
2        Signal Ground
3        Transmitted Data(out)
5        Received Data(in)
6        Data Terminal Ready(out)
1        Data Set Ready(in)
----------------------------------------
Flow Control: 6
Note: This assumes a reversing modular
cable is used
```

```
Equinox Systems
210002 Modular Splitter(DS Switches)
Port: 210002(8 leads)     RJ45
Gender: Female              PinConfig: C60

Pin   Function(Direction)
----------------------------------------
3        Signal Ground
5        Transmitted Data(out)
1        Received Data(in)
4        Request To Send(out)
6        Data Terminal Ready(out)
8        Print Control(out)
2        Data Carrier Detect(in)
7        Ring Indicator(in)
----------------------------------------
Flow Control: 8    XON/XOFF
Note: This assumes no reversing cable
```

```
Equinox Systems
210002 Modular Splitter(DS Switches)
Port:  8 lead rev-cable   RJ45
Gender: Male              PinConfig: C61

Pin   Function(Direction)
--------------------------------------
6        Signal Ground
4        Transmitted Data(out)
8        Received Data(in)
1        Print Control(out)
3        Data Terminal Ready(out)
5        Request To Send(out)
2        Ring Indicator(in)
7        Data Carrier Detect(in)
--------------------------------------
Flow Control: 1   XON/XOFF
Note:  This assumes a 8 lead reversing
cable
```

```
Equinox Systems
DS-5, DS-15 Data PBX
Port:  Supv. Printer port  DB25S
Gender: Female            PinConfig: C14

Pin   Function(Direction)
--------------------------------------
1        Protective Ground
2        Transmit Data(In)
3        Receive Data(In)
4        Request to Send(In)
5        Clear to Send(Out)
6        Data Set Ready(Out)
7        Signal Ground
8        Data Carrier Detect(Out)
20       Data Terminal Ready(In)
--------------------------------------
Flow Control: 20
Note:
```

```
Equinox Systems
DS & LM Products
Port:  DB25 Adapter(2/3/7)DB25S
Gender: Female            PinConfig: C19

Pin   Function(Direction)
--------------------------------------
7        Signal Ground
2        Transmitted Data(out)
3        Received Data(in)
--------------------------------------
Flow Control:     XON/XOFF
Note:  Other adapters are available to
support full control
```

```
Equinox Systems
DS-5, DS-15 Data PBX(210017 Modular
Splitter)
Port:  210036 Adapter     DB25S
Gender: Female            PinConfig: C14

Pin   Function(Direction)
--------------------------------------
2        Transmit Data(In)
3        Receive Data(Out)
5        Clear to Send(Out)
6        Data Set Ready(Out)
7        Signal Ground
8        Data Carrier Detect(Out)
20       Data Terminal Ready(In)
--------------------------------------
Flow Control: 20
Note:  Use either a 4 or 6 conductor
modular reversing cable.  Splitters used
with 24 Line RS & IRS cards
```

```
Equinox Systems
DS-5, DS-15 Data PBX(210017 Modular
Splitter)
Port:  210036 Adapter     DB25P
Gender: Male              PinConfig: C14

Pin   Function(Direction)
--------------------------------------
2        Transmit Data(In)
3        Receive Data(Out)
5        Clear to Send(Out)
6        Data Set Ready(Out)
7        Signal Ground
8        Data Carrier Detect(Out)
20       Data Terminal Ready(In)
--------------------------------------
Flow Control: 20
Note:  Use either a 4 or 6 conductor
modular reversing cable.  Splitters used
with 24 Line RS & IRS cards
```

```
Equinox Systems
DS-5, DS-15 Data PBX(210017 Modular
Splitter)
Port:  210036 Adapter     DB25S
Gender: Female            PinConfig: C14

Pin   Function(Direction)
--------------------------------------
2        Transmit Data(In)
3        Receive Data(Out)
5        Clear to Send(Out)
6        Data Set Ready(Out)
7        Signal Ground
8        Data Carrier Detect(Out)
20       Data Terminal Ready(In)
--------------------------------------
Flow Control: 20
Note:  Use either a 4 or 6 conductor
modular reversing cable.  Splitters used
with 24 Line RS & IRS cards
```

```
Equinox Systems
DS-5, DS-15 Data PBX(8 Line Sync DCE
Distr. Panel)
Port: 8-line Sync DCE        DB25P
Gender: Male                 PinConfig: C14

Pin   Function(Direction)
-----------------------------------------
2      Transmit Data(In)
3      Receive Data(Out)
5      Clear to Send(Out)
6      Data Set Ready(Out)
7      Signal Ground
8      Data Carrier Detect(Out)
20     Data Terminal Ready(In)
22     Ring Indicator(Out)
25     BUSY(In)
-----------------------------------------
Flow Control: 20
Note:  Distribution panels provide DB-25
ports Male or female ports are available
```

```
Equinox Systems
DS-5, DS-15 Data PBX(8-Line Sync DTE
Distr. Panel)
Port: 8 line Sync DTE        DB25P
Gender: Male                 PinConfig: C01

Pin   Function(Direction)
-----------------------------------------
2      Transmit Data(Out)
3      Receive Data(In)
4      Request to Send(Out)
5      Clear to Send(In)
6      Data Set Ready(In)
7      Signal Ground
8      Data Carrier Detect(In)
15     Transmit Clock(In)
17     Receive Clock(In)
20     Data Terminal Ready(Out)
24     External Transmit Clock(Out)
25     BUSY(Out)
-----------------------------------------
Flow Control: 20
Note:  Distribution panels provide
multiple DB-25 ports. Male or female
ports are available
```

```
Equinox Systems
DS-5, DS-15 Data PBX(DCE Fan-Out Cable)
Port:  DCE-Data Only FanoutDB25P
Gender:  Male                PinConfig: C06

Pin   Function(Direction)
-----------------------------------------
2      Transmit Data(In)
3      Receive Data(Out)
7      Signal Ground
-----------------------------------------
Flow Control:
Note:  Fanout cables convert 50 pin
connectors on Line Boards or MUXes to
DB25 connectors(male or female)
```

```
Equinox Systems
DS-5, DS-15 Data PBX(Distribution Panel
Wiring)
Port: DTE-5 Control SignalDB25P
Gender:  Male                PinConfig: C01

Pin   Function(Direction)
-----------------------------------------
2      Transmit Data(Out)
3      Receive Data(In)
4      Request to Send(Out)
7      Signal Ground
8      Data Carrier Detect(In)
20     Data Terminal Ready(Out)
22     Ring Indicator(In)
25     BUSY(Out)
-----------------------------------------
Flow Control: 20
Note:  Distribution panels provide
multiple DB-25 ports. Male or female
ports are available
```

```
Equinox Systems
DS-5, DS-15 Data PBX(DTE Fan-Out Cable)
Port: DTE-2 Control SignalDB25P
Gender:  Male                PinConfig: C01

Pin   Function(Direction)
-----------------------------------------
2      Transmit Data(Out)
3      Receive Data(In)
4      Request to Send(Out)
7      Signal Ground
8      Data Carrier Detect(In)
20     Data Terminal Ready(Out)
-----------------------------------------
Flow Control: 20
Note:  Fanout cables convert 50 pin
connectors on Line Boards or MUXes to
DB25 connectors(male or female)
```

```
Equinox Systems
DS-5, DS-15 Data PBX(DTE Fan-Out Cable)
Port: DTE-5 Control SignalDB25P
Gender:  Male                PinConfig: C01

Pin   Function(Direction)
-----------------------------------------
2      Transmit Data(Out)
3      Receive Data(In)
4      Request to Send(Out)
7      Signal Ground
8      Data Carrier Detect(In)
20     Data Terminal Ready(Out)
22     Ring Indicator(In)
25     BUSY(Out)
-----------------------------------------
Flow Control: 20
Note:  Fanout cables convert 50 pin
connectors on Line Boards or MUXes to
DB25 connectors(male or female)
```

```
Equinox Systems
DS-5, DS-15 Data PBX-210002 Modular
Splitter
Port:  Female-210008 Adap. DB25S
Gender:  Female              PinConfig: C14

Pin    Function(Direction)
------------------------------------------
2        Transmit Data(In)
3        Receive Data(Out)
5        Clear to Send(Out)
6        Data Set Ready(Out)
7        Signal Ground
8        Data Carrier Detect(Out)
20       Data Terminal Ready(In)
22       Ring Indicator(Out)
25       BUSY(In)
------------------------------------------
Flow Control: 8
Note:  Use 8 conductor reversing modular
cables to connect splitter/adapters.
Works w/12 Line CS
```

```
Equinox Systems
DS-5, DS-15 Data PBX-210002 Modular
Splitter
Port:  Male-210003 Adapter DB25P
Gender:  Male                PinConfig: C01

Pin    Function(Direction)
------------------------------------------
2        Transmit Data(Out)
3        Receive Data(In)
4        Request to Send(Out)
7        Signal Ground
8        Data Carrier Detect(In)
20       Data Terminal Ready(Out)
22       Ring Indicator(In)
25       BUSY(Out)
------------------------------------------
Flow Control: 8
Note:  Use 8 conductor reversing modular
cables to connect splitter/adapters.
Works w/24 Line RS/IRS
```

```
Equinox Systems
DS-5, DS-15 Data PBX-210002 Modular
Splitter
Port:  Male-210004 Adapter DB25P
Gender:  Male                PinConfig: C14

Pin    Function(Direction)
------------------------------------------
2        Transmit Data(In)
3        Receive Data(Out)
5        Clear to Send(Out)
6        Data Set Ready(Out)
7        Signal Ground
8        Data Carrier Detect(Out)
20       Data Terminal Ready(In)
22       Ring Indicator(Out)
25       BUSY(In)
------------------------------------------
Flow Control: 8
Note:  Use 8 conductor reversing modular
cables to connect splitter/adapters.
Works w/24 Line RS/IRS
```

```
Equinox Systems
DS-5, DS-15 Data PBX-210116 Modular
Splitter
Port:  Female-210027 Adapt.DB25S
Gender:  Female              PinConfig: C01

Pin    Function(Direction)
------------------------------------------
2        Transmit Data(Out)
3        Receive Data(In)
4        Request to Send(Out)
6        Data Set Ready(In)
7        Signal Ground
8        Data Carrier Detect(In)
20       Data Terminal Ready(Out)
------------------------------------------
Flow Control: 20
Note:  Use 4 or 6 conductor reversing
modular cables to connect
splitter/adapters.  Works w/24 Line
RS/IRS
```

```
Equinox Systems
DS-5, DS-15 Data PBX-210116 Modular
Splitter
Port:  Female-210037 Adapt.DB25S
Gender:  Female              PinConfig: C14

Pin    Function(Direction)
------------------------------------------
2        Transmit Data(In)
3        Receive Data(Out)
5        Clear to Send(Out)
6        Data Set Ready(Out)
7        Signal Ground
8        Data Carrier Detect(Out)
20       Data Terminal Ready(In)
------------------------------------------
Flow Control: 20
Note:  Use 4 or 6 conductor reversing
modular cables to connect
splitter/adapters.  Works w/24 Line
RS/IRS
```

```
Equinox Systems
DS-5, DS-15 Data PBX-210116 Modular
Splitter
Port:  Male-210026 Adapter DB25P
Gender:  Male                PinConfig: C01

Pin    Function(Direction)
------------------------------------------
2        Transmit Data(Out)
3        Receive Data(In)
4        Request to Send(Out)
6        Data Set Ready(In)
7        Signal Ground
8        Data Carrier Detect(In)
20       Data Terminal Ready(Out)
------------------------------------------
Flow Control: 20
Note:  Use 4 or 6 conductor reversing
modular cables to connect
splitter/adapters.  Works w/24 Line
RS/IRS
```

```
Equinox Systems
DS-5, DS-15 Data PBX-210116 Modular
Splitter
Port: Male-210036 Adapter DB25P
Gender: Male                    PinConfig: C14

Pin    Function(Direction)
--------------------------------------------
2         Transmit Data(In)
3         Receive Data(Out)
5         Clear to Send(Out)
6         Data Set Ready(Out)
7         Signal Ground
8         Data Carrier Detect(Out)
20        Data Terminal Ready(In)
--------------------------------------------
Flow Control: 20
Note: Use 4 or 6 conductor reversing
modular cables to connect
splitter/adapters.  Works w/24 Line
RS/IRS
```

```
Equinox Systems
DS-5, DS-15 Data PBX-210117 Modular
Splitter
Port: Male-210026 Adapter DB25P
Gender: Male                    PinConfig: C01

Pin    Function(Direction)
--------------------------------------------
2         Transmit Data(Out)
3         Receive Data(In)
4         Request to Send(Out)
6         Data Set Ready(In)
7         Signal Ground
8         Data Carrier Detect(In)
20        Data Terminal Ready(Out)
--------------------------------------------
Flow Control: 20
Note: Use 4 or 6 conductor reversing
modular cables to connect
splitter/adapters.  Works w/24 Line
RS/IRS
```

```
Equinox Systems
LM-48 Local Multiplexor(DCE male fanout
#690077)
Port: DCE-Male fanout      DB25P
Gender: Male                    PinConfig: C14

Pin    Function(Direction)
--------------------------------------------
2         Transmit Data(In)
3         Receive Data(Out)
5         Clear to Send(Out)
6         Data Set Ready(Out)
7         Signal Ground
8         Data Carrier Detect(Out)
20        Data Terminal Ready(In)
--------------------------------------------
Flow Control: 20
Note: These 8 ports are provided by a
fanout cable #690077.  There is a female
version(#690044)
```

```
Equinox Systems
LM-48 Local Multiplexor(DTE fanout cable
#690076)
Port: DTE-fanout(female) DB25S
Gender: Female                  PinConfig: C01

Pin    Function(Direction)
--------------------------------------------
2         Transmit Data(Out)
3         Receive Data(In)
4         Request to Send(Out)
7         Signal Ground
8         Data Carrier Detect(In)
20        Data Terminal Ready(Out)
--------------------------------------------
Flow Control: 20
Note: These 8 ports are provided by a
fanout cable #690076 that converts the 50
pin telco connector
```

```
Equinox Systems
LM-48 Local Multiplexor(DTE fanout cable
#690075)
Port: DTE-fanout(male)     DB25P
Gender: Male                    PinConfig: C01

Pin    Function(Direction)
--------------------------------------------
2         Transmit Data(Out)
3         Receive Data(In)
4         Request to Send(Out)
7         Signal Ground
8         Data Carrier Detect(In)
20        Data Terminal Ready(Out)
--------------------------------------------
Flow Control: 20
Note: These 8 ports are provided by a
fanout cable #690075 that converts the 50
pin telco connector
```

```
Equinox Systems
LM-48 Local Multiplexor(HP fanout cable
#690043)
Port: HP-fanout(male)      DB25P
Gender: Male                    PinConfig: C01

Pin    Function(Direction)
--------------------------------------------
2         Transmit Data(Out)
3         Receive Data(In)
4         Request to Send(Out)
7         Signal Ground
8         Data Carrier Detect(In)
20        Data Terminal Ready(Out)
--------------------------------------------
Flow Control: 20
Note: These 8 ports provided by a fanout
cable #690043 that converts the 50 pin
telco connector for HP
```

Equinox Systems **LM-48 Local Multiplexor-DCE Fanout Cable** **- #690044** Port: DCE Fanout cable DB25S Gender: Female PinConfig: C14 Pin Function(Direction) --- 2 Transmit Data(In) 3 Receive Data(Out) 5 Clear to Send(Out) 6 Data Set Ready(Out) 7 Signal Ground 8 Data Carrier Detect(Out) 20 Data Terminal Ready(In) --- Flow Control: 20 Note: These ports are provided by a fanout cable(690044) that provides 8 DCE ports from a 50-pin connector	**Equinox Systems** **LM-48 T1 Local Multiplexer** Port: Adapter(210027) DB25S Gender: Female PinConfig: C01 Pin Function(Direction) --- 2 Transmit Data(Out) 3 Receive Data(In) 4 Request to Send(Out) 6 Data Set Ready(In) 7 Signal Ground 8 Data Carrier Detect(In) 20 Data Terminal Ready(Out) --- Flow Control: 8 Note: Adapters connect to modular splitter w/reversing 6 lead cable. 4 lead cable can also be used
Equinox Systems **LM-48 T1 Local Multiplexer** Port: Adapter(210026) DB25P Gender: Male PinConfig: C01 Pin Function(Direction) --- 2 Transmit Data(Out) 3 Receive Data(In) 4 Request to Send(Out) 6 Data Set Ready(In) 7 Signal Ground 8 Data Carrier Detect(In) 20 Data Terminal Ready(Out) --- Flow Control: 8 Note: Adapters connect to modular splitter w/reversing 6 lead cable. 4 lead cable can also be used	**Equinox Systems** **LM-48 T1 Local Multiplexer** Port: Adapter(210037) DB25S Gender: Female PinConfig: C14 Pin Function(Direction) --- 2 Transmit Data(In) 3 Receive Data(Out) 4 Request to Send(In) 5 Clear to Send(Out) 6 Data Set Ready(Out) 7 Signal Ground 8 Data Carrier Detect(Out) 20 Data Terminal Ready(In) --- Flow Control: 20 Note: Adapters connect to modular splitter w/reversing 6 lead cable. 4 lead cable can also be used.
Equinox Systems **LM-48 T1 Local Multiplexer** Port: Adapter(210036) DB25P Gender: Male PinConfig: C14 Pin Function(Direction) --- 2 Transmit Data(In) 3 Receive Data(Out) 4 Request to Send(In) 5 Clear to Send(Out) 6 Data Set Ready(Out) 7 Signal Ground 8 Data Carrier Detect(Out) 20 Data Terminal Ready(In) --- Flow Control: 20 Note: Adapters connect to modular splitter w/reversing 6 lead cable. 4 lead cable can also be used	**Equinox Systems** **LM-48 T1 Local Multiplexer** Port: Adapter(210025) DB25S Gender: Female PinConfig: C14 Pin Function(Direction) --- 2 Transmit Data(In) 3 Receive Data(Out) 4 Request to Send(In) 6 Data Set Ready(Out) 7 Signal Ground 8 Data Carrier Detect(Out) 20 Data Terminal Ready(In) --- Flow Control: 20 Note: Adapters connect to modular splitter w/reversing 6 lead cable. 4 lead cable can be used w/o 6/8/20

```
Equinox Systems                        Equinox Systems
LM-48 T1 Local Multiplexer             Megaport Board-210016 Modular Splitter
Port:  Adapter(210024)      DB25P      Port:  6 lead Modular      RJ11
Gender:  Male          PinConfig: C14  Gender:  Female       PinConfig: C56

Pin   Function(Direction)              Pin   Function(Direction)
------------------------------------   ------------------------------------
2      Transmit Data(In)               3      Protective Ground
3      Receive Data(Out)               5      Signal Ground
4      Request to Send(In)             4      Transmitted Data(out)
6      Data Set Ready(Out)             2      Received Data(in)
7      Signal Ground                   1      Print Control(out)
8      Data Carrier Detect(Out)        6      Print Control(in)
20     Data Terminal Ready(In)         ------------------------------------
------------------------------------   Flow Control: 1   XON/XOFF
Flow Control: 20                       Note:  This does not assume a reversing
Note:  Adapters connect to modular     cable
splitter w/reversing 6 lead cable. 4 lead
cable can be used w/o 6/8/20
------------------------------------   ------------------------------------
Equinox Systems                        HullSpeed Data Products
Megaport Board-210016 Modular Splitter MSI-4, MSI-8 Modem Sharing devices
Port:  6 lead rev-cable   RJ11         Port:  DCE(Master)         DB25P
Gender:  Male          PinConfig: C57  Gender:  Male         PinConfig: C14

Pin   Function(Direction)              Pin   Function(Direction)
------------------------------------   ------------------------------------
4      Protective Ground               2      Transmit Data(In)
2      Signal Ground                   3      Receive Data(Out)
3      Transmitted Data(out)           4      Request to Send(In)
5      Received Data(in)               5      Clear to Send(Out)
6      Data Terminal Ready(out)        6      Data Set Ready(Out)
1      Data Set Ready(in)              7      Signal Ground
------------------------------------   8      Carrier Detect(Out)
Flow Control: 6                        15     Transmit Clock(Out)
Note:  This assumes a reversing modular 17    Receive Clock(Out)
cable is used                          20     Data Terminal Ready(In)
                                       ------------------------------------
                                       Flow Control:
                                       Note:
------------------------------------   ------------------------------------
HullSpeed Data Products                Inmac
MSI-4, MSI-8 Modem Sharing devices     Clear Signal Smart Switch 64
Port:  DTE ports          DB25S        Port:  6 lead rev-cable   RJ11
Gender:  Female       PinConfig: C05   Gender:  Male         PinConfig: C71

Pin   Function(Direction)              Pin   Function(Direction)
------------------------------------   ------------------------------------
2      Transmit Data(Out)              2      Signal Ground
3      Receive Data(In)               5      Transmitted Data(out)
4      Request to Send(Out)            3      Received Data(in)
5      Clear to Send(In)               6      Data Terminal Ready(out)
6      Data Set Ready(In)              1      Clear To Send(in)
7      Signal Ground                   ------------------------------------
8      Carrier Detect(In)              Flow Control: 6   XON/XOFF
15     Transmit Clock(In)              Note:  This port entry assumes a
17     Receive Clock(In)               reversing cable is used
------------------------------------
Flow Control:
Note:
```

inmac
Clear Signal Smart Switch 64
Port: RJ-11(6 lead)   RJ11
Gender: Female   PinConfig: C54

Pin   Function(Direction)
----
5   Signal Ground
2   Transmitted Data(out)
4   Received Data(in)
1   Print Control(out)
6   Clear To Send(in)

Flow Control: 1   XON/XOFF
Note: This port entry assumes no
reversing cable

---

inmac
Jetshare II Card
Port: RJ11   RJ11
Gender: Female   PinConfig: C62

Pin   Function(Direction)
----
2   Signal Ground
5   Transmitted Data(out)
3   Received Data(in)
4   Data Terminal Ready(out)

Flow Control: 4   XON/XOFF
Note: This assumes no reversing cable

---

inmac
Laser Print Switch(Clear Signal)
Port: Input Port (1-8)   DB25S
Gender: Female   PinConfig: P11

Pin   Function(Direction)
----
1   Protective Ground
2   Data Out(Out)
3   Data In(In)
5   Clear to Send(In)
7   Signal Ground
20   Data Terminal Ready(Out)

Flow Control: 20   XON/XOFF
Note: Don't confuse this with the
Printer Port

---

inmac
Net Controller Plus(Clear Signal)
Port: DTE   DB25S
Gender: Female   PinConfig: C11

Pin   Function(Direction)
----
2   Transmit Data(Out)
3   Receive Data(In)
4   Request to Send(Out)
5   Clear to Send(In)
7   Signal Ground
8   Data Carrier Detect(In)
20   Data Terminal Ready(Out)

Flow Control: 5   XON/XOFF
Note: Lead 5 must be on for this port to
send data Hardware flow control is the
default.

---

inmac
Serial Smart Switch
Port: Computer Ports   DB25S
Gender: Female   PinConfig: C08

Pin   Function(Direction)
----
1   Protective Ground
2   Transmit Data(Out)
3   Receive Data(In)
4   Request to Send(Out)
7   Signal Ground
20   Data Terminal Ready(Out)

Flow Control: 20,4   XON/XOFF
Note: 2 or 4 port models are available.
Note that this is the computer port, not
the printer port

---

inmac
Serial Smart Switch
Port: Printer   DB25S
Gender: Female   PinConfig: C01

Pin   Function(Direction)
----
1   Protective Ground
2   Transmit Data(Out)
3   Receive Data(In)
4   Request to Send(Out)
5   Clear to Send(In)
6   Data Set Ready(In)
7   Signal Ground
20   Data Terminal Ready(Out)

Flow Control: 5 & 6   XON/XOFF
Note: Leads 5/6 should be connected to
the printer's flow control lead.

```
inmac
Smart Switch 64 (Clear Signal)
Port:  Ports 1-8(DB-25)    DB25S
Gender: Female             PinConfig: C14

Pin   Function(Direction)
-------------------------------------------
1      Frame Ground
2      Data In(In)
3      Data Out(Out)
5      Clear to Send(Out)
6      Data Set Ready(Out)
7      Signal Ground
8      Data Carrier Detect(Out)
20     Data Terminal Ready(In)
-------------------------------------------
Flow Control: 20            XON/XOFF
Note:  An RS-232 DCE Port splitter
provides the above ports by connecting to
the 8-port Serial Module
```

```
inmac
SS-8 & SS-16 Smart Switch(Any port to Any
port)
Port:  RS-232              DB25S
Gender: Female             PinConfig: C07

Pin   Function(Direction)
-------------------------------------------
1      Chassis Ground
2      Data Out(Out)
3      Data In(In)
5      Clear to Send(In)
7      Signal Ground
20     Data Terminal Ready(Out)
-------------------------------------------
Flow Control: 5             XON/XOFF
Note:  This port is setup to attach a
modem(Button out) Button out is for DTE.
Leads 6 & 8 are on(output)
```

```
inmac
SS-8 & SS-16 Smart Switch(Any port to Any
port)
Port:  RS-232              DB25S
Gender: Female             PinConfig: C14

Pin   Function(Direction)
-------------------------------------------
1      Chassis Ground
2      Data In(In)
3      Data Out(Out)
5      Clear to Send(Out)
6      Data Set Ready(Out)
7      Signal Ground
8      Data Carrier Detect(Out)
20     Data Terminal Ready(In)
-------------------------------------------
Flow Control: 20            XON/XOFF
Note:  This port is set for attachment of
DTE(Button in) Button in out position
sets it to attach a modem
```

```
inmac
Laser Print Switch(Clear Signal)
Port:  Serial Output       DB25S
Gender: Female             PinConfig: C14

Pin   Function(Direction)
-------------------------------------------
1      Frame Ground
2      Data In(In)
3      Data Out(Out)
5      Clear to Send(Out)
6      Data Set Ready(Out)
7      Signal Ground
8      Data Carrier Detect(Out)
20     Data Terminal Ready(In)
-------------------------------------------
Flow Control: 20            XON/XOFF
Note:  Lead 20 must on to release data.
Leads 5/6/8 are held high.
```

```
IPC America
POS-I, POS-II, POS-III Point of Sale
Terminal
Port:  Serial 1/2 9-pin    DB9P
Gender: Male               PinConfig: C16

Pin   Function(Direction)
-------------------------------------------
1      Carrier Detect(In)
2      Receive Data(In)
3      Transmit Data(Out)
4      Data Terminal Ready(Out)
5      Signal Ground
6      Data Set Ready(In)
7      Request to Send(Out)
8      Clear to Send(In)
9      Ring Indicator(In)
-------------------------------------------
Flow Control: 6 & 8
Note:  The flow control leads of the
attached device should be connected to
leads 6 & 8
```

```
PERCON Incorporated
Series 10 Bar Code And Mag Stripe Decoder
Port:  RS-232              DB9S
Gender: Female             PinConfig: C42

Pin   Function(Direction)
-------------------------------------------
9      Signal Ground
2      Transmitted Data(out)
3      Received Data(in)
4      Request To Send(out)
5      Clear To Send(in)
-------------------------------------------
Flow Control: 4   XON/XOFF
Note:
```

Rose Electronics
Caretaker, Caretake Plus Switch
Port: RS-232 port   DB25S
Gender: Female   PinConfig: C01

Pin   Function(Direction)
----
2   Transmit Data(Out)
3   Receive Data(In)
4   Request to Send(Out)
6   Data Set Ready(In)
7   Signal Ground
20   Data Terminal Ready(Out)

Flow Control: 20, 6   XON/XOFF
Note:

Rose Electronics
MSN-4S1P/8S1P SWITCHES
Port: RJ45   RJ45
Gender: Female   PinConfig: C41

Pin   Function(Direction)
----
5   Signal Ground
4   Transmitted Data(out)
6   Received Data(in)
3   Data Terminal Ready(out)
2   Data Set Ready(in)

Flow Control: 3   XON/XOFF
Note: This entry assumes no reversing
cable

Rose Electronics
MSN-12S1P/16S1P SWITCH
Port: RJ45   RJ45
Gender: Female   PinConfig: C41

Pin   Function(Direction)
----
5   Signal Ground
4   Transmitted Data(out)
6   Received Data(in)
3   Data Terminal Ready(out)
2   Data Set Ready(in)

Flow Control: 3   XON/XOFF
Note: This entry assumes no reversing
cable

Rose Electronics
MSU-3SP/6SP/9SP SWITCH
Port: RJ45   RJ45
Gender: Female   PinConfig: C41

Pin   Function(Direction)
----
5   Signal Ground
4   Transmitted Data(out)
6   Received Data(in)
3   Data Terminal Ready(out)
2   Data Set Ready(in)

Flow Control: 3   XON/XOFF
Note: This entry assumes no reversing
cable

Rose Electronics
Master Switch(Standard series)
Port: RS-232(DB-25)   DB25S
Gender: Female   PinConfig: C01

Pin   Function(Direction)
----
2   Transmit Data(Out)
3   Receive Data(In)
4   Request to Send(Out)
6   Data Set Ready(In)
7   Signal Ground
20   Data Terminal Ready(Out)

Flow Control: 20, 6   XON/XOFF
Note:

Rose Electronics
Porter Switch
Port: RS-232 port   DB25S
Gender: Female   PinConfig: C01

Pin   Function(Direction)
----
2   Transmit Data(Out)
3   Receive Data(In)
4   Request to Send(Out)
6   Data Set Ready(In)
7   Signal Ground
20   Data Terminal Ready(Out)

Flow Control: 20, 6   XON/XOFF
Note:

Sharp
JX100 Scanner
Port: RS-232   DB9S
Gender: Female   PinConfig: C48

Pin   Function(Direction)
----
5   Signal Ground
2   Transmitted Data(out)
3   Received Data(in)

Flow Control: XON/XOFF
Note:

Star Gate Technologies
DCEFCON Adapter
Port: RJ12-DB25 Adapter   DB25S
Gender: Female   PinConfig: C14

Pin   Function(Direction)
----
2   Transmit Data(In)
3   Receive Data(Out)
4   Request to Send(In)
5   Clear to Send(Out)
7   Signal Ground
20   Data Terminal Ready(In)

Flow Control: 20   XON/XOFF
Note: Part No. 399020-01

```
Star Gate Technologies                    Star Gate Technologies
DCEFCON Adapter                           DCEMCON Adapter
Port:  RJ12-DB25 Adapter   DB25S          Port:  RJ12-DB25 Adapter   DB25P
Gender:  Female            PinConfig: C14 Gender:  Male              PinConfig: C14

Pin   Function(Direction)                 Pin   Function(Direction)
---------------------------------------   ---------------------------------------
2      Transmit Data(In)                  2      Transmit Data(In)
3      Receive Data(Out)                  3      Receive Data(Out)
4      Request to Send(In)                4      Request to Send(In)
5      Clear to Send(Out)                 5      Clear to Send(Out)
7      Signal Ground                      7      Signal Ground
20     Data Terminal Ready(In)            20     Data Terminal Ready(In)
---------------------------------------   ---------------------------------------
Flow Control: 20          XON/XOFF        Flow Control: 20          XON/XOFF
Note:  Part No. 399020-01                 Note:  Part No. 399019-01
```

```
Star Gate Technologies                    Star Gate Technologies
DTEMCON Connector                         DTEMODF Connector
Port:  RJ12-DB25P adapter  DB25P          Port:  RJ12-DB25P adapter  DB25S
Gender:  Male              PinConfig: C05 Gender:  Female            PinConfig: C05

Pin   Function(Direction)                 Pin   Function(Direction)
---------------------------------------   ---------------------------------------
2      Transmit Data(Out)                 2      Transmit Data(Out)
3      Receive Data(In)                   3      Receive Data(In)
4      Request to Send(Out)               4      Request to Send(Out)
5      Clear to Send(Out)                 5      Clear to Send(Out)
7      Signal Ground                      7      Signal Ground
8      Data Carrier Detect(Out)           8      Data Carrier Detect(Out)
---------------------------------------   ---------------------------------------
Flow Control: 4           XON/XOFF        Flow Control: 4           XON/XOFF
Note:  Part# 399022-01                    Note:  Part# 399026-01
```

```
Star Gate Technologies                    VIR Inc.
DTEMODM Connector                         Interactive Switch Patch
Port:  RJ12-DB25P adapter  DB25P          Port:  CNTL.IN             DB25P
Gender:  Male              PinConfig: C11 Gender:  Male              PinConfig: C06

Pin   Function(Direction)                 Pin   Function(Direction)
---------------------------------------   ---------------------------------------
2      Transmit Data(Out)                 2      Transmit Data(In)
3      Receive Data(In)                   3      Receive Data(Out)
4      Request to Send(Out)               7      Signal Ground
5      Clear to Send(Out)                 ---------------------------------------
7      Signal Ground                      Flow Control:             XON/XOFF
8      Data Carrier Detect(Out)           Note:
20     Data Terminal Ready(Out)
---------------------------------------
Flow Control: 20          XON/XOFF
Note:  Part# 399027-01
```

```
Western Telematic Inc.                    Western Telematic Inc.
LASERNET QwikShare sharing device         LASERNET QwikShare sharing device
Port:  SA-16F PC Adapter   DB25S          Port:  SA-2M Adapter       DB25P
Gender:  Female            PinConfig: C10 Gender:  Male              PinConfig: C14

Pin   Function(Direction)                 Pin   Function(Direction)
---------------------------------------   ---------------------------------------
2      Receive Data(In)                   2      Transmit Data(In)
3      Transmit Data(Out)                 3      Transmit Data(Out)
5      Clear to Send(Out)                 5      Clear to Send(Out)
6      Data Set Ready(Out)                6      Data Set Ready(Out)
7      Signal Ground                      7      Signal Ground
---------------------------------------   20     Data Terminal Ready(In)
Flow Control: 5                           ---------------------------------------
Note:                                     Flow Control: 20
                                          Note:
```

```
WESTERN TELEMATIC INC.
LASERNET QwikShare sharing device
Port: Snap Adapter(male) DB25P
Gender: Male              PinConfig: C14

Pin   Function(Direction)
----------------------------------------------
2       Receive Data(In)
3       Transmit Data(Out)
5       Clear to Send(Out)
6       Data Set Ready(Out)
7       Signal Ground
20      Data Terminal Ready(In)
----------------------------------------------
Flow Control: 20
Note:
```

```
Western Telematic Inc.
PSU-41A port sharing unit
Port: Input Serial port   DB25S
Gender: Female            PinConfig: P11

Pin   Function(Direction)
----------------------------------------------
1       Protective Ground
2       Data Out(Out)
3       Data In(In)
5       Clear to Send(In)
7       Signal Ground
20      Data Terminal Ready(Out)
----------------------------------------------
Flow Control: 20          XON/XOFF
Note: This is one of multiple input
ports, note difference between this and
output port.
```

```
Western Telematic Inc.
PSU-41A port sharing unit
Port: Output serial port  DB25S
Gender: Female            PinConfig: C14

Pin   Function(Direction)
----------------------------------------------
1       Frame Ground
2       Data In(In)
3       Data Out(Out)
5       Clear to Send(Out)
6       Data Set Ready(Out)
7       Signal Ground
8       Data Carrier Detect(Out)
20      Data Terminal Ready(In)
----------------------------------------------
Flow Control: 20          XON/XOFF
Note: Note this is an output serial
port, not the input ports.  Leads 6 & 8
are always high.
```

```
Western Telematic Inc.
PSU-41B port sharing unit
Port: Input Serial port   DB25S
Gender: Female            PinConfig: P11

Pin   Function(Direction)
----------------------------------------------
1       Protective Ground
2       Data Out(Out)
3       Data In(In)
5       Clear to Send(In)
7       Signal Ground
20      Data Terminal Ready(Out)
----------------------------------------------
Flow Control: 20          XON/XOFF
Note: This is one of multiple input
ports, note difference between this and
output port.
```

```
Western Telematic Inc.
PSU-41B port sharing unit
Port: Output serial port  DB25S
Gender: Female            PinConfig: C14

Pin   Function(Direction)
----------------------------------------------
1       Frame Ground
2       Data In(In)
3       Data Out(Out)
5       Clear to Send(Out)
6       Data Set Ready(Out)
7       Signal Ground
8       Data Carrier Detect(Out)
20      Data Terminal Ready(In)
----------------------------------------------
Flow Control: 20          XON/XOFF
Note: Note this is an output serial
port, not the input ports.
```

```
Western Telematic Inc.
PSU-42C port sharing unit
Port: Input Serial ports  DB25S
Gender: Female            PinConfig: P11

Pin   Function(Direction)
----------------------------------------------
1       Protective Ground
2       Data Out(Out)
3       Data In(In)
5       Clear to Send(In)
7       Signal Ground
14      +5V (Out)
20      Data Terminal Ready(Out)
----------------------------------------------
Flow Control: 20          XON/XOFF
Note: There are multiple input
ports(above), note difference between
these and output serial ports
```

```
Western Telematic Inc.                  Western Telematic Inc.
PSU-42C port sharing unit               PSU-42P port sharing unit
Port: Output Serial Ports DB25P         Port: Output Serial port  DB25S
Gender: Male              PinConfig: C14 Gender: Female           PinConfig: C14

Pin  Function(Direction)                Pin  Function(Direction)
------------------------------          ------------------------------
1      Protective Ground                1      Protective Ground
2      Data In(In)                      2      Data In(In)
3      Data Out(Out)                    3      Data Out(Out)
5      Clear to Send(Out)               5      Clear to Send(Out)
6      Data Set Ready(Out)              7      Signal Ground
7      Signal Ground                    20     Data Terminal Ready(In)
8      Data Carrier Detect(Out)         ------------------------------
20     Data Terminal Ready(In)          Flow Control: 20        XON/XOFF
------------------------------                                  ACK/NAK
Flow Control: 20        XON/XOFF        Note: Lead 20 should be connected to the
Note: Don't confuse this port with the  printer/plotter output hardware flow
input ports Leads 6&8 are alway high    control lead
--------------------------------------------------------------------
Western Telematic Inc.                  Western Telematic Inc.
PSU-81A port sharing unit               PSU-81A port sharing unit
Port: Input Serial port   DB25S         Port: Output serial port  DB25S
Gender: Female            PinConfig: P11 Gender: Female           PinConfig: C14

Pin  Function(Direction)                Pin  Function(Direction)
------------------------------          ------------------------------
1      Protective Ground                1      Frame Ground
2      Data Out(Out)                    2      Data In(In)
3      Data In(In)                      3      Data Out(Out)
5      Clear to Send(In)                5      Clear to Send(Out)
7      Signal Ground                    6      Data Set Ready(Out)
20     Data Terminal Ready(Out)         7      Signal Ground
------------------------------          8      Data Carrier Detect(Out)
Flow Control: 20        XON/XOFF        20     Data Terminal Ready(In)
Note: This is one of multiple input     ------------------------------
ports, note difference between this and Flow Control: 20        XON/XOFF
output port.                            Note: Note this is an output serial
                                        port, not the input ports.  Leads 6 & 8
                                        are always high.
--------------------------------------------------------------------
Western Telematic Inc.                  Western Telematic Inc.
PSU-81B port sharing unit               PSU-81B port sharing unit
Port: Input Serial port   DB25S         Port: Output serial port  DB25S
Gender: Female            PinConfig: P11 Gender: Female           PinConfig: C14

Pin  Function(Direction)                Pin  Function(Direction)
------------------------------          ------------------------------
1      Protective Ground                1      Frame Ground
2      Data Out(Out)                    2      Data In(In)
3      Data In(In)                      3      Data Out(Out)
5      Clear to Send(In)                5      Clear to Send(Out)
7      Signal Ground                    6      Data Set Ready(Out)
20     Data Terminal Ready(Out)         7      Signal Ground
------------------------------          8      Data Carrier Detect(Out)
Flow Control: 20        XON/XOFF        20     Data Terminal Ready(In)
Note: This is one of multiple input     ------------------------------
ports, note difference between this and Flow Control: 20        XON/XOFF
output port.                            Note: Note this is an output serial
                                        port, not the input ports.
```

```
Western Telematic Inc.                    Western Telematic Inc.
PSU-82C port sharing unit                 PSU-82C port sharing unit
Port:  Input Serial ports  DB25S          Port:  Output Serial Ports DB25P
Gender:  Female            PinConfig: P11 Gender:  Male              PinConfig: C14

Pin   Function(Direction)                 Pin   Function(Direction)
-----------------------------------       -----------------------------------
1     Protective Ground                   1     Protective Ground
2     Data Out(Out)                       2     Data In(In)
3     Data In(In)                         3     Data Out(Out)
5     Clear to Send(In)                   5     Clear to Send(In)
7     Signal Ground                       6     Data Set Ready(Out)
14    +5V (Out)                           7     Signal Ground
20    Data Terminal Ready(Out)            8     Data Carrier Detect(Out)
-----------------------------------       20    Data Terminal Ready(In)
Flow Control: 20          XON/XOFF        -----------------------------------
Note:  There are multiple input          Flow Control: 20          XON/XOFF
ports(above), note difference between     Note:  Don't confuse this port with the
these and output serial ports            input ports Leads 6&8 are alway high
```

```
Western Telematic Inc.                    Western Telematic Inc.
PSU-82SP port sharing unit                PSU-82SP port sharing unit
Port:  Input Serial ports  DB25S          Port:  Output Serial Port  DB25P
Gender:  Female            PinConfig: P11 Gender:  Male              PinConfig: C01

Pin   Function(Direction)                 Pin   Function(Direction)
-----------------------------------       -----------------------------------
1     Protective Ground                   1     Protective Ground
2     Data Out(Out)                       2     Data Out(Out)
3     Data In(In)                         3     Data In(In)
5     Clear to Send(In)                   4     Request to Send(Out)
7     Signal Ground                       5     Clear to Send(In)
20    Data Terminal Ready(Out)            7     Signal Ground
-----------------------------------       20    Data Terminal Ready(Out)
Flow Control: 20          XON/XOFF        -----------------------------------
Note:  Multiple input serial ports are    Flow Control: 5           XON/XOFF
provided.  Insure that you don't confuse  Note:  Don't confuse this port with the
the output port with this                 input ports Lead 4 is alway high, lead 5
                                          must be on to send
```

```
Western Telematic, Inc.                   Western Telematic, Inc.
INC-64 RS-232 Port Splitter(RS-232R or W) QwikShare Printer Sharing System
Port:  RS-232            DB25S             Port:  SA-16F Adapter      DB25S
Gender:  Female         PinConfig: C14     Gender:  Female           PinConfig: C14

Pin   Function(Direction)                 Pin   Function(Direction)
-----------------------------------       -----------------------------------
1     Frame Ground                        2     Transmit Data(In)
2     Data In(In)                         3     Receive Data(Out)
3     Data Out(Out)                       4     Request to Send(In)
5     Clear to Send(Out)                  5     Clear to Send(Out)
6     Data Set Ready(Out)                 6     Data Set Ready(Out)
7     Signal Ground                       7     Signal Ground
8     Data Carrier Detect(Out)            8     Data Carrier Detect(Out)
20    Data Terminal Ready(In)             20    Data Terminal Ready(In)
-----------------------------------       -----------------------------------
Flow Control: 5, 20                       Flow Control:             XON/XOFF
Note:  Lead CTS will be on when ready to  Note:  This port is on the Snap Adapter
receive. This splitter attaches to a      than converts the QwikShare RJ11C port to
serial module                             a DB25 for a PC(Above)
```

```
Xyplex
1100, 1500, 1800 MAXserver(RJ-45 to
female adapter)
Port:  1-16                      DB25S
Gender: Female             PinConfig: C14

Pin   Function(Direction)
--------------------------------------------
2     Transmit Data(In)
3     Receive Data(Out)
4     Request to Send(In)
5     Clear to Send(Out)
6     Data Set Ready(Out)
7     Signal Ground
8     Data Carrier Detect(Out)
20    Data Terminal Ready(In)
22    Ring Indicator(Out)
--------------------------------------------
Flow Control: 8              XON/XOFF
Note:  A reversing-cable & this adapter
provide a DB25 port for DTE connections
```

```
Xyplex
1100, 1500, 1800 MAXserver(RJ-45 to male
adapter)
Port:  1-16                      DB25P
Gender: Male               PinConfig: C01

Pin   Function(Direction)
--------------------------------------------
2     Transmit Data(Out)
3     Receive Data(In)
4     Request to Send(Out)
5     Clear to Send(In)
6     Data Set Ready(In)
7     Signal Ground
8     Data Carrier Detect(In)
20    Data Terminal Ready(Out)
22    Ring Indicator(In)
--------------------------------------------
Flow Control: 6              XON/XOFF
Note:  A straight-through modular cable &
this adapter provide a DB25 port for DCE
connections
```

printers + plotters

```
Advanced Matrix Technology
Accel-500 Printer
Port:  DCE(RS-232)          DB25S
Gender:  Female             PinConfig: C14

Pin   Function(Direction)
-------------------------------------------
1        Chassis Ground
2        Transmit Data(In)
3        Receive Data(Out)
4        Request to Send(In)
5        Clear to Send(Out)
6        Data Set Ready(Out)
7        Signal Ground
8        Data Carrier Detect(Out)
20       Data Terminal Ready(In)
-------------------------------------------
Flow Control: 5           XON/XOFF
Note:  Lead 5 is an output flow control
lead.  This port is optionable to be DTE,
instead of above(DCE)
```

```
Advanced Matrix Technology
Accel-500 Printer
Port:  DTE(RS-232)          DB25S
Gender:  Female             PinConfig: P03

Pin   Function(Direction)
-------------------------------------------
1        Chassis Ground
2        Transmit Data(Out)
3        Receive Data(In)
4        Request to Send(Out)
5        Clear to Send(In)
6        Data Set Ready(In)
7        Signal Ground
11       Data Terminal Ready(Out)
20       Data Terminal Ready(Out)
25       Data Terminal Ready(Out)
-------------------------------------------
Flow Control: 20,11,25    XON/XOFF
Note:  11 & 20 are the same as 20, except
polarity can be switched.  This port is
DTE, optionable as DCE
```

```
Advanced Technologies Intl.
0880/DW-2, DW-3 Printers
Port:  RS-232               DB25S
Gender:  Female             PinConfig: P03

Pin   Function(Direction)
-------------------------------------------
1        Protective Ground
2        Transmit Data(Out)
3        Receive Data(In)
4        Request to Send(Out)
5        Clear to Send(In)
6        Data Set Ready(In)
7        Signal Ground
8        Data Carrier Detect(In)
20       Data Terminal Ready(Out)
-------------------------------------------
Flow Control: 20           XON/XOFF
Note:
```

```
Advanced Technologies Intl.
1570/DW-2, DW-3, 2670/DW-2,DW-3  Printers
Port:  RS-232               DB25S
Gender:  Female             PinConfig: P03

Pin   Function(Direction)
-------------------------------------------
1        Protective Ground
2        Transmit Data(Out)
3        Receive Data(In)
4        Request to Send(Out)
5        Clear to Send(In)
6        Data Set Ready(In)
7        Signal Ground
8        Data Carrier Detect(In)
20       Data Terminal Ready(Out)
-------------------------------------------
Flow Control: 20           XON/XOFF
Note:
```

```
Advanced Technologies Intl.
LC-6026 Printer
Port:  RS-232               DB25S
Gender:  Female             PinConfig: P03

Pin   Function(Direction)
-------------------------------------------
1        Protective Ground
2        Transmit Data(Out)
3        Receive Data(In)
4        Request to Send(Out)
5        Clear to Send(In)
6        Data Set Ready(In)
7        Signal Ground
8        Data Carrier Detect(In)
20       Data Terminal Ready(Out)
-------------------------------------------
Flow Control: 20           XON/XOFF
Note:
```

```
Analog Technology Corp.
8220 Printer
Port:  Serial               DB25S
Gender:  Female             PinConfig: P08

Pin   Function(Direction)
-------------------------------------------
2        Transmit Data(Out)
3        Receive Data(In)
4        Request to Send(Out)
5        Clear to Send(In)
6        Data Set Ready(In)
7        Signal Ground
20       Data Terminal Ready(Out)
-------------------------------------------
Flow Control: 20           XON/XOFF
ACK/NAK
Note:  Leads DSR/CTS can be optioned to
be ignored, else, they must be on for
printer to receive data
```

```
Apple
LaserWriter IINT, IINTX Printers
Port: RS-232(25 pin)        DB25S
Gender: Female              PinConfig: P03

Pin   Function(Direction)
------------------------------------------
1       Protective Ground
2       Transmit Data(Out)
3       Receive Data(In)
4       Request to Send(Out)
5       Clear to Send(In)
6       Data Set Ready(In)
7       Signal Ground
8       Data Carrier Detect(In)
20      Data Terminal Ready(Out)
22      Ring Indicator(In)
------------------------------------------
Flow Control: 20            XON/XOFF
Note:
```

```
Apple
LaserWriter, LaserWriter Plus Printers
Port: RS-232(25 pin)        DB25S
Gender: Female              PinConfig: P03

Pin   Function(Direction)
------------------------------------------
1       Protective Ground
2       Transmit Data(Out)
3       Receive Data(In)
4       Request to Send(Out)
5       Clear to Send(In)
6       Data Set Ready(In)
7       Signal Ground
8       Data Carrier Detect(In)
20      Data Terminal Ready(Out)
22      Ring Indicator(In)
------------------------------------------
Flow Control: 20            XON/XOFF
Note:
```

```
AT&T
495 Printer
Port: RS-232               DB25S
Gender: Female             PinConfig: P03

Pin   Function(Direction)
------------------------------------------
1       Protective Ground
2       Transmit Data(Out)
3       Receive Data(In)
4       Request to Send(Out)
5       Clear to Send(In)
7       Signal Ground
11      Secondary Req. to Send(Out)
19      Secondary Req. to Send(Out)
20      Data Terminal Ready(Out)
------------------------------------------
Flow Control: 20,4,11,19   XON/XOFF
ACK/NAK
Note: Serial port is mounted on the
personality cartridge
```

```
Axonix
LiteWrite, ThinWrite 100 Printers
Port: RS-232               DB25S
Gender: Female             PinConfig: P03

Pin   Function(Direction)
------------------------------------------
1       Frame Ground
2       Transmit Data(Out)
3       Receive Data(In)
4       Request to Send(Out)
6       Data Set Ready(In)
7       Signal Ground
11      Secondary Req. to Send(Out)
20      Data Terminal Ready(Out)
------------------------------------------
Flow Control: 20,11        XON/XOFF
Note: Lead 11 is inverted to be on when
the printer is busy.
```

```
Brother Intl
HL-4,HL-8e, HL-8PS, HR-40 Printers
Port: RS-232               DB25S
Gender: Female             PinConfig: P11

Pin   Function(Direction)
------------------------------------------
1       Frame Ground
2       Transmit Data(Out)
3       Receive Data(In)
6       Data Set Ready(In)
7       Signal Ground
8       Carrier Detect(In)
20      Data Terminal Ready(Out)
------------------------------------------
Flow Control: 20           XON/XOFF
Note:
```

```
Brother Intl
M-1809, M-1824L, M-1924L, M-1909 Printers
Port: RS-232               DB25S
Gender: Female             PinConfig: P11

Pin   Function(Direction)
------------------------------------------
1       Frame Ground
2       Transmit Data(Out)
3       Receive Data(In)
6       Data Set Ready(In)
7       Signal Ground
8       Carrier Detect(In)
20      Data Terminal Ready(Out)
------------------------------------------
Flow Control: 20           XON/XOFF
Note:
```

```
Brother Intl
M-2518, M-4018 Printers
Port:  RS-232              DB25S
Gender:  Female            PinConfig: P11

Pin   Function(Direction)
-------------------------------------------
1     Frame Ground
2     Transmit Data(Out)
3     Receive Data(In)
6     Data Set Ready(In)
7     Signal Ground
8     Carrier Detect(In)
20    Data Terminal Ready(Out)
-------------------------------------------
Flow Control: 20           XON/XOFF
Note:
```

```
C-TECH Electronics
C-510/515 Printers
Port:  RS-232              DB25S
Gender:  Female            PinConfig: P03

Pin   Function(Direction)
-------------------------------------------
1     Frame Ground
2     SD  (Out)
3     Receive Data(In)
4     Request to Send(Out)
5     Clear to Send(In)
6     Data Set Ready(In)
7     Signal Ground
8     Carrier Detect(Out)
20    Data Terminal Ready(Out)
25    Fault(Out)
-------------------------------------------
Flow Control: 20           XON/XOFF
Note:  Leads 2/4/5/6/8 are not used when
hardware flow control is used(RDY/BSY).
```

```
C-TECH Electronics
C-610+, C-645 Printers
Port:  RS-232              DB25S
Gender:  Female            PinConfig: P03

Pin   Function(Direction)
-------------------------------------------
1     Frame Ground
2     SD  (Out)
3     Receive Data(In)
4     Request to Send(Out)
5     Clear to Send(In)
6     Data Set Ready(In)
7     Signal Ground
8     Carrier Detect(Out)
20    Data Terminal Ready(Out)
25    Fault(Out)
-------------------------------------------
Flow Control: 20,4,25      XON/XOFF
Note:  Leads 4 & 25 are set to HIGH as
default
```

```
C.Itoh
C-240, C-245, C-715A Printers
Port:  RS-232              DB25S
Gender:  Female            PinConfig: P03

Pin   Function(Direction)
-------------------------------------------
1     Frame Ground
2     Transmit Data(Out)
3     Receive Data(In)
4     Request to Send(Out)
5     Clear to Send(In)
6     Data Set Ready(In)
7     Signal Ground
8     Carrier Detect(In)
14    Fault(Out)
20    Data Terminal Ready(Out)
-------------------------------------------
Flow Control: 20           XON/XOFF
Note:
```

```
C.Itoh
C-310 P/R Printers
Port:  RS-232              DB25S
Gender:  Female            PinConfig: P03

Pin   Function(Direction)
-------------------------------------------
1     Frame Ground
2     Transmit Data(Out)
3     Receive Data(In)
4     Request to Send(Out)
5     Clear to Send(In)
6     Data Set Ready(In)
7     Signal Ground
8     Carrier Detect(In)
14    Fault(Out)
20    Data Terminal Ready(Out)
-------------------------------------------
Flow Control: 20,14        XON/XOFF
Note:
```

```
C.ITOH
CI 4000 Model 10 Printer
Port:  RS-232              DB25S
Gender:  Female            PinConfig: P05

Pin   Function(Direction)
-------------------------------------------
1     Protective Ground
2     Transmit Data(Out)
3     Receive Data(In)
4     Request to Send(Out)
5     Clear to Send(In)
6     Data Set Ready(In)
7     Signal Ground
8     Rec.Line Signal Detect(In)
11    Busy(Out)
20    Data Terminal Ready(Out)
23    +12V(Out)
25    +5V (Out)
-------------------------------------------
Flow Control: 11           XON/XOFF
Note:  Leads 5/6/8 should be on for the
printer to operate
```

```
C.Itoh
CI 4000 Model 20 Printer
Port:  RS-232(male)          DB25P
Gender:  Male                PinConfig: P03

Pin    Function(Direction)
----------------------------------------
1      Frame Ground
2      Transmit Data(Out)
3      Receive Data(In)
4      Request to Send(Out)
5      Clear to Send(In)
6      Data Set Ready(In)
7      Signal Ground
8      Carrier Detect(In)
14     Fault(Out)
20     Data Terminal Ready(Out)
25     +5V (Out)
----------------------------------------
Flow Control: 20             XON/XOFF
Note:
```

```
C.ITOH
CI 5000 Printer
Port:  RS-232(DB-25)         DB25S
Gender:  Female              PinConfig: P05

Pin    Function(Direction)
----------------------------------------
1      Protective Ground
2      Transmit Data(Out)
3      Receive Data(In)
4      Request to Send(Out)
5      Clear to Send(In)
6      Data Set Ready(In)
7      Signal Ground
8      Data Carrier Detect(In)
11     Busy(Out)
20     Data Terminal Ready(Out)
23     +12V(Out)
25     +5V (Out)
----------------------------------------
Flow Control: 11             XON/XOFF
Note:  This printer has 3 ports-parallel,
RS-232 & RS-423 The above is the RS-232
port
```

```
C.ITOH
CI-400, CI-800 Printers
Port:  RS-232                DB25S
Gender:  Female              PinConfig: P05

Pin    Function(Direction)
----------------------------------------
1      Protective Ground
2      Transmit Data(Out)
3      Receive Data(In)
4      Request to Send(Out)
5      Clear to Send(In)
6      Data Set Ready(In)
7      Signal Ground
11     Busy(Out)
20     Data Terminal Ready(Out)
25     +5V (Out)
----------------------------------------
Flow Control: 11             XON/XOFF
ACK/NAK
Note:  Leads 5/6 should be on for the
printer to operate
```

```
C.ITOH
LIPS 10+ Laser Printer
Port:  RS-232                DB25S
Gender:  Female              PinConfig: P03

Pin    Function(Direction)
----------------------------------------
1      Protective Ground
2      Transmit Data(Out)
3      Receive Data(In)
4      Request to Send(Out)
5      Clear to Send(In)
6      Data Set Ready(In)
7      Signal Ground
8      Rec.Line Signal Detect(In)
20     Data Terminal Ready(Out)
----------------------------------------
Flow Control: 20             XON/XOFF
ACK/NAK
Note:
```

```
C.ITOH Electronics
C-815 Printer
Port:  RS-232                DB25S
Gender:  Female              PinConfig: P03

Pin    Function(Direction)
----------------------------------------
1      Chassis Ground
2      Transmit Data(Out)
3      Receive Data(In)
4      Request to Send(Out)
5      Clear to Send(In)
7      Signal Ground
11     Reverse Channel(Out)
20     Data Terminal Ready(Out)
----------------------------------------
Flow Control: 20,11    XON/XOFF
Note:  Lead 4 is always high. Lead 5 is
monitored for attached computer's state
```

```
DEC
LA34 Printer
Port:  RS-232                DB25S
Gender:  Female              PinConfig: P03

Pin    Function(Direction)
----------------------------------------
1      Protective Ground
2      Transmit Data(Out)
3      Receive Data(In)
4      Request to Send(Out)
5      Clear to Send(In)
6      Data Set Ready(In)
7      Signal Ground
8      Data Carrier Detect(In)
20     Data Terminal Ready(Out)
----------------------------------------
Flow Control: 20             XON/XOFF
Note:
```

```
DH Print
4000 Document/Ticket Printer
Port: RS-232              DB25S
Gender: Female            PinConfig: P09

Pin   Function(Direction)
--------------------------------------------
3        Receive Data(In)
4        Request to Send(Out)
7        Signal Ground
20       Data Terminal Ready(Out)
--------------------------------------------
Flow Control: 4
Note:
```

```
DH Print
4411 Journal Validate Printer
Port: RS-232              DB25S
Gender: Female            PinConfig: P09

Pin   Function(Direction)
--------------------------------------------
1        Chassis Ground
2        Transmit Data(Out)
3        Receive Data(In)
4        Request to Send(Out)
7        Signal Ground
20       Data Terminal Ready(Out)
--------------------------------------------
Flow Control: 4
Note: Insure that the polarity of lead 4
is high for the normal print conditions,
& off for busy
```

```
Eaton Corporation
4130 Receipt Cutter Printer
Port: RS-232              DB25S
Gender: Female            PinConfig: P09

Pin   Function(Direction)
--------------------------------------------
2        Transmit Data(Out)
3        Receive Data(In)
4        Request to Send(Out)
7        Signal Ground
20       Data Terminal Ready(Out)
--------------------------------------------
Flow Control: 4
Note: Insure lead 4 is optioned for
proper polarity, high when good printer
condition, low when busy
```

```
Epson America
2000/4000/4500 Action Printers w/8143
interface
Port: RS-232              DB25S
Gender: Female            PinConfig: P11

Pin   Function(Direction)
--------------------------------------------
1        Frame Ground
2        Transmit Data(Out)
3        Receive Data(In)
7        Signal Ground
20       Data Terminal Ready(Out)
--------------------------------------------
Flow Control: 20          XON/XOFF
Note:
```

```
Epson America
8143 Serial Interface Board
Port: RS-232              DB25S
Gender: Female            PinConfig: P11

Pin   Function(Direction)
--------------------------------------------
1        Frame Ground
2        Transmit Data(Out)
3        Receive Data(In)
7        Signal Ground
20       Data Terminal Ready(Out)
--------------------------------------------
Flow Control: 20          XON/XOFF
Note:
```

```
Epson America
ActionPrinters L-750, L-1000, Apex 80
Port: RS-232 Optional Int.DB25S
Gender: Female            PinConfig: P07

Pin   Function(Direction)
--------------------------------------------
1        Chassis Ground
2        Transmit Data(Out)
3        Receive Data(In)
6        Data Set Ready(In)
7        Signal Ground
8        Data Carrier Detect(In)
11       Reverse Channel(Out)
20       Data Terminal Ready(Out)
--------------------------------------------
Flow Control: 11,20       XON/XOFF
Note:
```

```
Epson America
Apex T-1000 Printer w/8143 interface
Port: RS-232              DB25S
Gender: Female            PinConfig: P11

Pin   Function(Direction)
--------------------------------------------
1        Frame Ground
2        Transmit Data(Out)
3        Receive Data(In)
7        Signal Ground
20       Data Terminal Ready(Out)
--------------------------------------------
Flow Control: 20          XON/XOFF
Note:
```

```
Epson America
DFX-5000 Printer
Port: RS-232              DB25S
Gender: Female            PinConfig: P11

Pin   Function(Direction)
--------------------------------------------
1        Frame Ground
2        Transmit Data(Out)
3        Receive Data(In)
7        Signal Ground
11       Data Terminal Ready(Out)
20       Data Terminal Ready(Out)
--------------------------------------------
Flow Control: 20,11       XON/XOFF
Note:
```

```
Epson America
EPL-6000 Printer
Port: RS-232              DB25S
Gender: Female            PinConfig: P03

Pin   Function(Direction)
----------------------------------------
1     Frame Ground
2     Transmit Data(Out)
3     Receive Data(In)
4     Request to Send(Out)
5     Clear to Send(In)
6     Data Set Ready(In)
7     Signal Ground
11    Reverse Channel(Out)
20    Data Terminal Ready(Out)
25    +5V (Out)
----------------------------------------
Flow Control: 20,11       XON/XOFF
Note: This port can also be optioned for
RS-422 signals
```

```
Epson
EX-800/1000 Printer
Port: RS-232(DIN)         DIN(6)
Gender: Female            PinConfig: P19

Pin   Function(Direction)
----------------------------------------
6     Protective Ground
5     Signal Ground
1     Transmitted Data(out)
3     Received Data(in)
2     Data Terminal Ready(out)
4     Data Set Ready(in)
----------------------------------------
Flow Control: 2
Note:
```

```
Epson America
EX-800/1000/1050/2400 printers w/8143
interface
Port: RS-232              DB25S
Gender: Female            PinConfig: P11

Pin   Function(Direction)
----------------------------------------
1     Frame Ground
2     Transmit Data(Out)
3     Receive Data(In)
7     Signal Ground
20    Data Terminal Ready(Out)
----------------------------------------
Flow Control: 20          XON/XOFF
Note:
```

```
Epson America
FX-100/100+/185/286 Printer
Port: RS-232 Optional Int.DB25S
Gender: Female            PinConfig: P07

Pin   Function(Direction)
----------------------------------------
1     Chassis Ground
2     Transmit Data(Out)
3     Receive Data(In)
6     Data Set Ready(In)
7     Signal Ground
8     Data Carrier Detect(In)
11    Reverse Channel(Out)
20    Data Terminal Ready(Out)
----------------------------------------
Flow Control: 11,20       XON/XOFF
Note:
```

```
Epson America
FX-850/1050 Printer w/8143 interface
Port: RS-232              DB25S
Gender: Female            PinConfig: P11

Pin   Function(Direction)
----------------------------------------
1     Frame Ground
2     Transmit Data(Out)
3     Receive Data(In)
7     Signal Ground
20    Data Terminal Ready(Out)
----------------------------------------
Flow Control: 20          XON/XOFF
Note:
```

```
Epson America
FX-80/80+/85/86e Printers
Port: RS-232 Optional Int.DB25S
Gender: Female            PinConfig: P07

Pin   Function(Direction)
----------------------------------------
1     Chassis Ground
2     Transmit Data(Out)
3     Receive Data(In)
6     Data Set Ready(In)
7     Signal Ground
8     Data Carrier Detect(In)
11    Reverse Channel(Out)
20    Data Terminal Ready(Out)
----------------------------------------
Flow Control: 11,20       XON/XOFF
Note:
```

```
Epson America
LQ-1000/1010 w/8143 interface
Port: RS-232              DB25S
Gender: Female            PinConfig: P11

Pin   Function(Direction)
-------------------------------------------
1        Frame Ground
2        Transmit Data(Out)
3        Receive Data(In)
7        Signal Ground
20       Data Terminal Ready(Out)
-------------------------------------------
Flow Control: 20          XON/XOFF
Note:  The printer comes with a standard
6 Mini-DIN serial port.  This port is an
optional board
```

```
Epson America
LQ-1050/1500/2500, JX-80 Printers
Port: RS-232 Optional Int.DB25S
Gender: Female            PinConfig: P07

Pin   Function(Direction)
-------------------------------------------
1        Chassis Ground
2        Transmit Data(Out)
3        Receive Data(In)
6        Data Set Ready(In)
7        Signal Ground
8        Data Carrier Detect(In)
11       Reverse Channel(Out)
20       Data Terminal Ready(Out)
-------------------------------------------
Flow Control: 11,20       XON/XOFF
Note:
```

```
Epson America
LQ-2550 Printer
Port: RS-232              DB25S
Gender: Female            PinConfig: P11

Pin   Function(Direction)
-------------------------------------------
1        Frame Ground
2        Transmit Data(Out)
3        Receive Data(In)
7        Signal Ground
11       Reverse Channel(Out)
20       Data Terminal Ready(Out)
-------------------------------------------
Flow Control: 20, 11      XON/XOFF
Note:
```

```
Epson America
LQ-500/510/800/860 Printers w/8143
Interface Board
Port: RS-232              DB25S
Gender: Female            PinConfig: P11

Pin   Function(Direction)
-------------------------------------------
1        Frame Ground
2        Transmit Data(Out)
3        Receive Data(In)
7        Signal Ground
11       Reverse Channel(Out)
20       Data Terminal Ready(Out)
-------------------------------------------
Flow Control: 20,11       XON/XOFF
Note:
```

```
Epson America
LQ-850/950 Printers
Port: RS-232 Optional Int.DB25S
Gender: Female            PinConfig: P07

Pin   Function(Direction)
-------------------------------------------
1        Chassis Ground
2        Transmit Data(Out)
3        Receive Data(In)
6        Data Set Ready(In)
7        Signal Ground
8        Data Carrier Detect(In)
11       Reverse Channel(Out)
20       Data Terminal Ready(Out)
-------------------------------------------
Flow Control: 11,20       XON/XOFF
Note:
```

```
Epson
LQ-800/850/950/1000/1050/2500  Printer
Port: RS-232(DIN)         DIN(6)
Gender: Female            PinConfig: P19

Pin   Function(Direction)
-------------------------------------------
6        Protective Ground
5        Signal Ground
1        Transmitted Data(out)
3        Received Data(in)
2        Data Terminal Ready(out)
4        Data Set Ready(in)
-------------------------------------------
Flow Control: 2   XON/XOFF
Note:
```

```
Epson America
LX-80/86, LX-800/810, Printers
Port: RS-232 Optional Int.DB25S
Gender: Female              PinConfig: P07

Pin   Function(Direction)
-------------------------------------------
1       Chassis Ground
2       Transmit Data(Out)
3       Receive Data(In)
6       Data Set Ready(In)
7       Signal Ground
8       Data Carrier Detect(In)
11      Reverse Channel(Out)
20      Data Terminal Ready(Out)
-------------------------------------------
Flow Control: 11,20        XON/XOFF
Note:
```

```
Epson America
MX-100 TYPE II, TYPE III Printers
Port: RS-232 Optional Int.DB25S
Gender: Female              PinConfig: P07

Pin   Function(Direction)
-------------------------------------------
1       Chassis Ground
2       Transmit Data(Out)
3       Receive Data(In)
6       Data Set Ready(In)
7       Signal Ground
8       Data Carrier Detect(In)
11      Reverse Channel(Out)
20      Data Terminal Ready(Out)
-------------------------------------------
Flow Control: 11,20        XON/XOFF
Note:
```

```
Epson America
MX-80/80F/T TYPEs I/III Printers
Port: RS-232 Optional Int.DB25S
Gender: Female              PinConfig: P07

Pin   Function(Direction)
-------------------------------------------
1       Chassis Ground
2       Transmit Data(Out)
3       Receive Data(In)
6       Data Set Ready(In)
7       Signal Ground
8       Data Carrier Detect(In)
11      Reverse Channel(Out)
20      Data Terminal Ready(Out)
-------------------------------------------
Flow Control: 11,20        XON/XOFF
Note:
```

```
Epson America
RX-100/100+/286 Printers
Port: RS-232 Optional Int.DB25S
Gender: Female              PinConfig: P07

Pin   Function(Direction)
-------------------------------------------
1       Chassis Ground
2       Transmit Data(Out)
3       Receive Data(In)
6       Data Set Ready(In)
7       Signal Ground
8       Data Carrier Detect(In)
11      Reverse Channel(Out)
20      Data Terminal Ready(Out)
-------------------------------------------
Flow Control: 11,20        XON/XOFF
Note:
```

```
Epson America
RX-80, 80F/T, 80F/T+ Printers
Port: RS-232 Optional Int.DB25S
Gender: Female              PinConfig: P07

Pin   Function(Direction)
-------------------------------------------
1       Chassis Ground
2       Transmit Data(Out)
3       Receive Data(In)
6       Data Set Ready(In)
7       Signal Ground
8       Data Carrier Detect(In)
11      Reverse Channel(Out)
20      Data Terminal Ready(Out)
-------------------------------------------
Flow Control: 11,20        XON/XOFF
Note:
```

```
Epson America
SQ-2000 Printer
Port: RS-232 Optional Int.DB25S
Gender: Female              PinConfig: P07

Pin   Function(Direction)
-------------------------------------------
1       Chassis Ground
2       Transmit Data(Out)
3       Receive Data(In)
6       Data Set Ready(In)
7       Signal Ground
8       Data Carrier Detect(In)
11      Reverse Channel(Out)
20      Data Terminal Ready(Out)
-------------------------------------------
Flow Control: 11,20        XON/XOFF
Note:
```

```
Epson                              Florida Digital
SQ-2500 Printer                    130, 3000, 6000 Printers
Port:  Serial(DIN)      DIN(6)     Port:  Serial           DB25S
Gender: Female    PinConfig: P19   Gender: Female    PinConfig: P03

Pin  Function(Direction)          Pin  Function(Direction)
-------------------------------   -------------------------------
6    Protective Ground            1    Frame Ground
5    Signal Ground                2    Transmit Data(Out)
1    Transmitted Data(out)        3    Receive Data(In)
3    Received Data(in)            4    Request to Send(Out)
-------------------------------   5    Clear to Send(In)
                                  6    Data Set Ready(In)
Flow Control:   XON/XOFF          7    Signal Ground
Note:                             11   BUSY(Out)
                                  20   Data Terminal Ready(Out)
                                  -------------------------------
                                  Flow Control: 20,11    XON/XOFF
                                  ACK/NAK
                                  Note:  Lead 20 must be optioned(off) to
                                  enable hardware flow control with lead
                                  20.
```

```
Fortis                             Fortis Information Systems
DH-45 Printer                      DM-5/20/40  Printer
Port:  Serial(25-pin)   DB25S      Port:  Serial-DIN 6     DIN(6)
Gender: Female    PinConfig: P03   Gender: Female    PinConfig: P19

Pin  Function(Direction)          Pin  Function(Direction)
-------------------------------   -------------------------------
1    Frame Ground                 6    Protective Ground
2    Transmit Data(Out)           5    Signal Ground
3    Receive Data(In)             1    Transmitted Data(out)
4    Request to Send(Out)         3    Received Data(in)
5    Clear to Send(In)            -------------------------------
6    Data Set Ready(In)
7    Signal Ground                Flow Control:   XON/XOFF
8    Carrier Detect(In)           Note:
20   Data Terminal Ready(Out)
-------------------------------
Flow Control: 20,11    XON/XOFF
Note: Lead 11 is used as flow control,
like lead 20, but it is reversed
polarity(Low when busy)
```

```
Fortis Information Systems         Fortis Information Systems
DM-1310DM-1310A, 2010-2015 Printers DM-2210/2215/3215 Printer
Port:  Serial-DIN 6     DIN(6)     Port:  Serial-DIN 6     DIN(6)
Gender: Female    PinConfig: P19   Gender: Female    PinConfig: P19

Pin  Function(Direction)          Pin  Function(Direction)
-------------------------------   -------------------------------
6    Protective Ground            6    Protective Ground
5    Signal Ground                5    Signal Ground
1    Transmitted Data(out)        1    Transmitted Data(out)
3    Received Data(in)            3    Received Data(in)
-------------------------------   -------------------------------
Flow Control:   XON/XOFF          Flow Control:   XON/XOFF
Note:                             Note:
```

```
Fortis Information Systems
DP-600P/600S/600W Printer
Port:  Serial-DIN 6        DIN(6)
Gender:  Female            PinConfig: P19

Pin   Function(Direction)
-------------------------------------
6     Protective Ground
5     Signal Ground
1     Transmitted Data(out)
3     Received Data(in)
-------------------------------------
Flow Control:    XON/XOFF
Note:
```

```
Fortis Information Systems
DQ-4015/4110, 4210/4215 Printers
Port:  Serial-DIN 6        DIN(6)
Gender:  Female            PinConfig: P19

Pin   Function(Direction)
-------------------------------------
6     Protective Ground
5     Signal Ground
1     Transmitted Data(out)
3     Received Data(in)
-------------------------------------
Flow Control:    XON/XOFF
Note:
```

```
Fortis
DX-15,DX-15XL,DX-21,DX-25, DX-41 Printers
Port:  Serial(25-pin)      DB25S
Gender:  Female            PinConfig: P03

Pin   Function(Direction)
-------------------------------------
1     Frame Ground
2     Transmit Data(Out)
3     Receive Data(In)
4     Request to Send(Out)
5     Clear to Send(In)
6     Data Set Ready(In)
7     Signal Ground
8     Carrier Detect(In)
20    Data Terminal Ready(Out)
-------------------------------------
Flow Control: 20,11        XON/XOFF
Note:  Lead 11 is used as flow control,
like lead 20, but it is reversed
polarity(Low when busy)
```

```
Fortis
HR-1,HR-15/15XL,HR-20,HR-25,HR-35,HR-40
Printers
Port:  Serial(25-pin)      DB25S
Gender:  Female            PinConfig: P03

Pin   Function(Direction)
-------------------------------------
1     Frame Ground
2     Transmit Data(Out)
3     Receive Data(In)
4     Request to Send(Out)
5     Clear to Send(In)
6     Data Set Ready(In)
7     Signal Ground
8     Carrier Detect(In)
20    Data Terminal Ready(Out)
-------------------------------------
Flow Control: 20,11        XON/XOFF
Note:  Lead 11 is used as flow control,
like lead 20, but it is reversed
polarity(Low when busy)
```

```
Fortis
TWIN 5, TWIN 6 Printers
Port:  Serial(25-pin)      DB25S
Gender:  Female            PinConfig: P03

Pin   Function(Direction)
-------------------------------------
1     Frame Ground
2     Transmit Data(Out)
3     Receive Data(In)
4     Request to Send(Out)
5     Clear to Send(In)
6     Data Set Ready(In)
7     Signal Ground
8     Carrier Detect(In)
20    Data Terminal Ready(Out)
-------------------------------------
Flow Control: 20,11        XON/XOFF
Note:  Lead 11 is used as flow control,
like lead 20, but it is reversed
polarity(Low when busy)
```

```
Genicom Corporation
3410XLS, 3410XLQ, Printers
Port:  RS-232              DB25S
Gender:  Female            PinConfig: P03

Pin   Function(Direction)
-------------------------------------
1     Protective Ground
2     Transmit Data(Out)
3     Receive Data(In)
4     Request to Send(Out)
5     Clear to Send(In)
6     Data Set Ready(In)
7     Signal Ground
9     +V  (Out)
10    -V  (Out)
19    Secondary Req.to Send(Out)
20    Data Terminal Ready(Out)
-------------------------------------
Flow Control: 20,4,19      XON/XOFF
Note:  Lead 20 can be optioned for
different indications
```

```
Genicom                                 Genicom Corporation
5010 Printer                            1040 Printer
Port: RS-232          DB25S             Port: RS-232          DB25S
Gender: Female        PinConfig: P03    Gender: Female        PinConfig: P03

Pin  Function(Direction)                Pin  Function(Direction)
-----------------------------------     -----------------------------------
1    Protective Ground                  1    Protective Ground
2    Transmit Data(Out)                 2    Transmit Data(Out)
3    Receive Data(In)                   3    Receive Data(In)
4    Request to Send(Out)               4    Request to Send(Out)
5    Clear to Send(In)                  5    Clear to Send(In)
7    Signal Ground                      6    Data Set Ready(In)
11   Secondary Req.to Send(Out)         7    SGR
19   Secondary Req.to Send(Out)         8    Data Carrier Detect(In)
20   Data Terminal Ready(Out)           11   Secondary Req.to Send(Out)
-----------------------------------     14   Secondary Req.to Send(Out)
Flow Control: 20,4,11,19  XON/XOFF      20   Data Terminal Ready(Out)
ACK/NAK                                 -----------------------------------
Note: Serial port is mounted on the    Flow Control: 20          XON/XOFF
personality cartridge                   Note: Leads 11 & 14 go high when printer
                                        is busy, while lead 20 goes low when
                                        printer is busy
```

```
Genicom Corporation                     Genicom Corporation
2030 Printer                            3210 Printer
Port: Serial          DB25P             Port: RS-232          DB25P
Gender: Male          PinConfig: C01    Gender: Male          PinConfig: P08

Pin  Function(Direction)                Pin  Function(Direction)
-----------------------------------     -----------------------------------
1    Protective Ground                  1    Chassis Ground
2    Transmit Data(Out)                 2    Transmit Data(Out)
3    Receive Data(In)                   3    Receive Data(In)
4    Request to Send(Out)               4    Request to Send(Out)
5    Clear to Send(In)                  5    Clear to Send(In)
6    Data Set Ready(In)                 7    Signal Ground
7    Signal Ground                      20   Data Terminal Ready(Out)
8    Data Carrier Detect(In)            -----------------------------------
9    +V  (Out)                          Flow Control: 20,4        XON/XOFF
10   -V  (Out)                          Note: 20 & 4 behave the same. Lead 5
20   Data Terminal Ready(Out)           enables use of XON/XOFF(Must be on)
22   Ring Indicator(In)
-----------------------------------
Flow Control: 5 & 6       XON/XOFF
Note:
```

```
Genicom Corporation                     Genicom Corporation
3310 Color Printer                      3310 Color Printer
Port: Serial-Lead 20 busy DB25S         Port: Serial-Lead 19 busy DB25S
Gender: Female        PinConfig: P03    Gender: Female        PinConfig: P01

Pin  Function(Direction)                Pin  Function(Direction)
-----------------------------------     -----------------------------------
1    Protective Ground                  1    Protective Ground
2    Transmit Data(Out)                 2    Transmit Data(Out)
3    Receive Data(In)                   3    Receive Data(In)
4    Request to Send(Out)               4    Request to Send(Out)
5    Clear to Send(In)                  5    Clear to Send(In)
6    Data Set Ready(In)                 6    Data Set Ready(In)
7    Signal Ground                      7    Signal Ground
9    +V  (Out)                          9    +V  (Out)
10   -V  (Out)                          10   -V  (Out)
19   Secondary Req.to Send(Out)         19   Secondary Req.to Send(Out)
20   Data Terminal Ready(Out)           20   Data Terminal Ready(Out)
-----------------------------------     -----------------------------------
Flow Control: 20,19,4     XON/XOFF      Flow Control: 19,20,4     XON/XOFF
Note: Options above set to use lead 20  Note: Options above set to use lead 19
as flow control                         as flow control
```

```
Genicom Corporation
3310 Color Printer
Port:  Serial-Lead 4 busy  DB25S
Gender:  Female              PinConfig: P09

Pin    Function(Direction)
---------------------------------------------
1      Protective Ground
2      Transmit Data(Out)
3      Receive Data(In)
4      Request to Send(Out)
5      Clear to Send(In)
6      Data Set Ready(In)
7      Signal Ground
9      +V  (Out)
10     -V  (Out)
19     Secondary Req.to Send(Out)
20     Data Terminal Ready(Out)
---------------------------------------------
Flow Control: 4,19,20     XON/XOFF
Note:  Options above set to use lead 4
as flow control
```

```
Genicom Corporation
3800 Printer
Port:  Serial-Lead 20 busy  DB25S
Gender:  Female              PinConfig: P03

Pin    Function(Direction)
---------------------------------------------
1      Protective Ground
2      Transmit Data(Out)
3      Receive Data(In)
4      Request to Send(Out)
5      Clear to Send(In)
6      Data Set Ready(In)
7      Signal Ground
9      +V  (Out)
10     -V  (Out)
11     Secondary Req.to Send(Out)
13     Secondary Cl'r to Send(In)
19     Secondary Req.to Send(Out)
20     Data Terminal Ready(Out)
25     Secondary Req.to Send(Out)
---------------------------------------------
Flow Control: 20,19,4,25   XON/XOFF
ACK/NAK
Note:  Options above set to use lead 20
as flow control
```

```
Genicom Corporation
3800 Printer
Port:  Serial-Lead 19 busy  DB25S
Gender:  Female              PinConfig: P01

Pin    Function(Direction)
---------------------------------------------
1      Protective Ground
2      Transmit Data(Out)
3      Receive Data(In)
4      Request to Send(Out)
5      Clear to Send(In)
6      Data Set Ready(In)
7      Signal Ground
9      +V  (Out)
10     -V  (Out)
11     Secondary Req.to Send(Out)
13     Secondary Cl'r to Send(In)
19     Secondary Req.to Send(Out)
20     Data Terminal Ready(Out)
25     Secondary Req.to Send(Out)
---------------------------------------------
Flow Control: 19,20,4,25   XON/XOFF
ACK/NAK
Note:  Options above set to use lead 19
as flow control
```

```
Genicom Corporation
3800 Printer
Port:  Serial-Lead 4 busy  DB25S
Gender:  Female              PinConfig: P09

Pin    Function(Direction)
---------------------------------------------
1      Protective Ground
2      Transmit Data(Out)
3      Receive Data(In)
4      Request to Send(Out)
5      Clear to Send(In)
6      Data Set Ready(In)
7      Signal Ground
9      +V  (Out)
10     -V  (Out)
13     Secondary Cl'r to Send(In)
19     Secondary Req.to Send(Out)
20     Data Terminal Ready(Out)
25     Secondary Req.to Send(Out)
---------------------------------------------
Flow Control: 4,19,20,25   XON/XOFF
ACK/NAK
Note:  Options above set to use lead 4
as flow control
```

```
Genicom Corporation
4410 Printer
Port:  Serial-Lead 11 busy DB25S
Gender: Female              PinConfig: P05

Pin   Function(Direction)
------------------------------------------
1        Protective Ground
2        Transmit Data(Out)
3        Receive Data(In)
4        Request to Send(Out)
5        Clear to Send(In)
6        Data Set Ready(In)
7        Signal Ground
11       Secondary Req.to Send(Out)
19       Secondary Req.to Send(Out)
20       Data Terminal Ready(Out)
------------------------------------------
Flow Control: 11,20,4,19   XON/XOFF
ACK/NAK
Note:  Options above set to use lead 11
as flow control
```

```
Genicom Corporation
4410, 4440 Printers
Port:  Serial-Lead 20 busy DB25S
Gender: Female              PinConfig: P03

Pin   Function(Direction)
------------------------------------------
1        Protective Ground
2        Transmit Data(Out)
3        Receive Data(In)
4        Request to Send(Out)
5        Clear to Send(In)
6        Data Set Ready(In)
7        Signal Ground
11       Secondary Req.to Send(Out)
19       Secondary Req.to Send(Out)
20       Data Terminal Ready(Out)
------------------------------------------
Flow Control: 20,19,4,11   XON/XOFF
ACK/NAK
Note:  Options above set to use lead
20,4,11, or 19  as flow control leads
```

```
Genicom Corporation
4410, 4440 Printers
Port:  Serial-Lead 19 busy DB25S
Gender: Female              PinConfig: P01

Pin   Function(Direction)
------------------------------------------
1        Protective Ground
2        Transmit Data(Out)
3        Receive Data(In)
4        Request to Send(Out)
5        Clear to Send(In)
6        Data Set Ready(In)
7        Signal Ground
11       Secondary Req.to Send(Out)
19       Secondary Req.to Send(Out)
20       Data Terminal Ready(Out)
------------------------------------------
Flow Control: 19,20,4,11   XON/XOFF
ACK/NAK
Note:  Options above set to use lead 19
as flow control
```

```
Genicom Corporation
4410, 4440 Printers
Port:  Serial-Lead 4 busy  DB25S
Gender: Female              PinConfig: P09

Pin   Function(Direction)
------------------------------------------
1        Protective Ground
2        Transmit Data(Out)
3        Receive Data(In)
4        Request to Send(Out)
5        Clear to Send(In)
6        Data Set Ready(In)
7        Signal Ground
11       Secondary Req.to Send(Out)
19       Secondary Req.to Send(Out)
20       Data Terminal Ready(Out)
------------------------------------------
Flow Control: 4,19,20,11   XON/XOFF
ACK/NAK
Note:  Options above set to use lead 4
as flow control
```

```
Genicom Corporation
4440 Printer
Port:  Serial-Lead 11 busy DB25S
Gender: Female              PinConfig: P05

Pin   Function(Direction)
------------------------------------------
1        Protective Ground
2        Transmit Data(Out)
3        Receive Data(In)
4        Request to Send(Out)
5        Clear to Send(In)
6        Data Set Ready(In)
7        Signal Ground
11       Secondary Req.to Send(Out)
19       Secondary Req.to Send(Out)
20       Data Terminal Ready(Out)
------------------------------------------
Flow Control: 11,19,4,20   XON/XOFF
Note:  Options above set to use lead 11
as flow control
```

```
Hewlett Packard
7595/7596B Plotters
Port:  RS-232              DB25S
Gender: Female              PinConfig: P03

Pin   Function(Direction)
------------------------------------------
1        Frame Ground
2        Transmit Data(Out)
3        Receive Data(In)
4        Request to Send(Out)
5        Clear to Send(In)
6        Data Set Ready(In)
7        Signal Ground
8        Data Carrier Detect(In)
20       Data Terminal Ready(Out)
23       DSRS(In)
------------------------------------------
Flow Control: 20              XON/XOFF
Note:
```

```
Hewlett Packard
DraftMaster RX/SX Plotters
Port: RS-232            DB25S
Gender: Female          PinConfig: P03

Pin   Function(Direction)
--------------------------------------------
1     Frame Ground
2     Transmit Data(Out)
3     Receive Data(In)
4     Request to Send(Out)
5     Clear to Send(In)
6     Data Set Ready(In)
7     Signal Ground
8     Data Carrier Detect(In)
17    Transmit Clock(In)
20    Data Terminal Ready(Out)
--------------------------------------------
Flow Control: 20        XON/XOFF
Note:
```

```
Hewlett Packard
DraftPro DXL/EXL Plotters
Port: RS-232            DB25S
Gender: Female          PinConfig: P03

Pin   Function(Direction)
--------------------------------------------
1     Frame Ground
2     Transmit Data(Out)
3     Receive Data(In)
4     Request to Send(Out)
5     Clear to Send(In)
6     Data Set Ready(In)
7     Signal Ground
8     Data Carrier Detect(In)
14    Supervisory Trans.Data(Out)
16    Supervisory Rec. Data(In)
20    Data Terminal Ready(Out)
--------------------------------------------
Flow Control: 20        XON/XOFF
Note:
```

```
Hewlett-Packard
7575A/7576A Plotters
Port: RS-232            DB25S
Gender: Female          PinConfig: P03

Pin   Function(Direction)
--------------------------------------------
1     Protective Ground
2     Transmit Data(Out)
3     Receive Data(In)
4     Request to Send(Out)
5     Clear to Send(In)
6     Data Set Ready(In)
7     Signal Ground
8     Rec.Line Signal Detect(In)
14    Supervisory Trans.Data(Out)
16    Supervisory Rec. Data(In)
20    Data Terminal Ready(Out)
--------------------------------------------
Flow Control: 20        XON/XOFF
Note:
```

```
Hewlett-Packard
DeskJet Printer
Port: RS-232            DB25S
Gender: Female          PinConfig: P11

Pin   Function(Direction)
--------------------------------------------
1     Protective Ground
2     Transmit Data(Out)
3     Receive Data(In)
7     Signal Ground
20    Data Terminal Ready(Out)
--------------------------------------------
Flow Control: 20        XON/XOFF
Note:
```

```
Hewlett-Packard
HP 7550A Plotter
Port: Computer/Modem    DB25P
Gender: Male            PinConfig: P08

Pin   Function(Direction)
--------------------------------------------
1     Protective Ground
2     Transmit Data(Out)
3     Receive Data(In)
4     Request to Send(Out)
5     Clear to Send(In)
6     Data Set Ready(In)
7     Signal Ground
20    Data Terminal Ready(Out)
--------------------------------------------
Flow Control: 20        XON/XOFF
Note: Leads 5 & 6 should be included in
your cable for completeness only.
```

```
Hewlett-Packard
LaserJet II/IID Printers
Port: RS-232            DB25S
Gender: Female          PinConfig: P11

Pin   Function(Direction)
--------------------------------------------
1     Chassis Ground
2     Transmit Data(Out)
3     Receive Data(In)
7     Signal Ground
20    Data Terminal Ready(Out)
--------------------------------------------
Flow Control: 20        XON/XOFF
Note:
```

```
Hewlett-Packard
LaserJet IIP printer
Port:  Serial              DB25S
Gender:  Female            PinConfig: P08

Pin   Function(Direction)
---------------------------------------
1        Protective Ground
2        Transmit Data(Out)
3        Receive Data(In)
4        Request to Send(Out)
7        Signal Ground
20       Data Terminal Ready(Out)
---------------------------------------
Flow Control: 20           XON/XOFF
Note:  This port can be optioned for RS-
422 operation
```

```
Hewlett-Packard
LaserJet+(Option 300)
Port:  Serial              DB25S
Gender:  Female            PinConfig: P11

Pin   Function(Direction)
---------------------------------------
1        Chassis Ground
2        Transmit Data(Out)
3        Receive Data(In)
7        Signal Ground
20       Data Terminal Ready(Out)
---------------------------------------
Flow Control: 20           XON/XOFF
Note:  This port may be optioned for RS-
422 operation
```

```
Hewlett-Packard
PaintJet, QuietJet, ThinkJet  Printers
Port:  RS-232              DB25S
Gender:  Female            PinConfig: P11

Pin   Function(Direction)
---------------------------------------
1        Protective Ground
2        Transmit Data(Out)
3        Receive Data(In)
7        Signal Ground
20       Data Terminal Ready(Out)
---------------------------------------
Flow Control: 20           XON/XOFF
Note:
```

```
Hewlett-Packard
RuggedWriter 480 Printer
Port:  RS-232              DB25S
Gender:  Female            PinConfig: P11

Pin   Function(Direction)
---------------------------------------
1        Protective Ground
2        Transmit Data(Out)
3        Receive Data(In)
7        Signal Ground
20       Data Terminal Ready(Out)
---------------------------------------
Flow Control: 20           XON/XOFF
Note:
```

```
Houston Instrument
DMP-29/40/51/52/60 Plotter
Port:  RS-232              DB25P
Gender:  Male              PinConfig: C19

Pin   Function(Direction)
---------------------------------------
7        Signal Ground
2        Transmitted Data(out)
3        Received Data(in)
---------------------------------------
Flow Control:    XON/XOFF
Note:  This entry assumes only leads
2/3/7 are used
```

```
Houston Instrument
DMP-29, 40, 50 Plotters
Port:  RS-232(full control)DB25P
Gender:  Male              PinConfig: P08

Pin   Function(Direction)
---------------------------------------
1        Chassis Ground
2        Transmit Data(Out)
3        Receive Data(In)
4        Request to Send(Out)
5        Clear to Send(In)
7        Signal Ground
14       Receive Data(In)
16       Transmit Data(Out)
20       Data Terminal Ready(Out)
---------------------------------------
Flow Control: 20,4         XON/XOFF
Note:
```

Houston Instrument
DMP-51, 52 MP Plotters
Port: RS-232(full control)DB25P
Gender: Male   PinConfig: P08

Pin   Function(Direction)
----
1   Chassis Ground
2   Transmit Data(Out)
3   Receive Data(In)
4   Request to Send(Out)
7   Signal Ground
20   Data Terminal Ready(Out)

Flow Control: 20,4   XON/XOFF
Note:

Houston Instrument
DMP-60 DL Plotter
Houston Instrument
DMP-60, 60DL Plotters
Port: RS-232(full control)DB25P
Gender: Male   PinConfig: P08

Pin   Function(Direction)
----
1   Chassis Ground
2   Transmit Data(Out)
3   Receive Data(In)
4   Request to Send(Out)
5   Clear to Send(In)
7   Signal Ground
14   Receive Data(In)
16   Transmit Data(Out)
20   Data Terminal Ready(Out)

Flow Control: 20,4   XON/XOFF
Note:

Ithaca Peripherals
PcOS Model 250 Printers
Port: Serial(Optional)   DB25S
Gender: Female   PinConfig: P03

Pin   Function(Direction)
----
1   Protective Ground
2   Transmit Data(Out)
3   Receive Data(In)
4   Request to Send(Out)
6   Data Set Ready(In)
7   Signal Ground
11   Supervisory Trans.Data(Out)
13   Signal Ground
20   Data Terminal Ready(Out)

Flow Control: 20,11   XON/XOFF
Note:

Ithaca Peripherals
PcOS Model 51/52/53 Printers
Port: Option#2(Serial)   DB25S
Gender: Female   PinConfig: P11

Pin   Function(Direction)
----
1   Protective Ground
3   Receive Data(In)
7   Signal Ground
11   Supervisory Trans.Data(Out)
13   Signal Ground
20   Data Terminal Ready(Out)

Flow Control: 20,11
Note: Option#2 does not support
XON/XOFF. If your computer requires
XON/XOFF, obtain Option#1

Ithaca Peripherals
PcOS Model 51/52%3 Printers
Port: Serial(Option#1)   DB25S
Gender: Female   PinConfig: P03

Pin   Function(Direction)
----
1   Protective Ground
2   Transmit Data(Out)
3   Receive Data(In)
4   Request to Send(Out)
6   Data Set Ready(In)
7   Signal Ground
11   Supervisory Trans.Data(Out)
13   Signal Ground
20   Data Terminal Ready(Out)

Flow Control: 20,11   XON/XOFF
Note: Option 1 supports XON/XOFF(above)
Option #2 does not support XON/OFF, but
rather DTR/Busy

Kipp & Zonen
BD 80 & CAD Reporter Printer/Plotters
Port: RS-232   DB25S
Gender: Female   PinConfig: P08

Pin   Function(Direction)
----
1   Protective Ground
2   Transmit Data(Out)
3   Receive Data(In)
4   Request to Send(Out)
5   Clear to Send(In)
6   Data Set Ready(In)
7   Signal Ground
20   Data Terminal Ready(Out)

Flow Control: 20   XON/XOFF
Note:

```
Kokak
Diconix 150 Plus Printer
Port:  RS-232              DB25S
Gender:  Female            PinConfig: P03

Pin    Function(Direction)
-------------------------------------------
1      Frame Ground
2      Transmit Data(Out)
3      Receive Data(In)
4      Request to Send(Out)
5      Clear to Send(In)
6      Data Set Ready(In)
7      Signal Ground
8      Carrier Detect(In)
20     Data Terminal Ready(Out)
-------------------------------------------
Flow Control: 20           XON/XOFF
ACK/NAK
Note:
```

```
Kyocera Unison
F-1000A, F-2000A, 2010/3010 Printers
Port:  RS-232              DB25S
Gender:  Female            PinConfig: P11

Pin    Function(Direction)
-------------------------------------------
1      Protective Ground
2      Transmit Data(Out)
3      Receive Data(In)
7      Signal Ground
20     Data Terminal Ready(Out)
-------------------------------------------
Flow Control: 20           XON/XOFF
ACK/NAK
Note:  The polarity of lead 20 can be
pos. or neg true. Most require positive.
Lead 4 is active "low"
```

```
Kyocera Unison
F-800A, Q-8010 Printers
Port:  RS-232              DB25S
Gender:  Female            PinConfig: P11

Pin    Function(Direction)
-------------------------------------------
1      Protective Ground
2      Transmit Data(Out)
3      Receive Data(In)
7      Signal Ground
20     Data Terminal Ready(Out)
-------------------------------------------
Flow Control: 20           XON/XOFF
ACK/NAK
Note:  The polarity of lead 20 can be
pos. or neg true. Most require positive.
Lead 4 is active "low"
```

```
NCR Corporation
6417 Printer
Port:  RS-232C             DB25S
Gender:  Female            PinConfig: P03

Pin    Function(Direction)
-------------------------------------------
1      Frame Ground
2      Transmit Data(Out)
3      Receive Data(In)
4      Request to Send(Out)
6      Data Set Ready(In)
7      Signal Ground
11     Reverse Channel(Out)
20     Data Terminal Ready(Out)
-------------------------------------------
Flow Control: 20,11        XON/XOFF
Note:
```

```
NCR Corporation
6421 Printer
Port:  RS-232C             DB25S
Gender:  Female            PinConfig: P05

Pin    Function(Direction)
-------------------------------------------
1      Protective Ground
2      Transmit Data(Out)
3      Receive Data(In)
4      Request to Send(Out)
5      Clear to Send(In)
6      Data Set Ready(In)
7      Signal Ground
8      Data Carrier Detect(In)
11     Reverse Channel(Out)
14     Fault(Out)
19     Reverse Channel(Out)
20     Data Terminal Ready(Out)
-------------------------------------------
Flow Control: 11,19,20     XON/XOFF
Note:  Lead 14 is off when a printer
error occurs Leads 11 & 19 are reverse
channel, while 20 is DTR
```

```
NCR Corporation
6424 Printer
Port:  RS-232C             DB25S
Gender:  Female            PinConfig: P03

Pin    Function(Direction)
-------------------------------------------
1      Frame Ground
2      Transmit Data(Out)
3      Receive Data(In)
4      Request to Send(Out)
5      Clear to Send(In)
6      Data Set Ready(In)
7      Signal Ground
8      Data Carrier Detect(In)
11     Reverse Channel(Out)
20     Data Terminal Ready(Out)
-------------------------------------------
Flow Control: 20,11        XON/XOFF
ACK/NAK
Note:
```

```
NCR Corporation                          NCR Corporation
6430 Printer                             6435, 6436-20, 6436-501 Printers
Port: RS-232C          DB25S             Port: RS-232C          DB25S
Gender: Female         PinConfig: P03    Gender: Female         PinConfig: P03

Pin   Function(Direction)                Pin   Function(Direction)
----------------------------------       ----------------------------------
1     Protective Ground                  1     Protective Ground
2     Transmit Data(Out)                 2     Transmit Data(Out)
3     Receive Data(In)                   3     Receive Data(In)
4     Request to Send(Out)               4     Request to Send(Out)
5     Clear to Send(In)                  5     Clear to Send(In)
6     Data Set Ready(In)                 6     Data Set Ready(In)
7     Signal Ground                      7     Signal Ground
8     Data Carrier Detect(In)            8     Data Carrier Detect(In)
11    Secondary Req.to Send(Out)         11    Busy(Out)
15    Transmit Clock(In)                 19    Busy(Out)
17    Receive Clock(In)                  20    Data Terminal Ready(Out)
19    Secondary Req.to Send(Out)         ----------------------------------
20    Data Terminal Ready(Out)           Flow Control: 20,11,19    XON/XOFF
22    Ring Indicator(In)                 Note:  This port can be optioned to be
24    External Transmit Clock(Out)       either RS-422 or RS-232 via dip switches
----------------------------------
Flow Control: 20,11,19    XON/XOFF
Note:  An RS449 port is available! RS449
is either a 37 or 9 pin connector
```

```
NCR Corporation                          NCR Corporation
6444 Printer                             6450 Printer
Port: RS-232C          DB25S             Port: RS-232C          DB25S
Gender: Female         PinConfig: P03    Gender: Female         PinConfig: P03

Pin   Function(Direction)                Pin   Function(Direction)
----------------------------------       ----------------------------------
1     Protective Ground                  1     Protective Ground
2     Transmit Data(Out)                 2     Transmit Data(Out)
3     Receive Data(In)                   3     Receive Data(In)
4     Request to Send(Out)               4     Request to Send(Out)
5     Clear to Send(In)                  5     Clear to Send(In)
6     Data Set Ready(In)                 6     Data Set Ready(In)
7     Signal Ground                      7     Signal Ground
9     +12V(Out)                          11    Secondary Req.to Send(Out)
10    -12V(Out)                          19    Secondary Req.to Send(Out)
11    Secondary Req.to Send(Out)         20    Data Terminal Ready(Out)
19    Secondary Req.to Send(Out)         ----------------------------------
20    Data Terminal Ready(Out)           Flow Control: 20,11,19    XON/XOFF
----------------------------------       ACK/NAK
Flow Control: 20,11,19    XON/XOFF       Note:
ACK/NAK
Note:  Leads 9 & 10 provide power sources
```

```
NEC Corporation                        OCE' Graphics
8815 Spinwriter                        G1022 Plotter
Port: RS-232          DB25S            Port: RS-232          DB25S
Gender: Female        PinConfig: P01   Gender: Female        PinConfig: P08

Pin   Function(Direction)              Pin   Function(Direction)
-----------------------------------    -----------------------------------
2     Transmit Data(Out)               1     Frame Ground
3     Receive Data(In)                 2     Transmit Data(Out)
4     Request to Send(Out)             3     Receive Data(In)
5     Clear to Send(In)                4     Request to Send(Out)
6     Data Set Ready(In)               5     Clear to Send(In)
7     Signal Ground                    6     Data Set Ready(In)
8     Data Carrier Detect(In)          7     Signal Ground
19    Reverse Channel(Out)             14    Supervisory Trans.Data(Out)
20    Data Terminal Ready(Out)         16    Supervisory Rec. Data(In)
                                       17    External Transmit Clock(In)
-----------------------------------    20    Data Terminal Ready(Out)
Flow Control: 19      XON/XOFF         23    Data Rate Select(In)
Note: Leads 5, 6, & 8 must be on for   -----------------------------------
printer operation                      Flow Control: 20      XON/XOFF
                                       ACK/NAK
                                       Note:
```

```
OCE' Graphics                          OCE' Graphics
G1824-C Plotters                       G1824-C Plotter
Port: Port A(DTE)     DB25S            Port: Port B(DCE)     DB25S
Gender: Female        PinConfig: P10   Gender: Female        PinConfig: C14

Pin   Function(Direction)              Pin   Function(Direction)
-----------------------------------    -----------------------------------
1     Protective Ground                1     Protective Ground
2     Transmit Data(Out)               2     Transmit Data(In)
3     Receive Data(In)                 3     Receive Data(Out)
4     Request to Send(Out)             4     Request to Send(In)
5     Clear to Send(In)                5     Clear to Send(Out)
6     Data Set Ready(In)               6     Data Set Ready(Out)
7     Signal Ground                    7     Signal Ground
8     Data Carrier Detect(In)          8     Data Carrier Detect(Out)
20    Data Terminal Ready(Out)         20    Data Terminal Ready(In)
-----------------------------------    -----------------------------------
Flow Control:         XON/XOFF         Flow Control:         XON/XOFF
ACK/NAK                                ACK/NAK
Note:                                  Note:
```

```
OCE' Graphics                          OCE' Graphics
G1824-S, G1830, G1834/35-CR/SR Plotters G1824-S, G1830, G1834/35-CR/SR Plotters
Port: Port A(DTE)     DB25S            Port: Port B(DCE)     DB25S
Gender: Female        PinConfig: P10   Gender: Female        PinConfig: C14

Pin   Function(Direction)              Pin   Function(Direction)
-----------------------------------    -----------------------------------
1     Protective Ground                1     Protective Ground
2     Transmit Data(Out)               2     Transmit Data(In)
3     Receive Data(In)                 3     Receive Data(Out)
4     Request to Send(Out)             4     Request to Send(In)
5     Clear to Send(In)                5     Clear to Send(Out)
6     Data Set Ready(In)               6     Data Set Ready(Out)
7     Signal Ground                    7     Signal Ground
8     Data Carrier Detect(In)          8     Data Carrier Detect(Out)
20    Data Terminal Ready(Out)         20    Data Terminal Ready(In)
-----------------------------------    -----------------------------------
Flow Control:         XON/XOFF         Flow Control:         XON/XOFF
ACK/NAK                                ACK/NAK
Note:                                  Note:
```

```
OCE' Graphics
G1835-S & SR, G1845AC Plotters
Port:  Port A(DTE)          DB25S
Gender:  Female             PinConfig: P10

Pin   Function(Direction)
----------------------------------------
1       Protective Ground
2       Transmit Data(Out)
3       Receive Data(In)
4       Request to Send(Out)
5       Clear to Send(In)
6       Data Set Ready(In)
7       Signal Ground
8       Data Carrier Detect(In)
20      Data Terminal Ready(Out)
----------------------------------------
Flow Control:           XON/XOFF
ACK/NAK
Note:
```

```
OCE' Graphics
G1835-S & SR, G1845C/AC Plotters
Port:  Port B(DCE)          DB25S
Gender:  Female             PinConfig: C14

Pin   Function(Direction)
----------------------------------------
1       Protective Ground
2       Transmit Data(In)
3       Receive Data(Out)
4       Request to Send(In)
5       Clear to Send(Out)
6       Data Set Ready(Out)
7       Signal Ground
8       Data Carrier Detect(Out)
20      Data Terminal Ready(In)
----------------------------------------
Flow Control:           XON/XOFF
ACK/NAK
Note:
```

```
OCE' Graphics
G9844/G9845 Plotter
Port:  Port A(DTE)          DB25S
Gender:  Female             PinConfig: P10

Pin   Function(Direction)
----------------------------------------
1       Protective Ground
2       Transmit Data(Out)
3       Receive Data(In)
4       Request to Send(Out)
5       Clear to Send(In)
6       Data Set Ready(In)
7       Signal Ground
8       Data Carrier Detect(In)
20      Data Terminal Ready(Out)
----------------------------------------
Flow Control:           XON/XOFF
ACK/NAK
Note:
```

```
OCE' Graphics
G9844/G9845 Plotters
Port:  Port B(DCE)          DB25S
Gender:  Female             PinConfig: C14

Pin   Function(Direction)
----------------------------------------
1       Protective Ground
2       Transmit Data(In)
3       Receive Data(Out)
4       Request to Send(In)
5       Clear to Send(Out)
6       Data Set Ready(Out)
7       Signal Ground
8       Data Carrier Detect(Out)
20      Data Terminal Ready(In)
----------------------------------------
Flow Control:           XON/XOFF
ACK/NAK
Note:
```

```
Okidata
MicroLine 172, 182 Turbo Printers
Port:  RS-232(Option)       DB25S
Gender:  Female             PinConfig: P03

Pin   Function(Direction)
----------------------------------------
1       Protective Ground
2       Transmit Data(Out)
3       Receive Data(In)
4       Request to Send(Out)
6       Data Set Ready(In)
7       Signal Ground
11      Supervisory Trans.Data(Out)
20      Data Terminal Ready(Out)
----------------------------------------
Flow Control: 20,11,4       XON/XOFF
Note:
```

```
Okidata
MicroLine 182-I Printer
Port:  RS-232              DB25S
Gender:  Female            PinConfig: P03

Pin   Function(Direction)
----------------------------------------
1       Protective Ground
3       Receive Data(In)
4       Request to Send(Out)
7       Signal Ground
11      Supervisory Trans.Data(Out)
13      Signal Ground
20      Data Terminal Ready(Out)
----------------------------------------
Flow Control: 20,11,4
Note:  Polarity can be optioned along
with the lead that yields the hardware
flow control lead
```

```
Okidata                                    | Okidata
MicroLine 190 Plus Printer                 | Microline 320/321/380 Printers
Port: RS-232            DB25S              | Port: RS-232(Option)   DB25S
Gender: Female          PinConfig: P05     | Gender: Female         PinConfig: P03

Pin   Function(Direction)                  | Pin   Function(Direction)
-------------------------------------      | -------------------------------------
1     Protective Ground                    | 1     Protective Ground
3     Receive Data(In)                     | 2     Transmit Data(Out)
4     Request to Send(Out)                 | 3     Receive Data(In)
5     Clear to Send(In)                    | 4     Request to Send(Out)
6     Data Set Ready(In)                   | 6     Data Set Ready(In)
7     Signal Ground                        | 7     Signal Ground
11    Supervisory Trans.Data(Out)          | 11    Supervisory Trans.Data(Out)
20    Data Terminal Ready(Out)             | 20    Data Terminal Ready(Out)
-------------------------------------      | -------------------------------------
Flow Control: 11                           | Flow Control: 20,11,4    XON/XOFF
Note: This port provided by a Super Sped   | Note:
Serial Board                               |
```

```
Okidata                                    | Okidata
Microline 390/390 Plus Printers            | MicroLine 393 Printer
Port: R2-232            DB25S              | Port: RS-232            DB25S
Gender: Female          PinConfig: P03     | Gender: Female          PinConfig: P03

Pin   Function(Direction)                  | Pin   Function(Direction)
-------------------------------------      | -------------------------------------
1     Protective Ground                    | 1     Protective Ground
2     Transmit Data(Out)                   | 2     Transmit Data(Out)
3     Receive Data(In)                     | 3     Receive Data(In)
4     Request to Send(Out)                 | 4     Request to Send(Out)
6     Data Set Ready(In)                   | 6     Data Set Ready(In)
7     Signal Ground                        | 7     Signal Ground
11    SSD (Out)                            | 11    Supervisory Trans.Data(Out)
20    Data Terminal Ready(Out)             | 20    Data Terminal Ready(Out)
-------------------------------------      | -------------------------------------
Flow Control: 20,4,11    XON/XOFF          | Flow Control: 20        XON/XOFF
Note:                                      | Note:
```

```
Okidata                                    | Okidata
MicroLine 84 Step 2 Printer                | OkiLASER 400/800/820/840 Printers
Port: RS-232            DB25S              | Port: RS-232            DB25S
Gender: Female          PinConfig: P03     | Gender: Female          PinConfig: P03

Pin   Function(Direction)                  | Pin   Function(Direction)
-------------------------------------      | -------------------------------------
1     Protective Ground                    | 1     Protective Ground
2     Transmit Data(Out)                   | 2     Transmit Data(Out)
3     Receive Data(In)                     | 3     Receive Data(In)
4     Request to Send(Out)                 | 4     Request to Send(Out)
5     Clear to Send(In)                    | 6     Data Set Ready(In)
6     Data Set Ready(In)                   | 7     Signal Ground
7     Signal Ground                        | 11    SSD (Out)
8     Carrier Detect(Out)                  | 20    Data Terminal Ready(Out)
11    Supervisory Trans.Data(Out)          | -------------------------------------
20    Data Terminal Ready(Out)             | Flow Control: 20,11      XON/XOFF
-------------------------------------      | Note:
Flow Control: 20,11,4    XON/XOFF          |
Note: Polarity of lead 11 is optionable    |
to be either high or low for flow control  |
```

```
Okidata
Super Speed RS-232-C Board
Port:  RS-232              DB25S
Gender:  Female           PinConfig: P05

Pin    Function(Direction)
-------------------------------------------
1      Protective Ground
3      Receive Data(In)
4      Request to Send(Out)
5      Clear to Send(In)
6      Data Set Ready(In)
7      Signal Ground
11     Supervisory Trans.Data(Out)
20     Data Terminal Ready(Out)
-------------------------------------------
Flow Control: 11          XON/XOFF
Note:
```

```
Olympia
ESW 2500i Printer
Port:  RS-232              DB25S
Gender:  Female           PinConfig: P03

Pin    Function(Direction)
-------------------------------------------
1      Protective Ground
2      Transmit Data(Out)
3      Receive Data(In)
4      Request to Send(Out)
5      Clear to Send(In)
6      Data Set Ready(In)
7      Signal Ground
8      Data Carrier Detect(In)
20     Data Terminal Ready(Out)
-------------------------------------------
Flow Control: 20          XON/XOFF
Note:
```

```
Olympia
Laserstar 6 Printer
Port:  RS-232              DB25S
Gender:  Female           PinConfig: P03

Pin    Function(Direction)
-------------------------------------------
1      Protective Ground
2      Transmit Data(Out)
3      Receive Data(In)
4      Request to Send(Out)
5      Clear to Send(In)
6      Data Set Ready(In)
7      Signal Ground
8      Data Carrier Detect(In)
20     Data Terminal Ready(Out)
-------------------------------------------
Flow Control: 20          XON/XOFF
ACK/NAK
Note:
```

```
Olympia
NP 80/136, 80/136-24 SE Printers
Port:  Serial(DIN)        DIN(6)
Gender:  Female           PinConfig: P19

Pin    Function(Direction)
-------------------------------------------
6      Protective Ground
5      Signal Ground
1      Transmitted Data(out)
3      Received Data(in)
2      Data Terminal Ready(out)
4      Data Set Ready(in)
-------------------------------------------
Flow Control: 2    XON/XOFF
Note:
```

```
Olympia
NP 136 S Printer
Port:  RS-232(I/F Card)   DB25S
Gender:  Female           PinConfig: P05

Pin    Function(Direction)
-------------------------------------------
1      Protective Ground
2      Transmit Data(Out)
3      Receive Data(In)
4      Request to Send(Out)
5      Clear to Send(In)
6      Data Set Ready(In)
7      Signal Ground
8      Data Carrier Detect(In)
11     Reverse Channel(Out)
18     -12V(Out)
20     Data Terminal Ready(Out)
21     +12V(Out)
-------------------------------------------
Flow Control: 11          XON/XOFF
Note:
```

```
Olympia
NP 30, 60 Printers
Port:  RS-232(DCE-odd opt.)DB25S
Gender:  Female           PinConfig: C14

Pin    Function(Direction)
-------------------------------------------
1      Frame Ground
2      Receive Data(In)
3      Transmit Data(Out)
4      Clear to Send(In)
5      Request to Send(Out)
6      Data Terminal Ready(Out)
7      Signal Ground
8      Data Terminal Ready(Out)
20     Data Set Ready(In)
-------------------------------------------
Flow Control: 6,8         XON/XOFF
Note:  This port is optionable DCE/DTE.
On DIP switches 851/852, set odd switches
on(e.g.1/3/5//7) for DCE
```

```
Olympia
NP 30, 60 Printers
Port:  RS-232(DTE-even opt)DB25S
Gender:  Female            PinConfig: P03

Pin    Function(Direction)
------------------------------------------
1         Protective Ground
2         Transmit Data(Out)
3         Receive Data(In)
4         Request to Send(Out)
5         Clear to Send(In)
6         Data Set Ready(In)
7         Signal Ground
8         Data Carrier Detect(In)
20        Data Terminal Ready(Out)
------------------------------------------
Flow Control: 20          XON/XOFF
Note:  Option switches in 852 & 851
should have even switches on to provide
DTE interface(e.g. 2/4/6/8)
```

```
Olympia
NP 80 S Printer
Port:  RS-232(I/F Card)    DB25S
Gender:  Female            PinConfig: P05

Pin    Function(Direction)
------------------------------------------
1         Protective Ground
2         Transmit Data(Out)
3         Receive Data(In)
4         Request to Send(Out)
5         Clear to Send(In)
6         Data Set Ready(In)
7         Signal Ground
8         Data Carrier Detect(In)
11        Reverse Channel(Out)
18        -12V(Out)
20        Data Terminal Ready(Out)
21        +12V(Out)
------------------------------------------
Flow Control: 11          XON/XOFF
Note:
```

```
Panasonic
KX-E3000/E3008, E400/500/508 Typewriters
Port:  RS-232              DB25S
Gender:  Female            PinConfig: C01

Pin    Function(Direction)
------------------------------------------
2         Transmit Data(Out)
3         Receive Data(In)
4         Request to Send(Out)
5         Clear to Send(In)
6         Data Set Ready(In)
7         Signal Ground
8         Data Carrier Detect(In)
20        Data Terminal Ready(Out)
------------------------------------------
Flow Control: 5,6,8       XON/XOFF
ACK/NAK
Note:
```

```
Panasonic
KX-E600/601/603, E700/701/708 Typewriters
Port:  RS-232              DB25S
Gender:  Female            PinConfig: C01

Pin    Function(Direction)
------------------------------------------
2         Transmit Data(Out)
3         Receive Data(In)
4         Request to Send(Out)
5         Clear to Send(In)
6         Data Set Ready(In)
7         Signal Ground
8         Data Carrier Detect(In)
20        Data Terminal Ready(Out)
------------------------------------------
Flow Control: 5,6,8       XON/XOFF
ACK/NAK
Note:
```

```
Panasonic
KX-E7500, 7000 typewriter
Port:  KX-EIS1 serial opt. DB25S
Gender:  Female            PinConfig: P03

Pin    Function(Direction)
------------------------------------------
1         Frame Ground
2         Transmit Data(Out)
3         Receive Data(In)
4         Request to Send(Out)
5         CST (In)
6         Data Set Ready(In)
7         Signal Ground
8         Data Carrier Detect(In)
20        Data Terminal Ready(Out)
22        Ring Indicator(In)
------------------------------------------
Flow Control: 20          XON/XOFF
ACK/NAK
Note:
```

```
Personal Computer Products Inc.
LaserImage 1000/1030/2020 Printers
Port:  Serial              DB25S
Gender:  Female            PinConfig: P03

Pin    Function(Direction)
------------------------------------------
1         Frame Ground
2         Transmit Data(Out)
3         Receive Data(In)
4         Request to Send(Out)
5         Clear to Send(In)
6         Data Set Ready(In)
7         Signal Ground
8         Carrier Detect(In)
20        Data Terminal Ready(Out)
------------------------------------------
Flow Control: 20          XON/XOFF
ACK/NAK
Note:  This printer supports a simplified
interface using only leads 2,3,7, and 20
```

```
Personal Computer Products Inc.
LaserImage 3000-3X, 3020 Printers
Port:  Serial              DB25S
Gender: Female        PinConfig: P03

Pin  Function(Direction)
----------------------------------------
1     Frame Ground
2     Transmit Data(Out)
3     Receive Data(In)
4     Request to Send(Out)
5     Clear to Send(In)
6     Data Set Ready(In)
7     Signal Ground
8     Carrier Detect(In)
20    Data Terminal Ready(Out)
----------------------------------------
Flow Control: 20          XON/XOFF
ACK/NAK
Note:  This printer supports a simplified
interface using only leads 2,3,7, and 20
```

```
QMS Corporation
ColorScript 100 Model 10 printer
Port:  RS-232              DB25S
Gender: Female        PinConfig: P03

Pin  Function(Direction)
----------------------------------------
1     Chassis Ground
2     Transmit Data(Out)
3     Receive Data(In)
4     Request to Send(Out)
5     Clear to Send(In)
6     Data Set Ready(In)
7     Signal Ground
8     Data Carrier Detect(In)
20    Data Terminal Ready(Out)
----------------------------------------
Flow Control: 20,4        XON/XOFF
ACK/NAK
Note:  Leads 20, 4, and 6 are optional
leads. The default flow control protocol
is XON/XOFF
```

```
Qume
CrystalPrint Publisher Printer
Port:  RS232               DB25S
Gender: Female        PinConfig: P11

Pin  Function(Direction)
----------------------------------------
1     Protective Ground
2     Transmit Data(Out)
3     Receive Data(In)
6     Data Carrier Detect(In)
7     Signal Ground
20    Data Terminal Ready(Out)
----------------------------------------
Flow Control: 20          XON/XOFF
Note:  An RS-422 port is also standard on
the printer
```

```
QUME
CrystalPrint VIII, Series II Printers
Port:  RS-232              DB25S
Gender: Female        PinConfig: P03

Pin  Function(Direction)
----------------------------------------
1     Chassis Ground
2     Transmit Data(Out)
3     Receive Data(In)
4     Request to Send(Out)
5     Clear to Send(In)
6     Data Set Ready(In)
7     Signal Ground
8     Data Carrier Detect(In)
20    Data Terminal Ready(Out)
----------------------------------------
Flow Control: 20          XON/XOFF
Note:
```

```
Qume
LaserTEN, LaserTEN PLUS Printers
Port:  101631 Module(DCE) DB25S
Gender: Female        PinConfig: C14

Pin  Function(Direction)
----------------------------------------
1     Chassis Ground
2     Transmit Data(In)
3     Receive Data(Out)
4     Request to Send(In)
5     Clear to Send(Out)
6     Data Set Ready(Out)
7     Signal Ground
8     Data Carrier Detect(Out)
20    Data Terminal Ready(In)
----------------------------------------
Flow Control: 6           XON/XOFF
ACK/NAK
Note:  This module provides null-modem
function & port emulates DCE.  Other
modules provide DTE port
```

```
Qume
LaserTEN, LaserTEN PLUS Printers
Port:  RS232 Module(DTE)   DB25S
Gender: Female        PinConfig: P03

Pin  Function(Direction)
----------------------------------------
1     Chassis Ground
2     Transmit Data(Out)
3     Receive Data(In)
4     Request to Send(Out)
5     Clear to Send(In)
6     Data Set Ready(In)
7     Signal Ground
8     Data Carrier Detect(In)
20    Data Terminal Ready(Out)
----------------------------------------
Flow Control: 20          XON/XOFF
ACK/NAK
Note:  This port emulates DTE & is
provided by a module. Other
modules(101631) provide a DCE interface
```

```
QUME
ScripTEN Printer
Port:  RS-232           DB25S
Gender: Female          PinConfig: P03

Pin    Function(Direction)
------------------------------------------
1          Chassis Ground
2          Transmit Data(Out)
3          Receive Data(In)
4          Request to Send(Out)
5          Clear to Send(In)
6          Data Set Ready(In)
7          Signal Ground
8          Data Carrier Detect(In)
20         Data Terminal Ready(Out)
------------------------------------------
Flow Control: 20        XON/XOFF
Note:
```

```
Qume
Sprint 11 PLUS 40/55/90/130 Printers
Port:  RS-232(Model 2)  DB25S
Gender: Female          PinConfig: P03

Pin    Function(Direction)
------------------------------------------
1          Chassis Ground
2          Transmit Data(Out)
3          Receive Data(In)
4          Request to Send(Out)
5          Clear to Send(In)
6          Data Set Ready(In)
7          Signal Ground
8          Data Carrier Detect(In)
20         Data Terminal Ready(Out)
------------------------------------------
Flow Control: 20        XON/XOFF
Note:
```

```
Qume
Sprint 11 PLUS WIDETRACK
Printer(interface module)
Port:  RS-232(Model 1)  DB25S
Gender: Female          PinConfig: P03

Pin    Function(Direction)
------------------------------------------
1          Chassis Ground
2          Transmit Data(Out)
3          Receive Data(In)
4          Request to Send(Out)
5          Clear to Send(In)
6          Data Set Ready(In)
7          Signal Ground
8          Data Carrier Detect(In)
20         Data Terminal Ready(Out)
------------------------------------------
Flow Control: 20        XON/XOFF
Note: The QUME Connection is available
in a buffered version(Model 2) in
addition to above(Model 1)
```

```
QUME
the QUME Connection-Model 1
Port:  RS-232           DB25P
Gender: Male            PinConfig: P03

Pin    Function(Direction)
------------------------------------------
1          Chassis Ground
2          Transmit Data(Out)
3          Receive Data(In)
4          Request to Send(Out)
5          Clear to Send(In)
6          Data Set Ready(In)
7          Signal Ground
8          Carrier Detect(In)
20         Data Terminal Ready(Out)
------------------------------------------
Flow Control: 20        XON/XOFF
Note:
```

```
QUME
the QUME Connection-Model 2
Port:  RS-232           DB25P
Gender: Male            PinConfig: P03

Pin    Function(Direction)
------------------------------------------
1          Chassis Ground
2          Transmit Data(Out)
3          Receive Data(In)
4          Request to Send(Out)
5          Clear to Send(In)
6          Data Set Ready(In)
7          Signal Ground
8          Carrier Detect(In)
20         Data Terminal Ready(Out)
------------------------------------------
Flow Control: 20        XON/XOFF
Note:
```

```
Seikosha
BP-5460FA Printer
Port:  Serial           DB25S
Gender: Female          PinConfig: P05

Pin    Function(Direction)
------------------------------------------
1          Protective Ground
2          Transmit Data(Out)
3          Receive Data(In)
4          Request to Send(Out)
5          Clear to Send(In)
6          Data Set Ready(In)
7          Signal Ground
8          Data Carrier Detect(In)
11         Secondary Req.to Send(Out)
20         Data Terminal Ready(Out)
------------------------------------------
Flow Control: 11, 20    XON/XOFF
ACK/NAK
Note:  Default options don't support
5/6/8.  To enable cut J1/J2/J3 & connect
a jumper @ J5/J4/J6
```

```
Seikosha
BP-5460FA Printer
Port:  Serial(factory set) DB25S
Gender:  Female            PinConfig: P04

Pin    Function(Direction)
-----------------------------------------
1      Protective Ground
2      Transmit Data(Out)
3      Receive Data(In)
4      Request to Send(Out)
7      Signal Ground
11     Secondary Req. to Send(Out)
20     Data Terminal Ready(Out)
-----------------------------------------
Flow Control: 11, 20      XON/XOFF
ACK/NAK
Note:  Leads 5/6/8 can be enabled through
jumpering.  But the above assume the
factory settings(off)
```

```
Seikosha
SBP-10AI, SL-230AI Printers
Port:  Serial            DB25S
Gender:  Female            PinConfig: P05

Pin    Function(Direction)
-----------------------------------------
1      Protective Ground
2      Transmit Data(Out)
3      Receive Data(In)
4      Request to Send(Out)
5      Clear to Send(In)
6      Data Set Ready(In)
7      Signal Ground
8      Data Carrier Detect(In)
11     Secondary Req.to Send(Out)
20     Data Terminal Ready(Out)
-----------------------------------------
Flow Control: 11, 20      XON/XOFF
ACK/NAK
Note:
```

```
Seikosha
SK-3000AI, 3005AI Printers
Port:  Serial            DB25S
Gender:  Female            PinConfig: P03

Pin    Function(Direction)
-----------------------------------------
1      Protective Ground
2      Transmit Data(Out)
3      Receive Data(In)
4      Request to Send(Out)
5      Clear to Send(In)
6      Data Set Ready(In)
7      Signal Ground
8      Data Carrier Detect(In)
11     Secondary Req.to Send(Out)
20     Data Terminal Ready(Out)
-----------------------------------------
Flow Control: 20, 11      XON/XOFF
ACK/NAK
Note:  Defaults don't use 5/6/8/11.  To
change move JP4 to JP3,JP6 to JP5,JP2 to
JP1.  For 11, JP8 to JP7
```

```
Seikosha
SK-3000AI, 3005AI Printers
Port:  Serial(Factory set) DB25S
Gender:  Female            PinConfig: P08

Pin    Function(Direction)
-----------------------------------------
1      Protective Ground
2      Transmit Data(Out)
3      Receive Data(In)
4      Request to Send(Out)
7      Signal Ground
20     Data Terminal Ready(Out)
-----------------------------------------
Flow Control: 20, 11      XON/XOFF
ACK/NAK
Note:  Leads 5/6/8/11 can be enabled
through jumpering. But the above assumes
the factory settings(off)
```

```
SP-1000AP/1600AS Printers
Port:  Serial            DB25S
Gender:  Female            PinConfig: P11

Pin    Function(Direction)
-----------------------------------------
2      Transmit Data(Out)
3      Receive Data(In)
7      Signal Ground
11     Secondary Req.to Send(Out)
20     Data Terminal Ready(Out)
-----------------------------------------
Flow Control: 20,11       XON/XOFF
Note:  To enable 11 as flow control,
connect jumper J3
```

```
Sharp
JX-9500 Printer
Port:  RS-232            DB25S
Gender:  Female            PinConfig: P08

Pin    Function(Direction)
-----------------------------------------
1      Frame Ground
2      Transmit Data(Out)
3      Receive Data(In)
4      Request to Send(Out)
6      Data Set Ready(In)
7      Signal Ground
20     Data Terminal Ready(Out)
-----------------------------------------
Flow Control: 20         XON/XOFF
Note:
```

```
Shinwa of America Inc.
MH4010/4045, CBP-136 Printers
Port: Serial(S)           DB25S
Gender: Female            PinConfig: P03

Pin   Function(Direction)
-------------------------------------
1         Protective Ground
2         Transmit Data(Out)
3         Receive Data(In)
4         Request to Send(Out)
6         Data Set Ready(In)
7         Signal Ground
8         Data Carrier Detect(In)
20        Data Terminal Ready(Out)
-------------------------------------
Flow Control: 20,4        XON/XOFF
Note:  Leads 4 & 20 behave the same
```

```
Shinwa of America, Inc.
EL2410, SL2410, SQ2410 Printers
Port: Serial(S)           DB25S
Gender: Female            PinConfig: P03

Pin   Function(Direction)
-------------------------------------
1         Protective Ground
2         Transmit Data(Out)
3         Receive Data(In)
4         Request to Send(Out)
6         Data Set Ready(In)
7         Signal Ground
8         Data Carrier Detect(In)
20        Data Terminal Ready(Out)
-------------------------------------
Flow Control: 20,4        XON/XOFF
Note:  Leads 4 & 20 behave the same
```

```
Shinwa of America, Inc.
VP 130/160/180, & LP Printers
Port: Serial(S)           DB25S
Gender: Female            PinConfig: P03

Pin   Function(Direction)
-------------------------------------
1         Protective Ground
2         Transmit Data(Out)
3         Receive Data(In)
4         Request to Send(Out)
6         Data Set Ready(In)
7         Signal Ground
8         Data Carrier Detect(In)
20        Data Terminal Ready(Out)
-------------------------------------
Flow Control: 20,4        XON/XOFF
Note:  Leads 4 & 20 behave the same
```

```
star micronics
4010X buffered serial board
Port: Serial              DB25S
Gender: Female            PinConfig: P03

Pin   Function(Direction)
-------------------------------------
1         Chassis Ground
2         Transmit Data(Out)
3         Receive Data(In)
4         Request to Send(Out)
5         Clear to Send(In)
7         Signal Ground
11        Reverse Channel(Out)
20        Data Terminal Ready(Out)
-------------------------------------
Flow Control: 20,11       XON/XOFF
ACK/NAK
Note:  Lead 5 is not checked by the
printer
```

```
star micronics
Delta 10/15, Gemini 10/15 Printers
Port: Serial              DB25S
Gender: Female            PinConfig: P03

Pin   Function(Direction)
-------------------------------------
1         Chassis Ground
2         Transmit Data(Out)
3         Receive Data(In)
4         Request to Send(Out)
5         Clear to Send(In)
6         Data Set Ready(In)
7         Signal Ground
8         Data Carrier Detect(In)
11        Reverse Channel(Out)
20        Data Terminal Ready(Out)
-------------------------------------
Flow Control: 20,11       XON/XOFF
Note:  Leads 6 & 8 are ignored by the
printer
```

```
star micronics
Gemini 10X/15X Printers
Port: Serial              DB25S
Gender: Female            PinConfig: P03

Pin   Function(Direction)
-------------------------------------
1         Chassis Ground
2         Transmit Data(Out)
3         Receive Data(In)
4         Request to Send(Out)
5         Clear to Send(In)
7         Signal Ground
11        Reverse Channel(Out)
20        Data Terminal Ready(Out)
-------------------------------------
Flow Control: 20,11       XON/XOFF
Note:  Lead 5 is not checked by the
printer
```

```
star micronics
NB-15, NB24-10/15, ND-10/15 Printers
Port: Serial                   DB25S
Gender: Female            PinConfig: P03

Pin   Function(Direction)
------------------------------------------
1     Chassis Ground
2     Transmit Data(Out)
3     Receive Data(In)
4     Request to Send(Out)
5     Clear to Send(In)
6     Data Set Ready(In)
7     Signal Ground
8     Data Carrier Detect(In)
11    Reverse Channel(Out)
20    Data Terminal Ready(Out)
------------------------------------------
Flow Control: 20,11         XON/XOFF
Note:  Leads 6 & 8 are ignored by the
printer
```

```
star micronics
NL-10, NP-10, NR-10/15 Printers
Port: Serial                   DB25S
Gender: Female            PinConfig: P03

Pin   Function(Direction)
------------------------------------------
1     Chassis Ground
2     Transmit Data(Out)
3     Receive Data(In)
4     Request to Send(Out)
5     Clear to Send(In)
6     Data Set Ready(In)
7     Signal Ground
8     Data Carrier Detect(In)
11    Reverse Channel(Out)
20    Data Terminal Ready(Out)
------------------------------------------
Flow Control: 20,11         XON/XOFF
Note:  Lead 6 & 8 are ignored
```

```
star micronics
NX-10/15, NX-1000/1500, Rainbow Printers
Port: Serial                   DB25S
Gender: Female            PinConfig: P03

Pin   Function(Direction)
------------------------------------------
1     Chassis Ground
2     Transmit Data(Out)
3     Receive Data(In)
4     Request to Send(Out)
5     Clear to Send(In)
7     Signal Ground
11    Reverse Channel(Out)
20    Data Terminal Ready(Out)
------------------------------------------
Flow Control: 20,11         XON/XOFF
Note:  The printer does not check lead 5
```

```
star micronics
NX-2400/2410/2415 Printer
Port: Serial                   DB25S
Gender: Female            PinConfig: P03

Pin   Function(Direction)
------------------------------------------
1     Chassis Ground
2     Transmit Data(Out)
3     Receive Data(In)
4     Request to Send(Out)
5     Clear to Send(In)
7     Signal Ground
11    Reverse Channel(Out)
20    Data Terminal Ready(Out)
------------------------------------------
Flow Control: 20,11         XON/XOFF
Note:  Lead 5 is not checked by the
printer
```

```
star micronics
Powertype Printer
Port: Serial                   DB25S
Gender: Female            PinConfig: P03

Pin   Function(Direction)
------------------------------------------
1     Chassis Ground
2     Transmit Data(Out)
3     Receive Data(In)
4     Request to Send(Out)
5     Clear to Send(In)
6     Data Set Ready(In)
7     Signal Ground
8     Data Carrier Detect(In)
11    Reverse Channel(Out)
20    Data Terminal Ready(Out)
------------------------------------------
Flow Control: 20,11         XON/XOFF
Note:  Leads 6 & 8 are ignored by the
printer
```

```
star micronics
Radix 10/15 Printers
Port: Serial                   DB25S
Gender: Female            PinConfig: P03

Pin   Function(Direction)
------------------------------------------
1     Chassis Ground
2     Transmit Data(Out)
3     Receive Data(In)
4     Request to Send(Out)
5     Clear to Send(In)
6     Data Set Ready(In)
7     Signal Ground
8     Data Carrier Detect(In)
11    Reverse Channel(Out)
20    Data Terminal Ready(Out)
------------------------------------------
Flow Control: 20,11         XON/XOFF
Note:  Leads 6 & 8 are ignored by the
printer
```

```
star micronics
SB-10, SD-10/15, SG-10/15, SR-10/15
Printers
Port:  Serial           DB25S
Gender: Female          PinConfig: P03

Pin    Function(Direction)
----------------------------------------
1      Chassis Ground
2      Transmit Data(Out)
3      Receive Data(In)
4      Request to Send(Out)
5      Clear to Send(In)
6      Data Set Ready(In)
7      Signal Ground
8      Data Carrier Detect(In)
11     Reverse Channel(Out)
20     Data Terminal Ready(Out)
----------------------------------------
Flow Control: 20,11     XON/XOFF
Note:  Leads 6 & 8 are ignored by the
printer
```

```
star micronics
SBI-2048 buffered board(Gemini 10/15)
Port:  Serial           DB25S
Gender: Female          PinConfig: P03

Pin    Function(Direction)
----------------------------------------
1      Chassis Ground
2      Transmit Data(Out)
3      Receive Data(In)
4      Request to Send(Out)
5      Clear to Send(In)
6      Data Set Ready(In)
7      Signal Ground
8      Data Carrier Detect(In)
11     Reverse Channel(Out)
20     Data Terminal Ready(Out)
----------------------------------------
Flow Control: 20,11     XON/XOFF
ACK/NAK
Note:  Leads 6 & 8 are ignored by the
printer
```

```
star micronics
Unbuffered board(Gemini 10/15)
Port:  Serial           DB25S
Gender: Female          PinConfig: P03

Pin    Function(Direction)
----------------------------------------
1      Chassis Ground
2      Transmit Data(Out)
3      Receive Data(In)
4      Request to Send(Out)
5      Clear to Send(In)
6      Data Set Ready(In)
7      Signal Ground
8      Data Carrier Detect(In)
11     Reverse Channel(Out)
20     Data Terminal Ready(Out)
----------------------------------------
Flow Control: 20,11     XON/XOFF
ACK/NAK
Note:  Leads 6 & 8 are ignored by the
printer
```

```
star micronics
XB-2410/2415, XR-1000/1500 Printers
Port:  Serial           DB25S
Gender: Female          PinConfig: P03

Pin    Function(Direction)
----------------------------------------
1      Chassis Ground
2      Transmit Data(Out)
3      Receive Data(In)
4      Request to Send(Out)
5      Clear to Send(In)
7      Signal Ground
11     Reverse Channel(Out)
20     Data Terminal Ready(Out)
----------------------------------------
Flow Control: 20,11     XON/XOFF
Note:  Lead 5 is not checked by the
printer
```

```
Symbol Technologies
PS 1000 Bar Code Printer
Port:  RS-232           DB9S
Gender: Female          PinConfig: P20

Pin    Function(Direction)
----------------------------------------
5      Signal Ground
3      Transmitted Data(out)
2      Received Data(in)
7      Request To Send(out)
8      Clear To Send(in)
----------------------------------------
Flow Control: 7  XON/XOFF
Note:
```

```
syntest Corporation
SP 200/400, SP 2000/2100 Printers
Port:  RS-232           DB25S
Gender: Female          PinConfig: P05

Pin    Function(Direction)
----------------------------------------
1      Protective Ground
2      Transmit Data(Out)
3      Receive Data(In)
4      Request to Send(Out)
5      Clear to Send(In)
6      Data Set Ready(In)
7      Signal Ground
11     Busy(Out)
20     Data Terminal Ready(Out)
----------------------------------------
Flow Control: 11        XON/XOFF
Note:
```

```
Tandem Computers
5515/5516/5518 Printers
Port:  RS-232          DB25S
Gender:  Female        PinConfig: P03

Pin   Function(Direction)
----------------------------------------
1     Protective Ground
2     Transmit Data(Out)
3     Receive Data(In)
4     Request to Send(Out)
5     Clear to Send(In)
6     Data Set Ready(In)
7     Signal Ground
8     Data Carrier Detect(In)
15    Transmit Clock(In)
17    Receive Clock(In)
20    Data Terminal Ready(Out)
----------------------------------------
Flow Control: 20          XON/XOFF
Note:
```

```
Tandem Computers
5573 LASER-LX Printer
Port:  RS-232          DB25S
Gender:  Female        PinConfig: P03

Pin   Function(Direction)
----------------------------------------
2     Transmit Data(Out)
3     Receive Data(In)
4     Request to Send(Out)
5     Clear to Send(In)
6     Data Set Ready(In)
7     Signal Ground
8     Data Carrier Detect(In)
20    Data Terminal Ready(Out)
----------------------------------------
Flow Control: 20          XON/XOFF
Note:
```

```
Texas Instruments
OmniLaser 2015/2106/2108/2115 Printers
Port:  RS-232          DB25S
Gender:  Female        PinConfig: P05

Pin   Function(Direction)
----------------------------------------
1     Protective Ground
2     Transmit Data(Out)
3     Receive Data(In)
4     Request to Send(Out)
5     Clear to Send(In)
6     Data Set Ready(In)
7     Signal Ground
8     Data Carrier Detect(In)
11    Busy(Out)
20    Data Terminal Ready(Out)
----------------------------------------
Flow Control: 11,20       XON/XOFF
Note:
```

```
Toshiba America
P321SL/SLC Printers
Port:  RS-232(Ready/Busy)  DB25S
Gender:  Female            PinConfig: P11

Pin   Function(Direction)
----------------------------------------
1     Frame Ground
3     Receive Data(In)
7     Signal Ground
14    Fault(Out)
19    Data Terminal Ready(Out)
20    Data Terminal Ready(Out)
----------------------------------------
Flow Control: 20          XON/XOFF
ACK/NAK
Note:  This port can be optioned for
XON/XOFF, with different pinning
requirements
```

```
Toshiba America
P321SL/SLC, P341SL Printers
Port:  RS-232(XON/XOFF)    DB25S
Gender:  Female            PinConfig: P10

Pin   Function(Direction)
----------------------------------------
1     Frame Ground
2     Transmit Data(Out)
3     Receive Data(In)
4     Request to Send(Out)
7     Signal Ground
14    Fault(Out)
19    Data Terminal Ready(Out)
20    Data Terminal Ready(Out)
----------------------------------------
Flow Control:             XON/XOFF
ACK/NAK
Note:  This port can be optioned for
hardware flow control, with different
pinning requirements
```

```
Toshiba America
P351 Model 2 Printer
Port:  RS-232(Ready/Busy)  DB25S
Gender:  Female            PinConfig: P11

Pin   Function(Direction)
----------------------------------------
1     Frame Ground
3     Receive Data(In)
5     Clear to Send(In)
6     Data Set Ready(In)
7     Signal Ground
8     Data Carrier Detect(In)
14    Fault(Out)
19    Data Terminal Ready(Out)
20    Data Terminal Ready(Out)
----------------------------------------
Flow Control: 20          XON/XOFF
ACK/NAK
Note:  This port can be optioned for
XON/XOFF, with different pinning
requirements
```

```
Toshiba America
P351 Model 2 Printer
Port: RS-232(XON/XOFF)      DB25S
Gender: Female              PinConfig: P10

Pin   Function(Direction)
---------------------------------------
1     Frame Ground
2     Transmit Data(Out)
3     Receive Data(In)
4     Request to Send(Out)
5     Clear to Send(In)
6     Data Set Ready(In)
7     Signal Ground
8     Data Carrier Detect(In)
14    Fault(Out)
19    Data Terminal Ready(Out)
20    Data Terminal Ready(Out)
---------------------------------------
Flow Control:              XON/XOFF
ACK/NAK
Note: This port can be optioned for
hardware flow control, with different
pinning requirements
```

```
Toshiba America
P351C Printer
Port: RS-232(Ready/Busy)   DB25S
Gender: Female             PinConfig: P03

Pin   Function(Direction)
---------------------------------------
1     Frame Ground
3     Receive Data(In)
4     Request to Send(Out)
6     Data Set Ready(In)
7     Signal Ground
8     Carrier Detect(In)
14    Fault(Out)
20    Data Terminal Ready(Out)
---------------------------------------
Flow Control: 20           XON/XOFF
ACK/NAK
Note: This port can be optioned for
XON/XOFF, with different pinning
requirements
```

```
Toshiba America
P351C Printer
Port: RS-232(XON/XOFF)      DB25S
Gender: Female              PinConfig: P10

Pin   Function(Direction)
---------------------------------------
1     Frame Ground
2     Transmit Data(Out)
3     Receive Data(In)
4     Request to Send(Out)
6     Data Set Ready(In)
7     Signal Ground
8     Carrier Detect(In)
14    Fault(Out)
20    Data Terminal Ready(Out)
---------------------------------------
Flow Control:              XON/XOFF
ACK/NAK
Note: This port can be optioned for
hardware flow control, with different
pinning requirements
```

```
Toshiba America
P351SX Printer
Port: RS-232(Ready/Busy)   DB25S
Gender: Female             PinConfig: P11

Pin   Function(Direction)
---------------------------------------
1     Frame Ground
3     Receive Data(In)
6     Data Set Ready(In)
7     Signal Ground
8     Carrier Detect(In)
14    Fault(Out)
19    Data Terminal Ready(Out)
20    Data Terminal Ready(Out)
---------------------------------------
Flow Control: 20           XON/XOFF
ACK/NAK
Note: This port can be optioned for
XON/XOFF, with different pinning
requirements
```

```
Toshiba America
P351SX Printer
Port: RS-232(XON/XOFF)      DB25S
Gender: Female              PinConfig: P10

Pin   Function(Direction)
---------------------------------------
1     Frame Ground
2     Transmit Data(Out)
3     Receive Data(In)
4     Request to Send(Out)
6     Data Set Ready(In)
7     Signal Ground
8     Carrier Detect(In)
14    Fault(Out)
19    Data Terminal Ready(Out)
20    Data Terminal Ready(Out)
---------------------------------------
Flow Control:              XON/XOFF
ACK/NAK
Note: This port can be optioned for
hardware flow control, with different
pinning requirements
```

```
Videojet Systems Intl.
Videojet 120L Coder/Printer
Port: RS-232               DB25S
Gender: Female             PinConfig: P08

Pin   Function(Direction)
---------------------------------------
1     Protective Ground
2     Transmit Data(Out)
3     Receive Data(In)
4     Request to Send(Out)
5     Clear to Send(In)
6     Data Set Ready(In)
7     Signal Ground
20    Data Terminal Ready(Out)
---------------------------------------
Flow Control: 20
Note:
```

terminals

```
ADDS
1010 Terminal
Port: EIA                    DB25S
Gender: Female               PinConfig: P08

Pin   Function(Direction)
----------------------------------------
1     Protective Ground
2     Transmit Data(Out)
3     Receive Data(In)
4     Request to Send(Out)
5     Clear to Send(In)
7     Signal Ground
20    Data Terminal Ready(Out)
----------------------------------------
Flow Control: 20             XON/XOFF
Note:
```

```
ADDS
2020/2025 Terminal
Port: AUX                    DB25P
Gender: Male                 PinConfig: C14

Pin   Function(Direction)
----------------------------------------
1     Frame Ground
2     Receive Data(In)
3     Transmit Data(Out)
4     Request to Send(In)
5     Clear to Send(Out)
6     Data Set Ready(Out)
7     Signal Ground
20    Data Terminal Ready(In)
----------------------------------------
Flow Control: 20             XON/XOFF
Note:
```

```
ADDS
2020/2025 Terminal
Port: HOST                   DB25S
Gender: Female               PinConfig: P03

Pin   Function(Direction)
----------------------------------------
1     Frame Ground
2     Transmit Data(Out)
3     Receive Data(In)
4     Request to Send(Out)
5     Clear to Send(In)
7     Signal Ground
8     Carrier Detect(In)
20    Data Terminal Ready(Out)
----------------------------------------
Flow Control: 20             XON/XOFF
Note:
```

```
ADDS
3320/4000 Terminal
Port: AUX                    DB25S
Gender: Female               PinConfig: C14

Pin   Function(Direction)
----------------------------------------
1     Protective Ground
2     Receive Data(In)
3     Transmit Data(Out)
4     Clear to Send(In)
5     Clear to Send(Out)
6     Data Terminal Ready(Out)
7     Signal Ground
20    Data Terminal Ready(In)
----------------------------------------
Flow Control: 20             XON/XOFF
Note:
```

```
ADDS
3320 Terminal
Port: EIA(RS-232)            DB25S
Gender: Female               PinConfig: P03

Pin   Function(Direction)
----------------------------------------
1     Protective Ground
2     Transmit Data(Out)
3     Receive Data(In)
4     Request to Send(Out)
5     Clear to Send(In)
6     Data Set Ready(In)
7     Signal Ground
8     Carrier Detect(In)
12    Serial In(In)
17    RD+ (In)
18    RD- (In)
20    Data Terminal Ready(Out)
23    Data Rate Select(Out)
24    TD+ (Out)
25    TD- (Out)
----------------------------------------
Flow Control: 20             XON/XOFF
Note:
```

```
ADDS
4000 Terminal
Port: EIA                    DB25S
Gender: Female               PinConfig: P08

Pin   Function(Direction)
----------------------------------------
1     Protective Ground
2     Transmit Data(Out)
3     Receive Data(In)
4     Request to Send(Out)
5     Clear to Send(In)
7     Signal Ground
20    Data Terminal Ready(Out)
----------------------------------------
Flow Control: 20             XON/XOFF
Note:
```

```
AT&T
705 Terminal
Port:  Port 2              DB25S
Gender:  Female            PinConfig: C11

Pin   Function(Direction)
----------------------------------------
1       Frame Ground
2       Transmit Data(Out)
3       Receive Data(In)
4       Request to Send(Out)
5       Clear to Send(In)
7       Signal Ground
8       Data Carrier Detect(In)
20      Data Terminal Ready(Out)
----------------------------------------
Flow Control: 5 & 8        XON/XOFF
Note:  Leads 5 & 8 should be on to send &
receive data.
```

```
C.ITOH
CIT 334 Terminal
Port:  2/3/7 only          DB25S
Gender:  Female            PinConfig: P16

Pin   Function(Direction)
----------------------------------------
1       Protective Ground
7       Signal Ground
2       Transmitted Data(out)
3       Received Data(in)
----------------------------------------
Flow Control:    XON/XOFF
Note:  Full control is supported, but
this entry uses only 2/3/7
```

```
C.ITOH
334 Terminal
Port:  DB25                DB25S
Gender:  Female            PinConfig: C01

Pin   Function(Direction)
----------------------------------------
1       Frame Ground
2       Transmit Data(Out)
3       Receive Data(In)
4       Request to Send(Out)
5       Clear to Send(In)
6       Data Set Ready(In)
7       Signal Ground
8       Data Carrier Detect(In)
12      Speed Select(In)
20      Data Terminal Ready(Out)
23      Speed Select(Out)
----------------------------------------
Flow Control: 6 & 8        XON/XOFF
Note:  Option the port for "Full Modem
Control" to use all of the above control
signals
```

```
C.ITOH
CIT 101XL Terminal
Port:  AUX                 DB25S
Gender:  Female            PinConfig: P06

Pin   Function(Direction)
----------------------------------------
1       Protective Ground
2       Transmit Data(Out)
3       Receive Data(In)
6       Data Set Ready(In)
7       Signal Ground
20      Data Terminal Ready(Out)
----------------------------------------
Flow Control: 6            XON/XOFF
Note:
```

```
C.ITOH
CIT 101XL Terminal
Port:  COMM                DB25P
Gender:  Male              PinConfig: C01

Pin   Function(Direction)
----------------------------------------
1       Frame Ground
2       Transmit Data(Out)
3       Receive Data(In)
4       Request to Send(Out)
5       Clear to Send(In)
6       Data Set Ready(In)
7       Signal Ground
8       Data Carrier Detect(In)
12      Speed Select(In)
20      Data Terminal Ready(Out)
22      Ring Indicator(In)
23      Speed Select(Out)
----------------------------------------
Flow Control: 6 & 8        XON/XOFF
Note:
```

```
C.ITOH
CIT344 Terminal
Port:  DB25                DB25S
Gender:  Female            PinConfig: C01

Pin   Function(Direction)
----------------------------------------
1       Frame Ground
2       Transmit Data(Out)
3       Receive Data(In)
4       Request to Send(Out)
5       Clear to Send(In)
6       Data Set Ready(In)
7       Signal Ground
8       Data Carrier Detect(In)
12      Speed Select(In)
20      Data Terminal Ready(Out)
23      Speed Select(Out)
----------------------------------------
Flow Control: 6 & 8        XON/XOFF
Note:  Option this port for "Full Modem
Control" to get the above control signals
```

```
Dell Computer Corp.               Esprit Systems
MT-15 Terminal                    ESP 6110+ Terminal
Port: RS-232(both ports) DB25P    Port: MAIN(leads 2/3/7) DB25S
Gender: Male        PinConfig: C01 Gender: Female     PinConfig: C19

Pin   Function(Direction)         Pin   Function(Direction)
------------------------------    ------------------------------
2     Transmit Data(Out)          7     Signal Ground
3     Receive Data(In)            2     Transmitted Data(out)
4     Request to Send(Out)        3     Received Data(in)
5     Clear to Send(In)           ------------------------------
6     Data Set Ready(In)          Flow Control:    XON/XOFF
7     Signal Ground               Note: This particular configuration uses
8     Data Carrier Detect(In)     only leads 2/3/7, full control is
20    Data Terminal Ready(Out)    optionable
22    Ring Indicator(In)
------------------------------
Flow Control: 5 & 6
Note:  Leads 5 & 6 must be on to send &
receive data. Connect 5 & 6 to other
device's flow control lead
```

```
Esprit Systems                    Esprit Systems
ESP 6110+ Terminal                ESP 6110+ Terminal
Port: AUX          DB25S          Port: COMM/RS-232      DB25S
Gender: Female  PinConfig: C21    Gender: Female    PinConfig: C01

Pin   Function(Direction)         Pin   Function(Direction)
------------------------------    ------------------------------
1     Protective Ground           1     Frame Ground
7     Signal Ground               2     Transmit Data(Out)
3     Transmitted Data(out)       3     Receive Data(In)
2     Received Data(in)           4     Request to Send(Out)
5     Clear To Send(out)          5     Clear to Send(In)
6     Data Set Ready(out)         6     Data Set Ready(In)
8     Data Carrier Detect(out)    7     Signal Ground
4     Request To Send(in)         8     Data Carrier Detect(In)
11    Print Control(in)           20    Data Terminal Ready(Out)
------------------------------    23    Speed Select(Out)
Flow Control:    XON/XOFF         ------------------------------
Note:                             Flow Control: 11        XON/XOFF
                                  Note: Lead 11 words for flow control
                                  only if an aux port is installed.  Leads
                                  5/6/8 can be disabled.
```

```
Esprit Systems                    Esprit Systems
ESP 6310 Terminal                 ESP 6310 Terminal
Port: AUX          DB25S          Port: EIA          DB25S
Gender: Female  PinConfig: C02    Gender: Female  PinConfig: P10

Pin   Function(Direction)         Pin   Function(Direction)
------------------------------    ------------------------------
1     Protective Ground           1     Protective Ground
2     Receive Data(In)            2     Transmit Data(Out)
3     Transmit Data(Out)          3     Receive Data(In)
4     Request to Send(In)         4     Request to Send(Out)
5     CSTS(Out)                   5     Clear to Send(In)
6     Data Set Ready(Out)         6     Data Set Ready(In)
7     Signal Ground               7     Signal Ground
8     Data Carrier Detect(Out)    8     Data Carrier Detect(In)
11    Secondary Cl'r to Send(In)  20    Data Terminal Ready(Out)
20    Data Terminal Ready(In)     ------------------------------
------------------------------    Flow Control:        XON/XOFF
Flow Control: 11        XON/XOFF  Note: This port can be optioned to use
Note:                             only 1/2/3/7, or an RS-422 option can be
                                  added.
```

```
Esprit Systems
LANTerm & LANTerm 2 Terminal
Port: RS-232(9-pin)        DB9P
Gender: Male               PinConfig: C16

Pin   Function(Direction)
-------------------------------------
1        Carrier Detect(In)
2        Receive Data(In)
3        Transmit Data(Out)
4        Data Terminal Ready(Out)
5        Signal Ground
6        Data Set Ready(In)
7        Request to Send(Out)
8        Clear to Send(In)
9        Ring Indicator(In)
-------------------------------------
Flow Control: 6 & 8        XON/XOFF
Note: The flow control leads of the
attached device should be connected to
leads 6 & 8
```

```
Esprit Systems
OPUS 2 Terminal
Port: Main(RS-232_         DB25S
Gender: Female             PinConfig: P03

Pin   Function(Direction)
-------------------------------------
1        Protective Ground
2        Transmit Data(Out)
3        Receive Data(In)
4        Request to Send(Out)
5        Clear to Send(In)
7        Signal Ground
8        Data Carrier Detect(In)
20       Data Terminal Ready(Out)
-------------------------------------
Flow Control: 20           XON/XOFF
Note:
```

```
Esprit Systems
OPUS 220 Terminal
Port: AUX                  DB25S
Gender: Female             PinConfig: C01

Pin   Function(Direction)
-------------------------------------
1        Protective Ground
2        Transmit Data(Out)
3        Receive Data(In)
4        Request to Send(Out)
6        Data Set Ready(In)
20       Data Terminal Ready(Out)
-------------------------------------
Flow Control: 6            XON/XOFF
Note:
```

```
Esprit Systems
OPUS 220 Terminal
Port: MAIN                 DB25S
Gender: Female             PinConfig: P10

Pin   Function(Direction)
-------------------------------------
1        Protective Ground
2        Transmit Data(Out)
3        Receive Data(In)
4        Request to Send(Out)
5        Clear to Send(In)
6        Data Set Ready(In)
7        Signal Ground
8        Carrier Detect(In)
12       Data Rate Select(In)
20       Data Terminal Ready(Out)
23       Data Rate Select(Out)
-------------------------------------
Flow Control:              XON/XOFF
Note: Terminal can be optioned to use
only 1/2/3/7.
```

```
Esprit Systems
OPUS 3n1+ Terminal
Port: AUX-Printer Mode     DB25S
Gender: Female             PinConfig: C14

Pin   Function(Direction)
-------------------------------------
1        Protective Ground
2        Receive Data(In)
3        Transmit Data(Out)
6        Data Set Ready(Out)
7        Signal Ground
8        Data Carrier Detect(Out)
20       Data Terminal Ready(In)
-------------------------------------
Flow Control: 20           XON/XOFF
Note: This port can be optioned as a
dual host port, or as a printer
port(above)
```

```
Esprit Systems
OPUS 3n1+ Terminal
Port: MAIN(2/3/7 option)   DB25S
Gender: Female             PinConfig: P10

Pin   Function(Direction)
-------------------------------------
1        Protective Ground
2        Transmit Data(Out)
3        Receive Data(In)
4        Request to Send(Out)
5        Clear to Send(In)
6        Data Set Ready(In)
7        Signal Ground
8        Data Carrier Detect(In)
20       Data Terminal Ready(Out)
-------------------------------------
Flow Control:              XON/XOFF
Note: This port can be optioned to use
only leads 2, 3, & 7
```

```
Esprit Systems
OPUS 3n1+ Terminal
Port: Main(Full Control)  DB25S
Gender: Female            PinConfig: PO3

Pin   Function(Direction)
------------------------------------------
1     Frame Ground
2     Transmit Data(Out)
3     Receive Data(In)
4     Request to Send(Out)
5     Clear to Send(In)
6     Data Set Ready(In)
7     Signal Ground
8     Data Carrier Detect(In)
20    Data Terminal Ready(Out)
------------------------------------------
Flow Control: 20          XON/XOFF
Note: This port can be optioned to used
only leads 2/3/7
```

```
Informer Computer Terminals
174M Communication Controller
Port: ACIA 0-7            DB25S
Gender: Female            PinConfig: PO6

Pin   Function(Direction)
------------------------------------------
1     Frame Ground
2     Transmit Data(Out)
3     Receive Data(In)
6     Clear to Send(In)
7     Signal Ground
9     +12V(Out)
10    -12V(Out)
20    Data Terminal Ready(Out)
------------------------------------------
Flow Control:             XON/XOFF
Note:
```

```
Informer Computer Terminals
174M Communication Controller
Port: SYNCH/O HOST        DB25S
Gender: Female            PinConfig: PO6

Pin   Function(Direction)
------------------------------------------
1     Frame Ground
2     Transmit Data(Out)
3     Receive Data(In)
4     Request to Send(In)
5     Clear to Send(In)
6     Data Set Ready(In)
7     Signal Ground
8     Data Carrier Detect(In)
9     +12V(Out)
10    -12V(Out)
15    Transmit Clock(In)
17    Receive Clock(In)
20    Data Terminal Ready(Out)
------------------------------------------
Flow Control:             XON/XOFF
Note:
```

```
Informer
200-101/102, 207/209/213/231ME  Terminals
Port: (COM2)PRINTER       DB9S
Gender: Female            PinConfig: C51

Pin   Function(Direction)
------------------------------------------
1     Protective Ground
7     Signal Ground
2     Transmitted Data(out)
5     Print Control(in)
------------------------------------------
Flow Control:    XON/XOFF
Note:
```

```
Informer
371 Port Expander
Port: PRINTER             DB15S
Gender: Female            PinConfig: C51

Pin   Function(Direction)
------------------------------------------
1     Protective Ground
7     Signal Ground
2     Transmitted Data(out)
5     Print Control(in)
------------------------------------------
Flow Control:    XON/XOFF
Note:
```

```
Informer Computer Terminals
200-101/102/178 Workstation
Port: COM1-Host           DB25S
Gender: Female            PinConfig: PO6

Pin   Function(Direction)
------------------------------------------
1     Frame Ground
2     Transmit Data(Out)
3     Receive Data(In)
4     Request to Send(In)
5     Clear to Send(In)
7     Signal Ground
20    Data Terminal Ready(Out)
------------------------------------------
Flow Control:             XON/XOFF
Note:
```

Informer Computer Terminals 200-376, 213, 213ME Workstations Port: COM1-Host DB25S Gender: Female PinConfig: P06	Informer Computer Terminals 207/209 Portable Terminals Port: COM 1 DB25S Gender: Female PinConfig: P10

Informer Computer Terminals
200-376, 213, 213ME Workstations
Port: COM1-Host   DB25S
Gender: Female   PinConfig: P06

Pin   Function(Direction)
----
1   Frame Ground
2   Transmit Data(Out)
3   Receive Data(In)
4   Request to Send(In)
5   Clear to Send(In)
6   Data Set Ready(In)
7   Signal Ground
8   Data Carrier Detect(In)
9   +12V(Out)
10   -12V(Out)
15   Transmit Clock(In)
17   Receive Clock(In)
20   Data Terminal Ready(Out)

Flow Control:
Note:

Informer Computer Terminals
207/209 Portable Terminals
Port: COM 1   DB25S
Gender: Female   PinConfig: P10

Pin   Function(Direction)
----
1   Frame Ground
2   Transmit Data(Out)
3   Receive Data(In)
4   Request to Send(Out)
5   Clear to Send(In)
6   Data Set Ready(In)
7   Signal Ground
8   Data Carrier Detect(Out)
9   +12V(Out)
10   -12V(Out)
15   Transmit Clock(In)
17   Receive Clock(In)
20   Data Terminal Ready(Out)

Flow Control: XON/XOFF
Note:

Informer Computer Terminals
220/221 Portable Terminal
Port: EIA   DB9P
Gender: Male   PinConfig: C16

Pin   Function(Direction)
----
1   Carrier Detect(In)
2   Receive Data(In)
3   Transmit Data(Out)
4   Data Terminal Ready(Out)
5   Signal Ground
6   Data Set Ready(In)
7   Request to Send(Out)
8   Clear to Send(In)
9   Ring Indicator(In)

Flow Control: 6 & 8
Note: The flow control leads of the
attached device should be connected to
leads 6 & 8

Informer Computer Terminals
371E Port Expander
Port: CONSOLE   DB15S
Gender: Female   PinConfig: C19

Pin   Function(Direction)
----
7   Signal Ground
2   Transmitted Data(out)
3   Received Data(in)

Flow Control: XON/XOFF
Note:

Informer Computer Terminals
378 Workstation
Port: COM1-Host   DB25S
Gender: Female   PinConfig: P06

Pin   Function(Direction)
----
1   Frame Ground
2   Transmit Data(Out)
3   Receive Data(In)
4   Request to Send(In)
5   Clear to Send(In)
6   Data Set Ready(In)
7   Signal Ground
8   Data Carrier Detect(In)
9   +12V(Out)
10   -12V(Out)
20   Data Terminal Ready(Out)

Flow Control: XON/XOFF
Note:

Informer
ALI911 Terminal
Port: RS-232   DB25P
Gender: Male   PinConfig: C32

Pin   Function(Direction)
----
1   Protective Ground
4   Signal Ground
2   Transmitted Data(out)
3   Received Data(in)

Flow Control: XON/XOFF
Note:

```
Liberty Electronics                      Liberty Electronics
Freedom One/One Turbo/One Plus Terminals Freedom One/One Plus/Turbo, 120 Terminals
Port: AUX              DB25S             Port: MAIN              DB25S
Gender: Female         PinConfig: P21   Gender: Female          PinConfig: P03

Pin   Function(Direction)               Pin   Function(Direction)
-------------------------------------   -------------------------------------
1     Protective Ground                 1     Chassis Ground
7     Signal Ground                     2     Transmit Data(Out)
3     Transmitted Data(out)             3     Receive Data(In)
2     Received Data(in)                 4     Request to Send(Out)
5     Clear To Send(out)                5     Clear to Send(In)
6     Data Set Ready(out)               6     Data Set Ready(In)
8     Data Carrier Detect(out)          7     Signal Ground
4     Request To Send(in)               8     Data Carrier Detect(In)
19    Print Control(in)                 20    Data Terminal Ready(Out)
20    Data Terminal Ready(in)           -------------------------------------
-------------------------------------   Flow Control: 20        XON/XOFF
Flow Control: 6   XON/XOFF              Note:
Note:
```

```
Link                                    Link
Link 125 Terminal                       Link 125/220 Terminal
Port: AUX              DB25S             Port: MAIN              DB25S
Gender: Female         PinConfig: C14   Gender: Female          PinConfig: P03

Pin   Function(Direction)               Pin   Function(Direction)
-------------------------------------   -------------------------------------
1     Frame Ground                      1     Frame Ground
2     Transmit Data(In)                 2     Transmit Data(Out)
3     Receive Data(Out)                 3     Receive Data(In)
4     Request to Send(In)               4     Request to Send(Out)
5     Clear to Send(Out)                5     Clear to Send(In)
6     Data Set Ready(Out)               6     Data Set Ready(In)
7     Signal Ground                     7     Signal Ground
8     Data Carrier Detect(Out)          8     Data Carrier Detect(In)
20    Data Terminal Ready(In)           20    Data Terminal Ready(Out)
-------------------------------------   -------------------------------------
Flow Control: 20      XON/XOFF          Flow Control: 20        XON/XOFF
Note:                                   Note:
```

```
Link                                    Link
MC27 Terminal                           MC27 Terminal
Port: AUX              DB25S             Port: MAIN              DB25S
Gender: Female         PinConfig: C02   Gender: Female          PinConfig: P03

Pin   Function(Direction)               Pin   Function(Direction)
-------------------------------------   -------------------------------------
1     Frame Ground                      1     Frame Ground
2     Transmit Data(In)                 2     Transmit Data(Out)
3     Receive Data(Out)                 3     Receive Data(In)
4     Request to Send(In)               4     Request to Send(Out)
5     Clear to Send(Out)                5     Clear to Send(In)
6     Data Set Ready(Out)               6     Data Set Ready(In)
7     Signal Ground                     7     Signal Ground
8     Data Carrier Detect(Out)          8     Data Carrier Detect(In)
11    Secondary Req.to Send(In)         11    DRSO
20    Data Terminal Ready(In)           15    Transmit Clock(In)
-------------------------------------   17    Receive Clock(In)
Flow Control: 20      XON/XOFF          20    Data Terminal Ready(Out)
Note:                                   -------------------------------------
                                        Flow Control: 20        XON/XOFF
                                        Note:
```

```
Mannesmann Tally Corporation
MT-1612 Printer Terminal
Port: RS-232
Gender: Female            DB25S
 PinConfig: P05

Pin   Function(Direction)
-------------------------------------
1      Protective Ground
2      Transmit Data(Out)
3      Receive Data(In)
4      Request to Send(Out)
5      Clear to Send(In)
6      Data Set Ready(In)
7      Signal Ground
8      Rec.Line Signal Detect(In)
11     Secondary Req.to Send(Out)
19     Secondary Req.to Send(Out)
20     Data Terminal Ready(Out)
22     Ring Indicator(In)
-------------------------------------
Flow Control: 11 19        XON/XOFF
Note:
```

```
NCR
TOWERVIEW X-Station Workstation
Port: RS-232(DB-9)         DB9S
Gender: Female             PinConfig: C16

Pin   Function(Direction)
-------------------------------------
1      Carrier Detect(In)
2      Receive Data(In)
3      Transmit Data(Out)
4      Data Terminal Ready(Out)
5      Signal Ground
6      Data Set Ready(In)
7      Request to Send(Out)
8      Clear to Send(In)
-------------------------------------
Flow Control: 6 & 8
Note: The flow control leads of the
attached device should be connected to
leads 6 & 8
```

```
NCR
TOWERVIEW X-Station w/C3412-K010-V001)
Port: RS-232 DB25 adapter DB25S
Gender: Female             PinConfig: C01

Pin   Function(Direction)
-------------------------------------
2      Transmit Data(Out)
3      Receive Data(In)
4      Request to Send(Out)
5      Clear to Send(In)
6      Data Set Ready(In)
7      Signal Ground
8      Data Carrier Detect(In)
20     Data Terminal Ready(Out)
-------------------------------------
Flow Control: 5 & 6        XON/XOFF
Note: An adapter is used to convert the
9-pin w-station port to be DB-25
```

```
Qume
QVT 101 PLUS Terminal
Port: AUX                  DB25S
Gender: Female             PinConfig: C14

Pin   Function(Direction)
-------------------------------------
1      Chassis Ground
2      Receive Data(In)
3      Transmit Data(Out)
6      Data Set Ready(Out)
7      Signal Ground
20     Data Terminal Ready(In)
-------------------------------------
Flow Control: 20           XON/XOFF
Note:
```

```
Qume
QVT 101, 119, PLUS Terminals
Port: EIA(HOST)            DB25S
Gender: Female             PinConfig: P03

Pin   Function(Direction)
-------------------------------------
1      Chassis Ground
2      Transmit Data(Out)
3      Receive Data(In)
4      Request to Send(Out)
5      Clear to Send(In)
6      Data Set Ready(In)
7      Signal Ground
8      Data Carrier Detect(In)
20     Data Terminal Ready(Out)
-------------------------------------
Flow Control: 20           XON/XOFF
Note: RS-422 is also supported from this
port using leads 15/17/24/25
```

```
Qume
QVT 119. 190 PLUS Terminals
Port: AUX                  DB25S
Gender: Female             PinConfig: C14

Pin   Function(Direction)
-------------------------------------
1      Chassis Ground
2      Receive Data(In)
3      Transmit Data(Out)
5      Clear to Send(Out)
6      Data Set Ready(Out)
7      Signal Ground
20     Data Terminal Ready(In)
-------------------------------------
Flow Control: 20           XON/XOFF
Note:
```

```
Qume
QVT 190 Terminal
Port: EIA(Host)              DB25S
Gender: Female               PinConfig: P03

Pin   Function(Direction)
-----------------------------------------
1     Chassis Ground
2     Transmit Data(Out)
3     Receive Data(In)
4     Request to Send(Out)
5     Clear to Send(In)
6     Data Set Ready(In)
7     Signal Ground
8     Data Carrier Detect(In)
20    Data Terminal Ready(Out)
-----------------------------------------
Flow Control: 20             XON/XOFF
Note:  This port also supports RS-422,
using leads 12/13/24/25.
```

```
Qume
QVT 203/323EV PLUS Terminal
Port: AUX                    DB25S
Gender: Female               PinConfig: C01

Pin   Function(Direction)
-----------------------------------------
1     Chassis Ground
2     Transmit Data(Out)
3     Receive Data(In)
4     Request to Send(Out)
6     Data Set Ready(In)
7     Signal Ground
20    Data Terminal Ready(Out)
-----------------------------------------
Flow Control: 20             XON/XOFF
Note:
```

```
Qume
QVT 203/323EV PLUS Terminal
Port: EIA(HOST)              DB25S
Gender: Female               PinConfig: P01

Pin   Function(Direction)
-----------------------------------------
1     Chassis Ground
2     Transmit Data(Out)
3     Receive Data(In)
4     Request to Send(Out)
5     Clear to Send(In)
6     Data Set Ready(In)
7     Signal Ground
8     Data Carrier Detect(In)
12    Speed Select(In)
19    Secondary Req.to Send(Out)
20    Data Terminal Ready(Out)
23    Speed Select(Out)
-----------------------------------------
Flow Control: 19             XON/XOFF
Note:  RS-422 is also supported from this
port using leads 17/21/24/25
```

```
Tandem Computers
5520(EIA Adapter Cable)
Port:  EIA Adapt.Cable       DB25S
Gender: Female               PinConfig: P08

Pin   Function(Direction)
-----------------------------------------
1     Protective Ground
2     Transmit Data(Out)
3     Receive Data(In)
4     Request to Send(Out)
5     Clear to Send(In)
6     Data Set Ready(In)
7     Signal Ground
20    Data Terminal Ready(Out)
-----------------------------------------
Flow Control: 20             XON/XOFF
Note:
```

```
Tandem Computers
6520 Terminal
Port: MAIN                   DB25S
Gender: Female               PinConfig: P03

Pin   Function(Direction)
-----------------------------------------
1     Protective Ground
2     Transmit Data(Out)
3     Receive Data(In)
4     Request to Send(Out)
5     Clear to Send(In)
6     Data Set Ready(In)
7     Signal Ground
8     Data Carrier Detect(In)
15    Transmit Clock(In)
17    Receive Clock(In)
20    Data Terminal Ready(Out)
-----------------------------------------
Flow Control: 20             XON/XOFF
Note:
```

```
Tandem Computers
6526 Terminal
Port: AUX1                   DB25S
Gender: Female               PinConfig: C01

Pin   Function(Direction)
-----------------------------------------
1     Frame Ground
2     Transmit Data(Out)
3     Receive Data(In)
4     Request to Send(Out)
5     Clear to Send(In)
6     Data Set Ready(In)
7     Signal Ground
8     Data Carrier Detect(In)
20    Data Terminal Ready(Out)
-----------------------------------------
Flow Control: 5              XON/XOFF
Note:  Printers should connect their
output flow control lead to pin 5 of this
port
```

```
Tandem Computers
6526 Terminal
Port: AUX2                  DB25S
Gender: Female              PinConfig: C01

Pin   Function(Direction)
------------------------------------
1     Frame Ground
2     Transmit Data(Out)
3     Receive Data(In)
4     Request to Send(Out)
5     Clear to Send(In)
6     Data Set Ready(In)
7     Signal Ground
8     Data Carrier Detect(In)
20    Data Terminal Ready(Out)
------------------------------------
Flow Control: 5            XON/XOFF
Note:  Printers connected to this port,
must have their output hardware flow
control lead connect to pin 5
```

```
Tandem Computers
6526 Terminal
Port: CPU                   DB25S
Gender: Female              PinConfig: C01

Pin   Function(Direction)
------------------------------------
1     Frame Ground
2     Transmit Data(Out)
3     Receive Data(In)
4     Request to Send(Out)
5     Clear to Send(In)
6     Data Set Ready(In)
7     Signal Ground
8     Data Carrier Detect(In)
15    Transmit Clock(In)
17    Receive Clock(In)
20    Data Terminal Ready(Out)
------------------------------------
Flow Control: 5,6, & 8     XON/XOFF
Note:
```

```
Tandem Computers
6530 Terminal
Port: MAIN                  DB25S
Gender: Female              PinConfig: P03

Pin   Function(Direction)
------------------------------------
1     Protective Ground
2     Transmit Data(Out)
3     Receive Data(In)
4     Request to Send(Out)
5     Clear to Send(In)
6     Data Set Ready(In)
7     Signal Ground
8     Data Carrier Detect(In)
15    Transmit Clock(In)
17    Receive Clock(In)
20    Data Terminal Ready(Out)
------------------------------------
Flow Control: 20           XON/XOFF
Note:
```

```
Tandem Computers
6820 Terminal
Port: MAIN                  DB25S
Gender: Female              PinConfig: P03

Pin   Function(Direction)
------------------------------------
1     Protective Ground
2     Transmit Data(Out)
3     Receive Data(In)
4     Request to Send(Out)
5     Clear to Send(In)
6     Data Set Ready(In)
7     Signal Ground
8     Data Carrier Detect(In)
15    Transmit Clock(In)
17    Receive Clock(In)
20    Data Terminal Ready(Out)
------------------------------------
Flow Control: 20           XON/XOFF
Note:
```

```
Tektronix
4200 Terminals
Port: RS-232                DB25P
Gender: Male                PinConfig: P03

Pin   Function(Direction)
------------------------------------
1     Protective Ground
2     Transmit Data(Out)
3     Receive Data(In)
4     Request to Send(Out)
5     Clear to Send(In)
6     Data Set Ready(In)
7     Signal Ground
8     Data Carrier Detect(In)
12    Secondary DCD(In)
15    Transmit Clock(In)
17    Receive Clock(In)
19    Secondary Req.to Send(Out)
20    Data Terminal Ready(Out)
------------------------------------
Flow Control: 20           XON/XOFF
Note:
```

```
Texas Instruments
LT220 Terminal
Port: RS-232                DB9P
Gender: Male                PinConfig: C16

Pin   Function(Direction)
------------------------------------
1     Carrier Detect(In)
2     Receive Data(In)
3     Transmit Data(Out)
4     Data Terminal Ready(Out)
5     Signal Ground
6     Data Set Ready(In)
7     Request to Send(Out)
8     Clear to Send(In)
------------------------------------
Flow Control: 6 & 8
Note:  The flow control leads of the
attached device should be connected to
leads 6 & 8
```

```
+---------------------------------------+---------------------------------------+
| Wang Laboratories                     | Wyse Technology                       |
| 2110 & 2110A Terminal                 | WY75/WY350/WY50+/WY50  Terminal       |
| Port: RS-232          DB25S           | Port: MODEM(2/3/7 only) DB25S         |
| Gender: Female        PinConfig: C01  | Gender: Female        PinConfig: C19  |
|                                       |                                       |
| Pin  Function(Direction)              | Pin   Function(Direction)             |
| ------------------------------------- | ------------------------------------- |
| 1    Protective Ground                | 7     Signal Ground                   |
| 2    Transmit Data(Out)               | 2     Transmitted Data(out)           |
| 3    Receive Data(In)                 | 3     Received Data(in)               |
| 4    Request to Send(Out)             | ------------------------------------- |
| 5    Clear to Send(In)                | Flow Control:   XON/XOFF              |
| 6    Data Set Ready(In)               | Note:                                 |
| 7    Signal Ground                    |                                       |
| 8    Carrier Detect(In)               |                                       |
| 20   Data Terminal Ready(Out)         |                                       |
| 22   Ring Indicator(In)               |                                       |
| ------------------------------------- |                                       |
| Flow Control: 5,6        XON/XOFF     |                                       |
| Note: Leads 5 & 6 must be on          |                                       |
+---------------------------------------+---------------------------------------+
| Wyse Technology                       | Wyse Technology                       |
| WY85 Terminal                         | WY150/WY120/WY30/WY60  Terminal       |
| Port: Printer         DB9P            | Port: MODEM(2/3/7 only)  DB25S        |
| Gender: Male          PinConfig: P22  | Gender: Female        PinConfig: C19  |
|                                       |                                       |
| Pin  Function(Direction)              | Pin   Function(Direction)             |
| ------------------------------------- | ------------------------------------- |
| 1    Protective Ground                | 7     Signal Ground                   |
| 7    Signal Ground                    | 2     Transmitted Data(out)           |
| 2    Transmitted Data(out)            | 3     Received Data(in)               |
| 3    Received Data(in)                | ------------------------------------- |
| 4    Request To Send(out)             | Flow Control:   XON/XOFF              |
| 5    Data Terminal Ready(out)         | Note:                                 |
| 6    Data Set Ready(in)               |                                       |
| ------------------------------------- |                                       |
| Flow Control: 5  XON/XOFF             |                                       |
| Note:                                 |                                       |
+---------------------------------------+---------------------------------------+
| Wyse Technology                       | Wyse Technology                       |
| WY120/WY150/WY50+ Terminals           | WY160 Terminal                        |
| Port: Modem(full control) DB25S       | Port: Serial 1 - 25 pin   DB25S       |
| Gender: Female        PinConfig: P03  | Gender: Female        PinConfig: P03  |
|                                       |                                       |
| Pin  Function(Direction)              | Pin   Function(Direction)             |
| ------------------------------------- | ------------------------------------- |
| 1    Frame Ground                     | 1     Frame Ground                    |
| 2    Transmit Data(Out)               | 2     Transmit Data(Out)              |
| 3    Receive Data(In)                 | 3     Receive Data(In)                |
| 4    Request to Send(Out)             | 4     Request to Send(Out)            |
| 5    Clear to Send(In)                | 5     Clear to Send(In)               |
| 6    Data Set Ready(In)               | 6     Data Set Ready(In)              |
| 7    Signal Ground                    | 7     Signal Ground                   |
| 8    Data Carrier Detect(In)          | 8     Data Carrier Detect(In)         |
| 20   Data Terminal Ready(Out)         | 20    Data Terminal Ready(Out)        |
| ------------------------------------- | ------------------------------------- |
| Flow Control: 20        XON/XOFF      | Flow Control: 20        XON/XOFF      |
| Note: This interface supports optioning| Note: This interface supports optioning|
| to use only leads 2/3/7.  Use different| to use only leads 2/3/7.  Use different|
| pinout entry for this.                | pinout entry for this.                |
+---------------------------------------+---------------------------------------+
```

```
Wyse Technology
WY160 Terminal
Port:  Serial 2 - 9 pin    DB9P
Gender:  Male              PinConfig: C16

Pin   Function(Direction)
-----------------------------------------------
1         Carrier Detect(In)
2         Receive Data(In)
3         Transmit Data(Out)
4         Data Terminal Ready(Out)
5         Signal Ground
6         Data Set Ready(In)
7         Request to Send(Out)
8         Clear to Send(In)
-----------------------------------------------
Flow Control: 4            XON/XOFF
Note:  The flow control leads of the
attached device should be connected to
leads 6 & 8
```

```
Wyse Technology
WY185 Terminal
Port:  Modem A-Full ControlDB25S
Gender:  Female            PinConfig: P03

Pin   Function(Direction)
-----------------------------------------------
1         Frame Ground
2         Transmit Data(Out)
3         Receive Data(In)
4         Request to Send(Out)
5         Clear to Send(In)
6         Data Set Ready(In)
7         Signal Ground
8         Data Carrier Detect(In)
12        Speed Select(In)
20        Data Terminal Ready(Out)
23        Data Rate Select(Out)
-----------------------------------------------
Flow Control: 20           XON/XOFF
Note:  This interface supports optioning
to use only leads 2/3/7.  Use different
pinout entry for this.
```

```
Wyse Technology
WY370 Terminal
Port:  Port A RS-232(Full) DB25S
Gender:  Female            PinConfig: P03

Pin   Function(Direction)
-----------------------------------------------
1         Frame Ground
2         Transmit Data(Out)
3         Receive Data(In)
4         Request to Send(Out)
5         Clear to Send(In)
7         Signal Ground
8         Data Carrier Detect(In)
15        RD- (In)
17        RD+ (In)
19        TD- (Out)
20        Data Terminal Ready(Out)
25        TD+ (Out)
-----------------------------------------------
Flow Control: 20           XON/XOFF
Note:  This interface supports optioning
to use only leads 2/3/7.  Use different
pinout entry for this.
```

```
Wyse Technology
WY370 Terminal
Port:  Port B - RS-232     DB25S
Gender:  Female            PinConfig: P03

Pin   Function(Direction)
-----------------------------------------------
1         Frame Ground
2         Transmit Data(Out)
3         Receive Data(In)
4         Request to Send(Out)
5         Clear to Send(In)
7         Signal Ground
8         Data Carrier Detect(In)
20        Data Terminal Ready(Out)
-----------------------------------------------
Flow Control: 20           XON/XOFF
Note:  This interface supports optioning
to use only leads 2/3/7.  Use different
pinout entry for this.
```

```
Wyse Technology
WY50+ Terminal
Port:  AUX port            DB25S
Gender:  Female            PinConfig: C14

Pin   Function(Direction)
-----------------------------------------------
1         Frame Ground
2         Transmit Data(In)
3         Receive Data(Out)
6         Data Set Ready(Out)
7         Signal Ground
8         Data Carrier Detect(Out)
20        Data Terminal Ready(In)
-----------------------------------------------
Flow Control: 20           XON/XOFF
Note:
```

```
Wyse Technology
WY99GT Terminal
Port:  AUX port            DB25S
Gender:  Female            PinConfig: C01

Pin   Function(Direction)
-----------------------------------------------
1         Frame Ground
2         Transmit Data(Out)
3         Receive Data(In)
4         Request to Send(Out)
5         Clear to Send(In)
6         Data Set Ready(In)
7         Signal Ground
8         Data Carrier Detect(In)
9         +12V(Out)
10        -12V(Out)
20        Data Terminal Ready(Out)
-----------------------------------------------
Flow Control: 6            XON/XOFF
Note:
```

```
Wyse Technology
WY99GT Terminal
Port: Modem(full control) DB25P
Gender:  Male                PinConfig: P03

Pin   Function(Direction)
-----------------------------------------
1        Frame Ground
2        Transmit Data(Out)
3        Receive Data(In)
4        Request to Send(Out)
5        Clear to Send(In)
6        Data Set Ready(In)
7        Signal Ground
8        Data Carrier Detect(In)
12       Speed Select(In)
15       RD+ (In)
17       RD- (In)
19       TD+ (Out)
20       Data Terminal Ready(Out)
23       Speed Select(Out)
25       TD- (Out)
-----------------------------------------
Flow Control: 20          XON/XOFF
Note:  This interface also supports
optioning to use only leads 2/3/7.   It
supports RS422-RS423-RS232(above)
```

APPENDIX

G

interconnections between computers and peripherals

Appendix G outlines the connections of computers, ports boards, modems, buffers, terminal servers, terminals, and printers through an RS-232 port. When used in conjunction with Appendix F, the proper cables may be constructed to allow data exchange between devices. The following displays the step-by-step procedure for determining how the pins of RS-232 cables should be connected using Appendix F and G.

1. In Appendix F, locate the appropriate devices to be connected, noting their pin configuration, "PinConfig: XXX". If your device is not listed, compare its RS-232 pinouts with devices in Appendix F until an exact match is found.
2. Proceed to the appropriate cable graph table. Graph G-1 is for connecting printers and most terminals to buffers, boards, data switches, computers. PinConfigs Pxx to Cxx connections will be based on Graph G-1. Graph G-2 is for connecting computers to other computers, buffers, boards, terminals servers, data switches, or modems. This is used for connecting PinConfigs, Cxx to Cxx.
3. Find the pin configuration of the first device in the column labeled "Device-A" at the leftmost column of the table.
4. Find the pin configuration of the other computer, modem, printer, or terminal, "Device-B" across the top row of the table.
5. Note the graph number at the intersection of the column and row.
6. Find the appropriately labeled graph, Gxxxx or RGxxxx, in this appendix for a display of the cross connections necessary in the RS-232 cable. Construct the cable accordingly. Note the "G" versus "RG" nomenclature. The "G" indicates that the cable is viewed from left to right, with the cable end for Device-A on the left, and Device-B's end of the cable on the right. When the RG (reverse Graph) appears, use the same cable graph, but reverse the view, Device-A is on the right and Device-B is on the left.

As an example, to connect an Hewlett-Packard LaserJet Series II printer (P11) to an IBM PC(CO1), Graph G2870 would be used for the cable design. Note the gender provided on each configuration. These present the opposite of what the cable requirement will be. The LaserJet provides a female port, hence, the cable connector will be the opposite, male. The PC has a male DB-25 connector, thus requiring a female DB25 for its cable end.

It is important to note that when building RS-232 cables, many different combinations of pin configurations exist for a connection. The diagrams point out only one of many ways in which RS-232 leads may be connected. Neither the author nor the publisher claims responsibility for the accuracy of the diagrams of charts, as they were constructed from information supplied by the vendors. The vendors of these products often provide similar information for device connections. Use their recommendations when possible, as they have been thoroughly tested. This should also be done because, in some cases, more leads are present in these graphs than are actually needed. These leads are provided for completeness and more flexible use of the cables.

Many times, there are not enough control signals in either port for a complete connection. "N/A" in the graph tables indicates that the two devices cannot be connected with confidence of total functionality. A connection may be possible using total functionality. A connection may be possible using only the data leads and signal ground. However, the author did not include these to avoid potential confusion and mis-wiring. Consult the user documentation for use of a simplified interface, or contact the vendor if the interface is not listed in this appendix. Furthermore, these graphs are for asynchronous connections only. Refer to Chapter 5 for instructions on how to connect the timing leads for synchronous connections. However, the bulk of the devices in Appendix F support asynchronous operation only.

Another factor impacting the inclusion of certain control leads, is the flow control technique used. For example, often pin 19, 20 or 4 may be used to hold a given lead, such as data set ready, on or off. If hardware flow control will not be used, pin 4 or 20 would be selected, in which case pin 19 would not even be used. The selection should be based on the options for the particular installation. The cable diagrams herein provide for hardware flow control where supported, unless there are no control signals. By providing for hardware flow control, software flow control should also work using the same cable.

Furthermore, different configurations may be possible for ports. The way a port is configured affects the cable to be used. If a port may be set up to emulate either data communication equipment (DCE) or data terminal equipment (DTE), choose the configuration that allows for the most flexibility in your configuration. Double check your selection of the proper port from Appendix F.

When reviewing the graphs, the arrows and ":" have special meaning as in Table G-2.

In the GXXXX sample graphs, the ":" indicates that the leads are connected to the adjacent lead(s) that have a ":" in the same column, either directly above or below. View this as a local jumpering of two or more leads together. Leads 5, 6, and 8 for Device B would all be connected together in the example. They are then connected across to lead 20 of the other device. Also in the GXXXX example, lead 20 of Device B is connected locally to lead 6 at the same end of the cable, and also connected to lead 6 at the other end of the cable. Leads 6, at both ends, are input leads, represented by the arrows (←, →). Leads 1 and 7 are connected straight-through from cable-end to cable-end, while leads 2 and 3 are crossed from end to end. Protective Ground may not be required and is left out of most of the cable designs. Use this legend as your guide in interpreting the graphs. Remember that a "RG" graph reverses the Device-A and Device-B perspective.

TABLE G–2. Graphs & Reverse Graphs

GXXXX			RGXXXX		
1	————	1	1	————	1
7	————	7	7	————	7
3	←————	2	3	←————	2
2	————→	3	2	————→	3
20	—— : →	5	20	—— : →	5
	: →	6		: →	6
	: →	8		: →	8
6	← : ——	20	6	← : ——	20
	: →	6		: →	6
Device-A	Device-B		Device-B	Device-A	

Once the cable has been built, the options should be reviewed. Double-check to ensure that the speed, parity, character length, flow control technique, polarity of flow control signal, and other options are properly set. Once set, attach the cable between the devices, power up the devices, enable the ports, and test your systems for proper operation.

Graph G-1. Printer/Plotter/Terminal to Computer Devices Table

Device-A	Device-B ---------->										
	C1	C2	C3	C4	C5	C6	C7	C8	C9	C10	C11
P1	G2268	G2269	G2270	G2271	G2272	G2273	G2274	G2275	G2276	G2277	G2278
P2	G2335	G2336	G2337	G2338	G2339	G2340	G2341	G2342	G2343	G2344	G2345
P3	G2402	G2403	G2404	G2405	G2406	G2407	G2408	G2409	G2410	G2411	G2412
P4	G2469	G2470	G2471	G2472	G2473	G2474	G2475	G2476	G2477	G2478	G2479
P5	G2536	G2537	G2538	G2539	G2540	G2541	G2542	G2543	G2544	G2545	G2546
P6	G2603	G2604	G2605	G2606	G2607	G2608	G2609	G2610	G2611	G2612	G2613
P7	G2670	G2671	G2672	G2673	G2674	G2675	G2676	G2677	G2678	G2679	G2680
P8	G2736	G2737	G2738	G2739	G2740	G2741	G2742	G2743	G2744	G2745	G2746
P9	G2803	G2804	G2805	G2806	G2807	G2808	G2809	G2810	G2811	G2812	G2813
P10	G2402	G2403	G2404	G2405	G2406	G2407	G2408	G2409	G2410	G2411	G2412
P11	G2870	G2871	G2872	G2873	G2874	G2875	G2876	G2877	G2878	G2879	G2880
P12	G2937	G2938	G2939	G2940	G2941	G2942	G2943	G2944	G2945	G2946	G2947
P13	G3004	G3005	G3006	G3007	G3008	G3009	G3010	G3011	G3012	G3013	G3014
P14	G3071	G3072	G3073	G3074	G3075	G3076	G3077	G3078	G3079	G3080	G3081
P15	G3138	G3139	G3140	G3141	G3142	G3143	G3144	G3145	G3146	G3147	G3148
P16	G3321	G3322	G3323	G3324	G3325	G3326	G3327	G3328	G3329	G3330	G3331
P17	G3205	G3206	G3207	G3208	G3209	n/a	G3210	G3211	G3212	G3213	G3214
P18	G3254	G3255	G3256	G3257	G3258	G3259	G3260	G3261	G3262	G3263	G3264
P19	G3388	G3389	G3390	G3391	G3392	G3393	G3394	G3395	G3396	G3397	G3398
P20	G3455	G3456	G3457	G3458	G3459	G3460	G3461	G3462	G3463	G3464	G3465
P21	G3522	G3523	G3524	G3525	G3526	G3527	G3528	G3529	G3530	G3531	G3532
P22	G3589	G3590	G3591	G3592	G3593	G3594	G3595	G3596	G3597	G3598	G3599

Graph G-1. Printer/Plotter/Terminal to Computer Devices Table (*cont.*)

| Device-A | Device-B -------> | | | | | | | | | | |
	C12	C13	C14	C15	C16	C17	C18	C19	C20	C21	C22
P1	G2279	G2280	G2281	G2282	G2283	G2284	G2285	G2286	G2287	G2288	G2289
P2	G2346	G2347	G2348	G2349	G2350	G2351	G2352	G2353	G2354	G2355	G2356
P3	G2413	G2414	G2415	G2416	G2417	G2418	G2419	G2420	G2421	G2422	G2423
P4	G2480	G2481	G2482	G2483	G2484	G2485	G2486	G2487	G2488	G2489	G2490
P5	G2547	G2548	G2549	G2550	G2551	G2552	G2553	G2554	G2555	G2556	G2557
P6	G2614	G2615	G2616	G2617	G2618	G2619	G2620	G2621	G2622	G2623	G2624
P7	G2681	G2682	G2683	G2684	G2685	G2686	G2687	G2688	G2689	G2690	G2691
P8	G2747	G2748	G2749	G2750	G2751	G2752	G2753	G2754	G2755	G2756	G2757
P9	G2814	G2815	G2816	G2817	G2818	G2819	G2820	G2821	G2822	G2823	G2824
P10	G2881	G2882	G2883	G2884	G2885	G2886	G2887	G2888	G2889	G2890	G2891
P11	G2948	G2949	G2950	G2951	G2952	G2953	G2954	G2955	G2956	G2957	G2958
P12	G3015	G3016	G3017	G3018	G3019	G3020	G3021	G3022	G3023	G3024	G3025
P13	G3082	G3083	G3084	G3085	G3086	G3087	G3088	G3089	G3090	G3091	G3092
P14	G3149	G3150	G3151	G3152	G3153	G3154	G3155	G3156	G3157	G3158	G3159
P15	G3332	G3333	G3334	G3335	G3336	G3337	G3338	G3339	G3340	G3341	G3342
P16	G3212	G3213	G3215	G3216	G3217	G3218	G3219	G3220	G3221	G3221	G3222
P17	n/a	n/a	G3215	G3216	G3217	G3218	G3219	n/a	G3220	G3221	G3222
P18	G3265	G3266	G3267	G3268	G3269	G3270	G3271	G3272	G3273	G3274	G3275
P19	G3399	G3400	G3401	G3402	G3403	G3404	G3405	G3406	G3407	G3408	G3409
P20	G3466	G3467	G3468	G3469	G3470	G3471	G3472	G3473	G3474	G3475	G3476
P21	G3533	G3534	G3535	G3536	G3537	G3538	G3539	G3540	G3541	G3542	G3543
P22	G3600	G3601	G3602	G3603	G3604	G3605	G3606	G3607	G3608	G3609	G3610

Graph G-1. Printer/Plotter/Terminal to Computer Devices Table (*cont.*)

| Device-A | Device-B --------> | | | | | | | | | | |
	C23	C26	C28	C29	C30	C33	C34	C35	C36	C37	C38
P1	G2290	G2291	G2292	G2293	G2294	G2295	G2296	G2297	G2298	G2299	G2300
P2	G2357	G2358	G2359	G2360	G2361	G2362	G2363	G2364	G2365	G2366	G2367
P3	G2424	G2425	G2426	G2427	G2428	G2429	G2430	G2431	G2432	G2433	G2434
P4	G2491	G2492	G2493	G2494	G2495	G2496	G2497	G2498	G2499	G2500	G2501
P5	G2558	G2559	G2560	G2561	G2562	G2563	G2564	G2565	G2566	G2567	G2568
P6	G2625	G2626	G2627	G2628	G2629	G2630	G2631	G2632	G2633	G2634	G2635
P7	G2692	G2693	G2694	G2695	G2696	G2697	G2698	G2699	G2700	G2701	G2702
P8	G2758	G2759	G2760	G2761	G2762	G2763	G2764	G2765	G2766	G2767	G2768
P9	G2825	G2826	G2827	G2828	G2829	G2830	G2831	G2832	G2833	G2834	G2835
P10	G2424	G2425	G2426	G2427	G2428	G2429	G2430	G2431	G2432	G2433	G2434
P11	G2892	G2893	G2894	G2895	G2896	G2897	G2898	G2899	G2900	G2901	G2902
P12	G2959	G2960	G2961	G2962	G2963	G2964	G2965	G2966	G2967	G2968	G2969
P13	G3026	G3027	G3028	G3029	G3030	G3031	G3032	G3033	G3034	G3035	G3036
P14	G3093	G3094	G3095	G3096	G3097	G3098	G3099	G3100	G3101	G3102	G3103
P15	G3160	G3161	G3162	G3163	G3164	G3165	G3166	G3167	G3168	G3169	G3170
P16	G3343	G3344	G3345	G3346	G3347	G3348	G3349	G3350	G3351	G3352	G3353
P17	G3223	G3224	G3225	G3226	G3227	n/a	G3228	G3229	G3230	G3231	G3232
P18	G3276	G3277	G3278	G3279	G3280	G3281	G3282	G3283	G3284	G3285	G3286
P19	G3410	G3411	G3412	G3413	G3414	G3415	G3416	G3417	G3418	G3419	G3420
P20	G3477	G3478	G3479	G3480	G3481	G3482	G3483	G3484	G3485	G3486	G3487
P21	G3544	G3545	G3546	G3547	G3548	G3549	G3550	G3551	G3552	G3553	G3554
P22	G3611	G3612	G3613	G3614	G3615	G3616	G3617	G3618	G3619	G3620	G3621

Graph G-1. Printer/Plotter/Terminal to Computer Devices Table (*cont.*)

| Device-A | Device-B ----------> | | | | | | | | | | |
	C39	C40	C41	C42	C43	C44	C45	C46	C47	C48	C49
P1	G2301	G2302	G2303	G2304	G2305	G2306	G2307	G2308	G2309	G2310	G2311
P2	G2368	G2369	G2370	G2371	G2372	G2373	G2374	G2375	G2376	G2377	G2378
P3	G2435	G2436	G2437	G2438	G2439	G2440	G2441	G2442	G2443	G2444	G2445
P4	G2502	G2503	G2504	G2505	G2506	G2507	G2508	G2509	G2510	G2511	G2512
P5	G2569	G2570	G2571	G2572	G2573	G2574	G2575	G2576	G2577	G2578	G2579
P6	G2636	G2637	G2638	G2639	G2640	G2641	G2642	G2643	G2644	G2645	G2646
P7	G2703	G2704	G2705	G2706	G2707	G2708	G2709	G2710	G2711	G2712	G2713
P8	G2769	G2770	G2771	G2772	G2773	G2774	G2775	G2776	G2777	G2778	G2779
P9	G2836	G2837	G2838	G2839	G2840	G2841	G2842	G2843	G2844	G2845	G2846
P10	G2435	G2436	G2437	G2438	G2439	G2440	G2441	G2442	G2443	G2444	G2445
P11	G2903	G2904	G2905	G2906	G2907	G2908	G2909	G2910	G2911	G2912	G2913
P12	G2970	G2971	G2972	G2973	G2974	G2975	G2976	G2977	G2978	G2979	G2980
P13	G3037	G3038	G3039	G3040	G3041	G3042	G3043	G3044	G3045	G3046	G3047
P14	G3104	G3105	G3106	G3107	G3108	G3109	G3110	G3111	G3112	G3113	G3114
P15	G3171	G3172	G3173	G3174	G3175	G3176	G3177	G3178	G3179	G3180	G3181
P16	G3354	G3355	G3356	G3357	G3358	G3359	G3360	G3361	G3362	G3363	G3364
P17	G3233	G3234	G3235	G3236	G3237	G3238	G3239	G3240	G3241	n/a	G3242
P18	G3287	G3288	G3289	G3290	G3291	G3292	G3293	G3294	G3295	G3296	G3297
P19	G3421	G3422	G3423	G3424	G3425	G3426	G3427	G3428	G3429	G3430	G3431
P20	G3488	G3489	G3490	G3491	G3492	G3493	G3494	G3495	G3496	G3497	G3498
P21	G3555	G3556	G3557	G3558	G3559	G3560	G3561	G3562	G3563	G3564	G3565
P22	G3622	G3623	G3624	G3625	G3626	G3627	G3628	G3629	G3630	G3631	G3632

Graph G-1. Printer/Plotter/Terminal to Computer Devices Table (*cont.*)

Device-A	Device-B ---------->										
	C50	C51	C52	C53	C54	C55	C56	C57	C60	C61	C62
P1	G2312	G2313	G2314	G2315	G2316	G2317	G2318	G2319	G2320	G2321	G2322
P2	G2379	G2380	G2381	G2382	G2383	G2384	G2385	G2386	G2387	G2388	G2389
P3	G2446	G2447	G2448	G2449	G2450	G2451	G2452	G2453	G2454	G2455	G2456
P4	G2513	G2514	G2515	G2516	G2517	G2518	G2519	G2520	G2521	G2522	G2523
P5	G2580	G2581	G2582	G2583	G2584	G2585	G2586	G2587	G2588	G2589	G2590
P6	G2647	G2648	G2649	G2650	G2651	G2652	G2653	G2654	G2655	G2656	G2657
P7	G2714	G2715	G2716	G2717	G2718	G2719	G2720	G2721	G2722	G2723	G2724
P8	G2780	G2781	G2782	G2783	G2784	G2785	G2786	G2787	G2788	G2789	G2790
P9	G2847	G2848	G2849	G2850	G2851	G2852	G2853	G2854	G2855	G2856	G2857
P10	G2914	G2915	G2916	G2917	G2918	G2919	G2920	G2921	G2922	G2923	G2924
P11	G2981	G2982	G2983	G2984	G2985	G2986	G2987	G2988	G2989	G2990	G2991
P12	G3048	G3049	G3050	G3051	G3052	G3053	G3054	G3055	G3056	G3057	G3058
P13	G3115	G3116	G3117	G3118	G3119	G3120	G3121	G3122	G3123	G3124	G3125
P14	G3182	G3183	G3184	G3185	G3186	G3187	G3188	G3189	G3190	G3191	G3192
P15	G3249	G3366	G3367	G3368	G3369	G3370	G3371	G3372	G3373	G3374	G3375
P16	G3365	G3366	G3367	G3368	G3369	G3370	G3371	G3372	G3373	G3374	G3375
P17	G3243	n/a	G3244	G3245	G3246	G3247	G3248	G3249	G3250	G3251	G3252
P18	G3298	G3299	G3300	G3301	G3302	G3303	G3304	G3305	G3306	G3307	G3308
P19	G3432	G3433	G3434	G3435	G3436	G3437	G3438	G3439	G3440	G3441	G3442
P20	G3499	G3500	G3501	G3502	G3503	G3504	G3505	G3506	G3507	G3508	G3509
P21	G3566	G3567	G3568	G3569	G3570	G3571	G3572	G3573	G3574	G3575	G3576
P22	G3633	G3634	G3635	G3636	G3637	G3638	G3639	G3640	G3641	G3642	G3643

Graph G-1.   Printer/Plotter/Terminal to Computer Devices Table (*cont.*)

Device-A	Device-B -------->											
	C63	C64	C65	C66	C67	C68	C69	C70	C71	C72	C73	C74
P1	G2323	G2324	G2325	G2326	G2327	G2328	G2329	G2330	G2331	G2332	G2333	G2334
P2	G2390	G2391	G2392	G2393	G2394	G2395	G2396	G2397	G2398	G2399	G2400	G2401
P3	G2457	G2458	G2459	G2460	G2461	G2462	G2463	G2464	G2465	G2466	G2467	G2468
P4	G2524	G2525	G2526	G2527	G2528	G2529	G2530	G2531	G2532	G2533	G2534	G2535
P5	G2591	G2592	G2593	G2594	G2595	G2596	G2597	G2598	G2599	G2600	G2601	G2602
P6	G2658	G2659	G2660	G2661	G2662	G2663	G2664	G2665	G2666	G2667	G2668	G2669
P7	G2725	G2726	G2727	G2728	G2729	G2730	G2731	G2732	G2733	G2734	G2735	G2736
P8	G2791	G2792	G2793	G2794	G2795	G2796	G2797	G2798	G2799	G2800	G2801	G2802
P9	G2858	G2859	G2860	G2861	G2862	G2863	G2864	G2865	G2866	G2867	G2868	G2869
P10	G2457	G2458	G2459	G2460	G2461	G2462	G2463	G2464	G2465	G2466	G2467	G2468
P11	G2925	G2926	G2927	G2928	G2929	G2930	G2931	G2932	G2933	G2934	G2935	G2936
P12	G2992	G2993	G2994	G2995	G2996	G2997	G2998	G2999	G3000	G3001	G3002	G3003
P13	G3059	G3060	G3061	G3062	G3063	G3064	G3065	G3066	G3067	G3068	G3069	G3070
P14	G3126	G3127	G3128	G3129	G3130	G3131	G3132	G3133	G3134	G3135	G3136	G3137
P15	G3193	G3194	G3195	G3196	G3197	G3198	G3199	G3200	G3201	G3202	G3203	G3204
P16	G3376	G3377	G3378	G3379	G3380	G3381	G3382	G3383	G3384	G3385	G3386	G3387
P17	G3253	G3656	G3657	G3658	G3659	G3660	G3661	G3662	G3663	G3664	G3665	G3666
P18	G3309	G3310	G3311	G3312	G3313	G3314	G3315	G3316	G3317	G3318	G3319	G3320
P19	G3443	G3444	G3445	G3446	G3447	G3448	G3449	G3450	G3451	G3452	G3453	G3454
P20	G3510	G3511	G3512	G3513	G3514	G3515	G3516	G3517	G3518	G3519	G3520	G3521
P21	G3577	G3578	G3579	G3580	G3581	G3582	G3583	G3584	G3585	G3586	G3587	G3588
P22	G3644	G3645	G3646	G3647	G3648	G3649	G3650	G3651	G3652	G3653	G3654	G3655

Graph G-2. Computer/Boards/Buffers/Data Switches/Modems to Other Computer Devices

| | Device - B ------------------->> | | | | | | | | | | |
Device-A	C1	C2	C3	C4	C5	C6	C7	C8	C9	C10	C11
C1	G450	G451	G452	G453	G454	G455	G456	G457	G458	G459	G460
C2	RG451	G470	G471	G472	G473	G474	G475	G476	G477	G478	G479
C3	RG452	RG471	G489	G490	G491	G492	G493	G494	G495	G496	G497
C4	RG453	RG472	RG490	G507	G508	G509	G510	G511	G512	G513	G514
C5	RG454	RG473	RG491	RG508	G524	G525	G526	G527	G528	G529	G530
C6	RG455	RG474	RG492	RG509	RG525	G540	G541	G542	G543	G544	G545
C7	RG456	RG475	RG493	RG510	RG526	RG541	G555	G556	G557	G558	G559
C8	RG457	RG476	RG494	RG511	RG527	RG542	RG556	G616	G617	G618	G619
C9	RG458	RG477	RG495	RG512	RG528	RG543	RG557	RG617	G477	G478	G479
C10	RG459	RG478	RG496	RG513	RG529	RG544	RG558	RG618	RG478	G676	G677
C11	RG460	RG479	RG497	RG514	RG530	RG545	RG559	RG619	RG479	RG677	G760
C12	RG461	RG480	RG498	RG515	RG531	RG546	RG560	RG620	RG480	RG678	RG761
C13	RG462	RG481	RG499	RG516	RG532	RG547	RG561	RG621	RG481	RG679	RG762
C14	RG463	RG482	RG500	RG517	RG533	RG548	RG562	RG622	RG482	RG680	RG763
C15	RG464	RG483	RG501	RG518	RG534	RG549	RG563	RG623	RG483	RG681	RG764
C16	RG465	RG484	RG502	RG519	RG535	RG550	RG564	RG624	RG484	RG682	RG765
C17	RG466	RG485	RG503	RG520	RG536	RG551	RG565	RG625	RG485	RG683	RG766
C18	RG467	RG486	RG504	RG521	RG537	RG552	RG566	RG626	RG486	RG684	RG767
C19	RG468	RG487	RG505	RG522	RG538	RG553	RG567	RG627	RG487	RG685	RG768
C20	RG168	RG215	RG262	RG309	RG356	RG403	RG568	RG628	RG488	RG686	RG769
C21	RG169	RG216	RG263	RG310	RG357	RG404	RG569	RG629	RG489	RG687	RG770
C22	RG170	RG217	RG264	RG311	RG358	RG405	RG570	RG630	RG490	RG688	RG771
C23	RG469	RG488	RG506	RG523	RG539	RG554	RG571	RG631	RG488	RG689	RG769

Graph G-2. Computer/Boards/Buffers/Data Switches/Modems to Other Computer Devices *(cont.)*

Device-A	Device - B ------------------>>										
	C12	C13	C14	C15	C16	C17	C18	C19	C20	C21	C22
C1	G461	G462	G463	G464	G465	G466	G467	G468	G168	G169	G170
C2	G480	G481	G482	G483	G484	G485	G486	G487	G215	G216	G217
C3	G498	G499	G500	G501	G502	G503	G504	G505	G262	G263	G264
C4	G515	G516	G517	G518	G519	G520	G521	G522	G309	G310	G311
C5	G531	G532	G533	G534	G535	G536	G537	G538	G356	G357	G358
C6	G546	G547	G548	G549	G550	G551	G552	G553	G403	G404	G405
C7	G560	G561	G562	G563	G564	G565	G566	G567	G568	G569	G570
C8	G620	G621	G622	G623	G624	G625	G626	G627	G628	G629	G630
C9	G480	G481	G482	G483	G484	G485	G486	G487	G488	G489	G490
C10	G678	G679	G680	G681	G682	G683	G684	G685	G686	G687	G688
C11	G761	G762	G763	G764	G765	G766	G767	G768	G769	G770	G771
C12	n/a	n/a	G981	G982	G983	G984	G985	n/a	G986	G987	G988
C13	n/a	n/a	G1029	G1030	G1031	G1032	G1033	n/a	G1034	G1035	G1036
C14	RG981	RG1029	G2268	G2269	G2270	G2271	G2272	G2273	G2274	G2275	G2276
C15	RG982	RG1030	RG2269	G928	G929	G930	G931	G932	G933	G934	G935
C16	RG983	RG1031	RG2270	RG929	G1077	G1078	G1079	G1080	G1081	G1082	G1083
C17	RG984	RG1032	RG2271	RG930	RG1078	G1129	G1130	G1131	G1132	G1133	G1134
C18	RG985	RG1033	RG2272	RG931	RG1079	RG1130	G1180	G1181	G1182	G1183	G1184
C19	n/a	n/a	RG2273	RG932	RG1080	RG1131	RG1181	G1230	G1232	G1233	G1234
C20	RG986	RG1034	RG2274	RG933	RG1081	RG1132	RG1182	RG1232	G2322	G2323	G2324
C21	RG987	RG1035	RG2275	RG934	RG1082	RG1133	RG1183	RG1233	RG2323	G1371	G1372
C22	RG988	RG1036	RG2276	RG935	RG1083	RG1134	RG1184	RG1234	RG2324	RG1372	G1280
C23	RG989	RG1037	RG2277	RG933	RG1081	RG1135	RG1185	RG1231	RG2325	RG1370	RG1279

Graph G-2. Computer/Boards/Buffers/Data Switches/Modems to Other Computer Devices *(cont.)*

Device-A	Device - B ---------->>										
	C23	C26	C28	C29	C30	C33	C34	C35	C36	C37	C38
C1	G469	G171	G172	G173	G174	G175	G176	G177	G178	G179	G180
C2	G488	G218	G219	G220	G221	G222	G223	G224	G225	G226	G227
C3	G506	G265	G266	G267	G268	G269	G270	G271	G272	G273	G274
C4	G523	G312	G313	G314	G315	G316	G317	G318	G319	G320	G321
C5	G539	G359	G360	G361	G362	G363	G364	G365	G366	G367	G368
C6	G554	G406	G407	G408	G409	G410	G411	G412	G413	G414	G415
C7	G571	G572	G573	G574	G575	G576	G577	G578	G579	G580	G581
C8	G631	G632	G633	G634	G635	G636	G637	G638	G639	G640	G641
C9	G488	G218	G219	G220	G221	G222	G223	G224	G225	G226	G227
C10	G689	G690	G691	G692	G693	G694	G695	G696	G697	G698	G699
C11	G769	G773	G774	G775	G776	G777	G778	G779	G780	G781	G782
C12	G989	G990	G991	G992	G993	n/a	G994	G995	G996	G997	G998
C13	G1037	G1038	G1039	G1040	G1041	n/a	G1042	G1043	G1044	G1045	G1046
C14	G2277	G2278	G2279	G2280	G2281	G2282	G2283	G2284	G2285	G2286	G2287
C15	G933	G937	G938	G939	G940	G941	G942	G943	G944	G945	G946
C16	G1081	G1085	G1086	G1087	G1088	G1089	G1090	G1091	G1092	G1093	G1094
C17	G1135	G1136	G1137	G1138	G1139	G1140	G1141	G1142	G1143	G1144	G1145
C18	G1185	G1186	G1187	G1188	G1189	G1190	G1191	G1192	G1193	G1194	G1195
C19	G1231	G1235	G1236	G1237	G1238	G1239	G1240	G1241	G1242	G1243	G1244
C20	G2325	G2326	G2327	G2328	G2329	G2330	G2331	G2332	G2333	G2334	G2335
C21	G1370	G1373	G1374	G1375	G1376	G1377	G1378	G1379	G1380	G1381	G1382
C22	G1279	G1281	G1282	G1283	G1284	G1285	G1286	G1287	G1288	G1289	G1290
C23	G1325	G1326	G1327	G1328	G1329	G1330	G1331	G1332	G1333	G1334	G1335

Graph G-2. Computer/Boards/Buffers/Data Switches/Modems to Other Computer Devices (cont.)

Device-A	Device - B ----------->>										
	C39	C40	C41	C42	C43	C44	C45	C46	C47	C48	C49
C1	G181	G182	G183	G184	G185	G186	G187	G188	G189	G190	G191
C2	G228	G229	G230	G231	G232	G233	G234	G235	G236	G237	G238
C3	G275	G276	G277	G278	G279	G280	G281	G282	G283	G284	G285
C4	G322	G323	G324	G325	G326	G327	G328	G329	G330	G331	G332
C5	G369	G370	G371	G372	G373	G374	G375	G376	G377	G378	G379
C6	G416	G417	G418	G419	G420	G421	G422	G423	G424	G425	G426
C7	G582	G583	G584	G585	G586	G587	G588	G589	G590	G591	G592
C8	G642	G643	G644	G645	G646	G647	G648	G649	G650	G651	G652
C9	G228	G229	G230	G231	G232	G233	G234	G235	G236	G237	G238
C10	G700	G701	G702	G703	G704	G705	G706	G707	G708	G709	G710
C11	G783	G784	G785	G786	G787	G788	G789	G790	G791	G792	G793
C12	G999	G1000	G1001	G1002	G1003	G1004	G1005	G1006	G1007	G1008	n/a
C13	G1047	G1048	G1049	G1050	G1051	G1052	G1053	G1054	G1055	G1056	n/a
C14	G2288	G2289	G2290	G2291	G2292	G2293	G2294	G2295	G2296	G2297	G2298
C15	G947	G948	G949	G950	G951	G952	G953	G954	G955	G956	G957
C16	G1095	G1096	G1097	G1098	G1099	G1100	G1101	G1102	G1103	G1104	G1105
C17	G1146	G1147	G1148	G1149	G1150	G1151	G1152	G1153	G1154	G1155	G1156
C18	G1196	G1197	G1198	G1199	G1200	G1201	G1202	G1203	G1204	G1205	G1206
C19	G1245	G1246	G1247	G1248	G1249	G1250	G1251	G1252	G1253	G1254	G1255
C20	G2336	G2337	G2338	G2339	G2340	G2341	G2342	G2343	G2344	G2345	G2346
C21	G1383	G1384	G1385	G1386	G1387	G1388	G1389	G1390	G1391	G1392	G1393
C22	G1291	G1292	G1293	G1294	G1295	G1296	G1297	G1298	G1299	G1300	G1301
C23	G1336	G1337	G1338	G1339	G1340	G1341	G1342	G1343	G1344	G1345	G1346

Graph G-2. Computer/Boards/Buffers/Data Switches/Modems to Other Computer Devices (*cont.*)

Device-A	Device - B --->>										
	C50	C51	C52	C53	C54	C55	C56	C57	C60	C61	C62
C1	G192	G193	G194	G195	G196	G197	G198	G199	G200	G201	G202
C2	G239	G240	G241	G242	G243	G244	G245	G246	G247	G248	G249
C3	G286	G287	G288	G289	G290	G291	G292	G293	G294	G295	G296
C4	G333	G334	G335	G336	G337	G338	G339	G340	G341	G342	G343
C5	G380	G381	G382	G383	G384	G385	G386	G387	G388	G389	G390
C6	G427	G428	G429	G430	G431	G432	G433	G434	G435	G436	G437
C7	G593	G594	G595	G596	G597	G598	G599	G600	G601	G602	G603
C8	G653	G654	G655	G656	G657	G658	G659	G660	G661	G662	G663
C9	G239	G240	G241	G242	G243	G244	G245	G246	G247	G248	G249
C10	G711	G712	G713	G714	G715	G716	G717	G718	G719	G720	G721
C11	G794	G795	G796	G797	G798	G799	G800	G801	G802	G803	G804
C12	G1009	n/a	G1010	G1011	n/a	G1012	n/a	G1013	G1014	G1015	G1016
C13	G1057	n/a	G1058	G1059	n/a	G1060	n/a	G1061	G1062	G1063	G1064
C14	G2299	G2300	G2301	G2302	G2303	G2304	G2305	G2306	G2307	G2308	G2309
C15	G958	G959	G960	G961	G962	G963	G964	G965	G966	G967	G968
C16	G1106	G1107	G1108	G1109	G1110	G1111	G1112	G1113	G1114	G1115	G1116
C17	G1157	G1158	G1159	G1160	G1161	G1162	G1163	G1164	G1165	G1166	G1167
C18	G1207	G1208	G1209	G1210	G1211	G1212	G1213	G1214	G1215	G1216	G1217
C19	G1256	G1257	G1258	G1259	G1260	G1261	G1262	G1263	G1264	G1265	G1266
C20	G2347	G2348	G2349	G2350	G2351	G2352	G2353	G2354	G2355	G2356	G2357
C21	G1394	G1395	G1396	G1397	G1398	G1399	G1400	G1401	G1402	G1403	G1404
C22	G1302	G1303	G1304	G1305	G1306	G1307	G1308	G1309	G1310	G1311	G1312
C23	G1347	G1348	G1349	G1350	G1351	G1352	G1353	G1354	G1355	G1356	G1357

Graph G-2. Computer/Boards/Buffers/Data Switches/Modems to Other Computer Devices (*cont.*)

Device-A	Device - B ------------>> C63	C64	C65	C66	C67	C68	C69	C70	C71	C72	C73	C74
C1	G203	G204	G205	G206	G207	G208	G209	G210	G211	G212	G213	G214
C2	G250	G251	G252	G253	G254	G255	G256	G257	G258	G259	G260	G261
C3	G297	G298	G299	G300	G301	G302	G303	G304	G305	G306	G307	G308
C4	G344	G345	G346	G347	G348	G349	G350	G351	G352	G353	G354	G355
C5	G391	G392	G393	G394	G395	G396	G397	G398	G399	G400	G401	G402
C6	G438	G439	G440	G441	G442	G443	G444	G445	G446	G447	G448	G449
C7	G604	G605	G606	G607	G608	G609	G610	G611	G612	G613	G614	G615
C8	G664	G665	G666	G667	G668	G669	G670	G671	G672	G673	G674	G675
C9	G250	G251	G252	G253	G254	G255	G256	G257	G258	G259	G260	G261
C10	G722	G723	G724	G725	G726	G727	G728	G729	G730	G731	G732	G733
C11	G805	G806	G807	G808	G809	G810	G811	G812	G813	G814	G815	G816
C12	G1017	G1018	G1019	G1020	G1021	G1022	G1023	G1024	G1025	G1026	G1027	G1028
C13	G1065	G1066	G1067	G1068	G1069	G1070	G1071	G1072	G1073	G1074	G1075	G1076
C14	G2310	G2311	G2312	G2313	G2314	G2315	G2316	G2317	G2318	G2319	G2320	G2321
C15	G969	G970	G971	G972	G973	G974	G975	G976	G977	G978	G979	G980
C16	G1117	G1118	G1119	G1120	G1121	G1122	G1123	G1124	G1125	G1126	G1127	G1128
C17	G1168	G1169	G1170	G1171	G1172	G1173	G1174	G1175	G1176	G1177	G1178	G1179
C18	G1218	G1219	G1220	G1221	G1222	G1223	G1224	G1225	G1226	G1227	G1228	G1229
C19	G1267	G1268	G1269	G1270	G1271	G1272	G1273	G1274	G1275	G1276	G1277	G1278
C20	G2358	G2359	G2360	G2361	G2362	G2363	G2364	G2365	G2366	G2367	G2368	G2369
C21	G1405	G1406	G1407	G1408	G1409	G1410	G1411	G1412	G1413	G1414	G1415	G1416
C22	G1313	G1314	G1315	G1316	G1317	G1318	G1319	G1320	G1321	G1322	G1323	G1324
C23	G1358	G1359	G1360	G1361	G1362	G1363	G1364	G1365	G1366	G1367	G1368	G1369

Graph G-2. Computer/Boards/Buffers/Data Switches/Modems to Other Computer Devices (cont.)

Device-A	Device - B										
	C1	C2	C3	C4	C5	C6	C7	C8	C9	C10	C11
C26	RG171	RG218	RG265	RG312	RG359	RG406	RG572	RG632	RG218	RG690	RG773
C28	RG172	RG219	RG266	RG313	RG360	RG407	RG573	RG633	RG219	RG691	RG774
C29	RG173	RG220	RG267	RG314	RG361	RG408	RG574	RG634	RG220	RG692	RG775
C30	RG174	RG221	RG268	RG315	RG362	RG409	RG575	RG635	RG221	RG693	RG776
C33	RG175	RG222	RG269	RG316	RG363	RG410	RG576	RG636	RG222	RG694	RG777
C34	RG176	RG223	RG270	RG317	RG364	RG411	RG577	RG637	RG223	RG695	RG778
C35	RG177	RG224	RG271	RG318	RG365	RG412	RG578	RG638	RG224	RG696	RG779
C36	RG178	RG225	RG272	RG319	RG366	RG413	RG579	RG639	RG225	RG697	RG780
C37	RG179	RG226	RG273	RG320	RG367	RG414	RG580	RG640	RG226	RG698	RG781
C38	RG180	RG227	RG274	RG321	RG368	RG415	RG581	RG641	RG227	RG699	RG782
C39	RG181	RG228	RG275	RG322	RG369	RG416	RG582	RG642	RG228	RG700	RG783
C40	RG182	RG229	RG276	RG323	RG370	RG417	RG583	RG643	RG229	RG701	RG784
C41	RG183	RG230	RG277	RG324	RG371	RG418	RG584	RG644	RG230	RG702	RG785
C42	RG184	RG231	RG278	RG325	RG372	RG419	RG585	RG645	RG231	RG703	RG786
C43	RG185	RG232	RG279	RG326	RG373	RG420	RG586	RG646	RG232	RG704	RG787
C44	RG186	RG233	RG280	RG327	RG374	RG421	RG587	RG647	RG233	RG705	RG788
C45	RG187	RG234	RG281	RG328	RG375	RG422	RG588	RG648	RG234	RG706	RG789
C46	RG188	RG235	RG282	RG329	RG376	RG423	RG589	RG649	RG235	RG707	RG790
C47	RG189	RG236	RG283	RG330	RG377	RG424	RG590	RG650	RG236	RG708	RG791
C48	RG190	RG237	RG284	RG331	RG378	RG425	RG591	RG651	RG237	RG709	RG792
C49	RG191	RG238	RG285	RG332	RG379	RG426	RG592	RG652	RG238	RG710	RG793
C50	RG192	RG239	RG286	RG333	RG380	RG427	RG593	RG653	RG239	RG711	RG794
C51	RG193	RG240	RG287	RG334	RG381	RG428	RG594	RG654	RG240	RG712	RG795

Graph G-2. Computer/Boards/Buffers/Data Switches/Modems to Other Computer Devices (*cont.*)

Device-A	Device - B --------------------->>										
	C12	C13	C14	C15	C16	C17	C18	C19	C20	C21	C22
C26	RG990	RG1038	RG2278	RG937	RG1085	RG1136	RG1186	RG1235	RG2326	RG1373	RG1281
C28	RG991	RG1039	RG2279	RG938	RG1086	RG1137	RG1187	RG1236	RG2327	RG1374	RG1282
C29	RG992	RG1040	RG2280	RG939	RG1087	RG1138	RG1188	RG1237	RG2328	RG1375	RG1283
C30	RG993	RG1041	RG2281	RG940	RG1088	RG1139	RG1189	RG1238	RG2329	RG1376	RG1284
C33	n/a	n/a	RG2282	RG941	RG1089	RG1140	RG1190	RG1239	RG2330	RG1377	RG1285
C34	RG994	RG1042	RG2283	RG942	RG1090	RG1141	RG1191	RG1240	RG2331	RG1378	RG1286
C35	RG995	RG1043	RG2284	RG943	RG1091	RG1142	RG1192	RG1241	RG2332	RG1379	RG1287
C36	RG996	RG1044	RG2285	RG944	RG1092	RG1143	RG1193	RG1242	RG2333	RG1380	RG1288
C37	RG997	RG1045	RG2286	RG945	RG1093	RG1144	RG1194	RG1243	RG2334	RG1381	RG1289
C38	RG998	RG1046	RG2287	RG946	RG1094	RG1145	RG1195	RG1244	RG2335	RG1382	RG1290
C39	RG999	RG1047	RG2288	RG947	RG1095	RG1146	RG1196	RG1245	RG2336	RG1383	RG1291
C40	RG1000	RG1048	RG2289	RG948	RG1096	RG1147	RG1197	RG1246	RG2337	RG1384	RG1292
C41	RG1001	RG1049	RG2290	RG949	RG1097	RG1148	RG1198	RG1247	RG2338	RG1385	RG1293
C42	RG1002	RG1050	RG2291	RG950	RG1098	RG1149	RG1199	RG1248	RG2339	RG1386	RG1294
C43	RG1003	RG1051	RG2292	RG951	RG1099	RG1150	RG1200	RG1249	RG2340	RG1387	RG1295
C44	RG1004	RG1052	RG2293	RG952	RG1100	RG1151	RG1201	RG1250	RG2341	RG1388	RG1296
C45	RG1005	RG1053	RG2294	RG953	RG1101	RG1152	RG1202	RG1251	RG2342	RG1389	RG1297
C46	RG1006	RG1054	RG2295	RG954	RG1102	RG1153	RG1203	RG1252	RG2343	RG1390	RG1298
C47	RG1007	RG1055	RG2296	RG955	RG1103	RG1154	RG1204	RG1253	RG2344	RG1391	RG1299
C48	RG1008	RG1056	RG2297	RG956	RG1104	RG1155	RG1205	RG1254	RG2345	RG1392	RG1300
C49	n/a	n/a	RG2298	RG957	RG1105	RG1156	RG1206	RG1255	RG2346	RG1393	RG1301
C50	RG1009	RG1057	RG2299	RG958	RG1106	RG1157	RG1207	RG1256	RG2347	RG1394	RG1302
C51	n/a	n/a	RG2300	RG959	RG1107	RG1158	RG1208	RG1257	RG2348	RG1395	RG1303

Graph G-2. Computer/Boards/Buffers/Data Switches/Modems to Other Computer Devices (cont.)

| Device-A | Device - B ------------------------------->> | | | | | | | | | | |
	C23	C26	C28	C29	C30	C33	C34	C35	C36	C37	C38
C26	RG1326	G1417	G1418	G1419	G1420	G1421	G1422	G1423	G1424	G1425	G1426
C28	RG1327	RG1418	G1461	G1462	G1463	G1464	G1465	G1466	G1467	G1468	G1469
C29	RG1328	RG1419	RG1462	G1504	G1505	G1506	G1507	G1508	G1509	G1510	G1511
C30	RG1329	RG1420	RG1463	RG1505	G1582	G1583	G1584	G1585	G1586	G1587	G1588
C33	RG1330	RG1421	RG1464	RG1506	RG1583	G1623	G1624	G1625	G1626	G1627	G1628
C34	RG1331	RG1422	RG1465	RG1507	RG1584	RG1624	G817	G818	G819	G820	G821
C35	RG1332	RG1423	RG1466	RG1508	RG1585	RG1625	RG818	G856	G857	G858	G859
C36	RG1333	RG1424	RG1467	RG1509	RG1586	RG1626	RG819	RG857	G1663	G1664	G1665
C37	RG1334	RG1425	RG1468	RG1510	RG1587	RG1627	RG820	RG858	RG1664	G1546	G1547
C38	RG1335	RG1426	RG1469	RG1511	RG1588	RG1628	RG821	RG859	RG1665	RG1546	G1700
C39	RG1336	RG1427	RG1470	RG1512	RG1589	RG1629	RG822	RG860	RG1666	RG1547	RG1701
C40	RG1337	RG1428	RG1471	RG1513	RG1590	RG1630	RG823	RG861	RG1667	RG1548	RG1702
C41	RG1338	RG1429	RG1472	RG1514	RG1591	RG1631	RG824	RG862	RG1668	RG1549	RG1703
C42	RG1339	RG1430	RG1473	RG1515	RG1592	RG1632	RG825	RG863	RG1669	RG1550	RG1704
C43	RG1340	RG1431	RG1474	RG1516	RG1593	RG1633	RG826	RG864	RG1670	RG1551	RG1705
C44	RG1341	RG1432	RG1475	RG1517	RG1594	RG1634	RG827	RG865	RG1671	RG1552	RG1706
C45	RG1342	RG1433	RG1476	RG1518	RG1595	RG1635	RG828	RG866	RG1672	RG1553	RG1707
C46	RG1343	RG1434	RG1477	RG1519	RG1596	RG1636	RG829	RG867	RG1673	RG1554	RG1708
C47	RG1344	RG1435	RG1478	RG1520	RG1597	RG1637	RG830	RG868	RG1674	RG1555	RG1709
C48	RG1345	RG1436	RG1479	RG1521	RG1598	RG1638	RG831	RG869	RG1675	RG1556	RG1710
C49	RG1346	RG1437	RG1480	RG1522	RG1599	RG1639	RG832	RG870	RG1676	RG1557	RG1711
C50	RG1347	RG1438	RG1481	RG1523	RG1600	RG1640	RG833	RG871	RG1677	RG1558	RG1712
C51	RG1348	RG1439	RG1482	RG1524	RG1601	RG1641	RG834	RG872	RG1678	RG1560	RG1713

Graph G-2. Computer/Boards/Buffers/Data Switches/Modems to Other Computer Devices (*cont.*)

| Device-A | Device - B ------------------------------->> | | | | | | | | | | |
	C39	C40	C41	C42	C43	C44	C45	C46	C47	C48	C49
C26	G1427	G1428	G1429	G1430	G1431	G1432	G1433	G1434	G1435	G1436	G1437
C28	G1470	G1471	G1472	G1473	G1474	G1475	G1476	G1477	G1478	G1479	G1480
C29	G1512	G1513	G1514	G1515	G1516	G1517	G1518	G1519	G1520	G1521	G1522
C30	G1589	G1590	G1591	G1592	G1593	G1594	G1595	G1596	G1597	G1598	G1599
C33	G1629	G1630	G1631	G1632	G1633	G1634	G1635	G1636	G1637	G1638	G1639
C34	G822	G823	G824	G825	G826	G827	G828	G829	G830	G831	G832
C35	G860	G861	G862	G863	G864	G865	G866	G867	G868	G869	G870
C36	G1666	G1667	G1668	G1669	G1670	G1671	G1672	G1673	G1674	G1675	G1676
C37	G1548	G1549	G1550	G1551	G1552	G1553	G1554	G1555	G1556	G1557	G1558
C38	G1701	G1702	G1703	G1704	G1705	G1706	G1707	G1708	G1709	G1710	G1711
C39	G894	G895	G896	G897	G898	G899	G900	G901	G902	G903	G904
C40	RG895	G1735	G1736	G1737	G1738	G1739	G1740	G1741	G1742	G1743	G1744
C41	RG896	RG1736	G1768	G1769	G1770	G1771	G1772	G1773	G1774	G1775	G1776
C42	RG897	RG1737	RG1769	G1800	G1801	G1802	G1803	G1804	G1805	G1806	G1807
C43	RG898	RG1738	RG1770	RG1801	G1831	G1832	G1833	G1834	G1835	G1836	G1837
C44	RG899	RG1739	RG1771	RG1802	RG1832	G1861	G1862	G1863	G1864	G1865	G1866
C45	RG900	RG1740	RG1772	RG1803	RG1833	RG1862	G1890	G1891	G1892	G1893	G1894
C46	RG901	RG1741	RG1773	RG1804	RG1834	RG1863	RG1891	G1918	G1919	G1920	G1921
C47	RG902	RG1742	RG1774	RG1805	RG1835	RG1864	RG1892	RG1919	G734	G735	G736
C48	RG903	RG1743	RG1775	RG1806	RG1836	RG1865	RG1893	RG1920	RG735	G1946	G1947
C49	RG904	RG1744	RG1776	RG1807	RG1837	RG1866	RG1894	RG1921	RG736	RG1947	G1971
C50	RG905	RG1745	RG1777	RG1808	RG1838	RG1867	RG1895	RG1922	RG737	RG1948	RG1972
C51	RG906	RG1746	RG1778	RG1809	RG1839	RG1868	RG1896	RG1923	RG738	RG1949	RG1973

Graph G-2. Computer/Boards/Buffers/Data Switches/Modems to Other Computer Devices *(cont.)*

| Device-A | Device - B | >>>>>>>>>>>> | | | | | | | | | | |
	C50	C51	C52	C53	C54	C55	C56	C57	C60	C61	C62
C26	G1438	G1439	G1440	G1441	G1442	G1443	G1444	G1445	G1446	G1447	G1448
C28	G1481	G1482	G1483	G1484	G1485	G1486	G1487	G1488	G1489	G1490	G1491
C29	G1523	G1524	G1525	G1526	G1527	G1528	G1529	G1530	G1531	G1532	G1533
C30	G1600	G1601	G1602	G1603	G1604	G1605	G1606	G1607	G1608	G1609	G1610
C33	G1640	G1641	G1642	G1643	G1644	G1645	G1646	G1647	G1648	G1649	G1650
C34	G833	G834	G835	G836	G837	G838	G839	G840	G841	G842	G843
C35	G871	G872	G873	G874	G875	G876	G877	G878	G879	G880	G881
C36	G1677	G1678	G1679	G1680	G1681	G1682	G1683	G1684	G1685	G1686	G1687
C37	G1559	G1560	G1561	G1562	G1563	G1564	G1565	G1566	G1567	G1568	G1569
C38	G1712	G1713	G1714	G1715	G1716	G1717	G1718	G1719	G1720	G1721	G1722
C39	G905	G906	G907	G908	G909	G910	G911	G912	G913	G914	G915
C40	G1745	G1746	G1747	G1748	G1749	G1750	G1751	G1752	G1753	G1754	G1755
C41	G1777	G1778	G1779	G1780	G1781	G1782	G1783	G1784	G1785	G1786	G1787
C42	G1808	G1809	G1810	G1811	G1812	G1813	G1814	G1815	G1816	G1817	G1818
C43	G1838	G1839	G1840	G1841	G1842	G1843	G1844	G1845	G1846	G1847	G1848
C44	G1867	G1868	G1869	G1870	G1871	G1872	G1873	G1874	G1875	G1876	G1877
C45	G1895	G1896	G1897	G1898	G1899	G1900	G1901	G1902	G1903	G1904	G1905
C46	G1922	G1923	G1924	G1925	G1926	G1927	G1928	G1929	G1930	G1931	G1932
C47	G737	G738	G739	G740	G741	G742	G743	G744	G745	G746	G747
C48	G1948	G1949	G1950	G1951	G1952	G1953	G1954	G1955	G1956	G1957	G1958
C49	G1972	G1973	G1974	G1975	G1976	G1977	G1978	G1979	G1980	G1981	G1982
C50	G1995	G1996	G1997	G1998	G1999	G2000	G2001	G2002	G2003	G2004	G2005
C51	RG1996	n/a	G2018	G2019	n/a	G2020	n/a	G2021	G2022	G2023	G2024

Graph G-2. Computer/Boards/Buffers/Data Switches/Modems to Other Computer Devices (*cont.*)

| Device-A | Device - B --------->> | | | | | | | | | | | |
	C63	C64	C65	C66	C67	C68	C69	C70	C71	C72	C73	C74
C26	G1449	G1450	G1451	G1452	G1453	G1454	G1455	G1456	G1457	G1458	G1459	G1460
C28	G1492	G1493	G1494	G1495	G1496	G1497	G1498	G1499	G1500	G1501	G1502	G1503
C29	G1534	G1535	G1536	G1537	G1538	G1539	G1540	G1541	G1542	G1543	G1544	G1545
C30	G1611	G1612	G1613	G1614	G1615	G1616	G1617	G1618	G1619	G1620	G1621	G1622
C33	G1651	G1652	G1653	G1654	G1655	G1656	G1657	G1658	G1659	G1660	G1661	G1662
C34	G844	G845	G846	G847	G848	G849	G850	G851	G852	G853	G854	G855
C35	G882	G883	G884	G885	G886	G887	G888	G889	G890	G891	G892	G893
C36	G1688	G1689	G1690	G1691	G1692	G1693	G1694	G1695	G1696	G1697	G1698	G1699
C37	G1570	G1571	G1572	G1573	G1574	G1575	G1576	G1577	G1578	G1579	G1580	G1581
C38	G1723	G1724	G1725	G1726	G1727	G1728	G1729	G1730	G1731	G1732	G1733	G1734
C39	G916	G917	G918	G919	G920	G921	G922	G923	G924	G925	G926	G927
C40	G1756	G1757	G1758	G1759	G1760	G1761	G1762	G1763	G1764	G1765	G1766	G1767
C41	G1788	G1789	G1790	G1791	G1792	G1793	G1794	G1795	G1796	G1797	G1798	G1799
C42	G1819	G1820	G1821	G1822	G1823	G1824	G1825	G1826	G1827	G1828	G1829	G1830
C43	G1849	G1850	G1851	G1852	G1853	G1854	G1855	G1856	G1857	G1858	G1859	G1860
C44	G1878	G1879	G1880	G1881	G1882	G1883	G1884	G1885	G1886	G1887	G1888	G1889
C45	G1906	G1907	G1908	G1909	G1910	G1911	G1912	G1913	G1914	G1915	G1916	G1917
C46	G1933	G1934	G1935	G1936	G1937	G1938	G1939	G1940	G1941	G1942	G1943	G1944
C47	G748	G749	G750	G751	G752	G753	G754	G755	G756	G757	G758	G759
C48	G1959	G1960	G1961	G1962	G1963	G1964	G1965	G1966	G1967	G1968	G1969	G1970
C49	G1983	G1984	G1985	G1986	G1987	G1988	G1989	G1990	G1991	G1992	G1993	G1994
C50	G2006	G2007	G2008	G2009	G2010	G2011	G2012	G2013	G2014	G2015	G2016	G2017
C51	G2025	G2026	G2027	G2028	G2029	G2030	G2031	G2032	G2033	G2034	G2035	G2036

Graph G-2. Computer/Boards/Buffers/Data Switches/Modems to Other Computer Devices *(cont.)*

Device-A	Device - B ---------->> C1	C2	C3	C4	C5	C6	C7	C8	C9	C10	C11
C52	RG194	RG241	RG288	RG335	RG382	RG429	RG595	RG655	RG241	RG713	RG796
C53	RG195	RG242	RG289	RG336	RG383	RG430	RG596	RG656	RG242	RG714	RG797
C54	RG196	RG243	RG290	RG337	RG384	RG431	RG597	RG657	RG243	RG715	RG798
C55	RG197	RG244	RG291	RG338	RG385	RG432	RG598	RG658	RG244	RG716	RG799
C56	RG198	RG245	RG292	RG339	RG386	RG433	RG599	RG659	RG245	RG717	RG800
C57	RG199	RG246	RG293	RG340	RG387	RG434	RG600	RG660	RG246	RG718	RG801
C60	RG200	RG247	RG294	RG341	RG388	RG435	RG601	RG661	RG247	RG719	RG802
C61	RG201	RG248	RG295	RG342	RG389	RG436	RG602	RG662	RG248	RG720	RG803
C62	RG202	RG249	RG296	RG343	RG390	RG437	RG603	RG663	RG249	RG721	RG804
C63	RG203	RG250	RG297	RG344	RG391	RG438	RG604	RG664	RG250	RG722	RG805
C64	RG204	RG251	RG298	RG345	RG392	RG439	RG605	RG665	RG251	RG723	RG806
C65	RG205	RG252	RG299	RG346	RG393	RG440	RG606	RG666	RG252	RG724	RG807
C66	RG206	RG253	RG300	RG347	RG394	RG441	RG607	RG667	RG253	RG725	RG808
C67	RG207	RG254	RG301	RG348	RG395	RG442	RG608	RG668	RG254	RG726	RG809
C68	RG208	RG255	RG302	RG349	RG396	RG443	RG609	RG669	RG255	RG727	RG810
C69	RG209	RG256	RG303	RG350	RG397	RG444	RG610	RG670	RG256	RG728	RG811
C70	RG210	RG257	RG304	RG351	RG398	RG445	RG611	RG671	RG257	RG729	RG812
C71	RG211	RG258	RG305	RG352	RG399	RG446	RG612	RG672	RG258	RG730	RG813
C72	RG212	RG259	RG306	RG353	RG400	RG447	RG613	RG673	RG259	RG731	RG814
C73	RG213	RG260	RG307	RG354	RG401	RG448	RG614	RG674	RG260	RG732	RG815
C74	RG214	RG261	RG308	RG355	RG402	RG449	RG615	RG675	RG261	RG733	RG816

Graph G-2. Computer/Boards/Buffers/Data Switches/Modems to Other Computer Devices (*cont.*)

Device-A	Device - B - - - - - - - - - - - - - - - - - >>										
	C12	C13	C14	C15	C16	C17	C18	C19	C20	C21	C22
C52	RG1010	RG1058	RG2301	RG960	RG1108	RG1159	RG1209	RG1258	RG2349	RG1396	RG1304
C53	RG1011	RG1059	RG2302	RG961	RG1109	RG1160	RG1210	RG1259	RG2350	RG1397	RG1305
C54	n/a	n/a	RG2303	RG962	RG1110	RG1161	RG1211	RG1260	RG2351	RG1398	RG1306
C55	RG1012	RG1060	RG2304	RG963	RG1111	RG1162	RG1212	RG1261	RG2352	RG1399	RG1307
C56	n/a	n/a	RG2305	RG964	RG1112	RG1163	RG1213	RG1262	RG2353	RG1400	RG1308
C57	RG1013	RG1061	RG2306	RG965	RG1113	RG1164	RG1214	RG1263	RG2354	RG1401	RG1309
C60	RG1014	RG1062	RG2307	RG966	RG1114	RG1165	RG1215	RG1264	RG2355	RG1402	RG1310
C61	RG1015	RG1063	RG2308	RG967	RG1115	RG1166	RG1216	RG1265	RG2356	RG1403	RG1311
C62	RG1016	RG1064	RG2309	RG968	RG1116	RG1167	RG1217	RG1266	RG2357	RG1404	RG1312
C63	RG1017	RG1065	RG2310	RG969	RG1117	RG1168	RG1218	RG1267	RG2358	RG1405	RG1313
C64	RG1018	RG1066	RG2311	RG970	RG1118	RG1169	RG1219	RG1268	RG2359	RG1406	RG1314
C65	RG1019	RG1067	RG2312	RG971	RG1119	RG1170	RG1220	RG1269	RG2360	RG1407	RG1315
C66	RG1020	RG1068	RG2313	RG972	RG1120	RG1171	RG1221	RG1270	RG2361	RG1408	RG1316
C67	RG1021	RG1069	RG2314	RG973	RG1121	RG1172	RG1222	RG1271	RG2362	RG1409	RG1317
C68	RG1022	RG1070	RG2315	RG974	RG1122	RG1173	RG1223	RG1272	RG2363	RG1410	RG1318
C69	RG1023	RG1071	RG2316	RG975	RG1123	RG1174	RG1224	RG1273	RG2364	RG1411	RG1319
C70	RG1024	RG1072	RG2317	RG976	RG1124	RG1175	RG1225	RG1274	RG2365	RG1412	RG1320
C71	RG1025	RG1073	RG2318	RG977	RG1125	RG1176	RG1226	RG1275	RG2366	RG1413	RG1321
C72	RG1026	RG1074	RG2319	RG978	RG1126	RG1177	RG1227	RG1276	RG2367	RG1414	RG1322
C73	RG1027	RG1075	RG2320	RG979	RG1127	RG1178	RG1228	RG1277	RG2368	RG1415	RG1323
C74	RG1028	RG1076	RG2321	RG980	RG1128	RG1179	RG1229	RG1278	RG2369	RG1416	RG1324

Graph G-2. Computer/Boards/Buffers/Data Switches/Modems to Other Computer Devices *(cont.)*

Device-A	Device - B ----------------->>										
	C23	C26	C28	C29	C30	C33	C34	C35	C36	C37	C38
C52	RG1349	RG1440	RG1483	RG1525	RG1602	RG1642	RG835	RG873	RG1679	RG1561	RG1714
C53	RG1350	RG1441	RG1484	RG1526	RG1603	RG1643	RG836	RG874	RG1680	RG1562	RG1715
C54	RG1351	RG1442	RG1485	RG1527	RG1604	RG1644	RG837	RG875	RG1681	RG1563	RG1716
C55	RG1352	RG1443	RG1486	RG1528	RG1605	RG1645	RG838	RG876	RG1682	RG1564	RG1717
C56	RG1353	RG1444	RG1487	RG1529	RG1606	RG1646	RG839	RG877	RG1683	RG1565	RG1718
C57	RG1354	RG1445	RG1488	RG1530	RG1607	RG1647	RG840	RG878	RG1684	RG1566	RG1719
C60	RG1355	RG1446	RG1489	RG1531	RG1608	RG1648	RG841	RG879	RG1685	RG1567	RG1720
C61	RG1356	RG1447	RG1490	RG1532	RG1609	RG1649	RG842	RG880	RG1686	RG1568	RG1721
C62	RG1357	RG1448	RG1491	RG1533	RG1610	RG1650	RG843	RG881	RG1687	RG1569	RG1722
C63	RG1358	RG1449	RG1492	RG1534	RG1611	RG1651	RG844	RG882	RG1688	RG1570	RG1723
C64	RG1359	RG1450	RG1493	RG1535	RG1612	RG1652	RG845	RG883	RG1689	RG1571	RG1724
C65	RG1360	RG1451	RG1494	RG1536	RG1613	RG1653	RG846	RG884	RG1690	RG1572	RG1725
C66	RG1361	RG1452	RG1495	RG1537	RG1614	RG1654	RG847	RG885	RG1691	RG1573	RG1726
C67	RG1362	RG1453	RG1496	RG1538	RG1615	RG1655	RG848	RG886	RG1692	RG1574	RG1727
C68	RG1363	RG1454	RG1497	RG1539	RG1616	RG1656	RG849	RG887	RG1693	RG1575	RG1728
C69	RG1364	RG1455	RG1498	RG1540	RG1617	RG1657	RG850	RG888	RG1694	RG1576	RG1729
C70	RG1365	RG1456	RG1499	RG1541	RG1618	RG1658	RG851	RG889	RG1695	RG1577	RG1730
C71	RG1366	RG1457	RG1500	RG1542	RG1619	RG1659	RG852	RG890	RG1696	RG1578	RG1731
C72	RG1367	RG1458	RG1501	RG1543	RG1620	RG1660	RG853	RG891	RG1697	RG1579	RG1732
C73	RG1368	RG1459	RG1502	RG1544	RG1621	RG1661	RG854	RG892	RG1698	RG1580	RG1733
C74	RG1369	RG1460	RG1503	RG1545	RG1622	RG1662	RG855	RG893	RG1699	RG1581	RG1734

Graph G-2. Computer/Boards/Buffers/Data Switches/Modems to Other Computer Devices (*cont.*)

Device-A	Device - B ----------------->> C39	C40	C41	C42	C43	C44	C45	C46	C47	C48	C49
C52	RG907	RG1747	RG1779	RG1810	RG1840	RG1869	RG1897	RG1924	RG739	RG1950	RG1974
C53	RG908	RG1748	RG1780	RG1811	RG1841	RG1870	RG1898	RG1925	RG740	RG1951	RG1975
C54	RG909	RG1749	RG1781	RG1812	RG1842	RG1871	RG1899	RG1926	RG741	RG1952	RG1976
C55	RG910	RG1750	RG1782	RG1813	RG1843	RG1872	RG1900	RG1927	RG742	RG1953	RG1977
C56	RG911	RG1751	RG1783	RG1814	RG1844	RG1873	RG1901	RG1928	RG743	RG1954	RG1978
C57	RG912	RG1752	RG1784	RG1815	RG1845	RG1874	RG1902	RG1929	RG744	RG1955	RG1979
C60	RG913	RG1753	RG1785	RG1816	RG1846	RG1875	RG1903	RG1930	RG745	RG1956	RG1980
C61	RG914	RG1754	RG1786	RG1817	RG1847	RG1876	RG1904	RG1931	RG746	RG1957	RG1981
C62	RG915	RG1755	RG1787	RG1818	RG1848	RG1877	RG1905	RG1932	RG747	RG1958	RG1982
C63	RG916	RG1756	RG1788	RG1819	RG1849	RG1878	RG1906	RG1933	RG748	RG1959	RG1983
C64	RG917	RG1757	RG1789	RG1820	RG1850	RG1879	RG1907	RG1934	RG749	RG1960	RG1984
C65	RG918	RG1758	RG1790	RG1821	RG1851	RG1880	RG1908	RG1935	RG750	RG1961	RG1985
C66	RG919	RG1759	RG1791	RG1822	RG1852	RG1881	RG1909	RG1936	RG751	RG1962	RG1986
C67	RG920	RG1760	RG1792	RG1823	RG1853	RG1882	RG1910	RG1937	RG752	RG1963	RG1987
C68	RG921	RG1761	RG1793	RG1824	RG1854	RG1883	RG1911	RG1938	RG753	RG1964	RG1988
C69	RG922	RG1762	RG1794	RG1825	RG1855	RG1884	RG1912	RG1939	RG754	RG1965	RG1989
C70	RG923	RG1763	RG1795	RG1826	RG1856	RG1885	RG1913	RG1940	RG755	RG1966	RG1990
C71	RG924	RG1764	RG1796	RG1827	RG1857	RG1886	RG1914	RG1941	RG756	RG1967	RG1991
C72	RG925	RG1765	RG1797	RG1828	RG1858	RG1887	RG1915	RG1942	RG757	RG1968	RG1992
C73	RG926	RG1766	RG1798	RG1829	RG1859	RG1888	RG1916	RG1943	RG758	RG1969	RG1993
C74	RG927	RG1767	RG1799	RG1830	RG1860	RG1889	RG1917	RG1944	RG759	RG1970	RG1994

Graph G-2. Computer/Boards/Buffers/Data Switches/Modems to Other Computer Devices (*cont.*)

Device-A	Device - B --------------->>										
	C50	C51	C52	C53	C54	C55	C56	C57	C60	C61	C62
C52	RG1997	RG2018	G2037	G2038	G2039	G2040	G2041	G2042	G2043	G2044	G2045
C53	RG1998	RG2019	RG2038	G2058	G2059	G2060	G2061	G2062	G2063	G2064	G2065
C54	RG1999	n/a	RG2039	RG2059	G2078	G2079	G2080	G2081	G2082	G2083	G2084
C55	RG2000	RG2020	RG2040	RG2060	RG2079	G2097	G2098	G2099	G2100	G2101	G2102
C56	RG2001	n/a	RG2041	RG2061	RG2080	RG2098	G2115	G2116	G2117	G2118	G2119
C57	RG2002	RG2021	RG2042	RG2062	RG2081	RG2099	RG2116	G2132	G2133	G2134	G2135
C60	RG2003	RG2022	RG2043	RG2063	RG2082	RG2100	RG2117	RG2133	G2148	G2149	G2150
C61	RG2004	RG2023	RG2044	RG2064	RG2083	RG2101	RG2118	RG2134	RG2149	G2163	G2164
C62	RG2005	RG2024	RG2045	RG2065	RG2084	RG2102	RG2119	RG2135	RG2150	RG2164	G2177
C63	RG2006	RG2025	RG2046	RG2066	RG2085	RG2103	RG2120	RG2136	RG2151	RG2165	RG2178
C64	RG2007	RG2026	RG2047	RG2067	RG2086	RG2104	RG2121	RG2137	RG2152	RG2166	RG2179
C65	RG2008	RG2027	RG2048	RG2068	RG2087	RG2105	RG2122	RG2138	RG2153	RG2167	RG2180
C66	RG2009	RG2028	RG2049	RG2069	RG2088	RG2106	RG2123	RG2139	RG2154	RG2168	RG2181
C67	RG2010	RG2029	RG2050	RG2070	RG2089	RG2107	RG2124	RG2140	RG2155	RG2169	RG2182
C68	RG2011	RG2030	RG2051	RG2071	RG2090	RG2108	RG2125	RG2141	RG2156	RG2170	RG2183
C69	RG2012	RG2031	RG2052	RG2072	RG2091	RG2109	RG2126	RG2142	RG2157	RG2171	RG2184
C70	RG2013	RG2032	RG2053	RG2073	RG2092	RG2110	RG2127	RG2143	RG2158	RG2172	RG2185
C71	RG2014	RG2033	RG2054	RG2074	RG2093	RG2111	RG2128	RG2144	RG2159	RG2173	RG2186
C72	RG2015	RG2034	RG2055	RG2075	RG2094	RG2112	RG2129	RG2145	RG2160	RG2174	RG2187
C73	RG2016	RG2035	RG2056	RG2076	RG2095	RG2113	RG2130	RG2146	RG2161	RG2175	RG2188
C74	RG2017	RG2036	RG2057	RG2077	RG2096	RG2114	RG2131	RG2147	RG2162	RG2176	RG2189

Graph G-2. Computer/Boards/Buffers/Data Switches/Modems to Other Computer Devices (cont.)

Device-A	Device - B ------------>> C63	C64	C65	C66	C67	C68	C69	C70	C71	C72	C73	C74
C52	G2046	G2047	G2048	G2049	G2050	G2051	G2052	G2053	G2054	G2055	G2056	G2057
C53	G2066	G2067	G2068	G2069	G2070	G2071	G2072	G2073	G2074	G2075	G2076	G2077
C54	G2085	G2086	G2087	G2088	G2089	G2090	G2091	G2092	G2093	G2094	G2095	G2096
C55	G2103	G2104	G2105	G2106	G2107	G2108	G2109	G2110	G2111	G2112	G2113	G2114
C56	G2120	G2121	G2122	G2123	G2124	G2125	G2126	G2127	G2128	G2129	G2130	G2131
C57	G2136	G2137	G2138	G2139	G2140	G2141	G2142	G2143	G2144	G2145	G2146	G2147
C60	G2151	G2152	G2153	G2154	G2155	G2156	G2157	G2158	G2159	G2160	G2161	G2162
C61	G2165	G2166	G2167	G2168	G2169	G2170	G2171	G2172	G2173	G2174	G2175	G2176
C62	G2178	G2179	G2180	G2181	G2182	G2183	G2184	G2185	G2186	G2187	G2188	G2189
C63	G2190	G2191	G2192	G2193	G2194	G2195	G2196	G2197	G2198	G2199	G2200	G2201
C64	RG2191	G2202	G2203	G2204	G2205	G2206	G2207	G2208	G2209	G2210	G2211	G2212
C65	RG2192	RG2203	G2213	G2214	G2215	G2216	G2217	G2218	G2219	G2220	G2221	G2222
C66	RG2193	RG2204	RG2214	G2223	G2224	G2225	G2226	G2227	G2228	G2229	G2230	G2231
C67	RG2194	RG2205	RG2215	RG2224	G2232	G2233	G2234	G2235	G2236	G2237	G2238	G2239
C68	RG2195	RG2206	RG2216	RG2225	RG2233	G2240	G2241	G2242	G2243	G2244	G2245	G2246
C69	RG2196	RG2207	RG2217	RG2226	RG2234	RG2241	G2247	G2248	G2249	G2250	G2251	G2252
C70	RG2197	RG2208	RG2218	RG2227	RG2235	RG2242	RG2248	G2253	G2254	G2255	G2256	G2257
C71	RG2198	RG2209	RG2219	RG2228	RG2236	RG2243	RG2249	RG2254	G2258	G2259	G2260	G2261
C72	RG2199	RG2210	RG2220	RG2229	RG2237	RG2244	RG2250	RG2255	RG2259	G2262	G2263	G2264
C73	RG2200	RG2211	RG2221	RG2230	RG2238	RG2245	RG2251	RG2256	RG2260	RG2263	G2265	G2266
C74	RG2201	RG2212	RG2222	RG2231	RG2239	RG2246	RG2252	RG2257	RG2261	RG2264	RG2266	G2267

```
Graphs G1 to
G167 are
reserved for
graphs used in
previous
editions of
the "RS-232
Made Easy"
series of
textbooks.
```

```
G168
1 -------- 1
7 -------- 8
2 ------> 4
3 <------ 2

20 ----:-> 5
      :-> 10
      :-> 7
5 <-:----- 12
6 <-:
8 <-:

4 ----:-> 11
```

```
G169
1 -------- 1
7 -------- 7
2 ------> 2
3 <------ 3

5 <-:----- 6
6 <-:
8 <-:

4 ----:-> 4
```

```
G170
7 -------- 4
2 ------> 3
3 <------ 2

20 ----:-> 1
      :-> 6
5 <-:----- 5
6 <-:
8 <-:
```

```
G171
7 -------- 5
2 ------> 7
3 <------ 4

20 ----:-> 2
      :-> 6
5 <-:----- 3
6 <-:
8 <-:
```

```
G172
7 -------- 3
2 ------> 5
3 <------ 4

20 ----:-> 8
      :-> 7
      :-> 6
5 <-:----- 2
6 <-:
8 <-:
```

```
G173
1 -------- 4
7 -------- 7
2 ------> 6
3 <------ 5

20 ----:-> 8
      :-> 2
      :-> 10
5 <-:----- 9
6 <-:
8 <-:

4 ----:-> 1
```

```
G174
1 -------- 3
7 -------- 6
2 ------> 5
3 <------ 4

20 ----:-> 7
      :-> 1
5 <-:----- 8
6 <-:
8 <-:
```

```
G175
7 -------- 8
2 ------> 2
3 <------ 1

4 --:
5 <-:
6 <-:
8 <-:
```

```
G176
7 -------- 8
2 ------> 6
3 <------ 1

20 ----:-> 7
      :-> 9
5 <-:----- 4
6 <-:
8 <-:
```

```
G177
7 -------- 7
2 ------> 3
3 <------ 2

20 ----:-> 5
      :-> 8
5 <-:----- 9
6 <-:
8 <-:
```

```
G178
7 -------- 5
2 ------> 3
3 <------ 2

5 <-:----- 6
6 <-:
8 <-:

4 ----:-> 4
      :-> 7
```

```
G179
1 -------- 2
7 -------- 7
2 ------> 3
3 <------ 8

20 ----:-> 5
      :-> 6
      :-> 1
5 <-:----- 9
6 <-:
8 <-:

4 ----:-> 10
```

```
G180
1 -------- 2
7 -------- 7
2 ------> 8
3 <------ 3

5 <-:----- 5
6 <-:
8 <-:

4 ----:-> 4
      :-> 9
```

```
G181
7 -------- 7
2 ------> 5
3 <------ 4

20 ------> 3
5 <-:----- 1
6 <-:
8 <-:
```

```
G182
7 -------- 4
2 ------> 6
3 <------ 3

5 <-:----- 2
6 <-:
8 <-:

4 ----:-> 1
      :-> 7
```

```
G183
7 -------- 5
2 ------> 6
3 <------ 4

20 ------> 2
5 <-:----- 3
6 <-:
8 <-:
```

```
G184
7 -------- 9
2 ------> 3
3 <------ 2

20 ------> 5
5 <-:----- 4
6 <-:
8 <-:
```

```
G185
7 -------- 3
2 ------> 4
3 <------ 2

20 ------> 5
5 <-:----- 1
6 <-:
8 <-:
```

```
G186
7 -------- 9
2 ------> 13
3 <------ 11

20 ------> 14
5 <-:----- 10
6 <-:
8 <-:
```

```
G187
7 -------- 5
2 ------> 2
3 <------ 3

20 ----:-> 8
      :-> 6
5 <-:----- 4
6 <-:
8 <-:
```

```
G188
7 -------- 5
2 ------> 2
3 <------ 3

20 ------> 8
5 <-:----- 7
6 <-:
8 <-:
```

```
G189
7 -------- 5
2 ------> 3
3 <------ 2

5 <-:----- 6
6 <-:
8 <-:
```

```
G190
7 -------- 5
2 ------> 3
3 <------ 2

4 --:
5 <-:
6 <-:
8 <-:
```

```
G191
1 -------- 3
7 -------- 4
2 ------> 5
3 <------ 2

20 ------> 6
5 <-:----- 1
6 <-:
8 <-:
```

```
G192
1 -------- 1
7 -------- 2
2 ------> 4
3 <------ 3

20 ------> 5
5 <-:----- 6
6 <-:
8 <-:
```

```
G193
1 -------- 1
7 -------- 7
3 <------ 2

4 --:
5 <-:
6 <-:
8 <-:
```

```
G194
1 -------- 1
7 -------- 7
2 ------> 5
3 <------ 3

20 ----:-> 8
      :-> 6
5 <-:----- 4
6 <-:
8 <-:
```

```
G195
7 -------- 4
2 ------> 5
3 <------ 3

20 ------> 2
5 <-:----- 6
6 <-:
8 <-:
```

```
G196
7 -------- 5
2 ------> 4
3 <------ 2

20 ------> 6
5 <-:----- 1
6 <-:
8 <-:
```

```
G197                  G198                  G199                  G200                  G201                  G202
7 ------- 1           1 ------- 3           1 ------- 4           7 ------- 3           7 ------- 6           7 ------- 2
2 ------> 4           7 ------- 5           7 ------- 2           2 ------> 1           2 ------> 8           2 ------> 3
3 <------ 2           2 ------> 2           2 ------> 5           3 <------ 5           3 <------ 4           3 <------ 5
                      3 <------ 4           3 <------ 3
20 ----:-> 6                                                      20 ------> 2          20 ------> 7          5 <-:----- 4
     :-> 8            5 <-:----- 1          20 ------> 1          5 ----:--- 8          5 <-:----- 1          6 <-:
5 <-:----- 3          6 <-:                 5 <-:----- 6          6 <-:                 6 <-:                 8 <-:
6 <-:                 8 <-:                 6 <-:                 8 <-:                 8 <-:
8 <-:                                       8 <-:
                                                                  4 ----:-> 7           4 ----:-> 2
```

```
G203                  G204                  G205                  G206                  G207                  G208
1 ------- 3           1 ------- 4           7 ------- 4           7 ------- 3           7 ------- 11          7 ------- 11
7 ------- 4           7 ------- 3           2 ------> 2           2 ------> 5           2 ------> 9           2 ------> 1
2 ------> 5           2 ------> 2           3 <------ 3           3 <------ 4           3 <------ 1           3 <------ 9
3 <------ 2           3 <------ 5
                                            20 ------> 6          20 ------> 1          20 ----:-> 10         5 <-:----- 3
20 ------> 1          20 ------> 6          5 <-:----- 1          5 <-:----- 6               :-> 3            6 <-:
5 <-:----- 6          5 <-:----- 1          6 <-:                 6 <-:                      :-> 12           8 <-:
6 <-:                 6 <-:                 8 <-:                 8 <-:                 5 <-:----- 2
8 <-:                 8 <-:                                                             6 <-:                 4 ----:-> 2
                                                                                        8 <-:                      :-> 4
```

```
G209                  G210                  G211                  G212                  G213                  G214
7 ------- 4           7 ------- 4           7 ------- 2           7 ------- 5           7 ------- 2           7 ------- 5
2 ------> 2           2 ------> 3           2 ------> 3           2 ------> 4           2 ------> 3           2 ------> 2
3 <------ 2           3 <------ 2           3 <------ 5           3 <------ 2           3 <------ 5           3 <------ 3

20 ------> 5          5 <-:----- 5          20 ------> 1          20 ------> 3          20 ------> 4          20 ----:-> 8
5 ----:--- 1          6 <-:                 5 <-:----- 6          5 <-:----- 1          5 <-:----- 6               :-> 6
6 <-:                 8 <-:                 6 <-:                 6 <-:                 6 <-:                 5 <-:----- 4
8 <-:                                       8 <-:                 8 <-:                 8 <-:                 6 <-:
                                                                                                              8 <-:
                                                                  4 ----:-> 6           4 ----:-> 1
```

```
G215                  G216                  G217                  G218                  G219                  G220
1 ------- 1           1 ------- 1           7 ------- 4           7 ------- 5           7 ------- 3           1 ------- 4
7 ------- 8           7 ------- 7           3 ------> 3           3 ------> 7           3 ------> 5           7 ------- 7
3 ------> 4           3 ------> 2           2 <------ 2           2 <------ 4           2 <------ 4           3 ------> 6
2 <------ 2           2 <------ 3                                                                             2 <------ 5
                                            4 <-:----- 5          4 <-:----- 3          4 <-:----- 1
4 <-:----- 3          4 <-:----- 5          20 <-:                20 <-:                20 <-:                4 <-:----- 3
20 <-:                20 <-:                                                                                  20 <-:
                      5 ----:-> 4           5 ----:-> 1           5 ----:-> 2           5 ----:-> 6
5 ----:-> 5                                      :-> 6                 :-> 6                 :-> 7           5 ----:-> 1
     :-> 7                                                                                    :-> 8               :-> 2
     :-> 10                                                                                                       :-> 8

6 ----:-> 11                                                                                                 6 ----:-> 10
```

```
G221                  G222                  G223                  G224                  G225                  G226
1 ------- 3           7 ------- 8           7 ------- 8           7 ------- 7           7 ------- 5           1 ------- 2
7 ------- 6           3 ------> 2           3 ------> 6           3 ------> 3           3 ------> 3           7 ------- 7
3 ------> 5           2 <------ 1           2 <------ 1           2 <------ 2           2 <------ 2           2 ------> 3
2 <------ 4                                                                                                   3 <------ 8

4 <-:----- 2          5 --:                 4 <-:----- 2          4 <-:----- 4          4 <-:----- 1          20 ----:-> 5
20 <-:                4 <-:                 20 <-:                20 <-:                20 <-:                     :-> 6
                      20 <-:                                                                                      :-> 1
5 ----:-> 1                                 5 ----:-> 7           5 ----:-> 5           5 ----:-> 4           5 <-:----- 9
     :-> 7                                       :-> 9                 :-> 8                 :-> 7           6 <-:
                                                                                                             8 <-:

                                                                                                             4 ----:-> 10
```

```
    G227                G228                G229                G230                G231                G232
1 ------- 2         7 ------- 7         7 ------- 4         7 ------- 5         7 ------- 9         7 ------- 3
7 ------- 7         2 -----> 5         2 -----> 6         2 -----> 6         2 -----> 3         2 -----> 4
2 -----> 8         3 <----- 4         3 <----- 3         3 <----- 4         3 <----- 2         3 <----- 2
3 <----- 3
                   20 -----> 3        5 <-:---- 2        20 -----> 2        20 -----> 5        20 -----> 5
5 <-:---- 5        5 <-:---- 1        6 <-:              5 <-:---- 3        5 <-:---- 4        5 <-:---- 1
6 <-:              6 <-:              8 <-:              6 <-:              6 <-:              6 <-:
8 <-:              8 <-:                                 8 <-:              8 <-:              8 <-:
                                      4 ----:-> 1
4 ----:-> 4                             :-> 7
  :-> 9


    G233                G234                G235                G236                G237                G238
7 ------- 9         7 ------- 5         7 ------- 5         7 ------- 5         7 ------- 5         1 ------- 3
3 -----> 13        3 -----> 2         3 -----> 2         3 -----> 3         3 -----> 3         7 ------- 4
2 <----- 11        2 <----- 3         2 <----- 3         2 <----- 2         2 <----- 2         3 -----> 5
                                                                                               2 <----- 2
4 <-:---- 10       4 <-:---- 4        4 <-:---- 7        4 <-:---- 6        5 --:
20 <-:             20 <-:             20 <-:             20 <-:             4 <-:              4 <-:---- 1
                                                                           20 <-:             20 <-:
5 ----:-> 14       5 ----:-> 6        5 ----:-> 8
                     :-> 8                                                                     5 ----:-> 6


    G239                G240                G241                G242                G243                G244
1 ------- 1         1 ------- 1         1 ------- 1         7 ------- 4         7 ------- 5         7 ------- 1
7 ------- 2         7 ------- 7         7 ------- 7         3 -----> 5         3 -----> 4         3 -----> 4
3 -----> 4         2 <----- 2         3 -----> 5         2 <----- 3         2 <----- 2         2 <----- 2
2 <----- 3                            2 <----- 3
                   5 --:                                 4 <-:---- 6        5 --:              4 <-:---- 3
4 <-:---- 6        4 <-:              4 <-:---- 2        20 <-:             4 <-:              20 <-:
20 <-:             20 <-:             20 <-:                                20 <-:
                                                         5 ----:-> 2                           5 ----:-> 6
5 ----:-> 5                           5 ----:-> 6                           6 ----:-> 6          :-> 8
                                        :-> 8


    G245                G246                G247                G248                G249                G250
1 ------- 3         1 ------- 4         7 ------- 3         7 ------- 6         7 ------- 2         1 ------- 3
7 ------- 5         7 ------- 2         3 -----> 1         3 -----> 8         3 -----> 3         7 ------- 4
3 -----> 2         3 -----> 5         2 <----- 5         2 <----- 4         2 <----- 5         3 -----> 5
2 <----- 4         2 <----- 3                                                                  2 <----- 2
                                      4 <-:---- 4        4 <-:---- 3        4 <-:---- 4
5 --:              4 <-:---- 6        20 <-:             20 <-:             20 <-:             4 <-:---- 6
4 <-:              20 <-:                                                                      20 <-:
20 <-:                                5 ----:-> 2        5 ----:-> 2
                   5 ----:-> 1          :-> 7             :-> 7                                5 ----:-> 1


    G251                G252                G253                G254                G255                G256
1 ------- 4         7 ------- 4         7 ------- 3         7 ------- 11        7 ------- 11        7 ------- 4
7 ------- 3         3 -----> 2         3 -----> 5         3 -----> 9         3 -----> 1         3 -----> 2
3 -----> 2         2 <----- 3         2 <----- 4         2 <----- 1         2 <----- 9         2 <----- 3
2 <----- 5
                   4 <-:---- 1        4 <-:---- 6        4 <-:---- 2        4 <-:---- 3        4 <-:---- 1
4 <-:---- 1        20 <-:             20 <-:             20 <-:             20 <-:             20 <-:
20 <-:
                   5 ---:-> 6         5 ----:-> 1        5 ----:-> 3        5 ----:-> 2        5 ----:-> 5
5 ----:-> 6                                               :-> 10             :-> 4
                                                          :-> 12
```

```
   G257                G258                G259                G260                G261                  G262
7 ------- 4         7 ------- 2         7 ------- 5         7 ------- 2         7 ------- 5          1 ------- 1
3 ------> 3         3 ------> 3         3 ------> 4         3 ------> 3         3 ------> 2          7 ------- 8
2 <------ 2         2 <------ 5         2 <------ 2         2 <------ 5         2 <------ 3          3 ------> 4
                                                                                                    2 <------ 2
4 <-:---- 5        4 <-:---- 6        4 <-:---- 1        4 <-:---- 6        4 <-:---- 4
20 <-:            20 <-:             20 <-:             20 <-:             20 <-:               8 <-:---- 12
                                                                                                   20 <-:
                  5 ----:-> 1        5 ----:-> 3        5 ----:-> 1        5 ----:-> 6          4 <------ 3
                                          :-> 6              :-> 4              :-> 8
                                                                                                   5 ----:-> 5
                                                                                                        :-> 7
                                                                                                        :-> 10
                                                                                                        :-> 11
```

```
   G263                G264                G265                G266                G267                  G268
1 ------- 1        7 ------- 4         7 ------- 5         7 ------- 3         1 ------- 4          1 ------- 3
7 ------- 7        3 ------> 3         3 ------> 7         3 ------> 5         7 ------- 7          7 ------- 6
3 ------> 2        2 <------ 2         2 <------ 4         2 <------ 4         3 ------> 6          3 ------> 5
2 <------ 3                                                                   2 <------ 5          2 <------ 4
                  8 <-:---- 5        8 <-:---- 3        8 <-:---- 2
8 <-:---- 6       20 <-:             20 <-:             20 <-:              8 <-:---- 9          8 <-:---- 8
20 <-:                                                                      20 <-:              20 <-:
                  5 --:              4 <------ 8        4 <------ 1
4 <------ 5       4 <-:                                                     4 <------ 3          4 <------ 2
                                     5 ----:-> 2        5 ----:-> 6
5 ----:-> 4                              :-> 6              :-> 7          5 ----:-> 1          5 ----:-> 1
                                                           :-> 8               :-> 2               :-> 7
                                                                              :-> 8
                                                                              :-> 10
```

```
   G269                G270                G271                G272                G273                  G274
7 ------- 8        7 ------- 8         7 ------- 7         7 ------- 5         1 ------- 2          1 ------- 2
3 ------> 2        3 ------> 6         3 ------> 3         3 ------> 3         7 ------- 7          7 ------- 7
2 <------ 1        2 <------ 1         2 <------ 2         2 <------ 2         3 ------> 3          3 ------> 8
                                                                             2 <------ 8          2 <------ 3
                  8 <-:---- 4        8 <-:---- 9        8 <-:---- 6
5 --:            20 <-:             20 <-:             20 <-:              8 <-:---- 9          8 <-:---- 5
4 <-:                                                                      20 <-:              20 <-:
8 <-:            4 <------ 2        4 <------ 4        4 <------ 1
20 <-:                                                                     4 <------ 4          4 <------ 1
                 5 ----:-> 7        5 ----:-> 5        5 ----:-> 4
                      :-> 9              :-> 8              :-> 7          5 ----:-> 1          5 ----:-> 4
                                                                              :-> 5               :-> 9
                                                                              :-> 6
                                                                              :-> 10
```

```
   G275                G276                G277                G278                G279                  G280
7 ------- 7        7 ------- 4         7 ------- 5         7 ------- 9         7 ------- 3          7 ------- 9
3 ------> 5        3 ------> 6         3 ------> 6         3 ------> 3         3 ------> 4          3 ------> 13
2 <------ 4        2 <------ 3         2 <------ 4         2 <------ 2         2 <------ 2          2 <------ 11

8 <-:---- 1       8 <-:---- 2        8 <-:---- 3        8 <-:---- 4        8 <-:---- 1          8 <-:---- 10
20 <-:            20 <-:             20 <-:             20 <-:             20 <-:               20 <-:

4 <------ 6       5 --:              5 --:              5 --:              5 --:                5 --:
                  4 <-:              4 <-:              4 <-:              4 <-:                4 <-:
5 ----:-> 3
```

```
   G281                 G282                 G283                 G284                 G285                 G286
7 ------- 5          7 ------- 5          7 ------- 5          7 ------- 5       1 ------- 3          1 ------- 1
3 ------> 2          3 ------> 2          3 ------> 3          3 ------> 3       7 ------- 4          7 ------- 2
2 <------ 3          2 <------ 3          2 <------ 2          2 <------ 2       3 ------> 5          3 ------> 4
                                                                                2 <------ 2          2 <------ 3
8 <-:---- 4          8 <-:---- 7          8 <-:---- 6          5 --:
20 <-:              20 <-:              20 <-:               4 <-:             8 <-:---- 1          8 <-:---- 6
                                                              8 <-:            20 <-:              20 <-:
4 <-:---- 7          5 --:              4 <-:---- 8          20 <-:
                    4 <-:                                                       5 --:                5 --:
5 ----:-> 6                                                                     4 <-:                4 <-:
   :-> 8
```

```
   G287                 G288                 G289                 G290                 G291                 G292
1 ------- 1          1 ------- 1          7 ------- 4          7 ------- 5       7 ------- 1          1 ------- 3
7 ------- 7          7 ------- 7          3 ------> 5          3 ------> 4       3 ------> 4          7 ------- 5
2 <------ 2          3 ------> 5          2 <------ 3          2 <------ 2       2 <------ 2          3 ------> 2
                    2 <------ 3                                                                      2 <------ 4
5 --:                                    8 <-:---- 6          8 <-:---- 1       8 <-:---- 3
4 <-:                8 <-:---- 4          20 <-:              20 <-:             20 <-:              8 <-:---- 1
8 <-:               20 <-:                                                                          20 <-:
20 <-:                                    5 --:                5 --:             4 <------ 5
                    4 <-:---- 2          4 <-:                4 <-:                                  5 --:
                                                                                5 ----:-> 6          4 <-:
                    5 ----:-> 6                                                     :-> 8
                       :-> 8
```

```
   G293                 G294                 G295                 G296                 G297                 G298
1 ------- 4          7 ------- 3          7 ------- 6          7 ------- 2       1 ------- 3          1 ------- 4
7 ------- 2          3 ------> 1          3 ------> 8          3 ------> 3       7 ------- 4          7 ------- 2
3 ------> 5          2 <------ 5          2 <------ 4          2 <------ 5       3 ------> 5          3 ------> 2
2 <------ 3                                                                      2 <------ 2          2 <------ 5
                    8 <-:---- 8          8 <-:---- 1          8 <-:---- 4
8 <-:---- 6          20 <-:              20 <-:              20 <-:             8 <-:---- 6          8 <-:---- 1
20 <-:                                                                          20 <-:              20 <-:
                    4 <------ 4          4 <------ 3          5 --:
5 --:                                                        4 <-:              5 --:                5 --:
4 <-:                5 ----:-> 2          5 ----:-> 2                            4 <-:                4 <-:
                       :-> 7                :-> 7
```

```
   G299                 G300                 G301                 G302                 G303                 G304
7 ------- 4          7 ------- 3          7 ------- 11         7 ------- 11      7 ------- 4          7 ------- 4
3 ------> 2          3 ------> 5          3 ------> 9          3 ------> 1       3 ------> 2          3 ------> 3
2 <------ 3          2 <------ 4          2 <------ 1          2 <------ 9       2 <------ 3          2 <------ 2
8 <-:---- 1          8 <-:---- 6          8 <-:---- 2          8 <-:---- 3       8 <-:---- 1          8 <-:---- 5
20 <-:              20 <-:              20 <-:              20 <-:             20 <-:              20 <-:
5 --:                5 --:                5 --:              4 <------ 10
4 <-:                4 <-:                4 <-:                                  4 <------ 6          5 --:
                                                            5 ----:-> 2                             4 <-:
                                                               :-> 4            5 ----:-> 5
```

```
   G305                 G306                 G307                 G308                 G309                 G310
7 ------- 2          7 ------- 5          7 ------- 2          7 ------- 5       1 ------- 1          1 ------- 1
3 ------> 3          3 ------> 4          3 ------> 3          3 ------> 2       7 ------- 8          7 ------- 7
2 <------ 5          2 <------ 2          2 <------ 5          2 <------ 3       2 ------> 4          2 ------> 2
                                                                                3 <------ 2          3 <------ 3
8 <-:---- 6          8 <-:---- 1          8 <-:---- 6          8 <-:---- 4                          5 <------ 5
20 <-:              20 <-:              20 <-:              20 <-:             5 <-:---- 12         6 <------ 6
                                                                                6 <-:                4 ------> 4
5 --:                5 --:                5 --:              4 <------ 7
4 <-:                4 <-:                4 <-:                                  20 <-:---- 3          20 <-:---- 8
                                                            5 ----:-> 6
                                                               :-> 8            4 ----:-> 5
                                                                                  :-> 7
                                                                                  :-> 10
                                                                                  :-> 11
```

```
 G311                  G312                  G313                  G314                G315                G316
7 ------ 4            7 ------ 5            7 ------ 3           1 ------ 4          1 ------ 3          7 ------ 8
2 ------> 3           2 ------> 7           2 ------> 5          7 ------ 7          7 ------ 6          2 ------> 2
3 <------ 2           3 <------ 4           3 <------ 4          2 ------> 6         2 ------> 5         3 <------ 1
                                                                3 <------ 5         3 <------ 4
5 <-:---- 5           5 <-:---- 3           5 <-:---- 2                                                4 --:
6 <-:                 6 <-:                 6 <-:                5 <-:---- 9         5 <-:---- 8        5 <-:
                                                                6 <-:               6 <-:              6 <-:
4 --:                 20 <-:---- 8          20 <-:---- 1                                                20 <-:
20 <-:                                                          20 <-:---- 3        20 <-:---- 2
                      4 ----:-> 2           4 ----:-> 6
                           :-> 6                 :-> 7          4 ----:-> 1         4 ----:-> 1
                                                 :-> 8              :-> 2                :-> 7
                                                                    :-> 8
                                                                    :-> 10

 G317                  G318                  G319                  G320                G321                G322
7 ------ 8            7 ------ 7            7 ------ 5           1 ------ 2          1 ------ 2          7 ------ 7
2 ------> 6           2 ------> 3           2 ------> 3          7 ------ 7          7 ------ 7          2 ------> 5
3 <------ 1           3 <------ 2           3 <------ 2          2 ------> 8         2 ------> 8         3 <------ 4
                                                                3 <------ 8         3 <------ 3
5 <-:---- 4           5 <-:---- 9           5 <-:---- 6                                                5 <-:---- 1
6 <-:                 6 <-:                 6 <-:                5 <-:---- 9         5 <-:---- 5        6 <-:
                                                                6 <-:               6 <-:
20 <-:---- 2          20 <-:---- 4          20 <-:---- 1                                                20 <-:---- 6
                                                                20 <-:---- 4        20 <-:---- 1
4 ----:-> 7           4 ----:-> 5           4 ----:-> 4                                                4 ----:-> 3
     :-> 9                 :-> 8                 :-> 7          4 ----:-> 1         4 ----:-> 4
                                                                    :-> 5                :-> 9
                                                                    :-> 6
                                                                    :-> 10

 G323                  G324                  G325                  G326                G327                G328
7 ------ 4            7 ------ 5            7 ------ 9           7 ------ 3          7 ------ 9          7 ------ 5
2 ------> 6           2 ------> 6           2 ------> 3          2 ------> 4         2 ------> 13        2 ------> 2
3 <------ 3           3 <------ 4           3 <------ 2          3 <------ 2         3 <------ 11        3 <------ 3
5 <-:---- 2           5 <-:---- 3           5 <-:---- 4         5 <-:---- 1         5 <-:---- 10        5 <-:---- 4
6 <-:                 6 <-:                 6 <-:                6 <-:               6 <-:              6 <-:
4 --:                 4 --:                 4 --:               4 --:               4 --:              20 <-:---- 7
20 <-:                20 <-:                20 <-:              20 <-:              20 <-:
                                                                                                       4 ----:-> 6
                                                                                                            :-> 8

 G329                  G330                  G331                  G332                G333                G334
7 ------ 5            7 ------ 5            7 ------ 5           1 ------ 3          1 ------ 1          1 ------ 1
2 ------> 2           2 ------> 3           2 ------> 3          7 ------ 4          7 ------ 2          7 ------ 7
3 <------ 3           3 <------ 2           3 <------ 2          2 ------> 5         2 ------> 4         3 <------ 2
                                                                3 <------ 2         3 <------ 3
5 <-:---- 7           5 <-:---- 6                                                                      4 --:
6 <-:                 6 <-:                 4 --:               5 <-:---- 1         5 <-:---- 6        5 <-:
                                            5 <-:               6 <-:               6 <-:              6 <-:
4 --:                 20 <-:---- 8          6 <-:                                                       20 <-:
20 <-:                                      20 <-:              4 --:               4 --:
                                                                20 <-:              20 <-:
```

```
 G335                    G336                    G337                    G338                    G339                    G340
1 ------- 1            7 ------- 4             7 ------- 5            7 ------- 1            1 ------- 3             1 ------- 4
7 ------- 7            2 ------> 5             2 ------> 4            2 ------> 4            7 ------- 5             7 ------- 2
2 ------> 5            3 <------ 3             3 <------ 2            3 <------ 2            2 ------> 2             2 ------> 5
3 <------ 3                                                                                 3 <------ 4             3 <------ 3

5 <-:---- 4           5 <-:---- 6             5 <-:---- 1            5 <-:---- 3                                    5 <-:---- 6
6 <-:                 6 <-:                   6 <-:                  6 <-:                  5 <-:---- 1             6 <-:
                                                                                            6 <-:
20 <-:---- 2          4 --:                   4 --:                  20 <-:---- 5                                   4 --:
                      20 <-:                  20 <-:                                        4 --:                   20 <-:
4 ----:-> 6                                                          4 ----:-> 6            20 <-:
   :-> 8                                                                :-> 8

 G341                    G342                    G343                    G344                    G345                    G346
7 ------- 3            7 ------- 6             7 ------- 2            1 ------- 3            1 ------- 4             7 ------- 4
2 ------> 1            2 ------> 8             2 ------> 3            7 ------- 4            7 ------- 3             2 ------> 2
3 <------ 5            3 <------ 4             3 <------ 5            2 ------> 5            2 ------> 2             3 <------ 3
                                                                     3 <------ 2            3 <------ 5
5 <-:---- 8           5 <-:---- 1             5 <-:---- 4                                   5 <-:---- 1            5 <-:---- 1
6 <-:                 6 <-:                   6 <-:                  5 <-:---- 6            6 <-:                  6 <-:
                                                                     6 <-:
20 <-:---- 4          20 <-:---- 3            4 --:                                         4 --:                  4 --:
                                              20 <-:                 4 --:                  20 <-:                 20 <-:
4 ----:-> 2           4 ----:-> 2                                    20 <-:
   :-> 7                 :-> 7

 G347                    G348                    G349                    G350                    G351                    G352
7 ------- 3            7 ------- 11            7 ------- 11           7 ------- 4            7 ------- 4             7 ------- 2
2 ------> 5            2 ------> 9             2 ------> 1            2 ------> 2            2 ------> 3             2 ------> 3
3 <------ 4            3 <------ 1             3 <------ 9            3 <------ 3            3 <------ 2             3 <------ 5
                                              5 <------ 10
5 <-:---- 6           5 <-:---- 2             6 <------ 3            5 <-:---- 1            5 <-:---- 5            5 <-:---- 6
6 <-:                 6 <-:                   4 ------> 2            6 <-:                  6 <-:                  6 <-:

4 --:                 4 --:                                         20 <-:---- 6           4 --:                  4 --:
20 <-:                20 <-:                  20 <-:---- 12                                 20 <-:                 20 <-:
                                                                    4 ----:-> 5

 G353                    G354                    G355                    G356                    G357                    G358
7 ------- 5            7 ------- 2             7 ------- 5            1 ------- 1            1 ------- 1             7 ------- 4
2 ------> 4            2 ------> 3             2 ------> 2            7 ------- 8            7 ------- 7             2 ------> 3
3 <------ 2            3 <------ 5             3 <------ 3            2 ------> 4            2 ------> 2             3 <------ 2
                                                                     3 <------ 2            3 <------ 3
5 <-:---- 1           5 <-:---- 6             5 <-:---- 4                                   5 <------ 5            5 <------ 5
6 <-:                 6 <-:                   6 <-:                  5 <------ 12           4 ------> 4

4 --:                 4 --:                   20 <-:---- 7           4 ----:-> 5                                   4 ----:-> 1
20 <-:                20 <-:                                            :-> 7                                         :-> 6
                                              4 ----:-> 6               :-> 10
                                                                        :-> 11

 G359                    G360                    G361                    G362                    G363                    G364
7 ------- 5            7 ------- 3             1 ------- 4            1 ------- 3            7 ------- 8             7 ------- 8
2 ------> 7            2 ------> 5             7 ------- 7            7 ------- 6            2 ------> 2             2 ------> 6
3 <------ 4            3 <------ 4             2 ------> 6            2 ------> 5            3 <------ 1             3 <------ 1
                                              3 <------ 5            3 <------ 4
5 <------ 3           5 <------ 2                                                                                  5 <------ 4
                                              5 <------ 9            5 <------ 8            4 --:
4 ----:-> 2           4 ----:-> 6                                                          5 <-:                  4 ----:-> 7
   :-> 6                 :-> 7                4 ----:-> 1            4 ----:-> 1                                      :-> 9
                        :-> 8                    :-> 2                 :-> 7
                                                 :-> 8
                                                 :-> 10
```

```
G365                 G366                 G367                 G368                 G369                 G370
7 ------- 7          7 ------- 5          1 ------- 2          1 ------- 2          7 ------- 7          7 ------- 4
2 ------> 3          2 ------> 3          7 ------- 7          7 ------- 7          2 ------> 5          2 ------> 6
3 <------ 2          3 <------ 2          2 ------> 3          2 ------> 8          3 <------ 4          3 <------ 3
                                          3 <------ 8          3 <------ 3
5 <----- 9           5 <------ 6                                                   5 <----- 1           5 <----- 2
                                          5 <------ 9          5 <------ 5
4 ----:-> 5          4 ----:-> 4                                                   4 ----:-> 3          4 ----:-> 1
     :-> 8                :-> 7           4 ----:-> 1          4 ----:-> 4                                    :-  7
                                               :-> 5               :-> 9
                                               :-> 6
                                               :-> 10
```

```
G371                 G372                 G373                 G374                 G375                 G376
7 ------- 5          7 ------- 9          7 ------- 3          7 ------- 9          7 ------- 5          7 ------- 5
2 ------> 6          2 ------> 3          2 ------> 4          2 ------> 13         2 ------> 2          2 ------> 2
3 <------ 4          3 <------ 2          3 <------ 2          3 <------ 11         3 <------ 3          3 <------ 3

5 <------ 3          5 <------ 4          5 <------ 1          5 <------ 10         5 <------ 4          5 <------ 7

4 ----:-> 2          4 ----:-> 5          4 ----:-> 5          4 ----:-> 14         4 ----:-> 6          4 ----:-> 8
                                                                                         :- 8
```

```
G377                 G378                 G379                 G380                 G381                 G382
7 ------- 5          7 ------- 5          1 ------- 3          1 ------- 1          1 ------- 1          1 ------- 1
2 ------> 3          2 ------> 3          7 ------- 4          7 ------- 2          7 ------- 7          7 ------- 7
3 <------ 2          3 <------ 2          2 ------> 5          2 ------> 4          3 <------ 2          2 ------> 5
                                          3 <------ 2          3 <------ 3                               3 <------ 3
5 <------ 6          4 --:                                                          4 --:
                     5 <-:               5 <------ 1          5 <------ 6          5 <-:               5 <------ 4

                                         4 ----:-> 6          4 ----:-> 5                               4 ----:-> 6
                                                                                                             :-> 8
```

```
G383                 G384                 G385                 G386                 G387                 G388
7 ------- 4          7 ------- 5          7 ------- 1          1 ------- 3          1 ------- 4          7 ------- 3
2 ------> 5          2 ------> 4          2 ------> 4          7 ------- 5          7 ------- 2          2 ------> 1
3 <------ 3          3 <------ 2          3 <------ 2          2 ------> 2          2 ------> 5          3 <------ 5
                                                              3 <------ 4          3 <------ 3
5 <------ 6          5 <------ 1          5 <------ 3                                                   5 <------ 8
                                                              5 <------ 1          5 <------ 6
4 ----:-> 2          4 ----:-> 6          4 ----:-> 6                                                   4 ----:-> 2
                                               :-> 8                               4 ----:-> 1               :-> 7
```

```
G389                 G390                 G391                 G392                 G393                 G394
7 ------- 6          7 ------- 2          1 ------- 3          1 ------- 4          7 ------- 4          7 ------- 3
2 ------> 8          2 ------> 3          7 ------- 4          7 ------- 3          2 ------> 2          2 ------> 5
3 <------ 4          3 <------ 5          2 ------> 5          2 ------> 2          3 <------ 3          3 <------ 4
                                          3 <------ 2          3 <------ 5
5 <------ 1          5 <------ 4                                                   5 <------ 1          5 <------ 6
                                          5 <------ 6          5 <------ 1
4 ----:-> 2                                                                        4 ----:-> 6          4 ----:-> 1
     :-> 7                                4 ----:-> 1          4 ----:-> 6
```

```
G395                 G396                 G397                 G398                 G399                 G400
7 ------- 11         7 ------- 11         7 ------- 4          7 ------- 4          7 ------- 2          7 ------- 5
2 ------> 9          2 ------> 1          2 ------> 2          2 ------> 3          2 ------> 3          2 ------> 4
3 <------ 1          3 <------ 9          3 <------ 3          3 <------ 2          3 <------ 5          3 <------ 2
                     5 <------ 10
5 <------ 2          4 ------> 2          5 <------ 1          5 <------ 5          5 <------ 6          5 <------ 1

4 ----:-> 3               :-  3          4 ----:-> 5                               4 ----:-> 1          4 ----:-> 3
     :-> 10               :-> 4                                                                              :-> 6
     :-> 12
```

```
G401                 G402                 G403                 G404                 G405                 G406
7 ------- 2          7 ------- 5          7 ------- 8          7 ------- 7          7 ------- 4          7 ------- 5
2 ------> 3          2 ------> 2          3 ------> 4          3 ------> 2          3 ------> 3          3 ------> 7
3 <------ 5          3 ------> 3          2 <------ 2          2 <------ 3          2 <------ 2          2 <------ 4
5 <------ 6          5 <------ 4          :-- 3               :-- 5               :-- 5               :-- 3
4 ----:-> 1          4 ----:-> 6          :-> 5               :-> 4               :-> 1               :-> 2
   :-> 4                :-> 8            :-> 7                                    :-> 6               :-> 6
                                          :-> 10
                                          :-- 9
                                          :-> 11

G407                 G408                 G409                 G410                 G411                 G412
7 ------- 3          7 ------- 7          7 ------- 6          7 ------- 8          7 ------- 8          7 ------- 7
3 ------> 5          3 ------> 6          3 ------> 5          3 ------> 2          3 ------> 6          3 ------> 3
2 <------ 4          2 <------ 5          2 <------ 4          2 <------ 1          2 <------ 1          2 <------ 2
:-- 1               :-- 3               :- 2                                     :-- 2               :-- 4
:-> 6               :-> 1               :- 1                                     :-> 7               :-> 5
:-> 7               :-> 2               :- 7                                     :-> 9               :-> 8
:-> 8               :-> 8
:-- 2               :-- 9
                     :-> 10

G413                 G414                 G415                 G416                 G417                 G418
7 ------- 5          7 ------- 7          7 ------- 7          7 ------- 7          7 ------- 4          7 ------- 5
3 ------> 3          3 ------> 3          3 ------> 8          3 ------> 5          3 ------> 6          3 ------> 6
2 <------ 2          2 <------ 8          2 <------ 3          2 <------ 4          2 <------ 5          2 <------ 4
:-- 1               :-- 4               :-- 1               :-- 1               :-- 2               :-- 3
:-> 4               :-> 1               :-> 4               :-> 3               :-> 1               :-> 2
:-> 7               :-> 5               :-> 9                                    :-> 7
                     :-> 6
                     :-- 9
                     :-> 10

G419                 G420                 G421                 G422                 G423                 G424
7 ------- 9          7 ------- 3          7 ------- 9          7 ------- 5          7 ------- 5          7 ------- 5
3 ------> 3          3 ------> 4          3 ------> 13         3 ------> 2          3 ------> 2          3 ------> 3
2 <------ 2          2 <------ 2          2 <------ 11         2 <------ 3          2 <------ 3          2 <------ 2
:-- 4               :-- 1               :-- 10              :-- 4               :-- 7
:-> 5               :-> 5               :-> 14              :-> 6               :-> 8
                                                             :-> 8

G425                 G426                 G427                 G428                 G429                 G430
7 ------- 5          7 ------- 4          7 ------- 2          7 ------- 7          7 ------- 7          7 ------- 4
3 ------> 3          3 ------> 5          3 ------> 4          2 <------ 2          3 ------> 5          3 ------> 5
2 <------ 2          2 <------ 2          2 <------ 3                               2 <------ 3          2 <------ 3
                     :-- 1               :-- 6                                    :-- 2               :-- 6
                     :-> 6               :-> 5                                    :-> 6               :-> 2
                                                                                  :-> 8

G431                 G432                 G433                 G434                 G435                 G436
7 ------- 5          7 ------- 1          7 ------- 5          7 ------- 2          7 ------- 3          7 ------- 6
3 ------> 4          3 ------> 4          3 ------> 2          3 ------> 5          3 ------> 1          3 ------> 8
2 <------ 2          2 <------ 2          2 <------ 4          2 <------ 3          2 <------ 5          2 <------ 4
                     :-- 3                                    :-- 6               :-- 4               :-- 3
                     :-> 6                                    :-> 1               :-> 2               :-> 2
                     :-> 8                                                        :-> 7               :-> 7
```

```
┌─────────────────────┬─────────────────────┬─────────────────────┬─────────────────────┬─────────────────────┬─────────────────────┐
│      G437           │      G438           │      G439           │      G440           │      G441           │      G442           │
│ 7 ------- 2         │ 7 ------- 4         │ 7 ------- 3         │ 7 ------- 4         │ 7 ------- 3         │ 7 ------- 11        │
│ 3 ------> 3         │ 3 ------> 5         │ 3 ------> 2         │ 3 ------> 2         │ 3 ------> 5         │ 3 ------> 9         │
│ 2 <------ 5         │ 2 <------ 2         │ 2 <------ 5         │ 2 <------ 3         │ 2 <------ 4         │ 2 <------ 1         │
│                     │                     │                     │                     │                     │                     │
│                     │  :-- 6              │  :-- 1              │  :-- 1              │  :-- 6              │  :-- 2              │
│                     │  :-> 1              │  :-> 6              │  :-> 6              │  :-> 1              │  :-> 3              │
│                     │                     │                     │                     │                     │  :-> 10             │
│                     │                     │                     │                     │                     │  :-> 12             │
├─────────────────────┼─────────────────────┼─────────────────────┼─────────────────────┼─────────────────────┼─────────────────────┤
│      G443           │      G444           │      G445           │      G446           │      G447           │      G448           │
│ 7 ------- 11        │ 7 ------- 4         │ 7 ------- 4         │ 7 ------- 2         │ 7 ------- 5         │ 7 ------- 2         │
│ 3 ------> 1         │ 3 ------> 2         │ 3 ------> 3         │ 3 ------> 3         │ 3 ------> 4         │ 3 ------> 3         │
│ 2 <------ 9         │ 2 <------ 3         │ 2 <------ 2         │ 2 <------ 5         │ 2 <------ 2         │ 2 <------ 5         │
│                     │                     │                     │                     │                     │                     │
│  :-- 3              │  :- 1               │                     │  :-- 6              │  :-- 1              │  :-- 6              │
│  :-> 2              │  :- 5               │                     │  :-> 1              │  :-> 3              │  :-> 1              │
│  :-> 4              │                     │                     │                     │  :-> 6              │  :-> 4              │
├─────────────────────┼─────────────────────┼─────────────────────┼─────────────────────┼─────────────────────┼─────────────────────┤
│      G449           │      G450           │      G451           │      G452           │      G453           │      G454           │
│ 7 ------- 5         │ 1 ------- 1         │ 1 ------- 1         │ 1 ------- 1         │ 1 ------- 1         │ 1 ------- 1         │
│ 3 ------> 2         │ 7 ------- 7         │ 7 ------- 7         │ 7 ------- 7         │ 7 ------- 7         │ 7 ------- 7         │
│ 2 <------ 3         │ 2 ------> 3         │ 2 ------> 2         │ 2 ------> 2         │ 2 ------> 3         │ 2 ------> 3         │
│                     │ 3 <------ 2         │ 3 <------ 3         │ 3 <------ 3         │ 3 <------ 2         │ 3 <------ 2         │
│  :-- 4              │                     │                     │                     │                     │                     │
│  :-> 6              │ 20 ----:-> 5        │ 5 <-:---- 6         │ 20 ------> 8        │ 20 ----:-> 5        │ 20 ----:-> 5        │
│  :-> 8              │      :-> 6          │ 6 <-:               │ 5 <-:---- 5         │      :-> 4          │      :-> 6          │
│                     │      :-> 8          │ 8 <-:               │ 6 <-:               │ 5 <-:---- 4         │ 5 <-:---- 4         │
│                     │ 5 <-:---- 20        │                     │ 8 <-:               │ 6 <-:               │ 6 <-:               │
│                     │ 6 <-:               │ 4 ----:-> 4         │                     │ 8 <-:               │ 8 <-:               │
│                     │ 8 <-:               │      :-> 20         │ 4 ----:-> 4         │                     │                     │
│                     │                     │                     │      :-> 20         │ 4 ----:-> 20        │                     │
├─────────────────────┼─────────────────────┼─────────────────────┼─────────────────────┼─────────────────────┼─────────────────────┤
│      G455           │      G456           │      G457           │      G458           │      G459           │      G460           │
│ 7 ------- 7         │ 7 ------- 5         │ 7 ------- 5         │ 1 ------- 1         │ 1 ------- 1         │ 1 ------- 1         │
│ 2 ------> 2         │ 2 ------> 4         │ 2 ------> 4         │ 7 ------- 7         │ 7 ------- 7         │ 7 ------- 7         │
│ 3 <------ 3         │ 3 <------ 3         │ 3 <------ 3         │ 2 ------> 2         │ 2 ------> 2         │ 2 ------> 3         │
│                     │                     │                     │ 3 <------ 3         │ 3 <------ 3         │ 3 <------ 2         │
│ 4 --:               │ 20 ------> 6        │ 5 <-:---- 1         │                     │                     │                     │
│ 5 <-:               │ 5 <-:---- 1         │ 6 <-:               │ 5 <-:---- 6         │ 5 <-:---- 6         │ 20 ----:-> 5        │
│ 6 <-:               │ 6 <-:               │ 8 <-:               │ 6 <-:               │ 6 <-:               │      :-> 8          │
│ 8 <-:               │ 8 <-:               │                     │ 8 <-:               │ 8 <-:               │                     │
│                     │                     │                     │                     │                     │ 5 <-:---- 4         │
│                     │                     │                     │ 4 ----:-> 4         │                     │ 6 <-:               │
│                     │                     │                     │      :-> 20         │                     │ 8 <-:               │
├─────────────────────┼─────────────────────┼─────────────────────┼─────────────────────┼─────────────────────┼─────────────────────┤
│      G461           │      G462           │      G463           │      G464           │      G465           │      G466           │
│ 1 ------- 1         │ 7 ------- 7         │ 1 ------- 1         │ 7 ------- 7         │ 7 ------- 5         │ 1 ------- 1         │
│ 7 ------- 7         │ 2 ------> 2         │ 7 ------- 7         │ 2 ------> 2         │ 2 ------> 2         │ 7 ------- 7         │
│ 2 ------> 2         │ 3 <------ 3         │ 2 ------> 2         │ 3 <------ 3         │ 3 <------ 3         │ 2 ------> 2         │
│ 3 <------ 3         │                     │ 3 <------ 3         │                     │                     │ 3 <------ 3         │
│                     │                     │                     │ 20 ----:-> 5        │ 20 ----:-> 8        │                     │
│                     │ 4 --:               │ 20 ------> 20       │      :-> 6          │      :-> 6          │ 5 <-:---- 8         │
│ 4 --:               │ 5 <-:               │                     │      :-> 8          │      :-> 1          │ 6 <-:               │
│ 5 <-:               │ 6 <-:               │ 5 <-:---- 5         │                     │                     │ 8 <-:               │
│ 6 <-:               │ 8 <-:               │ 6 <-:               │ 5 <-:---- 4         │ 5 <-:---- 4         │                     │
│ 8 <-:               │                     │ 8 <-:               │ 6 <-:               │ 6 <-:               │ 4 ----:-> 20        │
│                     │                     │                     │ 8 <-:               │ 8 <-:               │                     │
│                     │                     │ 4 ----:-> 4         │                     │                     │                     │
│                     │                     │      :-> 12         │                     │                     │                     │
└─────────────────────┴─────────────────────┴─────────────────────┴─────────────────────┴─────────────────────┴─────────────────────┘
```

```
G467                 G468                 G469                 G470                 G471                 G472
7 ------- 5          7 ------- 7          1 ------- 1          1 ------- 1          1 ------- 1          1 ------- 1
2 ------> 3          2 ------> 3          7 ------- 7          7 ------- 7          7 ------- 7          7 ------- 7
3 <----- 2          3 <----- 2          2 ------> 5          3 ------> 2          3 ------> 2          3 ------> 3
                                          3 <----- 3          2 <----- 3          2 <----- 3          2 <----- 2
20 ----:-> 7         4 --:                20 ------> 6
       :-> 4        5 <-:                5 <-:---- 4          4 <-:---- 5          4 <-:---- 5          4 <-:---- 4
5 <-:---- 6         6 <-:                6 <-:                20 <-:               20 <-:               20 <-:
6 <-:               8 <-:                8 <-:
8 <-:                                                          5 ----:-> 4          5 ----:-> 4          5 ----:-> 5
                                                                     :-> 20               :-> 8                :-> 6
                                                                                          :-> 20               :-> 20
```

```
G473                 G474                 G475                 G476                 G477                 G478
1 ------- 1          7 ------- 7          7 ------- 5          7 ------- 5          1 ------- 1          1 ------- 1
7 ------- 7          3 ------> 2          3 ------> 4          3 ------> 4          7 ------- 7          7 ------- 7
3 ------> 3          2 <----- 3          2 <----- 3          2 <----- 3          3 ------> 2          3 ------> 2
2 <----- 2                                                    4 <----- 7          2 <----- 3          2 <----- 3
                     5 --:                4 <-:---- 1          20 <----- 1
4 <-:---- 4         4 <-:                20 <-:                                    4 <-:---- 5          4 <-:---- 6
20 <-:               20 <-:                                                        20 <-:               20 <-:
                                          5 ----:-> 6
5 ----:-> 5                                                                        5 ----:-> 4
       :-> 6                                                                              :-> 20
```

```
G479                 G480                 G481                 G482                 G483                 G484
1 ------- 1          1 ------- 1          7 ------- 7          1 ------- 1          7 ------- 7          7 ------- 5
7 ------- 7          7 ------- 7          3 ------> 2          7 ------- 7          3 ------> 2          3 ------> 2
3 ------> 3          3 ------> 2          2 <----- 3          3 ------> 2          2 <----- 3          2 <----- 3
2 <----- 2          2 <----- 3                                2 <----- 3          4 <----- 4          4 <----- 7
4 <----- 4                                5 --:                                    5 ------> 5          20 <----- 4
20 <----- 20         5 --:                4 <-:                4 <-:---- 5          6 ------> 6          8 ------> 1
5 ------> 5          4 <-:                20 <-:               20 <-:               8 ------> 8          6 ------> 6
8 ------> 8          20 <-:                                                                              5 ------> 8
                                          6 ----:-> 5          5 ----:-> 4
                     6 ----:-> 20                                    :-> 12
                                                                     :-> 20
```

```
G485                 G486                 G487                 G488                 G489                 G490
1 ------- 1          7 ------- 5          7 ------- 7          1 ------- 1          1 ------- 1          1 ------- 1
7 ------- 7          3 ------> 3          3 ------> 3          7 ------- 7          7 ------- 7          7 ------- 7
3 ------> 2          2 <----- 2          2 <----- 2          3 ------> 5          3 ------> 2          3 ------> 3
2 <----- 3                                                    2 <----- 3          2 <----- 3          2 <----- 2
                     4 <-:---- 6          5 --:
4 <-:---- 8         20 <-:                4 <-:                4 <-:---- 4          5 ----:-> 8          5 ----:-> 5
20 <-:                                    20 <-:               20 <-:                     :-> 4                :-> 6
                     5 ----:-> 4                                                          :-> 20          8 <----- 4
5 ----:-> 20                :-> 7                              5 ----:-> 6          8 <-:---- 5
                                                                                    4   <-:
                                                                                    20  <-:
```

```
G491                 G492                 G493                 G494                 G495                 G496
1 ------- 1          7 ------- 7          7 ------- 5          7 ------- 5          1 ------- 1          1 ------- 1
7 ------- 7          3 ------> 2          3 ------> 4          3 ------> 4          7 ------- 7          7 ------- 7
3 ------> 3          2 <----- 3          2 <----- 3          2 <----- 3          3 ------> 2          3 ------> 2
2 <----- 2                                                                        2 <----- 3          2 <----- 3
                                          5 ------> 6
5 ----:-> 5          5 --:                8 <-:---- 1          4 <-:---- 1          8 <----- 6          8 <----- 6
       :-> 6        4 <-:                4 <-:                8 <-:
4 <----- 4          8 <-:                20 <-:                20 <-:               4 <-:---- 5          4 <-:---- 8
8 <-:               20 <-:                                                         20 <-:               20 <-:
20 <-:
                                                                                   5 ----:-> 4
                                                                                          :-> 20
```

```
G497                  G498                  G499                  G500                  G501                  G502
1 ------- 1           1 ------- 1           7 ------- 7           1 ------- 1           7 ------- 7           7 ------- 5
7 ------- 7           7 ------- 7           3 -----> 2           7 ------- 7           3 -----> 2           3 -----> 2
3 -----> 3           3 -----> 2           2 <------ 3           3 -----> 2           2 <------ 3           2 <------ 3
2 <------ 2           2 <------ 3                                 2 <------ 3
                                            5 --:                                      5 ----:-> 5           5 ----:-> 8
5 ----:-> 5           5 --:                 4 <-:                 5 ------> 20              :-> 6                 :-> 6
     :-> 8           4 <-:                 8 <-:                                         :-> 8                 :-> 1
4 <-:---- 4           8 <-:                 20 <-:                4 <-:---- 5           4 <-:---- 4           4 <-:---- 4
8 <-:                 20 <-:                                      8 <-:                 8 <-:                 8 <-:
20 <-:                                                            20 <-:                20 <-:                20 <-:
```

```
G503                  G504                  G505                  G506                  G507                  G508
1 ------- 1           7 ------- 5           7 ------- 7           1 ------- 1           1 ------- 1           1 ------- 1
7 ------- 7           3 -----> 3           3 -----> 3           7 ------- 7           7 ------- 7           7 ------- 7
3 -----> 2           2 <------ 2           2 <------ 2           3 -----> 5           2 -----> 3           2 -----> 3
2 <------ 3                                                       2 <------ 3           3 <------ 2           3 <------ 2
                      5 ----:-> 7                                                       4 ----:-> 5           4 ----:-> 5
8 <------ 8              :-> 6             5 --:                 5 ------> 6                :-> 6                 :-> 6
                      8 <------ 6           4 <-:                 8 <-:---- 4           5 <-:---- 4           5 <-:---- 4
5 --:                                       8 <-:                 4 <-:                 6 <-:                 6 <-:
4 <-:                 4 <-:---- 8           20 <-:                20 <-:                20 <-:                20 <-:
20 <-:                20 <-:
```

```
G509                  G510                  G511                  G512                  G513                  G514
7 ------- 7           7 ------- 5           7 ------- 5           1 ------- 1           1 ------- 1           1 ------- 1
2 -----> 2           2 -----> 4           2 -----> 4           7 ------- 7           7 ------- 7           7 ------- 7
3 <------ 3           3 <------ 3           3 <------ 3           2 -----> 2           2 -----> 2           2 -----> 3
                                                                 3 <------ 3           3 <------ 3           3 <------ 2
                      4 -----> 6
4 --:                 5 <-:---- 1           5 <-:---- 1           5 <-:---- 6           5 <-:---- 6           4 ----:-> 5
5 <-:                 6 <-:                 6 <-:                 6 <-:                 6 <-:                    :-> 8
6 <-:                 20 <-:                20 <-:                                                             5 <-:---- 4
20 <-:                                                            20 <-:---- 5           20 <-:---- 8           6 <-:
                                                                                                               20 <-:
                                                                 4 ----:-> 4
                                                                      :-> 20
```

```
G515                  G516                  G517                  G518                  G519                  G520
1 ------- 1           7 ------- 7           1 ------- 1           7 ------- 7           7 ------- 5           1 ------- 1
7 ------- 7           2 -----> 2           7 ------- 7           2 -----> 2           2 -----> 2           7 ------- 7
2 -----> 2           3 <------ 3           2 -----> 2           3 <------ 3           3 <------ 3           2 -----> 2
3 <------ 3                                 3 <------ 3                                                       3 <------ 3
                      4 --:                                      4 ----:-> 5           4 ----:-> 8
                      5 <-:                 4 -----> 20              :-> 6                 :-> 6             5 <-:---- 8
4 --:                 6 <-:                                           :-> 8                 :-> 1             6 <-:
5 <-:                 20 <-:                5 <-:---- 5           5 <-:---- 4           5 <-:---- 4
6 <-:                                       6 <-:                 6 <-:                 6 <-:                 4 --:
20 <-:                                       20 <-:                20 <-:                20 <-:                20 <-:
```

```
G521                  G522                  G523                  G524                  G525                  G526
7 ------- 5           7 ------- 7           1 ------- 1           1 ------- 1           7 ------- 7           7 ------- 5
2 -----> 3           2 -----> 3           7 ------- 7           7 ------- 7           2 -----> 2           2 -----> 4
3 <------ 2           3 <------ 2           2 -----> 5           2 -----> 3           3 <------ 3           3 <------ 3
                                            3 <------ 3           3 <------ 2
4 ----:-> 7                                                                            4 --:                 4 -----> 6
     :-> 4           4 --:                 4 -----> 6           4 ----:-> 5           5 <-:                 5 <-:---- 1
5 <-:---- 6           5 <-:                 5 <-:---- 4              :-> 6             6 <-:                 6 <-:
6 <-:                 6 <-:                 6 <-:                 5 <-:---- 4
                      20 <-:                20 <-:                6 <-:
20 <-:---- 8
```

```
     G527                  G528                  G529                  G530                  G531                  G532
7 ------- 5           1 ------- 1           1 ------- 1           1 ------- 1           1 ------- 1           7 ------- 7
2 ------> 4           7 ------- 7           7 ------- 7           7 ------- 7           7 ------- 7           2 ------> 2
3 <------ 3           2 ------> 2           2 ------> 2           2 ------> 3           2 ------> 2           3 <------ 3
                      3 <------ 3           3 <------ 3           3 <------ 2           3 <------ 3
5 <-:---- 1                                                                                                   4 --:
6 <-:                 5 <-:---- 6           5 <-:---- 6           4 ----:-> 5           4 --:                 5 <-:
                      6 <-:                 6 <-:                      :-> 8            5 <-:                 6 <-:
                                                                                        6 <-:
                      4 ----:-> 4                                 5 <-:---- 4
                           :-> 20                                 6 <-:
```

```
     G533                  G534                  G535                  G536                  G537                  G538
1 ------- 1           7 ------- 7           7 ------- 5           1 ------- 1           7 ------- 5           7 ------- 7
7 ------- 7           2 ------> 2           2 ------> 2           7 ------- 7           2 ------> 3           2 ------> 3
2 ------> 2           3 <------ 3           3 <------ 3           2 ------> 2           3 <------ 2           3 <------ 2
3 <------ 3                                                       3 <------ 3
                      4 ----:-> 5           4 ----:-> 8                                4 ----:-> 7           4 --:
4 ------> 20             :-   6                :-   6            5 <-:---- 8              :-   4            5 <-:
                        :-   8                :-   1            6 <-:                 5 <-:---- 6           6 <-:
5 <-:---- 5                                                                            6 <-:
6 <-:                 5 <-:---- 4           5 <-:---- 4          4 ----:-> 20
   :-- 8              6 <-:                 6 <-:
   :-> 4
   :-> 12
```

```
     G539                  G540                  G541                  G542                  G543                  G544
1 ------- 1           7 ------- 7           7 ------- 5           7 ------- 5           7 ------- 7           7 ------- 7
7 ------- 7           3 ------> 2           3 ------> 4           3 ------> 4           3 ------> 2           3 ------> 2
2 ------> 5           2 <------ 3           2 <------ 3           2 <------ 3           2 <------ 3           2 <------ 3
3 <------ 3
                                               :-- 1                                      :-- 5
4 ------> 6                                    :-> 6                                      :-> 4
5 <-:---- 4                                                                               :-> 20
6 <-:
```

```
     G545                  G546                  G547                  G548                  G549                  G550
7 ------- 7           7 ------- 7           7 ------- 7           7 ------- 7           7 ------- 7           7 ------- 5
3 ------> 3           3 ------> 2           3 ------> 2           3 ------> 2           3 ------> 2           3 ------> 2
2 <------ 2           2 <------ 3           2 <------ 3           2 <------ 3           2 <------ 3           2 <------ 3

   :-- 4                                                            :-- 5                 :- 4                 :- 4
   :-> 5                                                            :-> 4                 :- 5                 :- 1
   :-> 8                                                            :-> 12                :- 6                 :- 6
                                                                    :-> 20                :- 8                 :- 8
                                                                    :-- 8                                      :- 7
                                                                                                               :-
```

```
     G551                  G552                  G553                  G554                  G555                  G556
7 ------- 7           7 ------- 5           7 ------- 7           7 ------- 7           5 ------- 5           5 ------- 5
3 ------> 2           3 ------> 3           3 ------> 3           3 ------> 5           3 ------> 4           3 ------> 4
2 <------ 3           2 <------ 2           2 <------ 2           2 <------ 3           4 <------ 3           4 <------ 3

   :-- 8                 :- 6                                       :- 4                1 ------> 6
   :-> 20                :- 4                                       :- 6                6 <------ 1           6 <-:---- 1
                        :- 7
```

```
┌─────────────────────┬─────────────────────┬─────────────────────┬─────────────────────┬─────────────────────┬─────────────────────┐
│   G557              │   G558              │   G559              │   G560              │   G561              │   G562              │
│  5 ------- 7        │  5 ------- 7        │  5 ------- 7        │  5 ------- 7        │  5 ------- 7        │  5 ------- 7        │
│  3 -----> 2         │  3 -----> 2         │  3 -----> 3         │  3 -----> 2         │  3 -----> 2         │  3 -----> 2         │
│  4 <------ 3        │  4 <------ 3        │  4 <------ 2        │  4 <------ 3        │  4 <------ 3        │  4 <------ 3        │
│                     │                     │                     │                     │                     │                     │
│  6 <------ 6        │  6 <------ 6        │  1 ----:-> 5        │                     │                     │  1 ------> 20       │
│                     │                     │       :-> 8         │  1 --:              │  1 --:              │                     │
│  1 ----:-> 4        │                     │                     │  6 <-:              │  6 <-:              │  6 <-:----- 5       │
│       :-> 20        │                     │  6 <-:----- 4       │                     │                     │        :-- 8        │
│                     │                     │                     │                     │                     │        :-> 4        │
│                     │                     │                     │                     │                     │        :-> 12       │
├─────────────────────┼─────────────────────┼─────────────────────┼─────────────────────┼─────────────────────┼─────────────────────┤
│   G563              │   G564              │   G565              │   G566              │   G567              │   G568              │
│  5 ------- 7        │  5 ------- 5        │  5 ------- 7        │  5 ------- 5        │  5 ------- 7        │  5 ------- 8        │
│  3 -----> 2         │  3 -----> 2         │  3 -----> 2         │  3 -----> 3         │  3 -----> 3         │  3 -----> 4         │
│  4 <------ 3        │  4 <------ 3        │  4 <------ 3        │  4 <------ 2        │  4 <------ 2        │  4 <------ 2        │
│                     │                     │                     │                     │                     │                     │
│  1 ----:-> 5        │  1 ----:-> 8        │  6 <------ 8        │  1 ----:-> 7        │                     │  1 ----:-> 5        │
│       :- 6          │       :- 6          │                     │       :- 4          │  1 --:              │       :-> 10        │
│       :- 8          │       :- 1          │  1 ----:-> 20       │  6 <------ 6        │  6 <-:              │       :-> 7         │
│                     │                     │                     │                     │                     │  6 <------ 12       │
│  6 <-:----- 4       │  6 <-:----- 4       │                     │                     │                     │       :- 3          │
│                     │                     │                     │                     │                     │       :-> 11        │
├─────────────────────┼─────────────────────┼─────────────────────┼─────────────────────┼─────────────────────┼─────────────────────┤
│   G569              │   G570              │   G571              │   G572              │   G573              │   G574              │
│  5 ------- 7        │  5 ------- 4        │  5 ------- 7        │  5 ------- 5        │  5 ------- 3        │  5 ------- 7        │
│  3 -----> 2         │  3 -----> 3         │  3 -----> 5         │  3 -----> 7         │  3 -----> 5         │  3 -----> 6         │
│  4 <------ 3        │  4 <------ 2        │  4 <------ 3        │  4 <------ 4        │  4 <------ 4        │  4 <------ 5        │
│                     │                     │                     │                     │                     │                     │
│  6 <------ 6        │  1 ----:-> 1        │  1 ------> 6        │  1 ----:-> 2        │  1 ----:-> 8        │  1 ----:-> 8        │
│                     │       :-> 6         │  6 <------ 4        │       :-> 6         │       :-> 7         │       :-> 2         │
│  1 ----:-> 4        │  6 <------ 5        │                     │  6 <------ 3        │       :-> 6         │       :-> 10        │
│                     │                     │                     │                     │  6 <------ 2        │  6 <------ 9        │
│                     │                     │                     │                     │                     │       :- 3          │
│                     │                     │                     │                     │                     │       :-> 1         │
├─────────────────────┼─────────────────────┼─────────────────────┼─────────────────────┼─────────────────────┼─────────────────────┤
│   G575              │   G576              │   G577              │   G578              │   G579              │   G580              │
│  5 ------- 6        │  5 ------- 8        │  5 ------- 8        │  5 ------- 7        │  5 ------- 5        │  5 ------- 7        │
│  3 -----> 5         │  3 -----> 2         │  3 -----> 6         │  3 -----> 3         │  3 -----> 3         │  3 -----> 3         │
│  4 <------ 4        │  4 <------ 1        │  4 <------ 1        │  4 <------ 2        │  4 <------ 2        │  4 <------ 8        │
│                     │                     │                     │                     │                     │                     │
│  1 ----:-> 7        │                     │  1 ----:-> 7        │  1 ----:-> 5        │  6 <------ 6        │  1 ----:-> 5        │
│       :- 1          │  1 --:              │       :- 9          │       :- 8          │                     │       :-> 6         │
│  6 <------ 8        │  6 <-:              │  6 <------ 4        │  6 <------ 9        │  1 ----:-> 4        │       :-> 1         │
│                     │                     │                     │                     │       :- 7          │  6 <------ 9        │
│                     │                     │                     │                     │                     │       :- 4          │
│                     │                     │                     │                     │                     │       :-> 10        │
├─────────────────────┼─────────────────────┼─────────────────────┼─────────────────────┼─────────────────────┼─────────────────────┤
│   G581              │   G582              │   G583              │   G584              │   G585              │   G586              │
│  5 ------- 7        │  5 ------- 7        │  5 ------- 4        │  5 ------- 5        │  5 ------- 9        │  5 ------- 3        │
│  3 -----> 8         │  3 -----> 5         │  3 -----> 6         │  3 -----> 6         │  3 -----> 3         │  3 -----> 4         │
│  4 <------ 3        │  4 <------ 4        │  4 <------ 3        │  4 <------ 4        │  4 <------ 2        │  4 <------ 2        │
│                     │                     │                     │                     │                     │                     │
│  6 <------ 5        │  1 ------> 3        │  6 <------ 2        │  1 ------> 2        │  1 ------> 5        │  1 ------> 5        │
│                     │  6 <------ 1        │                     │  6 <------ 3        │  6 <------ 4        │  6 <------ 1        │
│  1 ----:-> 4        │                     │  1 ----:-> 1        │                     │                     │                     │
│       :-> 9         │                     │       :-> 7         │                     │                     │                     │
├─────────────────────┼─────────────────────┼─────────────────────┼─────────────────────┼─────────────────────┼─────────────────────┤
│   G587              │   G588              │   G589              │   G590              │   G591              │   G592              │
│  5 ------- 9        │  5 ------- 5        │  5 ------- 5        │  5 ------- 5        │  5 ------- 5        │  5 ------- 4        │
│  3 -----> 13        │  3 -----> 2         │  3 -----> 2         │  3 -----> 3         │  3 -----> 3         │  3 -----> 5         │
│  4 <------ 11       │  4 <------ 3        │  4 <------ 3        │  4 <------ 2        │  4 <------ 2        │  4 <------ 2        │
│                     │                     │                     │                     │                     │                     │
│  1 ------> 14       │  1 ----:-> 8        │  1 ------> 8        │  6 <------ 6        │                     │  1 ------> 6        │
│  6 <------ 10       │       :- 6          │  6 <------ 7        │                     │  1 --:              │  6 <------ 1        │
│                     │  6 <------ 4        │                     │                     │  6 <-:              │                     │
└─────────────────────┴─────────────────────┴─────────────────────┴─────────────────────┴─────────────────────┴─────────────────────┘
```

G593
5 ------- 2
3 ------> 4
4 <------ 3
 	
1 ------> 5
6 <------ 6
	G594
	5 ------- 7
	4 <------ 2
	
	1 --:
	6 <-:
		G595
		5 ------- 7
		3 ------> 5
		4 <------ 3
		
		1 ----:-> 8
		    :-> 6
		6 <------ 4
			G596
			5 ------- 4
			3 ------> 5
			4 <------ 3
			
			1 ------> 2
			6 <------ 6
				G597
				5 ------- 5
				3 ------> 4
				4 <------ 2
				
				1 ------> 6
				6 <------ 1
					G598
					5 ------- 1
					3 ------> 4
					4 <------ 2
					
					1 ----:-> 6
					    :-> 8
					6 <------ 3

G599
5 ------- 5
3 ------> 2
4 <------ 4
 	
6 <------ 1
	G600
	5 ------- 2
	3 ------> 5
	4 <------ 3
	
	1 ------> 1
	6 <------ 6
		G601
		5 ------- 3
		3 ------> 1
		4 <------ 5
		
		1 ------> 2
		6 <------ 8
		    :-- 4
		    :-> 7
			G602
			5 ------- 6
			3 ------> 8
			4 <------ 4
			
			1 ------> 7
			6 <------ 1
			    :-- 3
			    :-> 2
				G603
				5 ------- 2
				3 ------> 3
				4 <------ 5
				
				6 <------ 4
					G604
					5 ------- 4
					3 ------> 5
					4 <------ 2
					
					1 ------> 1
					6 <------ 6

G605
5 ------- 3
3 ------> 2
4 <------ 5
 	
1 ------> 6
6 <------ 1
	G606
	5 ------- 4
	3 ------> 2
	4 <------ 3
	
	1 ------> 6
	6 <------ 1
		G607
		5 ------- 3
		3 ------> 5
		4 <------ 4
		
		1 ------> 1
		6 <------ 6
			G608
			5 ------- 11
			3 ------> 9
			4 <------ 1
			
			1 ----:-> 10
			    :-> 3
			    :-> 12
			6 <------ 2
				G609
				5 ------- 11
				3 ------> 1
				4 <------ 9
				
				6 <------ 3
				
				1 ----:-> 2
				    :-> 4
					G610
					5 ------- 4
					3 ------> 2
					4 <------ 3
					
					1 ------> 5
					6 <------ 1

G611 5 ------- 4 3 ------> 3 4 <------ 2 6 <------ 5	**G612** 5 ------- 2 3 ------> 3 4 <------ 5 1 ------> 1 6 <------ 6	**G613** 5 ------- 5 3 ------> 4 4 <------ 2 1 ------> 3 6 <------ 1	**G614** 5 ------- 2 3 ------> 3 4 <------ 5 1 ------> 4 6 <------ 6	**G615** 5 ------- 5 3 ------> 2 4 <------ 3 1 ----:-> 8 :- 6 6 <------ 4	**G616** 5 ------- 5 3 ------> 4 4 <------ 3

G617
5 ------- 7
3 ------> 2
4 <------ 3
7 ------> 4
1 ------> 20
	G618
	5 ------- 7
	3 ------> 2
	4 <------ 3
		G619
		5 ------- 7
		3 ------> 3
		4 <------ 2
		
		1 ----:-> 5
		    :-> 8
			G620
			5 ------- 7
			3 ------> 2
			4 <------ 3
			1 ------> 20
				G621
				5 ------- 7
				3 ------> 2
				4 <------ 3
				1 ------> 5
					G622
					5 ------- 7
					3 ------> 2
					4 <------ 3
					7 ------> 4
					
					1 ----:-> 20
					    :-- 5

G623
5 ------- 7
3 ------> 2
4 <------ 3
 	
1 ----:-> 5
    :-> 6
    :-> 8
	G624
	5 ------- 5
	3 ------> 2
	4 <------ 3
	
	1 ----:-> 8
	    :-> 6
	    :-> 1
		G625
		5 ------- 7
		3 ------> 2
		4 <------ 3
		
		1 ----:-> 20
			G626
			5 ------- 5
			3 ------> 3
			4 <------ 2
			
			1 ----:-> 7
			    :-> 4
				G627
				5 ------- 7
				3 ------> 3
				4 <------ 2
					G628
					5 ------- 8
					3 ------> 4
					4 <------ 2
					
					1 ----:-> 5
					    :-> 10
					    :-> 7
					
					7 ----:-> 11

```
G629
5 ------- 7
3 ------> 2
4 <------ 3
7 ------> 4
```

```
G630
5 ------- 4
3 ------> 3
4 <------ 2
1 ----:-> 1
      :-> 6
```

```
G631
5 ------- 7
3 ------> 5
4 <------ 3
1 ------> 6
```

```
G632
5 ------- 5
3 ------> 7
4 <------ 4
1 ----:-> 2
      :-> 6
```

```
G633
5 ------- 3
3 ------> 5
4 <------ 4
1 ----:-> 8
      :-> 7
      :-> 6
```

```
G634
5 ------- 7
3 ------> 6
4 <------ 5
1 ----:-> 8
      :-> 2
      :-> 10
7 ----:-> 1
```

```
G635
5 ------- 6
3 ------> 5
4 <------ 4
1 ----:-> 7
      :-> 1
```

```
G636
5 ------- 8
3 ------> 2
4 <------ 1
```

```
G637
5 ------- 8
3 ------> 6
4 <------ 1
1 ----:-> 7
      :-> 9
```

```
G638
5 ------- 7
3 ------> 3
4 <------ 2
1 ----:-> 5
      :-> 8
```

```
G639
5 ------- 5
3 ------> 3
4 <------ 2
1 ----:-> 4
      :-> 7
```

```
G640
5 ------- 7
3 ------> 3
4 <------ 8
1 ----:-> 5
      :-> 6
      :-> 1
7 ----:-> 10
```

```
G641
5 ------- 7
3 ------> 8
4 <------ 3
1 ----:-> 4
      :-> 9
```

```
G642
5 ------- 7
3 ------> 5
4 <------ 4
1 ------> 3
```

```
G643
5 ------- 4
3 ------> 6
4 <------ 3
1 ----:-> 1
      :-> 7
```

```
G644
5 ------- 5
3 ------> 6
4 <------ 4
1 ------> 2
```

```
G645
5 ------- 9
3 ------> 3
4 <------ 2
1 ------> 5
```

```
G646
5 ------- 3
3 ------> 4
4 <------ 2
1 ------> 5
```

```
G647
5 ------- 9
3 ------> 13
4 <------ 11
1 ------> 14
```

```
G648
5 ------- 5
3 ------> 2
4 <------ 3
1 ----:-> 8
      :-> 6
```

```
G649
5 ------- 5
3 ------> 2
4 <------ 3
1 ------> 8
```

```
G650
5 ------- 5
3 ------> 3
4 <------ 2
```

```
G651
5 ------- 5
3 ------> 3
4 <------ 2
```

```
G652
5 ------- 4
3 ------> 5
4 <------ 2
1 ------> 6
```

```
G653
5 ------- 2
3 ------> 4
4 <------ 3
1 ------> 5
```

```
G654
5 ------- 7
4 <------ 2
```

```
G655
5 ------- 7
3 ------> 5
4 <------ 3
1 ----:-> 8
      :-> 6
```

```
G656
5 ------- 4
3 ------> 5
4 <------ 3
1 ------> 2
```

```
G657
5 ------- 5
3 ------> 4
4 <------ 2
```

```
G658
5 ------- 1
3 ------> 4
4 <------ 2
1 ----:-> 6
      :-> 8
```

```
G659
5 ------- 5
3 ------> 2
4 <------ 4
```

```
G660
5 ------- 2
3 ------> 5
4 <------ 3
1 ------> 1
```

```
G661
5 ------- 3
3 ------> 1
4 <------ 5
1 ------> 2
7 ----:-> 7
```

```
G662
5 ------- 6
3 ------> 8
4 <------ 4
1 ------> 7
7 ----:-> 2
```

```
G663
5 ------- 2
3 ------> 3
4 <------ 5
```

```
G664
5 ------- 4
3 ------> 5
4 <------ 2
1 ------> 1
```

```
G665
5 ------- 3
3 ------> 2
4 <------ 5
1 ------> 6
```

```
G666
5 ------- 4
3 ------> 2
4 <------ 3
1 ------> 6
```

```
G667
5 ------- 3
3 ------> 5
4 <------ 4
1 ------> 1
```

```
G668
5 ------- 11
3 ------> 9
4 <------ 1
1 ----:-> 10
      :-> 3
      :-> 12
```

```
G669
5 ------- 11
3 ------> 1
4 <------ 9
7 ------> 2
1 ------> 4
```

```
G670
5 ------- 4
3 ------> 2
4 <------ 3
1 ------> 5
```

G671
```
5 -------- 4
3 -------> 3
4 <------ 2
```

G672
```
5 -------- 2
3 -------> 3
4 <------ 5

1 ------> 1
```

G673
```
5 -------- 5
3 -------> 4
4 <------ 2

1 ------> 3

7 ----:-> 6
```

G674
```
5 -------- 2
3 -------> 3
4 <------ 5

1 ------> 4

7 ----:-> 1
```

G675
```
5 -------- 5
3 -------> 2
4 <------ 3

1 ----:-> 8
     :-> 6
1 -------- 1
```

G676
```
7 -------- 7
3 -------> 2
2 <------ 3
```

G677
```
1 -------- 1
7 -------- 7
3 -------> 3
2 <------ 2
8 -------> 5

6 ----:-> 8
```

G678
```
1 -------- 1
7 -------- 7
3 -------> 2
2 <------ 3

6 ----:-> 20
```

G679
```
7 -------- 7
3 -------> 2
2 <------ 3

6 ----:-> 5
```

G680
```
1 -------- 1
7 -------- 7
3 -------> 2
2 <------ 3

6 ----:-> 4
     :-> 20
```

G681
```
7 -------- 7
3 -------> 2
2 <------ 3
8 -------> 5
6 -------> 6

     :- 4
     :- 8
```

G682
```
7 -------- 5
3 -------> 2
2 <------ 3

6 ----:-> 1
     :-> 6
     :-> 8
```

G683
```
1 -------- 1
7 -------- 7
3 -------> 2
2 <------ 3

6 ----:-> 20
```

G684
```
7 -------- 5
3 -------> 3
2 <------ 2

6 ----:-> 4
     :-> 7
```

G685
```
7 -------- 7
3 -------> 3
2 <------ 3
```

G686
```
1 -------- 1
7 -------- 8
3 -------> 4
2 <------ 2

6 ----:-> 5
     :-> 7
     :-> 10

8 ----:-> 11
```

G687
```
1 -------- 1
7 -------- 7
3 -------> 2
2 <------ 3

6 ----:-> 4
```

G688
```
7 -------- 4
3 -------> 3
2 <------ 2

6 ----:-> 1
     :-> 6
```

G689
```
1 -------- 1
7 -------- 7
3 -------> 5
2 <------ 3

6 ----:-> 6
```

G690
```
7 -------- 5
3 -------> 7
2 <------ 4

6 ----:-> 2
     :-> 6
```

G691
```
7 -------- 3
3 -------> 5
2 <------ 4

6 ----:-> 6
     :-> 7
     :-> 8

8 ----:-> I
```

G692
```
1 -------- 4
7 -------- 7
3 -------> 6
2 <------ 5

6 ----:-> 1
     :-> 2
     :-> 8

8 ----:-> 10
```

G693
```
1 -------- 3
7 -------- 6
3 -------> 5
2 <------ 4

6 ----:-> 1
     :-> 7
```

G694
```
7 -------- 8
3 -------> 2
2 <------ 1
```

G695
```
7 -------- 8
3 -------> 6
2 <------ 1

6 ----:-> 7
     :-> 9
```

G696
```
7 -------- 7
3 -------> 3
2 <------ 2

6 ----:-> 5
     :-> 8
```

G697
```
7 -------- 5
3 -------> 3
2 <------ 2

6 ----:-> 4
     :-> 7
```

G698
```
1 -------- 2
7 -------- 7
3 -------> 3
2 <------ 8

6 ----:-> 1
     :-> 5
     :-> 6

8 ----:-> 10
```

G699
```
1 -------- 2
7 -------- 7
3 -------> 8
2 <------ 3

6 ----:-> 4
     :-> 9
```

G700
```
7 -------- 7
3 -------> 5
2 <------ 4

6 ----:-> 3
```

G701
```
7 -------- 4
3 -------> 6
2 <------ 3

6 ----:-> 1
     :-> 7
```

G702
```
7 -------- 5
3 -------> 6
2 <------ 4

6 ----:-> 2
```

G703
```
7 -------- 9
3 -------> 3
2 <------ 2

6 ----:-> 5
```

G704
```
7 -------- 3
3 -------> 4
2 <------ 2

6 ----:-> 5
```

G705
```
7 -------- 9
3 -------> 13
2 <------ 11

6 ----:-> 14
```

G706
```
7 -------- 5
3 -------> 2
2 <------ 3

6 ----:-> 6
     :-> 8
```

G707 7 ------- 5 3 ------> 2 2 <----- 3 6 ----:-> 8	**G708** 7 ------- 5 3 ------> 3 2 <----- 2	**G709** 7 ------- 5 3 ------> 3 2 <----- 2	**G710** 1 ------- 3 7 ------- 4 3 ------> 5 2 <----- 2	**G711** 1 ------- 1 7 ------- 2 3 ------> 4 2 <----- 3	**G712** 1 ------- 1 7 ------- 7 2 <----- 2

G713
1 ------- 1
7 ------- 7
3 ------> 5
2 <----- 3
 	
6 ----:-> 6
  :-> 8
	G714
	7 ------- 4
	3 ------> 5
	2 <----- 3
	
	6 ----:-> 2
		G715
		7 ------- 5
		3 ------> 4
		2 <----- 2
		
		6 ----:-> 6
			G716
			7 ------- 1
			3 ------> 4
			2 <----- 2
			
			6 ----:-> 6
			  :-> 8
				G717
				1 ------- 3
				7 ------- 5
				3 ------> 2
				2 <----- 4
					G718
					1 ------- 4
					7 ------- 2
					3 ------> 5
					2 <----- 3
					
					6 ----:-> 1

G719
7 ------- 3
3 ------> 1
2 <----- 5
 	
6 ----:-> 2
  :-> 7
	G720
	7 ------- 6
	3 ------> 8
	2 <----- 4
	
	6 ----:-> 2
	  :-> 7
		G721
		7 ------- 2
		3 ------> 3
		2 <----- 5
			G722
			1 ------- 3
			7 ------- 4
			3 ------> 5
			2 <----- 2
			6 ----:-> 1
				G723
				1 ------- 4
				7 ------- 3
				3 ------> 2
				2 <----- 5
				
				6 ----:-> 6
					G724
					7 ------- 4
					3 ------> 2
					2 <----- 3
					
					6 ----:-> 6

G725
7 ------- 3
3 ------> 5
2 <----- 4
 	
6 ----:-> 1
	G726
	7 ------- 11
	3 ------> 9
	2 <----- 1
	
	6 ----:-> 3
	  :-> 10
	  :-> 12
	
	8 ----:-> 1
		G727
		7 ------- 11
		3 ------> 1
		2 <----- 9
		
		6 ----:-> 2
		  :-> 4
			G728
			7 ------- 4
			3 ------> 2
			2 <----- 3
			
			6 ----:-> 5
				G729
				7 ------- 4
				3 ------> 3
				2 <----- 2
					G730
					7 ------- 2
					3 ------> 3
					2 <----- 5
					
					6 ----:-> 1

G731
7 ------- 5
3 ------> 4
2 <----- 2
 	
6 ----:-> 3
  :-> 6
	G732
	7 ------- 2
	3 ------> 3
	2 <----- 5
	
	6 ----:-> 1
	  :-> 4
		G733
		7 ------- 5
		3 ------> 2
		2 <----- 3
		
		6 ----:-> 6
		  :-> 8
			G734
			7 ------- 5
			2 ------> 3
			3 <----- 2
				G735
				7 ------- 5
				2 ------> 3
				3 <----- 2
					G736
					7 ------- 4
					2 ------> 5
					3 <----- 2

G737
7 ------- 2
2 ------> 4
3 <----- 3
	G738
	7 ------- 7
	3 <----- 2
		G739
		7 ------- 7
		2 ------> 5
		3 <----- 3
		
		6 ----:-> 6
		  :-> 8
			G740
			7 ------- 4
			2 ------> 5
			3 <----- 3
			
			6 ----:-> 2
				G741
				7 ------- 5
				2 ------> 4
				3 <----- 2
				
				6 ----:-> 6
					G742
					7 ------- 1
					2 ------> 4
					3 <----- 2
					
					6 ----:-> 6
					  :-> 8

G743
7 ------- 5
2 ------> 2
3 <----- 4
	G744
	7 ------- 2
	2 ------> 5
	3 <----- 3
	
	6 ----:-> 1
		G745
		7 ------- 3
		2 ------> 1
		3 <----- 5
		
		6 ----:-> 2
		  :-> 7
			G746
			7 ------- 6
			2 ------> 8
			3 <----- 4
			
			6 ----:-> 2
			  :-> 7
				G747
				7 ------- 2
				2 ------> 3
				3 <----- 5
					G748
					7 ------- 4
					2 ------> 5
					3 <----- 2
					6 ----:-> 1

```
  G749                 G750                 G751                 G752                 G753                 G754
7 ------- 3          7 ------- 4          7 ------- 3          7 ------- 11         7 ------- 11         7 ------- 4
2 ------> 2          2 ------> 2          2 ------> 5          2 ------> 9          2 ------> 1          2 ------> 2
3 <------ 5          3 <------ 3          3 <------ 4          3 <------ 1          3 <------ 9          3 <------ 3

6 ----:-> 6          6 ----:-> 6          6 ----:-> 1          6 ----:-> 3          6 ----:-> 2          6 ----:-> 5
                                                                   :-> 10                :-> 4
                                                                   :-> 12

                                                               8 ----:-> I
```

```
  G755                 G756                 G757                 G758                 G759                 G760
7 ------- 4          7 ------- 2          7 ------- 5          7 ------- 2          7 ------- 5          1 ------- 1
2 ------> 3          2 ------> 3          2 ------> 4          2 ------> 3          2 ------> 2          7 ------- 7
3 <------ 2          3 <------ 5          3 <------ 2          3 <------ 5          3 <------ 3          2 ------> 3
                                                                                                        3 <------ 2

                    6 ----:-> 1          6 ----:-> 3          6 ----:-> 1          6 ----:-> 6          20 ----:-> 5
                                             :-> 6                :-> 4                :-> 8                 :-> 8

                                                                                                        5 <-:---- 4
                                                                                                        8 <-:
```

```
  G761                 G762                 G763                 G764                 G765                 G766
1 ------- 1          7 ------- 7          1 ------- 1          7 ------- 7          7 ------- 5          1 ------- 1
7 ------- 7          2 ------> 2          7 ------- 7          2 ------> 2          2 ------> 2          7 ------- 7
2 ------> 2          3 <------ 3          2 ------> 2          3 <------ 3          3 <------ 3          2 ------> 2
3 <------ 3                              3 <------ 3                                                     3 <------ 3

4 --:               4 --:               20 ------> 20         20 ----:-> 5         20 ----:-> 8
5 <-:               5 <-:                                        :-> 6                :-> 6             5 <-:---- 8
8 <-:               8 <-:               5 <-:---- 5             :-> 8                :-> 1             8 <-:
                                        8 <-:
                                                             5 <-:---- 4          5 <-:---- 4          4 ----:-> 20
                                        4 ----:-> 4          8 <-:               8 <-:
                                            :-> 12
```

```
  G767                 G768                 G769                 G770                 G771                 G772
7 ------- 5          7 ------- 7          1 ------- 1          1 ------- 1          1 ------- 1          7 ------- 4
2 ------> 3          2 ------> 3          7 ------- 7          7 ------- 8          7 ------- 7          2 ------> 3
3 <------ 2          3 <------ 2          2 ------> 5          2 ------> 4          2 ------> 2          3 <------ 2
                                         3 <------ 3          3 <------ 2          3 <------ 3
20 ----:-> 7        4 --:                                                                              20 ----:-> 1
    :-> 4           5 <-:               20 ------> 6          20 ----:-> 5         5 <-:---- 6             :-> 6
5 <-:---- 6         8 <-:               5 <-:---- 4              :-> 10            8 <-:               5 <-:---- 5
8 <-:                                   8 <-:                    :-> 7                                8 <-:
                                                             5 <-:---- 12         4 ----:-> 4
                                                             8 <-:

                                                             4 ----:-> 11
```

```
  G773                 G774                 G775                 G776                 G777                 G778
7 ------- 5          7 ------- 3          1 ------- 4          1 ------- 3          7 ------- 8          7 ------- 8
2 ------> 7          2 ------> 5          7 ------- 7          7 ------- 6          2 ------> 2          2 ------> 6
3 <------ 4          3 <------ 4          2 ------> 6          2 ------> 5          3 <------ 1          3 <------ 1
                                         3 <------ 5          3 <------ 4
20 ----:-> 2        20 ----:-> 8                                                  4 --:               20 ----:-> 7
    :-> 6               :-> 7          20 ----:-> 8          20 ----:-> 7         5 <-:                   :-> 9
5 <-:---- 3            :-> 6               :-> 2                 :-> 1            8 <-:               5 <-:---- 4
8 <-:               5 <-:---- 2            :-> 10            5 <-:---- 8                              8 <-:
                    8 <-:               5 <-:---- 9          8 <-:
                                        8 <-:

                                        4 ----:-> 1
```

```
G779                  G780                  G781                  G782                  G783                  G784
7 ------- 7           7 ------- 5           1 ------- 2           1 ------- 2           7 ------- 7           7 ------- 4
2 ----> 3             2 ------- 3           7 ------- 7           7 ------- 7           2 -----> 5            2 -----> 6
3 <----- 2            3 <----- 2            2 -----> 3            2 -----> 8            3 <----- 4            3 <----- 3

20 ----:-> 5          5 <-:----- 6          3 <----- 8            3 <----- 3            20 ------> 3          5 <-:----- 2
    :-> 8             8 <-:                                                             5 <-:----- 1          8 <-:
5 <-:----- 9          4 ----:-> 4           20 ----:-> 5          5 <-:----- 5          8 <-:
8 <-:                     :-> 7                 :-> 6             8 <-:                                      4 ----:-> 1
                                                :-> 1             4 ----:-> 4                                    :-> 7
                                             5 <-:----- 9             :-> 9
                                             8 <-:
                                             4 ----:-> 10


G785                  G786                  G787                  G788                  G789                  G790
7 ------- 5           7 ------- 9           7 ------- 3           7 ------- 9           7 ------- 5           7 ------- 5
2 -----> 6            2 -----> 3            2 -----> 4            2 -----> 13           2 -----> 2            2 -----> 2
3 <----- 4            3 <----- 2            3 <----- 2            3 <----- 11           3 <----- 3            3 <----- 3

20 -----> 2           20 ------> 5          20 ------> 5          20 ------> 14         20 ----:-> 8          20 ------> 8
5 <-:----- 3          5 <-:----- 4          5 <-:----- 1          5 <-:----- 10             :-> 6            5 <-:----- 7
8 <-:                 8 <-:                 8 <-:                 8 <-:                 5 <-:----- 4          8 <-:
                                                                                       8 <-:


G791                  G792                  G793                  G794                  G795                  G796
7 ------- 5           7 ------- 5           1 ------- 3           1 ------- 1           1 ------- 1           1 ------- 1
2 -----> 3            2 -----> 3            7 ------- 4           7 ------- 2           7 ------- 7           7 ------- 7
3 <----- 2            3 <----- 2            2 -----> 5            2 -----> 4            3 <----- 2            2 -----> 5

5 <-:----- 6                               3 <----- 2            3 <----- 3                                 3 <----- 3
8 <-:                 4 --:                                                            4 --:
                      5 <-:                20 ------> 6          20 ------> 5          5 <-:                20 ----:-> 8
                      8 <-:                5 <-:----- 1          5 <-:----- 6          8 <-:                    :-> 6
                                           8 <-:                 8 <-:                                      5 <-:----- 4
                                                                                                            8 <-:


G797                  G798                  G799                  G800                  G801                  G802
7 ------- 4           7 ------- 5           7 ------- 1           1 ------- 3           1 ------- 4           7 ------- 3
2 -----> 5            2 -----> 4            2 -----> 4            7 ------- 5           7 ------- 2           2 -----> 1
3 <----- 3            3 <----- 2            3 <----- 2            2 -----> 2            2 -----> 5            3 <----- 5

20 ------> 2          20 ------> 6          20 ----:-> 6          3 <----- 4            3 <----- 3            20 ------> 2
5 <-:----- 6          5 <-:----- 1             :-> 8                                                         5 <-:----- 8
8 <-:                 8 <-:                5 <-:----- 3          5 <-:----- 1          20 ------> 1          8 <-:
                                           8 <-:                 8 <-:                 5 <-:----- 6
                                                                                       8 <-:                4 ----:-> 7


G803                  G804                  G805                  G806                  G807                  G808
7 ------- 6           7 ------- 2           1 ------- 3           1 ------- 4           7 ------- 4           7 ------- 3
2 -----> 8            2 -----> 3            7 ------- 4           7 ------- 3           2 -----> 2            2 -----> 5
3 <----- 4            3 <----- 5            2 -----> 5            2 -----> 2            3 <----- 3            3 <----- 4

20 ------> 7          5 <-:----- 4          3 <----- 2            3 <----- 5            20 ------> 6          20 ------> 1
5 <-:----- 1          8 <-:                                                            5 <-:----- 1          5 <-:----- 6
8 <-:                                       20 ------> 1          20 ------> 6          8 <-:                8 <-:
                                            5 <-:----- 6          5 <-:----- 1
4 ----:-> 2                                 8 <-:                 8 <-:


G809                  G810                  G811                  G812                  G813                  G814
7 ------- 11          7 ------- 11          7 ------- 4           7 ------- 4           7 ------- 2           7 ------- 5
2 -----> 9            2 -----> 1            2 -----> 2            2 -----> 3            2 -----> 3            2 -----> 4
3 <----- 1            3 ------- 9           3 <----- 3            3 <----- 2            3 <----- 5            3 <----- 2

20 ----:-> 10         5 <-:----- 3          20 ------> 5          5 <-:----- 5          20 ------> 1          20 ------> 3
    :-> 3             8 <-:                 5 <-:----- 1          8 <-:                 5 <-:----- 6          5 <-:----- 1
    :-> 12            4 ----:-> 2           8 <-:                                       8 <-:                8 <-:
5 <-:----- 2              :-> 4
8 <-:                                                                                                       4 ----:-> 6
```

```
 G815                  G816                  G817                  G818                  G819                  G820
7 ------- 2           7 ------- 5           8 ------- 8           8 ------- 7           8 ------- 5           8 ------- 7
2 ------> 3           2 ------> 2           1 ------> 6           1 ------> 3           1 ------> 3           1 ------> 3
3 <------ 5           3 <------ 3           6 <------ 1           6 <------ 2           6 <------ 2           6 <------ 8

20 -----> 4           20 ---:-> 8           4 ----:-> 7          4 ----:-> 5           7 <-:---- 6           4 ----:-> 5
5 <-:---- 6                :-> 6                 :-> 9                :-> 8           9 <-:                     :-> 6
8 <-:                 5 <-:---- 4           7 <-:---- 4          7 <-:---- 9                                     :-> 1
                      8 <-:                 9 <-:                9 <-:                2 ----:-> 4           7 <-:---- 9
4 ----:-> 1                                                                               :-> 7           9 <-:

                                                                                                           2 ----:-> 10

 G821                  G822                  G823                  G824                  G825                  G826
8 ------- 7           8 ------- 7           8 ------- 4           8 ------- 5           8 ------- 9           8 ------- 3
1 ------> 8           1 ------> 5           1 ------> 6           1 ------> 6           1 ------> 3           1 ------> 4
6 <------ 3           6 <------ 4           6 <------ 3           6 <------ 4           6 <------ 2           6 <------ 2

7 <-:---- 5           4 ------> 3           7 <-:---- 2          4 ------> 2           4 ------> 5           4 ------> 5
9 <-:                 7 <-:---- 1           9 <-:                7 <-:---- 3           7 <-:---- 4          7 <-:---- 1
                      9 <-:                                      9 <-:                9 <-:                9 <-:
2 ----:-> 4                                 2 ----:-> 1
     :-> 9                                       :-> 7

 G827                  G828                  G829                  G830                  G831                  G832
8 ------- 9           8 ------- 5           8 ------- 5           8 ------- 5           8 ------- 5           8 ------- 4
1 ------> 13          1 ------> 2           1 ------> 2           1 ------> 3           1 ------> 3           1 ------> 5
6 <------ 11          6 <------ 3           6 <------ 3           6 <------ 2           6 <------ 2           6 <------ 2

4 ------> 14          4 ----:-> 8           4 ------> 8          7 <-:---- 6           2 --:                4 ------> 6
7 <-:---- 10               :-> 6           7 <-:---- 7          9 <-:                7 <-:                7 <-:---- 1
9 <-:                 7 <-:---- 4           9 <-:                                     9 <-:                9 <-:
                      9 <-:

 G833                  G834                  G835                  G836                  G837                  G838
8 ------- 2           8 ------- 7           8 ------- 7           8 ------- 4           8 ------- 5           8 ------- 1
1 ------> 4           6 <------ 2           1 ------> 5           1 ------> 5           1 ------> 4           1 ------> 4
6 <------ 3                                 6 <------ 3           6 <------ 3           6 <------ 2           6 <------ 2

4 ------> 5           2 --:                4 ----:-> 8           4 ------> 2           4 ------> 6           4 ----:-> 6
7 <-:---- 6           7 <-:                     :-> 6           7 <-:---- 6           7 <-:---- 1               :-> 8
9 <-:                 9 <-:                7 <-:---- 4           9 <-:                9 <-:                7 <-:---- 3
                                           9 <-:                                                           9 <-:

 G839                  G840                  G841                  G842                  G843                  G844
8 ------- 5           8 ------- 2           8 ------- 3           8 ------- 6           8 ------- 2           8 ------- 4
1 ------> 2           1 ------> 5           1 ------> 1           1 ------> 8           1 ------> 3           1 ------> 5
6 <------ 4           6 <------ 3           6 <------ 5           6 <------ 4           6 <------ 5           6 <------ 2

7 <-:---- 1           4 ------> 1           4 ------> 2          4 ------> 7           7 <-:---- 4          4 ------> 1
9 <-:                 7 <-:---- 6           7 <-:---- 8          7 <-:---- 1           9 <-:                7 <-:---- 6
                      9 <-:                9 <-:                9 <-:                                      9 <-:

                                           2 ----:-> 7          2 ----:-> 2

 G845                  G846                  G847                  G848                  G849                  G850
8 ------- 3           8 ------- 4           8 ------- 3           8 ------- 11          8 ------- 11          8 ------- 4
1 ------> 2           1 ------> 2           1 ------> 5           1 ------> 9           1 ------> 1           1 ------> 2
6 <------ 5           6 <------ 3           6 <------ 4           6 <------ 1           6 <------ 9           6 <------ 3

4 ------> 6           4 ------> 6           4 ------> 1          4 ----:-> 10          7 <-:---- 3          4 ------> 5
7 <-:---- 1           7 <-:---- 1           7 <-:---- 6              :-> 3            9 <-:                7 <-:---- 1
9 <-:                 9 <-:                9 <-:                    :-> 12                                 9 <-:
                                                                7 <-:---- 2           2 ----:-> 2
                                                                9 <-:                      :-> 4
```

```
G851                 G852                 G853                 G854                 G855                 G856
8 ------- 4          8 ------- 2          8 ------- 5          8 ------- 2          8 ------- 5          7 ------- 7
1 ------> 3          1 ------> 3          1 ------> 4          1 ------> 3          1 ------> 2          2 ------> 3
6 <------ 2          6 <------ 5          6 <------ 2          6 <------ 5          6 <------ 3          3 <------ 2

7 <-:----- 5         4 ------> 1          4 ------> 3          4 ------> 4          4 ----:-> 8          9 ----:-> 5
9 <-:                7 <-:---- 6          7 <-:---- 1          7 <-:---- 6               :-> 6               :-> 8
                     9 <-:                9 <-:                9 <-:                7 <-:---- 4          5 <-:---- 9
                                          2 ----:-> 6          2 ----:-> 1          9 <-:                8 <-:


G857                 G858                 G859                 G860                 G861                 G862
7 ------- 5          7 ------- 7          7 ------- 7          7 ------- 7          7 ------- 4          7 ------- 5
2 ------> 3          2 ------> 3          2 ------> 8          2 ------> 5          2 ------> 6          2 ------> 6
3 <------ 2          3 <------ 8          3 <------ 3          3 <------ 4          3 <------ 3          3 <------ 4

5 <-:---- 6          9 ----:-> 5          5 <-:---- 5          9 ------> 3          5 <-:---- 2          9 ------> 2
8 <-:                     :-> 6           8 <-:               5 <-:---- 1          8 <-:               5 <-:---- 3
                          :-> 1                               8 <-:                                    8 <-:
4 ----:-> 4          5 <-:---- 9          4 ----:-> 4                               4 ----:-> 1
     :-> 7           8 <-:                     :-> 9                                     :-> 7

                     4 ----:-> 10


G863                 G864                 G865                 G866                 G867                 G868
7 ------- 9          7 ------- 3          7 ------- 9          7 ------- 5          7 ------- 5          7 ------- 5
2 ------> 3          2 ------> 4          2 ------> 13         2 ------> 2          2 ------> 2          2 ------> 3
3 <------ 2          3 <------ 2          3 <------ 11         3 <------ 3          3 <------ 3          3 <------ 2

9 ------> 5          9 ------> 5          9 ------> 14         9 ----:-> 8          9 ------> 8          5 <-:---- 6
5 <-:---- 4          5 <-:---- 1          5 <-:---- 10             :-> 6           5 <-:---- 7          8 <-:
8 <-:                8 <-:                8 <-:               5 <-:---- 4          8 <-:
                                                              8 <-:


G869                 G870                 G871                 G872                 G873                 G874
7 ------- 5          7 ------- 4          7 ------- 2          7 ------- 7          7 ------- 7          7 ------- 4
2 ------> 3          2 ------> 5          2 ------> 4          3 <------ 2          2 ------> 5          2 ------> 5
3 <------ 2          3 <------ 2          3 <------ 3                               3 <------ 3          3 <------ 3

4 --:                9 ------> 6          9 ------> 5          4 --:                9 ----:-> 8          9 ------> 2
5 <-:                5 <-:---- 1          5 <-:---- 6          5 <-:                     :-> 6           5 <-:---- 6
8 <-:                8 <-:                8 <-:                8 <-:                5 <-:---- 4          8 <-:
                                                                                   8 <-:


G875                 G876                 G877                 G878                 G879                 G880
7 ------- 5          7 ------- 1          7 ------- 5          7 ------- 2          7 ------- 3          7 ------- 6
2 ------> 4          2 ------> 4          2 ------> 2          2 ------> 5          2 ------> 1          2 ------> 8
3 <------ 2          3 <------ 2          3 <------ 4          3 <------ 3          3 <------ 5          3 <------ 4

9 ------> 6          9 ----:-> 6          5 <-:---- 1          9 ------> 1          9 ------> 2          9 ------> 7
5 <-:---- 1               :-> 8           8 <-:               5 <-:---- 6          5 <-:---- 8          5 <-:---- 1
8 <-:                5 <-:---- 3                              8 <-:                8 <-:                8 <-:
                     8 <-:
                                                                                   4 ----:-> 7          4 ----:-> 2


G881                 G882                 G883                 G884                 G885                 G886
7 ------- 2          7 ------- 4          7 ------- 3          7 ------- 4          7 ------- 3          7 ------- 11
2 ------> 3          2 ------> 5          2 ------> 2          2 ------> 2          2 ------> 5          2 ------> 9
3 <------ 5          3 <------ 2          3 <------ 5          3 <------ 3          3 <------ 4          3 <------ 1

5 <-:---- 4          9 ------> 1          9 ------> 6          9 ------> 6          9 ------> 1          9 ----:-> 10
8 <-:                5 <-:---- 6          5 <-:---- 1          5 <-:---- 1          5 <-:---- 6              :-> 3
                     8 <-:                8 <-:                8 <-:                8 <-:                    :-> 12
                                                                                                       5 <-:---- 2
                                                                                                       8 <-:
```

G887 7 ------- 11 2 -------> 1 3 <------ 9 5 <-:----- 3 8 <-: 4 ----:-> 2 :-> 4	**G888** 7 -------- 4 2 -------> 2 3 <------ 3 9 -------> 5 5 <-:----- 1 8 <-:	**G889** 7 -------- 4 2 -------> 3 3 <------ 2 5 <-:---- 5 8 <-:	**G890** 7 -------- 2 2 -------> 3 3 <------ 5 9 -------> 1 5 <-:----- 6 8 <-:	**G891** 7 ------- 5 2 -------> 4 3 <------ 2 9 -------> 3 5 <-:----- 1 8 <-: 4 ----:-> 6	**G892** 7 -------> 2 2 -------> 3 3 <------ 5 9 -------> 4 5 <-:----- 6 8 <-: 4 ----:-> 1

G893
7 -------- 5
2 -------> 2
3 <------ 3
 	
9 ----:-> 8
  :-> 6
5 <-:----- 4
8 <-:
	G894
	7 -------- 7
	4 -------> 5
	5 <------ 4
	
	1 ------> 3
	3 <-:----- 1
	8 <-:
		G895
		7 -------- 4
		4 -------> 6
		5 <------ 3
		
		3 <-:---- 2
		8 <-:
		
		6 ----:-> 1
		  :-> 7
			G896
			7 -------- 5
			4 -------> 6
			5 <------ 4
			
			1 ------> 2
			3 <-:----- 3
			8 <-:
				G897
				7 -------- 9
				4 -------> 3
				5 <------ 2
				
				1 -------> 5
				3 <-:----- 4
				8 <-:
					G898
					7 -------- 3
					4 -------> 4
					5 <------ 2
					
					1 -------> 5
					3 <-:----- 1
					8 <-:

G899 7 -------- 9 4 -------> 13 5 <------ 11 1 -------> 14 3 <-:----- 10 8 <-:	**G900** 7 -------- 5 4 -------> 2 5 <------ 3 1 ----:-> 8 :-> 6 3 <-:----- 4 8 <-:	**G901** 7 -------- 5 4 -------> 2 5 <------ 3 1 -------> 8 3 <-:----- 7 8 <-:	**G902** 7 -------- 5 4 -------> 3 5 <------ 2 3 <-:---- 6 8 <-:	**G903** 7 -------- 5 4 -------> 3 5 <------ 2 6 --: 3 <-: 8 <-:	**G904** 7 -------- 4 4 -------> 5 5 <------ 2 1 -------> 6 3 <-:----- 1 8 <-:

G905
7 -------- 2
4 -------> 4
5 <------ 3
 	
1 -------> 5
3 <-:----- 6
8 <-:
	G906
	7 -------- 7
	5 <------ 2
	
	6 --:
	3 <-:
	8 <-:
		G907
		7 -------- 7
		4 -------> 5
		5 <------ 3
		
		1 ----:-> 8
		  :-> 6
		3 <-:----- 4
		8 <-:
			G908
			7 -------- 4
			4 -------> 5
			5 <------ 3
			
			1 -------> 2
			3 <-:----- 6
			8 <-:
				G909
				7 -------- 5
				4 -------> 4
				5 <------ 2
				
				1 -------> 6
				3 <-:----- 1
				8 <-:
					G910
					7 -------- 1
					4 -------> 4
					5 <------ 2
					
					1 ----:-> 6
					  :-> 8
					3 <-:----- 3
					8 <-:

G911 7 -------- 5 4 -------> 2 5 <------ 4 3 <-:---- 1 8 <-:	**G912** 7 -------- 2 4 -------> 5 5 <------ 3 1 -------> 1 3 <-:----- 6 8 <-:	**G913** 7 -------- 3 4 -------> 1 5 <------ 5 1 -------> 2 3 <-:----- 8 8 <-: 6 ----:-> 7	**G914** 7 -------- 6 4 -------> 8 5 <------ 4 1 -------> 7 3 <-:----- 1 8 <-: 6 ----:-> 2	**G915** 7 -------- 2 4 -------> 3 5 <------ 5 3 <-:---- 4 8 <-:	**G916** 7 -------- 4 4 -------> 5 5 <------ 2 1 -------> 1 3 <-:----- 6 8 <-:

G917
7 -------- 3
4 -------> 2
5 <------ 5
 	
1 -------> 6
3 <-:----- 1
8 <-:
	G918
	7 -------- 4
	4 -------> 2
	5 <------ 3
	
	1 -------> 6
	3 <-:----- 1
	8 <-:
		G919
		7 -------- 3
		4 -------> 5
		5 <------ 4
		
		1 -------> 1
		3 <-:----- 6
		8 <-:
			G920
			7 -------- 11
			4 -------> 9
			5 <------ 1
			
			1 ----:-> 10
			  :-> 3
			  :-> 12
			3 <-:----- 2
			8 <-:
				G921
				7 -------- 11
				4 -------> 1
				5 <------ 9
				
				3 <-:---- 3
				8 <-:
				
				6 ----:-> 2
				  :-> 4
					G922
					7 -------- 4
					4 -------> 2
					5 <------ 3
					
					1 -------> 5
					3 <-:----- 1
					8 <-:

```
G923                 G924                 G925                 G926                 G927                 G928
7 ------- 4          7 ------- 2          7 ------- 5          7 ------- 2          7 ------- 5          7 ------- 7
4 ------> 3          4 ------> 3          4 ------> 4          4 ------> 3          4 ------> 2          3 ------> 2
5 <------ 2          5 <------ 5          5 <------ 2          5 <------ 5          5 <------ 3          2 <------ 3

3 <-:---- 5          1 ------> 1          1 ------> 3          1 ------> 4          1 ----:-> 8          4 ----:-> 5
8 <-:                3 <-:---- 6          3 <-:---- 1          3 <-:---- 6                :-> 6                :-> 6
                     8 <-:                8 <-:                8 <-:                3 <-:---- 4                :-> 8
                                                                                    8 <-:
                                          6 ----:-> 6          6 ----:-> 1                               5 <-:---- 4
                                                                                                         6 <-:
                                                                                                         8 <-:


G929                 G930                 G931                 G932                 G933                 G934
7 ------- 5          7 ------- 7          7 ------- 5          7 ------- 7          7 ------- 7          7 ------- 8
3 ------> 2          3 ------> 2          3 ------> 3          3 ------> 3          3 ----> 5            3 ------> 4
2 <------ 3          2 <------ 3          2 <------ 2          2 <------ 2          2 <------ 3          2 <------ 2

4 ----:-> 8          5 <-:---- 8          4 ----:-> 7          4 --:               4 ------> 6          5 <-:---- 12
      :-> 6          6 <-:                      :-> 4          5 <-:               5 <-:---- 4          6 <-:
      :-> 1                                5 <-:---- 6          6 <-:                6 <-:
                     4 --:                6 <-:                8 <-:                8 <-:                8 <-:---- 3
5 <-:---- 4          8 <-:
6 <-:                                     8 <-:---- 8                                                   4 ----:-> 5
8 <-:                                                                                                         :-> 7
                                                                                                              :-> 10
                                                                                                              :-> 11


G935                 G936                 G937                 G938                 G939                 G940
7 ------- 7          7 ------- 4          7 ------- 5          7 ------- 3          7 ------- 7          7 ------- 6
3 ------> 2          3 ------> 3          3 ------> 7          3 ------> 5          3 ------> 6          3 ------> 5
2 <------ 3          2 <------ 2          2 <------ 4          2 <------ 4          2 <------ 5          2 <------ 4
5 <------ 5
6 ------> 6          5 <-:---- 5          5 <-:---- 3          5 <-:---- 2          5 <-:---- 9          5 <-:---- 8
4 ------> 4          6 <-:                6 <-:                6 <-:                6 <-:                6 <-:

                     4 --:                8 <-:---- 8          8 <-:---- 1          8 <-:---- 3          8 <-:---- 2
8 <-:---- 8          8 <-:
                                          4 ----:-> 2          4 ----:-> 6          4 ----:-> 1          4 ----:-> 1
                                                :-> 6                :-> 7                :-> 2                :-> 7
                                                                     :-> 8                :-> 8
                                                                                          :-> 10


G941                 G942                 G943                 G944                 G945                 G946
7 ------- 8          7 ------- 8          7 ------- 7          7 ------- 5          7 ------- 7          7 ------- 7
3 ------> 2          3 ------> 6          3 ------> 3          3 ------> 3          3 ------> 3          3 ------> 8
2 <------ 1          2 <------ 1          2 <------ 2          2 <------ 2          2 <------ 8          2 <------ 3

4 --:                5 <-:---- 4          5 <-:---- 9          5 <-:---- 6          5 <-:---- 9          5 <-:---- 5
5 <-:                6 <-:                6 <-:                6 <-:                6 <-:                6 <-:
6 <-:
8 <-:                8 <-:---- 2          8 <-:---- 4          8 <-:---- 1          8 <-:---- 4          8 <-:---- 1

                     4 ----:-> 7          4 ----:-> 5          4 ----:-> 4          4 ----:-> 1          4 ----:-> 4
                           :-> 9                :-> 8                :-> 7                :-> 5                :-> 9
                                                                                         :-> 6
                                                                                         :-> 10
```

```
  G947                G948                G949                G950                G951                G952
7 ------- 7         7 ------- 4         7 ------- 5         7 ------- 9         7 ------- 3         7 ------- 9
3 ------> 5         3 ------> 6         3 ------> 6         3 ------> 3         3 ------> 4         3 ------> 13
2 <------ 4         2 <------ 3         2 <------ 4         2 <------ 2         2 <------ 2         2 <------ 11

5 <-:---- 1         5 <-:---- 2         5 <-:---- 3         5 <-:---- 4         5 <-:---- 1         5 <-:---- 10
6 <-:               6 <-:               6 <-:               6 <-:               6 <-:               6 <-:

8 <-:---- 6         4 --:               4 --:               4 --:               4 --:               4 --:
4 ----:-> 3         8 <-:               8 <-:               8 <-:               8 <-:               8 <-:


  G953                G954                G955                G956                G957                G958
7 ------- 5         7 ------- 5         7 ------- 5         7 ------- 5         7 ------- 4         7 ------- 2
3 ------> 2         3 ------> 2         3 ------> 3         3 ------> 3         3 ------> 5         3 ------> 4
2 <------ 3         2 <------ 3         2 <------ 2         2 <------ 2         2 <------ 2         2 <------ 3

5 <-:---- 4         5 <-:---- 7         5 <-:---- 6                            5 <-:---- 1         5 <-:---- 6
6 <-:               6 <-:               6 <-:                                   6 <-:               6 <-:

8 <-:---- 7         4 --:               8 <-:---- 8         4 --:              4 --:               4 --:
4 ----:-> 6         8 <-:                                   5 <-:              8 <-:               8 <-:
    :-> 8                                                   6 <-:
                                                            8 <-:


  G959                G960                G961                G962                G963                G964
7 ------- 7         7 ------- 7         7 ------- 4         7 ------- 5         7 ------- 1         7 ------- 5
2 <------ 2         3 ------> 5         3 ------> 5         3 ------> 4         3 ------> 4         3 ------> 2
                    2 <------ 3         2 <------ 3         2 <------ 2         2 <------ 2         2 <------ 4

4 --:               5 <-:---- 4         5 <-:---- 6         5 <-:---- 1         5 <-:---- 3         5 <-:---- 1
5 <-:               6 <-:               6 <-:               6 <-:               6 <-:               6 <-:
6 <-:
8 <-:               8 <-:---- 2         4 --:               4 --:              8 <-:---- 5         4 --:
                    4 ----:-> 6         8 <-:               8 <-:              4 ----:-> 6         8 <-:
                        :-> 8                                                      :-> 8


  G965                G966                G967                G968                G969                G970
7 ------- 2         7 ------- 3         7 ------- 6         7 ------- 2         7 ------- 4         7 ------- 3
3 ------> 5         3 ------> 1         3 ------> 8         3 ------> 3         3 ------> 5         3 ------> 2
2 <------ 3         2 <------ 5         2 <------ 4         2 <------ 5         2 <------ 2         2 <------ 5

5 <-:---- 6         5 <-:---- 8         5 <-:---- 1         5 <-:---- 4         5 <-:---- 6         5 <-:---- 1
6 <-:               6 <-:               6 <-:               6 <-:               6 <-:               6 <-:

4 --:               8 <-:---- 4         8 <-:---- 3         4 --:              4 --:               4 --:
8 <-:               4 ----:-> 2         4 ----:-> 2         8 <-:              8 <-:               8 <-:
                        :-> 7               :-> 7


  G971                G972                G973                G974                G975                G976
7 ------- 4         7 ------- 3         7 ------- 11        7 ------- 11        7 ------- 4         7 ------- 4
3 ------> 2         3 ------> 5         3 ------> 9         3 ------> 1         3 ------> 2         3 ------> 3
2 <------ 3         2 <------ 4         2 <------ 1         2 <------ 9         2 <------ 3         2 <------ 2
                                                           5 <------ 10
5 <-:---- 1         5 <-:---- 6         5 <-:---- 2        6 <------ 3         5 <-:---- 1         5 <-:---- 5
6 <-:               6 <-:               6 <-:              4 ------> 2         6 <-:               6 <-:

4 --:               4 --:               4 --:                                 8 <-:---- 6         4 --:
8 <-:               8 <-:               8 <-:              8 <-:---- 12        4 ----:-> 5         8 <-:
```

G977 7 ------- 2 3 ------> 3 2 <------ 5 5 <-:---- 6 6 <-: 4 --: 8 <-:	**G978** 7 ------- 5 3 ------> 4 2 <------ 2 5 <-:---- 1 6 <-: 4 --: 8 <-:	**G979** 7 ------- 2 3 ------> 3 2 <------ 5 5 <-:---- 6 6 <-: 4 --: 8 <-:

G980	**G981**	**G982**

7 ------- 5
3 ------> 2
2 <------ 3
 	
5 <-:---- 4
6 <-:
 	
8 <-:---- 7
 	
4 ----:-> 6
	1 ------- 1
	7 ------- 7
	3 ------> 2
	2 <------ 3
	
	20 <-:---- 5
	    :-- 8
	    :-> 4
	    :-> 20
		7 ------- 7
		3 ------> 2
		2 <------ 3
		
		20 <-:-:-- 4
		    :-> 5
		    :-> 6
		    :-> 8

G983	**G984**	**G985**	**G986**	**G987**	**G988**
7 ------- 5 3 ------> 2 2 <------ 3 20 <-:---- 4 :-- 7 :-> 1 :-> 6 :-> 8	1 ------- 1 7 ------- 7 3 ------> 2 2 <------ 3 20 <-:-:-- 8 :-> 20	7 ------- 5 3 ------> 3 2 <------ 2 20 <-:---- 6 :-- 8 :-> 4 :-> 7	1 ------- 1 7 ------- 8 3 ------> 4 2 <------ 2 20 <-:---- 3 :-- 9 :-> 5 :-> 7 :-> 10 :-- 12 :-> 11	1 ------- 1 7 ------- 7 3 ------> 2 2 <------ 3 20 <-:-:-- 5 :-> 6 :-> 4	7 ------- 4 3 ------> 3 2 <------ 2 20 <-:-:-- 5 :-> 6 :-> 1

G989	**G990**	**G991**	**G992**	**G993**	**G994**
1 ------- 1 7 ------- 7 3 ------> 5 2 <------ 3 20 <-:-:-- 4 :-> 6	7 ------- 5 3 ------> 7 2 <------ 4 20 <-:---- 3 :-- 8 :-> 2 :-> 6	7 ------- 3 3 ------> 5 2 <------ 4 20 <-:---- 1 :-- 2 :-> 6 :-> 7 :-> 8	1 ------- 4 7 ------- 7 3 ------> 6 2 <------ 5 20 <-:---- 3 :-- 9 :-> 1 :-> 2 :-> 8 :-> 10	1 ------- 3 7 ------- 6 3 ------> 5 2 <------ 4 20 <-:---- 2 :-- 8 :-> 1 :-> 7	7 ------ 8 3 ------> 6 2 <------ 1 20 <-:---- 2 :-- 4 :-> 7 :-> 9

G995	**G996**	**G997**	**G998**	**G999**	**G1000**
7 ------- 7 3 ------> 3 2 <------ 2 20 <-:---- 4 :-- 9 :-> 5 :-> 8	7 ------- 5 3 ------> 3 2 <------ 2 20 <-:---- 1 :-- 6 :-> 4 :-> 7	1 ------- 2 7 ------- 7 3 ------> 3 2 <------ 8 20 <-:---- 4 :-- 9 :-> 1 :-> 5 :-> 6 :-> 10	1 ------- 2 7 ------- 7 3 ------> 8 2 <------ 3 20 <-:---- 1 :-- 5 :-> 4 :-> 9	7 ------- 7 3 ------> 5 2 <------ 4 20 <-:---- 1 :-- 6 :-> 3	7 ------- 4 3 ------> 6 2 <------ 3 20 <-:-:-- 2 :-> 7

G1001	**G1002**	**G1003**	**G1004**	**G1005**	**G1006**
7 ------- 5 3 ------> 6 2 <------ 4 20 <-:-:-- 3 :-> 2	7 ------- 9 3 ------> 3 2 <------ 2 20 <-:-:-- 4 :-> 5	7 ------- 3 3 ------> 4 2 <------ 2 20 <-:-:-- 1 :-> 5	7 ------- 9 3 ------> 13 2 <------ 11 20 <-:-:-- 10 :-> 14	7 ------- 5 3 ------> 2 2 <------ 3 20 <-:---- 4 :-- 7 :-> 6 :-> 8	7 ------- 5 3 ------> 2 2 <------ 3 20 <-:-:-- 7 :-> 8

```
 G1007                    G1008                    G1009                    G1010                    G1011                    G1012
7 ------- 5              1 ------- 1              1 ------- 1              1 ------- 1              7 ------- 4              7 ------- 1
3 ------> 3              7 ------- 2              7 ------- 2              7 ------- 7              3 ------> 5              3 ------> 4
2 <------ 2              3 ------> 4              3 ------> 4              3 ------> 5              2 <------ 3              2 <------ 2
                         2 <------ 3              2 <------ 3              2 <------ 3
20 <-:---- 6                                                                                       20 <-:-:--- 6           20 <-:---- 3
                         20 <-:---- 6             20 <-:-:--- 6            20 <-:---- 2                  :-> 2                   :-- 5
                                                        :-> 5                  :-- 4                                            :-> 6
                                                                                :-> 6                                           :-> 8
                                                                                :-> 8                                           :-> 1


 G1013                    G1014                    G1015                    G1016                    G1017                    G1018
1 ------- 4              7 ------- 3              7 ------- 6              7 ------- 2              1 ------- 3              1 ------- 4
7 ------- 2              3 ------> 1              3 ------> 8              3 ------> 3              7 ------- 4              7 ------- 3
3 ------> 5              2 <------ 5              2 <------ 4              2 <------ 5              3 ------> 5              3 ------> 2
2 <------ 3                                                                                       2 <------ 2              2 <------ 5
                         20 <-:---- 4             20 <-:---- 3             20 <-:---- 4
20 <-:---- 6                  :-- 6                   :-- 5                                        20 <-:-:--- 6           20 <-:-:--- 1
                              :-> 2                   :-> 2                                            :-> 1                   :-> 6
                              :-> 7                   :-> 7


 G1019                    G1020                    G1021                    G1022                    G1023                    G1024
7 ------- 4              7 ------- 3              7 ------- 11             7 ------- 11             7 ------- 4              7 ------- 4
3 ------> 2              3 ------> 5              3 ------> 9              3 ------> 1              3 ------> 2              3 ------> 3
2 <------ 3              2 <------ 4              2 <------ 1              2 <------ 9              2 <------ 3              2 <------ 2

20 <-:-:--- 1           20 <-:-:--- 6            20 <-:-:--- 2            20 <-:---- 3             20 <-:---- 1             20 <-:---- 5
     :-> 6                   :-> 1                   :-> 3                     :-- 10                  :-- 6
                                                     :-> 10                    :-> 2                   :-> 5
                                                     :-> 12                    :-> 4


 G1025                    G1026                    G1027                    G1028                    G1029                    G1030
7 ------- 2              7 ------- 5              7 ------- 2              7 ------- 5              7 ------- 7              7 ------- 7
3 ------> 3              3 ------> 4              3 ------> 3              3 ------> 2              3 ------> 2              3 ------> 2
2 <------ 5              2 <------ 2              2 <------ 5              2 <------ 3              2 <------ 3              2 <------ 3

20 <-:-:--- 6           20 <-:---- 1             20 <-:---- 6             20 <-:---- 4             5 <-:---- 5             5 <-:-:--- 4
     :-> 1                   :-> 3                   :-> 1                     :-- 7                   :-- 8                   :-> 5
                             :-> 6                   :-> 4                     :-> 6                   :-> 4                   :-> 6
                                                                               :-> 8                   :-> 20                  :-> 8


 G1031                    G1032                    G1033                    G1034                    G1035                    G1036
7 ------- 5              7 ------- 7              7 ------- 5              7 ------- 8              7 ------- 7              7 ------- 4
3 ------> 2              3 ------> 2              3 ------> 3              3 ------> 4              3 ------> 2              3 ------> 3
2 <------ 3              2 <------ 3              2 <------ 2              2 <------ 2              2 <------ 3              2 <------ 2

5 <-:---- 4             5 <-:-:--- 8             5 <-:---- 6             5 <-:---- 3             5 <-:-:--- 5            5 <-:-:--- 5
     :-- 7                   :-> 20                   :-- 8                   :-- 9                   :-> 6                   :-> 6
     :-> 1                                            :-> 4                   :-> 5                   :-> 4                   :-> 1
     :-> 6                                            :-> 7                   :-> 7
     :-> 8
                                                                             :-> 10
                                                                             :-- 12
                                                                             :-> 11
```

```
G1037                  G1038                  G1039                  G1040                  G1041                  G1042
7 ------- 7            7 ------- 5            7 ------- 3            7 ------- 7            7 ------- 6            7 ------- 8
3 ------> 5            3 ------> 7            3 ------> 5            3 ------> 6            3 ------> 5            3 ------> 6
2 <------ 3            2 <------ 4            2 <------ 4            2 <------ 5            2 <------ 4            2 <------ 1

5 <-:-:-- 4            5 <-:---- 3            5 <-:---- 1            5 <-:---- 3            5 <-:---- 2            5 <-:---- 2
   :-> 6                  :-- 8                  :-- 2                  :-- 9                  :-- 8                  :-- 4
                         :-> 2                  :-> 6                  :-> 1                  :-> 1                  :-> 7
                         :-> 6                  :-> 7                  :-> 2                  :-> 7                  :-> 9
                                                :-> 8                  :-> 8
                                                                       :-> 10


G1043                  G1044                  G1045                  G1046                  G1047                  G1048
7 ------- 7            7 ------- 5            7 ------- 7            7 ------- 7            7 ------- 7            7 ------- 4
3 ------> 3            3 ------> 3            3 ------> 3            3 ------> 8            3 ------> 5            3 ------> 6
2 <------ 2            2 <------ 2            2 <------ 8            2 <------ 3            2 <------ 4            2 <------ 3

5 <-:---- 4            5 <-:---- 1            5 <-:---- 4            5 <-:---- 1            5 <-:---- 1            5 <-:-:-- 2
   :-- 9                  :-- 6                  :-- 9                  :-- 5                  :-- 6                  :-> 7
   :-> 5                  :-> 4                  :-> 1                  :-> 4                  :-> 3
   :-> 8                  :-> 7                  :-> 5                  :-> 9
                                                :-> 6
                                                :-> 10


G1049                  G1050                  G1051                  G1052                  G1053                  G1054
7 ------- 5            7 ------- 9            7 ------- 3            7 ------- 9            7 ------- 5            7 ------- 5
3 ------> 6            3 ------> 3            3 ------> 4            3 ------> 13           3 ------> 2            3 ------> 2
2 <------ 4            2 <------ 2            2 <------ 2            2 <------ 11           2 <------ 3            2 <------ 3

5 <-:-:-- 3            5 <-:-:-- 4            5 <-:-:-- 1            5 <-:-:--- 10          5 <-:---- 4            5 <-:-:-- 7
   :-> 2                  :-> 5                  :-> 5                   :-> 14                :-- 7                  :-> 8
                                                                                             :-> 6
                                                                                             :-> 8


G1055                  G1056                  G1057                  G1058                  G1059                  G1060
7 ------- 5            7 ------- 2            7 ------- 2            7 ------- 7            7 ------- 4            7 ------- 1
3 ------> 3            3 ------> 4            3 ------> 4            3 ------> 5            3 ------> 5            3 ------> 4
2 <------ 2            2 <------ 3            2 <------ 3            2 <------ 3            2 <------ 3            2 <------ 2

5 <-:---- 6            5 <-:---- 6            5 <-:-:-- 6            5 <-:---- 2            5 <-:-:-- 6            5 <-:---- 3
                                                :-> 5                  :-- 4                  :-> 2                  :-- 5
                                                                       :-> 6                                         :-> 6
                                                                       :-> 8                                         :-> 8
                                                                                                                     :-> 1


G1061                  G1062                  G1063                  G1064                  G1065                  G1066
7 ------- 2            7 ------- 3            7 ------- 6            7 ------- 2            7 ------- 4            7 ------- 3
3 ------> 5            3 ------> 1            3 ------> 8            3 ------> 3            3 ------> 5            3 ------> 2
2 <------ 3            2 <------ 5            2 <------ 4            2 <------ 5            2 <------ 2            2 <------ 5

5 <-:---- 6            5 <-:---- 4            5 <-:---- 3            5 <-:---- 4            5 <-:-:-- 6            5 <-:-:-- 1
                         :-- 6                  :-- 5                                        :-> 1                  :-> 6
                         :-> 2                  :-> 2
                         :-> 7                  :-> 7
```

```
  G1067                G1068                G1069                G1070                G1071                G1072
7 ------- 4          7 ------- 3          7 ------- 11         7 ------- 11         7 ------- 4          7 ------- 4
3 ------> 2          3 ------> 5          3 ------> 9          3 ------> 1          3 ------> 2          3 ------> 3
2 <------ 3          2 <------ 4          2 <------ 1          2 <------ 9          2 <------ 3          2 <------ 2

5 <-:-:-- 1          5 <-:-:-- 6          5 <-:-:-- 2          5 <-:--- 3          5 <-:--- 1          5 <-:---- 5
    :-> 6                :-> 1                :-> 3                :-- 10               :-- 6
                                              :-> 10               :-> 2                :-> 5
                                              :-> 12               :-> 4

  G1073                G1074                G1075                G1076                G1077                G1078
7 ------- 2          7 ------- 5          7 ------- 2          7 ------- 5          5 ------- 5          5 ------- 7
3 ------> 3          3 ------> 4          3 ------> 3          3 ------> 2          3 ------> 2          3 ------> 2
2 <------ 5          2 <------ 2          2 <------ 5          2 <------ 3          2 <------ 3          2 <------ 3

5 <-:-:-- 6          5 <-:---- 1          5 <-:--- 6          5 <-:--- 4          4 ----:-> 8          8 <-:---- 8
    :-> 1                :-> 3                :-> 1                :-- 7                :-> 6          6 <-:
                         :-> 6                :-> 4                :-> 6                :-> 1          8 <-:
                                                                  :-> 8          8 <-:---- 4          7 ----:-> 20
                                                                                 6 <-:
                                                                                 8 <-:

  G1079                G1080                G1081                G1082                G1083                G1084
5 ------- 5          5 ------- 7          5 ------- 7          5 ------- 8          5 ------- 7          5 ------- 4
3 ------> 3          3 ------> 3          3 ------> 5          3 ------> 4          3 ------> 2          3 ------> 3
2 <------ 2          2 <------ 2          2 <------ 3          2 <------ 2          2 <------ 3          2 <------ 2

4 ----:-> 7          7 --:               4 ------> 6          4 ----:-> 5          1 <-:--- 6          4 ----:-> 1
    :-> 4          1 <-:               1 <-:-:-- 4              :-> 10         6 <-:                   :-> 6
1 <-:---- 6          6 <-:               6 <-:                   :-> 7          8 <-:               1 <-:---- 5
6 <-:               8 <-:               8 <-:               1 <-:---- 12         7 ----:-> 4          6 <-:
8 <-:                                                       6 <-:                                    8 <-:
                                                            8 <-:
                                                            7 ----:-> 11

  G1085                G1086                G1087                G1088                G1089                G1090
5 ------- 5          5 ------- 3          5 ------- 7          5 ------- 6          5 ------- 8          5 ------- 8
3 ------> 7          3 ------> 5          3 ------> 6          3 ------> 5          3 ------> 2          3 ------> 6
2 <------ 4          2 <------ 4          2 <------ 5          2 <------ 4          2 <------ 1          2 <------ 1

4 ----:-> 2          4 ----:-> 8          4 ----:-> 8          4 ----:-> 7          7 --:               4 ----:-> 7
    :-> 6                :-> 7                :-> 2                :-> 1          1 <-:                   :-> 9
1 <-:---- 3              :-> 6                :-> 10         1 <-:---- 8          6 <-:               1 <-:---- 4
6 <-:               1 <-:---- 2          1 <-:---- 9          6 <-:               8 <-:               6 <-:
8 <-:               6 <-:               6 <-:               8 <-:                                    8 <-:
                    8 <-:               8 <-:
                                        7 ----:-> 1

  G1091                G1092                G1093                G1094                G1095                G1096
5 ------- 7          5 ------- 5          5 ------- 7          5 ------- 5          5 ------- 7          5 ------- 4
3 ------> 3          3 ------> 3          3 ------> 3          3 ------> 8          3 ------> 5          3 ------> 6
2 <------ 2          2 <------ 2          2 <------ 8          2 <------ 3          2 <------ 4          2 <------ 3

4 ----:-> 5          1 <-:--- 6          4 ----:-> 5          1 <-:--- 5          4 ------> 3          1 <-:--- 2
    :-> 8          6 <-:                   :-> 6          6 <-:               1 <-:-:-- 1          6 <-:
1 <-:---- 9          8 <-:                   :-> 1          8 <-:               6 <-:               8 <-:
6 <-:               7 ----:-> 4          1 <-:---- 9          7 ----:-> 4          8 <-:               7 ----:-> 1
8 <-:                   :-> 7          6 <-:                   :-> 9                                    :-> 7
                                        8 <-:
                                        7 ----:-> 10
```

```
  G1097                  G1098                  G1099                  G1100                  G1101                  G1102
5 ------- 5            5 ------- 9            5 ------- 3            5 ------- 9            5 ------- 5            5 ------- 5
3 ------> 6            3 ------> 3            3 ------> 4            3 ------> 13           3 ------> 2            3 ------> 2
2 <------ 4            2 <------ 2            2 <------ 2            2 <------ 11           2 <------ 3            2 <------ 3

4 ------> 2            4 ------> 5            4 ------> 5            4 ------> 14          4 ----:-> 8            4 ------> 8
8 <-:---- 3           1 <-:---- 4           1 <-:---- 1           1 <-:---- 10                :-> 6           1 <-:---- 7
6 <-:                 6 <-:                 6 <-:                 6 <-:                 1 <-:---- 4           6 <-:
1 <-:                 8 <-:                 8 <-:                 8 <-:                 6 <-:                 8 <-:
                                                                                        8 <-:
```

```
  G1103                  G1104                  G1105                  G1106                  G1107                  G1108
5 ------- 5            5 ------- 5            5 ------- 4            5 ------- 2            5 ------- 7            5 ------- 7
3 ------> 3            3 ------> 3            3 ------> 5            3 ------> 4            2 <------ 2            3 ------> 5
2 <------ 2            2 <------ 2            2 <------ 2            2 <------ 3                                  2 <------ 3

1 <-:---- 6                                 4 ------> 6            4 ------> 5            7 --:                 4 ----:-> 8
6 <-:                 7 --:                 1 <-:---- 1           1 <-:---- 6            1 <-:                      :-> 6
8 <-:                 1 <-:                 6 <-:                 6 <-:                 6 <-:                 1 <-:---- 4
                      6 <-:                 8 <-:                 8 <-:                 8 <-:                 6 <-:
                      8 <-:                                                                                   8 <-:
```

```
  G1109                  G1110                  G1111                  G1112                  G1113                  G1114
5 ------- 4            5 ------- 5            5 ------- 1            5 ------- 5            5 ------- 2            5 ------- 3
3 ------> 5            3 ------> 4            3 ------> 4            3 ------> 2            3 ------> 5            3 ------> 1
2 <------ 3            2 <------ 2            2 <------ 2            2 <------ 4            2 <------ 3            2 <------ 5

4 ------> 2            4 ------> 6            4 ----:-> 6           1 <-:---- 1            4 ------> 1            4 ------> 2
1 <-:---- 6           1 <-:---- 1                :-> 8            6 <-:                 1 <-:---- 6           1 <-:---- 8
6 <-:                 6 <-:                 1 <-:---- 3           8 <-:                 6 <-:                 6 <-:
8 <-:                 8 <-:                 6 <-:                                       8 <-:                 8 <-:
                                            8 <-:
                                                                                                              7 ----:-> 7
```

```
  G1115                  G1116                  G1117                  G1118                  G1119                  G1120
5 ------- 6            5 ------- 2            5 ------- 4            5 ------- 3            5 ------- 4            5 ------- 3
3 ------> 8            3 ------> 3            3 ------> 5            3 ------> 2            3 ------> 2            3 ------> 5
2 <------ 4            2 <------ 5            2 <------ 2            2 <------ 5            2 <------ 3            2 <------ 4

4 ------> 7            1 <-:---- 4           4 ------> 1            4 ------> 6            4 ------> 6            4 ------> 1
1 <-:---- 1           6 <-:                 1 <-:---- 6           1 <-:---- 1           1 <-:---- 1           1 <-:---- 6
6 <-:                 8 <-:                 6 <-:                 6 <-:                 6 <-:                 6 <-:
8 <-:                                       8 <-:                 8 <-:                 8 <-:                 8 <-:

7 ----:-> 2
```

```
  G1121                  G1122                  G1123                  G1124                  G1125                  G1126
5 ------- 11           5 ------- 11          5 ------- 4            5 ------- 4            5 ------- 2            5 ------- 5
3 ------> 9            3 ------> 1            3 ------> 2            3 ------> 3            3 ------> 3            3 ------> 4
2 <------ 1            2 <------ 9            2 <------ 3            2 <------ 2            2 <------ 5            2 <------ 2

4 ----:-> 10          1 <-:---- 3           4 ------> 5            1 <-:---- 5           4 ------> 1            4 ------> 3
     :-> 3            6 <-:                 1 <-:---- 1           6 <-:                 1 <-:---- 6           1 <-:---- 1
     :-> 12           8 <-:                 6 <-:                 8 <-:                 6 <-:                 6 <-:
1 <-:---- 2                                 8 <-:                                       8 <-:                 8 <-:
6 <-:                 7 ----:-> 2
8 <-:                      :-> 4                                                                               7 ----:-> 6
```

```
  G1127               G1128               G1129               G1130               G1131               G1132
5 ------- 2         5 ------- 5         7 ------- 7         7 ------- 5         7 ------- 7         7 ------- 8
3 ------> 3         3 ------> 2         3 ------> 2         3 ------> 3         3 ------> 3         3 ------> 4
2 <------ 5         2 <------ 3         2 <------ 3         2 <------ 2         2 <------ 2         2 <------ 2

4 ------> 4         4 ----:-> 8         20 <------ 8        8 ----:-> 7        8 --:              8 ----:-> 5
1 <-:----- 6            :-> 6                                   :-> 4          20 <-:                 :-> 10
6 <-:              1 <-:----- 4         8 ----:-> 20        20 <------ 6                               :-> 7
8 <-:              6 <-:                                                                         20 <------ 12
                   8 <-:                                                                             :-- 3
7 ----:-> 1                                                                                          :-> 11

  G1133               G1134               G1135               G1136               G1137               G1138
7 ------- 7         7 ------- 4         7 ------- 7         7 ------- 5         7 ------- 3         7 ------- 7
3 ------> 2         3 ------> 3         3 ------> 5         3 ------> 7         3 ------> 5         3 ------>20
2 <------ 3         2 <------ 2         2 <------ 3         2 <------ 4         2 <------ 4         2 <------ 7

20 <------ 6        8 ----:-> 1         8 ------- 6         8 ----:-> 2        8 ----:-> 8         8 ----:-> 8
                       :-> 6           20 <------ 4            :-> 6              :-> 7                :-> 2
8 ----:-> 4        20 <------ 5                           20 <------ 3            :-> 6                :-> 10
                                                                            20 <------ 2         20 <------ 9
                                                                                                    :-- 3
                                                                                                    :-> 8

  G1139               G1140               G1141               G1142               G1143               G1144
7 ------- 6         7 ------- 8         7 ------- 8         7 ------- 7         7 ------- 5         7 ------- 7
3 ------> 5         3 ------> 2         3 ------> 6         3 ------> 3         3 ------> 3         3 ------> 3
2 <------ 4         2 <------ 1         2 <------ 1         2 <------ 2         2 <------ 2         2 <------ 8

8 ----:-> 7         8 --:              8 ----:-> 7         8 ----:-> 5        20 <------ 6        8 ----:-> 7
    :-> 1           20 <-:                 :-> 9               :-> 8                                  :->20
20 <------ 8                           20 <------ 4        20 <------ 9        8 ----:-> 4             :-> 8
                                                                                  :-> 7          20 <------ 9
                                                                                                    :-- 2
                                                                                                    :-> 10

  G1145               G1146               G1147               G1148               G1149               G1150
7 ------- 7         7 ------- 7         7 ------- 4         7 ------- 5         7 ------- 9         7 ------- 3
3 ------> 8         3 ------> 5         3 ------> 6         3 ------> 6         3 ------> 3         3 ------> 4
2 <------ 3         2 <------ 4         2 <------ 3         2 <------ 4         2 <------ 2         2 <------ 2

20 <------ 5        8 ------> 3         20 <------ 2        8 ------> 2        8 ------> 5         8 ------> 5
                   20 <------ 1                           20 <------ 3        20 <------ 4        20 <------ 1
8 ----:-> 4                            8 ----:-> 1
    :-> 9                                  :-> 7

  G1151               G1152               G1153               G1154               G1155               G1156
7 ------- 9         7 ------- 5         7 ------- 5         7 ------- 5         7 ------- 5         7 ------- 4
3 ------> 13        3 ------> 2         3 ------> 2         3 ------> 3         3 ------> 3         3 ------> 5
2 <------ 11        2 <------ 3         2 <------ 3         2 <------ 2         2 <------ 2         2 <------ 2

8 ------> 14        8 ----:-> 8        8 ------> 8         20 <------ 6                           8 ------> 6
20 <------ 10         :-  6            20 <------ 7                            8 --:              20 <------ 1
                   20 <------ 4                                               20 <-:

  G1157               G1158               G1159               G1160               G1161               G1162
7 ------- 2         7 ------- 7         7 ------- 7         7 ------- 4         7 ------- 5         7 ------- 1
3 ------> 4         2 <------ 2         3 ------> 5         3 ------> 3         3 ------> 4         3 ------> 4
2 <------ 3                            2 <------ 3         2 <------ 3         2 <------ 2         2 <------ 2

8 ------> 5         8 --:              8 ----:-> 8        8 ------> 2         8 ------> 6         8 ----:-> 6
20 <------ 6        20 <-:                :-> 6           20 <------ 6        20 <------ 1            :-> 8
                                      20 <------ 4                                              20 <------ 3
```

```
  G1163                G1164                G1165                G1166                G1167                G1168
7 ------- 5          7 ------- 2          7 ------- 3          7 ------- 6          7 ------- 2          7 ------- 4
3 ------> 2          3 ------> 5          3 ------> 1          3 ------> 8          3 ------> 3          3 ------> 5
2 <------ 4          2 <------ 3          2 <------ 5          2 <------ 4          2 <------ 5          2 <------ 2

20 <------ 1         8 ------> 1          8 ------> 2          8 ------> 7          20 <------ 4         8 ------> 1
                     20 <------ 6         20 <------ 8         20 <------ 1                              20 <------ 6
                                          :-- 4               :-- 3
                                          :-> 7               :-> 2


  G1169                G1170                G1171                G1172                G1173                G1174
7 ------- 3          7 ------- 4          7 ------- 3          7 ------- 11         7 ------- 11         7 ------- 4
3 ------> 2          3 ------> 2          3 ------> 5          3 ------> 9          3 ------> 1          3 ------> 2
2 <------ 5          2 <------ 3          2 <------ 4          2 <------ 1          2 <------ 9          2 <------ 3

8 ------> 6          8 ------> 6          8 ------> 1          8 ----:-> 10         20 <------ 3         8 ------> 5
20 <------ 1         20 <------ 1         20 <------ 6         :-> 3                                     20 <------ 1
                                                              :-> 12               8 ----:-> 2
                                                              20 <------ 2         :-> 4


  G1175                G1176                G1177                G1178                G1179                G1180
7 ------- 4          7 ------- 2          7 ------- 5          7 ------- 2          7 ------- 5          5 ------- 5
3 ------> 3          3 ------> 3          3 ------> 4          3 ------> 3          3 ------> 2          2 ------> 3
2 <------ 2          2 <------ 5          2 <------ 2          2 <------ 5          2 <------ 3          3 <------ 2

20 <------ 5         8 ------> 1          8 ------> 3          8 ------> 4          8 ----:-> 8          6 ----:-> 7
                     20 <------ 6         20 <------ 1         20 <------ 6         :-> 6                :-> 4
                                                                                   20 <------ 4         7 <-:----- 6
                                                                                                        4 <-:


  G1181                G1182                G1183                G1184                G1185                G1186
5 ------- 7          5 ------- 7          5 ------- 8          5 ------- 7          5 ------- 4          5 ------- 5
2 ------> 3          2 ------> 5          2 ------> 4          2 ------> 2          2 ------> 3          2 ------> 7
3 <------ 2          3 <------ 3          3 <------ 2          3 <------ 3          3 <------ 2          3 <------ 4

8 --:               6 ------> 6          6 ----:-> 5          7 <-:----- 6         6 ----:-> 1          6 ----:-> 2
7 <-:               7 <-:----- 4         :-> 10               4 <-:                :-> 6                :-> 6
4 <-:               4 <-:                :-> 7                                     7 <-:----- 5         7 <-:----- 3
                                         7 <-:----- 12        8 ----:-> 4          4 <-:                4 <-:
                                         4 <-:

                                         8 ----:-> 11


  G1187                G1188                G1189                G1190                G1191                G1192
5 ------- 3          5 ------- 7          5 ------- 6          5 ------- 8          5 ------- 8          5 ------- 7
2 ------> 5          2 ------> 6          2 ------> 5          2 ------> 2          2 ------> 6          2 ------> 3
3 <------ 4          3 <------ 5          3 <------ 4          3 <------ 1          3 <------ 1          3 <------ 2

6 ----:-> 8          6 ----:-> 8          6 ----:-> 7                              6 ----:-> 7          6 ----:-> 5
:-> 7                :-> 2                :-> 1                8 --:               :-> 9                :-> 8
:-> 6                :-> 10               7 <-:----- 8        7 <-:                7 <-:----- 4         7 <-:----- 9
7 <-:----- 2         7 <-:----- 9         4 <-:               4 <-:                4 <-:                4 <-:
4 <-:                4 <-:

                     8 ----:-> 1
```

```
G1193
5 ------- 5
2 ------> 3
3 <------ 2

7 <-:---- 6
4 <-:
8 ----:-> 4
    :-> 7
```

```
G1194
5 ------- 7
2 ------> 3
3 <------ 8

6 ----:-> 5
    :-> 6
    :-> 1
7 <-:---- 9
4 <-:
8 ----:-> 10
```

```
G1195
5 ------- 7
2 ------> 8
3 <------ 3

7 <-:---- 5
4 <-:
8 ----:-> 4
    :-> 9
```

```
G1196
5 ------- 7
2 ------> 5
3 <------ 4

6 ------> 3
7 <-:---- 1
4 <-:
```

```
G1197
5 ------- 4
2 ------> 6
3 <------ 3

7 <-:---- 2
4 <-:
8 ----:-> 1
    :-> 7
```

```
G1198
5 ------- 5
2 ------> 6
3 <------ 4

6 ------> 2
4 <-:
7 <-:
```

```
G1199
5 ------- 9
2 ------> 3
3 <------ 2

6 ------> 5
7 <-:---- 4
4 <-:
```

```
G1200
5 ------- 3
2 ------> 4
3 <------ 2

6 ------> 5
7 <-:---- 1
4 <-:
```

```
G1201
5 ------- 9
2 ------> 13
3 <------ 11

6 ------> 14
7 <-:---- 10
4 <-:
```

```
G1202
5 ------- 5
2 ------> 2
3 <------ 3

6 ----:-> 8
    :-> 6
7 <-:---- 4
4 <-:
```

```
G1203
5 ------- 5
2 ------> 2
3 <------ 3

6 ------> 8
7 <-:---- 7
4 <-:
```

```
G1204
5 ------- 5
2 ------> 3
3 <------ 2

7 <-:---- 6
4 <-:
```

```
G1205
5 ------- 5
2 ------> 3
3 <------ 2

8 --:
7 <-:
4 <-:
```

```
G1206
5 ------- 4
2 ------> 5
3 <------ 2

6 ------> 6
7 <-:---- 1
4 <-:
```

```
G1207
5 ------- 2
2 ------> 4
3 <------ 3

6 ------> 5
7 <-:---- 6
4 <-:
```

```
G1208
5 ------- 7
3 <------ 2

8 --:
7 <-:
4 <-:
```

```
G1209
5 ------- 7
2 ------> 5
3 <------ 3

6 ----:-> 8
    :-> 6
7 <-:---- 4
4 <-:
```

```
G1210
5 ------- 4
2 ------> 5
3 <------ 3

6 ------> 2
7 <-:---- 6
4 <-:
```

```
G1211
5 ------- 5
2 ------> 4
3 <------ 2

6 ------> 6
7 <-:---- 1
4 <-:
```

```
G1212
5 ------- 1
2 ------> 4
3 <------ 2

6 ----:-> 6
    :-> 8
7 <-:---- 3
4 <-:
```

```
G1213
5 ------- 5
2 ------> 2
3 <------ 4

7 <-:---- 1
4 <-:
```

```
G1214
5 ------- 2
2 ------> 5
3 <------ 3

6 ------> 1
7 <-:---- 6
4 <-:
```

```
G1215
5 ------- 3
2 ------> 1
3 <------ 5

6 ------> 2
7 <-:---- 8
4 <-:

8 ----:-> 7
```

```
G1216
5 ------- 6
2 ------> 8
3 <------ 4

6 ------> 7
7 <-:---- 1
4 <-:

8 ----:-> 2
```

```
G1217
5 ------- 2
2 ------> 3
3 <------ 5

7 <-:---- 4
4 <-:
```

```
G1218
5 ------- 4
2 ------> 5
3 <------ 2

6 ------> 1
7 <-:---- 6
4 <-:
```

```
G1219
5 ------- 3
2 ------> 2
3 <------ 5

6 ------> 6
7 <-:---- 1
4 <-:
```

```
G1220
5 ------- 4
2 ------> 2
3 <------ 3

6 ------> 6
7 <-:---- 1
4 <-:
```

```
G1221
5 ------- 3
2 ------> 5
3 <------ 4

6 ------> 1
7 <-:---- 6
4 <-:
```

```
G1222
5 ------- 11
2 ------> 9
3 <------ 1

6 ----:-> 10
    :-> 3
    :-> 12
7 <-:---- 2
4 <-:
```

```
G1223
5 ------- 11
2 ------> 1
3 <------ 9

7 <-:---- 3
4 <-:
8 ----:-> 2
    :-> 4
```

```
G1224
5 ------- 4
2 ------> 2
3 <------ 3

6 ------> 5
7 <-:---- 1
4 <-:
```

```
G1225
5 ------- 4
2 ------> 3
3 <------ 2

7 <-:---- 5
4 <-:
```

```
G1226
5 ------- 2
2 ------> 3
3 <------ 4

6 ------> 1
7 <-:---- 6
4 <-:
```

```
G1227
5 ------- 5
2 ------> 4
3 <------ 2

6 ------> 3
7 <-:---- 1
4 <-:

8 ----:-> 6
```

```
G1228
5 ------- 2
2 ------> 3
3 <------ 5

6 ------> 4
7 <-:---- 6
4 <-:

8 ----:-> 1
```

```
G1229                  G1230                  G1231                  G1232                  G1233                  G1234
5 ------- 5            7 ------- 7            7 ------- 7            7 ------- 8            7 ------- 7            7 ------- 4
2 ------> 2            2 ------> 3            2 ------> 5            2 ------> 4            2 ------> 2            2 ------> 3
3 <------ 3            3 <------ 2            3 <------ 3            3 <------ 2            3 <------ 3            3 <------ 2

6 ----:-> 8                                   :-- 4                 :-- 3                 :-- 5                 :-- 5
    :-> 6                                     :- 6                  :-> 5                 :-> 4                 :-> 1
7 <-:----- 4                                                        :-> 7                                       :-> 6
4 <-:                                                               :-> 10
                                                                    :-- 9
                                                                    :-> 11


G1235                  G1236                  G1237                  G1238                  G1239                  G1240
7 ------- 5            7 ------- 3            7 ------- 7            7 ------- 6            7 ------- 8            7 ------- 8
2 ------> 7            2 ------> 5            2 ------> 6            2 ------> 5            2 ------> 2            2 ------> 6
3 <------ 4            3 <------ 4            3 <------ 5            3 <------ 4            3 <------ 1            3 <------ 1

:-- 3                 :-- 1                  :-- 3                 :- 2                                         :-- 2
:-> 2                 :-> 6                  :-> 1                 :- 1                                         :-> 7
:-> 6                 :-> 7                  :-> 2                 :- 7                                         :-> 9
                                             :-> 8
                      :-> 8
                      :-- 2                  :-- 9
                                             :-> 10


G1241                  G1242                  G1243                  G1244                  G1245                  G1246
7 ------- 7            7 ------- 5            7 ------- 7            7 ------- 7            7 ------- 7            7 ------- 4
2 ------> 3            2 ------> 3            2 ------> 3            2 ------> 8            2 ------> 5            2 ------> 6
3 <------ 2            3 <------ 2            3 <------ 8            3 <------ 3            3 <------ 4            3 <------ 3

:-- 4                 :-- 1                  :-- 4                 :-- 1                 :-- 1                 :-- 2
:-> 5                 :-> 4                  :-> 1                 :-> 4                 :-> 3                 :-> 1
:-> 8                 :-> 7                  :-> 5                 :-> 9                                       :-> 7
                                             :-> 6

                                             :-- 9
                                             :-> 10


G1247                  G1248                  G1249                  G1250                  G1251                  G1252
7 ------- 5            7 ------- 9            7 ------- 3            7 ------- 9            7 ------- 5            7 ------- 5
2 ------> 6            2 ------> 3            2 ------> 4            2 ------> 13           2 ------> 2            2 ------> 2
3 <------ 4            3 <------ 2            3 <------ 2            3 <------ 11           3 <------ 3            3 <------ 3

:-- 3                 :-- 4                  :-- 1                 :-- 10                :-- 4                 :-- 7
:-> 2                 :-> 5                  :-> 5                 :-> 14                :-> 6                 :-> 8
                                                                                        :-> 8


G1253                  G1254                  G1255                  G1256                  G1257                  G1258
7 ------- 5            7 ------- 5            7 ------- 4            7 ------- 2            7 ------- 7            7 ------- 7
2 ------> 3            2 ------> 3            2 ------> 5            2 ------> 4            3 <------ 2            2 ------> 5
3 <------ 2            3 <------ 2            3 <------ 2            3 <------ 3                                  3 <------ 3

                                             :-- 1                 :-- 6                                       :-- 2
                                             :-> 6                 :-> 5                                       :-> 6
                                                                                                               :-> 8


G1259                  G1260                  G1261                  G1262                  G1263                  G1264
7 ------- 4            7 ------- 5            7 ------- 1            7 ------- 5            7 ------- 2            7 ------- 3
2 ------> 5            2 ------> 4            2 ------> 4            2 ------> 2            2 ------> 5            2 ------> 1
3 <------ 3            3 <------ 2            3 <------ 2            3 <------ 4            3 <------ 3            3 <------ 5

:-- 6                                        :-- 3                                       :-- 6                 :-- 4
:-> 2                                        :-> 6                                       :-> 1                 :-> 2
                                             :-> 8                                                             :-> 7
```

```
G1265                 G1266                 G1267                 G1268                 G1269                 G1270
7 ------- 6           7 ------- 2           7 ------- 4           7 ------- 3           7 ------- 4           7 ------- 3
2 -----> 8            2 -----> 3            2 -----> 5            2 -----> 2            2 -----> 2            2 -----> 5
3 <------ 4           3 <------ 5           3 <------ 2           3 <------ 5           3 <------ 3           3 <------ 4

:-- 3                                       :-- 6                 :-- 1                 :-- 1                 :-- 6
:-> 2                                       :-> 1                 :-> 6                 :-> 6                 :-> 1
:-> 7
```

```
G1271                 G1272                 G1273                 G1274                 G1275                 G1276
7 ------- 11          7 ------- 11          7 ------- 4           7 ------- 4           7 ------- 2           7 ------- 5
2 -----> 9            2 -----> 1            2 -----> 2            2 -----> 3            2 -----> 3            2 -----> 4
3 <------ 1           3 <------ 9           3 <------ 3           3 <------ 2           3 <------ 5           3 <------ 2

:-- 2                 :-- 3                 :- 1                                        :-- 6                 :-- 1
:-> 3                 :-> 2                 :- 5                                        :-> 1                 :-> 3
:-> 10                :-> 4                                                                                   :-> 6
:-> 12
```

```
G1277                 G1278                 G1279                 G1280                 G1281                 G1282
7 ------- 2           7 ------- 5           4 ------- 7           4 ------- 4           4 ------- 5           4 ------- 3
2 -----> 3            2 -----> 2            2 -----> 5            2 -----> 3            2 -----> 7            2 -----> 5
3 <------ 5           3 <------ 3           3 <------ 3           3 <------ 2           3 <------ 4           3 <------ 4

:-- 6                 :-- 4                 5 -----> 6            6 <-:---- 5           6 <-:---- 3           6 <-:---- 2
:-> 1                 :-> 6                 6 <-:---- 4           1 <-:                 1 <-:                 1 <-:
:-> 4                 :-> 8                 1 <-:
                                                                  5 --:                 5 ----:-> 2           5 ----:-> 6
                                                                                        :-> 6                 :-> 7
                                                                                                              :-> 8
```

```
G1283                 G1284                 G1285                 G1286                 G1287                 G1288
4 ------- 7           4 ------- 6           4 ------- 8           4 ------- 8           4 ------- 7           4 ------- 5
2 -----> 6            2 -----> 5            2 -----> 2            2 -----> 6            2 -----> 3            2 -----> 3
3 <------ 5           3 <------ 4           3 <------ 1           3 <------ 1           3 <------ 2           3 <------ 2

6 <-:---- 9           6 <-:---- 8                                6 <-:---- 4           6 <-:---- 9           6 <-:---- 6
1 <-:                 1 <-:                 5 --:                 1 <-:                 1 <-:                 1 <-:
                                            6 <-:
5 ----:-> 1           5 ----:-> 1           1 <-:                 5 ----:-> 7           5 ----:-> 5           5 ----:-> 4
:-> 2                 :-> 7                                       :-> 9                 :-> 8                 :-> 7
:-> 8
:-> 10
```

```
G1289                 G1290                 G1291                 G1292                 G1293                 G1294
4 ------- 7           4 ------- 7           4 ------- 7           4 ------- 4           4 ------- 5           4 ------- 9
2 -----> 3            2 -----> 8            2 -----> 5            2 -----> 6            2 -----> 6            2 -----> 3
3 <------ 8           3 <------ 3           3 <------ 4           3 <------ 3           3 <------ 4           3 <------ 2

6 <-:---- 9           6 <-:---- 5           6 <-:---- 1           6 <-:---- 2           6 <-:---- 3           6 <-:---- 4
1 <-:                 1 <-:                 1 <-:                 1 <-:                 1 <-:                 1 <-:

5 ----:-> 1           5 ----:-> 4           5 ----:-> 3
:-> 5                 :-> 9
:-> 6
:-> 10
```

G1295	G1296	G1297	G1298	G1299	G1300
4 ------- 3 2 -----> 4 3 <----- 2 6 <-:---- 1 1 <-:	4 ------- 9 2 -----> 13 3 <----- 11 6 <-:---- 10 1 <-:	4 ------- 5 2 -----> 2 3 <----- 3 6 <-:---- 4 1 <-: 5 ----:-> 6 :-> 8	4 ------- 5 2 -----> 2 3 <----- 3 6 <-:---- 7 1 <-:	4 -----> 5 2 -----> 3 3 <----- 2 6 <-:---- 6 1 <-:	4 -----> 5 2 -----> 3 3 <----- 2 5 --: 6 <-: 1 <-:

G1301	G1302	G1303	G1304	G1305	G1306
4 ------- 4 2 -----> 5 3 <----- 2 6 <-:---- 1 1 <-:	4 ------- 2 2 -----> 4 3 <----- 3 6 <-:---- 6 1 <-:	4 ------- 7 3 <----- 2 5 --: 6 <-: 1 <-:	4 ------- 7 2 -----> 5 3 <----- 3 6 <-:---- 4 1 <-: 5 ----:-> 6 :-> 8	4 ------- 4 2 -----> 5 3 <----- 3 6 <-:---- 6 1 <-:	4 ------- 5 2 -----> 4 3 <----- 2 6 <-:---- 1 1 <-:

G1307	G1308	G1309	G1310	G1311	G1312

4 ------- 1
2 -----> 4
3 <----- 2
 	
6 <-:---- 3
1 <-:
 	
5 ----:-> 6
    :-> 8
	4 ------- 5
	2 -----> 2
	3 <----- 4
	
	6 <-:---- 1
	1 <-:
		4 ------- 2
		2 -----> 5
		3 <----- 3
		
		6 <-:---- 6
		1 <-:
			4 ------- 3
			2 -----> 1
			3 <----- 5
			
			6 <-:---- 8
			1 <-:
			
			5 ----:-> 2
			    :-> 7
				4 ------- 6
				2 -----> 8
				3 <----- 4
				
				6 <-:---- 1
				1 <-:
				
				5 ----:-> 2
				    :-> 7
					4 ------- 2
					2 -----> 3
					3 <----- 5
					
					6 <-:---- 4
					1 <-:

G1313	G1314	G1315	G1316	G1317	G1318
4 ------- 4 2 -----> 5 3 <----- 2 6 <-:---- 6 1 <-:	4 ------- 3 2 -----> 2 3 <----- 5 6 <-:---- 1 1 <-:	4 ------- 4 2 -----> 2 3 <----- 3 6 <-:---- 1 1 <-:	4 ------- 3 2 -----> 5 3 <----- 4 6 <-:---- 6 1 <-:	4 ------- 11 2 -----> 9 3 <----- 1 6 <-:---- 2 1 <-:	4 ------- 11 2 -----> 1 3 <----- 9 6 <----- 10 1 <----- 3 5 -----> 2

G1319	G1320	G1321	G1322	G1323	G1324
4 ------- 4 2 -----> 2 3 <----- 3 6 <-:---- 1 1 <-: 5 ----:-> 5	4 ------- 4 2 -----> 3 3 <----- 2 6 <-:---- 5 1 <-:	4 ------- 2 2 -----> 3 3 <----- 5 6 <-:---- 6 1 <-:	4 ------- 5 2 -----> 4 3 <----- 2 6 <-:---- 1 1 <-:	4 ------- 2 2 -----> 3 3 <----- 3 6 <-:---- 6 1 <-:	4 ------- 5 2 -----> 2 3 <----- 3 6 <-:---- 4 1 <-: 5 ----:-> 6

G1325	G1326	G1327	G1328	G1329	G1330

7 ------- 7
3 -----> 5
5 <----- 3
 	
4 -----> 6
6 <----- 4
	7 ------- 5
	3 -----> 7
	5 <----- 4
	
	4 ----:-> 2
	    :-> 6
	6 <----- 3
		7 ------- 3
		3 -----> 5
		5 <----- 4
		
		4 ----:-> 8
		    :-> 7
		    :-> 6
		6 <----- 2
			7 ------- 7
			3 -----> 6
			5 <----- 7
			
			4 ----:-> 8
			    :-> 5
			    :-> 10
			6 <----- 9
			    :-- 3
			    :-> 4
				7 ------- 6
				3 -----> 5
				5 <----- 4
				
				4 ----:-> 7
				    :-> 1
				6 <----- 8
					7 ------- 8
					3 -----> 2
					5 <----- 1
					
					4 --:
					6 <-:

G1331
7 ------- 8
3 ------> 6
5 <------ 1
 	
4 ----:-> 7
    :-> 9
6 <------ 4
	G1332
	7 ------- 7
	3 ------> 3
	5 <------ 2
	
	4 ----:-> 5
	    :-> 8
	6 <------ 9
		G1333
		7 ------- 5
		3 ------> 3
		5 <------ 2
		
		6 <------ 6
		4 ----:-> 4
		    :-> 7

G1334
7 ------- 7
3 ------> 3
5 <------ 4
 	
4 ----:-> 7
    :-> 6
    :-> 4
6 <------ 9
    :-- 5
    :-> 10
	G1335
	7 ------- 7
	3 ------> 8
	5 <------ 3
	
	6 <------ 5
	
	4 ----:-> 4
	    :-> 9
		G1336
		7 ------- 7
		3 ------> 5
		5 <------ 4
		
		4 ------> 3
		6 <------ 1

G1337 7 ------- 4 3 ------> 6 5 <------ 3 6 <------ 2 4 ----:-> 1 :-> 7	**G1338** 7 ------- 5 3 ------> 6 5 <------ 4 4 ------> 2 6 <------ 3	**G1339** 7 ------- 9 3 ------> 3 5 <------ 2 4 ------> 5 6 <------ 4
G1340 7 ------- 3 3 ------> 4 5 <------ 2 4 ------> 5 6 <------ 1	**G1341** 7 ------- 9 3 ------> 13 5 <------ 11 4 ------> 14 6 <------ 10	**G1342** 7 ------- 5 3 ------> 2 5 <------ 3 4 ----:-> 8 :- 6 6 <------ 4
G1343 7 ------- 5 3 ------> 2 5 <------ 3 4 ------> 8 6 <------ 7	**G1344** 7 ------- 5 3 ------> 3 5 <------ 2 6 <------ 6	**G1345** 7 ------- 5 3 ------> 3 5 <------ 2 4 --: 6 <-:
G1346 7 ------- 4 3 ------> 5 5 <------ 2 4 ------> 6 6 <------ 1	**G1347** 7 ------- 2 3 ------> 4 5 <------ 3 4 ------> 5 6 <------ 6	**G1348** 7 ------- 7 5 <------ 2 4 --: 6 <-:
G1349 7 ------- 7 3 ------> 5 5 <------ 3 4 ----:-> 8 :-> 6 6 <------ 4	**G1350** 7 ------- 4 3 ------> 5 5 <------ 3 4 ------> 2 6 <------ 6	**G1351** 7 ------- 5 3 ------> 4 5 <------ 2 4 ------> 6 6 <------ 1
G1352 7 ------- 1 3 ------> 4 5 <------ 2 4 ----:-> 6 :-> 8 6 <------ 3	**G1353** 7 ------- 5 3 ------> 2 5 <------ 4 6 <------ 1	**G1354** 7 ------- 2 3 ------> 5 5 <------ 3 4 ------> 1 6 <------ 6

G1355
7 ------- 3
3 ------> 1
5 <------ 5
 	
4 ------> 2
6 <------ 8
    :-- 4
    :-> 7
	G1356
	7 ------- 6
	3 ------> 8
	5 <------ 4
	
	4 ------> 7
	6 <------ 1
	    :-- 3
	    :-> 2
		G1357
		7 ------- 2
		3 ------> 3
		5 <------ 5
		
		6 <------ 4

G1358 7 ------- 4 3 ------> 5 5 <------ 2 4 ------> 1 6 <------ 6	**G1359** 7 ------- 3 3 ------> 2 5 <------ 5 4 ------> 6 6 <------ 1	**G1360** 7 ------- 4 3 ------> 2 5 <------ 3 4 ------> 6 6 <------ 1

G1361
7 ------- 3
3 ------> 5
5 <------ 4
 	
4 ------> 1
6 <------ 6
	G1362
	7 ------- 11
	3 ------> 9
	5 <------ 1
	
	4 ----:-> 10
	    :-> 3
	    :-> 12
	6 <------ 2
		G1363
		7 ------- 11
		3 ------> 1
		5 <------ 9
		
		6 <------ 3
		
		4 ----:-> 2
		    :-> 4

G1364 7 ------- 4 3 ------> 2 5 <------ 3 4 ------> 5 6 <------ 1	**G1365** 7 ------- 4 3 ------> 3 5 <------ 2 6 <------ 5	**G1366** 7 ------- 2 3 ------> 3 5 <------ 5 4 ------> 1 6 <------ 6

G1367
7 ------- 5
3 ------> 4
5 <------ 2
 	
4 ------> 3
6 <------ 1
	G1368
	7 ------- 2
	3 ------> 3
	5 <------ 5
	
	4 ------> 4
	6 <------ 6
		G1369
		7 ------- 5
		3 ------> 2
		5 <------ 3
		
		4 ----:-> 8
		    :-> 6
		6 <------ 4
			G1370
			2 <------ 3
			
			4 <-:---- 4
			11 <-:
			
			5 ----:-> 6
				G1371
				1 ------- 1
				7 ------- 7
				3 ------> 2
				2 <------ 3
				
				4 <-:---- 5
				11 <-:
				5 ----:-> 4
					G1372
					7 ------- 4
					3 ------> 3
					2 <------ 2
					
					4 <-:---- 5
					11 <-:
					
					5 ----:-> 1
					    :-> 6

G1373
7 ------- 5
3 ------> 7
2 <------ 4
 	
4 <-:---- 3
11 <-:
 	
5 ----:-> 2
    :-> 6
	G1374
	7 ------- 3
	3 ------> 5
	2 <------ 4
	
	4 <-:---- 1
	11 <-:
	
	5 ----:-> 6
	    :-> 7
	    :-> 8
		G1375
		1 ------- 4
		7 ------- 7
		3 ------> 6
		2 <------ 5
		
		4 <-:---- 3
		11 <-:
		
		5 ----:-> 1
		    :-> 2
		    :-> 8
		
		6 ----:-> 10
			G1376
			1 ------- 3
			7 ------- 6
			3 ------> 5
			2 <------ 4
			
			4 <-:---- 2
			11 <-:
			
			5 ----:-> 1
			    :-> 7
				G1377
				7 ------- 8
				3 ------> 2
				2 <------ 1
				
				5 --:
				4 <-:
				11 <-:
					G1378
					7 ------- 8
					3 ------> 6
					2 <------ 1
					
					4 <-:---- 2
					11 <-:
					
					5 ----:-> 7
					    :-> 9

G1379
7 ------- 7
3 ------> 3
2 <------ 2
 	
4 <-:---- 4
11 <-:
 	
5 ----:-> 5
    :-> 8
	G1380
	7 ------- 5
	3 ------> 3
	2 <------ 2
	
	4 <-:---- 1
	11 <-:
	
	5 ----:-> 4
	    :-> 7
		G1381
		1 ------- 2
		7 ------- 7
		2 ------> 3
		3 <------ 8
		
		11 ----:-> 5
		     :-> 6
		     :-> 1
		5 <-:---- 9
		6 <-:
		8 <-:
		
		4 ----:-> 10
			G1382
			1 ------- 2
			7 ------- 7
			2 ------> 8
			3 <------ 3
			
			5 <-:---- 5
			6 <-:
			8 <-:
			
			4 ----:-> 4
			    :-> 9
				G1383
				7 ------- 7
				2 ------> 5
				3 <------ 4
				
				11 ------> 3
				5 <-:---- 1
				6 <-:
				8 <-:
					G1384
					7 ------- 4
					2 ------> 6
					3 <------ 3
					
					5 <-:---- 2
					6 <-:
					8 <-:
					
					4 ----:-> 1
					    :-> 7

G1385 7 ------- 5 2 ------> 6 3 <------ 4 11 ------> 2 5 <-:---- 3 6 <-: 8 <-:	**G1386** 7 ------- 9 2 ------> 3 3 <------ 2 11 ------> 5 5 <-:---- 4 6 <-: 8 <-:	**G1387** 7 ------- 3 2 ------> 4 3 <------ 2 11 ------> 5 5 <-:---- 1 6 <-: 8 <-:	**G1388** 7 ------- 9 3 ------> 13 2 <------ 11 4 <-:---- 10 11 <-: 5 ----:-> 14	**G1389** 7 ------- 5 3 ------> 2 2 <------ 3 4 <-:---- 4 11 <-: 5 ----:-> 6 :-> 8	**G1390** 7 ------- 5 3 ------> 2 2 <------ 3 4 <-:---- 7 11 <-: 5 ----:-> 8
G1391 7 ------- 5 3 ------> 3 2 <------ 2 4 <-:---- 6 11 <-:	**G1392** 7 ------- 5 3 ------> 3 2 <------ 2 5 --: 4 <-: 11 <-:	**G1393** 1 ------- 3 7 ------- 4 3 ------> 5 2 <------ 2 4 <-:---- 1 11 <-: 5 ----:-> 6	**G1394** 1 ------- 1 7 ------- 2 3 ------> 4 2 <------ 3 4 <-:---- 6 11 <-: 5 ----:-> 5	**G1395** 1 ------- 1 7 ------- 7 2 <------ 2 5 --: 4 <-: 11 <-:	**G1396** 1 ------- 1 7 ------- 7 3 ------> 5 2 <------ 3 4 <-:---- 2 11 <-: 5 ----:-> 6 :-> 8

```
G1397                  G1398                  G1399                  G1400                  G1401                  G1402
7 ------- 4            7 ------- 5            7 ------- 1            1 ------- 3            1 ------- 4            7 ------- 3
3 ------> 5            3 ------> 4            3 ------> 4            7 ------- 5            7 ------- 2            3 ------> 1
2 <------ 3            2 <------ 2            2 <------ 2            3 ------> 2            3 ------> 5            2 <------ 5
                                                                    2 <------ 4            2 <------ 3
4 <-:----- 6          5 --:                  4 <-:----- 3                                 4 <-:----- 6          4 <-:----- 4
11 <-:                 4 <-:                 11 <-:                 5 --:                 11 <-:                11 <-:
                      11 <-:                                        4 <-:
5 ----:-> 2                                  5 ----:-> 6           11 <-:                 5 ----:-> 1           5 ----:-> 2
                      6 ----:-> 6               :-> 8                                                              :-> 7
```

```
G1403                  G1404                  G1405                  G1406                  G1407                  G1408
7 ------- 6            7 ------- 2            1 ------- 3            1 ------- 4            7 ------- 4            7 ------- 3
3 ------> 8            3 ------> 3            7 ------- 4            7 ------- 4            3 ------> 2            3 ------> 5
2 <------ 4            2 <------ 5            3 ------> 5            3 ------> 2            2 <------ 3            2 <------ 4
                                             2 <------ 2            2 <------ 5
4 <-:----- 3          4 <-:----- 4                                                        4 <-:----- 1          4 <-:----- 6
11 <-:                11 <-:                 4 <-:----- 6          4 <-:----- 1           11 <-:                11 <-:
                                             11 <-:                11 <-:
5 ----:-> 2                                                                               5 ----:-> 6           5 ----:-> 1
   :-> 7                                     5 ----:-> 1           5 ----:-> 6
```

```
G1409                  G1410                  G1411                  G1412                  G1413                  G1414
7 ------- 11           7 ------- 11           7 ------- 4            7 ------- 4            7 ------- 2            7 ------- 5
3 ------> 9            3 ------> 1            3 ------> 2            3 ------> 3            3 ------> 3            3 ------> 4
2 <------ 1            2 <------ 9            2 <------ 3            2 <------ 2            2 <------ 5            2 <------ 2

4 <-:----- 2          4 <-:----- 3          4 <-:----- 1          4 <-:----- 5          4 <-:----- 6          4 <-:----- 1
11 <-:                11 <-:                11 <-:                11 <-:                11 <-:                11 <-:

5 ----:-> 3           5 ----:-> 2           5 ----:-> 5                                 5 ----:-> 1           5 ----:-> 3
   :-> 10                :-> 4                                                                                   :-> 6
   :-> 12
```

```
G1415                  G1416                  G1417                  G1418                  G1419                  G1420
7 ------- 2            7 ------- 5            5 ------- 5            5 ------- 3            5 ------- 7            5 ------- 6
3 ------> 3            3 ------> 2            4 ------> 7            4 ------> 5            4 ------> 6            4 ------> 5
2 <------ 5            2 <------ 3            7 <------ 4            7 <------ 4            7 <------ 5            7 <------ 4

4 <-:----- 6          4 <-:----- 4          3 ----:-> 2           3 ----:-> 8           3 ----:-> 8           3 ----:-> 7
11 <-:                11 <-:                   :-> 6                  :-> 7                  :-> 2                  :-> 1
                                             2 <-:----- 3             :-> 6                  :-> 10                 :-> 8
5 ----:-> 1           5 ----:-> 6           6 <-:                 2 <-:----- 2          2 <-:----- 9          2 <-:-----
   :-> 4                 :-> 8                                     6 <-:                 6 <-:                 6 <-:

                                                                                         8 ----:-> 1
```

```
G1421                  G1422                  G1423                  G1424                  G1425                  G1426
5 ------- 8            5 ------- 8            5 ------- 7            5 ------- 5            5 ------- 7            5 ------- 7
4 ------> 2            4 ------> 6            4 ------> 3            4 ------> 3            4 ------> 3            4 ------> 8
7 <------ 1            7 <------ 1            7 <------ 2            7 <------ 2            7 <------ 8            7 <------ 3

8 --:                 3 ----:-> 7           3 ----:-> 5           2 <-:----- 6          3 ----:-> 5           2 <-:----- 5
2 <-:                    :-> 9                 :-> 8              6 <-:                    :-> 6              6 <-:
6 <-:                 2 <-:----- 4          2 <-:----- 9                                    :-> 1
                      6 <-:                 6 <-:                 8 ----:-> 4           2 <-:----- 9          8 ----:-> 4
                                                                    :-> 7              6 <-:                    :-> 9

                                                                                         8 ----:-> 10
```

G1427 5 ------- 7 4 ------> 5 7 <------ 4 3 ------> 3 2 <-:---- 1 6 <-:	**G1428** 5 ------- 4 4 ------> 6 7 <------ 3 2 <-:---- 2 6 <-: 8 ----:-> 1 :-> 7	**G1429** 5 ------- 5 4 ------> 6 7 <------ 4 3 ------> 2 6 <-: 2 <-:
G1430 5 ------- 9 4 ------> 3 7 <------ 2 3 ------> 5 2 <-:---- 4 6 <-:	**G1431** 5 ------- 3 4 ------> 4 7 <------ 2 3 ------> 5 2 <-:---- 1 6 <-:	**G1432** 5 ------- 9 4 ------> 13 7 <------ 11 3 ------> 14 2 <-:---- 10 6 <-:
G1433 5 ------- 5 4 ------> 2 7 <------ 3 3 ----:-> 8 :-> 6 2 <-:---- 4 6 <-:	**G1434** 5 ------- 5 4 ------> 2 7 <------ 3 3 ------> 8 2 <-:---- 7 6 <-:	**G1435** 5 ------- 5 4 ------> 3 7 <------ 2 2 <-:---- 6 6 <-:
G1436 5 ------- 5 4 ------> 3 7 <------ 2 8 --: 2 <-: 6 <-:	**G1437** 5 ------- 4 4 ------> 5 7 <------ 2 3 ------> 6 2 <-:---- 1 6 <-:	**G1438** 5 ------- 2 4 ------> 4 7 <------ 3 3 ------> 5 2 <-:---- 6 6 <-:
G1439 5 ------- 7 7 <------ 2 8 --: 2 <-: 6 <-:	**G1440** 5 ------- 7 4 ------> 5 7 <------ 3 3 ----:-> 8 :-> 6 2 <-:---- 4 6 <-:	**G1441** 5 ------- 4 4 ------> 5 7 <------ 3 3 ------> 2 2 <-:---- 6 6 <-:
G1442 5 ------- 5 4 ------> 4 7 <------ 2 3 ------> 6 2 <-:---- 1 6 <-:	**G1443** 5 ------- 1 4 ------> 4 7 <------ 2 3 ----:-> 6 :-> 8 2 <-:---- 3 6 <-:	**G1444** 5 ------- 5 4 ------> 2 7 <------ 4 2 <-:---- 1 6 <-:
G1445 5 ------- 2 4 ------> 5 7 <------ 3 3 ------> 1 2 <-:---- 6 6 <-:	**G1446** 5 ------- 3 4 ------> 1 7 <------ 5 3 ------> 2 2 <-:---- 8 6 <-: 8 ----:-> 7	**G1447** 5 ------- 6 4 ------> 8 7 <------ 4 3 ------> 7 2 <-:---- 1 6 <-: 8 ----:-> 2
G1448 5 ------- 2 4 ------> 3 7 <------ 5 2 <-:---- 4 6 <-:	**G1449** 5 ------- 4 4 ------> 5 7 <------ 2 3 ------> 1 2 <-:---- 6 6 <-:	**G1450** 5 ------- 3 4 ------> 2 7 <------ 5 3 ------> 6 2 <-:---- 1 6 <-:

G1451
5 ------- 4
4 ------> 2
7 <------ 3
 	
3 ------> 6
2 <-:---- 1
6 <-:
	G1452
	5 ------- 3
	4 ------> 5
	7 <------ 4
	
	3 ------> 1
	2 <-:---- 6
	6 <-:
		G1453
		5 ------- 11
		4 ------> 9
		7 <------ 1
		
		3 ----:-> 10
		    :-> 3
		    :-> 12
		2 <-:---- 2
		6 <-:

G1454 5 ------- 11 4 ------> 1 7 <------ 9 2 <-:---- 3 6 <-: 8 ----:-> 2 :-> 4	**G1455** 5 ------- 4 4 ------> 2 7 <------ 3 3 ------> 5 2 <-:---- 1 6 <-:	**G1456** 5 ------- 4 4 ------> 3 7 <------ 2 2 <-:---- 5 6 <-:
G1457 5 ------- 2 4 ------> 3 7 <------ 5 3 ------> 1 2 <-:---- 6 6 <-:	**G1458** 5 ------- 5 4 ------> 4 7 <------ 2 3 ------> 3 2 <-:---- 1 6 <-: 8 ----:-> 6	**G1459** 5 ------- 2 4 ------> 3 7 <------ 5 3 ------> 4 2 <-:---- 6 6 <-: 8 ----:-> 1

G1460
5 ------- 5
4 ------> 2
7 <------ 3
 	
3 ----:-> 8
    :-> 6
2 <-:---- 4
6 <-:
	G1461
	3 ------- 3
	4 ------> 5
	5 <------ 4
	
	2 ----:-> 8
	    :-> 7
	    :-> 6
	6 <-:---- 2
	7 <-:
	8 <-:
		G1462
		3 ------- 7
		4 ------> 6
		5 <------ 5
		
		2 ----:-> 8
		    :-> 2
		    :-> 10
		6 <-:---- 9
		7 <-:
		8 <-:
		
		1 ----:-> 1

```
G1463                 G1464                 G1465                 G1466                 G1467                 G1468
3 ------- 6           3 ------- 8           3 ------- 8           3 ------- 7           3 ------- 5           3 ------- 7
4 ------> 5           4 ------> 2           4 ------> 6           4 ------> 3           4 ------> 3           4 ------> 3
5 <------ 4           5 <------ 1           5 <------ 1           5 <------ 2           5 <------ 2           5 <------ 8

2 ----:-> 7                                 2 ----:-> 7           2 ----:-> 5           6 <-:---- 6           2 ----:-> 5
     :-> 1                                       :-> 9                :-> 8           7 <-:                      :-> 6
6 <-:---- 8           1 --:                 6 <-:---- 4           6 <-:---- 9           8 <-:                      :-> 1
7 <-:                 6 <-:                 7 <-:                 7 <-:                                       6 <-:---- 9
8 <-:                 7 <-:                 8 <-:                 8 <-:                 1 ----:-> 4           7 <-:
                      8 <-:                                                                 :-> 7           8 <-:

                                                                                                            1 ----:-> 10

G1469                 G1470                 G1471                 G1472                 G1473                 G1474
3 ------- 7           3 ------- 7           3 ------- 4           3 ------- 5           3 ------- 9           3 ------- 3
4 ------> 8           4 ------> 5           4 ------> 6           4 ------> 6           4 ------> 3           4 ------> 4
5 <------ 3           5 <------ 4           5 <------ 3           5 <------ 4           5 <------ 2           5 <------ 2

6 <-:---- 5           2 ------> 3           6 <-:---- 2           2 ----:-> 2           2 ------> 5           2 ------> 5
7 <-:                 6 <-:---- 1           7 <-:                 8 <-:---- 3           6 <-:---- 4           6 <-:---- 1
8 <-:                 7 <-:                 8 <-:                 7 <-:                 7 <-:                 7 <-:
                      8 <-:                                       6 <-:                 8 <-:                 8 <-:
1 ----:-> 4                                 1 ----:-> 1
     :-> 9                                       :-> 7

G1475                 G1476                 G1477                 G1478                 G1479                 G1480
3 ------- 9           3 ------- 5           3 ------- 5           3 ------- 5           3 ------- 5           3 ------- 4
4 ------> 13          4 ------> 2           4 ------> 2           4 ------> 3           4 ------> 3           4 ------> 5
5 <------ 11          5 <------ 3           5 <------ 3           5 <------ 2           5 <------ 2           5 <------ 2

2 ------> 14          2 ----:-> 8           2 ------> 8           6 <-:---- 6           1 --:                 2 ------> 6
6 <-:---- 10               :-> 6           6 <-:---- 7           7 <-:                 6 <-:                 6 <-:---- 1
7 <-:                 6 <-:---- 4           7 <-:                 8 <-:                 7 <-:                 7 <-:
8 <-:                 7 <-:                 8 <-:                                       8 <-:                 8 <-:
                      8 <-:

G1481                 G1482                 G1483                 G1484                 G1485                 G1486
3 ------- 2           3 ------- 7           3 ------- 7           3 ------- 4           3 ------- 5           3 ------- 1
4 ------> 4           5 <------ 2           4 ------> 5           4 ------> 5           4 ------> 4           4 ------> 4
5 <------ 3                                 5 <------ 3           5 <------ 3           5 <------ 2           5 <------ 2

2 ------> 5           1 --:                 2 ----:-> 8           2 ------> 2           2 ------> 6           2 ----:-> 6
6 <-:---- 6           6 <-:                      :-> 6           6 <-:---- 6           6 <-:---- 1                :-> 8
7 <-:                 7 <-:                 6 <-:---- 4           7 <-:                 7 <-:                 6 <-:---- 3
8 <-:                 8 <-:                 7 <-:                 8 <-:                 8 <-:                 7 <-:
                                            8 <-:                                                            8 <-:

G1487                 G1488                 G1489                 G1490                 G1491                 G1492
3 ------- 5           3 ------- 2           3 ------- 3           3 ------- 6           3 ------- 2           3 ------- 4
4 ------> 2           4 ------> 5           4 ------> 1           4 ------> 8           4 ------> 3           4 ------> 5
5 <------ 4           5 <------ 3           5 <------ 5           5 <------ 4           5 <------ 5           5 <------ 2

6 <-:---- 1           2 ------> 1           2 ------> 2           2 ------> 7           6 <-:---- 4           2 ------> 1
7 <-:                 6 <-:---- 6           6 <-:---- 8           6 <-:---- 1           7 <-:                 6 <-:---- 6
8 <-:                 7 <-:                 7 <-:                 7 <-:                 8 <-:                 7 <-:
                      8 <-:                 8 <-:                 8 <-:                                       8 <-:

                                            1 ----:-> 7           1 ----:-> 2
```

```
  G1493                  G1494                  G1495                  G1496                  G1497                  G1498
3 ------- 3            3 ------- 4            3 ------- 3            3 ------- 11           3 ------- 11           3 ------- 4
4 -----> 2            4 -----> 2            4 -----> 5            4 -----> 9            4 -----> 1            4 -----> 2
5 <------ 5            5 <------ 3            5 <------ 4            5 <------ 1            5 <------ 9            5 <------ 3

2 -----> 6            2 -----> 6            2 -----> 1            2 ----:-> 10          6 <-:---- 3            2 -----> 5
6 <-:---- 1            6 <-:---- 1            6 <-:---- 6                :-> 3            7 <-:                  6 <-:---- 1
7 <-:                  7 <-:                  7 <-:                      :-> 12           8 <-:                  7 <-:
8 <-:                  8 <-:                  8 <-:                 6 <-:---- 2                                   8 <-:
                                                                     7 <-:                  1 ----:-> 2
                                                                     8 <-:                      :-> 4


  G1499                  G1500                  G1501                  G1502                  G1503                  G1504
3 ------- 4            3 ------- 2            3 ------- 5            3 ------- 2            3 ------- 5            7 ------- 7
4 -----> 3            4 -----> 3            4 -----> 4            4 -----> 3            4 -----> 2            5 -----> 6
5 <------ 2            5 <------ 5            5 <------ 2            5 <------ 5            5 <------ 3            6 <------ 5

6 <-:---- 5            2 -----> 1            2 -----> 3            2 -----> 4            2 ----:-> 8            9 ----:-> 8
7 <-:                  6 <-:---- 6            6 <-:---- 1            6 <-:---- 6                :-> 6                :-> 2
8 <-:                  7 <-:                  7 <-:                  7 <-:                  6 <-:---- 4                :-> 10
                       8 <-:                  8 <-:                  8 <-:                  7 <-:                 10 <-:---- 9
                                                                                            8 <-:                  2 <-:
                                              1 ----:-> 6            1 ----:-> 1                                   8 <-:

                                                                                                                  3 ----:-> 1


  G1505                  G1506                  G1507                  G1508                  G1509                  G1510
7 ------- 6            7 ------- 8            7 ------- 8            7 ------- 7            7 ------- 5            7 ------- 7
5 -----> 5            5 -----> 2            5 -----> 6            5 -----> 3            5 -----> 3            5 -----> 3
6 <------ 4            6 <------ 1            6 <------ 1            6 <------ 2            6 <------ 2            6 <------ 8

9 ----:-> 7                                   9 ----:-> 7            9 ----:-> 5           10 <-:---- 6            9 ----:-> 5
    :-> 1            3 --:                      :-> 9                  :-> 8             2 <-:                      :-> 6
10 <-:---- 8          10 <-:                 10 <-:---- 4           10 <-:---- 9            8 <-:                      :-> 1
2 <-:                  2 <-:                  2 <-:                  2 <-:                                        10 <-:---- 9
8 <-:                  8 <-:                  8 <-:                  8 <-:                  3 ----:-> 4            2 <-:
                                                                                                :-> 7            8 <-:

                                                                                                                  3 ----:-> 10


  G1511                  G1512                  G1513                  G1514                  G1515                  G1516
7 ------- 7            7 ------- 7            7 ------- 4            7 ------- 5            7 ------- 9            7 ------- 3
5 -----> 8            5 -----> 5            5 -----> 6            5 -----> 6            5 -----> 3            5 -----> 4
6 <------ 3            6 <------ 4            6 <------ 3            6 <------ 4            6 <------ 2            6 <------ 2

10 <-:---- 5           9 -----> 3           10 <-:---- 2            9 -----> 2            9 -----> 5            9 -----> 5
2 <-:                 10 <-:---- 1           2 <-:                  8 <-:---- 3           10 <-:---- 4           10 <-:---- 1
8 <-:                  2 <-:                  8 <-:                  2 <-:                  2 <-:                  2 <-:
                       8 <-:                                        10 <-:                 8 <-:                  8 <-:
3 ----:-> 4                                   3 ----:-> 1
    :-> 9                                         :-> 7


  G1517                  G1518                  G1519                  G1520                  G1521                  G1522
7 ------- 9            7 ------- 5            7 ------- 5            7 ------- 5            7 ------- 5            7 ------- 4
5 -----> 13           5 -----> 2            5 -----> 2            5 -----> 3            5 -----> 3            5 -----> 5
6 <------ 11           6 <------ 3            6 <------ 3            6 <------ 2            6 <------ 2            6 <------ 2

9 -----> 14           9 ----:-> 8            9 -----> 8           10 <-:---- 6                                   9 -----> 6
10 <-:---- 10              :-> 6            10 <-:---- 7            2 <-:                  3 --:                 10 <-:---- 1
2 <-:                 10 <-:---- 4           2 <-:                  8 <-:                 10 <-:                 2 <-:
8 <-:                  2 <-:                  8 <-:                                        2 <-:                  8 <-:
                       8 <-:                                                               8 <-:
```

G1523
7 ------- 2
5 ------> 4
6 <------ 3
 	
9 ------> 5
10 <-:----- 6
2 <-:
8 <-:
	G1524
	7 ------- 7
	6 <------ 2
	
	3 --:
	10 <-:
	2 <-:
	8 <-:
		G1525
		7 ------- 7
		5 ------> 5
		6 <------ 3
		9 ----:-> 8
		    :-> 6
		10 <-:----- 4
		2 <-:
		8 <-:
			G1526
			7 ------- 4
			5 ------> 5
			6 <------ 3
			9 ------> 2
			10 <-:----- 6
			2 <-:
			8 <-:
				G1527
				7 ------- 5
				5 ------> 4
				6 <------ 2
				9 ------> 6
				10 <-:----- 1
				2 <-:
				8 <-:
					G1528
					7 ------- 1
					5 ------> 4
					6 <------ 2
					9 ----:-> 6
					    :-> 8
					10 <-:----- 3
					2 <-:
					8 <-:

G1529 7 ------- 5 5 ------> 2 6 <------ 4 10 <-:----- 1 2 <-: 8 <-:	**G1530** 7 ------- 2 5 ------> 5 6 <------ 3 9 ------> 1 10 <-:----- 6 2 <-: 8 <-:	**G1531** 7 ------- 3 5 ------> 1 6 <------ 5 9 ------> 2 10 <-:----- 8 2 <-: 8 <-: 3 ----:-> 7	**G1532** 7 ------- 6 5 ------> 8 6 <------ 4 9 ------> 7 10 <-:----- 1 2 <-: 8 <-: 3 ----:-> 2	**G1533** 7 ------- 2 5 ------> 3 6 <------ 5 10 <-:----- 4 2 <-: 8 <-:	**G1534** 7 ------- 4 5 ------> 5 6 <------ 2 9 ------> 1 10 <-:----- 6 2 <-: 8 <-:

G1535
7 ------- 3
5 ------> 2
6 <------ 5
9 ------> 6
10 <-:----- 1
2 <-:
8 <-:
	G1536
	7 ------- 4
	5 ------> 2
	6 <------ 3
	9 ------> 6
	10 <-:----- 1
	2 <-:
	8 <-:
		G1537
		7 ------- 3
		5 ------> 5
		6 <------ 4
		9 ------> 1
		10 <-:----- 6
		2 <-:
		8 <-:
			G1538
			7 ------- 11
			5 ------> 9
			6 <------ 1
			9 ----:-> 10
			    :-> 3
			    :-> 12
			10 <-:----- 2
			2 <-:
			8 <-:
				G1539
				7 ------- 11
				5 ------> 1
				6 <------ 9
				10 <-:----- 3
				2 <-:
				8 <-:
				
				3 ----:-> 2
				    :-> 4
					G1540
					7 ------- 4
					5 ------> 2
					6 <------ 3
					9 ------> 5
					10 <-:----- 1
					2 <-:
					8 <-:

G1541
7 ------- 4
5 ------> 3
6 <------ 2
 	
10 <-:----- 5
2 <-:
8 <-:
	G1542
	7 ------- 2
	5 ------> 3
	6 <------ 5
	9 ------> 1
	10 <-:----- 6
	2 <-:
	8 <-:
		G1543
		7 ------- 5
		5 ------> 4
		6 <------ 2
		9 ------> 3
		10 <-:----- 1
		2 <-:
		8 <-:
		
		3 ----:-> 6
			G1544
			7 ------- 2
			5 ------> 3
			6 <------ 5
			9 ------> 4
			10 <-:----- 6
			2 <-:
			8 <-:
			
			3 ----:-> 1
				G1545
				7 ------- 5
				5 ------> 2
				6 <------ 3
				9 ----:-> 8
				    :-> 6
				10 <-:----- 4
				2 <-:
				8 <-:
					G1546
					7 ------- 7
					8 ------> 3
					3 <------ 8
					9 ----:-> 5
					    :-> 6
					    :-> 1
					1 <-:----- 9
					6 <-:
					5 <-:
					
					4 ----:-> 10

G1547
7 ------- 7
8 ------> 8
3 <------ 3
1 <-:----- 5
6 <-:
5 <-:
 	
4 ----:-> 4
    :-> 9
	G1548
	7 ------- 7
	8 ------> 5
	3 <------ 4
	9 ------> 3
	1 <-:----- 1
	6 <-:
	5 <-:
		G1549
		7 ------- 4
		8 ------> 6
		3 <------ 3
		1 <-:----- 2
		6 <-:
		5 <-:
		
		4 ----:-> 1
		    :-> 7
			G1550
			7 ------- 5
			8 ------> 6
			3 <------ 4
			9 ------> 2
			5 <-:----- 3
			6 <-:
			1 <-:
				G1551
				7 ------- 9
				8 ------> 3
				3 <------ 2
				9 ------> 5
				1 <-:----- 4
				6 <-:
				5 <-:
					G1552
					7 ------- 3
					8 ------> 4
					3 <------ 2
					9 ------> 5
					1 <-:----- 1
					6 <-:
					5 <-:

```
G1553                 G1554                 G1555                 G1556                 G1557                 G1558
7 ------- 9           7 ------- 5           7 ------- 5           7 ------- 5           7 ------- 5           7 ------- 4
8 ------> 13          8 ------> 2           8 ------> 2           8 ------> 3           8 ------> 3           8 ------> 5
3 <------ 11          3 <------ 3           3 <------ 3           3 <------ 2           3 <------ 2           3 <------ 2

9 ------> 14          9 ----:-> 8           9 ------> 8           1 <-:----- 6          7 ------- 5           9 ------> 6
1 <-:----- 10             :-> 6            1 <-:----- 7          6 <-:                4 --:                 1 <-:----- 1
6 <-:                 1 <-:----- 4          6 <-:                5 <-:                1 <-:                6 <-:
5 <-:                 6 <-:                5 <-:                                       6 <-:                5 <-:
                      5 <-:                                                            5 <-:


G1559                 G1560                 G1561                 G1562                 G1563                 G1564
7 ------- 2           7 ------- 7           7 ------- 7           7 ------- 4           7 ------- 5           7 ------- 1
8 ------> 4           3 <------ 2           8 ------> 5           8 ------> 5           8 ------> 4           8 ------> 4
3 <------ 3                                 3 <------ 3           3 <------ 3           3 <------ 2           3 <------ 2

9 ------> 5           4 --:                 9 ----:-> 8           9 ------> 2           9 ------> 6           9 ----:-> 6
1 <-:----- 6          1 <-:                    :-> 6             1 <-:----- 6          1 <-:----- 1             :-> 8
6 <-:                6 <-:                1 <-:----- 4          6 <-:                6 <-:                1 <-:----- 3
5 <-:                5 <-:                6 <-:                5 <-:                5 <-:                6 <-:
                                            5 <-:                                                            5 <-:


G1565                 G1566                 G1567                 G1568                 G1569                 G1570
7 ------- 5           7 ------- 2           7 ------- 3           7 ------- 6           7 ------- 2           7 ------- 4
8 ------> 2           8 ------> 5           8 ------> 1           8 ------> 8           8 ------> 3           8 ------> 5
3 <------ 4           3 <------ 3           3 <------ 5           3 <------ 4           3 <------ 5           3 <------ 2

1 <-:----- 1          9 ------> 1           9 ------> 2           9 ------> 7           1 <-:----- 4          9 ------> 1
6 <-:                1 <-:----- 6          1 <-:----- 8          1 <-:----- 1          6 <-:                1 <-:----- 6
5 <-:                6 <-:                6 <-:                6 <-:                5 <-:                6 <-:
                      5 <-:                5 <-:                5 <-:                                       5 <-:
                                            4 ----:-> 7          4 ----:-> 2


G1571                 G1572                 G1573                 G1574                 G1575                 G1576
7 ------- 3           7 ------- 4           7 ------- 3           7 ------- 11          7 ------- 11         7 ------- 4
8 ------> 2           8 ------> 2           8 ------> 5           8 ------> 9           8 ------> 1           8 ------> 2
3 <------ 5           3 <------ 3           3 <------ 4           3 <------ 1           3 <------ 9           3 <------ 3

9 ------> 6           9 ------> 6           9 ------> 1           9 ----:-> 10          1 <-:----- 3          9 ------> 5
1 <-:----- 1          1 <-:----- 1          1 <-:----- 6             :-> 3             6 <-:                1 <-:----- 1
6 <-:                6 <-:                6 <-:                    :-> 12            5 <-:                6 <-:
5 <-:                5 <-:                5 <-:                1 <-:----- 2                                5 <-:
                                                               6 <-:                4 ----:-> 2
                                                               5 <-:                    :-> 4


G1577                 G1578                 G1579                 G1580                 G1581                 G1582
7 ------- 4           7 ------- 2           7 ------- 5           7 ------- 2           7 ------- 5           6 ------- 6
8 ------> 3           8 ------> 3           8 ------> 4           8 ------> 3           8 ------> 2           4 ------> 5
3 <------ 2           3 <------ 5           3 <------ 2           3 <------ 5           3 <------ 3           5 <------ 4

1 <-:----- 5          9 ------> 1           9 ------> 3           9 ------> 4           9 ----:-> 8           8 ----:-> 7
6 <-:                1 <-:----- 6          1 <-:----- 1          1 <-:----- 6             :-> 6                 :-> 1
5 <-:                6 <-:                6 <-:                6 <-:                1 <-:----- 4          7 <-:----- 8
                      5 <-:                5 <-:                5 <-:                6 <-:                1 <-:
                                            4 ----:-> 6          4 ----:-> 1          5 <-:
```

```
G1583                 G1584                 G1585                 G1586                 G1587                 G1588
6 ------- 8           6 ------- 8           6 ------- 7           6 ------- 5           6 ------- 7           6 ------- 7
4 ------> 2           4 ------> 6           4 ------> 3           4 ------> 3           4 ------> 3           4 ------> 8
5 <----- 1            5 <----- 1            5 <----- 2            5 <----- 2            5 <----- 8            5 <----- 3

2 --:                 8 ----:-> 7           8 ----:-> 5           7 <-:---- 6           8 ----:-> 5           7 <-:---- 5
7 <-:                       :-> 9                 :-> 8           1 <-:                       :-> 6           1 <-:
1 <-:                 7 <-:----- 4          7 <-:----- 9                                      :-> 1
                      1 <-:                 1 <-:                 2 ----:-> 4           7 <-:----- 9          2 ----:-> 4
                                                                        :-> 7          1 <-:                       :-> 9

                                                                                       2 ----:-> 10


G1589                 G1590                 G1591                 G1592                 G1593                 G1594
6 ------- 7           6 ------- 4           6 ------- 5           6 ------- 9           6 ------- 3           6 ------- 9
4 ------> 5           4 ------> 6           4 ------> 6           4 ------> 3           4 ------> 4           4 ------ 13
5 <----- 4            5 <----- 3            5 <----- 4            5 <----- 2            5 <----- 2            5 <----- 11

8 ------> 3           7 <-:---- 2           8 ------> 2           8 ------> 5           8 ------> 5           8 ------> 14
7 <-:----- 1          1 <-:                 1 <-:                 7 <-:----- 4          7 <-:---- 1           7 <-:---- 10
1 <-:                                        7 <-:                1 <-:                 1 <-:                 1 <-:
                      2 ----:-> 1
                            :-> 7


G1595                 G1596                 G1597                 G1598                 G1599                 G1600
6 ------- 5           6 ------- 5           6 ------- 5           6 ------- 5           6 ------- 4           6 ------- 2
4 ------> 2           4 ------> 2           4 ------> 3           4 ------> 3           4 ------> 5           4 ------> 4
5 <----- 3            5 <----- 3            5 <----- 2            5 <----- 2            5 <----- 2            5 <----- 3

8 ----:-> 8           8 ------> 8           7 <-:---- 6          2 --:                 8 ------> 6           8 ------> 5
      :-> 6           7 <-:---- 7           1 <-:                7 <-:                 7 <-:----- 1          7 <-:---- 6
7 <-:----- 4          1 <-:                                      1 <-:                 1 <-:                 1 <-:
1 <-:


G1601                 G1602                 G1603                 G1604                 G1605                 G1606
6 ------- 7           6 ------- 7           6 ------- 4           6 ------- 5           6 ------- 1           6 ------- 5
5 <----- 2            4 ------> 5           4 ------> 5           4 ------> 4           4 ------> 4           4 ------> 2
                      5 <----- 3            5 <----- 3            5 <----- 2            5 <----- 2            5 <----- 4
2 --:
7 <-:                 8 ----:-> 8           8 ------> 2           8 ------> 6           8 ----:-> 6           7 <-:---- 1
1 <-:                       :-> 6           7 <-:---- 6           7 <-:---- 1                 :-> 8           1 <-:
                      7 <-:----- 4          1 <-:                 1 <-:                 7 <-:----- 3
                      1 <-:                                                             1 <-:


G1607                 G1608                 G1609                 G1610                 G1611                 G1612
6 ------- 2           6 ------- 3           6 ------- 6           6 ------- 2           6 ------- 4           6 ------- 3
4 ------> 5           4 ------> 1           4 ------> 8           4 ------> 3           4 ------> 5           4 ------> 2
5 <----- 3            5 <----- 5            5 <----- 4            5 <----- 5            5 <----- 2            5 <----- 5

8 ------> 1           8 ------> 2           8 ------> 7           7 <-:---- 4           8 ------> 1           8 ------> 6
7 <-:----- 6          7 <-:----- 8          7 <-:---- 1           1 <-:                 7 <-:----- 6          7 <-:---- 1
1 <-:                 1 <-:                 1 <-:                                       1 <-:                 1 <-:

                      2 ----:-> 7           2 ----:-> 2


G1613                 G1614                 G1615                 G1616                 G1617                 G1618
6 ------- 4           6 ------- 3           6 ------- 11          6 ------- 11          6 ------- 4           6 ------- 4
4 ------> 2           4 ------> 5           4 ------> 9           4 ------> 1           4 ------> 2           4 ------> 3
5 <----- 3            5 <----- 4            5 <----- 1            5 <----- 9            5 <----- 3            5 <----- 2

8 ------> 6           8 ------> 1           8 ----:-> 10          7 <-:---- 3           8 ------> 5           7 <-:---- 5
7 <-:----- 1          7 <-:----- 6                :-> 3           1 <-:                 7 <-:---- 1           1 <-:
1 <-:                 1 <-:                       :-> 12                                1 <-:
                                             7 <-:----- 2         2 ----:-> 2
                                             1 <-:                      :-> 4
```

G1619
`6 ------- 2`
`4 ------> 3`
`5 <------ 5`
 	
`8 ------> 1`
`7 <-:----- 6`
`1 <-:`
	G1620
	`6 ------- 5`
	`4 ------> 4`
	`5 <------ 2`
	
	`8 ------> 3`
	`7 <-:----- 1`
	`1 <-:`
	
	`2 ----:-> 6`
		G1621
		`6 ------- 2`
		`4 ------> 3`
		`5 <------ 5`
		
		`8 ------> 4`
		`7 <-:----- 6`
		`1 <-:`
		
		`2 ----:-> 1`
			G1622
			`6 ------- 5`
			`4 ------> 2`
			`5 <------ 3`
			
			`8 ----:-> 8`
			`        :-> 6`
			`7 <-:----- 4`
			`1 <-:`
				G1623
				`8 ------- 8`
				`1 ------> 2`
				`2 <------ 1`
					G1624
					`8 ------- 8`
					`1 ------> 6`
					`2 <------ 1`
					
					`:-- 2`
					`:-> 7`
					`:-> 9`

G1625
`8 ------- 7`
`1 ------> 3`
`2 <------ 2`
 	
`:-- 4`
`:-> 5`
`:-> 8`
	G1626
	`8 ------- 5`
	`1 ------> 3`
	`2 <------ 2`
	
	`:-- 1`
	`:-> 4`
	`:-> 7`
		G1627
		`8 ------- 7`
		`1 ------> 3`
		`2 <------ 8`
		
		`:-- 4`
		`:-> 1`
		`:-> 5`
		`:-> 6`
		
		`:-- 9`
		`:-> 10`
			G1628
			`8 ------- 7`
			`1 ------> 8`
			`2 <------ 3`
			
			`:-- 1`
			`:-> 4`
			`:-> 9`
				G1629
				`8 ------- 7`
				`1 ------> 5`
				`2 <------ 4`
				
				`:-- 1`
				`:-> 3`
					G1630
					`8 ------- 4`
					`1 ------> 6`
					`2 <------ 3`
					
					`:-- 2`
					`:-> 5`
					`:-> 7`

G1631
`8 ------- 5`
`1 ------> 6`
`2 <------ 4`
 	
`:-- 3`
`:-> 2`
	G1632
	`8 ------- 9`
	`1 ------> 3`
	`2 <------ 2`
	
	`:-- 4`
	`:-> 5`
		G1633
		`8 ------- 3`
		`1 ------> 4`
		`2 <------ 2`
		
		`:-- 1`
		`:-> 5`
			G1634
			`8 ------- 9`
			`1 ------> 13`
			`2 <------ 11`
			
			`:-- 10`
			`:-> 14`
				G1635
				`8 ------- 5`
				`1 ------> 2`
				`2 <------ 3`
				
				`:-- 4`
				`:-> 6`
				`:-> 8`
					G1636
					`8 ------- 5`
					`1 ------> 2`
					`2 <------ 3`
					
					`:-- 7`
					`:-> 8`

G1637
`8 ------- 5`
`1 ------> 3`
`2 <------ 2`
	G1638
	`8 ------- 5`
	`1 ------> 3`
	`2 <------ 2`
		G1639
		`8 ------- 4`
		`1 ------> 5`
		`2 <------ 2`
		
		`:-- 1`
		`:-> 6`
			G1640
			`8 ------- 2`
			`1 ------> 4`
			`2 <------ 3`
			
			`:-- 6`
			`:-> 5`
				G1641
				`8 ------- 7`
				`2 <------ 2`
					G1642
					`8 ------- 7`
					`1 ------> 5`
					`2 <------ 3`
					
					`:-- 2`
					`:-> 6`
					`:-> 8`

G1643
`8 ------- 4`
`1 ------> 5`
`2 <------ 3`
 	
`:-- 6`
`:-> 2`
	G1644
	`8 ------- 5`
	`1 ------> 4`
	`2 <------ 2`
		G1645
		`8 ------- 1`
		`1 ------> 4`
		`2 <------ 2`
		
		`:-- 3`
		`:-> 6`
		`:-> 8`
			G1646
			`8 ------- 5`
			`1 ------> 2`
			`2 <------ 4`
				G1647
				`8 ------- 2`
				`1 ------> 5`
				`2 <------ 3`
				
				`:-- 6`
				`:-> 1`
					G1648
					`8 ------- 3`
					`1 ------> 1`
					`2 <------ 5`
					
					`:-- 4`
					`:-> 2`
					`:-> 7`

G1649
`8 ------- 6`
`1 ------> 8`
`2 <------ 4`
 	
`:-- 3`
`:-> 2`
`:-> 7`
	G1650
	`8 ------- 2`
	`1 ------> 3`
	`2 <------ 5`
		G1651
		`8 ------- 4`
		`1 ------> 5`
		`2 <------ 2`
		
		`:-- 6`
		`:-> 1`
			G1652
			`8 ------- 3`
			`1 ------> 2`
			`2 <------ 5`
			
			`:-- 1`
			`:-> 6`
				G1653
				`8 ------- 4`
				`1 ------> 2`
				`2 <------ 3`
				
				`:-- 1`
				`:-> 6`
					G1654
					`8 ------- 3`
					`1 ------> 5`
					`2 <------ 4`
					
					`:-- 6`
					`:-> 1`

```
 G1655                  G1656                  G1657                  G1658                  G1659                  G1660
8 ------- 11          8 ------- 11          8 ------- 4           8 ------- 4           8 ------- 2           8 ------- 5
1 ------> 9           1 ------> 1           1 ------> 2           1 ------> 3           1 ------> 3           1 ------> 4
2 <------ 1           2 <------ 9           2 <------ 3           2 <------ 2           2 <------ 5           2 <------ 2

   :-- 2                 :-- 3                 :-- 1                                       :-- 6                 :-- 1
   :-> 3                 :-> 2                 :-- 5                                       :-> 1                 :-> 3
   :-> 10                :-> 4                                                                                   :-> 6
   :-> 12


 G1661                  G1662                  G1663                  G1664                  G1665                  G1666
8 ------- 2           8 ------- 5           5 ------- 5           1 ------- 2           1 ------- 2           5 ------- 7
1 ------> 3           1 ------> 2           2 ------> 3           5 ------- 7           5 ------- 7           3 ------> 5
2 <------ 5           2 <------ 3           3 <------ 2           3 ------> 3           3 ------> 8           2 <------ 4
                                                                 2 <------ 8           2 <------ 3
   :-- 6                 :-- 4                                                                                4 ----:-> 3
   :-> 1                 :-> 6              7 <-:----- 1          4 ----:-> 5          8 <-:----- 5          8 <-:----- 1
   :-> 4                 :-> 8              4 <-:                      :-> 6           6 <-:                 6 <-:
                                            8 ----:-> 4          8 <-:----- 9          1 <-:                 1 <-:
                                                 :-> 7           6 <-:
                                                                 1 <-:                 7 ----:-> 4
                                                                                            :-> 9
                                                                 7 ----:-> 10


 G1667                  G1668                  G1669                  G1670                  G1671                  G1672
5 ------- 4           5 ------- 5           5 ------- 9           5 ------- 3           5 ------- o           5 ------- 5
3 ------- 6           3 ------- 6           3 ------> 3           3 ------> 4           2 ------> 13          2 ------> 2
2 <------ 3           2 <------ 4           2 <------ 2           2 <------ 2           3 <------ 11          3 <------ 3

8 <-:----- 2          4 ------- 2          4 ------> 5          4 ------> 5           7 <-:----- 10         7 <-:----- 4
6 <-:                 8 <-:----- 3         8 <-:----- 4         8 <-:----- 1          4 <-:                 4 <-:
1 <-:                 6 <-:                6 <-:                6 <-:
                      1 <-:                1 <-:                1 <-:                 8 ----:-> 14         8 ----:-> 6
7 ----:-> 1                                                                                                     :-> 8
     :-> 7


 G1673                  G1674                  G1675                  G1676                  G1677                  G1678
5 ------- 5           5 ------- 5           5 ------- 5           1 ------- 3           1 ------- 1           1 ------- 1
2 ------> 2           2 ------> 3           2 ------> 3           5 ------- 4           5 ------- 2           5 ------- 7
3 <------ 3           3 <------ 2           3 <------ 2           2 ------> 5           2 ------> 4           3 <------ 2
                                                                 3 <------ 2           3 <------ 3
7 <-:----- 7          7 <-:----- 6         8 --:                                                            8 --:
4 <-:                 4 <-:                7 <-:                 7 <-:----- 1          7 <-:----- 6         7 <-:
                                           4 <-:                4 <-:                 4 <-:                4 <-:
8 ----:-> 8
                                                                8 ----:-> 6          8 ----:-> 5


 G1679                  G1680                  G1681                  G1682                  G1683                  G1684
1 ------- 1           5 ------- 4           5 ------- 5           5 ------- 1           1 ------- 3           1 ------- 4
5 ------- 7           2 ------> 5           2 ------> 4           2 ------> 4           5 ------- 5           5 ------- 2
2 ------> 5           3 <------ 3           3 <------ 2           3 <------ 2           2 ------> 2           2 ------> 5
3 <------ 3                                                                            3 <------ 4           3 <------ 3
                      7 <-:----- 6         8 --:                7 <-:----- 3
7 <-:----- 2          4 <-:                7 <-:                4 <-:                 8 --:                 7 <-:----- 6
4 <-:                                       4 <-:                                      7 <-:                4 <-:
                      8 ----:-> 2                               8 ----:-> 6          4 <-:
8 ----:-> 6                                6 ----:-> 6               :-> 8                                 8 ----:-> 1
     :-> 8
```

```
      G1685                    G1686                    G1687                    G1688                    G1689                    G1690
5 ------- 3            5 ------- 6            5 ------- 2            1 ------- 3            1 ------- 4            5 ------- 4
2 ------> 1            2 ------> 8            2 ------> 3            5 ------- 4            5 ------- 3            2 ------> 2
3 <------ 5            3 <------ 4            3 <------ 5            2 ------> 5            2 ------> 2            3 <------ 3
                                                                    3 <------ 2            3 <------ 5

7 <-:---- 4            7 <-:---- 3            7 <-:---- 4                                                        7 <-:---- 1
4 <-:                  4 <-:                  4 <-:                  7 <-:---- 6            7 <-:---- 1            4 <-:
                                                                    4 <-:                  4 <-:
8 ----:-> 2            8 ----:-> 2                                                                               8 ----:-> 6
   :-> 7                  :-> 7                                     8 ----:-> 1            8 ----:-> 6
```

```
      G1691                    G1692                    G1693                    G1694                    G1695                    G1696
5 ------- 3            5 ------- 11           5 ------- 11           5 ------- 4            5 ------- 4            5 ------- 2
2 ------> 5            2 ------> 9            2 ------> 1            2 ------> 2            2 ------> 3            2 ------> 3
3 <------ 4            3 <------ 1            3 <------ 9            3 <------ 3            3 <------ 2            3 <------ 5

7 <-:---- 6            7 <-:---- 2            7 <-:---- 3            7 <-:---- 1            7 <-:---- 5            7 <-:---- 6
4 <-:                  4 <-:                  4 <-:                  4 <-:                  4 <-:                  4 <-:

8 ----:-> 1            8 ----:-> 3            8 ----:-> 2            8 ----:-> 5                                  8 ----:-> 1
                         :-> 10                 :-> 4
                         :-> 12
```

```
      G1697                    G1698                    G1699                    G1700                    G1701                    G1702
5 ------- 5            5 ------- 2            5 ------- 5            1 ------- 2            7 ------- 7            7 ------- 4
2 ------> 4            2 ------> 3            2 ------> 2            7 ------- 7            8 ------> 5            8 ------> 6
3 <------ 2            3 <------ 5            3 <------ 3            8 ------- 8            3 <------ 4            3 <------ 3
                                                                    3 <------ 3
7 <-:---- 1            7 <-:---- 6            7 <-:---- 4                                  9 ------> 3            5 <-:---- 2
4 <-:                  4 <-:                  4 <-:                  5 <-:---- 5            5 <-:---- 1            6 <-:
                                                                    6 <-:                  6 <-:                  1 <-:
8 ----:-> 3            8 ----:-> 1            8 ----:-> 6            1 <-:                  1 <-:
   :-> 6                  :-> 4                  :-> 8                                                            4 ----:-> 1
                                                                    4 ----:-> 4                                     :-> 7
                                                                       :-> 9
```

```
      G1703                    G1704                    G1705                    G1706                    G1707                    G1708
7 ------- 5            7 ------- 9            7 ------- 3            7 ------- 9            7 ------- 5            7 ------- 5
8 ------> 6            8 ------> 3            8 ------> 4            3 ------> 13           3 ------> 2            3 ------> 2
3 <------ 4            3 <------ 2            3 <------ 2            8 <------ 11           8 <------ 3            8 <------ 3

9 ------> 2            9 ------> 5            9 ------> 5
5 <-:---- 3            5 <-:---- 4            5 <-:---- 1            4 <-:---- 10          4 <-:---- 4            4 <-:---- 7
6 <-:                  6 <-:                  6 <-:                  9 <-:                  9 <-:                  9 <-:
1 <-:                  1 <-:                  1 <-:
                                                                    5 ----:-> 14          5 ----:-> 6            5 ----:-> 8
                                                                                             :-> 8
```

```
      G1709                    G1710                    G1711                    G1712                    G1713                    G1714
7 ------- 5            7 ------- 5            1 ------- 3            1 ------- 1            1 ------- 1            1 ------- 1
3 ------> 3            3 ------> 3            7 ------- 4            7 ------- 2            7 ------- 7            7 ------- 7
8 <------ 2            8 <------ 2            3 ------> 5            3 ------> 4            8 <------ 2            3 ------> 5
                                             8 <------ 2            8 <------ 3                                  8 <------ 3

4 <-:---- 6            5 --:                                                              5 --:
9 <-:                  4 <-:                 4 <-:---- 1            4 <-:---- 6            4 <-:                 4 <-:---- 2
                       9 <-:                 9 <-:                 9 <-:                  9 <-:                 9 <-:

                                             5 ----:-> 6            5 ----:-> 5                                 5 ----:-> 6
                                                                                                                  :-> 8
```

```
 G1715                 G1716                 G1717                 G1718                 G1719                 G1720
7 ------- 4           7 ------- 5           7 ------- 1           1 ------- 3           1 ------- 4           7 ------- 3
3 ------> 5           3 ------> 4           3 ------> 4           7 ------- 5           7 ------- 2           3 ------> 1
8 <------ 3           8 <------ 2           8 <------ 2           3 ------> 2           3 ------> 5           8 <------ 5
                                                                  8 <------ 4           8 <------ 3
4 <-:---- 6           5 --:                4 <-:---- 3                                 4 <-:---- 6           4 <-:---- 4
9 <-:                 4 <-:                9 <-:                 5 --:                 9 <-:                9 <-:
                      9 <-:                                      4 <-:
5 ----:-> 2                                5 ----:-> 6           9 <-:                5 ----:-> 1           5 ----:-> 2
                      6 ----:-> 6              :-> 8                                                            :-> 7

 G1721                 G1722                 G1723                 G1724                 G1725                 G1726
7 ------- 6           7 ------- 2           1 ------- 3           1 ------- 4           7 ------- 4           7 ------- 3
3 ------> 8           3 ------> 3           7 ------- 4           7 ------- 3           3 ------> 2           3 ------> 5
8 <------ 4           8 <------ 5           3 ------> 5           3 ------> 2           8 <------ 3           8 <------ 4
                                            8 <------ 2           8 <------ 5
4 <-:---- 3           4 <-:---- 4                                                      4 <-:---- 1           4 <-:---- 6
9 <-:                 9 <-:                4 <-:---- 6           4 <-:---- 1           9 <-:                9 <-:
                                            9 <-:                9 <-:
5 ----:-> 2                                                                            5 ----:-> 6           5 ----:-> 1
   :-> 7                                    5 ----:-> 1           5 ----:-> 6

 G1727                 G1728                 G1729                 G1730                 G1731                 G1732
7 ------- 11          7 ------- 11          7 ------- 4           7 ------- 4           7 ------- 2           7 ------- 5
3 ------> 9           3 ------> 1           3 ------> 2           3 ------> 3           3 ------> 3           3 ------> 4
8 <------ 1           8 <------ 9           8 <------ 3           8 <------ 2           8 <------ 5           8 <------ 2

4 <-:---- 2           4 <-:---- 3           4 <-:---- 1           4 <-:---- 5           4 <-:---- 6           4 <-:---- 1
9 <-:                 9 <-:                9 <-:                9 <-:                9 <-:                9 <-:

5 ----:-> 3           5 ----:-> 2           5 ----:-> 5                                5 ----:-> 1           5 ----:-> 3
   :-> 10                :-> 4                                                                                  :-> 6
   :-> 12

 G1733                 G1734                 G1735                 G1736                 G1737                 G1738
7 ------- 2           7 ------- 5           4 ------- 4           4 ------- 5           4 ------- 9           4 ------- 3
3 ------> 3           3 ------> 2           3 ------> 6           3 ------> 6           3 ------> 3           3 ------> 4
8 <------ 5           8 <------ 3           6 <------ 3           6 <------ 4           6 <------ 2           6 <------ 2

4 <-:---- 6           4 <-:---- 4           7 <------ 2           2 ------> 2           2 ------> 5           2 ------> 5
9 <-:                9 <-:                                      7 <------ 3           7 <------ 4           7 <------ 1
                                            2 ----:-> 1
5 ----:-> 1           5 ----:-> 6              :-> 7
   :-> 4                :-> 8

 G1739                 G1740                 G1741                 G1742                 G1743                 G1744
4 ------- 9           4 ------- 5           4 ------- 5           4 ------- 5           4 ------- 5           4 ------- 4
3 ------> 13          3 ------> 2           3 ------> 2           3 ------> 3           3 ------> 3           3 ------> 5
6 <------ 11          6 <------ 3           6 <------ 3           6 <------ 2           6 <------ 2           6 <------ 2

2 ------> 14          2 ----:-> 8           2 ------> 8           7 <------ 6                                2 ------> 6
7 <------ 10             :- 6              7 <------ 7                                 2 --:                7 <------ 1
                      7 <------ 4                                                      7 <-:

 G1745                 G1746                 G1747                 G1748                 G1749                 G1750
4 ------- 2           4 ------- 7           4 ------- 7           4 ------- 4           4 ------- 5           4 ------- 1
3 ------> 4           6 <------ 2           3 ------> 5           3 ------> 5           3 ------> 4           3 ------> 4
6 <------ 3                                 6 <------ 3           6 <------ 3           6 <------ 2           6 <------ 2

2 ------> 5           2 --:                2 ----:-> 8           2 ------> 2           2 ------> 6           2 ----:-> 6
7 <------ 6           7 <-:                   :-> 6              7 <------ 6           7 <------ 1              :-> 8
                                            7 <------ 4                                                     7 <------ 3
```

```
 G1751                 G1752                 G1753                 G1754                 G1755                 G1756
4 ------- 5          4 ------- 2          4 ------- 3          4 ------- 6          4 ------- 2          4 ------- 4
3 ------> 2          3 ------> 5          3 ------> 1          3 ------> 8          3 ------> 3          3 ------> 5
6 <------ 4          6 <------ 3          6 <------ 5          6 <------ 4          6 <------ 5          6 <------ 2

7 <------ 1          2 ------> 1          2 ------> 2          2 ------> 7          7 <------ 4          2 ------> 1
                     7 <------ 6          7 <------ 8          7 <------ 1                               7 <------ 6
                                          :-- 4                :-- 3
                                          :-> 7                :-> 2
```

```
 G1757                 G1758                 G1759                 G1760                 G1761                 G1762
4 ------- 3          4 ------- 4          4 ------- 3          4 ------- 11         4 ------- 11         4 ------- 4
3 ------> 2          3 ------> 2          3 ------> 5          3 ------> 9          3 ------> 1          3 ------> 2
6 <------ 5          6 <------ 3          6 <------ 4          6 <------ 1          6 <------ 9          6 <------ 3

2 ------> 6          2 ------> 6          2 ------> 1          2 ----:-> 10        7 <------ 3          2 ------> 5
7 <------ 1          7 <------ 1          7 <------ 6              :-> 3                                7 <------ 1
                                                                 :-> 12           2 ----:-> 2
                                                             7 <------ 2              :-> 4
```

```
 G1763                 G1764                 G1765                 G1766                 G1767                 G1768
4 ------- 4          4 ------- 2          4 ------- 5          4 ------- 2          4 ------- 5          5 ------- 5
3 ------> 3          3 ------> 3          3 ------> 4          3 ------> 3          3 ------> 2          4 ------> 6
6 <------ 2          6 <------ 5          6 <------ 2          6 <------ 5          6 <------ 3          6 <------ 4

7 <------ 5          2 ------> 1          2 ------> 3          2 ------> 4          2 ----:-> 8          3 ------> 2
                     7 <------ 6          7 <------ 1          7 <------ 6              :-> 6            2 <------ 3
                                                                                  7 <------ 4
```

```
 G1769                 G1770                 G1771                 G1772                 G1773                 G1774
5 ------- 9          5 ------- 3          5 ------- 9          5 ------- 5          5 ------- 5          5 ------- 5
4 ------> 3          4 ------> 4          4 ------> 13         4 ------> 2          4 ------> 2          4 ------> 3
6 <------ 2          6 <------ 2          6 <------ 11         6 <------ 3          6 <------ 3          6 <------ 2

3 ------> 5          3 ------> 5          3 ------> 14         3 ----:-> 8          3 ------> 8          2 <------ 6
2 <------ 4          2 <------ 1          2 <------ 10             :-- 6            2 <------ 7
                                                             2 <------ 4
```

```
 G1775                 G1776                 G1777                 G1778                 G1779                 G1780
5 ------- 5          5 ------- 4          5 ------- 2          5 ------- 7          5 ------- 7          5 ------- 4
4 ------> 3          4 ------> 5          4 ------> 4          6 <------ 2          4 ------> 5          4 ------> 5
6 <------ 2          6 <------ 2          6 <------ 3                               6 <------ 3          6 <------ 3

3 --:                3 ------> 6          3 ------> 5          3 --:                3 ----:-> 8          3 ------> 2
2 <-:                2 <------ 1          2 <------ 6          2 <-:                    :-> 6            2 <------ 6
                                                                                  2 <------ 4
```

```
 G1781                 G1782                 G1783                 G1784                 G1785                 G1786
5 ------- 5          5 ------- 1          5 ------- 5          5 ------- 2          5 ------- 3          5 ------- 6
4 ------> 4          4 ------> 4          4 ------> 2          4 ------> 5          4 ------> 1          4 ------> 8
6 <------ 2          6 <------ 2          6 <------ 4          6 <------ 3          6 <------ 5          6 <------ 4

3 ------> 6          3 ----:-> 6          2 <------ 1          3 ------> 1          3 ------> 2          3 ------> 7
2 <------ 1              :-> 8                                2 <------ 6          2 <------ 8          2 <------ 1
                     2 <------ 3                                                  :-- 4                :-- 3
                                                                                 :-> 7                :-> 2
```

```
G1787                 G1788                 G1789                 G1790                 G1791                 G1792
5 ------- 2           5 ------- 4           5 ------- 3           5 ------- 4           5 ------- 3           5 ------- 11
4 ------> 3           4 ------> 5           4 ------> 2           4 ------> 2           4 ------> 5           4 ------> 9
6 <------ 5           6 <------ 2           6 <------ 5           6 <------ 3           6 <------ 4           6 <------ 1

2 <------ 4           3 ------> 1           3 ------> 6           3 ------> 6           3 ------> 1           3 ----:-> 10
                      2 <------ 6           2 <------ 1           2 <------ 1           2 <------ 6               :-> 3
                                                                                                                :-> 12
                                                                                                            2 <------ 2
```

```
G1793                 G1794                 G1795                 G1796                 G1797                 G1798
5 ------- 11          5 ------- 4           5 ------- 4           5 ------- 2           5 ------- 5           5 ------- 2
4 ------> 1           4 ------> 2           4 ------> 3           4 ------> 3           4 ------> 2           4 ------> 3
6 <------ 9           6 <------ 3           6 <------ 2           6 <------ 5           6 <------ 2           6 <------ 5

2 <------ 3           3 ------> 5           2 <------ 5           3 ------> 1           3 ------> 3           3 ------> 4
                      2 <------ 1                                 2 <------ 6           2 <------ 1           2 <------ 6
3 ----:-> 2
     :-> 4
```

```
G1799                 G1800                 G1801                 G1802                 G1803                 G1804
5 ------- 5           9 ------- 9           9 ------- 3           9 ------- 9           9 ------- 5           9 ------- 5
4 ------> 2           2 ------> 3           2 ------> 4           2 ------> 13          2 ------> 2           2 ------> 2
6 <------ 3           6 <------ 2           6 <------ 2           6 <------ 11          6 <------ 3           6 <------ 3

3 ----:-> 8           4 ------> 5           4 ------> 5          4 ------> 14           4 ----:-> 8           4 ------> 8
     :-> 6            5 <------ 4           5 <------ 1          5 <------ 10               :-  6            5 <------ 7
2 <------ 4                                                                            5 <------ 4
```

```
G1805                 G1806                 G1807                 G1808                 G1809                 G1810
9 ------- 5           9 ------- 5           9 ------- 4           9 ------- 2           9 ------- 7           9 ------- 7
2 ------> 3           2 ------> 3           2 ------> 5           2 ------> 4           6 <------ 2           2 ------> 5
6 <------ 2           6 <------ 2           6 <------ 2           6 <------ 3                                 6 <------ 3

5 <------ 6                                 4 ------> 6           4 ------> 5           4 --:                4 ----:-> 8
                      4 --:                 5 <------ 1           5 <------ 6           5 <-:                    :-> 6
                      5 <-:                                                                                  5 <------ 4
```

```
G1811                 G1812                 G1813                 G1814                 G1815                 G1816
9 ------- 4           9 ------- 5           9 ------- 1           9 ------- 5           9 ------- 2           9 ------- 3
2 ------> 5           2 ------> 4           2 ------> 4           2 ------> 2           2 ------> 5           2 ------> 1
6 <------ 3           6 <------ 2           6 <------ 2           6 <------ 4           6 <------ 2           6 <------ 5

4 ------> 2           4 ------> 6           4 ----:-> 6           5 <------ 1           4 ------> 1           4 ------> 2
5 <------ 6           5 <------ 1               :-> 8                                  5 <------ 6           5 <------ 8
                                            5 <------ 3                                                         :-- 4
                                                                                                               :-> 7
```

```
G1817                 G1818                 G1819                 G1820                 G1821                 G1822
9 ------- 6           9 ------- 2           9 ------- 4           9 ------- 3           9 ------- 4           9 ------- 3
2 ------> 8           2 ------> 3           2 ------> 5           2 ------> 2           2 ------> 2           2 ------> 5
6 <------ 4           6 <------ 5           6 <------ 2           6 <------ 5           6 <------ 3           6 <------ 4

4 ------> 7           5 <------ 4           4 ------> 1           4 ------> 6           4 ------> 6           4 ------> 1
5 <------ 1                                 5 <------ 6           5 <------ 1           5 <------ 1           5 <------ 6
    :-- 3
    :-> 2
```

```
G1823                 G1824                 G1825                 G1826                 G1827                 G1828
9 ------- 11          9 ------- 11          9 ------- 4           9 ------- 4           9 ------- 2           9 ------- 5
2 ------> 9           2 ------> 1           2 ------> 2           2 ------> 3           2 ------> 3           2 ------> 4
6 <------ 1           6 <------ 9           6 <------ 3           6 <------ 2           6 <------ 5           6 <------ 2
4 ----:-> 10          5 <------ 3           4 ------> 5           5 <------ 5           4 ------> 1           4 ------> 3
    :-> 3             4 ----:-> 2           5 <------ 1                                 5 <------ 6           5 <------ 1
    :-> 12                :-> 4
5 <------ 2

G1829                 G1830                 G1831                 G1832                 G1833                 G1834
9 ------- 2           9 ------- 5           3 ------- 3           3 ------- 9           3 ------- 5           3 ------- 5
2 ------> 3           2 ------> 2           2 ------> 4           2 ------> 13          2 ------> 2           2 ------> 2
6 <------ 5           6 <------ 3           4 <------ 2           4 <------ 11          4 <------ 3           4 <------ 3
4 ------> 4           4 ----:-> 8           1 ------> 5           1 ------> 14          1 ----:-> 8           1 ------> 8
5 <------ 6               :-> 6             5 <------ 1           5 <------ 10              :- 6              5 <------ 7
                     5 <------ 4                                                       5 <------ 4

G1835                 G1836                 G1837                 G1838                 G1839                 G1840
3 ------- 5           3 ------- 5           3 ------- 4           3 ------- 2           3 ------- 7           3 ------- 7
2 ------> 3           2 ------> 3           2 ------> 5           2 ------> 4           4 <------ 2           2 ------> 5
4 <------ 2           4 <------ 2           4 <------ 2           4 <------ 3                                 4 <------ 3
5 <------ 6                                 1 ------> 6           1 ------> 5           1 --:                1 ----:-> 8
                     1 --:                 5 <------ 1           5 <------ 6           5 <-:                    :-> 6
                     5 <-:                                                                                  5 <------ 4

G1841                 G1842                 G1843                 G1844                 G1845                 G1846
3 ------- 4           3 ------- 5           3 ------- 1           3 ------- 5           3 ------- 2           3 ------- 3
2 ------> 5           2 ------> 4           2 ------> 4           2 ------> 2           2 ------> 5           2 ------> 1
4 <------ 3           4 <------ 2           4 <------ 2           4 <------ 4           4 <------ 3           4 <------ 5
1 ------> 2           1 ------> 6           1 ----:-> 6          5 <------ 1           1 ------> 1           1 ------> 2
5 <------ 6           5 <------ 1               :-> 8                                 5 <------ 6           5 <------ 8
                                          5 <------ 3                                                          :- 4
                                                                                                              :-> 7

G1847                 G1848                 G1849                 G1850                 G1851                 G1852
3 ------- 6           3 ------- 2           3 ------- 4           3 ------- 3           3 ------- 4           3 ------- 3
2 ------> 8           2 ------> 3           2 ------> 5           2 ------> 2           2 ------> 2           2 ------> 5
4 <------ 4           4 <------ 5           4 <------ 2           4 <------ 5           4 <------ 3           4 <------ 4
1 ------> 7           5 <------ 4           1 ------> 1           1 ------> 6           1 ------> 6           1 ------> 1
5 <------ 1                                5 <------ 6           5 <------ 1           5 <------ 1           5 <------ 6
    :-- 3
    :-> 2

G1853                 G1854                 G1855                 G1856                 G1857                 G1858
3 ------- 11          3 ------- 11          3 ------- 4           3 ------- 4           3 ------- 2           3 ------- 5
2 ------> 9           2 ------> 1           2 ------> 2           2 ------> 3           2 ------> 3           2 ------> 4
4 <------ 1           4 <------ 9           4 <------ 3           4 <------ 2           4 <------ 5           4 <------ 2
1 ----:-> 10          5 <------ 3           1 ------> 5          5 <------ 5           1 ------> 1           1 ------> 3
    :-> 3             1 ----:-> 2           5 <------ 1                                5 <------ 6           5 <------ 1
    :-> 12                :-> 4
5 <------ 2
```

```
G1859                 G1860                 G1861                 G1862                 G1863                 G1864
3 ------- 2           3 ------- 5           9 ------- 9           9 ------- 5           9 ------- 5           9 ------- 5
2 ------> 3           2 ------> 2           11 ------> 13         11 ------> 2          11 ------> 2          11 ------> 3
4 <------ 5           4 <------ 3           13 <------ 11         13 <------ 3          13 <------ 3          13 <------ 2

1 ------> 4           1 ----:-> 8           10 ------> 14         10 ----:-> 8          10 ------> 8          14 <------ 6
5 <------ 6                 :-> 6           14 <------ 10               :   6           14 <------ 7
                      5 <------ 4                                14 <------ 4


G1865                 G1866                 G1867                 G1868                 G1869                 G1870
9 ------- 5           9 ------- 4           9 ------- 2           9 ------- 7           9 ------- 7           9 ------- 4
11 ------> 3          11 ------> 5          11 ------> 4          13 <------ 2          11 ------> 5          11 ------> 5
13 <------ 2          13 <------ 2          13 <------ 3                               13 <------ 3          13 ------- 3

10 --:                10 ------> 6          10 ------> 5          10 --:                10 ----:-> 8          10 ------> 2
14 <-:                14 <------ 1          14 <------ 6          14 <-:                      :-> 6           14 <------ 6
                                                                                       14 <------ 4


G1871                 G1872                 G1873                 G1874                 G1875                 G1876
9 ------- 5           9 ------- 1           9 ------- 5           9 ------- 2           9 ------- 3           9 ------- 6
11 ------> 4          11 ------> 4          11 ------> 2          11 ------> 5          11 ------> 1          11 ------> 8
13 <------ 2          13 <------ 3          13 <------ 4          13 <------ 3          13 <------ 5          13 <------ 4

10 ------> 6          10 ----:-> 6          14 <------ 1          10 ------> 1          10 ------> 2          10 ------> 7
14 <------ 1                :-> 8                                 14 <------ 6          14 <------ 8          14 <------ 1
                      14 <------ 3                                                            :-- 4                :-- 3
                                                                                             :-> 7                :-> 2


G1877                 G1878                 G1879                 G1880                 G1881                 G1882
9 ------- 2           9 ------- 4           9 ------- 3           9 ------- 4           9 ------- 3           9 ------- 11
11 ------> 3          11 ------> 5          11 ------> 2          11 ------> 2          11 ------> 5          11 ------> 9
13 <------ 5          13 <------ 2          13 <------ 5          13 <------ 3          13 <------ 4          13 <------ 1

14 <------ 4          10 ------> 1          10 ------> 6          10 ------> 6          10 ------> 1          10 ----:-> 10
                      14 <------ 6          14 <------ 1          14 <------ 1          14 <------ 6                :-> 3
                                                                                                                   :-> 12
                                                                                                            14 <------ 2


G1883                 G1884                 G1885                 G1886                 G1887                 G1888
9 ------- 11          9 ------- 4           9 ------- 4           9 ------- 2           9 ------- 5           9 ------- 2
11 ------> 1          11 ------> 2          11 ------> 3          11 ------> 3          11 ------> 4          11 ------> 3
13 <------ 9          13 <------ 3          13 <------ 2          13 <------ 5          13 <------ 3          13 <------ 5

14 <------ 3          10 ------> 5          14 <------ 5          10 ------> 1          10 ------> 3          10 ------> 4
                      14 <------ 1                               14 <------ 6          14 <------ 1          14 <------ 6
10 ----:-> 2
       :-> 4


G1889                 G1890                 G1891                 G1892                 G1893                 G1894
9 ------- 5           5 ------- 5           5 ------- 5           5 ------- 5           5 ------- 5           5 ------- 4
11 ------> 2          3 ------> 2           3 ------> 2           3 ------> 3           3 ------> 3           3 ------> 5
13 <------ 3          2 <------ 3           2 <------ 3           2 <------ 2           2 <------ 2           2 <------ 2

10 ----:-> 8          4 ----:-> 8           4 ------> 8           8 <-:--- 6           7 --:                4 ------> 6
       :-> 6                :-> 6           8 <-:--- 7            6 <-:                8 <-:                8 <-:--- 1
14 <------ 4          8 <-:--- 4            6 <-:                                      6 <-:                6 <-:
                      6 <-:
```

```
G1895                    G1896                    G1897                    G1898                    G1899                    G1900
5 ------- 2              5 ------- 7              5 ------- 7              5 ------- 4              5 ------- 5              5 ------- 1
3 -----> 4              2 <----- 2              3 -----> 5              3 -----> 5              3 -----> 4              3 -----> 4
2 <----- 3                                       2 <----- 3              2 <----- 3              2 <----- 2              2 <----- 2

4 -----> 5              7 --:                    4 ----:-> 8             4 -----> 2              4 -----> 6             4 ----:-> 6
8 <-:----- 6            8 <-:                         :-> 6              8 <-:----- 6            8 <-:----- 1                 :-> 8
6 <-:                   6 <-:                    8 <-:----- 4            6 <-:                   6 <-:                   8 <-:----- 3
                                                 6 <-:                                                                   6 <-:


G1901                    G1902                    G1903                    G1904                    G1905                    G1906
5 ------- 5              5 ------- 2              5 ------- 3              5 ------- 6              5 ------- 2              5 ------- 4
3 -----> 2              3 -----> 5              3 -----> 1              3 -----> 8              3 -----> 3              3 -----> 5
2 <----- 4              2 <----- 3              2 <----- 5              2 <----- 4              2 <----- 5              2 <----- 2

8 <-:----- 1            4 -----> 1              4 -----> 2              4 -----> 7             8 <-:----- 4            4 -----> 1
6 <-:                   8 <-:----- 6            8 <-:----- 8            8 <-:----- 1            6 <-:                   8 <-:----- 6
                        6 <-:                   6 <-:                   6 <-:                                           6 <-:

                                                7 ----:-> 7             7 ----:-> 2


G1907                    G1908                    G1909                    G1910                    G1911                    G1912
5 ------- 3              5 ------- 4              5 ------- 3              5 ------- 11             5 ------- 11             5 ------- 4
3 -----> 2              3 -----> 2              3 -----> 5              3 -----> 9              3 -----> 1              3 -----> 2
2 <----- 5              2 <----- 3              2 <----- 4              2 <----- 1              2 <----- 9              2 <----- 3

4 -----> 6              4 -----> 6              4 -----> 1              4 ----:-> 10            8 <-:----- 3            4 -----> 5
8 <-:----- 1            8 <-:----- 1            8 <-:----- 6                 :-> 3              6 <-:                   8 <-:----- 1
6 <-:                   6 <-:                   6 <-:                        :-> 12                                     6 <-:
                                                                        8 <-:----- 2            7 ----:-> 2
                                                                        6 <-:                        :-> 4


G1913                    G1914                    G1915                    G1916                    G1917                    G1918
5 ------- 4              5 ------- 2              5 ------- 5              5 ------- 2              5 ------- 5              5 ------- 5
3 -----> 3              3 -----> 3              3 -----> 4              3 -----> 3              3 -----> 2              3 -----> 2
2 <----- 2              2 <----- 5              2 <----- 2              2 <----- 5              2 <----- 3              2 <----- 3

8 <-:----- 5            4 -----> 1              4 -----> 3              4 -----> 4              4 ----:-> 8             7 -----> 8
6 <-:                   8 <-:----- 6            8 <-:----- 1            8 <-:----- 6                 :-> 6              8 <----- 7
                        6 <-:                   6 <-:                   6 <-:                   8 <-:----- 4
                                                                                                6 <-:
                        7 ----:-> 6             7 ----:-> 6             7 ----:-> 1


G1919                    G1920                    G1921                    G1922                    G1923                    G1924
5 ------- 5              5 ------- 5              5 ------- 4              5 ------- 2              5 ------- 7              5 ------- 7
3 -----> 3              3 -----> 3              3 -----> 5              3 -----> 4              2 <----- 2              3 -----> 5
2 <----- 2              2 <----- 2              2 <----- 2              2 <----- 3                                       2 <----- 3

8 <----- 6                                      7 -----> 6              7 -----> 5             7 --:                    7 ----:-> 8
                        7 --:                    8 <----- 1              8 <----- 6              8 <-:                        :-> 6
                        8 <-:                                                                                            8 <----- 4


G1925                    G1926                    G1927                    G1928                    G1929                    G1930
5 ------- 4              5 ------- 5              5 ------- 1              5 ------- 5              5 ------- 2              5 ------- 3
3 -----> 5              3 -----> 4              3 -----> 4              3 -----> 2              3 -----> 5              3 -----> 1
2 <----- 3              2 <----- 2              2 <----- 2              2 <----- 4              2 <----- 3              2 <----- 5

7 -----> 2              7 -----> 6              7 ----:-> 6             8 <----- 1              7 -----> 1              7 -----> 2
8 <----- 6              8 <----- 1                   :-> 8                                       8 <----- 6              8 <----- 8
                                                8 <----- 3                                                              :-- 4
                                                                                                                        :-> 7
```

```
 G1931              G1932              G1933              G1934              G1935              G1936
5 ------- 6        5 ------- 2        5 ------- 4        5 ------- 3        5 ------- 4        5 ------- 3
3 ------> 8        3 ------> 3        3 ------> 5        3 ------> 2        3 ------> 2        3 ------> 5
2 <------ 4        2 <------ 5        2 <------ 2        2 <------ 5        2 <------ 3        2 <------ 4

7 ------> 7        8 <------ 4        7 ------> 1        7 ------> 6        7 ------> 6        7 ------> 1
8 <------ 1                           8 <------ 6        8 <------ 1        8 <------ 1        8 <------ 6
   :-- 3
   :-> 2
```

```
 G1937              G1938              G1939              G1940              G1941              G1942
5 ------- 11       5 ------- 11       5 ------- 4        5 ------- 4        5 ------- 2        5 ------- 5
3 ------> 9        3 ------> 1        3 ------> 2        3 ------> 3        3 ------> 3        3 ------> 4
2 <------ 1        2 <------ 9        2 <------ 3        2 <------ 2        2 <------ 5        2 <------ 2

7 ----:-> 10       8 <------ 3        7 ------> 5        8 <------ 5        7 ------> 1        7 ------> 3
   :-> 3                              8 <------ 1                           8 <------ 6        8 <------ 1
   :-> 12          7 ----:-> 2
8 <------ 2           :-> 4
```

```
 G1943              G1944              G1946              G1947              G1948              G1949
5 ------- 2        5 ------- 5        5 ------- 5        5 ------- 4        5 ------- 2        5 ------- 7
3 ------> 3        3 ------> 2        2 ------> 3        2 ------> 5        2 ------> 4        3 <------ 2
2 <------ 5        2 <------ 3        3 <------ 2        3 <------ 2        3 <------ 3

7 ------> 4        7 ----:-> 8                             :-- 1              :-- 6
8 <------ 6           :-> 6                                :-> 6              :-> 5
                  8 <------ 4
```

```
 G1950              G1951              G1952              G1953              G1954              G1955
5 ------- 7        5 ------- 4        5 ------- 5        5 ------- 1        5 ------- 5        5 ------- 2
2 ------> 5        2 ------> 5        2 ------> 4        2 ------> 4        2 ------> 2        2 ------> 5
3 <------ 3        3 <------ 3        3 <------ 2        3 <------ 2        3 <------ 4        3 <------ 3

   :-- 2              :-- 6                                :-- 3                                 :-- 6
   :-> 6              :-> 2                                :-> 6                                 :-> 1
   :-> 8                                                   :-> 8
```

```
 G1956              G1957              G1958              G1959              G1960              G1961
5 ------- 3        5 ------- 6        5 ------- 2        5 ------- 4        5 ------- 3        5 ------- 4
2 ------> 1        2 ------> 8        2 ------> 3        2 ------> 5        2 ------> 2        2 ------> 2
3 <------ 5        3 <------ 4        3 <------ 5        3 <------ 2        3 <------ 5        3 <------ 3

   :-- 4              :-- 3                                :-- 6              :-- 1              :-- 1
   :-> 2              :-> 2                                :-> 1              :-> 6              :-> 6
   :-> 7              :-> 7
```

```
 G1962              G1963              G1964              G1965              G1966              G1967
5 ------- 3        5 ------- 11       5 ------- 11       5 ------- 4        5 ------- 4        5 ------- 2
2 ------> 5        2 ------> 9        2 ------> 2        2 ------> 2        2 ------> 3        2 ------> 3
3 <------ 4        3 <------ 1        3 <------ 9        3 <------ 3        3 <------ 2        3 <------ 5

   :-- 6              :-- 2              :-- 3              :- 1                                 :-- 6
   :-> 1              :-> 3              :-> 2              :- 5                                 :-> 1
                     :-> 10             :-> 4
                     :-> 12
```

```
 G1968              G1969              G1970              G1971              G1972              G1973
5 ------- 5        5 ------- 2        5 ------- 5        4 ------- 4        4 ------- 2        4 ------- 7
2 ------> 4        2 ------> 3        2 ------> 2        2 ------> 5        2 ------> 4        5 <------ 2
3 <------ 2        3 <------ 5        3 <------ 3        5 <------ 2        5 <------ 3

   :-- 1              :-- 6              :-- 4           1 ------> 6        1 ------> 5        1 --:
   :-> 3              :-> 1              :-> 6           6 <------ 1        6 <------ 6        6 <-:
   :-> 6              :-> 4              :-> 8
```

```
G1974                G1975                G1976                G1977                G1978                G1979
4 -------- 7         4 -------- 4         4 -------- 5         4 -------- 1         4 -------- 5         4 -------- 2
2 ------> 5          2 ------> 5          2 ------> 4          2 ------> 4          2 ------> 2          2 ------> 5
5 <------ 3          5 <------ 3          5 <------ 2          5 <------ 2          5 <------ 4          5 <------ 3

1 ----:-> 8          1 ------> 2          1 ------> 6          1 ----:-> 6          6 <------ 1          1 ------> 1
     :-> 6           6 <------ 6          6 <------ 1               :-> 8                                6 <------ 6
6 <------ 4                                                   6 <------ 3


G1980                G1981                G1982                G1983                G1984                G1985
4 -------- 3         4 -------- 6         4 -------- 2         4 -------- 4         4 -------- 3         4 -------- 4
2 ------> 1          2 ------> 8          2 ------> 3          2 ------> 5          2 ------> 2          2 ------> 2
5 <------ 5          5 <------ 4          5 <------ 5          5 <------ 2          5 <------ 5          5 <------ 3

1 ------> 2          1 ------> 7          6 <------ 4          1 ------> 1          1 ------> 6          1 ------> 6
6 <------ 8          6 <------ 1                               6 <------ 6          6 <------ 1          6 <------ 1
  :-- 4                :-- 3
  :-> 7                :-> 2


G1986                G1987                G1988                G1989                G1990                G1991
4 -------- 3         4 -------- 11        4 -------- 11        4 -------- 4         4 -------- 4         4 -------- 2
2 ------> 5          2 ------> 9          2 ------> 1          2 ------> 2          2 ------> 3          2 ------> 3
5 <------ 4          5 <------ 1          5 <------ 9          5 <------ 3          5 <------ 2          5 <------ 5

1 ------> 1          1 ----:-> 10         6 <------ 3          1 ------> 5          6 <------ 5          1 ------> 1
6 <------ 6               :-> 3                                6 <------ 1                               6 <------ 6
                         :-> 12          1 ----:-> 2
6 <------ 2                                   :-> 4


G1992                G1993                G1994                G1995                G1996                G1997
4 -------- 5         4 -------- 2         4 -------- 5         2 -------- 2         2 -------- 7         3 -------- 7
2 ------> 4          2 ------> 3          2 ------> 2          3 ------> 4          4 <------ 2          3 ------> 5
5 <------ 2          5 <------ 5          5 <------ 3          4 <------ 3                               4 <------ 3

1 ------> 3          1 ------> 4          1 ----:-> 8          6 ------> 5          6 --:               6 ----:-> 8
6 <------ 1          6 <------ 6               :-> 6           5 <------ 6          5 <-:                    :-> 6
                                         6 <------ 4                                                   5 <------ 4


G1998                G1999                G2000                G2001                G2002                G2003
2 -------- 4         2 -------- 5         2 -------- 1         2 -------- 5         2 -------- 4         2 -------- 3
3 ------> 5          3 ------> 4          3 ------> 4          3 ------> 2          3 ------> 5          3 ------> 1
4 <------ 3          4 <------ 2          4 <------ 2          4 <------ 4          4 <------ 3          4 <------ 5

6 ------> 2          6 ------> 6          6 ----:-> 6          5 <------ 1          6 ------> 1          6 ------> 2
5 <------ 6          5 <------ 1               :-> 8                                5 <------ 6          5 <------ 8
                                         5 <------ 3                                                      :-- 4
                                                                                                          :-> 7


G2004                G2005                G2006                G2007                G2008                G2009
2 -------- 6         2 -------- 2         2 -------- 4         2 -------- 3         2 -------- 4         2 -------- 3
3 ------> 8          3 ------> 3          3 ------> 5          3 ------> 2          3 ------> 2          3 ------> 5
4 <------ 4          4 <------ 5          4 <------ 2          4 <------ 5          4 <------ 3          4 <------ 4

6 ------> 7          5 <------ 4          6 ------> 1          6 ------> 6          6 ------> 6          6 ------> 1
5 <------ 1                               5 <------ 6          5 <------ 1          5 <------ 1          5 <------ 6
  :-- 3
  :-> 2
```

G2010 2 ------- 11 3 ------> 9 4 <------ 1 6 ----:-> 10 　　　:-> 3 　　　:-> 12 5 <------ 2	**G2011** 2 ------- 11 3 ------> 1 4 <------ 9 5 <------ 3 6 ----:-> 2 　　　:-> 4	**G2012** 2 ------- 4 3 ------> 2 4 <------ 3 6 ------> 5 5 <------ 1	**G2013** 2 ------- 4 3 ------> 3 4 <------ 2 5 <------ 5	**G2014** 2 ------- 2 3 ------> 3 4 <------ 5 6 ------> 1 5 <------ 6	**G2015** 2 ------- 5 3 ------> 4 4 <------ 2 6 ------> 3 5 <------ 1
G2016 2 ------- 2 3 ------> 3 4 <------ 5 6 ------> 4 5 <------ 6	**G2017** 2 ------- 5 3 ------> 2 4 <------ 3 6 ----:-> 8 　　　:-> 6 5 <------ 4	**G2018** 7 ------- 7 2 ------> 5 5 <-:---- 2 　　:-- 4 　　:-> 6 　　:-> 8	**G2019** 7 ------- 4 2 ------> 5 5 <-:-:-- 6 　　　:-> 2	**G2020** 7 ------- 1 2 ------> 4 5 <-:---- 3 　　:-- 5 　　:-> 6 　　:-> 8 　　:-> 1	**G2021** 7 ------- 2 2 ------> 5 5 <-:---- 6
G2022 7 ------- 3 2 ------> 1 5 <-:---- 4 　　:-- 6 　　:-> 2 　　:-> 7	**G2023** 7 ------- 6 2 ------> 8 5 <-:---- 3 　　:-- 5 　　:-> 2 　　:-> 7	**G2024** 7 ------- 2 2 ------> 3 5 <-:---- 4	**G2025** 7 ------- 4 2 ------> 5 5 <-:-:-- 6 　　　:-> 1	**G2026** 7 ------- 3 2 ------> 2 5 <-:-:-- 1 　　　:-> 6	**G2027** 7 ------- 4 2 ------> 2 5 <-:-:-- 1 　　　:-> 6
G2028 7 ------- 3 2 ------> 5 5 <-:-:-- 6 　　:-> 1	**G2029** 7 ------- 11 2 ------> 9 5 <-:-:-- 2 　　　:-> 3 　　　:-> 10 　　　:-> 12	**G2030** 7 ------- 11 2 ------> 1 5 <-:---- 3 　　:-- 10 　　:-> 2 　　:-> 4	**G2031** 7 ------- 4 2 ------> 2 5 <-:---- 1 　　:-- 6 　　:-> 5	**G2032** 7 ------- 4 2 ------> 3 5 <-:---- 5	**G2033** 7 ------- 2 2 ------> 3 5 <-:-:-- 6 　　　:-> 1
G2034 7 ------- 5 2 ------> 4 5 <-:---- 1 　　:-> 3 　　:-> 6	**G2035** 7 ------- 2 2 ------> 3 5 <-:---- 6 　　:-> 1 　　:-> 4	**G2036** 7 ------- 5 2 ------> 2 5 <-:---- 4 　　:-- 7 　　:-> 6 　　:-> 8	**G2037** 7 ------- 7 3 ------> 5 5 <------ 3 4 ----:-> 8 　　　:-> 6 8 <-:---- 4 6 <-:	**G2038** 7 ------- 4 3 ------> 5 5 <------ 3 4 ------> 2 8 <-:---- 6 6 <-:	**G2039** 7 ------- 5 3 ------> 4 5 <------ 2 4 ------> 6 8 <-:---- 1 6 <-:
G2040 7 ------- 1 3 ------> 4 5 <------ 2 4 ----:-> 6 　　　:-> 8 8 <-:---- 3 6 <-:	**G2041** 7 ------- 5 3 ------> 2 5 <------ 4 8 <-:---- 1 6 <-:	**G2042** 7 ------- 2 3 ------> 5 5 <------ 3 4 ------> 1 8 <-:---- 6 6 <-:	**G2043** 7 ------- 3 3 ------> 1 5 <------ 5 4 ------> 2 8 <-:---- 8 6 <-: 2 ----:-> 7	**G2044** 7 ------- 6 3 ------> 8 5 <------ 4 4 ------> 7 8 <-:---- 1 6 <-: 2 ----:-> 2	**G2045** 7 ------- 2 3 ------> 3 5 <------ 5 8 <-:---- 4 6 <-:

```
    G2046              G2047              G2048              G2049              G2050              G2051
7 ------- 4        7 ------- 3        7 ------- 4        7 ------- 3        7 ------- 11       7 ------- 11
3 ------> 5        3 ------> 2        3 ------> 2        3 ------> 5        3 ------> 9        3 ------> 1
5 <------ 2        5 <------ 5        5 <------ 3        5 <------ 4        5 <------ 1        5 <------ 9

4 ------> 1        4 ------> 6        4 ------> 6        4 ------> 1        4 ----:-> 10       8 <-:---- 3
8 <-:---- 6        8 <-:---- 1        8 <-:---- 1        8 <-:---- 6            :-> 3         6 <-:
6 <-:              6 <-:              6 <-:              6 <-:                  :-> 12
                                                                            8 <-:---- 2        2 ----:-> 2
                                                                            6 <-:                  :-> 4
```

```
    G2052              G2053              G2054              G2055              G2056              G2057
7 ------- 4        7 ------- 4        7 ------- 2        7 ------- 5        7 ------- 2        7 ------- 5
3 ------> 2        3 ------> 3        3 ------> 3        3 ------> 4        3 ------> 3        3 ------> 2
5 <------ 3        5 <------ 2        5 <------ 5        5 <------ 2        5 <------ 5        5 <------ 3

4 ------> 5        8 <-:---- 5        4 ------> 1        4 ------> 3        4 ------> 4        4 ----:-> 8
8 <-:---- 1        6 <-:              8 <-:---- 6        8 <-:---- 1        8 <-:---- 6            :-> 6
6 <-:                                 6 <-:              6 <-:              6 <-:              8 <-:---- 4
                                                                                               6 <-:
                                      2 ----:-> 6        2 ----:-> 6        2 ----:-> 1
```

```
    G2058              G2059              G2060              G2061              G2062              G2063
4 ------- 4        4 ------- 5        4 ------- 1        4 ------- 5        4 ------- 2        4 ------- 3
3 ------> 5        3 ------> 4        3 ------> 4        3 ------> 2        3 ------> 5        3 ------> 1
5 <------ 3        5 <------ 2        5 <------ 2        5 <------ 4        5 <------ 3        5 <------ 5

1 <-:---- 6        1 <-:---- 1        1 <-:---- 3        1 <-:---- 1        1 <-:---- 6        1 <-:---- 8
2 <-:              2 <-:              2 <-:              2 <-:              2 <-:              2 <-:

                                      6 ----:-> 6                                             6 ----:-> 2
                                          :-> 8                                                   :-> 7
```

```
    G2064              G2065              G2066              G2067              G2068              G2069
4 ------- 6        4 ------- 2        4 ------- 4        4 ------- 3        4 ------- 4        4 ------- 3
3 ------> 8        3 ------> 3        3 ------> 5        3 ------> 2        3 ------> 2        3 ------> 5
5 <------ 4        5 <------ 5        5 <------ 2        5 <------ 5        5 <------ 3        5 <------ 4

1 <-:---- 1        1 <-:---- 4        1 <-:---- 6        1 <-:---- 1        1 <-:---- 1        1 <-:---- 6
2 <-:              2 <-:              2 <-:              2 <-:              2 <-:              2 <-:

6 ----:-> 2
    :-> 7
```

```
    G2070              G2071              G2072              G2073              G2074              G2075
4 ------- 11       4 ------- 11       4 ------- 4        4 ------- 4        4 ------- 2        4 ------- 5
3 ------> 9        3 ------> 1        3 ------> 2        3 ------> 3        3 ------> 3        3 ------> 4
5 <------ 1        5 <------ 9        5 <------ 3        5 <------ 2        5 <------ 5        5 <------ 2
                   1 <------ 10
1 <-:---- 2        2 <------ 3        1 <-:---- 1        1 <-:---- 5        1 <-:---- 6        1 <-:---- 1
2 <-:              6 ------> 2        2 <-:              2 <-:              2 <-:              2 <-:

                                      6 ----:-> 5
```

```
    G2076              G2077              G2078              G2079              G2080              G2081
4 ------- 2        4 ------- 5        5 ------- 5        5 ------- 1        5 ------- 5        5 ------- 2
3 ------> 3        3 ------> 2        2 ------> 4        2 ------> 4        2 ------> 2        2 ------> 5
5 <------ 5        5 <------ 3        4 <------ 2        4 <------ 2        4 <------ 4        4 <------ 3

1 <-:---- 6        1 <-:---- 4        1 ------> 6        1 ----:-> 6        6 <------ 1        1 ------> 1
2 <-:              2 <-:              6 <------ 1            :-> 8                            6 <------ 6
                                                         6 <------ 3
                   6 ----:-> 6
```

```
G2082                G2083                G2084                G2085                G2086                G2087
5 ------- 3          5 ------- 6          5 ------- 2          5 ------- 4          5 ------- 3          5 ------- 4
2 ------> 1          2 ------> 8          2 ------> 3          2 ------> 5          2 ------> 2          2 ------> 2
4 <------ 5          4 <------ 4          4 <------ 5          4 <------ 2          4 <------ 5          4 <------ 3

1 ------> 2          1 ------> 7                               1 ------> 1          1 ------> 6          1 ------> 6
6 <------ 8          6 <------ 1          6 <------ 4          6 <------ 6          6 <------ 1          6 <------ 1
  :-- 4                :-- 3
  :-> 7                :-> 2


G2088                G2089                G2090                G2091                G2092                G2093
5 ------- 3          5 ------- 11         5 ------- 11         5 ------- 4          5 ------- 4          5 ------- 2
2 ------> 5          2 ------> 9          2 ------> 1          2 ------> 2          2 ------> 3          2 ------> 3
4 <------ 4          4 <------ 1          4 <------ 9          4 <------ 3          4 <------ 2          4 <------ 5

1 ------> 1          1 ----:-> 10                             1 ------> 5                               1 ------> 1
6 <------ 6            :-> 3             6 <------ 3           6 <------ 1          6 <------ 5          6 <------ 6
                      :-> 12
                    6 <------ 2          1 ----:-> 2
                                           :-> 4


G2094                G2095                G2096                G2097                G2098                G2099
5 ------- 5          5 ------- 2          5 ------- 5          5 ------- 1          5 ------- 5          5 ------- 2
2 ------> 4          2 ------> 3          2 ------> 2          2 ----> 4           2 ------> 2          2 ------> 5
4 <------ 2          4 <------ 5          4 <------ 3          4 <------ 2          4 <------ 4          4 <------ 3

1 ------> 3          1 ------> 4          1 ----:-> 8          3 ----:-> 6         6 <-:----- 1         3 ------> 1
6 <------ 1          6 <------ 6            :-> 6                :-> 8             8 <-:               6 <-:----- 6
                                         6 <------ 4           6 <-:----- 3                           8 <-:
                                                               8 <-:


G2100                G2101                G2102                G2103                G2104                G2105
5 ------- 3          5 ------- 6          5 ------- 2          5 ------- 4          5 ------- 3          5 ------- 4
2 ------> 1          2 ------> 8          2 ------> 3          2 ------> 5          2 ------> 2          2 ------> 2
4 <------ 5          4 <------ 4          4 <------ 5          4 <------ 2          4 <------ 5          4 <------ 3

3 ------> 2          3 ------> 7          6 <-:----- 4         3 ------> 1          3 ------> 6          3 ------> 6
6 <-:----- 8         6 <-:----- 1         8 <-:               6 <-:----- 6         6 <-:----- 1         6 <-:----- 1
8 <-:               8 <-:                                     8 <-:               8 <-:               8 <-:

5 ----:-> 7         5 ----:-> 2


G2106                G2107                G2108                G2109                G2110                G2111
5 ------- 3          5 ------- 11         5 ------- 11         5 ------- 4          5 ------- 4          5 ------- 2
2 ------> 5          2 ------> 9          2 ------> 1          2 ------> 2          2 ------> 3          2 ------> 3
4 <------ 4          4 <------ 1          4 <------ 9          4 <------ 3          4 <------ 2          4 <------ 5

3 ------> 1          3 ----:-> 10         6 <-:----- 3         3 ------> 5          6 <-:----- 5         3 ------> 1
6 <-:----- 6           :-> 3             8 <-:               6 <-:----- 1         8 <-:               6 <-:----- 6
8 <-:                 :-> 12                                 8 <-:                                   8 <-:
                    6 <-:----- 2         5 ----:-> 2
                    8 <-:                  :-> 4


G2112                G2113                G2114                G2115                G2116                G2117
5 ------- 5          5 ------- 2          5 ------- 5          5 ------- 5          5 ------- 2          5 ------- 3
2 ------> 4          2 ------> 3          2 ------> 2          4 ------> 2          4 ------> 5          4 ------> 1
4 <------ 2          4 <------ 5          4 <------ 3          2 <------ 4          2 <------ 3          2 <------ 5

3 ------> 3          3 ------> 4          3 ----:-> 8          6 <------ 1          1 ------> 1          1 ------> 2
6 <-:----- 1         6 <-:----- 6           :-> 6                                 6 <------ 6          6 <------ 8
8 <-:               8 <-:                6 <-:----- 4                                                    :-- 4
                                         8 <-:                                                          :-> 7
5 ----:-> 6         5 ----:-> 1
```

```
G2118                 G2119                 G2120                 G2121                 G2122                 G2123
5 ------ 6            5 ------- 2           5 ------- 4           5 ------- 3           5 ------- 4           5 ------- 3
4 ------> 8           4 ------> 3           4 ------> 5           4 ------> 2           4 ------> 2           4 ------> 5
2 <------ 4           2 <------ 5           2 <------ 2           2 <------ 5           2 <------ 3           2 <------ 4

1 ------> 7           6 <----- 4            1 ------> 1           1 ------> 6           1 ------> 6           1 ------> 1
6 <------ 1                                 6 <------ 6           6 <------ 1           6 <------ 1           6 <------ 6
     :-- 3
     :-> 2
```

```
G2124                 G2125                 G2126                 G2127                 G2128                 G2129
5 ------- 11          5 ------- 11          5 ------- 4           5 ------- 4           5 ------- 2           5 ------- 5
4 ------> 9           4 ------> 1           4 ------> 2           4 ------> 3           4 ------> 3           4 ------> 4
2 <------ 1           2 <------ 9           2 <------ 3           2 <------ 2           2 <------ 5           2 <------ 2

1 ----:-> 10          6 <------ 3           1 ------> 5           6 <------ 5           1 ------> 1           1 ------> 3
     :-> 3                                  6 <------ 1                                 6 <------ 6           6 <------ 1
     :-> 12           1 ----:-> 2
6 <------ 2                :-> 4
```

```
G2130                 G2131                 G2132                 G2133                 G2134                 G2135
5 ------- 2           4 ------> 5           2 ------- 2           2 ------- 3           2 ------- 6           2 ------- 2
4 ------> 3           2 <------ 2           3 ------> 5           3 ------> 1           3 ------> 8           3 ------> 3
2 <------ 5           2 <------ 3           5 <------ 3           5 <------ 5           5 <------ 4           5 <------ 5

1 ------> 4           1 ----:-> 8           6 ------> 1           6 ------> 2           6 ------> 7           1 <------ 4
6 <------ 6                :-> 6            1 <------ 6           1 <------ 8           1 <------ 1
                      6 <------ 4                                      :-- 4                :-- 3
                                                                      :-> 7                :-> 2
```

```
G2136                 G2137                 G2138                 G2139                 G2140                 G2141
2 ------- 4           2 ------- 3           2 ------- 4           2 ------- 3           2 ------- 11          2 ------- 11
3 ------> 5           3 ------> 2           3 ------> 2           3 ------> 5           3 ------> 9           3 ------> 1
5 <------ 2           5 <------ 5           5 <------ 3           5 <------ 4           5 <------ 1           5 <------ 9

6 ------> 1           6 ------> 6           6 ------> 6           6 ------> 1           6 ----:-> 10          1 <------ 3
1 <------ 6           1 <------ 1           1 <------ 1           1 <------ 6                :-> 3
                                                                                            :-> 12            6 ----:-> 2
                                                                                       1 <------ 2                :-> 4
```

```
G2142                 G2143                 G2144                 G2145                 G2146                 G2147
2 ------- 4           2 ------- 4           2 ------- 2           2 ------- 5           2 ------- 2           2 ------- 5
3 ------> 2           3 ------> 3           3 ------> 3           3 ------> 4           3 ------> 3           3 ------> 2
5 <------ 3           5 <------ 2           5 <------ 5           5 <------ 2           5 <------ 5           5 <------ 3

6 ------> 5           1 <------ 5           6 ------> 1           6 ------> 3           6 ------> 4           6 ----:-> 8
1 <------ 1                                 1 <------ 6           1 <------ 1           1 <------ 6                :-> 6
                                                                                                            1 <------ 4
```

```
G2148                 G2149                 G2150                 G2151                 G2152                 G2153
3 ------- 3           3 ------- 6           3 ------- 2           3 ------- 4           3 ------- 3           3 ------- 4
5 ------> 1           5 ------> 8           5 ------> 3           5 ------> 5           5 ------> 2           5 ------> 2
1 <------ 5           1 <------ 4           1 <------ 5           1 <------ 2           1 <------ 5           1 <------ 3

8 ------> 2           8 ------> 7           2 <-:---- 4           8 ------> 1           8 ------> 6           8 ------> 6
2 <-:---- 8           2 <-:---- 1                                2 <-:---- 6           2 <-:---- 1           2 <-:---- 1
                      4 ----:-> 2
4 ----:-> 7
```

```
G2154
3 ------- 3
5 ------> 5
1 <------ 4

8 ------> 1
2 <-:---- 6
```

```
G2155
3 ------- 11
5 ------> 9
1 <------ 1

8 ----:-> 10
    :-> 3
    :-> 12
2 <-:---- 2
```

```
G2156
3 ------- 11
5 ------> 1
1 <------ 9

2 <-:---- 3
4 ----:-> 2
    :-> 4
```

```
G2157
3 ------> 4
5 ------> 2
1 <------ 3

8 ------> 5
2 <-:---- 1
```

```
G2158
3 ------> 4
5 ------> 3
1 <------ 2

2 <-:---- 5
```

```
G2159
3 ------> 2
5 ------> 3
1 <------ 5

8 ------> 1
2 <-:---- 6
```

```
G2160
3 ------- 5
5 ------> 4
1 <------ 2

8 ------> 3
2 <-:---- 1

4 ----:-> 6
```

```
G2161
3 ------- 2
5 ------> 3
1 <------ 5

8 ------> 4
2 <-:---- 6

4 ----:-> 1
```

```
G2162
3 ------- 5
5 ------> 2
1 <------ 3

8 ----:-> 8
    :-> 6
2 <-:---- 4
```

```
G2162
3 ------- 5
5 ------> 2
1 <------ 3

8 ----:-> 8
    :-> 6
2 <-:---- 4
```

```
G2163
6 ------- 6
4 ------> 8
8 <------ 4

1 ------> 7
7 <------ 1

2 <-:---- 3

3 ----:-> 2
```

```
G2164
6 ------- 2
4 ------> 3
8 <------ 5

7 <------ 4

3 --:
2 <-:
```

```
G2165
6 ------- 4
4 ------> 5
8 <------ 2

1 ------> 1
7 <------ 6

3 --:
2 <-:
```

```
G2166
6 ------- 3
4 ------> 2
8 <------ 5

1 ------> 6
7 <------ 1

3 --:
2 <-:
```

```
G2167
6 ------- 4
4 ------> 2
8 <------ 3

1 ------> 6
7 <------ 1

3 --:
2 <-:
```

```
G2168
6 ------- 3
4 ------> 5
8 <------ 4

1 ------> 1
7 <------ 6

3 --:
2 <-:
```

```
G2169
6 ------- 11
4 ------> 9
8 <------ 1

1 ----:-> 10
    :-> 3
    :-> 12
7 <------ 2

3 --:
2 <-:
```

```
G2170
6 ------- 11
4 ------> 1
8 <------ 9

7 <------ 3

2 <-:---- 10

3 ----:-> 2
    :-> 4
```

```
G2171
6 ------- 4
4 ------> 2
8 <------ 3

1 ------> 5
7 <------ 1

2 <-:---- 6
```

```
G2172
6 ------- 4
4 ------> 3
8 <------ 2

7 <------ 5

3 --:
2 <-:
```

```
G2173
6 ------- 2
4 ------> 3
8 <------ 5

1 ------> 1
7 <------ 6

3 --:
2 <-:
```

```
G2174
6 ------- 5
4 ------> 4
8 <------ 2

1 ------> 3
7 <------ 1

3 --:
2 <-:

5 ----:-> 6
```

```
G2175
6 ------- 2
4 ------> 3
8 <------ 5

1 ------> 4
7 <------ 6

3 --:
2 <-:

5 ----:-> 1
```

```
G2176
6 ------- 5
4 ------> 2
8 <------ 3

1 ----:-> 8
    :-> 6
7 <------ 4

2 <-:---- 7
```

```
G2177
2 ------- 2
5 ------> 3
3 <------ 5
```

```
G2178
2 ------- 4
5 ------> 5
3 <------ 2

4 ------> 1
```

```
G2179
2 ------- 3
5 ------> 2
3 <------ 5

4 ------> 6
```

```
G2180
2 ------- 4
5 ------> 2
3 <------ 3

4 ------> 6
```

```
G2181
2 ------- 3
5 ------> 5
3 <------ 4

4 ------> 1
```

```
G2182
2 ------- 11
5 ------> 9
3 <------ 1

4 ----:-> 10
    :-> 3
    :-> 12
```

```
G2183
2 ------- 11
5 ------> 1
3 <------ 9

4 ----:-> 2
    :-> 4
```

```
G2184
2 ------- 4
5 ------> 2
3 <------ 3

4 ------> 5
```

```
G2185
2 ------- 4
5 ------> 3
3 <------ 2
```

```
G2186
2 ------- 2
5 ------> 3
3 <------ 5

4 ------> 1
```

```
G2187
2 ------- 5
5 ------> 4
3 <------ 2

4 ------> 3
    :-- 1
    :-> 6
```

```
G2188
2 ------- 2
5 ------> 3
3 <------ 5

4 ------> 4
    :-- 6
    :-> 1
```

```
G2189
2 ------- 5
5 ------> 2
3 <------ 3

4 ----:-> 8
      :-> 6
3 ------- 3
```

```
G2190
4 ------- 4
2 ------> 5
5 <------ 2

6 ------> 1
1 <------ 6
```

```
G2191
3 ------- 4
4 ------- 3
2 ------> 2
5 <------ 5

6 ------> 6
1 <------ 1
```

```
G2192
4 ------- 4
2 ------> 2
5 <------ 3

6 ------> 6
1 <------ 1
```

```
G2193
4 ------- 3
2 ------> 5
5 <------ 4

6 ------> 1
1 <------ 6
```

```
G2194
4 ------- 11
2 ------> 9
5 <------ 1

6 ----:-> 10
      :-> 3
      :-> 12
1 <------ 2
```

```
G2195
4 ------- 11
2 ------> 1
5 <------ 9

1 <------ 3

6 ----:-> 2
      :-> 4
```

```
G2196
4 ------- 4
2 ------> 2
5 <------ 3

6 ------> 5
1 <------ 1
```

```
G2197
4 ------- 4
2 ------> 3
5 <------ 2

1 <------ 5
```

```
G2198
4 ------- 2
2 ------> 3
5 <------ 5

6 ------> 1
1 <------ 6
```

```
G2199
4 ------- 5
2 ------> 4
5 <------ 2

6 ------> 3
1 <------ 1
```

```
G2200
4 ------- 2
2 ------> 3
5 <------ 5

6 ------> 4
1 <------ 6
```

```
G2201
4 ------- 5
2 ------> 2
5 <------ 3

6 ----:-> 8
      :-> 6
1 <------ 4
```

```
G2202
4 ------- 4
3 ------- 3
5 ------> 2
2 <------ 5

1 ------> 6
6 <------ 1
```

```
G2203
3 ------- 4
5 ------> 2
2 <------ 3

1 ------> 6
6 <------ 1
```

```
G2204
3 ------- 3
5 ------> 5
2 <------ 4

1 ------> 1
6 <------ 6
```

```
G2205
3 ------- 11
5 ------> 9
2 <------ 1

1 ----:-> 10
      :-> 3
      :-> 12
6 <------ 2
```

```
G2206
3 ------- 11
5 ------> 1
2 <------ 9

6 <------ 3

1 ----:-> 2
      :-> 4
```

```
G2207
3 ------- 4
5 ------> 2
2 <------ 3

1 ------> 5
6 <------ 1
```

```
G2208
3 ------- 4
5 ------> 3
2 <------ 2

6 <------ 5
```

```
G2209
3 ------- 2
5 ------> 3
2 <------ 5

1 ------> 1
6 <------ 6
```

```
G2210
3 ------- 5
5 ------> 4
2 <------ 2

1 ------> 3
6 <------ 1
```

```
G2211
3 ------- 2
5 ------> 3
2 <------ 5

1 ------> 4
6 <------ 6
```

```
G2212
3 ------- 5
5 ------> 2
2 <------ 3

1 ----:-> 8
      :-> 6
6 <------ 4
```

```
G2213
4 ------- 4
3 ------> 2
2 <------ 3

1 ------> 6
6 <------ 1
```

```
G2214
4 ------- 3
3 ------> 5
2 <------ 4

1 ------> 1
6 <------ 6
```

```
G2215
4 ------- 11
3 ------> 9
2 <------ 1

1 ----:-> 10
      :-> 3
      :-> 12
6 <------ 2
```

```
G2216
4 ------- 11
3 ------> 1
2 <------ 9

6 <------ 3

1 ----:-> 2
      :-> 4
```

```
G2217
4 ------- 4
3 ------> 2
2 <------ 3

1 ------> 5
6 <------ 1
```

```
G2218
4 ------- 4
3 ------> 3
2 <------ 2

6 <------ 5
```

```
G2219
4 ------- 2
3 ------> 3
2 <------ 5

1 ------> 1
6 <------ 6
```

```
G2220
4 ------- 5
3 ------> 4
2 <------ 2

1 ------> 3
6 <------ 1
```

```
G2221
4 ------- 2
3 ------> 3
2 <------ 5

1 ------> 4
6 <------ 6
```

```
G2222
4 ------- 5
3 ------> 2
2 <------ 3

1 ----:-> 8
      :-> 6
6 <------ 4
```

```
G2223
3 ------- 3
4 ------> 5
5 <------ 4

6 ------> 1
1 <------ 6
```

```
G2224
3 ------- 11
4 ------> 9
5 <------ 1

6 ----:-> 10
      :-> 3
      :-> 12
1 <------ 2
```

```
G2225                 G2226                 G2227                 G2228                 G2229                 G2230
3 ------- 11          3 ------- 4           3 ------- 4           3 ------- 2           3 ------- 5           3 ------- 2
4 ------> 1           4 ------> 2           4 ------> 3           4 ------> 3           4 ------> 4           4 ------> 3
5 <------ 9           5 <------ 3           5 <------ 2           5 <------ 5           5 <------ 2           5 <------ 5

1 <------ 3           6 ------> 5           1 <------ 5           6 ------> 1           6 ------> 3           6 ------> 4
                      1 <------ 1                                 1 <------ 6           1 <------ 1           1 <------ 6
6 ----:-> 2
   :-> 4
```

```
G2231                 G2232                 G2233                 G2234                 G2235                 G2236
3 ------- 5           11 ------- 11         11 ------- 11         11 ------- 4          11 ------- 4          11 ------- 2
4 ------> 2           1 ------> 9           1 ------> 1           1 ------> 2           1 ------> 3           1 ------> 3
5 <------ 3           9 <------ 1           9 <------ 9           9 <------ 3           9 <------ 2           9 <------ 5

6 ----:-> 8           2 ----:-> 10          10 <-:---- 3         2 ------> 5           10 <-:---- 5         2 ------> 1
   :-> 6                 :-> 3              3 <-:                 10 <-:---- 1          3 <-:                10 <-:---- 6
1 <------ 4              :-> 12             12 <-:                3 <-:                 12 <-:               3 <-:
                      10 <-:---- 2                                12 <-:                                     12 <-:
                      3 <-:                 2 ----:-> 2
                      12 <-:                   :-> 4
```

```
G2237                 G2238                 G2239                 G2240                 G2241                 G2242
11 ------- 5          11 ------- 2          11 ------- 5          11 ------- 11         11 ------- 4          11 ------- 4
1 ------> 4           1 ------> 3           1 ------> 2           9 ------> 1           9 ------> 2           9 ------> 3
9 <------ 2           9 <------ 5           9 <------ 3           1 <------ 9           1 <------ 3           1 <------ 2

2 ------> 3           2 ------> 4           2 ----:-> 8          2 <-:---- 3           2 <-:---- 1          2 <-:---- 5
10 <-:---- 1          10 <-:---- 6             :-> 6             4 <-:                 4 <-:                4 <-:
3 <-:                 3 <-:                 10 <-:---- 4
12 <-:                12 <-:                3 <-:                 3 ----:-> 2           3 ----:-> 5
                                            12 <-:                  :-> 4
```

```
G2243                 G2244                 G2245                 G2246                 G2247                 G2248
11 ------- 2          11 ------- 5          11 ------- 2          11 ------- 5          4 ------- 4           4 ------- 4
9 ------> 3           9 ------> 4           9 ------> 3           9 ------> 2           3 ------> 2           3 ------> 3
1 <------ 5           1 <------ 2           1 <------ 5           1 <------ 3           2 <------ 3           2 <------ 2

2 <-:---- 6           2 <-:---- 1          2 <-:---- 6           2 <-:---- 4           1 ------> 5           5 <------ 5
4 <-:                 4 <-:                4 <-:                 4 <-:                 5 <------ 1

3 ----:-> 1           3 ----:-> 3          3 ----:-> 1          3 ----:-> 6
                         :-> 6                :-> 4                :-> 8
```

```
G2249                 G2250                 G2251                 G2252                 G2253                 G2254
4 ------- 2           4 ------- 5           4 ------- 2           4 ------- 5           4 ------- 4           4 ------- 2
3 ------> 3           3 ------> 4           3 ------> 3           3 ------> 2           2 ------> 3           2 ------> 3
2 <------ 5           2 <------ 2           2 <------ 5           2 <------ 3           3 <------ 2           3 <------ 5

1 ------> 1           1 ------> 3           1 ------> 4           1 ----:-> 8                                5 ------> 1
5 <------ 6           5 <------ 1           5 <------ 6             :-> 6
                                                                 5 <------ 4
                      6 ----:-> 6           6 ----:-> 1
```

```
G2255                 G2256                 G2257                 G2258                 G2259                 G2260
4 ------- 5           4 ------- 2           4 ------- 5           2 ------- 2           2 ------- 5           2 ------- 2
2 ------> 4           2 ------> 3           2 ------> 2           5 ------> 3           5 ------> 4           5 ------> 3
3 <------ 2           3 <------ 5           3 <------ 3           3 <------ 5           3 <------ 2           3 <------ 5

5 ------> 3           5 ------> 4           5 ----:-> 8          6 ------> 1           6 ------> 3           6 ------> 4
 :-- 1                 :-- 6                  :-> 6             1 <------ 6           1 <------ 1           1 <------ 6
 :-> 6                 :-> 1
```

```
G2261                G2262                G2263                G2264                G2265                G2266
2 ------- 5          5 ------- 5          5 ------- 2          5 ------- 5          2 ------- 2          2 ------- 5
5 ------> 2          2 ------> 4          2 ------> 3          2 ------> 2          5 ------> 3          5 ------> 2
3 <------ 3          4 <------ 2          4 <------ 5          4 <------ 3          3 <------ 5          3 <------ 3

6 ----:-> 8          1 ------> 3          1 ------> 4          1 ----:-> 8          6 ------> 4          6 ----:-> 8
     :-> 6           3 <------ 1          3 <------ 6               :-> 6           4 <------ 6               :-> 6
1 <------ 4                                                   3 <------ 4                               4 <------ 4

                                                             6 <-:---- 7                               1 <-:---- 7


G2267                G2268                G2269                G2270                G2271                G2272
5 ------- 5          1 ------- 1          7 ------- 7          7 ------- 5          1 ------- 1          7 ------- 5
3 ------> 2          7 ------- 7          3 ------> 2          3 ------> 2          7 ------- 7          3 ------> 3
2 <------ 3          3 ------> 2          2 <------ 3          2 <------ 3          3 ------> 2          2 <------ 2
                     2 <------ 3          4 <------ 4          4 <------ 7          2 <------ 3
4 ----:-> 8                               5 ------> 5          20 <------ 4                              4 <-:---- 6
     :-> 6           4 <-:---- 5          6 ------> 6          8 ------> 1          4 <-:---- 8          20 <-:
8 <-:---- 4          20 <-:               8 --:--> 8           6 ------> 6          20 <-:
6 <-:                                     20 <-:               5 ------> 8                               5 ----:-> 4
                     5 ----:-> 4                                                    5 ----:-> 20              :-> 7
                          :-> 20


G2273                G2274                G2275                G2276                G2277                G2278
7 ------- 7          1 ------- 1          1 ------- 1          7 ------- 4          1 ------- 1          7 ------- 5
3 ------> 3          7 ------- 8          7 ------- 7          3 ------> 3          7 ------- 7          3 ------> 7
2 <------ 2          3 ------> 4          3 ------> 2          2 <------ 2          3 ------> 5          2 <------ 4
                     2 <------ 2          2 <------ 3                               2 <------ 3
                                                             4 <-:---- 5                               4 <-:---- 3
                     4 <-:---- 3          4 <-:---- 5          20 <-:               4 <-:---- 4          20 <-:
                     20 <-:               20 <-:                                    20 <-:
                                                             5 ----:-> 1                               5 ----:-> 2
                     5 ----:-> 5          5 ----:-> 4              :-> 6            5 ----:-> 6              :-> 6
                          :-> 7
                          :-> 10
                     8 ----:-> 11


G2279                G2280                G2281                G2282                G2283                G2284
7 ------- 3          1 ------- 4          1 ------- 3          7 ------- 8          7 ------- 8          7 ------- 7
3 ------> 5          7 ------- 7          7 ------- 6          3 ------> 2          3 ------> 6          3 ------> 3
2 <------ 4          3 ------> 6          3 ------> 5          2 <------ 1          2 <------ 1          2 <------ 2
                     2 <------ 5          2 <------ 4
4 <-:---- 1                                                   5 --:                4 <-:---- 2          4 <-:---- 4
20 <-:               4 <-:---- 3          4 <-:---- 2          4 <-:                20 <-:               20 <-:
                     20 <-:               20 <-:               20 <-:
5 ----:-> 6                                                                         5 ----:-> 7          5 ----:-> 5
     :-> 7           5 ----:-> 1          5 ----:-> 1                                    :-> 9                :-> 8
     :-> 8                :-> 2                :-> 7
                          :-> 8
                     8 ----:-> 10
```

```
 G2285                  G2286                  G2287                  G2288                  G2289                  G2290
7 ------- 5            1 ------- 2            1 ------- 2            7 ------ 7            7 ------- 4            7 ------- 5
3 ------> 3            7 ------- 7            7 ------- 7            3 -----> 5            3 ------> 6            3 ------> 6
2 <------ 2            3 ------> 3            3 ------> 8            2 <----- 4            2 <------ 3            2 <------ 4
                      2 <------ 8            2 <------ 3
4 <-:---- 1                                                         4 <-:---- 1          4 <-:---- 2          4 <-:---- 3
20 <-:                 4 <-:---- 4            4 <-:---- 1           20 <-:                20 <-:                20 <-:
                      20 <-:                 20 <-:
5 ----:-> 4                                                         5 ----:-> 3          5 ----:-> 1          5 ----:-> 2
   :-> 7              5 ----:-> 1            5 ----:-> 4                                     :-> 7
                         :-> 5                 :-> 9
                         :-> 6

                      8 ----:-> 10


 G2291                  G2292                  G2293                  G2294                  G2295                  G2296
7 ------- 9            7 ------- 3            7 ------- 9            7 ------- 5            7 ------- 5            7 ------- 5
3 ------> 3            3 ------> 4            3 ------> 13           3 ------> 2            3 ------> 2            3 ------> 3
2 <------ 2            2 <------ 2            2 <------ 11           2 <------ 3            2 <------ 3            2 <------ 2

4 <-:---- 4            4 <-:---- 1            4 <-:---- 10          4 <-:---- 4           4 <-:---- 7          4 <-:---- 6
20 <-:                20 <-:                 20 <-:                 20 <-:                20 <-:                20 <-:

5 ----:-> 5           5 ----:-> 5           5 ----:-> 14          5 ----:-> 6           5 ----:-> 8
                                                                      :-> 8


 G2297                  G2298                  G2299                  G2300                  G2301                  G2302
7 ------- 5            1 ------- 3            1 ------- 1            1 ------- 1            1 ------- 1            7 ------- 4
3 ------> 3            7 ------- 4            7 ------- 2            7 ------- 7            7 ------- 7            3 ------> 5
2 <------ 2            3 ------> 5            3 ------> 4            2 <------ 2            3 ------> 5            2 <------ 3
                      2 <------ 2            2 <------ 3                                  2 <------ 3
5 --:                                                              5 --:                                       4 <-:---- 6
4 <-:                  4 <-:---- 1            4 <-:---- 6            4 <-:                 4 <-:---- 2          20 <-:
20 <-:                20 <-:                 20 <-:                 20 <-:                20 <-:
                                                                                                               5 ----:-> 2
                      5 ----:-> 6           5 ----:-> 5                                  5 ----:-> 6
                                                                                            :-> 8


 G2303                  G2304                  G2305                  G2306                  G2307                  G2308
7 ------- 5            7 ------- 1            1 ------- 3            1 ------- 4            7 ------- 3            7 ------- 6
3 ------> 4            3 ------> 4            7 ------- 5            7 ------- 2            3 ------> 1            3 ------> 8
2 <------ 2            2 <------ 2            3 ------> 2            3 ------> 5            2 <------ 5            2 <------ 4
                                             2 <------ 4            2 <------ 3
5 --:                 4 <-:---- 3                                                         4 <-:---- 4          4 <-:---- 3
4 <-:                 20 <-:                 5 --:                  4 <-:---- 6          20 <-:                20 <-:
20 <-:                                        4 <-:                20 <-:
                      5 ----:-> 6            20 <-:                                       5 ----:-> 2          5 ----:-> 2
8 ----:-> 6              :-> 8                                     5 ----:-> 1              :-> 7                :-> 7


 G2309                  G2310                  G2311                  G2312                  G2313                  G2314
7 ------- 2            1 ------- 3            1 ------- 4            7 ------- 4            7 ------- 3            7 ------- 11
3 ------> 3            7 ------- 4            7 ------- 3            3 ------> 2            3 ------> 5            3 ------> 9
2 <------ 5            3 ------> 5            3 ------> 2            2 <------ 3            2 <------ 4            2 <------ 1
                      2 <------ 2            2 <------ 5
4 <-:---- 4                                                         4 <-:---- 1          4 <-:---- 6          4 <-:---- 2
20 <-:                 4 <-:---- 6            4 <-:---- 1           20 <-:                20 <-:                20 <-:
                      20 <-:                 20 <-:
                                                                   5 ----:-> 6          5 ----:-> 1          5 ----:-> 3
                      5 ----:-> 1           5 ----:-> 6                                                          :-> 10
                                                                                                                :-> 12
```

```
  G2315                 G2316                 G2317                 G2318                 G2319                 G2320
7 ------ 11           7 ------ 4            7 ------ 4            7 ------ 2            7 ------ 5            7 ------ 2
3 ------> 1           3 ------> 2           3 ------> 3           3 ------> 3           3 ------> 4           3 ------> 3
2 <------ 9           2 <------ 3           2 <------ 2           2 <------ 5           2 <------ 2           2 <------ 5

4 <-:---- 3           4 <-:---- 1           4 <-:---- 5          4 <-:---- 6           4 <-:---- 1           4 <-:---- 6
20 <-:                20 <-:                20 <-:               20 <-:                20 <-:                20 <-:

5 ----:-> 2           5 ----:-> 5                                5 ----:-> 1           5 ----:-> 3           5 ----:-> 1
   :-> 4                                                                                  :-> 6                 :-> 4
```

```
  G2321                 G2322                 G2323                 G2324                 G2325                 G2326
7 ------ 5            1 ------ 1            1 ------ 1            8 ------ 4            1 ------ 1            8 ------ 5
3 ------> 2           8 ------ 8            8 ------ 7            2 ------> 3           8 ------ 7            2 ------> 7
2 <------ 3           2 ------> 4           2 ------> 2           4 <------ 2           2 ------> 5           4 <------ 4
                      4 <------ 2           4 <------ 3                                 4 <------ 3
                                                                  12 ----:-> 1                               12 ----:-> 2
4 <-:---- 4           12 ----:-> 5          5 <-:---- 6             :-> 6              12 ------> 6             :-> 6
20 <-:                   :-> 10             10 <-:               5 <-:---- 5           5 <-:---- 4           5 <-:---- 3
                         :-> 7              7 <-:                10 <-:                10 <-:                10 <-:
5 ----:-> 6           5 <-:---- 12                               7 <-:                7 <-:                 7 <-:
   :-> 8              10 <-:                11 <-:---- 5
                      7 <-:                                      3 --:                 3 --:                 11 <-:---- 8
                                            3 ----:-> 4          11 <-:                11 <-:
                      11 <-:---- 3

                      3 ----:-> 11
```

```
  G2327                 G2328                 G2329                 G2330                 G2331                 G2332
8 ------ 3            1 ------ 4            1 ------ 3            8 ------ 8            8 ------ 8            8 ------ 7
2 ------> 5           8 ------ 7            8 ------ 6            2 ------> 2           2 ------> 6           2 ------> 3
4 <------ 4           2 ------> 6           2 ------> 5           4 <------ 1           4 <------ 1           4 <------ 2
                      4 <------ 5           4 <------ 4
12 ----:-> 8                                                     3 --:                 12 ----:-> 7          12 ----:-> 5
   :-> 7              12 ----:-> 8          12 ----:-> 7         5 <-:                    :-> 9                 :-> 8
   :-> 6                 :-> 2                 :-> 1             7 <-:                 5 <-:---- 4           5 <-:
5 <-:---- 2              :-> 10             5 <-:---- 8          10 <-:                10 <-:                10 <-:
10 <-:               5 <-:---- 9            10 <-:                                     7 <-:                 7 <-:
7 <-:                10 <-:                 7 <-:                9 --:
                     7 <-:                                      11 <-:                 11 <-:---- 2          11 <-:---- 4
11 <-:---- 1                                11 <-:---- 2
                     11 <-:---- 3

                     3 ----:-> 1
```

```
  G2333                 G2334                 G2335                 G2336                 G2337                 G2338
8 ------ 5            1 ------ 2            1 ------ 2            8 ------ 7            8 ------ 4            8 ------ 5
2 ------> 3           8 ------ 7            8 ------ 7            2 ------> 5           2 ------> 6           2 ------> 6
4 <------ 2           2 ------> 3           2 ------> 8           4 <------ 4           4 <------ 3           4 <------ 4
                      4 <------ 8           4 <------ 3
5 <-:---- 6                                                      12 ------> 3          5 <-:---- 2          12 ------> 2
10 <-:               12 ----:-> 5          5 <-:---- 5           5 <-:---- 1          10 <-:               5 <-:---- 3
7 <-:                   :-> 6              10 <-:                10 <-:                7 <-:                10 <-:
                        :-> 1              7 <-:                 7 <-:                                      7 <-:
11 <-:---- 1          5 <-:---- 9                                                     3 --:
                     10 <-:                11 <-:---- 1          11 <-:---- 6         11 <-:                3 --:
3 ----:-> 4           7 <-:                                                                                11 <-:
   :-> 7                                    3 ----:-> 4                               9 ----:-> 1
                     11 <-:---- 4              :-> 9                                      :-> 7

                     3 ----:-> 10
```

```
   G2339                 G2340                 G2341                 G2342                 G2343                 G2344
8 ------- 9           8 ------- 3           8 ------- 9           8 ------- 5           8 ------- 5           8 ------- 5
2 ------> 3           2 ------> 4           2 ------> 13          2 ------> 2           2 ------> 2           2 ------> 3
4 <------ 2           4 <------ 2           4 <------ 11          4 <------ 3           4 <------ 3           4 <------ 2

12 ------> 5          12 ------> 5          12 ------> 14         12 ----:-> 8          12 ------> 8          5 <-:----- 6
5 <-:----- 4          5 <-:----- 1          5 <-:----- 10           :-> 6             5 <-:----- 7          10 <-:
10 <-:                10 <-:                10 <-:                5 <-:----- 4          10 <-:                7 <-:
7 <-:                 7 <-:                 7 <-:                 10 <-:                7 <-:
                                                                  7 <-:                                      11 <-:----- 8
3 --:                 3 --:                 3 --:                                      3 --:
11 <-:                11 <-:                11 <-:                11 <-:----- 7         11 <-:


   G2345                 G2346                 G2347                 G2348                 G2349                 G2350
8 ------- 5           1 ------- 3           1 ------- 1           1 ------- 1           1 ------- 1           8 ------- 4
2 ------> 3           8 ------- 4           8 ------- 2           8 ------- 7           8 ------- 7           2 ------> 5
4 <------ 2           2 ------> 5           2 ------> 4           4 <------ 2           2 ------> 5           4 <------ 3
                      4 <------ 2           4 <------ 3                                 4 <------ 3
3 --:                                                            3 --:                                       12 ------> 2
5 <-:                 12 ------> 6          12 ------> 5          5 <-:                 12 ----:-> 8          5 <-:----- 6
7 <-:                 5 <-:----- 1          5 <-:----- 6          7 <-:                    :-> 6             10 <-:
10 <-:                10 <-:                10 <-:                10 <-:                5 <-:----- 4          7 <-:
                      7 <-:                 7 <-:                                       10 <-:
9 --:                                                            9 --:                 7 <-:                3 --:
11 <-:                3 --:                 3 --:                 11 <-:                                      11 <-:
                      11 <-:                11 <-:                                      11 <-:----- 2


   G2351                 G2352                 G2353                 G2354                 G2355                 G2356
8 ------- 5           8 ------- 1           1 ------- 3           1 ------- 4           8 ------- 3           8 ------- 6
2 ------> 4           2 ------> 4           8 ------- 5           8 ------- 2           2 ------> 1           2 ------> 8
4 <------ 2           4 <------ 2           2 ------> 2           2 ------> 5           4 <------ 5           4 <------ 4
                                            4 <------ 4           4 <------ 3
12 ------> 6          12 ----:-> 6                                                     12 ------> 2          12 ------> 7
5 <-:----- 1             :-> 8             5 <-:----- 1          12 ------> 1          5 <-:----- 8          5 <-:----- 1
10 <-:                5 <-:----- 3          10 <-:                5 <-:----- 6          10 <-:                10 <-:
7 <-:                 10 <-:                7 <-:                 10 <-:                7 <-:                 7 <-:
                      7 <-:                                       7 <-:
3 --:                                       3 --:                                      11 <-:----- 4         11 <-:----- 3
11 <-:                11 <-:----- 5         11 <-:                3 --:
                                                                  11 <-:                3 ----:-> 7          3 ----:-> 2


   G2357                 G2358                 G2359                 G2360                 G2361                 G2362
8 ------- 2           1 ------- 3           1 ------- 4           8 ------- 4           8 ------- 3           8 ------- 11
2 ------> 3           8 ------- 4           8 ------- 3           2 ------> 2           2 ------> 5           2 ------> 9
4 <------ 5           2 ------> 5           2 ------> 2           4 <------ 3           4 <------ 4           4 <------ 1
                      4 <------ 2           4 <------ 5
5 <-:----- 4                                                     12 ------> 6          12 ------> 1          12 ----:-> 10
10 <-:                12 ------> 1          12 ------> 6          5 <-:----- 1          5 <-:----- 6            :-> 3
7 <-:                 5 <-:----- 6          5 <-:----- 1          10 <-:                10 <-:                  :-> 12
                      10 <-:                10 <-:                7 <-:                 7 <-:                 5 <-:----- 2
3 --:                 7 <-:                 7 <-:                                                             10 <-:
11 <-:                                                           3 --:                 3 --:                 7 <-:
                      3 --:                 3 --:                 11 <-:                11 <-:
                      11 <-:                11 <-:                                                            3 --:
                                                                                                             11 <-:
```

```
G2363                 G2364                 G2365                 G2366                 G2367                 G2368
8 ------ 11           8 ------- 4           8 ------- 4           8 ------- 2           8 ------- 5           8 ------- 2
2 ------> 1           2 ------> 2           2 ------> 3           2 ------> 3           2 ------> 4           2 ------> 3
4 <------ 9           4 <------ 3           4 <------ 2           4 <------ 5           4 <------ 2           4 <------ 5

5 <-:---- 3           12 ------> 5          5 <-:---- 5          12 ------> 1          12 ------> 3          12 ------> 4
10 <-:                5 <-:---- 1           10 <-:               5 <-:---- 6          5 <-:---- 1          5 <-:---- 6
7 <-:                 10 <-:                7 <-:                10 <-:               10 <-:               10 <-:
                      7 <-:                                      7 <-:                7 <-:                7 <-:
11 <-:---- 10
                      11 <-:---- 6          3 --:               3 --:                3 --:                3 --:
3 ----:-> 2                                 11 <-:               11 <-:               11 <-:               11 <-:
  :-> 4
                                                                                      9 ----:-> 6          9 ----:-> 1
```

```
G2369                 G2268                 G2269                 G2270                 G2271                 G2272
8 ------- 5           1 ------- 1           1 ------- 1           1 ------- 1           1 ------- 1           1 ------- 1
2 ------> 2           7 ------- 7           7 ------- 7           7 ------- 7           7 ------- 7           7 ------- 7
4 <------ 3           2 ------> 3           2 ------> 2           2 ------> 2           2 ------> 3           2 ------> 3
                      3 <------ 2           3 <------ 3           3 <------ 3           3 <------ 2           3 <------ 2
12 ----:-> 8
   :-> 6              19 ----:-> 5          5 <-:---- 6          19 ----:-> 8          19 ----:-> 5          19 ----:-> 5
5 <-:---- 4              :-> 6              6 <-:                   :-> 4                :-> 6                :-> 6
10 <-:                   :-> 8              8 <-:                   :-> 20               :-> 20           5 <-:---- 4
7 <-:                 5 <-:---- 20                                5 <-:---- 5          5 <-:---- 4          6 <-:
                      6 <-:                19 ----:-> 4          6 <-:                6 <-:                8 <-:
11 <-:---- 7          8 <-:                   :-> 20             8 <-:                8 <-:
```

```
G2273                 G2274                 G2275                 G2276                 G2277                 G2278
7 ------- 7           7 ------- 5           7 ------- 5           1 ------- 1           1 ------- 1           1 ------- 1
2 ------> 2           2 ------> 4           2 ------> 4           7 ------- 7           7 ------- 7           7 ------- 7
3 <------ 3           3 <------ 3           3 <------ 3           2 ------> 2           2 ------> 2           2 ------> 3
                                                                 3 <------ 3           3 <------ 3           3 <------ 2
4 --:                 19 ------> 6          5 <-:---- 1
5 <-:                 5 <-:---- 1           6 <-:                5 <-:---- 6          5 <-:---- 6          19 ----:-> 5
6 <-:                 6 <-:                 8 <-:                6 <-:                6 <-:                   :-> 8
8 <-:                 8 <-:                                      8 <-:                8 <-:
                                                                                                           5 <-:---- 4
                                                                 19 ----:-> 4                              6 <-:
                                                                    :-> 20                                 8 <-:
```

```
G2279                 G2280                 G2281                 G2282                 G2283                 G2284
1 ------- 1           7 ------- 7           1 ------- 1           7 ------- 7           7 ------- 5           1 ------- 1
7 ------- 7           2 ------> 2           7 ------- 7           2 ------> 2           2 ------> 2           7 ------- 7
2 ------> 2           3 <------ 3           2 ------> 2           3 <------ 3           3 <------ 3           2 ------> 2
3 <------ 3                                 3 <------ 3                                                      3 <------ 3
                      4 --:                                      19 ----:-> 5          19 ----:-> 8
                      5 <-:                 19 ----:-> 20            :-> 6                :-> 6              5 <-:---- 8
4 --:                 6 <-:                    :-> 4                :-> 8                :-> 1              6 <-:
5 <-:                 8 <-:                    :-> 12            5 <-:---- 4          5 <-:---- 4          8 <-:
6 <-:                                                            6 <-:                6 <-:
8 <-:                                        5 <-:---- 5          8 <-:                8 <-:               19 ----:-> 20
                                             6 <-:
                                             8 <-:
```

```
   G2285
7 ------- 5
2 -----> 3
3 <------ 2

19 ----:-> 7
      :-> 4
5 <-:----- 6
6 <-:
8 <-:
```

```
   G2286
7 ------- 7
2 -----> 3
3 <------ 2

4 --:
5 <-:
6 <-:
8 <-:
```

```
   G2287
1 ------- 1
7 ------- 8
2 -----> 4
3 <------ 2

19 ----:-> 5
      :-> 10
      :-> 7
5 <-:----- 12
6 <-:
8 <-:

4 ----:-> 11
```

```
   G2288
1 ------- 1
7 ------- 7
2 -----> 2
3 <------ 3

5 <:---- 6
6 <-:
8 <-:

19 ----:-> 4
```

```
   G2289
7 ------- 4
2 -----> 3
3 <------ 2

19 ----:-> 1
      :-> 6
5 <-:----- 5
6 <-:
8 <-:
```

```
   G2290
1 ------- 1
7 ------- 7
2 -----> 5
3 <------ 3

19 -----> 6
5 <-:----- 4
6 <-:
8 <-:
```

```
   G2291
7 ------- 5
2 -----> 7
3 <------ 4

19 ----:-> 2
      :-> 6
5 <-:----- 3
6 <-:
8 <-:
```

```
   G2292
7 ------- 3
2 -----> 5
3 <------ 4

19 ----:-> 8
      :-> 7
      :-> 6
5 <-:----- 2
6 <-:
8 <-:
```

```
   G2293
1 ------- 4
7 ------- 7
2 -----> 6
3 <------ 5

19 ----:-> 8
      :-> 2
      :-> 10
5 <-:----- 9
6 <-:
8 <-:

4 ----:-> 1
```

```
   G2294
1 ------- 3
7 ------- 6
2 -----> 5
3 <------ 4

19 ----:-> 7
      :-> 1
5 <-:----- 8
6 <-:
8 <-:
```

```
   G2295
7 ------- 8
2 -----> 2
3 <------ 1

4 --:
5 <-:
6 <-:
8 <-:
```

```
   G2296
7 ------- 8
2 -----> 6
3 <------ 1

19 ----:-> 7
      :-> 9
5 <-:----- 4
6 <-:
8 <-:
```

```
   G2297
7 ------- 7
2 -----> 3
3 <------ 2

19 ----:-> 5
      :-> 8
5 <-:----- 9
6 <-:
8 <-:
```

```
   G2298
7 ------- 5
2 -----> 3
3 <------ 2

5 <-:----- 6
6 <-:
8 <-:

19 ----:-> 4
      :-> 7
```

```
   G2299
1 ------- 2
7 ------- 7
2 -----> 3
3 <------ 8

19 ----:-> 5
      :-> 6
      :-> 1
5 <-:----- 9
6 <-:
8 <-:

4 ----:-> 10
```

```
   G2300
1 ------- 2
7 ------- 7
2 -----> 8
3 <------ 3

5 <-:----- 5
6 <-:
8 <-:

19 ----:-> 4
      :-> 9
```

```
   G2301
7 ------- 7
2 -----> 5
3 <------ 4

19 -----> 3
5 <-:----- 1
6 <-:
8 <-:
```

```
   G2302
7 ------- 4
2 -----> 6
3 <------ 3

5 <-:----- 2
6 <-:
8 <-:

19 ----:-> 1
      :-> 7
```

```
   G2303
7 ------- 5
2 -----> 6
3 <------ 4

19 -----> 2
5 <-:----- 3
6 <-:
8 <-:
```

```
   G2304
7 ------- 9
2 -----> 3
3 <------ 2

19 -----> 5
5 <-:----- 4
6 <-:
8 <-:
```

```
   G2305
7 ------- 3
2 -----> 4
3 <------ 2

19 -----> 5
5 <-:----- 1
6 <-:
8 <-:
```

```
   G2306
7 ------- 9
2 -----> 13
3 <------ 11

19 -----> 14
5 <-:----- 10
6 <-:
8 <-:
```

```
   G2307
7 ------- 5
2 -----> 2
3 <------ 3

19 ----:-> 8
      :-> 6
5 <-:----- 4
6 <-:
8 <-:
```

```
   G2308
7 ------- 5
2 -----> 2
3 <------ 3

19 -----> 8
5 <-:----- 7
6 <-:
8 <-:
```

```
   G2309
7 ------- 5
2 -----> 3
3 <------ 2

5 <-:----- 6
6 <-:
8 <-:
```

```
   G2310
7 ------- 5
2 -----> 3
3 <------ 2

19 --:
5 <-:
6 <-:
8 <-:
```

```
   G2311
1 ------- 3
7 ------- 7
2 -----> 5
3 <------ 2

19 -----> 6
5 <-:----- 1
6 <-:
8 <-:
```

```
   G2312
1 ------- 1
7 ------- 2
2 -----> 4
3 <------ 3

19 -----> 5
5 <-:----- 6
6 <-:
8 <-:
```

```
   G2313
1 ------- 1
7 ------- 7
3 <------ 2

19 --:
5 <-:
6 <-:
8 <-:
```

```
   G2314
1 ------- 1
7 ------- 7
2 -----> 5
3 <------ 3

19 ----:-> 8
      :-> 6
5 <-:----- 4
6 <-:
8 <-:
```

```
G2315                G2316                G2317                G2318                G2319                G2320
7 ------ 4           7 ------- 5          7 ------- 1          1 ------- 3          1 ------- 4          7 ------- 3
2 ------> 5          2 ------> 4          2 ------> 4          7 ------- 3          7 ------- 2          2 ------> 1
3 <------ 3          3 <------ 2          3 <------ 2          2 ------> 2          2 ------> 5          3 <------ 5
                                                              3 <------ 4          3 <------ 3
19 ------> 2         19 ------> 6         19 ----:-> 6                             19 ------> 1         19 ----:-> 2
5 <-:---- 6          5 <-:---- 1             :-> 8            5 <-:---- 1          5 <-:---- 6             :-> 7
6 <-:               6 <-:                5 <-:---- 3          6 <-:               6 <-:               5 <-:---- 8
8 <-:               8 <-:                6 <-:               8 <-:               8 <-:               6 <-:
                                         8 <-:                                                        8 <-:


G2321                G2322                G2323                G2324                G2325                G2326
7 ------- 6          7 ------- 2          1 ------- 3          1 ------- 4          7 ------- 4          7 ------- 3
2 ------> 8          2 ------> 3          7 ------- 4          7 ------- 3          2 ------> 2          2 ------> 5
3 <------ 4          3 <------ 5          2 ------> 5          2 ------> 2          3 <------ 3          3 <------ 4
                                         3 <------ 2          3 <------ 5
19 ----:-> 7         5 <-:---- 4         19 ------> 1         19 ------> 6         19 ------> 6         19 ------> 1
   :-> 2             6 <-:               5 <-:---- 6          5 <-:---- 1          5 <-:---- 1          5 <-:---- 6
5 <-:---- 1          8 <-:               6 <-:               6 <-:               6 <-:               6 <-:
6 <-:                                    8 <-:               8 <-:               8 <-:               8 <-:
8 <-:


G2327                G2328                G2329                G2330                G2331                G2332
7 ------- 11         7 ------- 11         7 ------- 4          7 ------- 4          7 ------- 2          7 ------- 5
2 ------> 9          2 ------> 1          2 ------> 2          2 ------> 3          2 ------> 3          2 ------> 4
3 <------ 1          3 <------ 9          3 <------ 3          3 <------ 2          3 <------ 5          3 <------ 2
19 ----:-> 10        5 <-:---- 3         19 ------> 5         5 <-:---- 5         19 ------> 1         19 ----:-> 3
   :-> 3             6 <-:               5 <-:---- 1          6 <-:               5 <-:---- 6             :-> 6
   :-> 12            8 <-:               6 <-:               8 <-:               6 <-:               5 <-:---- 1
5 <-:---- 2         19 ----:-> 2         8 <-:                                   8 <-:               6 <-:
6 <-:                  :-> 4                                                                         8 <-:
8 <-:


G2333                G2334                G2268                G2269                G2270                G2271
7 ------- 2          7 ------- 5          1 ------- 1          1 ------- 1          1 ------- 1          1 ------- 1
2 ------> 3          2 ------> 2          7 ------- 7          7 ------- 7          7 ------- 7          7 ------- 7
3 <------ 5          3 <------ 3          2 ------> 3          2 ------> 2          2 ------> 2          2 ------> 3
19 ----:-> 4        19 ----:-> 8         3 <------ 2          3 <------ 3          3 <------ 3          3 <------ 2
   :-> 1               :-> 6            19 ----:-> 5          5 <-:---- 6         19 ----:-> 8         19 ----:-> 5
5 <-:---- 6          5 <-:---- 4            :-> 6             6 <-:                  :-> 4                :-> 6
6 <-:                6 <-:                  :-> 8             8 <-:                  :-> 20               :-> 20
8 <-:                8 <-:               5 <-:---- 20        19 ----:-> 4          5 <-:---- 5          5 <-:---- 4
                                         6 <-:                  :-> 20             6 <-:               6 <-:
                                         8 <-:                                    8 <-:               8 <-:


G2272                G2273                G2274                G2275                G2276                G2277
1 ------- 1          7 ------- 7          7 ------- 5          7 ------- 5          1 ------- 1          1 ------- 1
7 ------- 7          2 ------> 2          2 ------> 4          2 ------> 4          7 ------- 7          7 ------- 7
2 ------> 3          3 <------ 3          3 <------ 3          3 <------ 3          2 ------> 2          2 ------> 2
3 <------ 2                                                                        3 <------ 3          3 <------ 3
19 ----:-> 5         4 --:               19 ------> 6         5 <-:---- 1          5 <-:---- 6          5 <-:---- 6
   :-> 6             5 <-:               5 <-:---- 1          6 <-:               6 <-:               6 <-:
5 <-:---- 4          6 <-:               6 <-:               8 <-:               8 <-:               8 <-:
6 <-:                8 <-:               8 <-:                                   19 ----:-> 4
8 <-:                                                                               :-> 20
```

```
G2278                    G2279                    G2280
1 ------- 1              1 ------- 1              7 ------- 7
7 ------- 7              7 ------- 7              2 ------> 2
2 ------> 3              2 ------> 2              3 <------ 3
3 <------ 2              3 <------ 3
                                                  4 --:
19 ----:-> 5             4 --:                    5 <-:
     :-> 8               5 <-:                    6 <-:
                         6 <-:                    8 <-:
5 <-:---- 4              8 <-:
6 <-:
8 <-:
```

```
G2281                    G2282                    G2283
1 ------- 1              7 ------- 7              7 ------- 5
7 ------- 7              2 ------> 2              2 ------> 2
2 ------> 2              3 <------ 3              3 <------ 3
3 <------ 3
                         19 ----:-> 5             19 ----:-> 8
19 ----:-> 20                :-> 6                     :-> 6
     :-> 4                   :-> 8                     :-> 1
     :-> 12
                         5 <-:---- 4              5 <-:---- 4
5 <-:---- 5              6 <-:                    6 <-:
6 <-:                    8 <-:                    8 <-:
8 <-:
```

```
G2284                    G2285                    G2286
1 ------- 1              7 ------- 5              7 ------- 7
7 ------- 7              2 ------> 3              2 ------> 3
2 ------> 2              3 <------ 2              3 <------ 2
3 <------ 3
                         19 ----:-> 7             4 --:
5 <-:---- 8                  :-> 4                5 <-:
6 <-:                                             6 <-:
8 <-:                    5 <-:---- 6              8 <-:
                         6 <-:
19 ----:-> 20            8 <-:
```

```
G2287                    G2288                    G2289
1 ------- 1              1 ------- 1              7 ------- 4
7 ------- 8              7 ------- 7              2 ------> 3
2 ------> 4              2 ------> 2              3 <------ 2
3 <------ 2              3 <------ 3
                                                  19 ----:-> 1
19 ----:-> 5             5 <-:---- 6                   :-> 6
     :-> 10              6 <-:                    5 <-:---- 5
     :-> 7               8 <-:                    6 <-:
                                                  8 <-:
5 <-:---- 12            19 ----:-> 4
6 <-:
8 <-:

4 ----:-> 11
```

```
G2290                    G2291                    G2292
1 ------- 1              7 ------- 5              7 ------- 3
7 ------- 7              2 ------> 7              2 ------> 5
2 ------> 5              3 <------ 4              3 <------ 4
3 <------ 3
                         19 ----:-> 2             19 ----:-> 8
19 ------> 6                 :-> 6                     :-> 7
5 <-:---- 4                 :-> 3                     :-> 6
6 <-:
8 <-:                    5 <-:---- 3              5 <-:---- 2
                         6 <-:                    6 <-:
                         8 <-:                    8 <-:
```

```
G2293                    G2294                    G2295
1 ------- 4              1 ------- 3              7 ------- 8
7 ------- 7              7 ------- 6              2 ------> 2
2 ------> 6              2 ------> 5              3 <------ 1
3 <------ 5              3 <------ 4
                                                  4 --:
19 ----:-> 8            19 ----:-> 7              5 <-:
     :-> 2                   :-> 1                6 <-:
     :-> 10             5 <-:---- 8               8 <-:
                         6 <-:
5 <-:---- 9              8 <-:
6 <-:
8 <-:

4 ----:-> 1
```

```
G2296                    G2297                    G2298
7 ------- 8              7 ------- 7              7 ------- 5
2 ------> 6              2 ------> 3              2 ------> 3
3 <------ 1              3 <------ 2              3 <------ 2

19 ----:-> 7           19 ----:-> 5              5 <-:---- 6
     :-> 9                   :-> 8                6 <-:
5 <-:---- 4                                       8 <-:
6 <-:                   5 <-:---- 9
8 <-:                   6 <-:                    19 ----:-> 4
                         8 <-:                        :-> 7
```

```
G2299                    G2300                    G2301
1 ------- 2              1 ------- 2              7 ------- 7
7 ------- 7              7 ------- 7              2 ------> 5
2 ------> 3              2 ------> 8              3 <------ 4
3 <------ 8              3 <------ 3
                                                  19 ------> 3
19 ----:-> 5            5 <-:---- 5               5 <-:---- 1
     :-> 6               6 <-:                    6 <-:
     :-> 1               8 <-:                    8 <-:
5 <-:---- 9
6 <-:                   19 ----:-> 4
8 <-:                        :-> 9

4 ----:-> 10
```

```
G2302                 G2303                 G2304
7 ------- 4           7 ------- 5           7 ------- 9
2 ------> 6           2 ------> 6           2 ------> 3
3 <------ 3           3 <------ 4           3 <------ 2

5 <-:----- 2          19 ------> 2          19 ------> 5
6 <-:                 5 <-:----- 3          5 <-:----- 4
8 <-:                 6 <-:                 6 <-:
                      8 <-:                 8 <-:
19 ----:-> 1
     :-> 7

G2305                 G2306                 G2307
7 ------- 3           7 ------- 9           7 ------- 5
2 ------> 4           2 ------> 13          2 ------> 2
3 <------ 2           3 <------ 11          3 <------ 3

19 ------> 5          19 ------> 14         19 ----:-> 8
5 <-:----- 1          5 <-:----- 10             :-> 6
6 <-:                 6 <-:                 5 <-:----- 4
8 <-:                 8 <-:                 6 <-:
                                            8 <-:

G2308                 G2309                 G2310
7 ------- 5           7 ------- 5           7 ------- 5
2 ------> 2           2 ------> 3           2 ------> 3
3 <------ 3           3 <------ 2           3 <------ 2

19 ----:-> 8          5 <-:----- 6          19 --:
5 <-:----- 7          6 <-:                 5 <-:
6 <-:                 8 <-:                 6 <-:
8 <-:                                       8 <-:

G2311                 G2312                 G2313
1 ------- 3           1 ------- 1           1 ------- 1
7 ------- 4           7 ------- 2           7 ------- 7
2 ------> 5           2 ------> 4           3 <------ 2
3 <------ 2           3 <------ 3
                                            19 --:
19 ------> 6          19 ------> 5          5 <-:
5 <-:----- 1          5 <-:----- 6          6 <-:
6 <-:                 6 <-:                 8 <-:
8 <-:                 8 <-:

G2314                 G2315                 G2316
1 ------- 1           7 ------- 4           7 ------- 5
7 ------- 7           2 ------> 5           2 ------> 4
2 ------> 5           3 <------ 3           3 <------ 2
3 <------ 3
                      19 ------> 2          19 ------> 6
19 ----:-> 8          5 <-:----- 6          5 <-:----- 1
     :-> 6            6 <-:                 6 <-:
5 <-:----- 4          8 <-:                 8 <-:
6 <-:
8 <-:

G2317                 G2318                 G2319
7 ------- 1           1 ------- 3           1 ------- 4
2 ------> 4           7 ------- 5           7 ------- 2
3 <------ 2           2 ------> 2           2 ------> 5
                      3 <------ 4           3 <------ 3
19 ----:-> 6
     :-> 8            5 <-:----- 1          19 ------> 1
5 <-:----- 3          6 <-:                 5 <-:----- 6
6 <-:                 8 <-:                 6 <-:
8 <-:                                       8 <-:

G2320                 G2321                 G2322
7 ------- 3           7 ------- 6           7 ------- 2
2 ------> 1           2 ------> 8           2 ------> 3
3 <------ 5           3 <------ 4           3 <------ 5

19 ----:-> 2          19 ----:-> 7          5 <-:----- 4
     :-> 7                :-> 2            6 <-:
5 <-:----- 8          5 <-:----- 1          8 <-:
6 <-:                 6 <-:
8 <-:                 8 <-:

G2323                 G2324                 G2325
1 ------- 3           1 ------- 4           7 ------- 4
7 ------- 4           7 ------- 3           2 ------> 2
2 ------> 5           2 ------> 2           3 <------ 3
3 <------ 2           3 <------ 5
                                            19 ------> 6
19 ------> 1          19 ------> 6          5 <-:----- 1
5 <-:----- 6          5 <-:----- 1          6 <-:
6 <-:                 6 <-:                 8 <-:
8 <-:                 8 <-:

G2326                 G2327                 G2328
7 ------- 3           7 ------- 11          7 ------- 11
2 ------> 5           2 ------> 9           2 ------> 1
3 <------ 4           3 <------ 1           3 <------ 9

19 ------> 1          19 ----:-> 10         5 <-:----- 3
5 <-:----- 6              :-> 3            6 <-:
6 <-:                     :-> 12           8 <-:
8 <-:                 5 <-:----- 2
                      6 <-:                 19 ----:-> 2
                      8 <-:                     :-> 4

G2329                 G2330                 G2331
7 ------- 4           7 ------- 4           7 ------- 2
2 ------> 2           2 ------> 3           2 ------> 3
3 <------ 3           3 <------ 2           3 <------ 5

19 ------> 5          5 <-:----- 5          19 ------> 1
5 <-:----- 1          6 <-:                 5 <-:----- 6
6 <-:                 8 <-:                 6 <-:
8 <-:                                       8 <-:
```

```
┌─────────────────────┬─────────────────────┬─────────────────────┬─────────────────────┬─────────────────────┬─────────────────────┐
│      G2332          │      G2333          │      G2334          │      G2335          │      G2336          │      G2337          │
│ 7 ------- 5         │ 7 ------- 2         │ 7 ------- 5         │ 1 ------- 1         │ 1 ------- 1         │ 1 ------- 1         │
│ 2 ------> 4         │ 2 ------> 3         │ 2 ------> 2         │ 7 ------- 7         │ 7 ------- 7         │ 7 ------- 7         │
│ 3 <------ 2         │ 3 <------ 5         │ 3 <------ 3         │ 2 ------> 3         │ 2 ------> 2         │ 2 ------> 2         │
│                     │                     │                     │ 3 <------ 2         │ 3 ------> 3         │ 3 <------ 3         │
│ 19 ---:-> 3         │ 19 ---:-> 4         │ 19 ---:-> 8         │                     │ 5 <------ 5         │                     │
│      :-> 6          │      :-> 1          │      :-> 6          │ 5 <------ 20        │ 4 ------> 4         │ 5 <------ 5         │
│ 5 <-:---- 1         │ 5 <-:---- 6         │ 5 <-:---- 4         │                     │                     │                     │
│ 6 <-:               │ 6 <-:               │ 6 <-:               │ 4 ----:-> 5         │   :-- 6             │ 4 ----:-> 4         │
│ 8 <-:               │ 8 <-:               │ 8 <-:               │      :-> 6          │   :-> 20            │      :-> 8          │
│                     │                     │                     │      :-> 8          │                     │      :-> 20         │
├─────────────────────┼─────────────────────┼─────────────────────┼─────────────────────┼─────────────────────┼─────────────────────┤
│      G2338          │      G2339          │      G2340          │      G2341          │      G2342          │      G2343          │
│ 1 ------- 1         │ 1 ------- 1         │ 7 ------- 7         │ 7 ------- 5         │ 7 ------- 5         │ 1 ------- 1         │
│ 7 ------- 7         │ 7 ------- 7         │ 2 ------> 2         │ 2 ------> 4         │ 2 ------> 4         │ 7 ------- 7         │
│ 2 ------> 3         │ 2 ------> 3         │ 3 <------ 3         │ 3 <------ 3         │ 3 <------ 3         │ 2 ------> 2         │
│ 3 <------ 2         │ 3 <------ 2         │                     │                     │                     │ 3 <------ 3         │
│                     │                     │ 4 --:               │ 4 ------> 6         │ 5 <-:---- 1         │                     │
│ 5 <------ 4         │ 4 ----:-> 5         │ 5 <-:               │ 5 <-:---- 1         │                     │ 5 <-:---- 6         │
│                     │      :-> 6          │                     │                     │                     │                     │
│ 4 ----:-> 5         │ 5 <-:---- 4         │                     │                     │                     │ 4 ----:-> 4         │
│      :-> 6          │                     │                     │                     │                     │      :-> 20         │
│      :-> 20         │                     │                     │                     │                     │                     │
├─────────────────────┼─────────────────────┼─────────────────────┼─────────────────────┼─────────────────────┼─────────────────────┤
│      G2344          │      G2345          │      G2346          │      G2347          │      G2348          │      G2349          │
│ 1 ------- 1         │ 1 ------- 1         │ 1 ------- 1         │ 7 ------- 7         │ 1 ------- 1         │ 7 ------- 7         │
│ 7 ------- 7         │ 7 ------- 7         │ 7 ------- 7         │ 2 ------> 2         │ 7 ------- 7         │ 2 ------> 2         │
│ 2 ------> 2         │ 2 ------> 3         │ 2 ------> 2         │ 3 <------ 3         │ 2 ------> 2         │ 3 <------ 3         │
│ 3 <------ 3         │ 3 <------ 2         │ 3 <------ 3         │                     │ 3 <------ 3         │                     │
│                     │                     │                     │ 4 --:               │                     │ 4 ----:-> 5         │
│ 5 <-:---- 6         │ 4 ----:-> 5         │ 4 --:               │ 5 <-:               │ 4 ------> 20        │   :-- 6             │
│                     │      :-> 8          │ 5 <-:               │                     │                     │   :-- 8             │
│                     │ 5 <-:---- 4         │                     │                     │ 5 <-:---- 5         │ 5 <-:---- 4         │
│                     │                     │                     │                     │   :-- 8             │                     │
│                     │                     │                     │                     │   :-> 4             │                     │
│                     │                     │                     │                     │   :-> 12            │                     │
├─────────────────────┼─────────────────────┼─────────────────────┼─────────────────────┼─────────────────────┼─────────────────────┤
│      G2350          │      G2351          │      G2352          │      G2353          │      G2354          │      G2355          │
│ 7 ------- 5         │ 1 ------- 1         │ 7 ------- 5         │ 7 ------- 7         │ 1 ------- 1         │ 1 ------- 1         │
│ 2 ------> 2         │ 7 ------- 7         │ 2 ------> 3         │ 2 ------> 3         │ 7 ------- 8         │ 7 ------- 7         │
│ 3 <------ 3         │ 2 ------> 2         │ 3 <------ 2         │ 3 <------ 2         │ 2 ------> 4         │ 2 ------> 2         │
│                     │ 3 ------> 3         │                     │                     │ 3 <------ 2         │ 3 <------ 3         │
│ 4 ----:-> 8         │                     │ 4 ----:-> 7         │ 4 --:               │                     │ 5 <------ 5         │
│   :-- 6             │ 5 <-:---- 8         │   :-- 4             │ 5 <-:               │ 5 <------ 12        │ 4 ------> 4         │
│   :-- 1             │                     │ 5 <-:---- 6         │                     │                     │                     │
│                     │ 4 ----:-> 20        │                     │                     │ 4 ----:-> 5         │                     │
│ 5 <-:---- 4         │                     │                     │                     │   :-> 7             │                     │
│                     │                     │                     │                     │   :-> 10            │                     │
│                     │                     │                     │                     │   :-> 11            │                     │
├─────────────────────┼─────────────────────┼─────────────────────┼─────────────────────┼─────────────────────┼─────────────────────┤
│      G2356          │      G2357          │      G2358          │      G2359          │      G2360          │      G2361          │
│ 7 ------- 4         │ 1 ------- 1         │ 7 ------- 5         │ 7 ------- 3         │ 1 ------- 4         │ 1 ------- 3         │
│ 2 ------> 3         │ 7 ------- 7         │ 2 ------> 7         │ 2 ------> 5         │ 7 ------- 7         │ 7 ------- 6         │
│ 3 <------ 2         │ 2 ------> 5         │ 3 <------ 4         │ 3 <------ 4         │ 2 ------> 6         │ 2 ------> 5         │
│                     │ 3 <------ 3         │                     │                     │ 3 <------ 5         │ 3 <------ 4         │
│ 5 <------ 5         │                     │ 5 <------ 3         │ 5 <------ 2         │                     │                     │
│                     │ 4 ------> 6         │                     │                     │ 5 <------ 9         │ 5 <------ 8         │
│ 4 ----:-> 1         │ 5 <-:---- 4         │ 4 ----:-> 2         │ 4 ----:-> 6         │                     │                     │
│   :-> 6             │                     │      :-> 6          │   :-> 7             │ 4 ----:-> 1         │ 4 ----:-> 1         │
│                     │                     │                     │   :-> 8             │   :-> 2             │   :-> 7             │
│                     │                     │                     │                     │   :-> 8             │                     │
│                     │                     │                     │                     │   :-> 10            │                     │
└─────────────────────┴─────────────────────┴─────────────────────┴─────────────────────┴─────────────────────┴─────────────────────┘
```

G2362	G2363	G2364	G2365	G2366	G2367

7 ------- 8
2 ------> 2
3 <------ 1
 	
4 --:
5 <-:
	7 ------- 8
	2 ------> 6
	3 <------ 1
	
	5 <------ 4
	4 ----:-> 7
	    :-> 9
		7 ------- 7
		2 ------> 3
		3 <------ 2
		
		5 <------ 9
		4 ----:-> 5
		    :-> 8
			7 ------- 5
			2 ------> 3
			3 <------ 2
			
			5 <------ 6
			4 ----:-> 4
			    :-> 7
				1 ------- 2
				7 ------- 7
				2 ------> 3
				3 <------ 8
				
				5 <------ 9
				4 ----:-> 1
				    :-> 5
				    :-> 6
				    :-> 10
					1 ------- 2
					7 ------- 7
					2 ------> 8
					3 <------ 3
					
					5 <------ 5
					4 ----:-> 4
					    :-> 9

G2368	G2369	G2370	G2371	G2372	G2373
7 ------- 7 2 ------> 5 3 <------ 4 5 <------ 1 4 ----:-> 3	7 ------- 4 2 ------> 4 3 <------ 3 5 <------ 2 4 ----:-> 1 :- 7	7 ------- 5 2 ------> 6 3 <------ 4 5 <------ 3 4 ----:-> 2	7 ------- 9 2 ------> 3 3 <------ 2 5 <------ 4 4 ----:-> 5	7 ------- 3 2 ------> 4 3 <------ 2 5 <------ 1 4 ----:-> 5	7 ------- 9 2 ------> 13 3 <------ 11 5 <------ 10 4 ----:-> 14
G2374	G2375	G2376	G2377	G2378	G2379
7 ------- 5 2 ------> 2 3 <------ 3 5 <------ 4 4 ----:-> 6 :- 8	7 ------- 5 2 ------> 2 3 <------ 3 5 <------ 7 4 ----:-> 8	7 ------- 5 2 ------> 3 3 <------ 2 5 <------ 6	7 ------- 5 2 ------> 3 3 <------ 2 4 --: 5 <-:	1 ------- 3 7 ------- 4 2 ------> 5 3 <------ 2 5 <------ 1 4 ----:-> 6	1 ------- 1 7 ------- 2 2 ------> 4 3 <------ 3 5 <------ 6 4 ----:-> 5
G2380	G2381	G2382	G2383	G2384	G2385

1 ------- 1
7 ------- 7
3 <------ 2
 	
4 --:
5 <-:
	1 ------- 1
	7 ------- 7
	2 ------> 5
	3 <------ 3
	
	5 <------ 4
	
	4 ----:-> 6
	  :-> 8
		7 ------- 4
		2 ------> 5
		3 <------ 3
		
		5 <------ 6
		
		4 ----:-> 2
			7 ------- 5
			2 ------> 4
			3 <------ 2
			
			5 <------ 1
			
			4 ----:-> 6
				7 ------- 1
				2 ------> 4
				3 <------ 2
				
				5 <------ 3
				
				4 ----:-> 6
				    :-> 8
					1 ------- 3
					7 ------- 5
					2 ------> 2
					3 <------ 4
					
					5 <------ 1

G2386	G2387	G2388	G2389	G2390	G2391

1 ------- 4
7 ------- 2
2 ------> 5
3 <------ 3
 	
5 <------ 6
 	
4 ----:-> 1
	7 ------- 3
	2 ------> 1
	3 <------ 5
	
	5 <------ 8
	
	4 ----:-> 2
	    :-> 7
		7 ------- 6
		2 ------> 8
		3 <------ 4
		
		5 <------ 1
		
		4 ----:-> 2
		    :-> 7
			7 ------- 2
			2 ------> 3
			3 <------ 5
			
			5 <------ 4
				1 ------- 3
				7 ------- 4
				2 ------> 5
				3 <------ 2
				
				5 <------ 6
				
				4 ----:-> 1
					1 ------- 4
					7 ------- 3
					2 ------> 2
					3 <------ 5
					
					5 <------ 1
					
					4 ----:-> 6

G2392	G2393	G2394	G2395	G2396	G2397

7 ------- 4
 2 ------> 2
 3 <------ 3
 	
 5 <------ 1
 	
 4 ----:-> 6
	7 ------- 3
	 2 ------> 5
	 3 <------ 4
	
	 5 <------ 6
	
	 4 ----:-> 1
		7 ------- 11
		 2 ------> 9
		 3 <------ 1
		
		 5 <------ 2
		
		 4 ----:-> 3
		       :-> 10
		       :-> 12
			7 ------- 11
			 2 ------> 1
			 3 <------ 9
			 5 <------ 10
			 4 ------> 2
			
			   :-- 3
			   :-> 4
				7 ------- 4
				 2 ------> 2
				 3 <------ 3
				
				 5 <------ 1
				
				 4 ----:-> 5
					7 ------- 4
					 2 ------> 3
					 3 <------ 2
					
					 5 <------ 5

G2398	G2399	G2400	G2401	G2402	G2403

7 ------- 2
 2 ------> 3
 3 <------ 5
 	
 5 <------ 6
 	
 4 ----:-> 1
	7 ------- 5
	 2 ------> 4
	 3 <------ 2
	
	 5 <------ 1
	
	 4 ----:-> 3
	       :-> 6
		7 ------- 2
		 2 ------> 3
		 3 <------ 5
		
		 5 <------ 6
		
		 4 ----:-> 1
		       :-> 4
			7 ------- 5
			 2 ------> 2
			 3 <------ 3
			
			 5 <------ 4
			
			 4 ----:-> 6
			       :-> 8
				1 ------- 1
				 7 ------- 7
				 2 ------> 3
				 3 <------ 2
				
				 20 ----:-> 5
				       :-> 6
				       :-> 8
				 5 <-:---- 20
				 6 <-:
				 8 <-:
					1 ------- 1
					 7 ------- 7
					 2 ------> 2
					 3 <------ 3
					
					 5 <-:---- 6
					 6 <-:
					 8 <-:
					 20 ----:-> 4
					       :-> 20

G2404	G2405	G2406	G2407	G2408	G2409

1 ------- 1
 7 ------- 7
 2 ------> 2
 3 <------ 3
 	
 20 ----:-> 8
       :-> 4
       :-> 20
 5 <-:---- 5
 6 <-:
 8 <-:
	1 ------- 1
	 7 ------- 7
	 2 ------> 3
	 3 <------ 2
	
	 20 ----:-> 5
	       :-> 6
	       :-> 20
	 5 <-:---- 4
	 6 <-:
	 8 <-:
		1 ------- 1
		 7 ------- 7
		 2 ------> 3
		 3 <------ 2
		
		 20 ----:-> 5
		       :-> 6
		 5 <-:---- 4
		 6 <-:
		 8 <-:
			7 ------- 7
			 2 ------> 2
			 3 <------ 3
			
			 4 --:
			 5 <-:
			 6 <-:
			 8 <-:
				7 ------- 5
				 2 ------> 4
				 3 <------ 3
				
				 20 ------> 6
				 5 <-:---- 1
				 6 <-:
				 8 <-:
					7 ------- 5
					 2 ------> 4
					 3 <------ 3
					
					 5 <-:---- 1
					 6 <-:
					 8 <-:

G2410	G2411	G2412	G2413	G2414	G2415

1 ------- 1
 7 ------- 7
 2 ------> 2
 3 <------ 3
 	
 5 <-:---- 6
 6 <-:
 8 <-:
 	
 20 ----:-> 4
       :-> 20
	1 ------- 1
	 7 ------- 7
	 2 ------> 2
	 3 <------ 3
	
	 5 <-:---- 6
	 6 <-:
	 8 <-:
		1 ------- 1
		 7 ------- 7
		 2 ------> 3
		 3 <------ 2
		
		 20 ----:-> 5
		       :-> 8
		
		 5 <-:---- 4
		 6 <-:
		 8 <-:
			1 ------- 1
			 7 ------- 7
			 2 ------> 2
			 3 <------ 3
			
			 4 --:
			 5 <-:
			 6 <-:
			 8 <-:
				7 ------- 7
				 2 ------> 2
				 3 <------ 3
				
				 4 --:
				 5 <-:
				 6 <-:
				 8 <-:
					1 ------- 1
					 7 ------- 7
					 2 ------> 2
					 3 <------ 3
					
					 20 ----:-> 20
					       :-> 4
					       :-> 12
					
					 5 <-:---- 5
					 6 <-:
					 8 <-:

G2416	G2417	G2418	G2419	G2420	G2421

`7 ------- 7`
`2 ----> 2`
`3 <----- 3`
 	
`20 ----:-> 5`
`      :-> 6`
`      :-> 8`
 	
`5 <-:----- 4`
`6 <-:`
`8 <-:`
	`7 ------- 5`
	`2 ----> 2`
	`3 <----- 3`
	
	`20 ----:-> 8`
	`      :-> 6`
	`      :-> 1`
	
	`5 <-:----- 4`
	`6 <-:`
	`8 <-:`
		`1 ------- 1`
		`7 ------- 7`
		`2 -----> 2`
		`3 <----- 3`
		
		`5 <-:----- 8`
		`6 <-:`
		`8 <-:`
		
		`20 ----:-> 20`
			`7 ------- 5`
			`2 -----> 3`
			`3 <----- 2`
			
			`20 ----:-> 7`
			`      :-> 4`
			`5 <-:----- 6`
			`6 <-:`
			`8 <-:`
				`7 ------- 7`
				`2 -----> 3`
				`3 <----- 2`
				
				`4 --:`
				`5 <-:`
				`6 <-:`
				`8 <-:`
					`1 ------- 1`
					`7 ------- 8`
					`2 -----> 4`
					`3 <----- 2`
					
					`20 ----:-> 5`
					`      :-> 10`
					`5 <-:----- 12`
					`6 <-:`
					`8 <-:`
					
					`4 ----:-> 11`

G2422	G2423	G2424	G2425	G2426	G2427

`1 ------- 1`
`7 ------- 7`
`2 -----> 2`
`3 <----- 3`
 	
`5 <-:----- 6`
`6 <-:`
`8 <-:`
 	
`20 ----:-> 4`
	`7 ------- 4`
	`2 -----> 3`
	`3 <----- 2`
	
	`20 ----:-> 1`
	`      :-> 6`
	`5 <-:----- 5`
	`6 <-:`
	`8 <-:`
		`1 ------- 1`
		`7 ------- 7`
		`2 -----> 5`
		`3 <----- 3`
		
		`20 -----> 6`
		`5 <-:----- 4`
		`6 <-:`
		`8 <-:`
			`7 ------- 5`
			`2 -----> 7`
			`3 <----- 4`
			
			`20 ----:-> 2`
			`      :-> 6`
			`5 <-:----- 3`
			`6 <-:`
			`8 <-:`
				`7 ------- 3`
				`2 -----> 5`
				`3 <----- 4`
				
				`20 ----:-> 8`
				`      :-> 7`
				`      :-> 6`
				`5 <-:----- 2`
				`6 <-:`
				`8 <-:`
					`1 ------- 4`
					`7 ------- 7`
					`2 -----> 6`
					`3 <----- 5`
					
					`20 ----:-> 8`
					`      :-> 2`
					`      :-> 10`
					`5 <-:----- 9`
					`6 <-:`
					`8 <-:`
					
					`4 ----:-> 1`

G2428	G2429	G2430	G2431	G2432	G2433

`1 ------- 3`
`7 ------- 6`
`2 -----> 5`
`3 <----- 4`
 	
`20 ----:-> 7`
`      :-> 1`
`5 <-:----- 8`
`6 <-:`
`8 <-:`
	`7 ------- 8`
	`2 -----> 2`
	`3 <----- 1`
	
	`4 --:`
	`5 <-:`
	`6 <-:`
	`8 <-:`
		`7 ------- 8`
		`2 -----> 6`
		`3 <----- 1`
		
		`20 ----:-> 7`
		`      :-> 9`
		`5 <-:----- 4`
		`6 <-:`
		`8 <-:`
			`7 ------- 7`
			`2 -----> 3`
			`3 <----- 2`
			
			`20 ----:-> 5`
			`      :-> 8`
			`5 <-:----- 9`
			`6 <-:`
			`8 <-:`
				`7 ------- 5`
				`2 -----> 3`
				`3 <----- 2`
				
				`5 <-:----- 6`
				`6 <-:`
				`8 <-:`
				
				`20 ----:-> 4`
				`      :-> 7`
					`1 ------- 2`
					`7 ------- 7`
					`2 -----> 3`
					`3 <----- 8`
					
					`20 ----:-> 5`
					`      :-> 6`
					`      :-> 1`
					`5 <-:----- 9`
					`6 <-:`
					`8 <-:`
					
					`4 ----:-> 10`

G2434	G2435	G2436	G2437	G2438	G2439

`1 ------- 2`
`7 ------- 7`
`2 -----> 8`
`3 <----- 3`
 	
`5 <-:----- 5`
`6 <-:`
`8 <-:`
 	
`20 ----:-> 4`
`      :-> 9`
	`7 ------- 7`
	`2 -----> 5`
	`3 <----- 4`
	
	`20 -----> 3`
	`5 <-:----- 1`
	`6 <-:`
	`8 <-:`
		`7 ------- 4`
		`2 -----> 6`
		`3 <----- 3`
		
		`5 <-:----- 2`
		`6 <-:`
		`8 <-:`
		
		`20 ----:-> 1`
		`      :-> 7`
			`7 ------- 5`
			`2 -----> 6`
			`3 <----- 4`
			
			`20 -----> 2`
			`5 <-:----- 3`
			`6 <-:`
			`8 <-:`
				`7 ------- 9`
				`2 -----> 3`
				`3 <----- 2`
				
				`20 -----> 5`
				`5 <-:----- 4`
				`6 <-:`
				`8 <-:`
					`7 ------- 3`
					`2 -----> 4`
					`3 <----- 2`
					
					`20 -----> 5`
					`5 <-:----- 1`
					`6 <-:`
					`8 <-:`

G2440
```
7 ------- 9
2 ------> 13
3 <------ 11
20 ------> 14
5 <-:---- 10
6 <-:
8 <-:
```

G2441
```
7 ------- 5
2 ------> 2
3 <------ 3
20 ----:
         :-> 6
5 <-:---- 4
6 <-:
8 <-:
```

G2442
```
7 ------- 5
2 ------> 2
3 <------ 3
20 ------> 8
5 <-:---- 7
6 <-:
8 <-:
```

G2443
```
7 ------- 5
2 ------> 3
3 <------ 2
5 <-:---- 6
6 <-:
8 <-:
```

G2444
```
7 ------- 5
2 ------> 3
3 <------ 2
20 --:
5 <-:
6 <-:
8 <-:
```

G2445
```
1 ------- 3
7 ------- 4
2 ------> 5
3 <------ 2
20 ------> 6
5 <-:---- 1
6 <-:
8 <-:
```

G2446
```
1 ------- 1
7 ------- 2
2 ------> 4
3 <------ 3
20 ------> 5
5 <-:---- 6
6 <-:
8 <-:
```

G2447
```
1 ------- 1
7 ------- 7
3 <------ 2
20 --:
5 <-:
6 <-:
8 <-:
```

G2448
```
1 ------- 1
7 ------- 7
2 ------> 5
3 <------ 3
20 ----:-> 8
         :-> 6
5 <-:---- 4
6 <-:
8 <-:
```

G2449
```
7 ------- 4
2 ------> 5
3 <------ 3
20 ------> 2
5 <-:---- 6
6 <-:
8 <-:
```

G2450
```
7 ------- 5
2 ------> 4
3 <------ 2
20 ------> 6
5 <-:---- 1
6 <-:
8 <-:
```

G2451
```
7 ------- 1
2 ------> 4
3 <------ 2
20 ----:-> 6
         :-> 8
5 <-:---- 3
6 <-:
8 <-:
```

G2452
```
1 ------- 3
7 ------- 5
2 ------> 2
3 <------ 4
5 <-:---- 1
6 <-:
8 <-:
```

G2453
```
1 ------- 4
7 ------- 2
2 ------> 5
3 <------ 3
20 ------> 1
5 <-:---- 6
6 <-:
8 <-:
```

G2454
```
7 ------- 3
2 ------> 1
3 <------ 5
20 ----:-> 2
         :-> 7
5 <-:---- 8
6 <-:
8 <-:
```

G2455
```
7 ------- 6
2 ------> 8
3 <------ 4
20 ----:-> 7
         :-> 2
5 <-:---- 1
6 <-:
8 <-:
```

G2456
```
7 ------- 2
2 ------> 3
3 <------ 5
5 <-:---- 4
6 <-:
8 <-:
```

G2457
```
1 ------- 3
7 ------- 4
2 ------> 5
3 <------ 2
20 ------> 1
5 <-:---- 6
6 <-:
8 <-:
```

G2458
```
1 ------- 4
7 ------- 3
2 ------> 2
3 <------ 5
20 ------> 6
5 <-:---- 1
6 <-:
8 <-:
```

G2459
```
7 ------- 4
2 ------> 2
3 <------ 3
20 ------> 6
5 <-:---- 1
6 <-:
8 <-:
```

G2460
```
7 ------- 3
2 ------> 5
3 <------ 4
20 ------> 1
5 <-:---- 6
6 <-:
8 <-:
```

G2461
```
7 ------- 11
2 ------> 9
3 <------ 1
20 ----:-> 10
         :-> 3
         :-> 12
5 <-:---- 2
6 <-:
8 <-:
```

G2462
```
7 ------- 11
2 ------> 1
3 <------ 9
5 <-:---- 3
6 <-:
8 <-:
20 ----:-> 2
         :-> 4
```

G2463
```
7 ------- 4
2 ------> 2
3 <------ 3
20 ------> 5
5 <-:---- 1
6 <-:
8 <-:
```

G2464
```
7 ------- 4
2 ------> 3
3 <------ 2
5 <-:---- 5
6 <-:
8 <-:
```

G2465
```
7 ------- 2
2 ------> 3
3 <------ 5
20 ------> 1
5 <-:---- 6
6 <-:
8 <-:
```

G2466
```
7 ------- 5
2 ------> 4
3 <------ 2
20 ----:-> 3
         :-> 6
5 <-:---- 1
6 <-:
8 <-:
```

G2467
```
7 ------- 2
2 ------> 3
3 <------ 5
20 ----:-> 4
         :-> 1
5 <-:---- 6
6 <-:
8 <-:
```

G2468
```
7 ------- 5
2 ------> 2
3 <------ 3
20 ----:-> 8
         :-> 6
5 <-:---- 4
6 <-:
8 <-:
```

G2469
```
1 ------- 1
7 ------- 7
2 ------> 3
3 <------ 2
11 ----:-> 5
         :-> 6
         :-> 8
```

G2470	G2471	G2472	G2473	G2474	G2475
1 ------- 1 7 ------- 7 2 ------> 2 3 <------ 3 11 ------> 4 　　　:-- 6 　　　:-> 20	1 ------- 1 7 ------- 7 2 ------> 2 3 <------ 3 11 ----:-> 4 　　　:-> 8 　　　:-> 20	1 ------- 1 7 ------- 7 2 ------> 3 3 <------ 2 11 ---:-> 5 　　　:-> 6 　　　:-> 20	1 ------- 1 7 ------- 7 2 ------> 3 3 <------ 2 11 ----:-> 5 　　　:-> 6	7 ------- 7 2 ------> 2 3 <------ 3 11 --:	7 ------- 5 2 ------> 4 3 <------ 3 11 ------> 6

G2476	G2477	G2478	G2479	G2480	G2481
7 ------- 5 2 ------> 4 3 <------ 3	1 ------- 1 7 ------- 7 2 ------> 2 3 <------ 3 11 ----:-> 4 　　　:-> 20	1 ------- 1 7 ------- 7 2 ------> 2 3 <------ 3	1 ------- 1 7 ------- 7 2 ------> 3 3 <------ 2 11 ----:-> 5 　　　:-> 8	1 ------- 1 7 ------- 7 2 ------> 2 3 <------ 3	7 ------- 7 2 ------> 2 3 <------ 3

G2482	G2483	G2484	G2485	G2486	G2487
1 ------- 1 7 ------- 7 2 ------> 2 3 <------ 3 11 ------> 20 　　　:-- 8 　　　:-> 4 　　　:-> 12	7 ------- 7 2 ------> 2 3 <------ 3 11 ----:-> 5 　　　:- 6 　　　:- 8	7 ------- 5 2 ------> 2 3 <------ 3 11 ----:-> 8 　　　:- 6 　　　:- 1	1 ------- 1 7 ------- 7 2 ------> 2 3 <------ 3 11 ----:-> 20	7 ------- 5 2 ------> 3 3 <------ 2 11 ----:-> 7 　　　:-> 4	7 ------- 7 2 ------> 3 3 <------ 2

G2488	G2489	G2490	G2491	G2492	G2493
1 ------- 1 7 ------- 8 2 ------> 4 3 <------ 2 11 ----:-> 5 　　　:-> 7 　　　:-> 10 　　　:-> 11	1 ------- 1 7 ------- 7 2 ------> 2 3 <------ 3 11 ------> 4	7 ------- 4 2 ------> 3 3 <------ 2 11 ----:-> 1 　　　:-> 6	1 ------- 1 7 ------- 7 2 ------> 5 3 <------ 3 11 ------> 6	7 ------- 5 2 ------> 7 3 <------ 4 11 ----:-> 2 　　　:-> 6	7 ------- 3 2 ------> 5 3 <------ 4 11 ----:-> 6 　　　:-> 7 　　　:-> 8

G2494	G2495	G2496	G2497	G2498	G2499
1 ------- 4 7 ------- 7 2 ------> 6 3 <------ 5 11 ----:-> 1 　　　:-> 2 　　　:-> 8 　　　:-> 10	1 ------- 3 7 ------- 6 2 ------> 5 3 <------ 4 11 ----:-> 1 　　　:-> 7	7 ------- 8 2 ------> 2 3 <------ 1	7 ------- 8 2 ------> 6 3 <------ 1 11 ----:-> 7 　　　:-> 9	7 ------- 7 2 ------> 3 3 <------ 2 11 ----:-> 5 　　　:-> 8	7 ------- 5 2 ------> 3 3 <------ 2 11 ----:-> 4 　　　:-> 7

```
 G2500              G2501              G2502              G2503              G2504              G2505

1 ------- 2        1 ------- 2        7 ------- 7        7 ------- 4        7 ------- 5        7 ------- 9
7 ------- 7        7 ------- 7        2 ------> 5        2 ------> 6        2 ------> 6        2 ------> 3
2 ------> 3        2 ------> 8        3 <------ 4        3 <------ 3        3 <------ 4        3 <------ 2
3 <------ 8        3 <------ 3                                                                
11 ----:-> 1                          11 ----:-> 3       11 ----:-> 1       11 ----:-> 2       11 ----:-> 5
     :-> 5         11 ----:-> 4                               :- 7
     :-> 6              :-> 9
     :-> 10


 G2506              G2507              G2508              G2509              G2510              G2511

7 ------- 3        7 ------- 9        7 ------- 5        7 ------- 5        7 ------- 5        7 ------- 5
2 ------> 4        2 ------> 13       2 ------> 2        2 ------> 2        2 ------> 3        2 ------> 3
3 <------ 2        3 <------ 11       3 <------ 3        3 <------ 3        3 <------ 2        3 <------ 2

11 ----:-> 5       11 ----:-> 14      11 ----:-> 6       11 ----:-> 8                          11 --:
                                           :- 8


 G2512              G2513              G2514              G2515              G2516              G2517

1 ------- 3        1 ------- 1        1 ------- 1        1 ------- 1        7 ------- 4        7 ------- 5
7 ------- 4        7 ------- 2        7 ------- 7        7 ------- 7        2 ------> 5        2 ------> 4
2 ------> 5        2 ------> 4        3 <------ 2        2 ------> 5        3 <------ 3        3 <------ 2
3 <------ 2        3 <------ 3                           3 <------ 3
                                      11 --:                               11 ----:-> 2       11 ----:-> 6
11 ----:-> 6       11 ----:-> 5                          11 ----:-> 6
                                                              :-> 8


 G2518              G2519              G2520              G2521              G2522              G2523

7 ------- 1        1 ------- 3        1 ------- 4        7 ------- 3        7 ------- 6        7 ------- 2
2 ------> 4        7 ------- 5        7 ------- 2        2 ------> 1        2 ------> 8        2 ------> 3
3 <------ 2        2 ------> 2        2 ------> 5        3 <------ 5        3 <------ 4        3 <------ 5
                  3 <------ 4        3 <------ 3
11 ----:-> 6                                            11 ----:-> 2       11 ----:-> 2
     :-> 8                           11 ----:-> 1            :-> 7              :-> 7


 G2524              G2525              G2526              G2527              G2528              G2529

1 ------- 3        1 ------- 4        7 ------- 4        7 ------- 3        7 ------- 11       7 ------- 11
7 ------- 4        7 ------- 3        2 ------> 2        2 ------> 5        2 ------> 9        2 ------> 1
2 ------> 5        2 ------> 2        3 <------ 3        3 <------ 4        3 <------ 1        3 <------ 9
3 <------ 2        3 <------ 5                                                                11 ------> 2
                                      11 ----:-> 6       11 ----:-> 1       11 ----:-> 3
11 ----:-> 1       11 ----:-> 6                                                 :-> 10             :-- 3
                                                                               :-> 12             :-> 4


 G2530              G2531              G2532              G2533              G2534              G2535

7 ------- 4        7 ------- 4        7 ------- 2        7 ------- 5        7 ------- 2        7 ------- 5
2 ------> 2        2 ------> 3        2 ------> 3        2 ------> 4        2 ------> 3        2 ------> 2
3 <------ 3        3 <------ 2        3 <------ 5        3 <------ 2        3 <------ 5        3 <------ 3

11 ----:-> 5                          11 ----:-> 1       11 ----:-> 3       11 ----:-> 1       11 ----:-> 6
                                                              :-> 6              :-> 4              :-> 8
```

G2536
```
1 ------- 1
7 ------- 7
2 ------> 3
3 <------ 2

11 ----:-> 5
       :-> 6
       :-> 8
5 <-:----- 20
6 <-:
8 <-:
```

G2537
```
1 ------- 1
7 ------- 7
2 ------> 2
3 <------ 3

5 <-:----- 6
6 <-:
8 <-:

11 ----:--> 4
       :-> 20
```

G2538
```
1 ------- 1
7 ------- 7
2 ------> 2
3 <------ 3

11 ----:-> 8
       :-> 4
       :-> 20
5 <-:----- 5
6 <-:
8 <-:
```

G2539
```
1 ------- 1
7 ------- 7
2 ------> 3
3 <------ 2

11 ----:-> 5
       :-> 6
       :-> 20
5 <-:----- 4
6 <-:
8 <-:
```

G2540
```
1 ------- 1
7 ------- 7
2 ------> 3
3 <------ 2

11 ----:-> 5
       :-> 6
5 <-:----- 4
6 <-:
8 <-:
```

G2541
```
7 ------- 7
2 ------> 2
3 <------ 3

4 --:
5 <-:
6 <-:
8 <-:
```

G2542
```
7 ------- 5
2 ------> 4
3 <------ 3

11 ------> 6
5 <-:----- 1
6 <-:
8 <-:
```

G2543
```
7 ------- 5
2 ------> 4
3 <------ 3

5 <-:----- 1
6 <-:
8 <-:
```

G2544
```
1 ------- 1
7 ------- 7
2 ------> 2
3 <------ 3

5 <-:----- 6
6 <-:
8 <-:

11 ----:-> 4
       :-> 20
```

G2545
```
1 ------- 1
7 ------- 7
2 ------> 2
3 <------ 3

5 <-:----- 6
6 <-:
8 <-:
```

G2546
```
1 ------- 1
7 ------- 7
2 ------> 3
3 <------ 2

11 ----:-> 5
       :-> 8
5 <-:----- 4
6 <-:
8 <-:
```

G2547
```
1 ------- 1
7 ------- 7
2 ------> 2
3 <------ 3

4 --:
5 <-:
6 <-:
8 <-:
```

G2548
```
7 ------- 7
2 ------> 2
3 <------ 3

4 --:
5 <-:
6 <-:
8 <-:
```

G2549
```
1 ------- 1
7 ------- 7
2 ------> 2
3 <------ 3

11 ----:-> 20
       :-> 4
       :-> 12
5 <-:----- 5
6 <-:
8 <-:
```

G2550
```
7 ------- 7
2 ------> 2
3 <------ 3

11 ----:-> 5
       :-> 6
       :-> 8
5 <-:----- 4
6 <-:
8 <-:
```

G2551
```
7 ------- 5
2 ------> 2
3 <------ 3

11 ----:-> 8
       :-> 6
       :-> 1
5 <-:----- 4
6 <-:
8 <-:
```

G2552
```
1 ------- 1
7 ------- 7
2 ------> 2
3 <------ 3

5 <-:----- 8
6 <-:
8 <-:

11 ----:-> 20
```

G2553
```
7 ------- 5
2 ------> 3
3 <------ 2

11 ----:-> 7
       :-> 4
5 <-:----- 6
6 <-:
8 <-:
```

G2554
```
7 ------- 7
2 ------> 3
3 <------ 2

4 --:
5 <-:
6 <-:
8 <-:
```

G2555
```
1 ------- 1
7 ------- 8
2 ------> 4
3 <------ 2

11 ----:-> 5
       :-> 10
       :-> 7
5 <-:----- 12
6 <-:
8 <-:

4 ----:-> 11
```

G2556
```
1 ------- 1
7 ------- 7
2 ------> 2
3 <------ 3

5 <-:----- 6
6 <-:
8 <-:

11 ----:-> 4
```

G2557
```
7 ------- 4
2 ------> 3
3 <------ 2

11 ----:-> 1
       :-> 6
5 <-:----- 5
6 <-:
8 <-:
```

G2558
```
1 ------- 1
7 ------- 7
2 ------> 5
3 <------ 3

11 ------> 6
5 <-:----- 4
6 <-:
8 <-:
```

G2559
```
7 ------- 5
2 ------> 7
3 <------ 4

11 ----:-> 2
       :-> 6
5 <-:----- 3
6 <-:
8 <-:
```

G2560	G2561	G2562	G2563	G2564	G2565

<pre>7 ------- 3
2 ------> 5
3 <------ 4
 	
11 ----:-> 8
    :-> 7
    :-> 6
5 <-:---- 2
6 <-:
8 <-:</pre>
	<pre>1 ------- 4
	7 ------- 7
	2 ------> 6
	3 <------ 5
	
	11 ----:-> 8
	       :-> 2
	       :-> 10
	5 <-:---- 9
	6 <-:
	8 <-:
	
	4 ----:-> 1</pre>
		<pre>1 ------- 3
		7 ------- 6
		2 ------> 5
		3 <------ 4
		
		11 ----:-> 7
		      :-> 1
		5 <-:---- 8
		6 <-:
		8 <-:</pre>
			<pre>7 ------- 8
			2 ------> 2
			3 <------ 1
			
			4 --:
			5 <-:
			6 <-:
			8 <-:</pre>
				<pre>7 ------- 8
				2 ------> 6
				3 <------ 1
				
				11 ----:-> 7
				       :-> 9
				5 <-:---- 4
				6 <-:
				8 <-:</pre>
					<pre>7 ------- 7
					2 ------> 3
					3 <------ 2
					
					11 ----:-> 5
					      :-> 8
					5 <-:---- 9
					6 <-:
					8 <-:</pre>

G2566	G2567	G2568	G2569	G2570	G2571

<pre>7 ------- 5
2 ------> 3
3 <------ 2
 	
5 <-:---- 6
6 <-:
8 <-:
 	
11 ----:-> 4
     :-> 7</pre>
	<pre>1 ------- 2
	7 ------- 7
	2 ------> 3
	3 <------ 8
	
	11 ----:-> 5
	      :-> 6
	      :-> 1
	5 <-:---- 9
	6 <-:
	8 <-:
	
	4 ----:-> 10</pre>
		<pre>1 ------- 2
		7 ------- 7
		2 ------> 8
		3 <------ 3
		
		5 <-:---- 5
		6 <-:
		8 <-:
		
		11 ----:-> 4
		     :-> 9</pre>
			<pre>7 ------- 7
			2 ------> 5
			3 <------ 4
			
			11 ------> 3
			5 <-:---- 1
			6 <-:
			8 <-:</pre>
				<pre>7 ------- 4
				2 ------> 6
				3 <------ 3
				
				5 <-:---- 2
				6 <-:
				8 <-:
				
				11 ----:-> 1
				     :-> 7</pre>
					<pre>7 ------- 5
					2 ------> 6
					3 <------ 4
					
					11 ----:-> 2
					5 <-:---- 3
					6 <-:
					8 <-:</pre>

G2572	G2573	G2574	G2575	G2576	G2577

<pre>7 ------- 9
2 ------> 3
3 <------ 2
 	
11 ------> 5
5 <-:---- 4
6 <-:
8 <-:</pre>
	<pre>7 ------- 3
	2 ------> 4
	3 <------ 2
	
	11 ------> 5
	5 <-:---- 1
	6 <-:
	8 <-:</pre>
		<pre>7 ------- 9
		2 ------> 13
		3 <------ 11
		
		11 ------> 14
		5 <-:---- 10
		6 <-:
		8 <-:</pre>
			<pre>7 ------- 5
			2 ------> 2
			3 <------ 3
			
			11 ----:-> 8
			     :-> 6
			5 <-:---- 4
			6 <-:
			8 <-:</pre>
				<pre>7 ------- 5
				2 ------> 2
				3 <------ 3
				
				11 ------> 8
				5 <-:---- 7
				6 <-:
				8 <-:</pre>
					<pre>7 ------- 5
					2 ------> 3
					3 <------ 2
					
					5 <-:---- 6
					6 <-:
					8 <-:</pre>

G2578	G2579	G2580	G2581	G2582	G2583

<pre>7 ------- 5
2 ------> 3
3 <------ 2
 	
11 --:
5 <-:
6 <-:
8 <-:</pre>
	<pre>1 ------- 3
	7 ------- 4
	2 ------> 5
	3 <------ 2
	
	11 ------> 6
	5 <-:---- 1
	6 <-:
	8 <-:</pre>
		<pre>1 ------- 1
		7 ------- 2
		2 ------> 4
		3 <------ 3
		
		11 ------> 5
		5 <-:---- 6
		6 <-:
		8 <-:</pre>
			<pre>1 ------- 1
			7 ------- 7
			3 <------ 2
			
			11 --:
			5 <-:
			6 <-:
			8 <-:</pre>
				<pre>1 ------- 1
				7 ------- 7
				2 ------> 5
				3 <------ 3
				
				11 ----:-> 8
				     :-> 6
				5 <-:---- 4
				6 <-:
				8 <-:</pre>
					<pre>7 ------- 4
					2 ------> 5
					3 <------ 3
					
					11 ------> 2
					5 <-:---- 6
					6 <-:
					8 <-:</pre>

```
  G2584              G2585              G2586              G2587              G2588              G2589

7 ------- 5        7 ------- 1        1 ------- 3        1 ------- 4        7 ------- 3        7 ------- 6
2 ------> 4        2 ------> 4        7 ------- 5        7 ------- 2        2 ------> 1        2 ------> 8
3 <------ 2        3 <------ 2        2 ------> 2        2 ------> 5        3 <------ 5        3 <------ 4
                                      3 <------ 4        3 <------ 3
11 ------> 6       11 ----:-> 6                          11 ------> 1       11 ----:-> 2       11 ----:-> 7
5 <-:---- 1           :-> 8        5 <-:---- 1        5 <-:---- 6           :-> 7           :-> 2
6 <-:              5 <-:---- 3        6 <-:              6 <-:              5 <-:---- 8        5 <-:---- 1
8 <-:              6 <-:              8 <-:              8 <-:              6 <-:              6 <-:
                   8 <-:                                                    8 <-:              8 <-:
```

```
  G2590              G2591              G2592              G2593              G2594              G2595

7 ------- 2        1 ------- 3        1 ------- 4        7 ------- 4        7 ------- 3        7 ------- 11
2 ------> 3        7 ------- 4        7 ------- 3        2 ------> 2        2 ------> 5        2 ------> 9
3 <------ 5        2 ------> 5        2 ------> 2        3 <------ 3        3 <------ 4        3 <------ 1
                   3 <------ 2        3 <------ 5
5 <-:---- 4                                             11 ------> 6       11 ------> 1       11 ----:-> 10
6 <-:              11 ------> 1       11 ------> 6       5 <-:---- 1        5 <-:---- 6           :-> 12
8 <-:              5 <-:---- 6        5 <-:---- 1        6 <-:              6 <-:              5 <-:---- 2
                   6 <-:              6 <-:              8 <-:              8 <-:              6 <-:
                   8 <-:              8 <-:                                                    8 <-:
```

```
  G2596              G2597              G2598              G2599              G2600              G2601

7 ------- 11       7 ------- 4        7 ------- 4        7 ------- 2        7 ------- 5        7 ------- 2
2 ------> 1        2 ------> 2        2 ------> 3        2 ------> 3        2 ------> 4        2 ------> 3
3 <------ 9        3 <------ 3        3 <------ 2        3 <------ 5        3 <------ 2        3 <------ 5

5 <-:---- 3        11 ------> 5       5 <-:---- 5        11 ------> 1       11 ----:-> 3       11 ----:-> 4
6 <-:              5 <-:---- 1        6 <-:              5 <-:---- 6           :-> 6           :-> 1
8 <-:              6 <-:              8 <-:              6 <-:              5 <-:---- 1        5 <-:---- 6
                   8 <-:                                 8 <-:              6 <-:              6 <-:
11 ----:-> 2                                                                8 <-:              8 <-:
   :-> 4
```

```
  G2602              G2603              G2604              G2605              G2606              G2607

7 ------- 5        1 ------- 1        1 ------- 1        1 ------- 1        1 ------- 1        1 ------- 1
2 ------> 2        7 ------- 7        7 ------- 7        7 ------- 7        7 ------- 7        7 ------- 7
3 <------ 3        2 ------> 3        2 ------> 2        2 ------> 2        2 ------> 3        2 ------> 3
                   3 <------ 2        3 <------ 3        3 <------ 3        3 <------ 2        3 <------ 2
11 ----:-> 8                          20 ------> 4
   :-> 6           20 ----:-> 5                          20 ----:-> 4       20 ----:-> 5       20 ----:-> 5
5 <-:---- 4           :-> 6              :-- 6              :-> 8              :-> 6              :-> 6
6 <-:                 :-> 8              :-> 20             :-> 20             :-> 20
8 <-:
```

```
  G2608              G2609              G2610              G2611              G2612              G2613

7 ------- 7        7 ------- 5        7 ------- 5        1 ------- 1        1 ------- 1        1 ------- 1
2 ------> 2        2 ------> 4        2 ------> 4        7 ------- 7        7 ------- 7        7 ------- 7
3 <------ 3        3 <------ 3        3 <------ 3        2 ------> 2        2 ------> 2        2 ------> 3
                                                         3 <------ 3        3 <------ 3        3 <------ 2
20 --:             20 ------> 6
                                                         20 ----:-> 4                          20 ----:-> 5
                                                            :-> 20                                :-> 8
```

G2614	G2615	G2616	G2617	G2618	G2619
1 ------- 1 7 ------- 7 2 ------> 2 3 <------ 3	7 ------- 7 2 ------> 2 3 <------ 3	1 ------- 1 7 ------- 7 2 ------> 2 3 <------ 3 20 ------> 20 :-- 8 :-> 4 :-> 12	7 ------- 7 2 ------> 2 3 <------ 3 20 ----:-> 5 :- 6 :- 8	7 ------- 5 2 ------> 2 3 <------ 3 20 ----:-> 8 :- 6 :- 1	1 ------- 1 7 ------- 7 2 ------> 2 3 <------ 3 20 ----:-> 20

G2620	G2621	G2622	G2623	G2624	G2625
7 ------- 5 2 ------> 3 3 <------ 2 20 ----:-> 7 :-> 4	7 ------- 7 2 ------> 3 3 <------ 2	1 ------- 1 7 ------- 8 2 ------> 4 3 <------ 2 20 ----:-> 5 :-> 7 :-> 10 :-> 11	1 ------- 1 7 ------- 7 2 ------> 2 3 <------ 3 20 ------> 4	7 ------- 4 2 ------> 3 3 <------ 2 20 ----:-> 1 :-> 6	1 ------- 1 7 ------- 7 2 ------> 5 3 <------ 3 20 ------> 6

G2626	G2627	G2628	G2629	G2630	G2631
7 ------- 5 2 ------> 7 3 <------ 4 20 ----:-> 2 :-> 6	7 ------- 3 2 ------> 5 3 <------ 4 20 ----:-> 6 :-> 7 :-> 8	1 ------- 4 7 ------- 7 2 ------> 6 3 <------ 5 20 ----:-> 1 :-> 2 :-> 8 :-> 10	1 ------- 3 7 ------- 6 2 ------> 5 3 <------ 4 20 ----:-> 1 :-> 7	7 ------- 8 2 ------> 2 3 <------ 1	7 ------- 8 2 ------> 6 3 <------ 1 20 ----:-> 7 :-> 9

G2632	G2633	G2634	G2635	G2636	G2637
7 ------- 7 2 ------> 3 3 <------ 2 20 ----:-> 5 :-> 8	7 ------- 5 2 ------> 3 3 <------ 2 20 ----:-> 4 :-> 7	1 ------- 2 7 ------- 7 2 ------> 3 3 <------ 8 20 ----:-> 1 :-> 5 :-> 6 :-> 10	1 ------- 2 7 ------- 7 2 ------> 8 3 <------ 3 20 ----:-> 4 :-> 9	7 ------- 7 2 ------> 5 3 <------ 4 20 ----:-> 3	7 ------- 4 2 ------> 6 3 <------ 3 20 ----:-> 1 :- 7

G2638	G2639	G2640	G2641	G2642	G2643
7 ------- 5 2 ------> 6 3 <------ 4 20 ----:-> 2	7 ------- 9 2 ------> 3 3 <------ 2 20 ----:-> 5	7 ------- 3 2 ------> 4 3 <------ 2 20 ----:-> 5	7 ------- 9 2 ------> 13 3 <------ 11 20 ----:-> 14	7 ------- 5 2 ------> 2 3 <------ 3 20 ----:-> 6 :- 8	7 ------- 5 2 ------> 2 3 <------ 3 20 ----:-> 8

G2644	G2645	G2646	G2647	G2648	G2649
7 ------- 5 2 ------> 3 3 <------ 2	7 ------- 5 2 ------> 3 3 <------ 2 20 --:	1 ------- 3 7 ------- 4 2 ------> 5 3 <------ 2 20 ----:-> 6	1 ------- 1 7 ------- 2 2 ------> 4 3 <------ 3 20 ----:-> 5	1 ------- 1 7 ------- 7 3 <------ 2 20 --:	1 ------- 1 7 ------- 7 2 ------> 5 3 <------ 3 20 ----:-> 6 :-> 8

G2650	G2651	G2652	G2653	G2654	G2655

7 ------- 4
2 ------> 5
3 <------ 3
 	
20 ----:-> 2
	7 ------- 5
	2 ------> 4
	3 <------ 2
	
	20 ----:-> 6
		7 ------- 1
		2 ------> 4
		3 <------ 2
		20 ----:-> 6
		    :-> 8
			1 ------- 3
			7 ------- 5
			2 ------> 2
			3 <------ 4
				1 ------- 4
				7 ------- 2
				2 ------> 5
				3 <------ 3
				
				20 ----:-> 1
					7 ------- 3
					2 ------> 1
					3 <------ 5
					20 ----:-> 2
					    :-> 7

G2656	G2657	G2658	G2659	G2660	G2661
7 ------- 6 2 ------> 8 3 <------ 4 20 ----:-> 2 :-> 7	7 ------- 2 2 ------> 3 3 <------ 5	1 ------- 3 7 ------- 4 2 ------> 5 3 <------ 2 20 ----:-> 1	1 ------- 4 7 ------- 3 2 ------> 2 3 <------ 5 20 ----:-> 6	7 ------- 4 2 ------> 2 3 <------ 3 20 ----:-> 6	7 ------- 3 2 ------> 5 3 <------ 4 20 ---:-> 1

G2662	G2663	G2664	G2665	G2666	G2667

7 ------- 11
2 ------> 9
3 <------ 1
20 ----:-> 3
    :-> 10
    :-> 12
	7 ------- 11
	2 ------> 1
	3 <------ 9
	20 ------> 2
	  :-- 3
	  :-> 4
		7 ------- 4
		2 ------> 2
		3 <------ 3
		
		20 ----:-> 5
			7 ------- 4
			2 ------> 3
			3 <------ 2
				7 ------- 2
				2 ------> 3
				3 <------ 5
				
				20 ----:-> 1
					7 ------- 5
					2 ------> 4
					3 <------ 2
					20 ---:-> 3
					    :-> 6

G2668	G2669	G2670	G2671	G2672	G2673

7 ------- 2
2 ------> 3
3 <------ 5
20 ----:-> 1
    :-> 4
	7 ------- 5
	2 ------> 2
	3 <------ 3
	20 ----:-> 6
	    :-> 8
		1 ------- 1
		7 ------- 7
		2 ------> 3
		3 <------ 2
		11 ----:-> 5
		    :-> 6
		    :-> 8
		8 <-:----- 20
		6 <-:
			1 ------- 1
			7 ------- 7
			2 ------> 2
			3 <------ 3
			8 <-:----- 6
			6 <-:
			11 ----:-> 4
			    :-> 20
				1 ------- 1
				7 ------- 7
				2 ------> 2
				3 <------ 3
				11 ----:-> 8
				    :-> 4
				    :-> 20
				8 <-:----- 5
				6 <-:
					1 ------- 1
					7 ------- 7
					2 ------> 3
					3 <------ 2
					11 ----:-> 5
					    :-> 6
					    :-> 20
					8 <-:----- 4
					6 <-:

G2674	G2675	G2676	G2677	G2678	G2679

1 ------- 1
7 ------- 7
2 ------> 3
3 <------ 2
11 ----:-> 5
    :-> 6
8 <-:----- 4
6 <-:
	7 ------- 7
	2 ------> 2
	3 <------ 3
	20 --:
	8 <-:
	6 <-:
		7 ------- 5
		2 ------> 4
		3 <------ 3
		11 ------> 6
		8 <-:----- 1
		6 <-:
			7 ------- 5
			2 ------> 4
			3 <------ 3
			
			8 <-:----- 1
			6 <-:
				1 ------- 1
				7 ------- 7
				2 ------> 2
				3 <------ 3
				8 <-:----- 6
				6 <-:
				11 ----:-> 4
				    :-> 20
					1 ------- 1
					7 ------- 7
					2 ------> 2
					3 <------ 3
					8 <-:----- 6
					6 <-:

```
 G2680              G2681              G2682              G2683              G2684              G2685

1 ------- 1        1 ------- 1        7 ------- 7        1 ------- 1        7 ------- 7        7 ------- 5
7 ------- 7        7 ------- 7        2 ------> 2        7 ------- 7        2 ------> 2        2 ------> 2
2 ------> 3        2 ------> 2        3 <------ 3        2 ------> 2        3 <------ 3        3 <------ 3
3 <------ 2        3 <------ 3                           3 <------ 3
                                     20 --:                                11 ----:-> 5       11 ----:-> 8
11 ----:-> 5                          8 <-:             11 ----:-> 20           :-> 6              :-> 6
      :-> 8        20 --:              6 <-:                  :-> 4              :-> 8              :-> 1
                   8 <-:                                      :-> 12
8 <-:---- 4        6 <-:                                                   8 <-:---- 4        8 <-:---- 4
6 <-:                                                  8 <-:---- 5        6 <-:              6 <-:
                                                       6 <-:


 G2686              G2687              G2688              G2689              G2690              G2691

1 ------- 1        7 ------- 5        7 ------- 7        1 ------- 1        1 ------- 1        7 ------- 4
7 ------- 7        2 ------> 3        2 ------> 3        7 ------- 8        7 ------- 7        2 ------> 3
2 ------> 2        3 <------ 2        3 <------ 2        2 ------> 4        2 ------> 2        3 <------ 2
3 <------ 3                                              3 <------ 2        3 <------ 3
                   11 ----:-> 7        20 --:                                                 11 ----:-> 1
8 <-:---- 8             :-> 4          8 <-:            11 ----:-> 5        8 <-:---- 6            :-> 6
6 <-:              8 <-:---- 6         6 <-:                 :-> 10         6 <-:              8 <-:---- 5
                   6 <-:                                     :-> 7                            6 <-:
11 ----:-> 20                                           8 <-:---- 12        11 ----:-> 4
                                                        6 <-:

                                                        20 ----:-> 11


 G2692              G2693              G2694              G2695              G2696              G2697

1 ------- 1        7 ------- 5        7 ------- 3        1 ------- 4        1 ------- 3        7 ------- 8
7 ------- 7        2 ------> 7        2 ------> 5        7 ------- 7        7 ------- 6        2 ------> 2
2 ------> 5        3 <------ 4        3 <------ 4        2 ------> 6        2 ------> 5        3 <------ 1
3 <------ 3                                              3 <------ 5        3 <------ 4
                   11 ----:-> 2       11 ----:-> 8                                            20 --:
11 ------> 6            :-> 6              :-> 7        11 ----:-> 8        11 ----:-> 7       8 <-:
8 <-:---- 4        8 <-:---- 3             :-> 6             :-> 2              :-> 1          6 <-:
6 <-:              6 <-:               8 <-:---- 2            :-> 10         8 <-:---- 8
                                       6 <-:           8 <-:---- 9          6 <-:
                                                       6 <-:

                                                       20 ----:-> 1


 G2698              G2699              G2700              G2701              G2702              G2703

7 ------- 8        7 ------- 7        7 ------- 5        1 ------- 2        1 ------- 2        7 ------- 7
2 ------> 6        2 ------> 3        2 ------> 3        7 ------- 7        7 ------- 7        2 ------> 5
3 <------ 1        3 <------ 2        3 <------ 2        2 ------> 3        2 ------> 8        3 <------ 4
                                                         3 <------ 8        3 <------ 3
11 ----:-> 7       11 ----:-> 5       8 <-:---- 6                                             11 ------> 3
      :-> 9             :-> 8         6 <-:             11 ----:-> 5        8 <-:---- 5        8 <-:---- 1
8 <-:---- 4        8 <-:---- 9                               :-> 6         6 <-:              6 <-:
6 <-:              6 <-:              11 ----:-> 4            :-> 1
                                            :-> 7        8 <-:---- 9        11 ----:-> 4
                                                         6 <-:                  :-> 9

                                                         20 ----:-> 10
```

G2704	G2705	G2706	G2707	G2708	G2709
7 ------- 4 2 ------> 6 3 <----- 3 8 <-:----- 2 6 <-: 11 ----:-> 1 　　　:-> 7	7 ------- 5 2 ------> 6 3 <----- 4 11 ------> 2 8 <-:----- 3 6 <-:	7 ------- 9 2 ------> 3 3 <----- 2 11 ------> 5 8 <-:----- 4 6 <-:	7 ------- 3 2 ------> 4 3 <----- 2 11 ------> 5 8 <-:----- 1 6 <-:	7 ------- 9 2 ------> 13 3 <----- 11 11 ------> 14 8 <-:----- 10 6 <-:	7 ------- 5 2 ------> 2 3 <----- 3 11 ----:-> 8 　　　:-> 6 8 <-:----- 4 6 <-:

G2710	G2711	G2712	G2713	G2714	G2715
7 ------- 5 2 ------> 2 3 <----- 3 11 ------> 8 8 <-:----- 7 6 <-:	7 ------- 5 2 ------> 3 3 <----- 2 8 <-:----- 6 6 <-:	7 ------- 5 2 ------> 3 3 <----- 2 11 --: 8 <-: 6 <-:	1 ------- 3 7 ------- 4 2 ------> 5 3 <----- 2 11 ------> 6 8 <-:----- 1 6 <-:	1 ------- 1 7 ------- 2 2 ------> 4 3 <----- 3 11 ------> 5 8 <-:----- 6 6 <-:	1 ------- 1 7 ------- 7 3 <----- 2 11 --: 8 <-: 6 <-:

G2716	G2717	G2718	G2719	G2720	G2721
1 ------- 1 7 ------- 7 2 ------> 5 3 <----- 3 11 ----:-> 8 　　　:-> 6 8 <-:----- 4 6 <-:	7 ------- 4 2 ------> 5 3 <----- 3 11 ------> 2 8 <-:----- 6 6 <-:	7 ------- 5 2 ------> 4 3 <----- 2 11 ------> 6 8 <-:----- 1 6 <-:	7 ------- 1 2 ------> 4 3 <----- 2 11 ----:-> 6 　　　:-> 8 8 <-:----- 3 6 <-:	1 ------- 3 7 ------- 5 2 ------> 2 3 <----- 4 8 <-:----- 1 6 <-:	1 ------- 4 7 ------- 2 2 ------> 5 3 <----- 3 11 ------> 1 8 <-:----- 6 6 <-:

G2722	G2723	G2724	G2725	G2726	G2727
7 ------- 3 2 ------> 1 3 <----- 5 11 ----:-> 2 　　　:-> 7 8 <-:----- 8 6 <-:	7 ------- 6 2 ------> 8 3 <----- 4 11 ----:-> 7 　　　:-> 2 8 <-:----- 1 6 <-:	7 ------- 2 2 ------> 3 3 <----- 5 8 <-:----- 4 6 <-:	1 ------- 3 7 ------- 4 2 ------> 5 3 <----- 2 11 ------> 1 8 <-:----- 6 6 <-:	1 ------- 4 7 ------- 3 2 ------> 2 3 <----- 5 11 ------> 6 8 <-:----- 1 6 <-:	7 ------- 4 2 ------> 2 3 <----- 3 11 ------> 6 8 <-:----- 1 6 <-:

G2728	G2729	G2730	G2731	G2732	G2733
7 ------- 3 2 ------> 5 3 <----- 4 11 ------> 1 8 <-:----- 6 6 <-:	7 ------- 11 2 ------> 9 3 <----- 1 11 ----:-> 10 　　　:-> 3 　　　:-> 12 8 <-:----- 2 6 <-:	7 ------- 11 2 ------> 1 3 <----- 9 8 <-:----- 3 6 <-: 11 ----:-> 2 　　　:-> 4	7 ------- 4 2 ------> 2 3 <----- 3 11 ------> 5 8 <-:----- 1 6 <-:	7 ------- 4 2 ------> 3 3 <----- 2 8 <-:----- 5 6 <-:	7 ------- 2 2 ------> 3 3 <----- 5 11 ------> 1 8 <-:----- 6 6 <-:

G2734	G2735	G2736	G2736	G2737	G2738

7 ------- 5
2 ------> 4
3 <----- 2
 	
11 ----:-> 3
    :-> 6
8 <-:----- 1
6 <-:
	7 ------- 2
	2 ------> 3
	3 <----- 5
	
	11 ----:-> 4
	    :-> 1
	8 <-:----- 6
	6 <-:
		7 ------- 5
		2 ------> 2
		3 <----- 3
		
		11 ----:-> 8
		    :-> 6
		8 <-:----- 4
		6 <-:
			1 ------- 1
			7 ------- 7
			2 ------> 3
			3 <----- 2
			
			20 ----:-> 5
			    :-> 6
			    :-> 8
				1 ------- 1
				7 ------- 7
				2 ------> 2
				3 <----- 3
				
				20 ----:-> 4
				    :-> 20
					1 ------- 1
					7 ------- 7
					2 ------> 2
					3 <----- 3
					
					20 ----:-> 8
					    :-> 20

G2739	**G2740**	**G2741**	**G2742**	**G2743**	**G2744**

1 ------- 1
7 ------- 7
2 ------> 3
3 <----- 2
 	
20 ----:-> 5
    :-> 6
    :-> 20
	1 ------- 1
	7 ------- 7
	2 ------> 3
	3 <----- 2
	
	20 ----:-> 5
	    :-> 6
		7 ------- 7
		2 ------> 2
		3 <----- 3
			7 ------- 5
			2 ------> 4
			3 <----- 3
			
			20 ------> 6
				7 ------- 5
				2 ------> 4
				3 <----- 3
					1 ------- 1
					7 ------- 7
					2 ------> 2
					3 <----- 3
					
					20 ----:-> 4
					    :-> 20

G2745	**G2746**	**G2747**	**G2748**	**G2749**	**G2750**

1 ------- 1
7 ------- 7
2 ------> 2
3 <----- 3
	1 ------- 1
	7 ------- 7
	2 ------> 3
	3 <----- 2
	
	20 ----:-> 5
	    :-> 8
		1 ------- 1
		7 ------- 7
		2 ------> 2
		3 <----- 3
			7 ------- 7
			2 ------> 2
			3 <----- 3
				1 ------- 1
				7 ------- 7
				2 ------> 2
				3 <----- 3
				
				20 ----:-> 20
				    :-> 4
				    :-> 12
					7 ------- 7
					2 ------> 2
					3 <----- 3
					
					20 ----:-> 5
					    :-> 6
					    :-> 8

G2751	**G2752**	**G2753**	**G2754**	**G2755**	**G2756**

7 ------- 5
2 ------> 2
3 <----- 3
 	
20 ----:-> 8
    :-> 6
    :-> 1
	1 ------- 1
	7 ------- 7
	2 ------> 2
	3 <----- 3
	
	20 ----:-> 20
		7 ------- 5
		2 ------> 3
		3 <----- 2
		
		20 ----:-> 7
		    :-> 4
			7 ------- 7
			2 ------> 3
			3 <----- 2
				1 ------- 1
				7 ------- 8
				2 ------> 4
				3 <----- 2
				
				20 ----:-> 5
				    :-> 10
				    :-> 7
				    :-> 11
					1 ------- 1
					7 ------- 7
					2 ------> 2
					3 <----- 3
					
					20 ----:-> 4

G2757	**G2758**	**G2759**	**G2760**	**G2761**	**G2762**

7 ------- 4
2 ------> 3
3 <----- 2
 	
20 ----:-> 1
    :-> 6
	1 ------- 1
	7 ------- 7
	2 ------> 5
	3 <----- 3
	
	20 ------> 6
		7 ------- 5
		2 ------> 7
		3 <----- 4
		
		20 ----:-> 2
		    :-> 6
			7 ------- 3
			2 ------> 5
			3 <----- 4
			
			20 ----:-> 8
			    :-> 7
			    :-> 6
				1 ------- 4
				7 ------- 7
				2 ------> 6
				3 <----- 5
				
				20 ----:-> 8
				    :-> 2
				    :-> 10
				    :-> 1
					1 ------- 3
					7 ------- 6
					2 ------> 5
					3 <----- 4
					
					20 ----:-> 7
					    :-> 1

G2763	G2764	G2765	G2766	G2767	G2768

7 ------- 8
2 ------> 2
3 <------ 1
 	
20 ----:-> 7
       :-> 9
	7 ------- 8
	2 ------> 6
	3 <------ 1
	
	20 ----:-> 7
	       :-> 9
		7 ------- 7
		2 ------> 3
		3 <------ 2
		
		20 ----:-> 5
		       :-> 8
			7 ------- 5
			2 ------> 3
			3 <------ 2
			
			20 ----:-> 4
			       :-> 7
				1 ------- 2
				7 ------- 7
				2 ------> 3
				3 <------ 8
				
				20 ----:-> 5
				       :-> 6
				       :-> 1
				       :-> 10
					1 ------- 2
					7 ------- 7
					2 ------> 8
					3 <------ 3
					
					20 ----:-> 4
					       :-> 9

G2769	G2770	G2771	G2772	G2773	G2774
7 ------- 7 2 ------> 5 3 <------ 4 20 ------> 3	7 ------- 4 2 ------> 6 3 <------ 3 20 ----:-> 1 :-> 7	7 ------- 5 2 ------> 6 3 <------ 4 20 ------> 2	7 ------- 9 2 ------> 3 3 <------ 2 20 ------> 5	7 ------- 3 2 ------> 4 3 <------ 2 20 ------> 5	7 ------- 9 2 ------> 13 3 <------ 11 20 ------> 14

G2775	G2776	G2777	G2778	G2779	G2780
7 ------- 5 2 ------> 2 3 <------ 3 20 ----:-> 8 :-> 6	7 ------- 5 2 ------> 2 3 <------ 3 20 ------> 8	7 ------- 5 2 ------> 3 3 <------ 2	7 ------- 5 2 ------> 3 3 <------ 2	1 ------- 3 7 ------- 4 2 ------> 5 3 <------ 2 20 ------> 6	1 ------- 1 7 ------- 2 2 ------> 4 3 <------ 3 20 ------> 5

G2781	G2782	G2783	G2784	G2785	G2786

1 ------- 1
7 ------- 7
3 <------ 2
	1 ------- 1
	7 ------- 7
	2 ------> 5
	3 <------ 3
	
	20 ----:-> 8
	       :-> 6
		7 ------- 4
		2 ------> 5
		3 <------ 3
		
		20 ------> 2
			7 ------- 5
			2 ------> 4
			3 <------ 2
			
			20 ------> 6
				7 ------- 1
				2 ------> 4
				3 <------ 2
				
				20 ----:-> 6
				       :-> 8
					1 ------- 3
					7 ------- 5
					2 ------> 2
					3 <------ 4

G2787	G2788	G2789	G2790	G2791	G2792

1 ------- 4
7 ------- 2
2 ------> 5
3 <------ 3
 	
20 ------> 1
	7 ------- 3
	2 ------> 1
	3 <------ 5
	
	20 ----:-> 2
	       :-> 7
		7 ------- 6
		2 ------> 8
		3 <------ 4
		
		20 ----:-> 7
		       :-> 2
			7 ------- 2
			2 ------> 3
			3 <------ 5
				1 ------- 3
				7 ------- 4
				2 ------> 5
				3 <------ 2
				
				20 ------> 1
					1 ------- 4
					7 ------- 3
					2 ------> 2
					3 <------ 5
					
					20 ------> 6

G2793	G2794	G2795	G2796	G2797	G2798

7 ------- 4
2 ------> 2
3 <------ 3
 	
20 ------> 6
	7 ------- 3
	2 ------> 5
	3 <------ 4
	
	20 ------> 1
		7 ------- 11
		2 ------> 9
		3 <------ 1
		
		20 ----:-> 10
		       :-> 3
		       :-> 12
			7 ------- 11
			2 ------> 1
			3 <------ 9
			20 ----:-> 2
			       :-> 4
				7 ------- 4
				2 ------> 2
				3 <------ 3
				
				20 ------> 5
					7 ------- 4
					2 ------> 3
					3 <------ 2

```
 G2799                 G2800                 G2801                 G2802                 G2803                 G2804

7 ------- 2           7 ------- 5           7 ------- 2           7 ------- 5           1 ------- 1           1 ------- 1
2 ------> 3           2 ------> 4           2 ------> 3           2 ------> 2           7 ------- 7           7 ------- 7
3 <------ 5           3 <------ 2           3 <------ 5           3 <------ 3           2 ------> 3           2 ------> 2
                                                                                       3 <------ 2           3 <------ 3
20 ------> 1          20 ----:-> 3          20 ----:-> 4          20 ----:-> 8
                           :-> 6                 :-> 1                 :-> 6          4 ----:-> 5           6 <-:---- 6
                                                                                           :-> 6           4 ----:-> 4
                                                                                           :-> 8                 :-> 20
                                                                                       6 <-:---- 20


 G2805                 G2806                 G2807                 G2808                 G2809                 G2810

1 ------- 1           1 ------- 1           1 ------- 1           7 ------- 7           7 ------- 5           7 ------- 5
7 ------- 7           7 ------- 7           7 ------- 7           2 ------> 2           2 ------> 4           2 ------> 4
2 ------> 2           2 ------> 3           2 ------> 3           3 <------ 3           3 <------ 3           3 <------ 3
3 <------ 3           3 <------ 2           3 <------ 2
                                                                 20 --:               4 ------> 6           6 <-:---- 1
4 ----:-> 8           4 ----:-> 5           4 ----:-> 5           5 <-:                5 <-:---- 1
     :-> 4                 :-> 6                 :-> 6            6 <-:
     :-> 20                :-> 20           6 <-:---- 4           8 <-:
6 <-:---- 5           6 <-:---- 4


 G2811                 G2812                 G2813                 G2814                 G2815                 G2816

1 ------- 1           1 ------- 1           1 ------- 1           1 ------- 1           7 ------- 7           1 ------- 1
7 ------- 7           7 ------- 7           7 ------- 7           7 ------- 7           2 ------> 2           7 ------- 7
2 ------> 2           2 ------> 2           2 ------> 3           2 ------> 2           3 <------ 3           2 ------> 2
3 <------ 3           3 <------ 3           3 <------ 2           3 <------ 3                                 3 <------ 3
                                                                                       20 --:
6 <-:---- 6           6 <-:---- 6           4 ----:-> 5           20 --:               6 <-:                4 ----:-> 20
                                                 :-> 8           6 <-:                                           :-> 4
4 ----:-> 4                                                                                                      :-> 12
     :-> 20                                6 <-:---- 4
                                                                                                             6 <-:---- 5


 G2817                 G2818                 G2819                 G2820                 G2821                 G2822

7 ------- 7           7 ------- 5           1 ------- 1           7 ------- 5           7 ------- 7           1 ------- 1
2 ------> 2           2 ------> 2           7 ------- 7           2 ------> 3           2 ------> 3           7 ------- 8
3 <------ 3           3 <------ 3           2 ------> 2           3 <------ 2           3 <------ 2           2 ------> 4
                                           3 <------ 3                                                       3 <------ 2
4 ----:-> 5           4 ----:-> 8                                4 ----:-> 7           20 --:
     :-> 6                 :-> 6           6 <-:---- 8                :-> 4            6 <-:                4 ----:-> 5
     :-> 8                 :-> 1                                 6 <-:---- 6                                     :-> 10
6 <-:---- 4           6 <-:---- 4          4 ----:-> 20                                                          :-> 7
                                                                                                            6 <-:---- 12
                                                                                                            20 ----:-> 11


 G2823                 G2824                 G2825                 G2826                 G2827                 G2828

1 ------- 1           7 ------- 4           1 ------- 1           7 ------- 5           7 ------- 3           1 ------- 4
7 ------- 7           2 ------> 3           7 ------- 7           2 ------> 7           2 ------> 5           7 ------- 7
2 ------> 2           3 <------ 2           2 ------> 5           3 <------ 4           3 <------ 4           2 ------> 6
3 <------ 3                                 3 <------ 3                                                      3 <------ 5
                     4 ----:-> 1                                4 ----:-> 2           4 ----:-> 8
6 <-:---- 6               :-> 6            4 ------> 6                :-> 6                 :-> 7           4 ----:-> 8
                     6 <-:---- 5           6 <-:---- 4           6 <-:---- 3                :-> 6                :-> 2
4 ----:-> 4                                                                           6 <-:---- 2                :-> 10
                                                                                                            6 <-:---- 9
                                                                                                            20 ----:-> 1
```

G2829	G2830	G2831	G2832	G2833	G2834

1 ------- 3
7 ------- 6
2 ------> 5
3 <------ 4
 	
4 ----:-> 7
    :-> 1
6 <-:---- 8
	7 ------- 8
	2 ------> 2
	3 <------ 1
	
	20 --:
	6 <-:
		7 ------- 8
		2 ------> 6
		3 <------ 1
		
		4 ----:-> 7
		    :-> 9
		6 <-:---- 4
			7 ------- 7
			2 ------> 3
			3 <------ 2
			
			4 ----:-> 5
			    :-> 8
			6 <-:---- 9
				7 ------- 5
				2 ------> 3
				3 <------ 2
				
				6 <-:---- 6
				
				4 ----:-> 4
				    :-> 7
					1 ------- 2
					7 ------- 7
					2 ------> 3
					3 <------ 8
					
					4 ----:-> 5
					    :-> 6
					    :-> 1
					6 <-:---- 9
					
					20 ----:-> 10

G2835	G2836	G2837	G2838	G2839	G2840

1 ------- 2
7 ------- 7
2 ------> 8
3 <------ 3
 	
6 <-:---- 5
 	
4 ----:-> 4
    :-> 9
	7 ------- 7
	2 ------> 5
	3 <------ 4
	
	4 ------> 3
	6 <-:---- 1
		7 ------- 4
		2 ------> 6
		3 <------ 3
		
		6 <-:---- 2
		
		4 ----:-> 1
		    :-> 7
			7 ------- 5
			2 ------> 6
			3 <------ 4
			
			4 ------> 2
			6 <-:---- 3
				7 ------- 9
				2 ------> 3
				3 <------ 2
				
				4 ------> 5
				6 <-:---- 4
					7 ------- 3
					2 ------> 4
					3 <------ 2
					
					4 ------> 5
					6 <-:---- 1

G2841	G2842	G2843	G2844	G2845	G2846
7 ------- 9 2 ------> 13 3 <------ 11 4 ------> 14 6 <-:---- 10	7 ------- 5 2 ------> 2 3 <------ 3 4 ----:-> 8 :-> 6 6 <-:---- 4	7 ------- 5 2 ------> 2 3 <------ 3 4 ------> 8 6 <-:---- 7	7 ------- 5 2 ------> 3 3 <------ 2 6 <-:---- 6	7 ------- 5 2 ------> 3 3 <------ 2 4 --: 6 <-:	1 ------- 3 7 ------- 4 2 ------> 5 3 <------ 2 4 ------> 6 6 <-:---- 1

G2847	G2848	G2849	G2850	G2851	G2852

1 ------- 1
7 ------- 2
2 ------> 4
3 <------ 3
 	
4 ------> 5
6 <-:---- 6
	1 ------- 1
	7 ------- 7
	3 <------ 2
	
	4 --:
	6 <-:
		1 ------- 1
		7 ------- 7
		2 ------> 5
		3 <------ 3
		
		4 ----:-> 8
		    :-> 6
		6 <-:---- 4
			7 ------- 4
			2 ------> 5
			3 <------ 3
			
			4 ------> 2
			6 <-:---- 6
				7 ------- 5
				2 ------> 4
				3 <------ 2
				
				4 ------> 6
				6 <-:---- 1
					7 ------- 1
					2 ------> 4
					3 <------ 2
					
					4 ----:-> 6
					    :-> 8
					6 <-:---- 3

G2853	G2854	G2855	G2856	G2857	G2858

1 ------- 3
7 ------- 5
2 ------> 2
3 <------ 4
 	
6 <-:---- 1
	1 ------- 4
	7 ------- 2
	2 ------> 5
	3 <------ 3
	
	4 ------> 1
	6 <-:---- 6
		7 ------- 3
		2 ------> 1
		3 <------ 5
		
		4 ----:-> 2
		    :-> 7
		6 <-:---- 8
			7 ------- 6
			2 ------> 8
			3 <------ 4
			
			4 ----:-> 7
			    :-> 2
			6 <-:---- 1
				7 ------- 2
				2 ------> 3
				3 <------ 5
				
				6 <-:---- 4
					1 ------- 3
					7 ------- 4
					2 ------> 5
					3 <------ 2
					
					4 ------> 1
					6 <-:---- 6

G2859	G2860	G2861	G2862	G2863	G2864

1 ------- 4
7 ------- 3
2 ------> 2
3 <------ 5
 	
4 ------> 6
6 <-:---- 1
	7 ------- 4
	2 ------> 2
	3 <------ 3
	
	4 ------> 6
	6 <-:---- 1
		7 ------- 3
		2 ------> 5
		3 <------ 4
		
		4 ------> 1
		6 <-:---- 6
			7 ------- 11
			2 ------> 9
			3 <------ 1
			
			4 ----:-> 10
			    :-> 3
			    :-> 12
			6 <-:---- 2
				7 ------- 11
				2 ------> 1
				3 <------ 9
				
				6 <-:---- 3
				
				4 ----:-> 2
				    :-> 4
					7 ------- 4
					2 ------> 2
					3 <------ 3
					
					4 ------> 5
					6 <-:---- 1

G2865	G2866	G2867	G2868	G2869	G2870

7 ------- 4
2 ------> 3
3 <----- 2
 	
6 <-:---- 5
	7 ------- 2
	2 ------> 3
	3 <----- 5
	
	4 ------> 1
	6 <-:---- 6
		7 ------- 5
		2 ------> 4
		3 <----- 2
		
		4 ----:-> 3
		    :-> 6
		6 <-:---- 1
			7 ------- 2
			2 ------> 3
			3 <----- 5
			
			4 ----:-> 4
			    :-> 1
			6 <-:---- 6
				7 ------- 5
				2 ------> 2
				3 <----- 3
				
				4 ----:-> 8
				    :-> 6
				6 <-:---- 4
					1 ------- 1
					7 ------- 7
					2 ------> 3
					3 <----- 2
					
					6 <----- 20
					
					20 ----:-> 5
					     :-> 6
					     :-> 8

G2871	G2872	G2873	G2874	G2875	G2876

1 ------- 1
7 ------- 7
2 ------> 2
3 <----- 3
6 <----- 5
20 ------> 4
 	
  :-- 6
  :-> 20
	1 ------- 1
	7 ------- 7
	2 ------> 2
	3 <----- 3
	
	6 <----- 5
	
	20 ----:-> 4
	    :-> 8
	    :-> 20
		1 ------- 1
		7 ------- 7
		2 ------> 3
		3 <----- 2
		
		6 <----- 4
		
		20 ----:-> 5
		    :-> 6
		    :-> 20
			1 ------- 1
			7 ------- 7
			2 ------> 3
			3 <----- 2
			
			20 ----:-> 5
			    :-> 6
			6 <-:---- 4
				7 ------- 7
				2 ------> 2
				3 <----- 3
				
				20 --:
				6 <-:
					7 ------- 5
					2 ------> 4
					3 <----- 3
					
					20 ------> 6
					6 <-:---- 1

G2877	G2878	G2879	G2880	G2881	G2882

7 ------- 5
2 ------> 4
3 <----- 3
 	
6 <-:---- 1
	1 ------- 1
	7 ------- 7
	2 ------> 2
	3 <----- 3
	
	6 <-:---- 6
	
	20 ----:-> 4
	    :-> 20
		1 ------- 1
		7 ------- 7
		2 ------> 2
		3 <----- 3
		
		6 <-:---- 6
			1 ------- 1
			7 ------- 7
			2 ------> 3
			3 <----- 2
			
			20 ----:-> 5
			    :-> 8
			
			6 <-:---- 4
				1 ------- 1
				7 ------- 7
				2 ------> 2
				3 <----- 3
				
				20 --:
				6 <-:
					7 ------- 7
					2 ------> 2
					3 <----- 3
					
					20 --:
					6 <-:

G2883	G2884	G2885	G2886	G2887	G2888

1 ------- 1
7 ------- 7
2 ------> 2
3 <----- 3
 	
20 ------> 20
 	
6 <-:---- 5
  :-- 8
  :-> 4
  :-> 12
	7 ------- 7
	2 ------> 2
	3 <----- 3
	
	20 ----:-> 5
	  :- 6
	  :- 8
	
	6 <-:---- 4
		7 ------- 5
		2 ------> 2
		3 <----- 3
		
		20 ----:-> 8
		  :- 6
		  :- 1
		
		6 <-:---- 4
			1 ------- 1
			7 ------- 7
			2 ------> 2
			3 <----- 3
			
			6 <-:---- 8
			
			20 ----:-> 20
				7 ------- 5
				2 ------> 3
				3 <----- 2
				
				20 ----:-> 7
				    :-- 4
				6 <-:---- 6
					7 ------- 7
					2 ------> 3
					3 <----- 2
					
					20 --:
					6 <-:

G2889	G2890	G2891	G2892	G2893	G2894

1 ------- 1
7 ------- 8
2 ------> 4
3 <----- 2
 	
6 <----- 12
 	
20 ----:-> 5
    :-> 7
    :-> 10
    :-> 11
	1 ------- 1
	7 ------- 7
	2 ------> 2
	3 <----- 3
	6 <----- 5
	20 ------> 4
		7 ------- 4
		7 ------- 7
		3 <----- 2
		
		6 <----- 5
		
		20 ----:-> 1
		    :-> 6
			1 ------- 1
			7 ------- 7
			2 ------> 5
			3 <----- 3
			
			20 ------> 6
			6 <-:---- 4
				7 ------- 5
				2 ------> 7
				3 <----- 4
				
				6 <----- 3
				
				20 ----:-> 2
				    :-> 6
					7 ------- 3
					2 ------> 5
					3 <----- 4
					
					6 <----- 2
					
					20 ----:-> 6
					    :-> 7
					    :-> 8

G2895	G2896	G2897	G2898	G2899	G2900

1 ------- 4
7 ------- 7
2 ------> 6
3 <------ 5
 	
6 <------ 9
 	
20 ----:-> 1
    :-> 2
    :-> 8
    :-> 10
	1 ------- 3
	7 ------- 6
	2 ------> 5
	3 <------ 4
	
	6 <------ 8
	
	20 ----:-> 1
	    :-> 7
		7 ------- 8
		2 ------> 2
		3 <------ 1
		
		20 --:
		6 <-:
			7 ------- 8
			2 ------> 6
			3 <------ 1
			
			6 <------ 4
			
			20 ----:-> 7
			    :-> 9
				7 ------- 7
				2 ------> 3
				3 <------ 2
				
				6 <------ 9
				
				20 ----:-> 5
				    :-> 8
					7 ------- 5
					2 ------> 3
					3 <------ 2
					
					6 <------ 6
					
					20 ----:-> 4
					    :-> 7

G2901	G2902	G2903	G2904	G2905	G2906

1 ------- 2
7 ------- 7
2 ------> 3
3 <------ 8
 	
6 <------ 9
 	
20 ----:-> 1
    :-> 5
    :-> 6
    :-> 10
	1 ------- 2
	7 ------- 7
	2 ------> 8
	3 <------ 3
	
	6 <------ 5
	
	20 ----:-> 4
	    :-> 9
		7 ------- 7
		2 ------> 5
		3 <------ 4
		
		6 <------ 1
		
		20 ----:-> 3
			7 ------- 4
			2 ------> 6
			3 <------ 3
			
			6 <------ 2
			
			20 ----:-> 1
			    :-- 7
				7 ------- 5
				2 ------> 6
				3 <------ 4
				
				6 <------ 3
				
				20 ----:-> 2
					7 ------- 9
					2 ------> 3
					3 <------ 2
					
					6 <------ 4
					
					20 ----:-> 5

G2907	G2908	G2909	G2910	G2911	G2912
7 ------- 3 2 ------> 4 3 <------ 2 6 <------ 1 20 ----:-> 5	7 ------- 9 2 ------> 13 3 <------ 11 6 <------ 10 20 ----:-> 14	7 ------- 5 2 ------> 2 3 <------ 3 6 <------ 4 20 ----:-> 6 :- 8	7 ------- 5 2 ------> 2 3 <------ 3 6 <------ 7 20 ----:-> 8	7 ------- 5 2 ------> 3 3 <------ 2 6 <------ 6	7 ------- 5 2 ------> 3 3 <------ 2 20 --: 6 <-:

G2913	G2914	G2915	G2916	G2917	G2918
1 ------- 3 7 ------- 4 2 ------> 5 3 <------ 2 6 <------ 1 20 ----:-> 6	1 ------- 1 7 ------- 2 2 ------> 4 3 <------ 3 6 <------ 6 20 ----:-> 5	1 ------- 1 7 ------- 7 3 <------ 2 20 --: 6 <-:	1 ------- 1 7 ------- 7 2 ------> 5 3 <------ 3 6 <------ 4 20 ----:-> 6 :-> 8	7 ------- 4 2 ------> 5 3 <------ 3 6 <------ 6 20 ----:-> 2	7 ------- 5 2 ------> 4 3 <------ 2 6 <------ 1 20 ----:-> 6

G2919	G2920	G2921	G2922	G2923	G2924

7 ------- 1
2 ------> 4
3 <------ 2
 	
6 <------ 3
 	
20 ----:-> 6
    :-> 8
	1 ------- 3
	7 ------- 5
	2 ------> 2
	3 <------ 4
	
	6 <------ 1
		1 ------- 4
		7 ------- 2
		2 ------> 5
		3 <------ 3
		
		6 <------ 6
		
		20 ----:-> 1
			7 ------- 3
			2 ------> 1
			3 <------ 5
			
			6 <------ 8
			
			20 ----:-> 2
			    :-> 7
				7 ------- 6
				2 ------> 8
				3 <------ 4
				
				6 <------ 1
				
				20 ----:-> 2
				    :-> 7
					7 ------- 2
					2 ------> 3
					3 <------ 5
					
					6 <------ 4

G2925
 	
1 ------- 3
7 ------- 4
2 -----> 5
3 <----- 2
 	
6 <----- 6
 	
20 ----:-> 1
	G2926
	
	1 ------- 4
	7 ------- 3
	2 -----> 2
	3 <----- 5
	
	6 <----- 1
	
	20 ----:-> 6
		G2927
		
		7 ------- 4
		2 -----> 2
		3 <----- 3
		
		6 <----- 1
		
		20 ----:-> 6
			G2928
			
			7 ------- 3
			2 -----> 5
			3 <----- 4
			
			6 <----- 6
			
			20 ----:-> 1
				G2929
				
				7 ------- 11
				2 -----> 9
				3 <----- 1
				
				6 <----- 2
				
				20 ----:-> 3
				    :-> 10
				    :-> 12
					G2930
					
					7 ------- 11
					2 -----> 1
					3 <----- 9
					6 <----- 10
					20 -----> 2
					
					   :-- 3
					   :-> 4

G2931
 	
7 ------- 4
2 -----> 2
3 <----- 3
 	
6 <----- 1
 	
20 ----:-> 5
	G2932
	
	7 ------- 4
	2 -----> 3
	3 <----- 2
	
	6 <----- 5
		G2933
		
		7 ------- 2
		2 -----> 3
		3 <----- 5
		
		6 <----- 6
		
		20 ----:-> 1
			G2934
			
			7 ------- 5
			2 -----> 4
			3 <----- 2
			
			6 <----- 1
			
			20 ----:-> 3
			    :-> 6
				G2935
				
				7 ------- 2
				2 -----> 3
				3 <----- 5
				
				6 <----- 6
				
				20 ----:-> 1
				    :-> 4
					G2936
					
					7 ------- 5
					2 -----> 2
					3 <----- 3
					
					6 <----- 4
					
					20 ----:-> 6
					    :-> 8

G2937
 	
1 ------- 1
7 ------- 7
2 -----> 3
3 <----- 2
 	
4 ----:-> 5
    :-> 6
    :-> 8
	G2938
	
	1 ------- 1
	7 ------- 7
	2 -----> 2
	3 <----- 3
	
	4 ----:-> 4
	    :-> 20
		G2939
		
		1 ------- 1
		7 ------- 7
		2 -----> 2
		3 <----- 3
		
		4 ----:-> 8
		    :-> 4
		    :-> 20
			G2940
			
			1 ------- 1
			7 ------- 7
			2 -----> 3
			3 <----- 2
			
			4 ----:-> 5
			    :-> 6
			    :-> 20
				G2941
				
				1 ------- 1
				7 ------- 7
				2 -----> 3
				3 <----- 2
				
				4 ----:-> 5
				    :-> 6
					G2942
					
					7 ------- 7
					2 -----> 2
					3 <----- 3

G2943
 	
7 ------- 5
2 -----> 4
3 <----- 3
 	
4 ------> 6
	G2944
	
	7 ------- 5
	2 -----> 4
	3 <----- 3
		G2945
		
		1 ------- 1
		7 ------- 7
		2 -----> 2
		3 <----- 3
		
		4 ----:-> 4
		    :-> 20
			G2946
			
			1 ------- 1
			7 ------- 7
			2 -----> 2
			3 <----- 3
				G2947
				
				1 ------- 1
				7 ------- 7
				2 -----> 3
				3 <----- 2
				
				4 ----:-> 5
				    :-> 8
					G2948
					
					1 ------- 1
					7 ------- 7
					2 -----> 2
					3 <----- 3

G2949
 	
7 ------- 7
2 -----> 2
3 <----- 3
	G2950
	
	1 ------- 1
	7 ------- 7
	2 -----> 2
	3 <----- 3
	
	4 ----:-> 20
	    :-> 4
	    :-> 12
		G2951
		
		7 ------- 7
		2 -----> 2
		3 <----- 3
		
		4 ----:-> 5
		    :-> 6
		    :-> 8
			G2952
			
			7 ------- 5
			2 -----> 2
			3 <----- 3
			
			4 ----:-> 8
			    :-> 6
			    :-> 1
				G2953
				
				1 ------- 1
				7 ------- 7
				2 -----> 2
				3 <----- 3
				
				4 ----:-> 20
					G2954
					
					7 ------- 5
					2 -----> 3
					3 <----- 2
					
					4 ----:-> 7
					    :-> 4

G2955
 	
7 ------- 7
2 -----> 3
3 <----- 2
	G2956
	
	1 ------- 1
	7 ------- 8
	2 -----> 4
	3 <----- 2
	
	4 ----:-> 5
	    :-> 10
	    :-> 7
	    :-> 11
		G2957
		
		1 ------- 1
		7 ------- 7
		2 -----> 2
		3 <----- 3
		
		4 ----:-> 4
			G2958
			
			7 ------- 4
			2 -----> 3
			3 <----- 2
			
			4 ----:-> 1
			    :-> 6
				G2959
				
				1 ------- 1
				7 ------- 7
				2 -----> 5
				3 <----- 3
				
				4 ------> 6
					G2960
					
					7 ------- 5
					2 -----> 7
					3 <----- 4
					
					4 ----:-> 2
					    :-> 6

G2961
```
7 ------- 3
2 ------> 5
3 <------ 4

4 ----:-> 8
     :-> 7
     :-> 6
```

G2962
```
1 ------- 4
7 ------- 7
2 ------> 6
3 <------ 5

4 ----:-> 8
     :-> 2
     :-> 10
     :-> 1
```

G2963
```
1 ------- 3
7 ------- 6
2 ------> 5
3 <------ 4

4 ----:-> 7
     :-> 1
```

G2964
```
7 ------- 8
2 ------> 2
3 <------ 1
```

G2965
```
7 ------- 8
2 ------> 6
3 <------ 1

4 ----:-> 7
     :-> 9
```

G2966
```
7 ------- 7
2 ------> 3
3 <------ 2

4 ----:-> 5
     :-> 8
```

G2967
```
7 ------- 5
2 ------> 3
3 <------ 2

4 ----:-> 4
     :-> 7
```

G2968
```
1 ------- 2
7 ------- 7
2 ------> 3
3 <------ 8

4 ----:-> 5
     :-> 6
     :-> 1
     :-> 10
```

G2969
```
1 ------- 2
7 ------- 7
2 ------> 8
3 <------ 3

4 ----:-> 4
     :-> 9
```

G2970
```
7 ------- 7
2 ------> 5
3 <------ 4

4 ------> 3
```

G2971
```
7 ------- 4
2 ------> 6
3 <------ 3

4 ----:-> 1
     :-> 7
```

G2972
```
7 ------- 5
2 ------> 6
3 <------ 4

4 ------> 2
```

G2973
```
7 ------- 9
2 ------> 3
3 <------ 2

4 ------> 5
```

G2974
```
7 ------- 3
2 ----:-> 4
3 <------ 2

4 ------> 5
```

G2975
```
7 ------- 9
2 ------> 13
3 <------ 11

4 ------> 14
```

G2976
```
7 ------- 5
2 ------> 2
3 <------ 3

4 ----:-> 8
     :-> 6
```

G2977
```
7 ------- 5
2 ------> 2
3 <------ 3

4 ------> 8
```

G2978
```
7 ------- 5
2 ------> 3
3 <------ 2
```

G2979
```
7 ------- 5
2 ------> 3
3 <------ 2
```

G2980
```
1 ------- 3
7 ------- 4
2 ------> 5
3 <------ 2

4 ------> 6
```

G2981
```
1 ------- 1
7 ------- 2
2 ------> 4
3 <------ 3

4 ------> 5
```

G2982
```
1 ------- 1
7 ------- 7
3 <------ 2
```

G2983
```
1 ------- 1
7 ------- 7
2 ------> 5
3 <------ 3

4 ----:-> 8
     :-> 6
```

G2984
```
7 ------- 4
2 ------> 5
3 <------ 3

4 ------> 2
```

G2985
```
7 ------- 5
2 ------> 4
3 <------ 2

4 ------> 6
```

G2986
```
7 ------- 1
2 ------> 4
3 <------ 2

4 ----:-> 6
     :-> 8
```

G2987
```
1 ------- 3
7 ------- 5
2 ------> 2
3 <------ 4
```

G2988
```
1 ------- 4
7 ------- 2
2 ------> 5
3 <------ 3

4 ------> 1
```

G2989
```
7 ------- 3
2 ------> 1
3 <------ 5

4 ----:-> 2
     :-> 7
```

G2990
```
7 ------- 6
2 ------> 8
3 <------ 4

4 ----:-> 7
     :-> 2
```

G2991
```
7 ------- 2
2 ------> 3
3 <------ 5
```

G2992
```
1 ------- 3
7 ------- 4
2 ------> 5
3 <------ 2

4 ------> 1
```

G2993
```
1 ------- 4
7 ------- 3
2 ------> 2
3 <------ 5

4 ------> 6
```

G2994
```
7 ------- 4
2 ------> 2
3 <------ 3

4 ------> 6
```

G2995
```
7 ------- 3
2 ------> 5
3 <------ 4

4 ------> 1
```

G2996
```
7 ------- 11
2 ------> 9
3 <------ 1

4 ----:-> 10
     :-> 3
     :-> 12
```

```
G2997                 G2998                 G2999                 G3000                 G3001                 G3002

7 ------- 11          7 ------- 4           7 ------- 4           7 ------- 2           7 ------- 5           7 ------- 2
2 ------> 1           2 ------> 2           2 ------> 3           2 ------> 3           2 ------> 4           2 ------> 3
3 <------ 9           3 <------ 3           3 <------ 2           3 <------ 5           3 <------ 2           3 <------ 5
4 ----:-> 2           4 ------> 5                                 4 ------> 1           4 ----:-> 3           4 ----:-> 4
     :-> 4                                                                                   :-> 6                 :-> 1
```

```
G3003                 G3004                 G3005                 G3006                 G3007                 G3008

7 ------- 5           1 ------- 1           1 ------- 1           1 ------- 1           1 ------- 1           1 ------- 1
2 ------> 2           7 ------- 7           7 ------- 7           7 ------- 7           7 ------- 7           7 ------- 7
3 <------ 3           2 ------> 3           2 ------> 2           2 ------> 2           2 ------> 3           2 ------> 3
4 ----:-> 8           3 <------ 2           3 <------ 3           3 <------ 3           3 <------ 2           3 <------ 2
     :-> 6            19 ----:-> 5          6 <-:----- 6          19 ----:-> 8          19 ----:-> 5          19 ----:-> 5
                           :-> 6            19 ----:-> 4               :-> 4                 :-> 6                 :-> 6
                           :-> 8                :-> 20                :-> 20          6 <-:----- 4          6 <-:----- 4
                      6 <-:----- 20                               6 <-:----- 5
```

```
G3009                 G3010                 G3011                 G3012                 G3013                 G3014

7 ------- 7           7 ------- 5           7 ------- 5           1 ------- 1           1 ------- 1           1 ------- 1
2 ------> 2           2 ------> 4           2 ------> 4           7 ------- 7           7 ------- 7           7 ------- 7
3 <------ 3           3 <------ 3           3 <------ 3           2 ------> 2           2 ------> 2           2 ------> 3
                      19 ------> 6          6 <-:----- 1          3 <------ 3           3 <------ 3           3 <------ 2
20 --:                5 <-:----- 1                               6 <-:----- 6          6 <-:----- 6          19 ----:-> 5
5 <-:                                                            19 ----:-> 4                                     :-> 8
6 <-:                                                                 :-> 20
8 <-:                                                                                                       6 <-:----- 4
```

```
G3015                 G3016                 G3017                 G3018                 G3019                 G3020

1 ------- 1           7 ------- 7           1 ------- 1           7 ------- 7           7 ------- 5           1 ------- 1
7 ------- 7           2 ------> 2           7 ------- 7           2 ------> 2           2 ------> 2           7 ------- 7
2 ------> 2           3 <------ 3           2 ------> 2           3 <------ 3           3 <------ 3           2 ------> 2
3 <------ 3                                 3 <------ 3           19 ----:-> 5          19 ----:-> 8          3 <------ 3
                      20 --:                19 ----:-> 20              :-> 6                 :-> 6           6 <-:----- 8
20 --:                6 <-:                      :-> 4                 :-> 8                 :-> 1           19 ----:-> 20
6 <-:                                            :-> 12          6 <-:----- 4          6 <-:----- 4
                                            6 <-:----- 5
```

```
G3021                 G3022                 G3023                 G3024                 G3025                 G3026

7 ------- 5           7 ------- 7           1 ------- 1           1 ------- 1           7 ------- 4           1 ------- 1
2 ------> 3           2 ------> 3           7 ------- 8           7 ------- 7           2 ------> 3           7 ------- 7
3 <------ 2           3 <------ 2           2 ------> 4           2 ------> 2           3 <------ 2           2 ------> 5
19 ----:-> 7          20 --:                3 <------ 2           3 <------ 3           19 ----:-> 1          3 <------ 3
6 <-:----- 6          6 <-:                 19 ----:-> 5          6 <-:----- 6              :-> 6           19 ------> 6
                                                 :-> 10           19 ----:-> 4          6 <-:----- 5          6 <-:----- 4
                                                 :-> 7
                                            6 <-:----- 12
                                            20 ----:-> 11
```

```
G3027                G3028                G3029                G3030                G3031                G3032

7 ------- 5          7 ------- 3          1 ------- 4          1 ------- 3          7 ------- 8          7 ------- 8
2 ------> 7          2 ------> 5          7 ------- 7          7 ------- 6          2 ------> 2          2 ------> 6
3 <------ 4          3 <------ 4          2 ------> 6          2 ------> 5          3 <------ 1          3 <------ 1
                                          3 <------ 5          3 <------ 4
19 ----:-> 2         19 ----:-> 8                                                  20 --:               19 ----:-> 7
    :-> 6                :-> 7            19 ----:-> 8         19 ----:-> 7         6 <-:                    :-> 9
6 <-:---- 3             :-> 6                :-> 2                :-> 1                                  6 <-:---- 4
                    6 <-:---- 2             :-> 10           6 <-:---- 8
                                         6 <-:---- 9

                                         20 ----:-> 1


G3033                G3034                G3035                G3036                G3037                G3038

7 ------- 7          7 ------- 5          1 ------- 2          1 ------- 2          7 ------- 7          7 ------- 4
2 ------> 3          2 ------> 3          7 ------- 7          7 ------- 7          2 ------> 5          2 ------> 6
3 <------ 2          3 <------ 2          2 ------> 3          2 ------> 8          3 <------ 4          3 <------ 3
                                          3 <------ 8          3 <------ 3
19 ----:-> 5         6 <-:---- 6                                                   19 ------> 3         6 <-:---- 2
    :-> 8                                 19 ----:-> 5         6 <-:---- 5          6 <-:---- 1
6 <-:---- 9         19 ----:-> 4             :-> 6                                                      19 ----:-> 1
                        :-> 7                :-> 1            19 ----:-> 4                                  :-> 7
                                         6 <-:---- 9              :-> 9

                                         20 ----:-> 10


G3039                G3040                G3041                G3042                G3043                G3044

7 ------- 5          7 ------- 9          7 ------- 3          7 ------- 9          7 ------- 5          7 ------- 5
2 ------> 6          2 ------> 3          2 ------> 4          2 ------> 13         2 ------> 2          2 ------> 2
3 <------ 4          3 <------ 2          3 <------ 2          3 <------ 11         3 <------ 3          3 <------ 3

19 ------> 2         19 ------> 5         19 ------> 5         19 ------> 14        19 ----:-> 8         19 ------> 8
6 <-:---- 3         6 <-:---- 4          6 <-:---- 1          6 <-:---- 10             :-> 6           6 <-:---- 7
                                                                                  6 <-:---- 4


G3045                G3046                G3047                G3048                G3049                G3050

7 ------- 5          7 ------- 5          1 ------- 3          1 ------- 1          1 ------- 1          1 ------- 1
2 ------> 3          2 ------> 3          7 ------- 4          7 ------- 2          7 ------- 7          7 ------- 7
3 <------ 2          3 <------ 2          2 ------> 5          2 ------> 4          3 <------ 2          2 ------> 5
                                          3 <------ 2          3 <------ 3                              3 <------ 3
6 <-:---- 6                                                                        19 --:
                    19 --:               19 ------> 6         19 ------> 5         6 <-:               19 ----:-> 8
                    6 <-:                6 <-:---- 1          6 <-:---- 6                                  :-> 6
                                                                                                       6 <-:---- 4


G3051                G3052                G3053                G3054                G3055                G3056

7 ------- 4          7 ------- 5          7 ------- 1          1 ------- 3          1 ------- 4          7 ------- 3
2 ------> 5          2 ------> 4          2 ------> 4          7 ------- 5          7 ------- 2          2 ------> 1
3 <------ 3          3 <------ 2          3 <------ 2          2 ------> 2          2 ------> 5          3 <------ 5
                                                              3 <------ 4          3 <------ 3
19 ------> 2         19 ------> 6         19 ----:-> 6                                                  19 ----:-> 2
6 <-:---- 6         6 <-:---- 1              :-> 8            6 <-:---- 1          19 ------> 1             :-> 7
                                         6 <-:---- 3                               6 <-:---- 6          6 <-:---- 8
```

```
G3057
7 -------- 6
2 ------> 8
3 <-:---- 4
19 ----:-> 7
      :-> 2
6 <-:---- 1
```

```
G3058
7 -------- 2
2 ------> 3
3 <------ 5
6 <-:---- 4
```

```
G3059
1 -------- 3
7 -------- 4
2 ------> 5
3 <------ 2
19 ------> 1
6 <-:---- 6
```

```
G3060
1 -------- 4
7 -------- 3
2 ------> 2
3 <------ 5
19 ------> 6
6 <-:---- 1
```

```
G3061
7 -------- 4
2 ------> 2
3 <------ 3
19 ------> 6
6 <-:---- 1
```

```
G3062
7 -------- 3
2 ------> 5
3 <------ 4
19 ------> 1
6 <-:---- 6
```

```
G3063
7 -------- 11
2 ------> 9
3 <------ 1
19 ----:-> 10
      :-> 3
      :-> 12
6 <-:---- 2
```

```
G3064
7 -------- 11
2 ------> 1
3 <------ 9
6 <-:---- 3
19 ----:-> 2
      :-> 4
```

```
G3065
7 -------- 4
2 ------> 2
3 <------ 3
19 ------> 5
6 <-:---- 1
```

```
G3066
7 -------- 4
2 ------> 3
3 <------ 2
6 <-:---- 5
```

```
G3067
7 -------- 2
2 ------> 3
3 <------ 5
19 ------> 1
6 <-:---- 6
```

```
G3068
7 -------- 5
2 ------> 4
3 <------ 2
19 ----:-> 3
      :-> 6
6 <-:---- 1
```

```
G3069
7 -------- 2
2 ------> 3
3 <------ 5
19 ----:-> 4
      :-> 1
6 <-:---- 6
```

```
G3070
7 -------- 5
2 ------> 2
3 <------ 3
19 ----:-> 8
      :-> 6
6 <-:---- 4
```

```
G3071
1 -------- 1
7 -------- 7
2 <------ 2
8 ----:-> 5
     :-> 6
     :-> 8
```

```
G3072
1 -------- 1
7 -------- 7
2 <------ 3
8 ----:-> 4
     :-> 20
```

```
G3073
1 -------- 1
7 -------- 7
2 <------ 3
8 ----:-> 8
     :-> 4
     :-> 20
```

```
G3074
1 -------- 1
7 -------- 7
2 <------ 2
8 ----:-> 5
     :-> 6
     :-> 20
```

```
G3075
1 -------- 1
7 -------- 7
2 <------ 2
8 ----:-> 5
     :-> 6
```

```
G3076
7 -------- 7
2 <------ 3
```

```
G3077
7 -------- 5
2 <------ 3
8 ------> 6
```

```
G3078
7 -------- 5
2 <------ 3
```

```
G3079
1 -------- 1
7 -------- 7
2 <------ 3
8 ----:-> 4
     :-> 20
```

```
G3080
1 -------- 1
7 -------- 7
2 <------ 3
```

```
G3081
1 -------- 1
7 -------- 7
2 <------ 2
8 ----:-> 5
     :-> 8
```

```
G3082
1 -------- 1
7 -------- 7
2 <------ 3
```

```
G3083
7 -------- 7
2 <------ 3
```

```
G3084
1 -------- 1
7 -------- 7
2 <------ 3
8 ----:-> 20
     :-> 4
     :-> 12
```

```
G3085
7 -------- 7
2 <------ 3
8 ----:-> 5
     :-> 6
     :-> 8
```

```
G3086
7 -------- 5
2 <------ 3
8 ----:-> 8
     :-> 6
     :-> 1
```

```
G3087
1 -------- 1
7 -------- 7
2 <------ 3
8 ----:-> 20
```

```
G3088
7 -------- 5
2 <------ 2
8 ----:-> 7
     :-> 4
```

```
G3089
7 -------- 7
2 <------ 2
```

```
G3090
1 -------- 1
7 -------- 8
2 <------ 2
8 ----:-> 5
     :-> 10
     :-> 7
     :-> 11
```

```
G3091
1 -------- 1
7 -------- 7
2 <------ 3
8 ----:-> 4
```

```
G3092
7 -------- 4
2 <------ 2
8 ----:-> 1
     :-> 6
```

G3093	G3094	G3095	G3096	G3097	G3098

1 ------- 1
7 ------- 7
2 <------ 3
 	
8 ------> 6
	7 ------- 5
	2 <------ 4
	
	8 ----:-> 2
	    :-> 6
		7 ------- 3
		2 <------ 4
		
		8 ----:-> 8
		    :-> 7
		    :-> 6
			1 ------- 4
			7 ------- 7
			2 <------ 5
			
			8 ----:-> 8
			    :-> 2
			    :-> 10
			    :-> 1
				1 ------- 3
				7 ------- 6
				2 <------ 4
				
				8 ----:-> 7
				    :-> 1
					7 ------- 8
					2 <------ 1

G3099	G3100	G3101	G3102	G3103	G3104

7 ------- 8
2 <------ 1
 	
8 ----:-> 7
    :-> 9
	7 ------- 7
	2 <------ 2
	
	8 ----:-> 5
	    :-> 8
		7 ------- 5
		2 <------ 2
		
		8 ---:-> 4
		    :-> 7
			1 ------- 2
			7 ------- 7
			2 <------ 8
			
			8 ----:-> 5
			    :-> 6
			    :-> 1
			    :-> 10
				1 ------- 2
				7 ------- 7
				2 <------ 3
				
				8 ----:-> 4
				    :-> 9
					7 ------- 7
					2 <------ 4
					
					8 ------> 3

G3105	G3106	G3107	G3108	G3109	G3110

7 ------- 4
2 <------ 3
 	
8 ----:-> 1
    :-> 7
	7 ------- 5
	2 <------ 4
	
	8 ------> 2
		7 ------- 9
		2 <------ 2
		
		8 ------> 5
			7 ------- 3
			2 <------ 2
			
			8 ------> 5
				7 ------- 9
				2 <------ 11
				
				8 ------> 14
					7 ------- 5
					2 <------ 3
					
					8 ----:-> 8
					    :-> 6

G3111	G3112	G3113	G3114	G3115	G3116
7 ------- 5 2 <------ 3 8 ------> 8	7 ------- 5 2 <------ 2	7 ------- 5 2 <------ 2	1 ------- 3 7 ------- 4 2 <------ 2 8 ------> 6	1 ------- 1 7 ------- 2 2 <------ 3 8 ------> 5	1 ------- 1 7 ------- 7 2 <------ 2

G3117	G3118	G3119	G3120	G3121	G3122

1 ------- 1
7 ------- 7
2 <------ 3
 	
8 ----:-> 8
    :-> 6
	7 ------- 4
	2 <------ 3
	
	8 ------> 2
		7 ------- 5
		2 <------ 2
		
		8 ------> 6
			7 ------- 1
			2 <------ 2
			
			8 ----:-> 6
			    :-> 8
				1 ------- 3
				7 ------- 5
				2 <------ 4
					1 ------- 4
					7 ------- 2
					2 <------ 3
					
					8 ------> 1

G3123	G3124	G3125	G3126	G3127	G3128

7 ------- 3
2 <------ 5
 	
8 ----:-> 2
    :-> 7
	7 ------- 6
	2 <------ 4
	
	8 ----:-> 7
	    :-> 2
		7 ------- 2
		2 <------ 5
			1 ------- 3
			7 ------- 4
			2 <------ 2
			
			8 ------> 1
				1 ------- 4
				7 ------- 3
				2 <------ 5
				
				8 ------> 6
					7 ------- 4
					2 <------ 3
					
					8 ------> 6

G3129	G3130	G3131	G3132	G3133	G3134

7 ------- 3
2 <------ 4
 	
8 ------> 1
	7 ------- 11
	2 <------ 1
	
	8 ----:-> 10
	    :-> 3
	    :-> 12
		7 ------- 11
		2 <------ 9
		8 ----:-> 2
		    :-> 4
			7 ------- 4
			2 <------ 3
			
			8 ------> 5
				7 ------- 4
				2 <------ 2
					7 ------- 2
					2 <------ 5
					
					8 ------> 1

```
G3135
7 ------- 5
2 <------ 2

8 ----:-> 3
     :-> 6
```

```
G3136
7 ------- 2
2 <------ 5

8 ----:-> 4
     :-> 1
```

```
G3137
7 ------- 5
2 <------ 3

8 ----:-> 8
     :-> 6
```

```
G3138
1 ------- 1
7 ------- 7
2 ------> 3
3 <------ 2

25 ----:-> 5
     :-> 6
     :-> 8
5 <-:----- 20
6 <-:
8 <-:
```

```
G3139
1 ------- 1
7 ------- 7
2 ------> 2
3 <------ 3

5 <-:---- 6
6 <-:
8 <-:

25 ----:-> 4
     :-> 20
```

```
G3140
1 ------- 1
7 ------- 7
2 ------> 2
3 <------ 3

25 ----:-> 8
       :-> 4
       :-> 20
5 <-:---- 5
6 <-:
8 <-:
```

```
G3141
1 ------- 1
7 ------- 7
2 ------> 2
3 <------ 2

25 ----:-> 5
     :-> 6
     :-> 20
5 <-:---- 4
6 <-:
8 <-:
```

```
G3142
1 ------- 1
7 ------- 7
2 ------> 3
3 <------ 2

25 ----:-> 5
     :-> 6
5 <-:----- 4
6 <-:
8 <-:
```

```
G3143
7 ------- 7
2 ------> 2
3 <------ 3

4 --:
5 <-:
6 <-:
8 <-:
```

```
G3144
7 ------- 5
2 ------> 4
3 <------ 3

25 ------> 6
5 <-:---- 1
6 <-:
8 <-:
```

```
G3145
7 ------- 5
2 ------> 4
3 <------ 3

5 <-:---- 1
6 <-:
8 <-:
```

```
G3146
1 ------- 1
7 ------- 7
2 ------> 2
3 <------ 3

5 <-:---- 6
6 <-:
8 <-:

25 ----:-> 4
     :-> 20
```

```
G3147
1 ------- 1
7 ------- 7
2 ------> 2
3 <------ 3

5 <-:---- 6
6 <-:
8 <-:
```

```
G3148
1 ------- 1
7 ------- 7
2 ------> 3
3 <------ 2

25 ----:-> 5
     :-> 8
5 <-:---- 4
6 <-:
8 <-:
```

```
G3149
1 ------- 1
7 ------- 7
2 ------> 2
3 <------ 3

4 --:
5 <-:
6 <-:
8 <-:
```

```
G3150
7 ------- 7
2 ------> 2
3 <------ 3

4 --:
5 <-:
6 <-:
8 <-:
```

```
G3151
1 ------- 1
7 ------- 7
2 ------> 2
3 <------ 3

25 ----:-> 20
     :-> 4
     :-> 12
5 <-:----- 5
6 <-:
8 <-:
```

```
G3152
7 ------- 7
2 ------> 2
3 <------ 3

25 ----:-> 5
       :-> 6
       :-> 8
5 <-:---- 4
6 <-:
8 <-:
```

```
G3153
7 ------- 5
2 ------> 2
3 <------ 3

25 ----:-> 8
     :-> 6
     :-> 1
5 <-:----- 4
6 <-:
8 <-:
```

```
G3154
1 ------- 1
7 ------- 7
2 ------> 2
3 <------ 3

5 <-:---- 8
6 <-:
8 <-:

25 ----:-> 20
```

```
G3155
7 ------- 5
2 ------> 3
3 <------ 2

25 ----:-> 7
       :-> 4
5 <-:----- 6
6 <-:
8 <-:
```

```
G3156
7 ------- 7
2 ------> 3
3 <------ 2

4 --:
5 <-:
6 <-:
8 <-:
```

```
G3157
1 ------- 1
7 ------- 8
2 ------> 4
3 <------ 2

25 ----:-> 5
       :-> 10
       :-> 7
5 <-:----- 12
6 <-:
8 <-:

4 ----:-> 11
```

```
G3158
1 ------- 1
7 ------- 7
2 ------> 2
3 <------ 3

5 <-:---- 6
6 <-:
8 <-:

25 ----:-> 4
```

G3159	G3160	G3161	G3162	G3163	G3164

<pre>7 ------- 4
2 ------> 3
3 <------ 2
 	
25 ----:-> 1
       :-> 6
5 <-:---- 5
6 <-:
8 <-:</pre>
	<pre>1 ------- 1
	7 ------- 7
	2 ------> 5
	3 <------ 3
	
	25 ----:-> 6
	5 <-:---- 4
	6 <-:
	8 <-:</pre>
		<pre>7 ------- 5
		2 ------> 7
		3 <------ 4
		
		25 ----:-> 2
		       :-> 6
		5 <-:---- 3
		6 <-:
		8 <-:</pre>
			<pre>7 ------- 3
			2 ------> 5
			3 <------ 4
			
			25 ----:-> 8
			       :-> 7
			       :-> 6
			5 <-:---- 2
			6 <-:
			8 <-:</pre>
				<pre>1 ------- 4
				7 ------- 7
				2 ------> 6
				3 <------ 5
				
				25 ----:-> 8
				       :-> 2
				       :-> 10
				5 <-:---- 9
				6 <-:
				8 <-:
				
				4 ----:-> 1</pre>
					<pre>1 ------- 3
					7 ------- 6
					2 ------> 5
					3 <------ 4
					
					25 ----:-> 7
					       :-> 1
					5 <-:---- 8
					6 <-:
					8 <-:</pre>

G3165	G3166	G3167	G3168	G3169	G3170

<pre>7 ------- 8
2 ------> 2
3 <------ 1
 	
4 --:
5 <-:
6 <-:
8 <-:</pre>
	<pre>7 ------- 8
	2 ------> 6
	3 <------ 1
	
	25 ----:-> 7
	       :-> 9
	5 <-:---- 4
	6 <-:
	8 <-:</pre>
		<pre>7 ------- 7
		2 ------> 3
		3 <------ 2
		
		25 ----:-> 5
		       :-> 8
		5 <-:---- 9
		6 <-:
		8 <-:</pre>
			<pre>7 ------- 5
			2 ------> 3
			3 <------ 2
			
			5 <-:---- 6
			6 <-:
			8 <-:
			
			25 ----:-> 4
			       :-> 7</pre>
				<pre>1 ------- 2
				7 ------- 7
				2 ------> 3
				3 <------ 8
				
				25 ----:-> 2
				       :-> 6
				       :-> 1
				5 <-:---- 9
				6 <-:
				8 <-:
				
				4 ----:-> 10</pre>
					<pre>1 ------- 2
					7 ------- 7
					2 ------> 8
					3 <------ 3
					
					5 <-:---- 5
					6 <-:
					8 <-:
					
					25 ----:-> 4
					       :-> 9</pre>

G3171	G3172	G3173	G3174	G3175	G3176

<pre>7 ------- 7
2 ------> 5
3 <------ 4
 	
25 ------> 3
5 <-:---- 1
6 <-:
8 <-:</pre>
	<pre>7 ------- 4
	2 ------> 6
	3 <------ 3
	
	5 <-:---- 2
	6 <-:
	8 <-:
	
	25 ----:-> 1
	       :-> 7</pre>
		<pre>7 ------- 5
		2 ------> 6
		3 <------ 4
		
		25 ------> 2
		5 <-:---- 3
		6 <-:
		8 <-:</pre>
			<pre>7 ------- 9
			2 ------> 3
			3 <------ 2
			
			25 ------> 5
			5 <-:---- 4
			6 <-:
			8 <-:</pre>
				<pre>7 ------- 3
				2 ------> 4
				3 <------ 2
				
				25 ------> 5
				5 <-:---- 1
				6 <-:
				8 <-:</pre>
					<pre>7 ------- 9
					2 ------> 13
					3 <------ 11
					
					25 ------> 14
					5 <-:---- 10
					6 <-:
					8 <-:</pre>

G3177	G3178	G3179	G3180	G3181	G3182

<pre>7 ------- 5
2 ------> 2
3 <------ 3
 	
25 ----:-> 8
       :-> 6
5 <-:---- 4
6 <-:
8 <-:</pre>
	<pre>7 ------- 5
	2 ------> 2
	3 <------ 3
	
	25 ------> 8
	5 <-:---- 7
	6 <-:
	8 <-:</pre>
		<pre>7 ------- 5
		2 ------> 3
		3 <------ 2
		
		5 <-:---- 6
		6 <-:
		8 <-:</pre>
			<pre>7 ------- 5
			2 ------> 3
			3 <------ 2
			
			25 --:
			5 <-:
			6 <-:
			8 <-:</pre>
				<pre>1 ------- 3
				7 ------- 4
				2 ------> 5
				3 <------ 2
				
				25 ------> 6
				5 <-:---- 1
				6 <-:
				8 <-:</pre>
					<pre>1 ------- 1
					7 ------- 2
					2 ------> 4
					3 <------ 3
					
					25 ------> 5
					5 <-:---- 6
					6 <-:
					8 <-:</pre>

```
G3183
1 ------- 1
7 ------- 7
3 <----- 2

25 --:
5 <-:
6 <-:
8 <-:
```

```
G3184
1 ------- 1
7 ------- 7
2 -----> 5
3 <----- 3

25 ----:-> 8
       :-> 6
5 <-:----- 4
6 <-:
8 <-:
```

```
G3185
7 ------- 4
2 -----> 5
3 <----- 3

25 ------> 2
5 <-:----- 6
6 <-:
8 <-:
```

```
G3186
7 ------- 5
2 -----> 4
3 <----- 2

25 ------> 6
5 <-:----- 1
6 <-:
8 <-:
```

```
G3187
7 ------- 1
2 -----> 4
3 <----- 2

25 ----:-> 6
       :-> 8
5 <-:----- 3
6 <-:
8 <-:
```

```
G3188
1 ------- 3
7 ------- 5
2 -----> 2
3 <----- 4

5 <-:----- 1
6 <-:
8 <-:
```

```
G3189
1 ------- 4
7 ------- 2
2 -----> 5
3 <----- 3

25 ------> 1
5 <-:----- 6
6 <-:
8 <-:
```

```
G3190
7 ------- 3
2 -----> 1
3 <----- 5

25 ----:-> 2
       :-> 7
5 <-:----- 8
6 <-:
8 <-:
```

```
G3191
7 ------- 6
2 -----> 8
3 <----- 4

25 ----:-> 7
       :-> 2
5 <-:----- 1
6 <-:
8 <-:
```

```
G3192
7 ------- 2
2 -----> 3
3 <----- 5

5 <-:----- 4
6 <-:
8 <-:
```

```
G3193
1 ------- 3
7 ------- 4
2 -----> 5
3 <----- 2

25 ------> 1
5 <-:----- 6
6 <-:
8 <-:
```

```
G3194
1 ------- 4
7 ------- 3
2 -----> 2
3 <----- 5

25 ------> 6
5 <-:----- 1
6 <-:
8 <-:
```

```
G3195
7 ------- 4
2 -----> 2
3 <----- 3

25 ------> 6
5 <-:----- 1
6 <-:
8 <-:
```

```
G3196
7 ------- 3
2 -----> 5
3 <----- 4

25 ------> 1
5 <-:----- 6
6 <-:
8 <-:
```

```
G3197
7 ------- 11
2 -----> 9
3 <----- 1

25 ----:-> 10
       :-> 3
       :-> 12
5 <-:----- 2
6 <-:
8 <-:
```

```
G3198
7 ------- 11
2 -----> 1
3 <----- 9

5 <-:----- 3
6 <-:
8 <-:

25 ----:-> 2
       :-> 4
```

```
G3199
7 ------- 4
2 -----> 2
3 <----- 3

25 ------> 5
5 <-:----- 1
6 <-:
8 <-:
```

```
G3200
7 ------- 4
2 -----> 3
3 <----- 2

5 <-:----- 5
6 <-:
8 <-:
```

```
G3201
7 ------- 2
2 -----> 3
3 <----- 5

25 ------> 1
5 <-:----- 6
6 <-:
8 <-:
```

```
G3202
7 ------- 5
2 -----> 4
3 <----- 2

25 ----:-> 3
       :-> 6
5 <-:----- 1
6 <-:
8 <-:
```

```
G3203
7 ------- 2
2 -----> 3
3 <----- 5

25 ----:-> 4
       :-> 1
5 <-:----- 6
6 <-:
8 <-:
```

```
G3204
7 ------- 5
2 -----> 2
3 <----- 3

25 ----:-> 8
       :-> 6
5 <-:----- 4
6 <-:
8 <-:
```

```
G3205
1 ------- 1
7 ------- 7
2 -----> 3
3 <----- 2

5 <-:----- 20
6 <-:
8 <-:
       :-> 4
       :-> 5
       :-> 6
       :-> 8
```

```
G3206
1 ------- 1
7 ------- 7
2 -----> 2
3 <----- 3

5 <-:----- 6
6 <-:
8 <-:
       :-- 5
       :-> 4
       :-> 20
```

```
G3207
1 ------- 1
7 ------- 7
2 -----> 2
3 <----- 3

5 <-:----- 5
6 <-:
8 <-:
```

```
G3208
1 ------- 1
7 ------- 7
2 -----> 3
3 <----- 2

5 <-:----- 4
6 <-:
8 <-:
```

```
G3209
1 ------- 1
7 ------- 7
2 -----> 3
3 <----- 2

5 <-:----- 4
6 <-:
8 <-:
```

```
G3210
7 ------- 5
2 -----> 4
3 <----- 3

5 <-:----- 1
6 <-:
8 <-:
```

```
G3211
7 ------- 5
2 -----> 4
3 <----- 3

5 <-:----- 1
6 <-:
8 <-:
```

```
G3212
1 ------- 1
7 ------- 7
2 -----> 2
3 <----- 3

5 <-:----- 6
6 <-:
8 <-:
       :-- 5
       :-> 4
       :-> 20
```

```
   G3213              G3214              G3215              G3216              G3217              G3218
1 ------- 1       1 ------- 1       1 ------- 1       7 ------- 7       7 ------- 5       1 ------- 1
7 ------- 7       7 ------- 7       7 ------- 7       2 ------> 2       2 ------> 2       7 ------- 7
2 ------> 2       2 ------> 3       2 ------> 2       3 <------ 3       3 <------ 3       2 ------> 2
3 <------ 3       3 <------ 2       3 <------ 3                                            3 <------ 3
5 <------ 8                                           5 <-:---- 4       5 <-:---- 4
6 <------ 6       5 <-:---- 4       5 <-:---- 6       6 <-:             6 <-:             5 <-:---- 8
                  6 <-:             6 <-:             8 <-:             8 <-:             6 <-:
                  8 <-:             8 <-:                                                 8 <-:
                                       :-- 5
                                       :-> 4
                                       :-> 20

   G3219              G3220              G3221              G3222              G3223              G3224
7 ------- 5       1 ------- 1       1 ------- 1       7 ------- 4       1 ------- 1       7 ------- 5
2 ------> 3       7 ------- 8       7 ------- 7       2 ------> 3       7 ------- 7       2 ------> 7
3 <------ 2       2 ------> 4       2 ------> 2       3 <------ 2       2 ------> 5       3 <------ 4
                  3 <------ 2       3 <------ 3                         3 <------ 3
5 <-:---- 6                                           5 <-:---- 5                         5 <-:---- 3
6 <-:             5 <-:---- 12      5 <-:---- 6       6 <-:             5 <-:---- 4        6 <-:
8 <-:             6 <-:             6 <-:             8 <-:             6 <-:              8 <-:
   :- 8           8 <-:             8 <-:                               8 <-:                :- 8
   :- 4              :-- 3             :-- 5                                                  :- 2
   :- 7              :-> 5             :-> 4                                                  :- 6
                    :-> 7
                    :-> 10
                    :-- 9
                    :-> 11

   G3225              G3226              G3227              G3228              G3229              G3230
7 ------- 3       1 ------- 4       1 ------- 3       7 ------- 8       7 ------- 7       7 ------- 5
2 ------> 5       7 ------- 7       7 ------- 6       2 ------> 6       2 ------> 3       2 ------> 3
3 <------ 4       2 ------> 6       2 ------> 5       3 <------ 1       3 <------ 2       3 <------ 2
                  3 <------ 5       3 <------ 4
5 <-:---- 2                                           5 <-:---- 4       5 <-:---- 9       5 <-:---- 6
6 <-:             5 <-:---- 9       5 <-:---- 8       6 <-:             6 <-:             6 <-:
8 <-:             6 <-:             6 <-:             8 <-:             8 <-:             8 <-:
   :- 1           8 <-:             8 <-:                :-- 2             :-- 4             :-- 1
   :- 6              :-- 3             :-- 2             :-> 7             :-> 5             :-> 4
   :- 7              :-> 1             :-> 1             :-> 9             :-> 8             :-> 7
   :- 8              :-> 2             :-> 7
                     :-> 8
                     :-> 10

   G3231              G3232              G3233              G3234              G3235              G3236
1 ------- 2       1 ------- 2       7 ------- 7       7 ------- 4       7 ------- 5       7 ------- 9
7 ------- 7       7 ------- 7       2 ------> 5       2 ------> 6       2 ------> 6       2 ------> 3
2 ------> 3       2 ------> 8       3 <------ 4       3 <------ 3       3 <------ 4       3 <------ 2
3 <------ 8       3 <------ 3
                                    5 <-:---- 1       5 <-:---- 2       5 <-:---- 3       5 <-:---- 4
5 <-:---- 9       5 <-:---- 5       6 <-:             6 <-:             6 <-:             6 <-:
6 <-:             6 <-:             8 <-:             8 <-:             8 <-:             8 <-:
8 <-:             8 <-:                                  :- 6
   :-- 4             :-- 1                               :- 3
   :-> 1             :-> 4
   :-> 5             :-> 9
   :-> 6
   :-> 10
```

```
  G3237                G3238                 G3239                G3240                G3241                G3242
7 ------- 3          7 ------- 9           7 ------- 5          7 ------- 5          7 ------- 5          1 ------- 3
2 ------> 4          2 ------> 13          2 ------> 2          2 ------> 2          2 ------> 3          7 ------- 4
3 <----- 2           3 <----- 11          3 <----- 3          3 <----- 3          3 <----- 2           2 ------> 5
                                                                                                        3 <----- 2
5 <-:---- 1          5 <-:---- 10          5 <-:---- 4         5 <-:---- 7          5 <-:---- 6
6 <-:                6 <-:                 6 <-:               6 <-:               6 <-:                5 <-:---- 1
8 <-:                8 <-:                 8 <-:               8 <-:               8 <-:                6 <-:
                                                :- 7                                                   8 <-:
                                                :- 6
                                                :- 8

  G3243                G3244                 G3245                G3246                G3247                G3248
1 ------- 1          1 ------- 1           7 ------- 4          7 ------- 5          7 ------- 1          1 ------- 3
7 ------- 2          7 ------- 7           2 ------> 5          2 ------> 4          2 ------> 4          7 ------- 5
2 ------> 4          2 ------> 5           3 <----- 3          3 <----- 2           3 <----- 2           2 ------> 2
3 <----- 3           3 <----- 3                                                                         3 <----- 4
                                           5 <-:---- 6         5 <-:---- 1          5 <-:---- 3
5 <-:---- 6          5 <-:---- 4           6 <-:               6 <-:               6 <-:                5 <-:---- 1
6 <-:                6 <-:                 8 <-:               8 <-:               8 <-:                6 <-:
8 <-:                8 <-:                                                                              8 <-:
                            :-- 2                                                         :-- 5
                            :-> 6                                                         :-> 6
                            :-> 8                                                         :-> 8

  G3249                G3250                 G3251                G3252                G3253                G3254
1 ------- 4          7 ------- 3           7 ------- 6          7 ------- 2          1 ------- 3
7 ------- 2          2 ------> 1           2 ------> 8          2 ------> 3          7 ------- 4          1 ------- 1
2 ------> 5          3 <----- 5           3 <----- 4          3 <----- 5          2 ------> 5          7 ------- 7
3 <----- 3                                                                         3 <----- 2           2 ------> 3
                     5 <-:---- 8          5 <-:---- 1         5 <-:---- 4                               3 <----- 2
5 <-:---- 6          6 <-:                6 <-:               6 <-:                5 <-:---- 6
6 <-:                8 <-:                8 <-:               8 <-:                6 <-:                14 ----:-> 5
8 <-:                                                                              8 <-:                       :-> 6
                            :-- 4                :-- 3                                                         :-> 8
                            :-> 2                :-> 2                                                  5 <-:---- 20
                            :-> 7                :-> 7                                                  6 <-:
                                                                                                       8 <-:

  G3255                G3256                 G3257                G3258                G3259                G3260
1 ------- 1          1 ------- 1           1 ------- 1          1 ------- 1          7 ------- 7          7 ------- 5
7 ------- 7          7 ------- 7           7 ------- 7          7 ------- 7          2 ------> 2          2 ------> 4
2 ------> 2          2 ------> 2           2 ------> 3          2 ------> 3          3 <----- 3          3 <----- 3
3 <----- 3           3 <----- 3           3 <----- 2          3 <----- 2
                                                                                   20 --:               14 ------> 6
5 <-:---- 6          14 ----:-> 8         14 ----:-> 5         14 ----:-> 5         5 <-:               5 <-:---- 1
6 <-:                      :-> 4                :-> 6                :-> 6          6 <-:               6 <-:
8 <-:                      :-> 20               :-> 20         5 <-:---- 4          8 <-:               8 <-:
                    5 <-:---- 5          5 <-:---- 4
14 ----:-> 4        6 <-:                6 <-:               6 <-:
       :-> 20       8 <-:                8 <-:               8 <-:

  G3261                G3262                 G3263                G3264                G3265                G3266
7 ------- 5          1 ------- 1           1 ------- 1          1 ------- 1          1 ------- 1          7 ------- 7
2 ------> 4          7 ------- 7           7 ------- 7          7 ------- 7          7 ------- 7          2 ------> 2
3 <----- 3           2 ------> 2           2 ------> 2          2 ------> 3          2 ------> 2          3 <----- 3
                     3 <----- 3           3 <----- 3          3 <----- 2           3 <----- 3
5 <-:---- 1                                                                                             20 --:
6 <-:                5 <-:---- 6          5 <-:---- 6         14 ----:-> 5          20 --:               5 <-:
8 <-:                6 <-:                6 <-:                      :-> 8          5 <-:               6 <-:
                     8 <-:                8 <-:                                     6 <-:               8 <-:
                                                              5 <-:---- 4          8 <-:
                     14 ----:-> 4                             6 <-:
                            :-> 20                            8 <-:
```

G3267
```
1 ------- 1
7 ------- 7
2 ------> 2
3 <------ 3

14 ----:-> 20
      :-> 4
      :-> 12

5 <-:----- 5
6 <-:
8 <-:
```

G3268
```
7 ------- 7
2 ------> 2
3 <------ 3

14 ----:-> 5
      :-> 6
      :-> 8

5 <-:----- 4
6 <-:
8 <-:
```

G3269
```
7 ------- 5
2 ------> 2
3 <------ 3

14 ----:-> 8
      :-> 6
      :-> 1

5 <-:----- 4
6 <-:
8 <-:
```

G3270
```
1 ------- 1
7 ------- 7
2 ------> 2
3 <------ 3

5 <-:----- 8
6 <-:
8 <-:

14 ----:-> 20
```

G3271
```
7 ------- 5
2 ------> 3
3 <------ 2

14 ----:-> 7
      :-> 4

5 <-:----- 6
6 <-:
8 <-:
```

G3272
```
7 ------- 7
2 ------> 3
3 <------ 2

20 --:
5 <-:
6 <-:
8 <-:
```

G3273
```
1 ------- 1
7 ------- 7
2 ------> 4
3 <------ 2

14 ----:-> 5
      :-> 10
      :-> 7

5 <-:----- 12
6 <-:
8 <-:

20 ----:-> 11
```

G3274
```
1 ------- 1
7 ------- 7
2 ------> 2
3 <------ 3

5 <-:----- 6
6 <-:
8 <-:

14 ----:-> 4
```

G3275
```
7 ------- 4
2 ------> 3
3 <------ 2

14 ----:-> 1
      :-> 6

5 <-:----- 5
6 <-:
8 <-:
```

G3276
```
1 ------- 1
7 ------- 7
2 ------> 5
3 <------ 3

14 ----:-> 6
5 <-:----- 4
6 <-:
8 <-:
```

G3277
```
7 ------- 5
2 ------> 7
3 <------ 4

14 ----:-> 2
      :-> 6

5 <-:----- 3
6 <-:
8 <-:
```

G3278
```
7 ------- 3
2 ------> 5
3 <------ 4

14 ----:-> 8
      :-> 7
      :-> 6

5 <-:----- 2
6 <-:
8 <-:
```

G3279
```
1 ------- 4
7 ------- 7
2 ------> 6
3 <------ 5

14 ----:-> 8
      :-> 2
      :-> 10

5 <-:----- 9
6 <-:
8 <-:

20 ----:-> 1
```

G3280
```
1 ------- 3
7 ------- 6
2 ------> 5
3 <------ 4

14 ----:-> 7
      :-> 1
5 <-:----- 8
6 <-:
8 <-:
```

G3281
```
7 ------- 8
2 ------> 2
3 <------ 1

20 --:
5 <-:
6 <-:
8 <-:
```

G3282
```
7 ------- 8
2 ------> 6
3 <------ 1

14 ----:-> 7
      :-> 9
5 <-:----- 4
6 <-:
8 <-:
```

G3283
```
7 ------- 7
2 ------> 3
3 <------ 2

14 ----:-> 5
      :-> 8
5 <-:----- 9
6 <-:
8 <-:
```

G3284
```
7 ------- 5
2 ------> 3
3 <------ 2

5 <-:----- 6
6 <-:
8 <-:

14 ----:-> 4
      :-> 7
```

G3285
```
1 ------- 2
7 ------- 7
2 ------> 3
3 <------ 8

14 ----:-> 5
      :-> 6
      :-> 1
5 <-:----- 9
6 <-:
8 <-:

20 ----:-> 10
```

G3286
```
1 ------- 2
7 ------- 7
2 ------> 8
3 <------ 3

5 <-:----- 5
6 <-:
8 <-:

14 ----:-> 4
      :-> 9
```

G3287
```
7 ------- 7
2 ------> 5
3 <------ 4

14 ------> 3
5 <-:----- 1
6 <-:
8 <-:
```

G3288
```
7 ------- 4
2 ------> 6
3 <------ 3

5 <-:----- 2
6 <-:
8 <-:

14 ----:-> 1
      :-> 7
```

G3289
```
7 ------- 5
2 ------> 6
3 <------ 4

14 ------> 2
5 <-:----- 3
6 <-:
8 <-:
```

G3290
```
7 ------- 9
2 ------> 3
3 <------ 2

14 ------> 5
5 <-:----- 4
6 <-:
8 <-:
```

G3291	G3292	G3293

`7 ------- 3`
`2 ------> 4`
`3 <------ 2`
 	
`14 ------> 5`
`5 <-:----- 1`
`6 <-:`
`8 <-:`
	`7 ------- 9`
	`2 ------> 13`
	`3 <------ 11`
	
	`14 ------> 14`
	`5 <-:----- 10`
	`6 <-:`
	`8 <-:`
		`7 ------- 5`
		`2 ------> 2`
		`3 <------ 3`
		
		`14 ----:-> 8`
		`      :-> 6`
		`5 <-:----- 4`
		`6 <-:`
		`8 <-:`

G3294	G3295	G3296

`7 ------- 5`
`2 ------> 2`
`3 <------ 3`
 	
`14 ------> 8`
`5 <-:----- 7`
`6 <-:`
`8 <-:`
	`7 ------- 5`
	`2 ------> 3`
	`3 <------ 2`
	
	`5 <-:----- 6`
	`6 <-:`
	`8 <-:`
		`7 ------- 5`
		`2 ------> 3`
		`3 <------ 2`
		
		`14 --:`
		`5 <-:`
		`6 <-:`
		`8 <-:`

G3297	G3298	G3299

`1 ------- 3`
`7 ------- 4`
`2 ------> 5`
`3 <------ 2`
 	
`14 ------> 6`
`5 <-:----- 1`
`6 <-:`
`8 <-:`
	`1 ------- 1`
	`7 ------- 2`
	`2 ------> 4`
	`3 <------ 3`
	
	`14 ------> 5`
	`5 <-:----- 6`
	`6 <-:`
	`8 <-:`
		`1 ------- 1`
		`7 ------- 7`
		`3 <------ 2`
		
		`14 --:`
		`5 <-:`
		`6 <-:`
		`8 <-:`

G3300	G3301	G3302

`1 ------- 1`
`7 ------- 7`
`2 ------> 5`
`3 <------ 3`
 	
`14 ----:-> 8`
`      :-> 6`
`5 <-:----- 4`
`6 <-:`
`8 <-:`
	`7 ------- 4`
	`2 ------> 5`
	`3 <------ 3`
	
	`14 ------> 2`
	`5 <-:----- 6`
	`6 <-:`
	`8 <-:`
		`7 ------- 5`
		`2 ------> 4`
		`3 <------ 2`
		
		`14 ------> 6`
		`5 <-:----- 1`
		`6 <-:`
		`8 <-:`

G3303	G3304	G3305

`7 ------- 1`
`2 ------> 4`
`3 <------ 2`
 	
`14 ----:-> 6`
`      :-> 8`
`5 <-:----- 3`
`6 <-:`
`8 <-:`
	`1 ------- 3`
	`7 ------- 5`
	`2 ------> 2`
	`3 <------ 4`
	
	`5 <-:----- 1`
	`6 <-:`
	`8 <-:`
		`1 ------- 4`
		`7 ------- 5`
		`2 ------> 5`
		`3 <------ 3`
		
		`14 ------> 1`
		`5 <-:----- 6`
		`6 <-:`
		`8 <-:`

G3306	G3307	G3308

`7 ------- 3`
`2 ------> 1`
`3 <------ 5`
 	
`14 ----:-> 2`
`      :-> 7`
`5 <-:----- 8`
`6 <-:`
`8 <-:`
	`7 ------- 6`
	`2 ------> 8`
	`3 <------ 4`
	
	`14 ----:-> 7`
	`      :-> 2`
	`5 <-:----- 1`
	`6 <-:`
	`8 <-:`
		`7 ------- 2`
		`2 ------> 3`
		`3 <------ 5`
		
		`5 <-:----- 4`
		`6 <-:`
		`8 <-:`

G3309	G3310	G3311

`1 ------- 3`
`7 ------- 4`
`2 ------> 5`
`3 <------ 2`
 	
`14 ------> 1`
`5 <-:----- 6`
`6 <-:`
`8 <-:`
	`1 ------- 4`
	`7 ------- 3`
	`2 ------> 2`
	`3 <------ 5`
	
	`14 ------> 6`
	`5 <-:----- 1`
	`6 <-:`
	`8 <-:`
		`7 ------- 4`
		`2 ------> 2`
		`3 <------ 3`
		
		`14 ------> 6`
		`5 <-:----- 1`
		`6 <-:`
		`8 <-:`

G3312	G3313	G3314

`7 ------- 3`
`2 ------> 5`
`3 <------ 4`
 	
`14 ------> 1`
`5 <-:----- 6`
`6 <-:`
`8 <-:`
	`7 ------- 11`
	`2 ------> 9`
	`3 <------ 1`
	
	`14 ----:-> 10`
	`      :-> 3`
	`      :-> 12`
	`5 <-:----- 2`
	`6 <-:`
	`8 <-:`
		`7 ------- 11`
		`2 ------> 1`
		`3 <------ 9`
		
		`5 <-:----- 3`
		`6 <-:`
		`8 <-:`
		
		`14 ----:-> 2`
		`      :-> 4`

G3315	G3316	G3317

`7 ------- 4`
`2 ------> 2`
`3 <------ 3`
 	
`14 ------> 5`
`5 <-:----- 1`
`6 <-:`
`8 <-:`
	`7 ------- 4`
	`2 ------> 3`
	`3 <------ 2`
	
	`5 <-:----- 5`
	`6 <-:`
	`8 <-:`
		`7 ------- 2`
		`2 ------> 3`
		`3 <------ 5`
		
		`14 ------> 1`
		`5 <-:----- 6`
		`6 <-:`
		`8 <-:`

G3318	G3319	G3320

`7 ------- 5`
`2 ------> 4`
`3 <------ 2`
 	
`14 ----:-> 3`
`      :-> 6`
`5 <-:----- 1`
`6 <-:`
`8 <-:`
	`7 ------- 2`
	`2 ------> 3`
	`3 <------ 5`
	
	`14 ----:-> 4`
	`      :-> 1`
	`5 <-:----- 6`
	`6 <-:`
	`8 <-:`
		`7 ------- 5`
		`2 ------> 2`
		`3 <------ 3`
		
		`14 ----:-> 8`
		`      :-> 6`
		`5 <-:----- 4`
		`6 <-:`
		`8 <-:`

G3321	G3322	G3323	G3324	G3325	G3326

<pre>1 ------- 1
7 ------- 7
2 ------> 3
3 <------ 2
 	
  :-- 4
  :-> 5
  :-> 6
  :-> 8
  :-- 20</pre>
	<pre>1 ------- 1
	7 ------- 7
	2 ------> 2
	3 <------ 3
	
	  :-- 5
	  :-> 4
	  :-> 20</pre>
		<pre>1 ------- 1
		7 ------- 7
		2 ------> 2
		3 <------ 3
		
		  :-- 5
		  :-> 4
		  :-> 8
		  :-> 20</pre>
			<pre>1 ------- 1
			7 ------- 7
			2 ------> 3
			3 <------ 2
			
			  :-- 4
			  :-> 5
			  :-> 6
			  :-> 20</pre>
				<pre>1 ------- 1
				7 ------- 7
				2 ------> 3
				3 <------ 2
				
				  :- 4
				  : 5
				  :- 6</pre>
					<pre>7 ------- 7
					2 ------> 2
					3 <------ 3
					7 ------- 5</pre>

G3327	G3328	G3329	G3330	G3331	G3332

<pre>2 ------> 4
3 <------ 3
 	
  :- 1
  :- 6</pre>
	<pre>7 ------- 5
	2 ------> 4
	3 <------ 3</pre>
		<pre>1 ------- 1
		7 ------- 7
		2 ------> 2
		3 <------ 3
		
		  :-- 5
		  :-> 4
		  :-> 20</pre>
			<pre>1 ------- 1
			7 ------- 7
			2 ------> 2
			3 <------ 3</pre>
				<pre>1 ------- 1
				7 ------- 7
				2 ------> 3
				3 <------ 2
				
				  :-- 4
				  :-> 5
				  :-> 8</pre>
					<pre>1 ------- 1
					7 ------- 7
					2 ------> 2
					3 <------ 3</pre>

G3333	G3334	G3335	G3336	G3337	G3338

<pre>7 ------- 7
2 ------> 2
3 <------ 3</pre>
	<pre>1 ------- 1
	7 ------- 7
	2 ------> 2
	3 <------ 3
	
	  :-- 5
	  :-> 4
	  :-> 20</pre>
		<pre>7 ------- 7
		2 ------> 2
		3 <------ 3
		
		  :- 4
		  :- 5
		  :- 6
		  :- 8</pre>
			<pre>7 ------- 5
			2 ------> 2
			3 <------ 3
			
			  :- 4
			  :- 1
			  :- 6
			  :- 8
			  :- 7</pre>
				<pre>1 ------- 1
				7 ------- 7
				2 ------> 2
				3 <------ 3
				
				  :-- 8
				  :-> 20</pre>
					<pre>7 ------- 5
					2 ------> 3
					3 <------ 2
					
					  :- 6
					  :- 4
					  :- 7</pre>

G3339	G3340	G3341	G3342	G3343	G3344

<pre>7 ------- 7
2 ------> 3
3 <------ 2</pre>
	<pre>7 ------- 7
	2 ------> 5
	3 <------ 3
	
	  :- 4
	  :- 6</pre>
		<pre>7 ------- 8
		2 ------> 4
		3 <------ 2
		
		  :-- 3
		  :-> 5
		  :-> 7
		  :-> 10
		  :-- 9
		  :-> 11</pre>
			<pre>7 ------- 7
			2 ------> 2
			3 <------ 3
			
			  :-- 5
			  :-> 4</pre>
				<pre>7 ------- 4
				2 ------> 3
				3 <------ 2
				
				  :-- 5
				  :-> 1
				  :-> 6</pre>
					<pre>7 ------- 5
					2 ------> 7
					3 <------ 4
					
					  :-- 3
					  :-> 2
					  :-> 6</pre>

G3345	G3346	G3347	G3348	G3349	G3350

<pre>7 ------- 3
2 ------> 5
3 <------ 4
 	
  :-- 1
  :-> 6
  :-> 7
 	
  :-> 8
  :-- 2</pre>
	<pre>7 ------- 7
	2 ------> 6
	3 <------ 5
	
	  :-- 3
	  :-> 1
	  :-> 2
	  :-> 8
	
	  :-- 9
	  :-> 10</pre>
		<pre>7 ------- 6
		2 ------> 5
		3 <------ 4
		
		  :- 2
		  :- 1
		  :- 7</pre>
			<pre>7 ------- 8
			2 ------> 2
			3 <------ 1</pre>
				<pre>7 ------- 8
				2 ------> 6
				3 <------ 1
				
				  :-- 2
				  :-> 7
				  :-> 9</pre>
					<pre>7 ------- 7
					2 ------> 3
					3 <------ 2
					
					  :-- 4
					  :-> 5
					  :-> 8</pre>

G3351	G3352	G3353	G3354	G3355	G3356
7 ------- 5 2 ------> 3 3 <------ 2 :-- 1 :-> 4 :-> 7	7 ------- 7 2 ------> 3 3 <------ 8 :-- 4 :-> 1 :-> 5 :-> 6 :-- 9 :-> 10	7 ------- 7 2 ------> 8 3 <------ 3 :-- 1 :-> 4 :-> 9	7 ------- 7 2 ------> 5 3 <------ 4 :-- 1 :-> 3	7 ------- 4 2 ------> 6 3 <------ 3 :-- 2 :-> 1 :-> 7	7 ------- 5 2 ------> 6 3 <------ 4 :-- 3 :-> 2

G3357	G3358	G3359	G3360	G3361	G3362
7 ------- 9 2 ------> 3 3 <------ 2 :-- 4 :-> 5	7 ------- 3 2 ------> 4 3 <------ 2 :-- 1 :-> 5	7 ------- 9 2 ------> 13 3 <------ 11 :-- 10 :-> 14	7 ------- 5 2 ------> 2 3 <------ 3 :-- 4 :-> 6 :-> 8	7 ------- 5 2 ------> 2 3 <------ 3 :-- 7 :-> 8	7 ------- 5 2 ------> 3 3 <------ 2

G3363	G3364	G3365	G3366	G3367	G3368
7 ------- 5 2 ------> 3 3 <------ 2	7 ------- 4 2 ------> 5 3 <------ 2 :-- 1 :-> 6	7 ------- 2 2 ------> 4 3 <------ 3 :-- 6 :-> 5	7 ------- 7 3 <------ 2	7 ------- 7 2 ------> 5 3 <------ 3 :-- 2 :-> 6 :-> 8	7 ------- 4 2 ------> 5 3 <------ 3 :-- 6 :-> 2

G3369	G3370	G3371	G3372	G3373	G3374
7 ------- 5 2 ------> 4 3 <------ 2	7 ------- 1 2 ------> 4 3 <------ 2 :-- 3 :-> 6 :-> 8	7 ------- 5 2 ------> 2 3 <------ 4	7 ------- 2 2 ------> 5 3 <------ 3 :-- 6 :-> 1	7 ------- 3 2 ------> 1 3 <------ 5 :-- 4 :-> 2 :-> 7	7 ------- 6 2 ------> 8 3 <------ 4 :-- 3 :-> 2 :-> 7

G3375	G3376	G3377	G3378	G3379	G3380
7 ------- 2 2 ------> 3 3 <------ 5	7 ------- 4 2 ------> 5 3 <------ 2 :-- 6 :-> 1	7 ------- 3 2 ------> 2 3 <------ 5 :-- 1 :-> 6	7 ------- 4 2 ------> 2 3 <------ 3 :-- 1 :-> 6	7 ------- 3 2 ------> 5 3 <------ 4 :-- 6 :-> 1	7 ------- 11 2 ------> 9 3 <------ 1 :-- 2 :-> 3 :-> 10 :-> 12

G3381	G3382	G3383	G3384	G3385	G3386
7 ------- 11 2 ------> 1 3 <------ 9 :-- 3 :-> 2 :-> 4	7 ------- 4 2 ------> 2 3 <------ 3 :- 1 :- 5	7 ------- 4 2 ------> 3 3 <------ 2	7 ------- 2 2 ------> 3 3 <------ 5 :-- 6 :-> 1	7 ------- 5 2 ------> 4 3 <------ 2 :-- 1 :-> 3 :-> 6	7 ------- 2 2 ------> 3 3 <------ 5 :-- 6 :-> 1 :-> 4

```
G3387                G3388                G3389                G3390                G3391                G3392

7 ------- 5          6 ------- 1          6 ------- 1          6 ------- 1          6 ------- 1          6 ------- 1
2 -----> 2          5 ------- 7          5 ------- 7          5 ------- 7          5 ------- 7          5 ------- 7
3 <------ 3          1 -----> 3          1 -----> 2          1 -----> 2          1 -----> 3          1 -----> 3
                     3 <------ 2          3 <------ 3          3 <------ 3          3 <------ 2          3 <------ 2
    :-- 4                                 4 <------ 5          4 <------ 5
    :-> 6            4 <------ 20         2 -----> 4          2 ----:-> 4          4 <------ 4          2 ----:-> 5
    :-> 8                                                           :-> 8          2 ----:-> 5                :-> 6
                     2 ----:-> 5              :-- 6               :-> 20                :-> 6          4 <-:---- 4
                           :-> 6              :-> 20                                     :-> 20
                           :-> 8                                                  
```

```
G3393                G3394                G3395                G3396                G3397                G3398

5 ------- 7          5 ------- 5          5 ------- 5          6 ------- 1          6 ------- 1          6 ------- 1
1 -----> 2          1 -----> 4          1 -----> 4          5 ------- 7          5 ------- 7          5 ------- 7
3 <------ 3          3 <------ 3          3 <------ 3          1 -----> 2          1 -----> 2          1 -----> 3
                                                              3 <------ 3          3 <------ 3          3 <------ 2
2 --:                2 ------> 6          4 <-:---- 1          4 <-:---- 6          4 <-:---- 6          2 ---:-> 5
4 <-:                4 <-:---- 1                                                                              :-> 8
                                                              2 ----:-> 4                               4 <-:---- 4
                                                                    :-> 20
```

```
G3399                G3400                G3401                G3402                G3403                G3404

6 ------- 1          5 ------- 7          6 ------- 1          5 ------- 7          5 ------- 5          6 ------- 1
5 ------- 7          1 -----> 2          5 ------- 7          1 -----> 2          1 -----> 2          5 ------- 7
1 -----> 2          3 <------ 3          1 -----> 2          3 <------ 3          3 <------ 3          1 -----> 2
3 <------ 3                              3 <------ 3                                                   3 <------ 3
                                                              2 ----:-> 5          2 ----:-> 8
                     2 --:               2 ------> 20              :-  6                :-  6          4 <-:---- 8
2 --:                4 <-:                                        :-  8                :-  1
4 <-:                                    4 <-:---- 5                                                   2 ----:-> 20
                                              :-- 8          4 <-:---- 4          4 <-:---- 4
                                              :-> 4
                                              :-> 12
```

```
G3405                G3406                G3407                G3408                G3409                G3410

5 ------- 5          5 ------- 7          6 ------- 1          6 ------- 1          5 ------- 4          6 ------- 1
1 -----> 3          1 -----> 3          5 ------- 8          5 ------- 7          1 -----> 3          5 ------- 7
3 <------ 2          3 <------ 2          1 -----> 4          1 -----> 2          3 <------ 2          1 -----> 5
                                         3 <------ 2          3 <------ 3                               3 <------ 3
2 ----:-> 7          2 --:               4 <------ 12         4 <------ 5          4 <------ 5
    :-  4            4 <-:                                    2 ------> 4                               2 ------> 6
4 <-:---- 6                              2 ----:-> 5                               2 ----:-> 1          4 <-:---- 4
                                               :-> 7                                     :-> 6
                                               :-> 10
                                               :-> 11
```

```
G3411                G3412                G3413                G3414                G3415                G3416

5 ------- 5          5 ------- 3          6 ------- 4          6 ------- 3          5 ------- 8          5 ------- 8
1 -----> 7          1 -----> 5          5 ------- 7          5 ------- 6          1 -----> 2          1 -----> 6
3 <------ 4          3 <------ 4          1 -----> 6          1 -----> 5          3 <------ 1          3 <------ 1
                                         3 <------ 5          3 <------ 4
4 <------ 3          4 <------ 2          4 <------ 9          4 <------ 8          2 --:               4 <------ 4
                                                                                   4 <-:
2 ----:-> 2          2 ----:-> 6          2 ---:-> 1          2 ---:-> 1                               2 ----:-> 7
      :-> 6                :-> 7                :-> 2                :-> 7                                    :-> 9
                           :-> 8                :-> 8
                                               :-> 10
```

```
G3417              G3418              G3419              G3420              G3421              G3422

5 ------- 7        5 ------- 5        6 ------- 2        6 ------- 2        5 ------- 7        5 ------- 4
1 -------> 3       1 -------> 3       5 ------- 7        5 ------- 7        1 -------> 5       1 -------> 6
3 <------- 2       3 <------- 2       1 -------> 3       1 -------> 8       3 <------- 4       3 <------- 3
                                      3 <------- 8       3 <------- 3
4 <------ 9        4 <------ 6        4 <------ 9        4 <------ 5        4 <------ 1        4 <------ 2

2 ----:-> 5        2 ----:-> 4        2 ----:-> 1        2 ----:-> 4        2 ----:-> 3        2 ----:-> 1
      :-> 8              :-> 7              :-> 5              :-> 9                                  :- 7
                                           :-> 6
                                           :-> 10
```

```
G3423              G3424              G3425              G3426              G3427              G3428

5 ------- 5        5 ------- 9        5 ------- 3        5 ------- 9        5 ------- 5        5 ------- 5
1 -------> 6       1 -------> 3       1 -------> 4       1 -------> 13      1 -------> 2       1 -------> 2
3 <------- 4       3 <------- 2       3 <------- 2       3 <------- 11      3 <------- 3       3 <------- 3
4 <------ 3        4 <------ 4        4 <------ 1        4 <------ 10       4 <------ 4        4 <------ 7

2 ----:-> 2        2 ----:-> 5        2 ----:-> 5        2 ----:-> 14       2 ----:-> 6        2 ----:-> 8
                                                                                 :- 8
```

```
G3429              G3430              G3431              G3432              G3433              G3434

5 ------- 5        5 ------- 5        6 ------- 3        6 ------- 1        6 ------- 1        6 ------- 1
1 -------> 3       1 -------> 3       5 ------- 4        5 ------- 2        5 ------- 7        5 ------- 7
3 <------- 2       3 <------- 2       1 -------> 5       1 -------> 4       3 <------- 2       1 -------> 5
4 <------ 6                          3 <------- 2       3 <------- 3                          3 <------- 3
                   2 --:             4 <------ 1        4 <------ 6        2 --:              4 <------ 4
                   4 <-:                                                  4 <-:
                                     2 ----:-> 6        2 ----:-> 5                          2 ----:-> 6
                                                                                                   :-> 8
```

```
G3435              G3436              G3437              G3438              G3439              G3440

5 ------- 4        5 ------- 5        5 ------- 1        6 ------- 3        6 ------- 4        5 ------- 3
1 -------> 5       1 -------> 4       1 -------> 4       5 ------- 5        5 ------- 2        1 -------> 1
3 <------- 3       3 <------- 2       3 <------- 2       1 -------> 2       1 -------> 5       3 <------- 5
                                                        3 <------- 4       3 <------- 3
4 <------ 6        4 <------ 1        4 <------ 3        4 <------ 1        4 <------ 6        4 <------ 8

2 ----:-> 2        2 ----:-> 6        2 ----:-> 6                          2 ----:-> 1        2 ----:-> 2
                                            :-> 8                                                   :-> 7
```

```
G3441              G3442              G3443              G3444              G3445              G3446

5 ------- 6        5 ------- 2        6 ------- 3        6 ------- 4        5 ------- 4        5 ------- 3
1 -------> 8       1 -------> 3       5 ------- 4        5 ------- 3        1 -------> 2       1 -------> 5
3 <------- 4       3 <------- 5       1 -------> 5       1 -------> 2       3 <------- 3       3 <------- 4
                                      3 <------- 2       3 <------- 5
4 <------ 1        4 <------ 4        4 <------ 6        4 <------ 1        4 <------ 1        4 <------ 6

2 ----:-> 2                          2 ----:-> 1        2 ----:-> 6        2 ----:-> 6        2 ----:-> 1
      :-> 7
```

G3447	G3448	G3449	G3450	G3451	G3452

5 ------- 11
1 ------> 9
3 <------ 1
4 <------ 2
 	
2 ----:-> 3
   :-> 10
   :-> 12
	5 ------- 11
	1 ------> 1
	3 <------ 9
	4 <------ 10
	2 ------> 2
	
	:-- 3
	:-> 4
		5 ------- 4
		1 ------> 2
		3 <------ 3
		
		4 <------ 1
		
		2 ----:-> 5
			5 ------- 4
			1 ------> 3
			3 <------ 2
			
			4 <------ 5
				5 ------- 2
				1 ------> 3
				3 <------ 5
				
				4 <------ 6
				
				2 ----:-> 1
					5 ------- 5
					1 ------> 4
					3 <------ 2
					
					4 <------ 1
					
					2 ----:-> 3
					   :-> 6

G3453	G3454	G3455	G3456	G3457	G3458

5 ------- 2
1 ------> 3
3 <------ 5
 	
4 <------ 6
 	
2 ----:-> 1
   :-> 4
	5 ------- 5
	1 ------> 2
	3 <------ 3
	
	4 <------ 4
	
	2 ----:-> 6
	   :-> 8
		5 ------- 7
		3 ------> 3
		2 <------ 2
		
		8 <------ 20
		
		7 ----:-> 5
		   :-> 6
		   :-> 8
			5 ------- 7
			3 ------> 2
			2 <------ 3
			8 <------ 5
			7 ------> 4
			
			·:-- 6
			 :-> 20
				5 ------- 7
				3 ------> 2
				2 <------ 3
				
				8 <------ 5
				
				7 ----:-> 4
				   :-> 8
				   :-> 20
					5 ------- 7
					3 ------> 3
					2 <------ 2
					
					8 <------ 4
					
					7 ----:-> 5
					   :-> 6
					   :-> 20

G3459	G3460	G3461	G3462	G3463	G3464

5 ------- 7
3 ------> 3
2 <------ 2
 	
7 ----:-> 5
   :-> 6
8 <-:---- 4
	5 ------- 7
	3 ------> 2
	2 <------ 3
	
	7 --:
	8 <-:
		5 ------- 5
		3 ------> 4
		2 <------ 3
		
		7 ------> 6
		8 <-:---- 1
			5 ------- 5
			3 ------> 4
			2 <------ 3
			
			8 <-:---- 1
				5 ------- 7
				3 ------> 2
				2 <------ 3
				
				8 <-:---- 6
				
				7 ----:-> 4
				   :-> 20
					5 ------- 7
					3 ------> 2
					2 <------ 3
					
					8 <-:---- 6

G3465	G3466	G3467	G3468	G3469	G3470

5 ------- 7
3 ------> 3
2 <------ 2
 	
7 ----:-> 5
   :-> 8
 	
8 <-:---- 4
	5 ------- 7
	3 ------> 2
	2 <------ 3
	
	7 --:
	8 <-:
		5 ------- 7
		3 ------> 2
		2 <------ 3
		
		7 --:
		8 <-:
			5 ------- 7
			3 ------> 2
			2 <------ 3
			
			7 ------> 20
			
			8 <-:---- 5
			   :-- 8
			   :-> 4
			   :-> 12
				5 ------- 7
				3 ------> 2
				2 <------ 3
				
				7 ----:-> 5
				   :- 6
				   :- 8
				
				8 <-:---- 4
					5 ------- 5
					3 ------> 2
					2 <------ 3
					
					7 ----:-> 8
					   :- 6
					   :- 1
					
					8 <-:---- 4

G3471	G3472	G3473	G3474	G3475	G3476

5 ------- 7
3 ------> 2
2 <------ 3
 	
8 <-:---- 8
 	
7 ----:-> 20
	5 ------- 5
	3 ------> 3
	2 <------ 2
	
	7 ----:-> 7
	   :- 4
	8 <-:---- 6
		5 ------- 7
		3 ------> 3
		2 <------ 2
		
		7 --:
		8 <-:
			5 ------- 8
			3 ------> 4
			2 <------ 2
			
			8 <------ 12
			
			7 ----:-> 5
			   :-> 7
			   :-> 10
			   :-> 11
				5 ------- 7
				3 ------> 2
				2 <------ 3
				8 <------ 5
				7 ------> 4
					5 ------- 4
					3 ------> 3
					2 <------ 2
					
					8 <------ 5
					
					7 ----:-> 1
					   :-> 6

G3477	G3478	G3479	G3480	G3481	G3482

5 ------- 7
3 ------> 5
2 <------ 3
 	
7 ------> 6
8 <-:---- 4
	5 ------- 5
	3 ------> 7
	2 <------ 4
	
	8 <------ 3
	
	7 ----:-> 2
	    :-> 6
		5 ------- 3
		3 ------> 5
		2 <------ 4
		
		8 <------ 2
		
		7 ----:-> 6
		    :-> 7
		    :-> 8
			5 ------- 7
			3 ------> 6
			2 <------ 5
			
			8 <------ 9
			
			7 ----:-> 1
			    :-> 2
			    :-> 8
			    :-> 10
				5 ------- 6
				3 ------> 5
				2 <------ 4
				
				8 <------ 8
				
				7 ----:-> 1
				    :-> 7
					5 ------- 8
					3 ------> 2
					2 <------ 1
					
					7 --:
					8 <-:

G3483	G3484	G3485	G3486	G3487	G3488

5 ------- 8
3 ------> 6
2 <------ 1
 	
8 <------ 4
 	
7 ----:-> 7
    :-> 9
	5 ------- 7
	3 ------> 3
	2 <------ 2
	
	8 <------ 9
	
	7 ----:-> 5
	    :-> 8
		5 ------- 5
		3 ------> 3
		2 <------ 2
		
		8 <------ 6
		
		7 ----:-> 4
		    :-> 7
			5 ------- 7
			3 ------> 3
			2 <------ 8
			
			8 <------ 9
			
			7 ----:-> 1
			    :-> 5
			    :-> 6
			    :-> 10
				5 ------- 7
				3 ------> 8
				2 <------ 3
				
				8 <------ 5
				
				7 ----:-> 4
				    :-> 9
					5 ------- 7
					3 ------> 5
					2 <------ 4
					
					8 <------ 1
					
					7 ----:-> 3

G3489	G3490	G3491	G3492	G3493	G3494

5 ------- 4
3 ------> 6
2 <------ 3
 	
8 <------ 2
 	
7 ----:-> 1
  :- 7
	5 ------- 5
	3 ------> 6
	2 <------ 4
	
	8 <------ 3
	
	7 ----:-> 2
		5 ------- 9
		3 ------> 3
		2 <------ 2
		
		8 <------ 4
		
		7 ----:-> 5
			5 ------- 3
			3 ------> 4
			2 <------ 2
			
			8 <------ 1
			
			7 ----:-> 5
				5 ------- 9
				3 ------> 13
				2 <------ 11
				
				8 <------ 10
				
				7 ----:-> 14
					5 ------- 5
					3 ------> 2
					2 <------ 3
					
					8 <------ 4
					
					7 ----:-> 6
					  :- 8

G3495	G3496	G3497	G3498	G3499	G3500
5 ------- 5 3 ------> 2 2 <------ 3 8 <------ 7 7 ----:-> 8	5 ------- 5 3 ------> 3 2 <------ 2 8 <------ 6	5 ------- 5 3 ------> 3 2 <------ 2 7 --: 8 <-:	5 ------- 4 3 ------> 5 2 <------ 2 8 <------ 1 7 ----:-> 6	5 ------- 2 3 ------> 4 2 <------ 3 8 <------ 6 7 ----:-> 5	5 ------- 7 2 <------ 2 7 --: 8 <-:

G3501	G3502	G3503	G3504	G3505	G3506

5 ------- 7
3 ------> 5
2 <------ 3
 	
8 <------ 4
 	
7 ----:-> 6
    :-> 8
	5 ------- 4
	3 ------> 5
	2 <------ 3
	
	8 <------ 6
	
	7 ----:-> 2
		5 ------- 5
		3 ------> 4
		2 <------ 2
		
		8 <------ 1
		
		7 ----:-> 6
			5 ------- 1
			3 ------> 4
			2 <------ 2
			
			8 <------ 3
			
			7 ----:-> 6
			    :-> 8
				5 ------- 5
				3 ------> 2
				2 <------ 4
				
				8 <------ 1
					5 ------- 2
					3 ------> 5
					2 <------ 3
					
					8 <------ 6
					
					7 ----:-> 1

```
G3507            G3508            G3509            G3510            G3511            G3512
5 ------- 3      5 ------- 6      5 ------- 2      5 ------- 4      5 ------- 3      5 ------> 4
3 ------> 1      3 ------> 8      3 ------> 3      3 ------> 5      3 ------> 2      3 ------> 2
2 <------ 5      2 <------ 4      2 <------ 5      2 <------ 2      2 <------ 5      2 <------ 3
8 <------ 8      8 <------ 1      8 <------ 4      8 <------ 6      8 <------ 1      8 <------ 1
7 ----:-> 2      7 ----:-> 2                       7 ----:-> 1      7 ----:-> 6      7 ----:-> 6
     :-> 7            :-> 7

G3513            G3514            G3515            G3516            G3517            G3518
5 ------- 3      5 ------- 11     5 ------- 11     5 ------- 4      5 ------- 4      5 ------- 2
3 ------> 5      3 ------> 9      3 ------> 1      3 ------> 2      3 ------> 3      3 ------> 3
2 <------ 4      2 <------ 1      2 <------ 9      2 <------ 3      2 <------ 2      2 <------ 5
8 <------ 6      8 <------ 2      8 <------ 10     8 <------ 1      8 <------ 5      8 <------ 6
7 ----:-> 1      7 ----:-> 3     7 ------> 2      7 ----:-> 5                       7 ----:-> 1
                     :-> 10        :-- 3
                     :-> 12        :-> 4

G3519            G3520            G3521            G3522            G3523            G3524
5 ------- 5      5 ------- 2      5 ------- 5      1 ------- 1      1 ------- 1      1 ------- 1
3 ------> 4      3 ------> 3      3 ------> 2      7 ------- 7      7 ------- 7      7 ------- 7
2 <------ 2      2 <------ 5      2 <------ 3      3 ------> 3      3 ------> 2      3 ------> 2
8 <------ 1      8 <------ 6      8 <------ 4      2 <------ 2      2 <------ 3      2 <------ 3
7 ----:-> 3      7 ----:-> 1      7 ----:-> 6     6 ----:-> 5      19 <-:----- 6    6 ----:-> 8
     :-> 6            :-> 4            :-> 8           :-> 6       4 <-:                :-> 4
                                                      :-> 8       20 <-:               :-> 20
                                                 19 <-:----- 20   6 ----:-> 4      19 <-:----- 5
                                                 4 <-:                :-> 20       4 <-:
                                                 20 <-:                            20 <-:

G3525            G3526            G3527            G3528            G3529            G3530
1 ------- 1      1 ------- 1      7 ------- 7      7 ------- 5      7 ------- 5      1 ------- 1
7 ------- 7      7 ------- 7      3 ------> 2      3 ------> 4      3 ------> 4      7 ------- 7
3 ------> 3      3 ------> 3      2 <------ 3      2 <------ 3      2 <------ 3      3 ------> 2
2 <------ 2      2 <------ 2      8 --:           6 ------> 6      19 <-:----- 1    2 <------ 3
6 ----:-> 5      6 ----:-> 5      19 <-:          19 <-:----- 1    4 <-:           19 <-:----- 6
     :-> 6            :-> 6       4 <-:           4 <-:           20 <-:           4 <-:
     :-> 20      19 <-:----- 4    20 <-:          20 <-:                           20 <-:
19 <-:----- 4    4 <-:                                                             6 ----:-> 4
4 <-:           20 <-:                                                                  :-> 20
20 <-:

G3531            G3532            G3533            G3534            G3535            G3536
1 ------- 1      1 ------- 1      1 ------- 1      7 ------- 7      1 ------- 1      7 ------- 7
7 ------- 7      7 ------- 7      7 ------- 7      3 ------> 2      7 ------- 7      3 ------> 2
3 ------> 2      3 ------> 3      3 ------> 2      2 <------ 3      3 ------> 2      2 <------ 3
2 <------ 3      2 <------ 2      2 <------ 3      8 --:           2 <------ 3      6 ----:-> 5
19 <-:----- 6    6 ----:-> 5      8 --:           19 <-:          6 ----:-> 20          :-> 6
4 <-:                :-> 8       19 <-:           4 <-:               :-> 4             :-> 8
20 <-:          19 <-:----- 4    4 <-:           20 <-:               :-> 12       19 <-:----- 4
                4 <-:           20 <-:                           19 <-:----- 5    4 <-:
                20 <-:                                           4 <-:           20 <-:
                                                                20 <-:
```

```
     G3537                  G3538                  G3539                  G3540                  G3541                  G3542

7 ------- 5           1 ------- 1           7 ------- 5           7 ------- 7           1 ------- 1           1 ------- 1
3 ------> 2           7 ------- 7           3 ------> 3           3 ------> 3           7 ------- 8           7 ------- 7
2 <------ 3           3 ------> 2           2 <------ 2           2 <------ 2           3 ------> 4           3 ------> 2
                      2 <------ 3                                                       2 <------ 2           2 <------ 3
6 ----:-> 8                                 6 ----:-> 7           8 --:
    :-> 6             19 <-:----- 8             :-> 4            19 <-:                 6 ----:-> 5           19 <-:----- 6
    :-> 1             4 <-:                19 <-:----- 6         4 <-:                      :-> 10            4 <-:
19 <-:----- 4         20 <-:               4 <-:                 20 <-:                     :-> 7            20 <-:
4 <-:                                       20 <-:                                     19 <-:----- 12
20 <-:               6 ----:-> 20                                                       4 <-:                6 ----:-> 4
                                                                                        20 <-:

                                                                                        8 ----:-> 11


     G3543                  G3544                  G3545                  G3546                  G3547                  G3548

7 ------- 4           1 ------- 1           7 ------- 5           7 ------- 3           1 ------- 4           1 ------- 3
3 ------> 3           7 ------- 7           3 ------> 7           3 ------> 5           7 ------- 7           7 ------- 6
2 <------ 2           3 ------> 5           2 <------ 4           2 <------ 4           3 ------> 6           3 ------> 5
                      2 <------ 3                                                       2 <------ 5           2 <- ----- 4
6 ----:-> 1                                 6 ----:-> 2           6 ----:-> 8
    :-> 6             6 ----:-> 6               :-> 6                :-> 7             6 ----:-> 8           6 ----:-> 7
19 <-:----- 5         19 <-:----- 4         19 <-:----- 3             :-> 6                :-> 2                :-> 1
4 <-:                4 <-:                  4 <-:                19 <-:----- 2              :-> 10           19 <-:----- 8
20 <-:               20 <-:                 20 <-:               4 <-:                 19 <-:----- 9         4 <-:
                                                                 20 <-:                4 <-:                20 <-:
                                                                                       20 <-:

                                                                                       8 ----:-> 1


     G3549                  G3550                  G3551                  G3552                  G3553                  G3554

7 ------- 8           7 ------- 8           7 ------- 7           7 ------- 5           1 ------- 2           1 ------- 2
3 ------> 2           3 ------> 6           3 ------> 3           3 ------> 3           7 ------- 7           7 ------- 7
2 <------ 1           2 <------ 1           2 <------ 2           2 <------ 2           3 ------> 3           3 ------> 8
                                                                                       2 <------ 8           2 <------ 3
8 --:                6 ----:-> 7           6 ----:-> 5           19 <-:----- 6
19 <-:                   :-> 9                 :-> 8             4 <-:                 6 ----:-> 5           19 <-:----- 5
4 <-:                19 <-:----- 4         19 <-:----- 9         20 <-:                    :-> 6            4 <-:
20 <-:               4 <-:                 4 <-:                                           :-> 1            20 <-:
                     20 <-:                20 <-:                6 ----:-> 4            19 <-:----- 9
                                                                    :-> 7              4 <-:                6 ----:-> 4
                                                                                       20 <-:                   :-> 9

                                                                                       8 ----:-> 10


     G3555                  G3556                  G3557                  G3558                  G3559                  G3560

7 ------- 7           7 ------- 4           7 ------- 5           7 ------- 9           7 ------- 3           7 ------- 9
3 ------> 5           3 ------> 6           3 ------> 6           3 ------> 3           3 ------> 4           3 ------> 13
2 <------ 4           2 <------ 3           2 <------ 4           2 <------ 2           2 <------ 2           2 <------ 11

6 ------> 3           19 <-:----- 2         6 ------> 2           6 ------> 5           6 ------> 5           6 ------> 14
19 <-:----- 1         4 <-:                19 <-:----- 3         19 <-:----- 4         19 <-:----- 1         19 <-:----- 10
4 <-:                20 <-:                 4 <-:                4 <-:                 4 <-:                4 <-:
20 <-:                                      20 <-:               20 <-:                20 <-:               20 <-:

                     6 ----:-> 1
                         :-> 7
```

G3561	G3562	G3563	G3564	G3565	G3566

`7 ------- 5`
`3 ------> 2`
`2 <------ 3`
 	
`6 ----:-> 8`
`    :-> 6`
`19 <-:---- 4`
`4 <-:`
`20 <-:`
	`7 ------- 5`
	`3 ------> 2`
	`2 <------ 3`
	
	`6 ------> 8`
	`19 <-:---- 7`
	`4 <-:`
	`20 <-:`
		`7 ------- 5`
		`3 ------> 3`
		`2 <------ 2`
		
		`19 <-:---- 6`
		`4 <-:`
		`20 <-:`
			`7 ------- 5`
			`3 ------> 3`
			`2 <------ 2`
			
			`6 --:`
			`19 <-:`
			`4 <-:`
			`20 <-:`
				`1 ------- 3`
				`7 ------- 4`
				`3 ------> 5`
				`2 <------ 2`
				
				`6 ------> 6`
				`19 <-:---- 1`
				`4 <-:`
				`20 <-:`
					`1 ------- 1`
					`7 ------- 2`
					`3 ------> 4`
					`2 <------ 3`
					
					`6 ------> 5`
					`19 <-:---- 6`
					`4 <-:`
					`20 <-:`

G3567	**G3568**	**G3569**	**G3570**	**G3571**	**G3572**

`1 ------- 1`
`7 ------- 7`
`2 <------ 2`
 	
`6 --:`
`19 <-:`
`4 <-:`
`20 <-:`
	`1 ------- 1`
	`7 ------- 7`
	`3 ------> 5`
	`2 <------ 3`
	
	`6 ----:-> 8`
	`      :-> 6`
	`19 <-:---- 4`
	`4 <-:`
	`20 <-:`
		`7 ------- 4`
		`3 ------> 5`
		`2 <------ 3`
		
		`6 ------> 2`
		`19 <-:---- 6`
		`4 <-:`
		`20 <-:`
			`7 ------- 5`
			`3 ------> 4`
			`2 <------ 2`
			
			`6 ------> 6`
			`19 <-:---- 1`
			`4 <-:`
			`20 <-:`
				`7 ------- 1`
				`3 ------> 4`
				`2 <------ 2`
				
				`6 ----:-> 6`
				`      :-> 8`
				`19 <-:---- 3`
				`4 <-:`
				`20 <-:`
					`1 ------- 3`
					`7 ------- 5`
					`3 ------> 2`
					`2 <------ 4`
					
					`19 <-:---- 1`
					`4 <-:`
					`20 <-:`

G3573	**G3574**	**G3575**	**G3576**	**G3577**	**G3578**

`1 ------- 4`
`7 ------- 2`
`3 ------> 5`
`2 <------ 3`
 	
`6 ------> 1`
`19 <-:---- 6`
`4 <-:`
`20 <-:`
	`7 ------- 3`
	`3 ------> 1`
	`2 <------ 5`
	
	`6 ----:-> 2`
	`      :-> 7`
	`19 <-:---- 8`
	`4 <-:`
	`20 <-:`
		`7 ------- 6`
		`3 ------> 8`
		`2 <------ 4`
		
		`6 ----:-> 7`
		`      :-> 2`
		`19 <-:---- 1`
		`4 <-:`
		`20 <-:`
			`7 ------- 2`
			`3 ------> 3`
			`2 <------ 5`
			
			`19 <-:---- 4`
			`4 <-:`
			`20 <-:`
				`1 ------- 3`
				`7 ------- 4`
				`3 ------> 5`
				`2 <------ 2`
				
				`6 ------> 1`
				`19 <-:---- 6`
				`4 <-:`
				`20 <-:`
					`1 ------- 4`
					`7 ------- 3`
					`3 ------> 2`
					`2 <------ 5`
					
					`6 ------> 6`
					`19 <-:---- 1`
					`4 <-:`
					`20 <-:`

G3579	**G3580**	**G3581**	**G3582**	**G3583**	**G3584**

`7 ------- 4`
`3 ------> 2`
`2 <------ 3`
 	
`6 ------> 6`
`19 <-:---- 1`
`4 <-:`
`20 <-:`
	`7 ------- 3`
	`3 ------> 5`
	`2 <------ 4`
	
	`6 ------> 1`
	`19 <-:---- 6`
	`4 <-:`
	`20 <-:`
		`7 ------- 11`
		`3 ------> 9`
		`2 <------ 1`
		
		`6 ----:-> 10`
		`      :-> 3`
		`      :-> 12`
		`19 <-:---- 2`
		`4 <-:`
		`20 <-:`
			`7 ------- 11`
			`3 ------> 1`
			`2 <------ 9`
			
			`19 <-:---- 3`
			`4 <-:`
			`20 <-:`
			
			`6 ----:-> 2`
			`      :-> 4`
				`7 ------- 4`
				`3 ------> 2`
				`2 <------ 3`
				
				`6 ------> 5`
				`19 <-:---- 1`
				`4 <-:`
				`20 <-:`
					`7 ------- 4`
					`3 ------> 3`
					`2 <------ 2`
					
					`19 <-:---- 5`
					`4 <-:`
					`20 <-:`

G3585	**G3586**	**G3587**	**G3588**	**G3589**	**G3590**

`7 ------- 2`
`3 ------> 3`
`2 <------ 5`
 	
`6 ------> 1`
`19 <-:---- 6`
`4 <-:`
`20 <-:`
	`7 ------- 5`
	`3 ------> 4`
	`2 <------ 2`
	
	`6 ----:-> 3`
	`      :-> 6`
	`19 <-:---- 1`
	`4 <-:`
	`20 <-:`
		`7 ------- 2`
		`3 ------> 3`
		`2 <------ 5`
		
		`6 ----:-> 4`
		`      :-> 1`
		`19 <-:---- 6`
		`4 <-:`
		`20 <-:`
			`7 ------- 5`
			`3 ------> 2`
			`2 <------ 3`
			
			`6 ----:-> 8`
			`      :-> 6`
			`19 <-:---- 4`
			`4 <-:`
			`20 <-:`
				`1 ------- 1`
				`7 ------- 7`
				`2 ------> 3`
				`3 <------ 2`
				
				`5 ----:-> 5`
				`      :-> 6`
				`      :-> 8`
				`6 <-:---- 20`
					`1 ------- 1`
					`7 ------- 7`
					`2 ------> 2`
					`3 <------ 3`
					
					`6 <-:---- 6`
					
					`5 ----:-> 4`
					`      :-> 20`

G3591	G3592	G3593	G3594	G3595	G3596

`1 ------- 1`
`7 ------- 7`
`2 ------> 2`
`3 <------ 3`
 	
`5 ----:-> 8`
`     :-> 4`
`     :-> 20`
`6 <-:---- 5`
	`1 ------- 1`
	`7 ------- 7`
	`2 ------> 3`
	`3 <------ 2`
	
	`5 ----:-> 5`
	`     :-> 6`
	`     :-> 20`
	`6 <-:---- 4`
		`1 ------- 1`
		`7 ------- 7`
		`2 ------> 3`
		`3 <------ 2`
		
		`5 ----:-> 5`
		`     :-> 6`
		`6 <-:---- 4`
			`7 ------- 7`
			`2 ------> 2`
			`3 <------ 3`
			
			`4 --:`
			`5 <-:`
			`6 <-:`
			`8 <-:`
				`7 ------- 5`
				`2 ------> 4`
				`3 <------ 3`
				
				`5 ------> 6`
				`5 <-:---- 1`
					`7 ------- 5`
					`2 ------> 4`
					`3 <------ 3`
					
					`6 <-:---- 1`

G3597	G3598	G3599	G3600	G3601	G3602

`1 ------- 1`
`7 ------- 7`
`2 ------> 2`
`3 <------ 3`
 	
`6 <-:---- 6`
 	
`5 ----:-> 4`
`     :-> 20`
	`1 ------- 1`
	`7 ------- 7`
	`2 ------> 2`
	`3 <------ 3`
	
	`6 <-:---- 6`
		`1 ------- 1`
		`7 ------- 7`
		`2 ------> 3`
		`3 <------ 2`
		
		`5 ----:-> 5`
		`     :-> 8`
		`6 <-:---- 4`
			`1 ------- 1`
			`7 ------- 7`
			`2 ------> 2`
			`3 <------ 3`
			
			`4 --:`
			`6 <-:`
				`7 ------- 7`
				`2 ------> 2`
				`3 <------ 3`
				
				`4 --:`
				`6 <-:`
					`1 ------- 1`
					`7 ------- 7`
					`2 ------> 2`
					`3 <------ 3`
					
					`5 ----:-> 20`
					`     :-> 4`
					`     :-> 12`
					
					`6 <-:---- 5`

G3603	G3604	G3605	G3606	G3607	G3608

`7 ------- 7`
`2 ------> 2`
`3 <------ 3`
 	
`5 ----:-> 5`
`     :-> 6`
`     :-> 8`
`6 <-:---- 4`
	`7 ------- 5`
	`2 ------> 2`
	`3 <------ 3`
	
	`5 ----:-> 8`
	`     :-> 6`
	`     :-> 1`
	`6 <-:---- 4`
		`1 ------- 1`
		`7 ------- 7`
		`2 ------> 2`
		`3 <------ 3`
		
		`6 <-:---- 8`
		
		`5 ----:-> 20`
			`7 ------- 5`
			`2 ------> 3`
			`3 <------ 2`
			
			`5 ----:-> 7`
			`     :-> 4`
			`6 <-:---- 6`
				`7 ------- 7`
				`2 ------> 3`
				`3 <------ 2`
				
				`4 --:`
				`6 <-:`
					`1 ------- 1`
					`7 ------- 8`
					`2 ------> 4`
					`3 <------ 2`
					
					`5 ----:-> 5`
					`     :-> 10`
					`     :-> 7`
					`6 <-:---- 12`
					`4 ----:-> 11`

G3609	G3610	G3611	G3612	G3613	G3614

`1 ------- 1`
`7 ------- 7`
`2 ------> 2`
`3 <------ 3`
 	
`6 <-:---- 6`
 	
`5 ----:-> 4`
	`7 ------- 4`
	`2 ------> 3`
	`3 <------ 2`
	
	`5 ----:-> 1`
	`     :-> 6`
	`6 <-:---- 5`
		`1 ------- 1`
		`7 ------- 7`
		`2 ------> 5`
		`3 <------ 3`
		
		`5 ------> 6`
		`6 <-:---- 4`
			`7 ------- 5`
			`2 ------> 7`
			`3 <------ 4`
			
			`5 ----:-> 2`
			`     :-> 6`
			`6 <-:---- 3`
				`7 ------- 3`
				`2 ------> 5`
				`3 <------ 4`
				
				`5 ----:-> 8`
				`     :-> 7`
				`     :-> 6`
				`6 <-:---- 2`
					`1 ------- 4`
					`7 ------- 7`
					`2 ------> 6`
					`3 <------ 5`
					
					`5 ----:-> 8`
					`     :-> 2`
					`     :-> 10`
					`6 <-:---- 9`
					
					`4 ----:-> 1`

G3615	G3616	G3617	G3618	G3619	G3620

`1 ------- 3`
`7 ------- 6`
`2 ------> 5`
`3 <------ 4`
 	
`5 ----:-> 7`
`     :-> 1`
`6 <-:---- 8`
	`7 ------- 8`
	`2 ------> 2`
	`3 <------ 1`
	
	`4 --:`
	`6 <-:`
		`7 ------- 8`
		`2 ------> 6`
		`3 <------ 1`
		
		`5 ----:-> 7`
		`     :-> 9`
		`6 <-:---- 4`
			`7 ------- 7`
			`2 ------> 3`
			`3 <------ 2`
			
			`5 ----:-> 5`
			`     :-> 8`
			`6 <-:---- 9`
				`7 ------- 5`
				`2 ------> 3`
				`3 <------ 2`
				
				`6 <-:---- 6`
				
				`5 ----:-> 4`
				`     :-> 7`
					`1 ------- 2`
					`7 ------- 7`
					`2 ------> 3`
					`3 <------ 8`
					
					`5 ----:-> 5`
					`     :-> 6`
					`     :-> 1`
					`6 <-:---- 9`
					
					`4 ----:-> 10`

```
G3621              G3622              G3623              G3624              G3625              G3626

1 ------- 2        7 ------- 7        7 ------- 4        7 ------- 5        7 ------- 9        7 ------- 3
7 ------- 7        2 ------> 5        2 ------> 6        2 ------> 6        2 ------> 3        2 ------> 4
2 ------> 8        3 <------ 4        3 <------ 3        3 <------ 4        3 <------ 2        3 <------ 2
3 <------ 3
                   5 ------> 3        6 <-:---- 2        5 ------> 2        5 ------> 5        5 ------> 5
6 <-:---- 5        6 <-:---- 1                           6 <-:---- 3        6 <-:---- 4        6 <-:---- 1
                                      5 ----:-> 1
5 ----:-> 4                               :-> 7
    :-> 9
```

```
G3627              G3628              G3629              G3630              G3631              G3632

7 ------- 9        7 ------- 5        7 ------- 5        7 ------- 5        7 ------- 5        1 ------- 3
2 ------> 13       2 ------> 2        2 ------> 2        2 ------> 3        2 ------> 3        7 ------- 4
3 <------ 11       3 <------ 3        3 <------ 3        3 <------ 2        3 <------ 2        2 ------> 5
                                                                                              3 <------ 2
5 ------> 14       5 ----:-> 8        5 ------> 8        6 <-:---- 6        5 --:
6 <-:---- 10           :-> 6         6 <-:---- 7                           6 <-:             5 ------> 6
                   6 <-:---- 4                                                               6 <-:---- 1
```

```
G3633              G3634              G3635              G3636              G3637              G3638

1 ------- 1        1 ------- 1        1 ------- 1        7 ------- 4        7 ------- 5        7 ------- 1
7 ------- 2        7 ------- 7        7 ------- 7        2 ------> 5        2 ------> 4        2 ------> 4
2 ------> 4        3 <------ 2        2 ------> 5        3 <------ 3        3 <------ 2        3 <------ 2
3 <------ 3                           3 <------ 3
                   5 --:                                5 ------> 2        5 ------> 6        5 ----:-> 6
5 ------> 5        6 <-:             5 ----:-> 8        6 <-:---- 6        6 <-:---- 1            :-> 8
6 <-:---- 6                              :-> 6                                                6 <-:---- 3
                                      6 <-:---- 4
```

```
G3639              G3640              G3641              G3642              G3643              G3644

1 ------- 3        1 ------- 4        7 ------- 3        7 ------- 6        7 ------- 2        1 ------- 3
7 ------- 5        7 ------- 2        2 ------> 1        2 ------> 8        2 ------> 3        7 ------- 4
2 ------> 2        2 ------> 5        3 <------ 5        3 <------ 4        3 <------ 5        2 ------> 5
3 <------ 4        3 <------ 3                                                                3 <------ 2
                                      5 ----:-> 2        5 ----:-> 7        6 <-:---- 4
6 <-:---- 1        5 ------> 1            :-> 7              :-> 2                            5 ------> 1
                   6 <-:---- 6        6 <-:---- 8        6 <-:---- 1                          6 <-:---- 6
```

```
G3645              G3646              G3647              G3648              G3649              G3650

1 ------- 4        7 ------- 4        7 ------- 3        7 ------- 11       7 ------- 11       7 ------- 4
7 ------- 3        2 ------> 2        2 ------> 5        2 ------> 9        2 ------> 1        2 ------> 2
2 ------> 2        3 <------ 3        3 <------ 4        3 <------ 1        3 <------ 9        3 <------ 3
3 <------ 5
                   5 ------> 6        5 ------> 1        5 ----:-> 10       6 <-:---- 3        5 ------> 5
5 ------> 6        6 <-:---- 1        6 <-:---- 6           :-> 3                             6 <-:---- 1
6 <-:---- 1                                                :-> 12          5 ----:-> 2
                                                        6 <-:---- 2            :-> 4
```

```
G3651              G3652              G3653              G3654              G3655              G3656
                                                                                             1 ------- 4
7 ------- 4        7 ------- 2        7 ------- 5        7 ------- 2        7 ------- 5        7 ------- 3
2 ------> 3        2 ------> 3        2 ------> 4        2 ------> 3        2 ------> 2        2 ------> 2
3 <------ 2        3 <------ 5        3 <------ 2        3 <------ 5        3 <------ 3        3 <------ 5

6 <-:---- 5        5 ------> 1        5 ----:-> 3        5 ----:-> 4        5 ----:-> 8        5 <-:---- 1
                   6 <-:---- 6           :-> 6              :-> 1              :-> 6          6 <-:
                                      6 <-:---- 1        6 <-:---- 6        6 <-:---- 4        8 <-:
```

G3657	G3658	G3659	G3660	G3661	G3662
7 ------- 4 2 ------> 2 3 <------ 3 5 <-:---- 1 6 <-: 8 <-:	7 ------- 3 2 ------> 5 3 <------ 4 5 <-:---- 6 6 <-: 8 <-:	7 ------- 11 2 ------> 9 3 <------ 1 5 <-:---- 2 6 <-: 8 <-:	7 ------- 11 2 ------> 1 3 <------ 9 5 <-:---- 3 6 <-: 8 <-: :-- 10 :-> 2 :-> 4	7 ------- 4 2 ------> 2 3 <------ 3 5 <-:---- 1 6 <-: 8 <-: :- 6 :- 5	7 ------- 4 2 ------> 3 3 <------ 2 5 <-:---- 5 6 <-: 8 <-:
G3663	G3664	G3665	G3666		
7 ------- 2 2 ------> 3 3 <------ 5 5 <-:---- 6 6 <-: 8 <-:	7 ------- 5 2 ------> 4 3 <------ 2 5 <-:---- 1 6 <-: 8 <-:	7 ------- 2 2 ------> 3 3 <------ 5 5 <-:---- 6 6 <-: 8 <-:	7 ------- 5 2 ------> 2 3 <------ 3 5 <-:---- 4 6 <-: 8 <-: :-- 7 :-> 6 :-> 8		

APPENDIX

H

industry standard and modular cables

If industry standard ports are provided on devices, cabling requirements can be often met by using industry standard cables. Examples of industry standard ports are IBM PC/XT compatible, IBM PC/AT, APPLE Macintosh Mini-DIN, HP 15 pin compatible, Hayes modem port, Centronics port (both printer and IBM PC), and the emerging modular ports. This appendix features some industry standard cables that are available to connect standard compliant ports. The following cables for IBM PCs are provided: null-modem cables, straight-through cables (25-pin), AT to modem and computers, PC to printer with hardware flow control, and IBM parallel cable. In addition, the emerging modular telephone-style ports are featured with some suggestions about cabling and wiring. For custom cables, refer to Appendices F and G for assistance in cable design.

NULL MODEM CABLES

Standard Null-Modem Cable (DB-25 to DB-25)

Function	Pin #		Pin #	Function
Chassis Ground	1	←——→	1	Chassis Ground
Signal Ground	7	←——→	7	Signal Ground
Transmit Data (out)	2	——→	3	Receive Data (in)
Receive Data (in)	3	←——	2	Transmit Data (out)
Request to Send (out)	4	—|—→	8	Data Carrier Detect (in)
Clear to Send (in)	5	←—|		
Data Carrier Detect (in)	8	←—|—	4	Request to Send (out)
		|—→	5	Clear to Send (in)
Data Terminal Ready (out)	20	——→	6	Data Set Ready (in)
Data Set Ready (in)	6	←——	20	Data Terminal Ready (out)

STANDARD IBM PC AND COMPATIBLES CABLES

Standard PS/2 and PC/XT to Modem Cable (DB-25S to DB-25P)

Function	Pin #		Pin #	Function
Transmit Data (out)	2	——→	2	Transmit Data (in)
Receive Data (in)	3	←——	3	Receive Data (out)
Request to Send (out)	4	——→	4	Request to Send (in)
Clear to Send (in)	5	←——	5	Clear to Send (out)
Data Set Ready (in)	6	←——	6	Data Set Ready (out)
Signal Ground	7	——	7	Signal Ground
Data Carrier Detect (in)	8	←——	8	Data Carrier Detect (out)
Data Terminal Ready (out)	20	——→	20	Data Terminal Ready (in)
Ring Indicator (in)	22	——→	22	Ring Indicator (out)

Standard PC/AT to Hayes Smartmodem Cable (DB-9S to DB-25P)

Function	Pin #		Pin #	Function
Transmit Data (out)	3	⟶	2	Transmit Data (in)
Receive Data (in)	2	⟵	3	Receive Data (out)
Request to Send (out)	7	⟶	4	Request to Send (in)
Clear to Send (in)	8	⟵	5	Clear to Send (out)
Data Set Ready (in)	6	⟵	6	Data Set Ready (out)
Signal Ground	5	——	7	Signal Ground
Data Carrier Detect (in)	1	⟵	8	Data Carrier Detect (out)
Data Terminal Ready (out)	4	⟶	20	Data Terminal Ready (in)
Ring Indicator (in)	9	⟵	22	Ring Indicator (out)

Standard PC/XT or PS/2 Null-Modem Cable (DB-25S to DB-25S)

Function	Pin #		Pin #	Function
Signal Ground	7	⟵⟶	7	Signal Ground
Transmit Data (out)	2	⟶	3	Receive Data (in)
Receive Data (in)	3	⟵	2	Transmit Data (out)
Request to Send (out)	4	— │ ⟶	8	Data Carrier Detect (in)
Clear to Send (in)	5	⟵ │		
Data Carrier Detect (in)	8	⟵ │ —	4	Request to Send (out)
		│ ⟶	5	Clear to Send (in)
Data Terminal Ready (out)	20	⟶	6	Data Set Ready (in)
Data Set Ready (in)	6	⟵	20	Data Terminal Ready (out)

Standard Null-Modem Cable—PC/AT to PC/AT (DB-9S to DB-9S)

Function	Pin #		Pin #	Function
Signal Ground	5	⟵⟶	5	Signal Ground
Transmit Data (out)	3	⟶	2	Receive Data (in)
Receive Data (in)	2	⟵	3	Transmit Data (out)
Request to Send (out)	7	— │ ⟶	1	Data Carrier Detect (in)
Clear to Send (in)	8	⟵ │		
Data Carrier Detect (in)	1	⟵ │ —	7	Request to Send (out)
		│ ⟶	8	Clear to Send (in)
Data Terminal Ready (out)	4	⟶	6	Data Set Ready (in)
Data Set Ready (in)	6	⟵	4	Data Terminal Ready (out)

Null-Modem Cable—PS/2 or PC/XT to PC/AT (DB-25S to DB-9S)

Function	Pin #	Pin #	Function
Signal Ground	7 ⟷ 5		Signal Ground
Transmit Data (out)	2 ⟶ 2		Receive Data (in)
Receive Data (in)	3 ⟵ 3		Transmit Data (out)
Request to Send (out)	4 —|⟶ 1		Data Carrier Detect (in)
Clear to Send (in)	5 ⟵|		
Data Carrier Detect (in)	8 ⟵|— 7		Request to Send (out)
	|⟶ 8		Clear to Send (in)
Data Terminal Ready (out)	20 ⟶ 6		Data Set Ready (in)
Data Set Ready (in)	6 ⟵ 4		Data Terminal Ready (out)

PC/AT and PS/2 or PC/XT to Printer Cable (using hardware flow control)

Function	DB-9SS	DB-25S	DB-25S/P	Function
	Pin #	Pin #	Pin #	
Transmit Data (out)	3	2 ⟶	3	Receive Data (in)
Receive Data (in)	2	3 ⟵	2	Transmit Data (out)
Clear to Send (in)	8	5 ⟵|—	20	Data Terminal Ready (out)
Data Set Ready (in)	6	6 ⟵|		
Data Carrier Detect (in)	1	8 ⟵|		
Signal Ground	5	7 —	7	Signal Ground
Chassis Ground	n/a	1 —	1	Chassis Ground

Notes: If your printer uses a different lead for hardware flow control, such 4, 11, 19, or 25, substitute this lead for lead 20 of the above cable design. Also, printers may require that some input control leads be on, such as 5, 6, 8. If so, connect lead 20 from the PS/2 and PC connector or lead 4 from a PC/AT connector across to all these input control leads. The gender for the printer connector will vary based on the printer.

IBM Parallel Cable (DB-25P to Cinch-36 pin)

Function	Pin #		Pin #	Function
Data strobe (out)	1	———	1	Data strobe (in)
Data bit 0 (out)	2	———→	2	Data bit 0 (in)
Data bit 1 (out)	3	———→	3	Data bit 1 (in)
Data bit 2 (out)	4	———→	4	Data bit 2 (in)
Data bit 3 (out)	5	———→	5	Data bit 3 (in)
Data bit 4 (out)	6	———→	6	Data bit 4 (in)
Data bit 5 (out)	7	———→	7	Data bit 5 (in)
Data bit 6 (out)	8	———→	8	Data bit 6 (in)
Data bit 7 (out)	9	———→	9	Data bit 7 (in)
Acknowledge (in)	10	←———	10	Acknowledge (out)
Busy (in)	11	←———	11	Busy (out)
Paper end (in)	12	←———	12	Paper end (out)
Select (in)	13	←———	13	Select (out)
Auto feed (out)	14	———→	14	Auto feed (in)
Error (in)	15	←———	32	Fault (out)
Init (out)	16	———→	31	Prime/Init/Reset (in)
Ground	18	–│ — │–	19	Ground
Ground	19	–│ │–	20	Ground
Ground	20	–│ │–	21	Ground
Ground	21	–│ │–	22	Ground
Ground	22	–│ │–	23	Ground
Ground	23	–│ │–	24	Ground
Ground	24	–│ │–	25	Ground
Ground	25	–│ │–	26	Ground
		– │–	27	Ground
		– │–	28	Ground
		– │–	29	Ground
		– │–	30	round

Note: Your cable may not need to include the leads for the Reset function and not all printers support it. Furthermore, the ground leads may need to be connected to lead 16 of the 36-pin connector.

IBM Parallel Port Pinout	
DB25 Pin #	*Function*
1	Strobe
2	Data bit 0
3	Data bit 1
4	Data bit 2
5	Data bit 3
6	Data bit 4
7	Data bit 5
8	Data bit 6
9	Data bit 7
10	Acknowledge
11	Busy
12	Paper end (out of paper)
13	Select
14	Auto feed
15	Error
16	Initialize printer (reset)
17	Select input
18-25	Ground

PC Parallel-to-Centronics Amphenol Cable Lead Layout

DB25	*Amphenol*
1	1
2	2
3	3
4	4
5	5
6	6
7	7
8	8
9	9
10	10
11	11
12	12
13	13
14	14
15	32
16	31
17	36
18	33
19	19
20	21
22	25
23	27
24	29
25	30

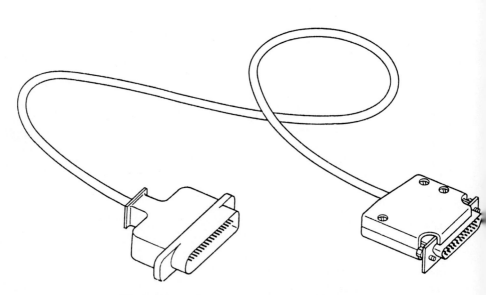

PC-to-printer DB-255 to Cinch-36 converter cable.

MODULAR CONNECTORS AND CABLES

More and more devices are using modular adapters to provide serial interfaces. These adapters are similar to the telephone jacks that are in your home. Modular adapters vary in size and consequently the number of leads/pins that can be provided. This next section features information for designing cables to connect devices with modular adapters, DB-25, DB-9, and Mini-DIN connectors.

Variations exist in the size and type of modular adapters available. Terms such as RJ-11 and RJ-45 are used to denote different ports and cables. Modular cable denotes the use of telephone cable similar to that used in your home. Commonly referred to as telco cables, due to their origin in the telephone companies, modular cables contain different numbers of wires. Typically, 2-, 3-, 4-pair cables are offered, with four, six, and eight wires, respectively. This refers to the number of conductors contained in the cable from end to end. Hence, a 2-pair cable offers four wires from end to end, while a 4-pair cable offers eight conductors. Your home telephone typically uses 2-pair cable, while most business installations use 4 pairs.

Modular connectors are the connectors at the ends of a modular cable. Typically RJ-11 denotes a smaller adapter, while RJ-45 is a slightly larger adapter. RJ-11 connectors are available for both four- and six-wire modular cables. Due to the use of RJ-11 connectors and adapters in the home, some people assume that RJ-11 automatically indicates 2 pair or four wire. This is not the case as 3-pair or six-wire cables are available with RJ-11 (six-pin) adapters on each end.

RJ-45 connectors can be attached to modular cables with any number of conductors up to ten. The connectors are categorized as a male gender. Typically, RJ-45 size connectors terminate each end of cables that are 4 pair, or contain eight conductors. However, 5-pair cables can use RJ-45 size connectors. Furthermore, 2-pair cables can be terminated with RJ-45 connectors. Be aware of this possibility. However, the most common use of the RJ-45 connectors is to terminate 4-pair cable.

Modular adapters are the receptacle where you connect the cables with their modular connectors. Modular adapters are denoted as female. Some devices now offer modular adapters instead of DB-25, DB-9, DB-15, or Mini-DIN connectors. Many port boards that are used in UNIX-based systems provide modular adapters for their serial ports, mainly for saving space and simplifying wiring connections. Examples are boards from Computone, DigiBoard, Comtrol, IMC, Equinox and Stallion. Other terminal and computers also use modular adapters for RS-232 interfaces. Refer to Appendix F for more devices that incorporate RJ-11 or RJ-45 adapters into their products. Appendix I lists the numbering of these adapters and the cable connectors.

With the introduction of modular adapters and modular cords, the interconnection with the different installed base of ports increases, as does the complexity. The number of leads in the port adapter determines cabling requirements. Not only the number, but also the placement of the various functions of the serial interface have a bearing on the cable requirements. The placement of the leads, such as Transmit Data, Receive Data, Signal Ground, and flow control leads will determine if 2-pair, 3-pair, 4-pair, or even 5-pair cable can be used.

Consider the possibility of an RJ-45 adapter that has eight leads. Refer to Appendix I for a depiction of this style adapter. Now assume the pinouts for the adapter exist as listed in Table H-1.

The layout of the functions and assignment by the vendor to the adapter pin numbers will dictate the type of modular cable that can be used. The modular connectors on a cable are symmetrical and centered. Plugging a 4-pair (eight-wire) cable into an adapter matches the inside eight leads of the adapter. Hence, the outermost conductors of a cable match up with leads 2 and 9 of the modular adapter/port. The innermost conductors of the modular cable plug into leads 5 and 6 of the adapter. The leads of a 2-pair cable make contact with the inside four leads of the RJ-45 adapter, and so on. Table H-2 depict the various cables and their adapter pin connections. There is no standard for placement of the RS-232 or RS-422 leads in a modular adapter, but there should be. Until this standard evolves, pay attention to the leads and their positions in the modular adapter.

TABLE H–1. Pinouts for a typical modular adapter

Signal Name	Pin #
Ring Indicator	1
Data Set Ready	2
Data Terminal Ready	3
Chassis Ground	4
Transmit Data	5
Received Data	6
Signal Ground	7
Clear to Send	8
Request to Send	9
Carrier Detect	10

TABLE H–2. RJ-45 adapter and 2-, 3-, 4-, and 5-pair cable connections

Adapter Signal Name	Pin #	Cable Conductors			
		5-pair	4-pair	3-pair	2-pair
Ring Indicator	1	X			
Data Set Ready	2	X	X		
Data Terminal Ready	3	X	X	X	
Chassis Ground	4	X	X	X	X
Transmit Data	5	X	X	X	X
Received Data	6	X	X	X	X
Signal Ground	7	X	X	X	X
Clear to Send	8	X	X	X	
Request to Send	9	X	X		
Carrier Detect	10	X			

Plugging straight-through modular cables into the modular adapter port provides the contacts as depicted in Table H-2. Vendors such as Black Box, TRW, and AMP provide cables with straight-through pinning. However, modular cables are also available that provide cross-pinning. See Figure H-1. In such cables, the outermost conductors are crossed from one end to the other. Also, the innermost conductors are crossed at each end. For example, in a 2-pair cable, conductor 1 at one end of the cable is crossed to conductor 4 at the other cable end. The same is true at both ends. Also conductor 2 at one cable end is crossed to conductor 3 at the other cable end. These two connections are repeated from both end's perspectives. In the case of a 4-pair modular cable, conductors 4 and 5, 3 and 6, 2 and 7, and 1 and 8 are crossed. Table H-3 depicts the straight through and cross-over–type modulars.

By using an adapter that is termed an in-line coupler, two cables can be connected to extend the distance of straight-through cables. However, note what happens if you connect two cables, both with crossed connectors such as depicted in Table H-4. The result is the equivalent of a straight-through cable. Refer to Appendix I for the modular adapter and cable pin numbering.

The assignment by the vendor of the RS-232 functions to the various leads dictate the cabling requirements. Different cables can be used depending on the connections of computers to computers, computers to printers, computers to terminals, or computers to modems.

Generally when software flow control is used, four wires at a minimum are required. When hardware flow control is used, the number of required leads varies. Generally, to connect a printer to a computer with hardware flow control, at least four or five leads are needed. When two computers with hardware flow control are to be connected, six leads at a minimum are required.

For example, should a printer using hardware flow control be connected to a computer, using RS-232, four or more leads may be required. The leads to be connected would be the data leads on each device (transmit to receive and vice versa), the signal grounds on each device straight-through. Finally, the output flow control lead from the printer would be cross connected to any input control leads on

TABLE H–3. Modular cable-pinning diagrams

4 Pair Cable Straight-through	4 Pair Cable Crossed-conductors	2 Pair Cable Straight-through	2 Pair Cable Crossed-conductors
1 —————— 1	1 —————— 8	1 —————— 1	1 —————— 4
2 —————— 2	2 —————— 7	2 —————— 2	2 —————— 3
3 —————— 3	3 —————— 6	3 —————— 3	3 —————— 2
4 —————— 4	4 —————— 5	4 —————— 4	4 —————— 1
5 —————— 5	5 —————— 4		
6 —————— 6	6 —————— 3		
7 —————— 7	7 —————— 2		
8 —————— 8	8 —————— 1		

TABLE H–4. Back-to-back cables with crossed conductors using in-line adapter

4-Pair Cable Crossed Pins	In-line Adapter	4-Pair Cable Crossed Pins
1 ——————— 8	——— * ———	8 ——————— 1
2 ——————— 7	——— * ———	7 ——————— 2
3 ——————— 6	——— * ———	6 ——————— 3
4 ——————— 5	——— * ———	5 ——————— 4
5 ——————— 4	——— * ———	4 ——————— 5
6 ——————— 3	——— * ———	3 ——————— 6
7 ——————— 2	——— * ———	2 ——————— 7
8 ——————— 1	——— * ———	1 ——————— 8

the computer side. Chances are that neither a straight-through or crossed-conductor cable would properly match up the leads. Consult Appendices F and G to determine which leads need to be connected. From this a modular cable can be constructed or purchased with the proper cross-connections if both devices are equipped with a modular adapter port.

However, most printers and modems incorporate DB-25-size ports, while some terminals, computers, and multiport boards incorporate RJ-11 or RJ-45 adapters. Factoring in the software or hardware flow control leads, a combination modular cord and modular adapters can be used to cable devices with different style connectors together. Figure H-1 depicts this type of cabling, with the computer end being a modular cable, while the printer end has modular-to-DB adapter. The modular adapter is a special adapter that has an RJ-11 or RJ-45 port on one side, with a DB-9, DB-15, or DB-25 connector on the other side. These are available with standard pinning connections as listed in Appendix J or as kits allowing the user to custom connect the pins. The end result is a cable configuration that can use standard modular cabling.

What if both devices incorporate DB-9, DB-15, or DB-25 connectors, either the same size or different? Modular cabling and adapters may still be used to connect the device ports. The modular/DB adapters are available with RJ-11C or RJ-45 connectors on the cable side of the adapter, with DB-9, DB-15, or DB-25 connectors on the device side. Select the appropriate adapter for each device based on the port size, noting the gender requirements. Consult Appendices F and G to design the pin crossovers. Do the appropriate crossovers in the adapters. Then use a modular cord that has a sufficient number of conductors to connect the device adapters. Table H-5 lists some of the possible connectors that are possible with modular cables and modular adapters. Be aware that some modular cables provide crossed conductors as cited in Table H-3.

Wall outlets for most office buildings are modular, either RJ-11C or RJ-45, or both. Behind these outlets is wiring that runs to a closet, a private branch exchange (PBX), or another outlet. Generally, these outlets are connected to a punch-down block or cross-connect panel that allows for jumpering to connect two outlets. Consult Figure H-2. Punch blocks are a quick solution to wiring within buildings.

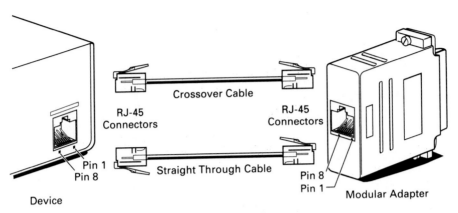

Figure H-1. Modular Cable and Modular/DB Adapter

They are typically concealed in wiring closets. Punch blocks have many rows of pins into which wires from the wall outlets are "punched down," hence the name. A special tool is available to perform the punch down. The punch blocks are then cabled to one another, or to a PBX.

There are a number of wiring plans that exist to provide cabling designs for wiring buildings and offices. Plans include certain pin numbers that have a certain color wire connected to them. Some building wiring installations conform to these plans, while others don't. Caution should be used prior to using any building wiring that does not conform to a specific plan. Without a documented plan, you will have to rely on pot luck. Also, don't assume that because the wall outlets are either RJ-11 or RJ-45 adapters, that they can be used for connecting computers and peripherals. Some of these are wired strictly for telephone use. Plugging a piece of computer equipment into a jack wired for telephone use can result in a shorting or blowing of components of the computer equipment. This is due to different voltages. Consult the building operations or MIS department to determine if the outlets can be used for connecting devices.

TABLE H–5.   Modular cable and adapter connections

Device A	Cable	Device B
DB-25	Modular	DB-25
DB-15	Modular	DB-15
DB-9	Modular	DB-9
DB-25	Modular	DB-9
DB-25	Modular	DB-15
DB-15	Modular	DB-9
DB-25	Modular	RJ
DB-15	Modular	RJ
DB-9	Modular	RJ
RJ	Modular	RJ

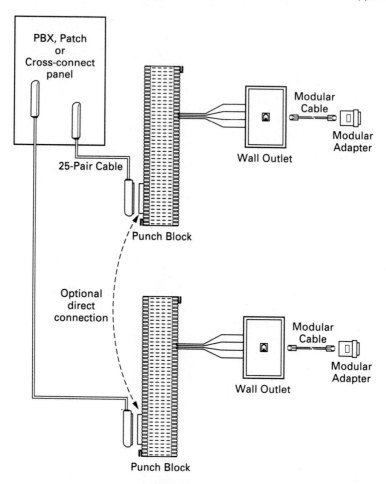

Figure H-2.

I

common connectors, pinouts, and numbering

This appendix contains tables and diagrams of common cables and connectors. Many times the user needs to know how many conductors are provided within a cable. Furthermore, information about which leads are provided based on the number of conductors in a cable is very useful. Table I-1 provides typical cable conductors for cables.

The remaining figures feature common ports, connectors, and pin numbering. Figures I-2 & I-3 provide the common cable connectors for DB-type and the Macintosh ports, along with their pin numbering. Figure I-3 depicts the assembly of both standard cable and connector, as well as a ribbon cable and connector. The assembley diagram for a DB-25 and Modular adapter if featured in Figure I-4. Figure I-5 outlines the pin numbering for modular connectors and adapters. Use this information in conjunction with the cable designs from Appendix F & G.

TABLE I-1   Typical RS-232 DB-25 Cable Conductors

# of Conductors	Pins provided	Typical use
4	2, 3, 7, 20	Interfacing with few or no input control leads, generally considered a simplified EIA interface
7	2, 3, 4, 6, 7, 8, 20	Computer to computer (asynchronous) Computer to printer/plotter (asynchronous) Computer to terminal (asynchronous)
12	1-8, 15, 17, 20, 22	Same as 7 conductor: Computer to computer (synchronous) Computer to modem (asynchronous) Computer to modem (synchronous with DCE timing) Terminal to modem (asynchronous) Printer to modem
16	1-8, 15, 17, 20-25	Same as 7 and 12 conductor: Computer to modem (synchronous with DTE timing) Computer to modem with data rate selection and signal quality detection used
25	1-25	All uses; however if a ribbon cable is used, cross-overs and jumpering are difficult

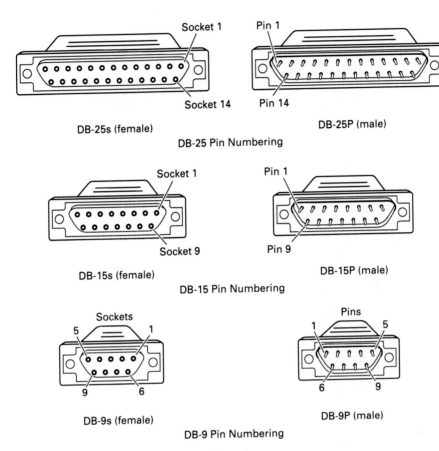

DB-25s (female) DB-25P (male)

DB-25 Pin Numbering

DB-15s (female) DB-15P (male)

DB-15 Pin Numbering

DB-9s (female) DB-9P (male)

DB-9 Pin Numbering

Figure I-1

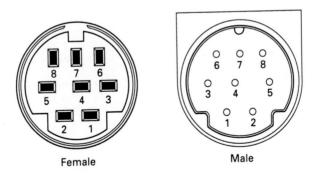

Female Male

Mini-Din pin numbering
for Apple Macintosh and other peripherals

Figure I-2

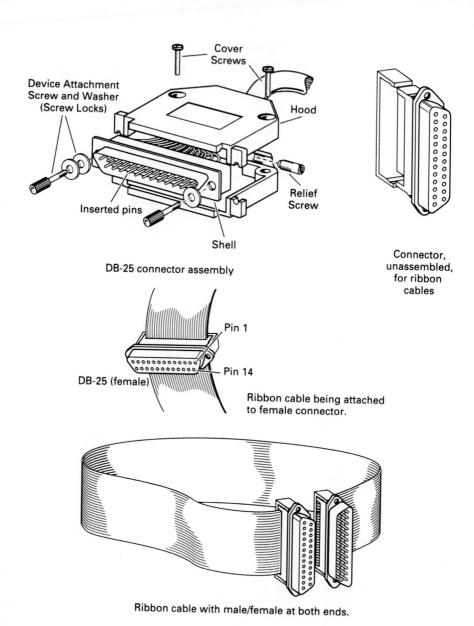

Cover Screws

Device Attachment
Screw and Washer
(Screw Locks)

Hood

Inserted pins

Relief
Screw

Shell

DB-25 connector assembly

Connector,
unassembled,
for ribbon
cables

Pin 1

DB-25 (female)

Pin 14

Ribbon cable being attached
to female connector.

Ribbon cable with male/female at both ends.

Figure I-3

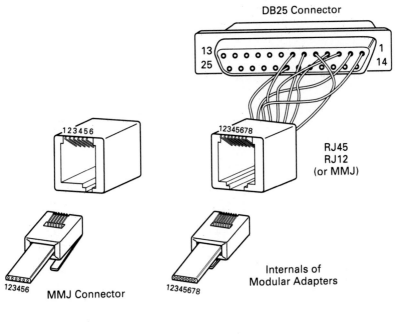

DB25 Connector

13
25

1
14

RJ45
RJ12
(or MMJ)

123456

12345678

MMJ Connector

12345678

Internals of
Modular Adapters

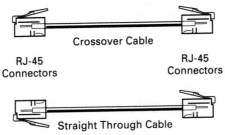

Crossover Cable

RJ-45
Connectors

RJ-45
Connectors

Straight Through Cable

Figure I-4

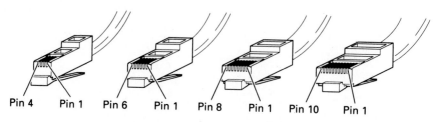

Pin 4   Pin 1   Pin 6   Pin 1   Pin 8   Pin 1   Pin 10   Pin 1

Modular Cords and Pin Numbering

Modular Adaptor Pin Numbering

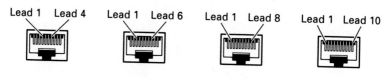

Lead 1   Lead 4   Lead 1   Lead 6   Lead 1   Lead 8   Lead 1   Lead 10

Modular Adaptor and Pin Numbering

Lead 1   Lead 4

RJ-11C Adaptor and Pin Numbering

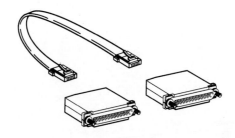

DB25-to-modular adapters

Figure I-5

J

TRW modular to DB-25 adapters

The following chart contains several modular to DB-25 adapters available from TRW. These provide eight-wire modular access to RS-232 input/output connectors. They are available with or without spring latches and come in four types.

Type 1 One piece hood with two mounting screws
Type 2 One-piece hood with latching blocks and mounting screws
Type 3 Two-piece hood with spring latches
Type 4 Two-piece hood with filler ends and two mounting screws

Socket Style Adapter (Female)

Part No.	Reference	Modular Jack Position								Jumpers	Type
		D-Subminiature Contact									
		1	2	3	4	5	6	7	8		
002-00010-9	FF-001	7(AB)	4(CA)	2(BA)	20(CD)	3(BB)	8(CF)	7(AB)	5(CB)	—	Type 1
002-00011-1	FF-002	7(AB)	4(CA)	2(BA)	20(CD)	3(BB)	8(CF)	7(AB)	5(CB)	—	Type 3
002-000012-4	FF-003	Unassembled Kit (requires plier-type termination tool.)									Type 5
002-00052-1	FF-004	—	8(CF)	1(AA)	2(BA)	7(AB)	3(BB)	8(CF)	—	4 to 5*	Type 1
002-00120-7	FF-005	—	20(CD), 6(CC)	1(AA)	3(BB)	7(AB)	2(BA)	20(CD), 6(CC)	—	4 to 5*	Type 1
002-00013-7	FF-006	1(AA)	4(CA)	3(BB)	8(CF)	2(BA)	20(CD)	7(AB)	5(CB)	—	Type 1
002-00016-2	FF-007	1(AA)	4(CA)	3(BB)	8(CF)	2(BA)	20(CD)	7(AB)	5(CB)	—	Type 4
002-00002-2	FF-008	1(AA)	5(CB)	2(BA)	20(CD)	3(BB)	8(CF)	7(AB)	4(CA)	—	Type 1
002-00016-5	FF-009	7(AB)	3(BB)	8(CF)	4(CA)	20(CD)	5(CB)	6(CC)	2(BA)	—	Type 1
002-00017-8	FF-010	1(AA)	4(CA)	3(BB)	8(CF)	2(BA)	20(CD), 6(CC)	7(AB)	5(CB)	—	Type 1
002-00018-3	FF-011	Unassembled Kit (requires plier-type termination tool.)									Type 1
002-00021-3	FF-012	7(AB)	4(CA)	2(BA)	20(CD)	3(BB)	6(CC), 8(CF)	7(AB)	5(CB)	—	Type 1
002-00003-5	FF-013	6(CC)	20(CD)	7(AB)	2(BA)	4(CA)	3(BB)	8(CF)	5(CB)	—	Type 1
002-00004-8	FF-015	2(BA)	3(BB)	4(CA)	6(CC)	8(CF)	7(AB)	9	20(CD)	—	Type 1
002-00006-3	FF-016	7(AB)	5(CB)	3(BB)	8(CF)	2(BA)	20(CD)	7(AB)	4(CA)	—	Type 1
002-00007-8	FF-018	20(CD)	7(AB)	5(CB)	3(BB)	4(CA)	2(BA)	8(CF)	1(AA)	—	Type 1
002-00008-9	FF-030	5(CB)	6(CC)	3(BB)	20(CD)	2(BA)	7(AB)	22(CE)	4(CA)	—	Type 1
002-00009-1	FF-031	4(CA)	20(CD)	2(BA)	6(CC)	3(BB)	7(AB)	22(CE)	5(CB)	—	Type 1

*D-Subminiature positions are jumpered together.

APPENDIX

K

rules for cable
design

RS232 CABLE DESIGN RULES

1. **CONNECT LIKE CATEGORIES OF LEADS TOGETHER.** Connect ground leads to ground leads, data to data, control to control, and timing to timing leads. Do not connect a control lead to a data lead. Separate the leads into the different categories as an aid to avoid misconnections.

2. **ALWAYS CONNECT AN "OUT" TO AN "IN" AND AN "IN" TO AN "OUT."** Simply put, this means that a lead that is provided by a device should be connected to one of the leads required by the device. Leads provided by a device should not be connected to another lead that is provided by a device, output to output. The direction of the leads is very important for proper cable design.

3. **A LEAD THAT IS INPUT SHOULD ONLY BE CONNECTED TO ANOTHER LEAD THAT IS AN INPUT IF BOTH OF THESE ARE CONNECTED TO AN OUTPUT LEAD.** The goal is to keep input leads on (high), using the leads that are output from a port. We may have to use one output lead to keep more than one input lead on. This is why you may need to connect multiple input leads together. This is the "jumpering" concept.

4. **IN SYNCHRONOUS CONNECTIONS, ONLY USE ONE SOURCE OF TIMING.** If multiple timing leads are available with a timing signal on them, use only one of them. The others should be driven off this single lead to get their timing. The goal is to minimize the number of timing sources to avoid clocks that are out of phase. In asynchronous connections, this rule is not applicable.

RS-422 CABLE DESIGN RULES

1. Connect the Signal Ground leads straight through from one port to the other.
2. Connect the Chassis/Protective Ground leads straight through from one port to the other (optional connection).
3. Connect the Transmit Data positive lead on one port to the Receive Data positive lead on the other port (TxD+ to RxD+).
4. Connect the Receive Data positive lead on one port to the Transmit Data positive lead on the other port (RxD+ to TxD+).
5. Connect the Transmit Data negative lead on one port to the Receive Data negative lead on the other port (TxD− to RxD−).
6. Connect the Receive Data negative lead on one port to the Transmit Data negative lead on the other port (RxD− to TxD−).
7. Connect the remaining control leads in the same manner as RS-232 connections, noting flow control requirements.

L

interfacing problems and remedies

Often the user faces problems getting two devices to work together. Once two devices are connected, they still may not function together properly. The next few sections summarize some of the symptoms that may be noticed when connecting devices. Furthermore, possible cures to clear the problem are proposed. This list is far from complete yet gives the user a place to begin in isolating the problems. These cures, separated by the categories, computers, modems, printers, and terminals, are covered in greater detail in the tutorial modules. First the symptoms and data-appearance problems will be covered, followed by some device-specific problems.

Common Connection Symptoms and Causes

Symptom	Causes
1. Garbled characters	Parity, speed, character length, stop bits, bad phone line
2. Lost data	Flow control
3. Double spacing	Translation of received carriage returns or line feeds
4. Overwriting	Translation of received carriage returns or line feeds
5. No display of typed characters	Far end is not echoplexing, duplex option
6. Double characters	Duplex option

Common Data Appearance Problems

If the data you receive look like . . .	Problem	Resolution
1. line1 . . . . . . (your output will vary) line2 . . . . . . (your output will vary) line3	Too many line feeds	Ensure that both CR and LF are not being performed with receipt of line ending sequence. Or disable one at the sending end of the connection.

2. line1 . . . .
     line2 . . . .
          line3 . . . .
	No carriage return is being performed	Enable receiving device to perform CR/LF upon receipt of line ending sequence.

3. Lines 1 and 2 and 3 overwriting each other causing illegible lines	No line feed is being performed	Change option so that receipt of line ending sequence is interpreted as CR/LF, instead of just a CR.
4. The qpoic ýrÜwn fox xwpeorlk fs	Mismatched options	Compare options of both ports to insure that the parity, speed char-length, # of stop bits match.
5. The qpoic broke fox xwpeorlk fslk	Bad phone line	Hang up and redial
6. Lost data or only partially received	Improper or no flow control	Ensure that both ports are set up for the same flow control
7. No data being displayed while you type	Duplex problem	Ensure that both ports gee-haw. If the attached device is not echoplexing, then your port should be set up for half-duplex.
8. DDoouubbllee CChhaarraacctteerrss	Duplex problem	The other device is set up to echoplex. Change your device to full-duplex, or no local display.

APPENDIX

M

ASCII character set

B7 B6 B5 → Bits B4 B3 B2 B1 ↓	Row / Column	0 0 0 Column 0	0 0 1 1	0 1 0 2	0 1 1 3	1 0 0 4	1 0 1 5	1 1 0 6	1 1 1 7
0 0 0 0	0	NUL CTRL (a) 0 0 0	DLE CTRL p 20 16 10	SP CTRL (sp) 40 32 20	0 60 48 30	(a) 100 64 40	P 120 80 50	` 140 96 60	p 160 112 70
0 0 0 1	1	SOH CTRL a 1 1 1	DC1 (XON) CTRL q 21 17 11	! 41 33 21	1 61 49 31	A 101 65 41	Q 121 81 51	a 141 97 61	q 161 113 71
0 0 1 0	2	STX CTRL b 2 2 2	DC2 CTRL r 22 18 12	" 42 34 22	2 62 50 32	B 102 66 42	R 122 82 52	b 142 98 62	r 162 114 72
0 0 1 1	3	EXT CTRL c 3 3 3	DC3 (XOFF) CTRL s 23 19 13	# 43 35 23	3 63 51 33	C 103 67 43	S 123 83 53	c 143 99 63	s 163 115 73
0 1 0 0	4	EOT CTRL d 4 4 4	DC4 CTRL t 24 20 14	$ 44 36 24	4 64 52 34	D 104 68 44	T 124 84 54	d 144 100 64	t 164 116 74
0 1 0 1	5	ENQ CTRL e 5 5 5	NAK CTRL u 25 21 15	% 45 37 25	5 65 53 35	E 105 69 45	U 125 85 55	e 145 101 65	u 165 117 75
0 1 1 0	6	ACK CTRL f 6 6 6	SYN CTRL v 26 22 16	& 46 38 26	6 66 54 36	F 106 70 46	V 126 86 56	f 146 102 66	v 166 118 76
0 1 1 1	7	BEL CTRL g 7 7 7	ETB CTRL w 27 23 17	' 47 39 27	7 67 55 37	G 107 71 47	W 127 87 57	g 147 103 67	w 167 119 77

ASCII code chart (columns 0–7, rows 8–15). Each cell lists the character followed by its octal, decimal, and hexadecimal values.

Bits B7 B6 B5 →	0 0 0 (Col 0)	0 0 1 (Col 1)	0 1 0 (Col 2)	0 1 1 (Col 3)	1 0 0 (Col 4)	1 0 1 (Col 5)	1 1 0 (Col 6)	1 1 1 (Col 7)
Row 8 — B4B3B2B1 = 1000	BS / CTRL h — 10 8 8	CAN / CTRL x — 30 24 18	(— 50 40 28	8 — 70 56 38	H — 110 72 48	X — 130 88 58	h — 150 104 68	x — 170 120 78
Row 9 — 1001	HT / CTRL i — 11 9 9	EM / CTRL y — 31 25 19	) — 51 41 29	9 — 71 57 39	I — 111 73 49	Y — 131 89 59	i — 151 105 69	y — 171 121 79
Row 10 — 1010	LF / CTRL j — 12 10 A	SUB / CTRL z — 32 26 1A	* — 52 42 2A	: — 72 58 3A	J — 112 74 4A	Z — 132 90 5A	j — 152 106 6A	z — 172 122 7A
Row 11 — 1011	VT / CTRL k — 13 11 B	ESC / CTRL [— 33 27 1B	+ — 53 43 2B	; — 73 59 3B	K — 113 75 4B	[— 133 91 5B	k — 153 107 6B	{ — 173 123 7B
Row 12 — 1100	FF / CTRL l — 14 12 C	FS / CTRL \ — 34 28 1C	, — 54 44 2C	< — 74 60 3C	L — 114 76 4C	\ — 134 92 5C	l — 154 108 6C	| — 174 124 7C
Row 13 — 1101	CR / CTRL m — 15 13 D	GS / CTRL] — 35 29 1D	= — 55 45 2D	= — 75 61 3D	M — 115 77 4D	] — 135 93 5D	m — 155 109 6D	} — 175 125 7D
Row 14 — 1110	SO / CTRL n — 16 14 E	RS / CTRL ` — 36 30 1E	. — 56 46 2E	> — 76 62 3E	N — 116 78 4E	^ — 136 94 5E	n — 156 110 6E	~ — 176 126 7E
Row 15 — 1111	SI / CTRL o — 17 15 F	US / CTRL - — 37 31 1F	/ — 57 47 2F	? — 77 63 3F	O — 117 79 4F	_ — 137 95 5F	o — 157 111 6F	DEL / CTRL (bs) — 177 127 7F

*Keyboard-generated characters.

431

Index